# DOROTHY IN WONDERLAND

# DOROTHY IN WONDERLAND

## A SYNCHRONISTIC JOURNEY TO THE SELF

Linda Tagliamonte

gatekeeper press™
Columbus, Ohio

Dorothy in Wonderland:
A Synchronistic Journey To The Self

Published by Gatekeeper Press
2167 Stringtown Rd, Suite 109
Columbus, OH 43123-2989
www.GatekeeperPress.com

The cover design, interior formatting, typesetting, and editorial work for this book are entirely the product of the author. Gatekeeper Press did not participate in and is not responsible for any aspect of these elements.

ISBN (paperback): 9781662901485
eISBN: 9781662901478

*For the Muse*

*For forty years*

# Contents

# Part One

*The Fool on the Precipice: Initiation*

A youth is about to stop off the edge of a precipice.
She symbolizes the Lifepower before it enters into
manifestation. Therefore, she represents inexperience—
which certainly can be foolish. She faces northwest, the
direction of the unknown. The sun behind her is still
rising, for the spiritual sun never reaches its zenith. The
wand over the youth's shoulder is a symbol of the will,
universal memory and instinct. The Fool is about to pass
into the cycle of life through which each soul must journey.
She must choose between good and evil. If she has no
philosophy, she is the Fool.

(excerpts from *A Complete guide to the TAROT*
by Eden Gray)

## The Queen of Swords

On a high throne, looking into a clouded sky, sits a queen with a raised sword in her left hand. "Let those approach who dare!" Her crown and the base of her throne are decorated with the Butterflies of the soul, and just under the arm of the throne we find a sylph, the elemental of the air. The Queen's face is chastened through suffering.

Reversed: Deceit, Malice. A woman of artifice and prudery. Clever stratagem. Proper and modest.

(excerpts from *A complete guide to the TAROT* by Eden Gray)

I, DOROTHY, HAVE been banished from the land of the religious. Branded. Labeled. Misunderstood. One less troublemaker. Or one less mirror to reflect back their Christian selves? Christian. I liked the word. They liked the word. Too bad neither of us could live it genuinely. But I don't fool myself into believing I ever could. I don't name myself that way. I just name myself Dorothy. Any name will do as it only describes a part of the self. This one has no meaning beyond its seven letters. It distinguishes me from all others, but it doesn't define me. That would be a major accomplishment. One I struggled for.

Yes, Dorothy will do. I have a strong identification with her. Dorothy was so secure in her homeland with her family and friends and then one day everything changed. The storm swept her far away to a strange land, the land of Oz.

Is that how I got here? In this modern-day land of Oz. Was I too, swept away by the storm? Caught in a tsunami? A victim of fate?

I lay prostrate on the floor of the craft shop porch. Weak. Thinking constantly of all that had happened. So much had happened. I couldn't understand it all. But it was over, or so I thought. If I could just relax my mind. Stop my thoughts. Release the pain. I waited for Bear and Lady.

Gazing at the small, white peaceful chapel set back in the distance, I decided to draw the country scene on the paper Connie had given me. Connie saw something more in me. Poor Connie. I really felt for her. Her brother's death had come so soon after her husband's death . . . Her husband, the man she admired and relied on for practical direction. She fell apart when he died. Even though underneath she was a truly educated woman, a thinker, she desperately needed his guidance to balance her outward scatterbrained personality. A compassionate woman, she felt the pain of others. I loved talking to her about Virginia, Vita, and Simone. Her background was literature, and she spoke about these women authors as if they were part of her personal experience. . . .

Oh, Connie, I always felt I failed you. What could I have done to relieve your pain? To bring you back to reality? Reality. As if that's a better place to be. I'm not sure anymore, but then I'm not so sure about anything anymore.

I started drawing and remembered it was a favorite past time of mine as a child. On Saturday mornings, I'd watch the John Nagy *Learn to Draw* show on TV. I had even sent away for the plastic covering that stuck to the TV screen. While the master was drawing, I copied the sketch on the plastic screen. I loved sitting in my pajamas right in front of the tube. Why didn't I continue drawing lessons? When did I start thinking that science and math were more relevant? Maybe that was the problem. Maybe I should have concentrated more on developing the right side of my brain. My thoughts followed the line of the pencil and I was drawn back to the graduation night of Catholic High School, that fated night that provided the final push to this new and foreign place. It was a big move, a five-year move.

It was a dreary, stormy night: June 21st, 1979; perhaps indicative of what was to follow? We stayed at my house till we had to leave for the Cathedral; a meaningless, huge, cold structure with endless ceiling and crowded masses of people. An appropriate place for this graduation. The place where Catholics go to experience community. I laugh. Christ would have laughed. This is what his simple, unadorned death had finally led to. The Cathedral, the center of worship, home of the bishop, our leader, and his priestly band of followers. This pompous group complete with "Most Reverend" credit cards. Lord, forgive my anger. I know tolerance is demanded but I couldn't tolerate this. This deception. This whoring of the original vision. The comfort, the houses in suburbia, the undeserved respect. And of course, the surrogate women to reflect the inflated image. Humble nuns accepting orders and following laws of a superstructure to which they are barred. A birth defect. No instrument to be representative of Christ. The requirements are stiff to get into this ball club. But it keeps the power where it should be. The buddy system works!

The Wolf and I were our usual flaming selves. We had arrived late and hurried downstairs to join the other faculty in the procession line. We were always entertaining and managed to get a laugh out of some of them (those who still remembered how to laugh). The more serious gave that look which said, "You are such children. Even here you carry on the clowning. Haven't you grown up yet? Don't you realize the seriousness of this night?" Actually, the more appropriate question was, "Don't you realize the ultimate joke of this night?"

Graduation was the presentation of the diploma signifying the mastery of high school reading, writing, and arithmetic. Yet, half of the students in this hall couldn't pass a junior high test. Forget high school level. They hadn't been taught to think. Education was a joke in our society. Learning was not a value unto itself. It only mattered to get the diploma, the degree, the job to earn money to buy cars, TVs, expensive clothes, stereos, games . . . How else to prove worth? To prove success?

One didn't need to think about the deeper meaning of life to acquire those things. The Why's . . . the Ultimates. The questions which had always provoked tension and growth had no meaning. Instead, this was the era of things, getting ahead, deception, drugs, violence, sports, rudeness. Things to fill in the gap. A substitute for thinking. Thinking provokes growth which is sometimes painful. It challenges the ideas of those we love. It demands struggle. It demands change. It demands personal involvement. It demands being at the edge. It does not provide the comforting pleasure and detachment that things provide. The nourishment of lazy minds. Minds afraid to ponder, afraid to wonder, afraid to look to inner answers. Answers which lead to personal action.

I laughed every time I heard Fr. Harold repeating the school motto, "There are no strangers here." The irony was that we were all strangers. Some more than others. Very few tried to break through to real communication and understanding and dare I say "love." Those of us who tried were regarded as threats. Something to be discarded. "We don't need what you have to offer." Those words still sting. Was it me? Or did they not see? Loss of power is threatening, especially if lost to a lay person. I love that term. Lay person. As if there were some special class of people who had the monopoly on being religious. I thought being religious had something to do with the way one treated others, not whether one refrained from sex or said daily prayers or went to church. The motto in the school seemed to be "Divide and keep control." The idea of people liking each other and working in a happy situation was not the concept of those in power. I naively thought it a nice philosophy to work toward. Naïve is certainly the word. It got me fired in the end. That attitude, along with my ideas of equality for girl students in this macho school was the real basis for my dismissal. I appealed the decision, and had the case gone to court, the school administration really could not substantiate its decision. I managed to get my job back, but it was futile. I knew I could never be effective anymore. I could never be myself. I would be walking on eggs. And of course, the doubt would manage to work its way through the core. One never knows. I was strong on the outside but inside, I was lava, soft, burning away at the lining.

I still see Fr. Harold, head of all the Diocesan schools, sitting in his comfortable chair behind the huge mahogany desk. We were discussing the closing of Saint Francis, the small Catholic girl's school, the brick mansion on the hill, where I had taught for six years. He looked rather smug and comfortable. "We just don't need what you have to offer up there in that secluded tower," he said as he puffed in the match flame while trying to light his pipe. His patience infuriated me. Patience being an excuse. If one proclaims patience, then things go on and it's not one's fault. One is being patient. One is allowing change to happen gradually, in its own time. Did Christ? Was he patient? Did he give it time? Or did he proclaim change? Radical action? A call to do something? Not using the normal channel but scourging out a new path, a dangerous, lonely, painful path to the self? Following the inner voice to the end? . . . following inner voices . . . Joan d' Arc . . .

I admired Joan d'Arc; her strength, her commitment, her craziness, her standing in the fire. I felt her once. It was at a teacher's workshop. After a week of intense all-day meetings, the group participants needed some play time. The group leader, a pantomime actor, invited us to test our skill. Across the street from the convention hall was an empty church. It had been gutted. We all marched over there, some more reluctantly than others. Alan explained the rules. I went first and was told to stand perfectly still in front of the others and think very deeply and seriously about a character from history. I was to communicate that personality without doing anything physical. I chose Joan d'Arc. I stood there, eyes closed, concentrating as hard as I could . . . I saw myself on the cross. *It was confusing. Hard to see. Smoke surrounded me. I felt the heat rising, rising closer to my tied feet. My breath got heavy. It was such an effort to pull my chest out for air. There was no air. Only gray smoke. Choking gray smoke. My chest sank into my body. It was easier this way. Keeping it close. It was hot. Unbearably hot. I wanted to scream. I wanted to let go. My body was sinking, melting down, the weight pulling on my arms, causing pain. I couldn't hold myself up any longer. I was giving away . . . pain registered on my face, brows turned inward and down. Tears ready to fall. So much tension in my arms, so much pull, stretched to the limit . . . I would have fallen had I continued.*

I stopped. Opened my eyes. Everyone was watching me. One woman immediately said, "Joan d'Arc, you were Joan d'Arc." She wasn't the only person who knew. One man voiced how stupid this exercise was, but later in private, he admitted to me that he also knew I was Joan d'Arc. It took a lot for him to share this.

A young woman went next. She closed her eyes. Her body assumed a gentle stance. My eyes focused on her face, her countenance. I saw a blue light enshroud her, a familiar blue hue. Where had I seen that shade of blue before? So soft, so gentle a color. Where? Thinking back . . . memories . . . Rome, the Vatican, yes, yes, *The Madonna and Child* had that same blue color, that same peacefulness, that same gentleness. She stopped and looked at us. I spoke first and said, "I saw a blue color emanating from you that reminded me of Michelangelo's *Madonna and Child.*"

She responded, "I imagined myself a mother looking at her first-born child."

That convinced me. There was so much more to this life than met the eye. So much more our minds could do . . . communication without words. The experiences of the rest of the year fed into this feeling.

* * *

After the graduation ceremony, the Wolf and I joined some faculty members for a final fling of bar hopping. Intuitively we both knew we would not be returning next year to teach. Out of character in dresses, we looked more attractive than usual. Everyone relished our comedy. We relished the attention. Sometimes we would get on this other wavelength, an other-worldly communication. Few could follow, but we were captivating regardless of whether we were understood. I wonder sometimes if we even understood.

We ended up in the back room of one of the bars. I asked Ken, a happily married chauvinistic man, to dance with me. Judging from his comments, I knew he thought me too masculine. I did have a rather aloof attitude, especially with men. Their attention was not important to me. The school was situated in an Italian ghetto and you can't get more chauvinistic than that! I didn't fit into the norm. But that night, my femininity was showing through. It usually came out when I was dancing or if I felt good in the clothes I was wearing.

Surprised, Ken commented, "You are a real woman, aren't you." I must admit I was flattered and just smiled. I knew my power. It is power. Don't be deceived into thinking otherwise. Maybe this is why we are the stronger sex. We can turn that power on or off as we choose. The shame is that many have chosen not to accept that power. If women learned to channel this deceptive power over men, they could change the world.

The Wolf was talking to Don. She took pleasure in teasing the opposite sex. They left the bar. I was upset but too drunk to do anything. Besides, I had no rights over her. I waited helplessly. Soon she returned and whispered in my ear, "Let's go to a gay bar." On the drive over she confessed, "Well, I'm sure now that I am gay. I couldn't do it with him."

"You tried to do it in his car?" I responded, infuriated.

"Yes, I only went so far, but in the end, I couldn't continue." The thought of her being even partially nude with him disgusted me. He must have been so frustrated. Wolf was an incredibly attractive woman. Thin, average height, light-skinned with long blonde hair. Don had been after her all school year. Though he was married, he was sleeping with another woman. He told her he loved her but couldn't leave his wife because of their child. He loved his wife as well. Now he loved Wolf. To me it was a mess. I never knew why Wolf had gotten as involved as she did. She said she found him attractive.

In the car, Wolf started dozing off as she was talking to me. "I want to go home," she said. "Will you take me home?" We were only about fifty miles from her house, and it was 2:00 am! She was supposed to sleep at my apartment, but I couldn't refuse her. I never could. My spirit dropped, but I turned the car around and headed for the highway. She drifted off. I cried, quiet, straight-faced tears. I didn't want her to see. I never wanted her to know her effect on me. About halfway to her house, she glanced over at me and said, "I guess that's what friends are for."

"Yes, friends," I replied and thought to myself, 'Do friends always cause this much pain?" I knew she cared about me. But caring and loving are not the same. I hated that phrase, "I care about you." Care just didn't make it. I understood why later when I fell in love with the Lioness and started caring about Wolf. Funny. It wasn't funny at the time. Feelings are so difficult. I think that's why I majored in science and math. Abstract, no feelings involved, just right and wrong answers. I found it hard to face, express, and accept my feelings. I didn't think I had any right to have them. I know now we all have a right to our feelings. They are there and we just must admit them. We can't always act upon them, but we are allowed to feel them.

I dropped her off and returned back home. She had asked me to stay at her place, but I couldn't, knowing her lover was there.

The next day, I received a phone call from some guy I had met at one of the bars.

"I'm from Boston," he said.

"Really," my interest heightened, "I've been thinking of moving to Boston and getting a waitressing job. I have some friends there I could live with."

"Do you know any places to apply?"

"No, not really."

"Well, I'm familiar with the city and could give you some suggestions. I have a lot of contacts and might be able to help you."

"That would be great."

"Let me have your phone number, and I'll call. We could get together to discuss." Foolishly, I gave him my number. Mistake number one, and it was a big one. It could have been the worst mistake I ever made as it could have been my last.

He asked to meet at the Friendly's Restaurant in East Hartford and then to go dancing. Excited about moving to Boston, I accepted his invitation. After I hung up the phone, I realized how hung over I still was. The last thing I felt like doing was dancing. I got this powerful intuitive feeling telling me, "You better not do this." Omen number one. I didn't have his phone number so I couldn't call him back to cancel. I felt bad about leaving him hanging at the restaurant, so I decided to go and only stay for supper.

Later that evening, I drove to the restaurant where we were to meet. I sat at the counter and waited, but he didn't show up. I wasn't familiar with this part of Hartford and asked the waitress if this was the only Friendly Restaurant in East Hartford.

"This isn't East Hartford. You have to drive a few blocks down this road to get to that shop," she said pointing to the street in front of the restaurant. Omen number two. I got back into the car and drove down the road and saw the restaurant. As I was getting out of my car, I saw him leaving the place. I tried to hurry so I could catch up to him but in doing so, I closed the door and my trench coat got caught in it. I couldn't open it to free my coat. Omen number three. Three adverse warnings, and yet stubbornly I continued in my pursuit of him. I finally opened the door and ran down the street. I caught up to him and called his name. He looked surprised and said in a harsh voice, "I didn't think you were keeping the date."

"I went to the wrong Friendly's. I'm sorry to keep you waiting. I want to have coffee with you, but I don't feel well enough to go dancing." He got upset, more than he should have, and insisted I go out with him later.

"No, I'm leaving after supper. Let's go back and have a hamburger. We can talk inside."

"I can't go back in there," he retorted in a mean voice. "I already ate. Let's go down the street to McDonald's."

I agreed, anything to calm him. It seemed innocent enough although at this point, I was a little concerned with his overly oppressive attitude. I didn't owe him anything. If I didn't feel good, he had no reason to get upset. We got in my car, and I drove down the road to McDonald's.

His whole physical stance started to bother me. Tall and strong looking with piercing blue eyes, he stretched his body taking up a lot of the room in my small Datsun. A nervous feeling emanated from him. I tried to make small talk, but this proved to be a bad idea.

"So how do you like your apartment?"

"It was robbed when I was in the hospital."

'Oh,' I thought, 'that's why he's so uptight.' "Did your insurance cover the loss?"

"I didn't have any."

"Why were you in the hospital?" Bad topic, I realized. He jumped back and forth in his seat in an agitated manner and said, "What do you mean? Mental or physical?" This was the creepiest and most uncomfortable conversation I had ever been involved in. His replies were sharp and not normal. He was getting angry for no apparent reason. From his presence, I felt this growing evil. It seemed to be filling the whole car. A heavy intense black cloud hung over me. I got quiet and kept driving without looking at him. I didn't know what to do. It was a relief when he pointed out that the McDonald's was just ahead. We had traveled quite a distance. His description of "down the road a piece" had not been accurate. I parked the car, and we went inside. He sprawled out in one of the booths while I went to the counter to order a hamburger and fries. I ate as he spoke continuously now.

"It doesn't matter how you play the game, but rather whether you win or lose. That's all that matters. Whether you win or lose." This confused me, and I tried to understand what he was trying to say. Was he talking about his job?

"What do you mean?" I asked.

"I am a loser."

"Why do you say that?"

"My family disowned me. You're the first woman I've spoken to in four months."

'Oh brother,' I thought.

He continued, "My friends are here today and gone tomorrow."

"Explain."

"They all got killed," he said and acted as if this should make perfect sense to me, adding, "This is big-time stuff with high stakes." He then leaned forward looking very intensely in my eyes and said, "You know I hurt women."

Now I was petrified but tried to project a calm attitude. With conviction, I said, "You don't really like to do that, do you?"

"Yes. If I want to get back at them." There was a big pause and then he continued, "I've killed twelve people over the last nine months. The cops don't even know. They're so stupid. You can get away with it so easy."

My God. My God. Three warnings, and I didn't heed them! How could I be so stupid? I was so scared that I felt paralyzed. I gathered all the courage I could muster and said, "I'm going to get some ketchup." Before he could respond, I bounced up and ran over to the counter. I got the manager's attention and said, "Look, I'm with this man whom I really don't know, and he just told me that he killed twelve people."

His response was typical. "Lady, you've got to be kidding!"

"Please listen. I know it sounds a little strange, but it's true. Call the police because I don't want to get back in the car with him." I could see he thought I was crazy. I was at the point of tears. He wasn't going to call the police. Just then I heard this shouting coming from the back room behind the counter.

"Ms. D! Ms. D!" It was Laurie, one of my students from the private girl's school, St. Francis. She was obviously an employee. I was so relieved.

"Laurie, tell your manager that I am your teacher and that I am sane." I told her my situation. She believed me and immediately called the police. I was shaking so she brought me into the back room. I sat and talked with Laurie and her two friends and was never so happy to see three people in my live. I finally calmed down, but I wasn't going to go back into the restaurant, not even to get my pocketbook. The police arrived, and the man got up and exited the restaurant when they pulled in the parking lot. He must have suspected something since it was taking a long time to get that ketchup!

I told the police what had happened, and they went to talk to him. They returned shortly and said he had been in a mental institution for four months, but his record was clear. They said they would take him home. Relief! Laurie and her friends followed me in their car over to Adele's house. I didn't want to go home yet.

On the drive over, I thought about how coincidental it was that Laurie was working at this particular Friendly's. Teaching at the private school had been such a happy time for me. The people there were my friends, even the students. We shared a special bond. Adele also taught at the school. We went to the same college and though we couldn't stand each other in college, during teaching, we became best friends.

Adele was an emotional English major and into arts, and I was an analytical math major and into sports. I still remember how angry I would get when Adele would come into the makeshift gym of square wooden tiles at the small Catholic girl's college in New England. We would be just finishing up a volleyball game when Adele in her black tights would sit in the middle of the floor signaling that our gym time was over. And she wouldn't move! No amount of pleading worked. We had to stop. Other times she would sit right in front of the mailboxes waiting for a letter from Jerry, her boyfriend. I was a senior at the time and didn't think it should be necessary for seniors to climb over underclasswomen to get their mail. Oh, she made me angry. When I heard she was hired as my counterpart for the junior high, I was concerned. I didn't think it would work, but on the contrary, we complimented each other. She made me laugh with her emotional outbreaks and total lack of scientific skills, and I entertained her with my interpretation of events as mythical realities. For Adele family was priority and for me adventure was priority. Through each other, we got a glimpse of the other life.

I related the events to Adele and she totally understood my anxiety. She didn't think my fears were irrational or overdone. "D, you must have been out of your mind with fear!"

"Adele I was so scared I couldn't even pick up a French fry! And you know how thin McDonald fries are!"

The next day, I was worried that this man still had my phone number. Could he trace my address? I told Sarah, my lover, about it. She told me I was stupid for giving our number to a stranger. I agreed. She insisted we change the phone number.

Two days later I received a phone call from a detective asking me about the MacDonald's event.

"Do you know where this man lives?"

"No, I don't but the police who came to the restaurant took him home so they should know."

"I talked with them already. They left him off at some corner. They never checked his apartment."

"They didn't take him home?" I shrieked. "Why didn't they check his apartment after I told the police he said he killed twelve people?"

"Well, when they questioned him about it, he said he was drunk the night he told you that. He was only teasing you, and you took him seriously."

"What? He told me that at the Friendly's." The police believed his story over mine. The male bond. They must have thought me a hysterical woman. The detective on the phone went on to tell me that nine women had been killed in that same area over the last year. My heart dropped. I tried to calm myself by thinking maybe he imagined himself as the killer. People in mental institutions must imagine all kinds of things. But I couldn't escape the horrifying thought that maybe he was telling the truth!

The next week at school I was a wreck. My relationship with Sarah was coming to an overdue end. I had just gotten rehired after two weeks of inner struggle over the firing. Now this added tension. I told Sr. Lidia, principal of St. Francis, about the killer experience, and sensing my distraught emotional state, she left the Bear's phone number in my mailbox with a note suggesting I contact her in Maine and go visit. I had taught with Bear at St. Francis.

I took this as a sign. I called the Bear. She suggested I visit at the end of the month as right now they had a lot of guests. I accepted the invitation but was a little disappointed about having to wait. I needed to get away right now. Funny, she called me back two hours later and invited me for the next weekend since a favorite student of mine was going to be visiting and she thought it would be fun for all of us to be together. I accepted relieved.

I left for Maine after school on Friday. It had been a week of meetings in preparation for the next school term, and at this time I was still considering returning to my job. Earlier that day I had met with Fr. O'Malley, the principal, to discuss my position. I had decided to apply for the full-time math position instead of continuing with the half math, half chemistry position I now had. I was a math major and after all I had been through with this school, I had no desire to burden myself next year with teaching huge chemistry classes. My idealistic concept of giving had been damaged by the firing. Fr. O'Malley listened, but would not give me an answer on my request.

"I'll do my best to give you what you want, but I can't guarantee anything."

I took this to mean that he preferred I keep the position I had. Understandably, it would be harder to find a teacher who could do both chemistry and math, but I was tired of being a sucker, especially when it wasn't appreciated so I replied, "Well, I can't guarantee that I will return next year."

"That's your option," he responded. "You will receive your contract sometime in July, and you have two weeks to sign it." There was no love lost between us—that was obvious. We were just dealing on strictly professional terms. I thanked him for the meeting, departed, and headed for the long journey north.

I reached Kennybunk just before dusk and got a motel room. It was the first night I slept comfortably after all that had happened. It was a relief being so far away from the maniac. I had visions of him following me in retaliation for calling the police. Maine seemed like a safe distance. Relaxing with my solitude and freedom, I realized this was the longest trip I had ever gone on alone. I was in high spirits.

I departed around 8:00 am and arrived at the Co-op where Bear worked before noon. I got out of the car and walked around the grounds but didn't see Bear or Lady. I walked onto the porch of the craft shop and felt exhausted. I lay down. Looking up at the sky, my mind wandered. I felt I had been drawn to this place. It was no coincidence. A voice, a force, a consciousness called my name. Was I under some control? What was I responding to? Certainly, something beyond myself, my reality. Or was my mind playing games? I do play games. It keeps life from becoming boring.

*          *          *

Finally Bear and Lady arrived. I was thrilled to see them. After exchanging hugs, Lady excused herself to do some errands in the craft shop. Bear and I talked. It was easy to talk to her. I always felt we had an honest relationship though we were never close friends. I admired her playful spirit. She would do things that were out of character for a nun. One night, we were drinking in an Irish bar, and Bear, feeling no pain, poured a bottle of beer down the backside pocket of some innocent male bystander just because she felt like doing it. Another night we were Greek dancing in my apartment and both of us fell on to a huge rubber plant. We were hysterical trying to repair it with scotch tape.

Besides this down-to-earth human side, Bear lived what I considered to be a true Christian life: simply with few material possessions and always amongst common people. She accepted the "way-outs" in this world, and if she believed in a truth, she defended it to the end. When St. Francis closed, and all the students and faculty were in terrible pain over the news, Bear marched down to where the Board of Trustees were comfortably having their coffee and donuts and invited them to come upstairs to see the emotional havoc their decision had caused.

"Come and see what the little guys are feeling," she announced boldly. Of course, they didn't come, but her action stood out in my mind. When she followed her own voice, she was untouchable, and that's how I choose to remember her.

"So D, how was your year at Catholic High?" she asked. That one simple question projected me into this other wavelength. All the pain surfaced. I hadn't had time to feel it yet. I was so busy fighting and trying to remain strong, but now the dam opened, and the currents flowed.

"Bear, that woman is truly evil," I said regarding the Queen of Swords, reversed. "She got me fired. She's a sick woman. She's into power and she doesn't care who she uses or destroys along the way." Bear nodded like she understood, and I continued, "Bear, I could have destroyed her, but when it came right down to it, I couldn't do it."

"Someone ought to destroy her. She's been doing it too long, and it just continues. The powers to be are blind to her. She's got them all nicely wrapped around her finger."

"Father O'Malley came to the school in the middle of the year so he must have relied on her input as to who to fire. They fired six of us for economic reasons, but how we six were chosen is puzzling. They told us around April way past the deadline for notification of nonrenewal of teachers' contracts. Fr. O'Malley called me down to his office and motioned that I sit across from him at the round coffee table in his office . . . "

"Well, Dorothy, I have some difficult news for you. We must make some cutbacks for next year, and your position is one of them. Not enough students have signed up for Consumer Chemistry so there doesn't seem to be a need for it."

I was surprised at his last remark, knowing the caliber of students at this school, so I questioned his figures. He jumped up, went to his desk, and fidgeted around some papers looking desperately for the information I requested.

"Uh, I don't seem to be able to locate those figures. But I'll get them for you later." He looked at me like he was so concerned and said, "I know this must come as a shock to you."

"Yes, I need time to think this over since I didn't expect to be dismissed this late in the year." The next words that came out of my mouth were a complete surprise even to me. In spite of the uncomfortable situation, I was calm and said, "Well, Father, I would like to keep the lines of communication between us open, and I will get back to you after I have given it some thought. I might like to discuss this further with you."

"Oh, yes, Dorothy. By all means! Come any time and I'll answer as best I can."

Then I added, "Just one question, Father. Tell me. Am I the type of person you want on to have on your faculty?"

"Oh yes, Dorothy, I am pleased with your work. There is no question of your professional performance. Your involvement and concern for the students are very evident. I know you took on the cheerleaders as an added responsibility in addition to everything else you are doing. It really is merely a matter of finance."

"Thank you, Father, and I will get back to you as I said." After shaking his hand, I left rather pleased with my reaction.

For the rest of the week, I mulled over my experiences of the school year trying desperately to understand the situation.

The first interview . . . it was not something I had been overly enthusiastic about. I was still suffering internally. The announcement of the closing of St. Francis was a shock. I was so happy there and felt that what we were doing as an educational institution was meaningful. We were very successful considering what was happening at other schools. We provided more than a book education. The school had evolved over the years from being an all-white, upper-class, elite private girls' school to a mixture of white, middle-class suburban girls and black inner-city girls. The interchange between the two cultures was the real value. It was where the Christian spirit lived. It worked! The two groups actually got along, learned from one another, and more than that- liked each other. These girls were special. Each in her own way. And the small community environment of the school encouraged the individuality of each student.

A prime example was the relationship between Alicia, a black girl with a voice bordering a Warwick/Flack combination and Jane, a suburban white girl who had taught herself to play the piano. They came to me, the junior class advisor, and jokingly asked about the possibility of putting on a concert to raise money for the class. I think they were surprised when I didn't immediately say no and more so that I got excited about it.

"Go ahead and start practicing and let's see what happens." Well, that's all the encouragement they needed. They practiced every day before school, during school, after school and who knows? They probably did some work over the phone at night! They practiced for months and got the rest of the class members involved to help in various ways. Just before they were ready to give the performance, the announcement of the closing of the school was made. It was hardest on this group of girls since they were juniors with only one more year before graduation. Feeling angry and hurt, they thought about giving up on the concert idea, but after talking it over with me and the rest of the class, they decided on the "let's show them we are bigger" attitude and continued with the plans.

The night was perfect. The girls creatively converted the blah auditorium into a convincing café complete with red and white checkered tablecloths, carnations, and dim lights. It was classy, and the show was a total success. The girls incorporated a slide presentation about the school during one of Alicia's songs. No one left dry eyed.

The closing affected everyone, even those with hard skins. The day the announcement was made I watched Theresa, one of my students, sit at her desk writing poetry. She was too upset to speak though this was not a girl prone to sappy emotion. She currently was involved in a court case for stabbing a girl from her neighborhood. She'd just as soon speak with her fists than dilly-dally with words. She was writing about how her home was being taken away. Theresa lived in a house with fourteen other people. No wonder she considered the school her home.

Lydia, who would have been valedictorian and senior class president, comforted me on the day the student body was told about the closing. The faculty had been told on a Thursday. A real treat this was. They herded us into the library after school for a mandatory meeting. In marched the Board of Trustees followed meekly by the Administration of the school. Most of the faculty thought that next year would be the decision year as to whether the school remained open. We always had financial problems. But it was April and a bit late to announce a closing for the following year. The news was more definitive than expected.

The President of the Board got up and said, "St. Francis will not be opening in September, and since we realize this is such short notice, the diocese has agreed to give our teachers preference in job openings." Period. No discussion. Silence.

I was sitting in a front row seat and after his words, I jumped up and out loud said, "Oh, my God! What about the juniors? I don't believe this!"

Everyone, including me, was surprised at my reaction. It just happened. I immediately left the room.

I thought to myself later, 'Imagine how faculty members who had been teaching at the school for forty or fifty years felt? I was only there six years.' But the school was more than a job. Those of us who stayed did so for philosophical reasons. The pay was terrible, but that was not our main concern.

The next morning the faculty was all upset. The students were called down later that morning to the auditorium and told. A period of dead silence followed, and then one by one they all started crying. I kept myself by the window and fought back tears from the moment the students began coming into the room. I couldn't look at any of them. Now tears were streaming down my face. Lydia motioned for me to come sit by her. I did. She took my hand and said, "It's ok, Ms. D, we'll get through."

The following Tuesday, a meeting was held for the parents to express their concerns. They were not happy! They wanted to know why they were not informed earlier of the situation so they could have tried to save the school. Answers were flimsy. The leaders just wanted to get the meeting over with the least amount of energy. It's strange, but I find that religious people, contrary to what one might expect, have the most difficulty in dealing with emotions. One would think that the philosophy of the group would strengthen such response. In my experience, religious people don't always believe what they say they do, nor do they always act upon these beliefs.

I suppose I expected something positive to happen at this meeting. The night before I had awakened with an overpowering vision of a pulsating, light-shining, green heart. It was the kind one sees superimposed over a picture of Christ, although it's usually red. The dream brought me energy and hope. I woke Sarah up at 6:00 am and told her we had to go speak with Sr. Donna, the head of the order running the school. It was like right now! We had to do it right now! Sarah thought I was crazy, but she came with me. She was good to me through this difficult time. I had been teaching at St. Francis before she started but I knew she loved the school just as much as I did. I really wished I loved her the way she needed to be loved, but sometimes she was just too hard on me. Sarah had a strong moral sense, and I didn't always live up to the expectations.

Sr. Donna met with us. The last time I had seen her was at the student meeting. She had pulled Sarah and me into a classroom with the intention of calming me down. I had just walked up to the principal and accused her of "selling us out to all the in competency!" Sr. Donna agreed a lot was wrong, but her message was to let this die and start anew somewhere else. She hadn't convinced me.

During the meeting, I told Sr. Donna everything that was wrong with the school. For the past twenty years or so, the Board of Trustees was chaired by the same man—The Godfather type. This type of leadership was not conducive to new ideas. And then there was the internal conflict among the Administration team. A trio team was imposed on the school the preceding year. They were inexperienced and were still just learning how to function as a team, let alone run a school! I had worked on recruitment that summer and learned that many interested parents who had requested brochures about the school were never contacted as a follow up. I felt this response should have been mandatory. I couldn't believe it wasn't done routinely. I learned then you never assume that higher ups are doing their jobs.

Sarah told Sr. Donna that for a long time now the school was continuing not due to the efforts of the nuns in charge but kept alive by the dedication of the lay staff. Most of us were single, had no community meeting to attend, like the nuns, and gave more time to the students. Our teaching was more than a 9-5 job. Sr. Donna didn't appreciate the comment!

Sr. Donna appeared understanding, but I could tell by her attitude that all was in vain. A press release had already been given about the closing, making it almost impossible to reverse the present course. Nothing happened after the parent's meeting. If they spoke against the decision, they would be held libel. I didn't know what to do. I was not moved to speak out. I thought the parents would follow a nun, but me . . . I wasn't so sure.

At school the next day, I just sat in a chair in the faculty room and cried. Doris, an older faculty member whom I loved and respected dearly said to me, "You really thought something would happen, didn't you?" I just looked at her and continued crying. Doris had been with the school for a long time. She was one of those dying breeds of gracious ladies who maintained her dignity throughout the ordeal though she probably suffered the most. Doris had wanted the school to be a training ground for women leaders. I think she saw me as one of the younger members who would carry on her work. And now to think it was ending this way.

Finally, when I accepted that it was over, I started writing a resume, but it wasn't really in my heart to do so. I thought about taking a year off. I did manage to get a brief resume out to schools, and later in the year I got the call from Catholic High saying that they were looking for a physics/math teacher. They were interested in talking to me. I called for an interview with the Queen of Swords, reversed, and she asked me to come right away. I had heard about her from some other faculty members, but I decided to remain objective and form my own opinions. We met that afternoon.

\*   \*   \*

How to describe my encounter with the Queen of Swords, reversed, the resident Wicked Witch of the South? My experiences with this woman were probably the deepest and most confusing I had had up to this point in my life. I'm still unsure about it. But this interaction caused me to change considerably. That I can say with certainly. I lost my naivete.

I arrived at the main office for my appointment with the Queen. She promptly came out and invited me to her office down the hall. She was of average height, slim with soft reddish-blonde hair. Her face reflected a sharp mind though her expressions sometimes hid or softened the thoughts within and there was something I didn't trust about the smile. She walked across the room displaying a light sensuality but having a definite sense of her capabilities. I found her rather attractive. Her clothes were stylish, not that "out of date" nun look. Friendly enough, she motioned that I sit in the chair in front of her then she left to get some files. I watched her. Both of us were a bit shy. We were respectful of the other's reputation in the diocese. Soon she came back into the room and stood behind the desk facing me. She spread her hands on either side of the desk with the fingernails barely touching the surface and started explaining the various curriculums to me. Then very quietly, she sat back in the reclined chair.

"There are two positions I think you might be interested in. One is an all-math position and the other is a combination of math/physics. The latter position is the one I had in mind for you. It involves a new program called COLT where the students only take two courses a semester but meet for two-hour sessions so they can complete a full year of credit. It is a highly individualized and concentrated approach. The students complete a series of Learning Activity Packets called LAPS."

"Are the LAPS already designed for this course?" I asked, concerned about my lack of experience in teaching physics.

"I think they are," she responded. "Yes."

"Then I'm definitely interested."

"I thought you would be, given your success with the individualized science program you designed at St. Francis."

"If the LAPS are done, I could easily pick up the physics since I have already taught chemistry and junior high physics."

"Good," she responded.

Up to this point, the conversation was going quite well, I thought. She went on to explain the program in more detail. Then I thought about Sarah who also needed a job. If I took the math/physics position, that left the math position a possibility for her. Knowing that the diocese was to give our teachers preference, I thought Sarah was a shoo-in. "I'm definitely interested in the math/physics position. There is another math teacher from St. Francis who was still looking for a job. Are you interested in speaking with her?" I asked.

"Really? Yes, give me her name and phone number," she responded handing me a piece of paper. I wrote Sarah's number, and she called right then and there and made an appointment with her. But something bothered me. Her response was too quick and too pleasing. Obviously, she knew I would be happy if she considered Sarah for the other job. For some reason, I felt she wanted me to accept her job right away. I couldn't imagine why.

I asked a few more questions and then we discussed my teaching load and the pay scale. "You will get credit for five of your years of experience. I feel badly that we can't offer you more money. Let me make an appointment with Fr. Donald, the principal, and you can discuss money with him. Also here are the name and number of the current physics teacher, Jean, whom I think will be helpful to you."

I left thinking everything was set. Both Sarah and I would have jobs for next year. As the math position involved teaching students of lesser ability, Sarah's strength and preference, I felt for sure she would get the job.

Boy was I wrong! Sarah had her interview also that afternoon and came back with bad feelings about it. The Queen was short with her and gave the impression that the position had already been filled. Contrary to the impression she gave me. Sarah felt that the interview was just a matter of formality. The "don't call us, we'll call you" kind.

I was confused and upset. I felt bad for Sarah. She had always been given a raw deal by the diocese although I considered her the better teacher as she had rapport with students yet maintained control in the classroom. This balance was something I had to work at. I was such an idealist and thought learning was special, not something you had to fight to get across. Sarah knew how to get to the students. While I taught subject matter, she taught kids. Sarah began her teaching career in a tough inner-city, Catholic grammar school run by the same order of nuns that ran St. Francis. By the time Sarah got to the school, most of the nuns had left for more prestigious jobs. She shared the seventh and eighth grade with Sr. Joan who was from another order of nuns. It was not an easy place to teach at. A lot of pressures. One day, Sarah found the principal washing her office cabinets with a sponge that she was dipping into a pail without water! Sr. Joan and Sarah tried to get her help, but the higher ups wouldn't listen. The school was experiencing financial difficulty, and the priest in charge (there is always a priest in charge!) was pushing to close the school. He convinced Sr. Joan and Sarah to support him. He told them that it was in the best interest of the students. Reluctantly and painfully, they gave their support seeing how ineffectual they were with the principal issue. In the end, it was Sr. Joan and Sarah who got screwed! The priest reversed his decision and kept the school open with one change. He eliminated the upper two grades which meant that only Sr. Joan and Sarah lost their jobs.

I was not wild about the methods of the diocese. An understatement actually! But I decided to remain open-minded. I went for my appointment with Fr. Donald the next day. It was a formality type meeting as I had already been hired in the eyes of the Queen. Fr. Donald was a half-hour late. I watched him whiz by me as he rushed into his office. He noticed me out of the corner of his eye but didn't say anything. Shortly, he came out and gave me a copy of the contract to read, which I did, most thoroughly. Thank God! About forty-five minutes later, I was called into his office.

We talked very little. He was pleasant but rather busy. "So, what do you think about faculty loyalty in terms of students?" he asked.

"Well, if you're asking me whether I would discuss a faculty member with a student, no I wouldn't. I would consider that highly unprofessional."

"What about loyalty to the school?"

"Well, I believe in loyalty, but I would never do anything I felt was in opposition to my conscience."

"Oh, no, I would never expect that you would do anything against your conscience, "he replied. Then we got on to the subject of money. Salary was dependent on a series of salary steps based on the years of teaching experience.

"Well, I think I'll put you on step two," he said.

"Father, I think I belong on step five as I have six years' experience." I felt justified in my response having just read the contract.

"Step five? No one comes in on step five!"

"But it says in the contract a teacher can maintain five years of teaching credit when entering the diocese."

He was a little startled since he had forgotten that he had just given me the contract to read as a means of keeping me busy.

"I'll have to call the diocesan office before making any definite agreement with you. I'll call you tomorrow," he said. I left thinking my boldness had probably just lost me the job. Spaced, I drove over to Adele's to talk about what I had done. Adele commended me on my courageous spirit and agreed that I had every right to the money. I could always rely on Adele. She had a similar spunky spirit. I can still picture the scene the day Adele got up and whacked this big, over-sized businessman who was sitting next to her at Friendly's. Rather obnoxiously, he had pushed his dirty dishes in front of her and began blowing cigar smoke into her face. Adele said nothing, but rather just acted. The poor fellow was in too much shock to do anything. Here was this small five-foot tall young woman, who was by no means in a calm mood, slapping him on the back with her pocketbook. We laugh about it, now but it could have been a dangerous situation for her had he retaliated.

"D, you have every right to the money you deserve. Don't let them bully you!"

I left Adele's with a renewed sense of courage and called Fr. Donald the next day. I asked him what he had found out.

"Oh yes, Dorothy, step two," he responded.

There was a pause on my part and then I said, "I can't accept that, Father."

"You can't?" he questioned, rather surprised at my remark.

"No. How can I accept that when I read in the contract that I was allowed five years of teaching experience?" Another pause.

"Oh . . . I'll call the diocesan office and call you right back." He did so and said, "Dorothy, you were right about the contract. The diocesan office agreed, and so you will start on step five."

I hung up the phone and screamed with delight! I was so pleased that I had held out and didn't compromise. I also realized that he never had any intentions of calling the diocesan office to discuss my salary. He just thought I would give in. You've got to watch these guys!

Later in the week, I picked up my teaching books to start preparing for classes. I called Jean, the physics teacher, to ask if we could meet so that I could get an idea of the available equipment and resources. Her response was rather cool on the phone. She was busy playing a lot of golf, but added, "I guess I could fit in a short meeting with you." After the Queen's assurance of her helpfulness, I was surprised at her reaction.

We met. Jean came across as a rather nervous, quick-moving individual. Very intelligent and efficient.

"I've been with this school long enough that they can't get away with anything on me," she said. A weird comment, but her whole manner was abrupt and scientific. She opened all the closets and drawers to show me where everything was kept. But she wasn't going out of her way to help me. I got the distinct impression that this lab was her domain, and I could use it, but I'd better know that it was her domain.

After she finished dashing here and there, I said, "I'm really glad to be working with you. I know a professor over at the College who is impressed with you and the things you do in your classes." She paused and looked at me.

"Really? Who?"

I named the professor, and we got to talking about the College. I confided my insecurities about teaching physics. She assured me that I could do it. We started talking on a whole different level and her attitude towards me changed drastically. I think she kind of felt sorry for me. Then I learned that Jean was not in favor of teaching physics in a COLT curriculum, but COLT happened to be the Queen's baby. I would be getting the cream of the crop as the Queen had convinced the top students to take COLT. Ironically, I was to have the elite students, though Jean was the more experienced teacher.

From that moment on, Jean and I got along very well. Kindred spirits, scientists with a humanitarian leaning, we both enjoyed reading similar type books. Thought she initially considered me the enemy she could not continue her cold attitude toward me. She grew to like me, and I, her. Later, she became one of the few people I could trust.

A year after I had left the diocesan school, I returned for a visit. By this time, I was blacklisted and not welcomed there anymore, but Jean was glad to see me. I ran behind the bushes and knocked on her classroom window. Jean sneaked me in. She couldn't get over my new attire. By this time, I had given up dresses and heels and was wearing army fatigues. A red, white, and blue scarf covered my head. She told me she had seen a film that summer about two gay women.

"You could have easily played the dike in the film!" she exclaimed.

"Yes, Jean, if I were a little taller."

Thank God for Jean. I learned the first week of school from the head of the science department that there were no ready-made LAPS for the physics course. Panic! What would I do now? Sarah said I should have gone in and questioned the Queen, but I decided to be the good little teacher and designed a LAP which I brought to the Queen and said, "I learned that there are no LAPS for physics but I developed this format. Is it all right with you?"

Slightly shocked and embarrassed, she responded favorably as she quickly glanced over the LAP. "Oh yes, it looks fine. I had no idea they weren't already developed." How could she not know the LAPS were not done? She was the academic dean. I let it go. We were both playing a game. Neither wanted to cause friction at this point. This was a big mistake on my part. Sarah was right. I should have demanded an explanation. I didn't. I guess I figured the Queen could never get on my back for not being the world's best physics teacher.

Swiftly, I involved myself in mainstream activities of the school. I became the advisor to the cheerleaders and started working on establishing a faculty committee. I discovered that a lack of communication existed between the administration and the faculty, causing some bad feelings. I served as faculty committee chairperson at my previous job, so I felt confident in presenting my ideas for such a committee. The faculty welcomed my suggestion and voted favorably on the proposal. Though I looked young, I had taught enough years to feel confident expressing my ideas at faculty meetings and was not afraid to address any topic. St. Francis had always appreciated my independent spirit. I moved from a source of strength that many of these faculty members did not possess. I did not fear losing my job. I felt that if you couldn't express personal truth in a job, the job wasn't worth having anyway.

I was super busy preparing three different math classes, setting up lab classes, and trying to stay at least two chapters ahead of the physics class. The school was overcrowded, but parents wanted to keep their kids out of the inner-city public schools which had large black populations. These parents were prejudiced. You could count the number of black students on one hand at Catholic High. As a matter of fact, most of the black students were girls from the St. Francis. This was probably the reason I was hired so quickly. The administration needed someone to help these girls transition into this different environment.

My classes were large. Algebra-in-two years (I had the second half) had close to forty students in it! That was a challenge. The abilities covered a wide range. I had ten boys who had flunked the first part, so I was constantly working privately with them while keeping the rest of the class at a normal pace. It was nuts! The students knew I wasn't experienced in teaching such low-level classes and gave me a hard time whenever they could. I think such behavior is a pride issue. Here you are the smart teacher who can whip off concepts that students find difficult, so they let you know that there are things they can do better than you. I tried to be patient, even kidded at times, and on some level, they liked me though they had a weird way of showing it. I was cool according to their standards, which was based a lot on the way I dressed. But some days, they drove me to the limit. I would scream at them which had the effect of upsetting me more than them. Even though it settled them down for a while, since they weren't used to hearing me scream, it didn't last long. Maybe it just wasn't worth teaching them what we were trying to teach. One doesn't need algebra to get through life.

I also taught a low-level Algebra, part 1. Another large group of mostly freshman boys. A real treat! They were just starting to feel their oats and thought they were cute. And why not? Their Italian mothers had been telling them that all their lives. That attitude is hard to deal with in a classroom. Many came from broken homes and continued their family struggles in the classroom. I became a substitute mother. And society thinks teachers are overpaid! No concept of what a teacher puts up with! It's not a 9-5 job. During the school term, all I would do is prepare for classes. Teachers deserve every penny they get. And sometimes they even manage to get the material across and feel good about themselves.

There's always the one redeeming student who keeps your spirit going. I had one girl who did exceptionally well in my Algebra part 1 class. In fact, she did so well that I wondered why she wasn't registered for a full year of algebra. I checked with her guidance counselor. The girl had tested low, but in her file was a note from her previous teacher suggesting that she be placed in a higher math class regardless of her test scores because she was an overachiever. Obviously, no one had bothered to read the note. I questioned the Queen about the situation. She blamed the old principal for the summer slip-up. I asked about the possibility of working with her after school to catch her up so that she could go on to Algebra 2 the following year. The Queen agreed to let me try. She and two other girls met with me during free periods and after school. The original girl did well enough on the final test to go ahead the next year.

One day I went into the Queen's office to ask how I was doing. I wanted to keep the lines of communication open between us.

"Is there anything I should be doing differently or are you happy with my work?" I asked. I could tell by her look that she was a little shocked that I had taken the initiative to see her, but I wanted to know where I stood with her.

"You're doing fine. But there is one thing."

"What's that?" I asked.

"Some faculty members have spoken to me about how hard it is to get close to you. It is obvious that you and Wolf had been friends before coming to Catholic High. These faculty members feel left out."

"That's interesting. I thought I was friendly to everyone. I appreciate your honesty." I was a little surprised to learn this. Wolf and I were good friends and did talk together often, but I didn't think we made others feel left out. We had been instrumental in organizing a faculty luncheon on St. Patrick's Day. Later, I thought how strange it was for grown faculty members to go to an Academic Dean about such an issue rather than just telling us.

One afternoon the Queen accompanied Wolf and me to lunch. The Queen had drunk a little too much and was free with her thoughts. We learned how she felt about Fr. Donald in no uncertain terms. She was not impressed with him at all. I was surprised at her breaking confidence. Maybe this was why Fr. Donald asked me about faculty loyalty during my initial interview?

The Queen came into my Algebra Part 1 class for a teacher evaluation one afternoon, just about twenty minutes before class was over. It was the worse time to come. By this time, the students get fidgety. I had given a quiz the day before, and half of the class flunked it, so I had divided the class into two groups. I had gone over the quiz with the half who had flunked and gave some advanced work to the other group. When she walked in, I had just finished going over the quiz and had asked this group to do some additional work before retaking the quiz. The successful group had finished their work by this time and wanted harder material, so I gave them some, but I hadn't gone over this material yet. I asked them to try and reason it out themselves. Well, they were confused as I knew they would be, and they kept trying to get my attention while I was concerned with catching the lower half up. The Queen walked in just as I was trying to satisfy all these different needs in the best way I could. Freshmen are not very patient students. Her evaluation was not good. She spoke of confusion in the classroom, but never gave me credit for attempting to meet the needs of the different groups. If she had asked before coming in, I could have explained what I was trying to do. And if she came in from the beginning, she would have gotten a better idea of what I could successfully accomplish in one class period.

I was upset over this evaluation but signed it after she reassured me that she would return to this class for a second evaluation. Sarah warned me about signing it. It didn't give an overall view of the class. Again, she was right.

Well, between going to basketball games every Tuesday and Friday night and sometimes a third night for a make-up game, riding the bus with the cheerleaders, doing physics LAPS, getting labs ready and preparing for three math classes, I was pretty strung out. I still hadn't gotten over the emotional upset of St. Francis closing. For whatever reason, I came down with mono that December. I was very sick and had to stay home for three weeks. For this disease, it was not a long time to stay home. I hated missing class time since it's hard on the students to have a substitute so I returned as soon as I could and slept between classes in the nurse's room. Just teaching one class would really tire me out.

That was the beginning of the end. One of the other math teachers had agreed to teaching two COLT math classes in the same time block. They were not easy subjects either—Math IV and Calculus! One of these courses by itself is a hand full. Two in one-time block is an absurdity! The parents complained, and the school had to do something to correct the problem. Guess who was chosen? The Queen called me to her office and asked if I could help with the Math IV class. I didn't know what to say. I was still weak from the mono and falling in bed around 7:00 pm nightly, but I took the book and told her I would look it over and get back to her. Teaching Math IV was appealing, but I knew it would require a lot of preparation, and I wasn't sure I was physically up for it. I knew I would treat it like all of my other classes and feel responsible for it. It wasn't fair to the students if I was too tired to keep up the pace. Sarah and I talked about it. I always felt guilty about saying no. Sarah made me realize that I had no reason to feel guilty. It was an administrative mistake to allow one teacher to take on such a responsibility. It was their problem to solve. Not mine.

After much thought and personal struggle, I went to see the Queen.

"I'm sorry, but I don't feel well enough to take on this added responsibility."

"I understand," she said. "I'll do the class myself."

I felt relieved and thought the matter was a closed book. Wrong. The next day the head of the math department, Sr. Ignatius, who was a personal friend of the Queen came to see me. "The Queen is over-burdened. Would you consider teaching the Math IV if I take away one of your other math classes?"

Added pressure. Now what was I to do? I felt terrible about walking out on one of my own classes. How could I leave them so late in the year? What would that say to these kids? "You're not as important as the Math IV class?"

"I'll think it over," I responded to Sr. Ignatius. I was a nervous wreck. It was obvious that I was in no physical shape to do this class. Sarah pointed that out to me in no uncertain terms. The next day I went to see the Queen. I restated my position. "I would love to help you out, but I just don't feel well enough at this time."

"No problem," she said.

Later in the day I went to see Sr. Ignatius and repeated my position to her.

"The Queen already told me that your doctor said you shouldn't do it," she said to me.

"The doctor?" I repeated sarcastically. "It wasn't the doctor! It was my decision." I thought, 'How did the doctor get involved'? For some reason, this upset me, and I went back to see the Queen.

"Why did you tell Sr. Ignatius that my doctor told me not to do the class. I never called the doctor. I thought I made it very clear as to the reason I was refusing to take on this class."

"I never told Sr. Ignatius that the doctor said you couldn't do the class," she retorted.

"What?" I responded in a riled tone since someone was not telling the truth.

"I didn't say that," she repeated.

"Then why did she tell me you did?"

"Are you calling me a liar?" she asked.

"Well, you lied to me before about the LAPS being done," I said, looking her right in the eyes. My voice reflected a power that I didn't usually use with her.

"But I thought they were done."

"How could you now not know for sure? You are the academic dean," I shouted.

She looked meekly at me, but I continued. "Also, you never came back to do a second evaluation of my classroom as you assured me you would." She cowered now and got this frightened look on her face. I knew she was at the point of tears.

"You don't realize the pressure of this job. I'm overworked!"

This caused me to back down, and quietly, I said, "I just don't like dishonesty. I tried to be supportive and up front with you all year." I added a few other comments and left.

We managed to maintain a working relationship for the rest of the year, but it was strained. Something had changed. A line had been crossed. I had crossed it. She was nice to me and always smiled at me, but I knew it wasn't real. I kept my distance. Only thirty years old, I was idealistic and demanded high standards from myself and those around me. Looking back as a fifty-year-old woman, I would say that at that time I was a zealot and impatient to a fault. I also see that although the Queen didn't always do what I considered was correct, she was probably doing the best she could have given her own set of pressures and goals. I realize now that I too have become a Queen of Swords. Back then I was looking at a potential part of myself.

Another incident occurred during the school year that bears telling. Fr. O'Malley replaced Fr. Donald in the middle of the year. I wasn't surprised, given the Queen's low image of Fr. Donald. Fr. O'Malley called me in to his office to discuss next year's teaching load. He asked if I would teach chemistry. I agreed, but asked to be relieved of the cheerleading responsibility, since I would require additional preparation time. He agreed.

"Is there anything else that you would like to discuss with me?" he asked.

"There is one issue I am concerned about."

"What's that?" he asked.

"The status of the girls in this school. I feel like they get short changed when it comes to their sports. There is always a lengthy announcement about the results of the boys' games, but many times nothing is said about the girls' games. How do you think that makes them feel about the importance of their sports? Also, the boys have a rather loose dress code compared to the girls. The boys are required to wear a tie and jacket of any material or color. Many get away with wearing corduroy jeans. Contrary, the girls must wear one specific color. The material of their vest and skirt is also specific. Blouse colors are limited. I feel this is not fair. What is this saying to the girls? Why is their freedom more restricted? In a Christian sense of justice, there should not be such a discrepancy. What does this do to the self-concept of the girls? We have a responsibility to that development as educators."

He listened to what I had to say, but I could tell he wasn't impressed and said, "I think you are making too much of a deal out of these topics."

"I don't think so," I responded.

Later, at one of our faculty meetings, Fr. O'Malley asked if there was anything else anyone wanted to bring up for consideration. I got up and repeated what I had said to him about the girls' sports and dress code. Surprisingly, some of the other faculty members rose and voiced support for my concerns. Some were male faculty. Confronted with a faculty that was at least half, if not more, women,

Fr. O'Malley changed his stance and suggested that a committee of parents, students, and teachers meet to correct the unequal situation.

It was now April, and I had been fired. In a match off between my good and bad, I felt my good tipped the scales and I felt justified in returning to Fr. O'Malley's office to pose a few questions to him.

"Father would you mind if I asked a few questions about my being laid off?"

"No, of course not," he responded trying to be so understanding.

"First, I'd like to know why I was the math teacher chosen to be dismissed."

"Well, you were the newest member of the department."

"That's not true Father. Ben was also a new member of the department and a first-year teacher compared to me with my six years of experience."

"I'm not exactly sure why he was not chosen. I'll have to check," he responded. I thought to myself, I know why he wasn't chosen, he's co-coach of the football team.

"Second, if there were to be fewer science courses next year, why wasn't I given a full math position?"

"I didn't think you had enough credits to teach math," he came back rather quickly.

"Not enough credits! I'm a full math major. I presently teach three math classes, and if anything, my science credits would be in question, though my experience would outweigh that. I taught science for six years, and I took graduate level courses . . ." Thinking to myself when did a Catholic school care whether one was qualified or not?

"Oh, I wasn't aware of that," he said.

"Besides, Ben isn't a math major. He's a business major, teaching math. If anyone should be let go for lack of credentials, it should be he."

As a rebuttal, he said, "The Queen told me you didn't feel academically capable of teaching the Math IV class." Fire filled my being and with strength in my voice,

I said, "I didn't tell her that. What I did say was that I could have done it academically, but physically I didn't feel up to it. I had just returned from having mono, and I couldn't say up late to do the necessary preparations. One does not just walk into a classroom cold!"

"Oh," he responded. Embarrassed, he didn't know what to say. My questions were good ones. He was treading on weak ice and cracks were forming.

"You've brought up some issues that I was not aware of. Let me look into it, and I'll get back to you with answers. Remember, I came in at the middle of the year."

"Yes, I know that," I said, thinking, 'So, who directed you?' "That would be fine." I left his office.

Two weeks later, he called me back into his office. By this time the other laid-off teachers had gotten lawyers and were starting legal procedures. He motioned for me to sit down and said, "Dorothy, I owe you an apology. You were right. I looked up the contracts and yours was signed before Ben's. Your credentials as a math major are excellent, more than enough credits. I was proceeding on information supplied to me and assumed it was correct. I would like to offer you your job back. Ben should be let go, and I have informed him already."

I was choked up. I felt for this man. It took a lot of courage for him to admit those things to me. I thanked him and said, "I just couldn't understand how the decision was made, and that's why I questioned you. For me, it was a matter of justice."

"I'm glad you did so. I want you to be on my faculty."

"Thank you. It was never my intention that Ben get fired, so I have to think about the offer."

"I understand your concern, but you have every right to the position, and Ben's fate should not be considered in your decision." In the Christian sense, I felt that this was a weird statement coming from a priest.

I got up and hugged him, and he hugged me back. There was a good feeling between us. I left, feeling victorious for me, but terrible for Ben. Later that day, I talked with Ben. He expressed no animosity and felt I should take my job back.

"I'm not sure I can do that," I said. As it turned out, a position teaching religion opened, and Ben got it. Credits were not a concern when football was primary!

I was on a high for a while, and then I started reviewing his response that he had relied on someone else's information. Whose? Who else could it be? It had to be the Queen. How could a new principal make such a decision without consulting the academic dean? I couldn't work there thinking such an exchange must have taken place. I was out of my mind at this point and boldly I went back to Fr. O'Malley the next day and said, "I want my job back, but I also want to know if it was the Queen who gave you the misleading information. If it was, I can't work for her."

He got very indignant and jumped out of his seat. "You don't have any right to ask such a question."

"I have every right if it was about me and my work situation."

"I'm not going to answer you. If you have a problem with the Queen, take it up with her."

"I will. But I don't want to accuse her if it's not true. I thought you could erase my suspicions."

"I consider this conversation over," he said as he got up and opened the door. "I corrected the wrong, and that is enough."

I was so mad when I left that office. I wanted a meeting with Fr. O'Malley, the Queen, Sr. Ignatius, and Fr. Harold, the head of the diocesan office. But I backed down. I didn't have the heart to put her in such a position, and I wasn't sure it wouldn't backfire on me. I was minor in the line of the tradition I would be attacking.

Instead, I went immediately to the Queen's office and confronted her with my suspicions. I can't believe the balls I had at this time in my life. I was afraid of no one and stopped at nothing. I was obnoxious.

"Was it you who told Fr. O'Malley that I was the newest member of the math faculty, that I didn't have sufficient math credits, and that I didn't feel academically capable of teaching Math IV?"

"No! It wasn't and Fr. O'Malley did not consult with me about who to fire."

"Then who did he consult with if it wasn't you?"

"I don't know, and furthermore, I'm fed up with you and your attitude! Every time you come into my office, it's to complain about something. You are so negative!"

She hit a weak spot, and quietly I responded, "I don't think that's exactly true. I've come into your office to discuss other matters. I sometimes come in for your help since I am new here." I felt drained. My energy level was low. She was smarter than I, more experienced than I, and knew how to hurt. She continued about her opinion of me, which wasn't very good at this point. When she was finished, I said, "I feel badly that you think of me as so negative. I don't think I'm negative in the classroom."

"No, not in the classroom, but everywhere else!" I thought it best that I leave and said, "I'm sorry I accused you of conspiring against me." I left, dejected. She was one up on me this time.

I knew I could never go back, not after all that had happened during the year. Fr. O'Malley's hesitation about not giving me the full math position indicated that my status had changed. My opinions would be ignored from here on in. That's if I even had the nerve to voice them. And I didn't want to be in a place where I couldn't be myself. Besides, I didn't know whom I could trust anymore. I couldn't exist like that. All the fight and spirit were drained from me. And that's not the way I wanted to be.

*       *       *

The closing of St. Francis and, more importantly, the firing caused
me to re-examine my life. I had been unhappy about my relationship
with Sarah for some time, but now I was taking steps to break it.
Frequently, I would go off on my own seeking independence.

I was thin. The thinnest I had ever been, even thinner than my
younger sister and that was a first. The mono had been responsible
for much of the weight loss as was the firing experience. I thought
nothing of going to Boston and buying thirty-dollar blouses. A lot
of money in the late 70's. I had shoes to compliment every outfit
of matching skirt, jacket and scarf. I was at the height of physical
confidence, though my academic confidence was wavering.

Independence. What a joke! One weekend I decided to go to the
Cape. I was living in the Hartford area and the Cape was about a
five- or six-hour ride. I got in my car and headed down the Wilbur
Cross Highway. While driving, I started thinking, what happens
if I get there and I feel depressed and there is no one to talk to?
Maybe I shouldn't go so far, the first time. I was only twenty-
nine and it was the worst year of my life. I was coming to grips
with a lot of myself. It wasn't easy. I needed to talk about things.
Constantly.

When I got to New Haven, I decided to get a motel. New Haven
of all places! So close to my hometown. If I got desperate, there were
plenty of people I could call. Some independence!

I just lay on the bed for a while and then started laughing
hysterically. I thought, 'Dorothy, here you are, Ms. Independence. In
your own room. Are you having a wonderful time?' Of course, I was
bored to death and lonely. I dressed and went to a popular restaurant
in the city. I sat at the bar and ordered a glass of wine. I was thinking
about Sarah.

The bartender came over to me and said, "It can't be that bad." I
just smiled. It was that bad.

Two well-dressed men came into the restaurant and sat next to
me. One was a little older and rather attractive. The younger man and
I exchanged glances. The two men started playing cards. I looked over
the younger man's shoulders to view his cards. He held them lower
so I could see better. He motioned for my opinion. When he followed
my suggestions, he won.

"You're a good luck charm," he said as he scooped up the other
man's money. He kept refilling my wine. I was getting drunk. The
younger man was looking very good to me, but I wasn't into having

a *ménage à trois*. The younger man, a doctor, got a buzz from his beeper.

"Emergency call." He frowned. Then he turned to me and whispered, "I have to leave, but I will be back later if you want to wait." To my relief, they both left. I finished my drink and called Wolf. I decided to be honest with her. I thought if I told her I loved her, the obsession would go away, and I would be free to love someone else. My feelings for Wolf always tainted my feelings for Sarah and Sarah knew it.

One night when a few friends were at our house, Sarah announced, "Dorothy really loves Wolf. I'm just the second choice." I was stunned. I had to run out. I grabbed my drink and flew out the apartment door. Wolf followed and jumped into my VW just as I was pulling out of the parking lot. I cried. She was kind to me and said, "I never knew."

"I didn't think you were ready to know."

"I was ready."

Wolf answered the phone. "Can you meet me?" I asked.

"I have a dinner date, but I can meet you later at the gay bar."

I hated being in the room alone, so I left early for the gay bar. It was too early for the downstairs women's bar to open, so I sat upstairs at the men's and had another drink. I was the only genetic woman at the bar. I felt strange. The man next to me was alone and he started talking to me.

"I feel funny being the only woman here," I confided.

He shrugged his shoulders as if to say, "Don't worry about it."

"I'm waiting for a woman friend."

"Your lover?" he asked.

"No, not exactly. I do love her, but she's with someone else. I figure if I tell her, it will free me." I was amazed that he understood. He told me about his life.

"I loved a man who didn't love me, too. I don't usually tell people. You know the fear of rejection thing. It's hard keeping such an important part of one's life so secret."

"Yes, so many secrets," I repeated. Even when Wolf got involved in her first gay relationship, she didn't tell Sarah or me, and we were best of friends.

The man had been a teacher who left his profession. "I liked my job enough," he said. "But one day I was in a faculty meeting and realized that someone could fall over dead and no one would notice. It was the height of boredom. I liked the teaching but couldn't stand the other stuff."

I told him about my teaching experience. I enjoyed speaking to the opposite sex and not worrying about sexual hassles.

Wolf arrived much, much later in the night. Too late. I was in no shape for a serious conversation. Everything came out distorted. We went downstairs to the women's bar. Wolf was stone sober, and I was polluted. This was not a good combination. I was crying before I started talking. Wine makes for a depressive drunk.

Awkwardly, I told her I loved her. It didn't come out the way I had planned.

"I love someone else," she replied.

"I know that. I don't expect anything to change. I just want to get it out of my system."

"Will this prevent you from loving someone else?"

"No."

Just then my male buddy came downstairs almost as if he sensed I needed relief. He joked with me. I introduced him to Wolf. She soon left and I went upstairs with him to dance. He held me close.

I managed to get back to my motel room though I am not sure how. I was sick all night. I kept getting up to vomit. At one point I was standing over the toilet next to the tub and next thing I knew I was on the floor. I must have passed out. I woke up with a terrible pain on my chin. I must have hit the tub edge as I fell. There was blood. I still have the scar.

The next morning, I felt like such a jerk. I wanted to see Wolf and explain that things were not as bad as they had sounded. I drove to her house, but this was a mistake. Two other women had spent the night, and Wolf couldn't talk. I sat at her kitchen table writing a letter to her on a brown paper bag.

After leaving her house, I returned to the motel, checked out, and went to my sister's house. I felt dumb not making it to the Cape, but she understood. It wasn't too long after that she took a motel room in New Haven to get away from a bad situation with her boyfriend.

Mar and I spent the day together. She listened to my woes from the night before and didn't judge. Sister bonding. Though we fought terribly when we were younger, now we were extremely close and understanding of one another. Mar knew everything about me. I once told her that I would never marry anyone unless I felt as comfortable with that person as I felt with her. We gave each other space and rarely made value judgements unless we were concerned about one another's safety. More importantly, we liked eating Chinese food together!

That night I decided to go to a play. A reading of a new play called

*Virginia* was scheduled for 8:00 pm at a local theater. It was about Virginia Woolf and Vita Sackville West. Right up my alley. I had read everything I could find about the Bloomsbury group. I left for the theatre, anticipating a quiet, thoughtful, relaxing night.

There weren't many people at the performance. Mostly singles. I took a seat in the middle of the right side. There was no scenery, only four chairs on the stage. Informally, the cast roamed in one by one. One actress dominated my attention. Of slight build, she was extremely attractive with beautiful dark hair brushed over an intensely colored scarf. She sat in the farthest seat to the right and faced in toward the other chairs. I was fascinated by her. Her movements were definite and intentional. Sensuously, she crossed her legs and slid down into the chair to gain more comfort. Periodically, she ran her hand through her long hair, or she would throw the scarf back over her shoulder. Detached but well aware of her beauty.

I kept my eyes on her the whole time. At one point, she turned and looked toward the audience. Our eyes met. It was a most unusual meeting. I felt my eyes pulsating with such intensity that for the endurance of the exchange nothing else existed in the space but our eyes. I was in a trance. There was a direct line of communication. I wondered if she felt the same, but not being able to stand it, I turned my eyes away and broke the spell.

The play began. She read the part of Vita. I wasn't surprised. The play was interesting but didn't really portray the true relationship between Virginia and Vita as I understood from all the books that I had read on the subject. Vita's part ended before the play was over and the actress walked off the stage. I was disappointed. I would never know if she had experienced the same intense resonance between our eyes.

At the end, the actors remained on stage to answer questions from the audience. I was stiff from sitting so I got up and stood in front of my seat. I couldn't believe what happened next. The Vita actress came into the theatre and stood right next to me. I was shaking. I complimented her on her reading. She thanked me and leaned over to say, "I don't agree with the way Vita was portrayed in this play."

"Neither do I," I responded. We talked about the relationship between these two characters, and I felt I was better read on the subject. She listened intently till another actor came over to her and said they were ready to leave. She walked out with him.

I still hadn't found out whether she felt the stage eye contact as I was too afraid to ask. How does one ask such a question? I wasn't even sure it was real. I hung around the theatre for a while and then left. I saw her again in the parking lot and asked if she needed a ride. It was an awkward, aggressive move. I don't know why I asked. She thanked me, but said she was all set.

The experience of this pulsating eye contact was not the last.

All of these experiences . . . St. Francis closing, admitting to Wolf that I loved her, falling out of love with Sarah, my interaction with the Queen of Swords, reversed, the firing and then meeting the weirdo . . . they were just too much for me. Me who didn't deal well with feelings to begin with! My head was swirling as I was telling Bear about everything. But I knew in some weird way she understood.

"Bear, how am I ever going to go back there?"

"I don't know, Dorothy. Maybe you won't." Just then Lady came back on the porch.

"Let's go. I'm ready," she said. It was obvious the Lady was in charge.

"Ok," Bear said as she grabbed my luggage and flung it on the back of her truck. "You're lucky. You just missed black fly and mud season. Consider it a blessing. You'll have to sit in the back since there's very little space in the front. Especially with all of Lady's stuff!"

"What stuff? That's for my art!" retorted Lady. I didn't want to get in the middle of their bickering, so I jumped on the back. It was a beautiful sunny day, and I didn't mind being in the elements. I really didn't know what to expect. Someone told me you had to canoe to get to Bear's community. But that turned out to be false. You could get there by crossing a lake, but there was also road access.

About three miles up the road, Bear turned off the main drag and onto a dirt road. A steep hill was ahead. Bear gunned it to prevent the small light truck from getting stuck in the mud. I was thrown back. I grabbed on to my bags and the side of the truck. The first hill was the worst. Further in, the road was rocky and primitive and surrounded by woods. It was so beautiful and peaceful. The road curved on and on for what seemed like miles, and I noticed a sign saying, "Caution, people and domestic animals ahead."

Finally, we stopped. We walked to an eight-sided house where Bear and Lady lived. It was simple but comfortable. The roof was white colored, and the sides were alternating wood panels of light and dark stain. One side was made up entirely of windows. Under the house in the crawl space, wood was stored for heating. There were a couple of lawn chairs in the front yard and white birch trees lined the back. The shape seemed to inherently emanate a sense of peace. It was reassuring to stand inside the structure and be able to view every side of the outdoor landscape by just turning around. The view was compelling. A lake sat in the distance through the tall trees, green leaves and blue sky. One could stand and look forever.

In the middle of the floor, comfortable chairs were positioned around the wood stove. Three single bedrooms with no doors lined the inside of the house opposite the windows. The ceiling was the best part. When you looked up, directly in the middle, you could see where the rafters met and were tied together. It was perfectly symmetrical. It was spiritual. It was hypnotic. I spaced out and stared up at the mystical focus for a long time.

Bear and Lady had been living here a whole year. The winter was cold, and since they had no electricity, running water, or indoor plumbing, I was impressed with their survival skills. The outhouse was enclosed only by a plastic covering.

This celibate community named Mandala was made up of three nuns, a priest, Lady and two young men. The foundress was a former Carmelite nun whom I shall call the Empress. She had been kicked out of her order for reasons unknown. The popular belief was that it had something to do with her desire to work among the local people rather than living a hermit life of prayer. The Empress believed that physical labor was good for the spirit and prayer accompanied hard work.

Mass was held daily at 7:00 am. Thursday was community night which meant supper followed by an intellectual discussion by the members. Saturday was workday. It was spent either yarding wood in preparation for the winter or building structures on the property. Every house was erected by the members of the community with the aid of volunteers. After work on Saturday, Mass was held, followed by a potluck supper. This meal was open to the people of the greater community at large. Sunday was a personal day. Other than that, the community seemed to have a rather loose structure.

Bear told me that I would like the Empress since we had a lot in common.

"You're both avid readers, and Doris Lessing is one of her favorite authors and I know she is one of yours." My interest heightened as I had just finished reading *Memoirs of a Survivor*. We sat by the wood stove sipping wine and exchanged news about common friends back in Connecticut. It was good to be with these friends. I forgot about all the hassles of the past year.

"We're in the process of clearing ground for a new building," relayed Bear.

"It's going to be a big barn for sheltering vehicles as well as a sleeping space for visitors. We are always swamped with visitors. Originally, this house was to be the visitor house till Lady and I moved in. The Empress and her house companion, the Hierophant, will be working on the barn site now. Do you want to go and meet them?"

"Yes, of course," I said. We walked out to where the two women were working. The Hierophant was standing rake in hand. The Empress was bent over pulling weed roots out of the ground. We approached, and I was the first to speak, "I hear you like Doris Lessing."

The Empress raised her head. Her hair was completely covered by a black French tam. She was wearing a loose white Chinese shirt with colored hand embroidery, baggy khaki cuffed pants and sneakers. She looked at me as she rose to a standing position. My mouth must have dropped open as she was the most beautiful woman I had ever seen. Her skin was soft and smooth, very fair colored with a rose tinge. Her face was round and her eyes, God her eyes, were large and deep set black. They penetrated. Her whole being was dream like. It exuded an invitation into a fairytale. Nothing was real from here on in. But I welcomed the journey. I could never say no to those eyes.

She didn't answer my question. She probably thought me bold or maybe she was just shy, but she did smile. I listened to her voice as she talked to Bear about the clearing job. It was quiet and soft with a slight Northern accent and remained perfectly in tune with the gentleness of her face.

Bear excused us as we had to arrange for sleeping accommodations.

Walking back toward the octagon house, I kept thinking of her face. It reminded me of a character from a Hesse novel. For some reason, I felt I had just met the female Goldmund, which would make me the female Narcissus. Or was it the other way around?

# Part Two

*The journey, the descent*

## The Empress

The Empress is the Earth Mother. A field of ripe wheat lies before her, sacred to the Egyptian goddess Isis; behind her is seen the stream of consciousness flowing between cypress trees, sacred to Venus. She wears a crown of twelve stars, each with six points, denoting dominion over the macrocosm. She typifies the productive, generative activities in the subconscious after it has been impregnated by seed ideas from the self-conscious. The subconscious has control over all the steps of development in the material world; therefore, the Empress represents the multiplicator of images.

(excerpts from *A Complete guide to the TAROT* by Eden Gray)

## The Hierophant

This master of sacred mysteries wears the triple crown of a Pope. The Hierophant represents traditional, orthodox teaching considered suitable to the Masses. He is ruling power of external religion. His preference is for the outer forms of religion, the ritual, the creed, the ceremony. The importance of social approval is strong as is his need to conform to society.

(excerpts from *A Complete guide to the TAROT*
by Eden Gray)

## The High Priestess

The High Priestess is the virgin daughter of the moon and wears on her head the symbol of a full moon, with a waxing and waning image of the moon on each side. She is the eternal feminine, sometimes called Isis or Artemis. She corresponds to all the virgin goddesses of the ancient world, even to Eve before her union with Adam. She is spiritual enlightenment, inner illumination. The High Priestess has the latent power to manifest. She is the link between the seen and unseen.

(excerpts from *A Complete guide to the TAROT*
by Eden Gray)

THE NEXT AFTERNOON I spent alone, lying on the wooden dock that jutted out from the lake cottage located at the bottom of a steep hill and shared by the Empress and the Hierophant. The dock was very unsteady with large breaks between sections. It took three jumps to reach the end where it was deep enough for diving. Huge rocks and makeshift carpentry had caused the disjointed path. Sitting at the edge of the dock, I could see the entire cottage. A large glassed door center room opened onto a patio deck that spanned the entire length of the house. A small raised peak of loft space sat on top. The bedrooms were to the left and a greenhouse to the right. Firewood, a canoe, and tools were stored beneath the patio decks. Though the house lacked color, the combination of weathered wood and glass framing the distinctive parts created an aura of rustic beauty.

To the right stood the home of the Hermit, the priest of the community. His house was small, mute red in color, and comfortably hidden among the tall trees. There was nothing overly distinct about it except that it was the only cottage with walk-in access to the lake. The lakeside brush had been cleared and beach sand had been brought in to fill the space. A huge rock straddled both the water and the land. The Hermit said morning Mass for the members of the community, but the rest of the time he remained in seclusion as much as possible. He kept busy chopping wood and working on his literary endeavors.

In between the two cottages sat another cottage whose owners were not connected to the community. The couple used the cottage on summer weekends, but the rest of the time it remained vacant. Its secluded small dock and water hole made it the ideal spot for a private morning bath.

The lake setting calmed me, unlike the changeable ocean that I had grown up with. The water was quiet and peaceful, sometimes lacking any motion at all. Its surface resembled a reflective piece of glass and mirrored my thoughts.

Lydia, my former student from St. Francis, came to visit on the weekend. While the others worked, we spent the day by the lake playing together, floating on the canoe. That night we were guests in Bear's octagon house. Lydia slept in one of the tiny bedrooms while I settled on a cot positioned beneath the lake-side windows. When I looked up, I could see the stars. The black night surrounded me giving the impression that I was outdoors. I listened to the quiet. No cars, no furnace, no appliances, no neighbors. Just dead silence periodically broken by the song of loons. The mating call carried across the water. It was an eerie sound, this song of the subconscious.

I had little contact with the Empress till the morning I was to leave. She invited me to her house for breakfast. Humbled by all that she had accomplished, I felt uncomfortable in the presence of such a powerful and influential woman. Her lack of material concerns embarrassed me as I sat wearing my $30.00 designer shirt and tight jeans. She cooked and I answered her questions. She listened attentively and interrupted only once to compliment me on fighting the unjust administrative decision. I realized then that I had found a friend in her and began to relax. We talked a long time about me and then about her work. I asked, "Is there any way I could become a part of what you are doing? I have no plans for the summer, and I have saved enough money to support myself for a while."

She welcomed my offer and replied, "We are trying to start a new project in one of the larger cities in Maine. There is a woman, an ex-teacher like yourself, who wants to run a Hospitality House, a shelter for the homeless. My community is supportive of this project. She tried living here but decided woods living was not for her. Would you be interested, as she would love to have help? Once we find the right spot, it will involve getting the house physically in shape. It is to be a sleeping facility for the needy so it will involve cooking, cleaning and later some counseling."

"I'm very interested if you think I could be helpful," I responded.

"I'm sure you can be. There is a planning meeting next Wednesday night and you could meet the Artist and ask her questions to get a better idea about whether you want to work on the project."

"I have a wedding to go to this weekend back in Connecticut but I'm sure I could be back in time for the Wednesday meeting," I replied with anticipation.

And I was. In three days, I moved all my things out of the apartment, brought them to my mother's, and was on my way back to Maine. The experience was an ordeal, a physical hell! Sarah stayed out of the apartment the entire time, making it easier for both of us. She knew as well as I did that it was time for me to leave, but that did not make the goodbye any easier. We still cared about each other, maybe even loved each other, but not enough to continue trying to correct what was wrong between us. I had tried. For the last five years I had not been happy, but I had stayed hoping we could work it out.

Our first two years together were special. At that time, I could never imagine myself feeling any different for her. But then doubt crept in, maybe it was family pressure. I can't say for sure. Maybe I needed more tenderness than she could give, and I still wasn't sure about my choice of lifestyle. I was tired of living behind closed doors. We slept in a twin bed our entire relationship. The other twin bed was merely in the room to divert any suspicion. After all, we were teachers, and gayness was not well accepted in the profession.

The last year together, I started dating men and spending time with other female friends. I'm sure that hurt her. She didn't understand especially since I had been the one to instigate the relationship. We were traveling in Europe the summer before senior year. I had rushed out for her birthday celebration and bought wine and cheese and bread. That night I sat on the end of the bed and told her I loved her. She looked at me with a shocked look. It wasn't something that would have crossed her mind. She didn't say anything, and we acted like nothing had been said. I felt dumb but I was sure she felt the same for me or I never would have said anything.

Though she said nothing, she thought about it for months. Sarah always thinks before acting. Not a trait of mine. During senior year, we shared a dorm room. After a lot of nights of giving each other back rubs, I fell asleep one night in her bunk bed. It was still very innocent. The next night, I went to sleep crying. She asked what was wrong. I couldn't respond. She told me to come up into her bed. I did. She held me.

"What does love mean to you?" she asked.

"It means putting the other person before yourself." I guess that fit with her definition. She let me caress her, kiss her, and then make love to her.

That night she made a life-time commitment. I didn't. So, when I told her two years later, I wanted to end the relationship, she was not happy. She should have let me go. It might have saved whatever feelings I had for her. And who knows, I might have gone crawling back to her after experiencing life without her. Instead, she got violently upset. She gritted her teeth and fire came out of her eyes. I got scared, deeply scared for her. I felt I was in the presence of evil. A monster of my own creation stood in front of me. I feared she might kill me, so I lied. I told her that I didn't mean it, and I would never leave her. My words calmed her, but she was a smart woman. Later, my inconsistent behavior provoked her, and she threatened to tell my parents about us. I wasn't ready for this disclosure. I continued to stay with her. I still remember one day looking out the picture window at our bird feeder. I wasn't happy with my job. I wasn't happy with Sarah. I wanted out so bad from all of it. With deep angry

tears I looked at the sky and kept asking why. Was I really meant
to suffer so? Was there some reason for all of this? Right then and
there, I gave up my will. "All right. All right. I'll try. I'll stop fighting.
I'll take a new course. I'll try it your way. I'll try to be happy." And
believe it or not, it worked. I became involved with my work, and my
relationship with Sarah improved. It wasn't perfect, but it was better.
I felt successful in what I was doing. I felt good about my teaching
ability. I think I began to grow up that day. And things went ok till
St. Francis closed, till I got fired, till I met the Wicked Witch. Then it
was too much. I needed to get out. Sarah knew it, too. She no longer
gave me any opposition.

My things were packed. I waited for my brother to come with
his truck. I looked back into the apartment from the doorway and
couldn't stand the empty feeling I got from not seeing my things
in their usual places. I couldn't imagine how Sarah was going to
feel comfortable living here with all the gaps. But then maybe she
welcomed the void. Maybe the presence of my things and me brought
more pain. We hadn't been physically involved for some time.

Our possessions really do reflect who we are. As do our job, and
friends. They constitute our essence. We like to think of ourselves
as so independent. But are we really? It was so hard for me to shake
the concept of not being a teacher anymore. Come September who
would I be? It was a painful decision to give up teaching. It was a
growing decision.

It was the height of the gas shortage crisis and my brother called,
"D, I can't make it. I can't get gas."

"You have to make it. My things are all packed and in the hallway.
I can't stay here anymore. I'll go crazy!"

My desperate reaction moved him, and he said, "Don't worry,
Dorothy. I'll get gas somehow and be there in an hour." And he was.
He'll never know how much that meant to me.

It took all day, but I made it back to Maine just in time to board
the van going to the Hospitality House meeting. The Empress drove.
She was quite adept in maneuvering all sorts of vehicles: jeeps, dump
trucks, plows, motorcycles and snow mobiles! It was her favorite past
time besides fixing them and chain sawing wood. We stopped for
supper at Ma and Pa Kettle's. Having eight kids already in the family,
six more for supper wasn't a big deal. "Eat or forever hold your peace"
was their motto. Ma and Pa Kettle worked for the Co-op which was
run by the members of the community. The Co-op consisted of a
craft store where local artists sold their goods, a learning center, a
pottery kiln, a weaving, leather, and wood shop and offices for the

community members. Ma Kettle did social outreach work and was never home. Pa Kettle did paperwork and was always home. They had switched roles after moving up to Maine from the big city. Pa was an ex-principal who couldn't take the stress of bureaucracy anymore. Ma had been the stay-at-home housewife raising all the kids.

Ma Kettle welcomed us. We sat around a huge old mahogany tabletop balancing on two wine barrels. None of the chairs matched. Neither did the plates, glasses, cups, or silverware. The food was placed on the table, and everyone helped themselves.

I tried to be social but did little more than push the food around in the plate that Ma Kettle had made for me. I was exhausted from the day of driving and the move. This was the first chance I had time to think. I spaced out into my own world as the voices bellowed around me. I began to drown. I thought about all I had left behind and questioned what in God's name I was doing here. Depression seeped into me. I was sinking badly.

When I looked up, I caught the Empress looking at me. She sat directly across from me, and her eyes were focused deeply into mine. There was a mysterious shining energy emanating out of her. A spiritual kiss initiated me into secret communication with the mystical spell. Without physical contact, she seemed to reach inside me and grab my inner being. I had the sensation of being lifted. It lasted only a short while. When it stopped, she smiled at me and I smiled back.

Who was this person? Where was this power coming from? It reminded me of the eye exchange with the Vita character in the play. What was similar about these two women? Or was this different? I said nothing and neither did she. Nor did either of us say anything when we got back into the van though we were the first to do so. I was quiet the rest of the night. I was totally baffled, but tremendously intrigued.

That night I met the Artist and learned from the public meeting that starting the Hospitality House was not going to be easy. The Artist was trying to convince her church parish to allow her use of the vacant rectory for the shelter. The rectory was next door to the parish school and parents were leery of having "vagrants" in such proximity to their children. The Artist reminded the Christians "these vagrants include battered mothers, homeless fire victims, and those temporarily out of work."

"They could also be members of this parish," added a supportive priest. But the parish was not impressed.

"We are not opposed to a Hospitality House. We just don't want it in our backyard," declared one parishioner.

The Artist was a vibrant woman. I enjoyed trying to keep up with her vertiginous thoughts. Despite the overwhelmingly negative response of the community, she declared, "I feel confident the House will be a reality. We need a new approach and plenty of patience!"

We made plans to meet on Sunday. She had rented a studio room in an office building in the center of Bangor and suggested we both live there while doing the groundwork for the shelter.

"It's really an office space so there is no plumbing, but my mother's house is within walking distance. There is a small bathroom with a toilet at the end of the hall. If we are careful, we can get away with staying overnight."

I was concerned about the lack of creature comforts. It didn't faze her.

"Have much to do. See you on Sunday," she said as she whisked away and started mingling with the crowd. She had a comment for everyone she passed. I liked the Artist and felt our backgrounds would make us compatible comrades. I could learn a lot from her direct and confident manner.

On the return trip, we stopped to get Dunkin donuts to bring back to Ma and Pa Kettle's. There wasn't a Dunkin Donut shop where the Kettles lived, so this was a real treat for everyone. I was beginning to get a sense of how primitive and down to earth this group really was.

The next few days I took as personal ones since I would be losing the solitude of the woods shortly. The Empress suggested that I read a book entitled *Knowing Woman* by Castillejo, a Jungian analyst. It was my first introduction to Jungian theory, and I was fascinated with the new concepts of the anima, animus, shadow, and subconscious. Intuitively, I knew that this line of reasoning would open me to a whole new understanding of life. It was only the beginning. I was stepping out from the edge of the precipice.

The night before my journey to the city was difficult. I was apprehensive about returning to city living. What if there wasn't enough physical labor for me? What if the Artist and I didn't get along? We were two people who had never seen each other before the Wednesday meeting, and now we were planning to live together in one room! To relieve my own tensions, I wrote a letter to the Empress. In it, I explained how this was a bad time in my life. I told her about my failure with Sarah. I wanted her to be aware of where I was coming from. I wrote, "I am a hero worshipper, and you have become the new hero. In a Don Quixote fashion, I tend to follow idealistic causes without any sense of the realistic implications. I am on the horse before I have a sense of the destination. I apologize for my present state of confusion, but I will do my best." I left the letter in her mailbox knowing she would not read it till I was well on my way.

The next morning, I waited for the Artist at Pizza Hut and soon she drove into the parking lot on a motorbike.

"I'm trying to cut down on living expenses. The car was just too much maintenance," she responded to my unasked question.

She was a heavy woman, but her choice of clothing seemed to compliment her shape.

"Gotta go. I have some errands to run. Here are the two keys to the apartment. One will let you in the main entrance, and the other is for the office space. Can you get another set made? Can you do it today? Make yourself at home and move your luggage in. Take whatever space you need. I'll be home later tonight," And then she threw me a paper with the directions and raced off.

The studio was quite charming, as was the building. It was an old brick three story structure with fancily framed, huge, tall windows. Small shops occupied the first floor and a wide staircase led to studio. Across the hall from the studio was a bathroom shared with the other five offices. I quickly realized my roommate was not the best housekeeper. Paintings and sketches were tacked sloppily on the walls and an easel sat in the middle of the floor along with brushes, paints, dirty clothes and a water bucket. A canvas painting of three figures was in progress. A piece of 4 x 8 plywood jutting out from the middle of the wall constituted a makeshift wall providing some privacy to each sleeping area. In between the "bedrooms" was a table upon which sat a small refrigerator and one chair for sitting was pushed underneath. A big green sofa faced the TV.

I carried up all my belongings and arranged my section of the room. Exhausted, I fell into the green chair for a rest. Everything was so foreign. I felt like a child discovering a new part of her house, frightened while making the journey, but determined to go on. I lay in the chair for a long time and began to realize I felt very much alone. I hoped I could keep my sanity until the house was opened. It started to rain. Worse, it began to thunder. I couldn't enjoy watching the storm since the windows faced another building. I didn't like thunderstorms anyway. I shut the light off and went to bed.

I woke up, startled, thinking that the Artist had no key to get in. It was already 10:00 pm, and she had said she would be home at around 9:00 pm. I raced downstairs to see if she was standing outside. No one was there. I waited for a while but thought that maybe she had gone to her mother's. Twenty minutes later, I heard a loud knocking at the door. It was she and from her pleasant facial expression, I knew it was the first time she had tried to get in.

"Hope the cot is comfortable," she said. "It was the best I could do."

"It's fine."

"Thought the board would give us a little privacy."

"Yes. It's fine."

"Oh, I'm so tired. So much to do tomorrow. I have a meeting on the summer program. I'm running it. Let's see, I need lists to pass out, pencils . . . "

"Is there anything I can help you with?" I interrupted.

"Yes. You can help with some of the classes. We need people to relieve teachers and do lunch. Why don't you come to the meeting with me? It's at the rectory. You'll meet the love of my life."

"Who's that?"

"Father Thomas."

"A priest?"

"Oh, he doesn't know. I just have this wild crush on him. He's so intelligent and so good looking. I go to him when I'm really upset, crying. He's so understanding."

"Don't you think it's a bit of a dead end?"

"I know nothing will happen, but I can dream. Besides, I have too much to do to worry about that now."

"You confuse me."

"Good!"

"Good? What is that supposed to mean?"

"Goodnight." She yawned. "I've got to get some sleep."

We were both quiet from that point on, but my mind refused to rest. It seemed to be working double time. In the middle of the night I had an enlightenment. I wanted to scream but remained outwardly calm though my insides were swirling. It was my animus who had directed the writing of that depressing, self-critical letter to the Empress. In a moment of weakness, he had come through, true to form and had done a job on me. I was frightened about moving to the city and he had used this channel to scream out that he needed a creative physical outlet. My job had always encouraged my thinking function, but my sensation function was underdeveloped. This could be the reason I had trouble with my sexual nature. I could sleep with people I didn't love or sometimes didn't even know. I preferred it this way. My principles were strong in every other aspect but this one.

I thought about the Queen of Swords, reversed, and suddenly realized that she had the same problem. I identified with her and forgave her. I understood the motivating power. She, too, was a victim and I wanted to tell her that I loved her. A wave of relief overcame me. All the tension released. No longer was there a heavy weight on my head.

Since the Empress had indirectly been responsible for the awakening, I wanted to share my discovery with her. The next day after the school meeting, I drove down to the Co-op and asked the Empress if I could speak with her. We sat on the porch. I was nervous, but as I talked, I felt relief. She listened quietly and emphasized the need to pray constantly. Though I somewhat agreed, it was hard for such a physical person as me to accept such an answer. I wished it could be that simple, but it wasn't! She was certainly more spiritual than I could ever be! The discussion did not meet my expectations. She left. Everyone was busy, and I didn't feel like I belonged. I got in my car and drove back to the city though I had intended on staying the night. Rejection never set well with me.

On the ride back, I fantasized . . . *We drove to her favorite get-away spot by a small pool of water. She listened while I talked, and then without speaking, she removed all her clothes and went swimming. With her eyes, she bid me do the same. I waded over to her. She rested her head on my breast and I gently kissed her lips. No words were spoken, only the shared nakedness of two human beings. A gift more powerful than words . . .*

That night I wrote in my journal, "I want to learn to speak without words."

During our conversation, the Empress had suggested that we write a book together about relationships between women, as Castillejo had intended to do but died before having a chance to do so. Women tend to deal harshly with one another. Is it because we identify with each other and see our own faults in the women we are closest to? One of the reasons I had left Catholic High was so Wolf could become her own person there. I left Sarah so she could find the love she needed. In the beginning of our relationship I knew she needed to accept love from a woman, and I needed to give it. We had fulfilled each other's needs. And now something else was required. My own mother was unable to show physical affection. Was I trying to make up for this deficiency? Could I really expect other women to want to give of themselves in this way?

Rejection from women was always painful for me. Wolf says she doesn't love me, yet she pours her heart out to me. She shares her inner most thoughts, even those she doesn't tell her lover. One afternoon after a drinking bout, we were sitting on the couch, and she started pulling up my pant leg. Quite untimely, though, Sarah walked in and Wolf left without saying a word.

. . . My first female encounter was at age five. A nurse and her twelve-year-old daughter, Jean, lived on the first floor. Jean was going through puberty. Her mother worked so Jean was alone a lot. An elderly woman down the hall checked in periodically to make sure Jean was ok. I became Jean's playmate to the displeasure of my mother who must have sensed something was askew. There was such a big age difference.

Jean liked to go down to the basement, a God-awful place. The low dark ceilings were draped with spider webs. Pieces of the cement and rock walls crumbled onto the dirt floor. Storage rooms jutted off the long corridor which seemed to go back forever. One solitary light bulb hung in the middle.

"Help me find my mother's bin. She wants me to bring up a folding chair for the porch," she said as she roamed in and out of the tiny cave like rooms. I followed a few yards behind getting more and more anxious as we went deeper into the black.

"Jean, it's too dark. Let go back. I'm scared," I yelled to her as she got further and further ahead leaving me alone in the dim lit corridor. And then I added, "I'm going back."

"No. It's just up ahead. Come here. Maybe it's in here . . . " she said as she slipped into another storage hollow. I was too far in to turn back, I stopped before the doorway she had entered. Soon Jean emerged with this trance like stare on her face and said, "I'm from the mice people and I'm going to get you."

"Jean. Stop it. You're scaring me," I shouted. But it didn't stop Jean. She kept coming toward me, repeating her threat. I turned and run as fast as I could to the exit door. I ran all the way up to our apartment. But I never told my mother.

The next time I saw Jean, I ignored her, but she said it was only a game and I was such a baby for getting so scared. She convinced me to come and play again. I refused to go down to the cellar anymore.

Sometimes we would play in her room which was full of toys. One day she locked the door. Her mother was cooking in the kitchen. Jean turned on the radio and started dancing around the room, leaping from bureau to bed. She twirled a long silky scarf behind her like an Indian woman in a slave dance. As she moved in her frenzied ballet, she removed her clothing piece by piece till all she had was the scarf covering her bottom privates. I watched. Mesmerized. Apprehensive but interested. I uttered some resistance about her mother being in the other room, but she motioned that I remain silent.

Soon, exhausted from the acrobatic motion, she fell to the floor lying on her back with her legs wide open and knees raised exposing her young tender cunt. Her fingers held back the lips covering the entrance to her vagina.

"Look inside and tell me what you see," she said to me. I looked but didn't know how to describe what I saw.

"It's dark," I replied.

"Use the flashlight from the draw," she ordered. I did but soon her mother called for dinner and I was able to escape to our apartment upstairs.

The Artist left early the next morning, and I spent the day walking around town. The words of the Empress about "giving your love away" seemed ridiculous to me. I didn't know a soul in this city so how was I supposed to "give my love away!" Later, I went to Mass and found the Artist there. She was upset as one of her sisters had borrowed her moped and fell off.

"If things don't pick up, I'm not going to make it here," I said to her.

"You have to be patient!" she stated, and we got into a semi-argument.

"We need to plan this house out very carefully. And why are you over-reacting? What's bothering you?" For a reason of which I am not quite sure, I confessed that I was gay.

"Is that a problem for you?" she asked.

"No, only in terms of my family. They don't know." This was not the truth of the matter, but I felt awkward discussing my gayness. I realized my gayness didn't make any difference in the way she treated me. I felt comfortable again.

"You should take a painting course at the University," she said to me as we relaxed by the TV. "There is very little you can do till we get a house site. And there is a lot of legal work I still have to do. The course will be good for you."

We talked about art and literature, and when we finally went to bed, I was pleasantly tired.

On Wednesday, she suggested that we go to the beach and just get to know one another. She took me to a secluded area. We had to walk about a quarter of a mile through a dark forest before getting to the shore. Rotting trunks lay everywhere. Dew sparkled on the grass and leaves. When we came to the opening, we encountered a cliff jutting into the ocean. On the left was sand, and on the right, an inland cove.

Miles of rocks lined the shore front. No one else was at the secret swimming hole, and I felt gifted to be sharing in this fairyland.

We laid our towels down, keeping a fair distance between us. Reflectively, I asked, "Do you think they face their sexuality out at the community? I'm not sure what's going on out there. Maybe intuitively I know, but no one explains. I'm so tired of playing games."

"Isn't not playing games just another game?" she asked. I didn't answer, but I thought to myself, I don't want to be in another dishonest situation.

. . . *"You know, Dorothy, I still have sexual desires even at my age. It doesn't change. Don't let anyone tell you differently. There is a part of me that has remained the same despite the years."* When Doris shared this with me, I knew it was coming from the deepest part of her, a part she rarely exposed. I felt honored to be trusted with such a personal confession. A stately, proud woman, she rarely discussed sex. Everything she did in her life was done with a sense of purpose. Religion was kept alive through her. We didn't always agree. We hardly ever agreed.

"The radical," she called me. But she listened to me, and I listened to her. I wanted to grow old like her, gracefully. She watched me. Maybe she saw her younger self in me. I saw my older self in her. I saw myself carrying on her life's work of educating women for influential positions. After I left teaching, our relationship became strained. I don't think she understood anymore what was happening to me. I was in the flux of change, and our positions on worldly topics seemed more at odds. I couldn't understand her position on the boat people and welfare. She was from a generation of Americans who made it on their own and took pride in their material accomplishments. I didn't think that was enough anymore. We had lost too much. We had sacrificed inner peace, deeper meaning. She saw me as dropping out. I saw me as starting again, choosing a difficult path. I wanted the women I educated not to be concerned with the superficial. Maybe that's why the community was so attractive to me. Maybe that's why sex was not an issue for them. . . .

In our own way, we warn others as to who we are. A big caution sign flashes, "This is who I am. Please don't do anything to hurt me." The man who told me he hurt women and killed nine people was warning me: "Don't stay with me as I may do something I don't really want to. Protect yourself. I like you but I can't help myself." Then my letter to the Empress. I was warning her. Her looks confused me. What did she intend by them? My physical orientation would misinterpret her embracing spiritual orientation as a physical attraction. The explanation about the animus was my mind's way of circumventing true feelings. It shifted the blame.

Self-discovery was new for me. I wasn't very experienced yet. I was still innocent, unaware of my power to manipulate, to cause results. Knowledge gave sense to this unjust confusion of existence. Where pain is real. Where some can justify inflicting suffering. Where love, compassion, truth, sensitivity, mercy, gentleness, kindness are the lesser-understood forces.

I had my first conscious experience with self-discovery after St. Francis closed. Sr. Emmaus gave a weekend retreat for the entire faculty. It was to be a healing retreat, but for me it was just the beginning of the realization of anger. My anger. One of the elder nuns, a successful principal who suffered all her life with a crippling disease, got up and said, "This must be the will of God. No one really wanted this decision. We prayed, and the voice of God answered."

This was enough to make me jump out of my seat and scream at her, "What will of God?! It was a decision made by people on the Board of Trustees. People made that decision! And whose voice were they listening to? Maybe we hear the voice differently."

Poor woman. The decision was obviously terribly painful for her, but given the facts presented, she could see no other choice. She relied on the good faith of the more influential board members. If there had been anything in her power to do, she would have done it.

Sr. Emmaus diverted the discussion and focused on me. "You can learn more about the voice if you care to give some attention to it. It requires input. Are you interested?" I backed down, embarrassed at my vicious attack on a woman I respected. The anger took me by surprise. I had tapped into some flowing hot spring within myself. At the end of the meeting, Sr. Emmaus approached me and invited me on a personal retreat. I accepted.

In June I met her for the retreat. The place had been perfect. The center was on a semi-private road in a small town in the southern part of the state. The building had once served as a residence for women preparing to enter the convent. There were many furnished single bedrooms each with desk, lamp, and comfortable chair. Simple but sufficient. Behind the building was a garden lined with bushes. Beyond the bushes, spread a huge open field with rocks and distant forest.

My room was on the second floor. The chapel and kitchen were on the first. Sr. Emmaus and I met briefly that night. She gave me a bible and asked what I hoped to get out of our cessions.

"I want to explore the will of God versus the will of one's self,"

I answered. She nodded and said, "I see myself as the instrument, but the answers must come from you. I will suggest passages from the Bible. I want you to do more than just read the words. I want you to concentrate on any words or phrases that impress you. I want you to pray on them and listen to your thoughts. Keep notes, and they will be the basis for our daily discussions. Understand?" I nodded. She continued, "I suggest you refrain from talking to others in the house. This is a time to be alone. Regulate this request with your own needs. In the good old days, silence was mandatory, but the new generation has other ideas," she smiled and got up indicating that our session was over.

The next morning, I took one of the lawn chairs and walked just beyond the bushes to the left. It was a small, protected area. I snuggled in, got comfortable, and began reading the first passage, Psalm 23: *"Besides restful waters he leads me" . . . leads me . . . leads me.* Most of the places I worked at were suggested to me by others. Others who cared about me. I was led. My high school chemistry teacher drove me to her alma mater and introduced me to the faculty. I chose this school based on my admiration for her and the teachers I met . . . then my first teaching job. I had to choose between a chemistry position at a non-parochial high school or the junior high position at St. Francis. The "Dear Dorothy, I'd love to have you on the faculty" letter from the principal who had been a prior student in one of my lab classes convinced me to take the junior high position. Doris had told me about the Catholic High position.

*"Restful waters."* I liked this image. I went frequently to the ocean when I needed to think, to be alone. I felt at one with an omnipresent spirit, some deep, mysterious source to draw power.

I felt discouraged at this point. I didn't understand the word prayer. I didn't think I was doing it right. *"Leads me"* means someone is ahead of me, leading me, waiting silently, going so far, looking back, waiting . . . I had a vision of someone ahead of me, footsteps . . . I was following footsteps. It was a person, but not anyone I knew. I wasn't afraid of this person, this gentle, quiet person . . . follow . . .

That was enough. I went back and had lunch.

In the afternoon I walked further out into the fields and sat on the ground near some rocks. I opened to Isaiah 43, laid my papers on the grass, kicked off my clunky two-inch, rubber-soled heels, and put my sweater and cup on the grass. *"Fear not for I am with you."* I couldn't get into the words. I was so aware of my beautiful surroundings. The sun was shining. Bugs were flying around my papers. I was too happy for this heavy stuff. I got up, walked around, then came back and reread the paragraph. I strolled about twenty-five feet away from my belongings, sat down in a new spot and glanced back at my shoes, cup, and papers which were being blown around. For a split second I had this sense that I was still over there. It was like being in two places at the same time. The words, "*I am with you,*" immediately made sense. I could understand how someone could be there without really being there. I thought I would let the papers blow about only so far and then I would go back and gather them.

Fear was such a real part of my life. It had to do with growing up Italian. It had to do with my mother's insecurities. Even out here in this beautiful, peaceful spot, I caught myself thinking that some dog might come out of the woods and chase me. I looked behind my shoulder periodically to make sure no one was sneaking up on me. As a young child I was afraid, especially at night. I slept in an L shaped room with a closet at the end of the room. Each night, my parents would put me into my bed and close the light. I lie awake obsessed by the shaking of the closet door handle. I knew there was a skeleton living in the closet waiting to jump out and get me. I called for my father. Donned in his long white underwear, he would look in the dark opening and assure me that the only things in the closet were my clothes. He'd leave but return shortly when my cries started again. This time he'd bring a flashlight and make me look in the closet with him. His voice of reassurance was a bit more forceful and I knew better than to wake him again. Worrying about the skeleton, I'd go to sleep.

It would give me a tremendous sense of peace if I really believed that God was with me always. I thought about the unsettled times in my life when I submitted, when I accepted rather than fought. Maybe I could do it again and believe that God was always with me. Then I would have no fear. Wasn't I really submitting to myself? Wasn't the will of God then within me?

I shared all my thoughts with Sr. Emmaus. Some of my questions were hard for her, but she was truly open to the direction of the spirit wherever it took us. She suggested I read John next. I did but didn't get any earth-shattering insights like I had the day before.

"That's normal," she said. "Sometimes people go through a whole retreat without any sense of accomplishment. You are very blessed in what you have experienced so far."

That night I read all of John to get a better sense of Christ's relationship with the Father. It was my favorite gospel. From the passages, I got a greater sense of the message of Christ and that it was tied up not so much in what we do but how we love. This understanding led to a forgiveness and acceptance of the school's mission coming to an end. All those terrible angry feelings over what had been done or not done disappeared. I slept well that night and, in the morning, I ran, taking time to sit by a stream and look at the wildflowers growing in the area.

Luke 7 and Matthew 14 occupied my thoughts on my last full day. I told Sr. Emmaus that I felt guilty at times for the gifts I had been given so I spent a lot of time with Matthew 14, 22-33. That's the passage where the disciples are out on the lake, and Christ walks out to them. Peter challenges Christ and says, *"If it is really you, tell me to come to you across the water."* Jesus says, *"Come."* Peter got his sign, which was a great gift, and he was fine till he started fearing his gift, and that's when he started sinking. Christ saved him but chided him for having little faith. The gift should have increased his faith, but Peter was typically human, always needing reassurance. Peter, more than the other disciples, displayed the full range of human emotions, and that's what I liked most about him.

After supper I retired to my room and tried to read Mathew 26, 36-46, the agony scene. With the high I was on from all the previous insight and the loss of those bad feelings, there was no way I could get into the agony! I had no better luck with Luke 24, 13-25. I gave the whole thing up and went out for an evening stroll.

I was scheduled to meet with Sr. Emmaus one last time before heading home. For me, things were resolved, but I waited for the appointed hour. I roamed around the old building visiting the chapel and checking out various rooms on the second floor and happened to walk into a small reading room. I sat down and fingered through the magazines on the coffee table. I picked one up and read an article on becoming a nun. As I laid the book down, I noticed a letter sticking out from the pile with the school name, St. Francis in the first paragraph. I felt that this was not my letter to read but I couldn't stop myself. The letter said now that St. Francis closing was final, there would be a meeting of any nuns interested in discussing possibilities for a new mission, a new school. A new school? A new mission? Red, bright red! I actually saw red all over! All around me. All the hurt and anger boiled up again. After all the lay faculty had given, these nuns had the nerve to start something new and not include us in the planning! This was typical. I put the letter down and went outside to run off the pain. I was furious! Why did I go into that room? Why, after I had felt so good? Why now? Why end this way? Then it dawned on me. Go back and read the agony. So, I did.

I returned to my room and reread the passage. Only this time

I wasn't reading words. I was living the agony. I knew how Christ must have felt knowing what was to come and asking his friends to just stay awake with him which they couldn't do. Was that too much to ask? He was accepting the rest of the burden. At his time of greatest need, his closest friends were only concerned about their own needs. Imagine the pain. To be broken with sorrow and alone. No friends. He was alone with his God. And all he could say was, "Yes." He forgave them.

In the cession I wasn't sure I should tell Sr. Emmaus what had happened that morning, but in justice to her, I did. I told her about the room, the letter, and what it led me to. She just listened with no reproach. She told me to keep using this method to read other parts of the Bible. I thanked her for her guidance and left . . .

"Dorothy wake up. It's time to go. You're getting a lot of sun."

"Huh. I must have fallen asleep," I muttered. The Artist was already packing her stuff and was halfway down the path before I realized where I was. We returned to the office building. It was Independence Day.

The next day I sat in the apartment alone. It had only been only a few days, but I was starting to go crazy being in the city. I didn't know what to do with myself. I wrote in the journal: "Who the hell cares that I'm sitting in this studio room alone? Am I being used? No one from the community would come live in the city. Why am I doing it? I have no friends except the Artist, and she's never home. Why don't I just take off?"

The Empress says we must continue talking, but she doesn't mean it. She's doing what she likes. They all are. Why do I keep myself in these unpleasant situations? Am I a masochist?

And what is the sacrifice at Mandala, the community of the Empress? There's less out there to clutter one's life. The lake is beautiful. It's quiet. It's peaceful. Is that why Simone Weil worked in the factories? Self-torture? What is the sacrifice? Sex?

I washed my hair and felt better.

The Artist came home. She was all excited. "There is the possibility that we may get a house. One of the church members is considering donating his rental house for our use!" That made me feel better.

"I'm feeling depressed and rejected," I said to her.

"You have a right to feel depressed. And when you're depressed, you're more sensitive to rejection. I'm consciously rejecting you, and so is Mandala. It's a hard circle to break into with four strong women."

"I don't understand."

"No matter. Let's go see the house," she said and was already out the door before I could ask any questions. I followed.

The house was located on the outskirts of the city. It was in a perfect location since there were no neighbors to contend with. The family that owned it wanted the house used for some Christian mission, and they were trying to choose the right one. They found an old religious picture in the attic and felt it was a sign.

Tammy, an ex-prisoner turned charismatic, was already living in the house. She was to work with whatever mission assumed residency. She came with the package.

"Well, I just don't want it to become Catholic," emphasized Tammy.

"We could still have a place where people could pray or have Mass. I could get one of our priests to drop in," said the Artist, who definitely wanted it to stay Catholic.

"What about a woman priest?" I asked sarcastically.

"I'm not into that. I want this to be in line with the established Church. Don't go making waves," said the Artist, glancing in my direction.

"Ever since I was saved, I believe in my practices, and I don't want any other beliefs to sway me," piped in Tammy.

The conversation was getting nowhere. We were hung up in our own prejudices, and the house was taking a back seat. The gay, the reborn-prisoner, and the church freak. A motley crew! We discussed the need to be honest, but it was obvious that it was going to take a lot of energy just to maintain a working relationship.

That night I treated myself to a classical concert at the University. Maybe I'd meet some nice attractive, professional gay woman. In the journal that night I wrote: No chance. Sat by myself. There are no sophisticated, professional gay women, or they are well hidden.

I spent Friday morning running errands for the Artist and typing for the summer school program. Early in the afternoon I took off for the woods. I should have stayed with the Artist since she was going to find out about the house on Saturday, but I decided to show my true colors early on in the relationship. Then she couldn't accuse me later of not being myself.

That night, the community hosted a party for twenty-five student volunteers. I helped with the cooking, and later was invited to sleep in the house of the Empress. Even though the Hierophant made me feel comfortable, I was not really at ease staying in that house.

After dinner, the volunteers started singing. I felt very removed from this young group. I was so aware of myself and the presence of the Empress. Every time she looked at me, I tried to remain detached. I sat back from the group on a small stool and she came over and stood by me, for what reason I didn't know. Neither one of us said a word.

Later, I met Indiana, a nurse from Boston, who was very quiet-a shy, deep, natural soul. She was tenting on the grounds.

The next morning, I was afraid to get out of bed before the Hierophant but managed the courage. It was a restless night. I felt tight. I slept huddled into myself, my ears feeling very hollow, like they were echoing. Maybe I should see a doctor, I thought. I still needed time to recover. Time to rest. The damage was deep, though reparable, I hoped.

That day I worked with Cleme, a friend of Bear. She went through a crisis at age thirty, too. It was good to talk to her. We built the fence for the barn, a great accomplishment.

Sunday, I worked all day on the barn. At supper, I was so calm that I looked forward to sleeping. We ate at the round house. The Empress avoided me, but before she left, she asked me about the Hospitality House, and I told her the latest setbacks.

"Don't stay in limbo too long," she warned.

She and the Hierophant left, but I stayed to chat with Bear. It was dark when I walked down to the lake house. I entered the cottage and saw the two of them sitting in lawn chairs in front of the huge glass door that opened to the porch. It was dusk, and their bodies formed a silhouette in contrast to the muted light of the window door. The Empress was sitting on the right. It was the first time I had seen her without a scarf on her head. I was dazzled. She had long, straight, jet-black hair that hung loosely down her side. She was leaning back in the chair, legs crossed. One leg stretched out in front of the window. Her head rested, tilted on one hand, her left arm bent resting on the chair while her free hand combed through the thick strands of hair. She threw it back over the chair. Black beauty I thought. She's a black beauty. I stood frozen in the suspended moment of silent radiance. I didn't dare move and break the spell.

The Hierophant invited me to join them. I walked over and sat in a chair triangular to the pair.

"So, what are your initial impressions of the community?" asked the Empress, continuing to throw back her hair.

"An individualistic community where people quietly exist," I replied. "What one does seems to be important here."

"Maybe too individualistic," she commented. I sensed she was referring to her problems with Lady. The Empress was harsh with

Lady at supper. From my limited observations, they appeared to be at odds with one another about the meaning of community. Playing the rainmaker, I asked, "What is the sacrifice here?" I was trying to point out that maybe her sacrifice and the Lady's were quite different and that she should be tolerant of that.

"Personal time," she answered. "Being available when you're not always ready to be. Not everyone agrees on this. I am not happy to say. What do you think I can do to change that attitude?"

"Sometimes just being honest with the person helps," I answered. She responded, "Yes, our discontent comes out in other ways, doesn't it?" I shook my head in agreement.

I should have told her that there seems to be much sharing in the community and a real concern for the local poor. Why didn't I give her positive feedback? Why does negativity come first?

The Empress was judgmental. She had a great capacity to work and unconsciously demanded it from others. She shouldn't demand more than one can give. The Empress empathized with the poor. She felt their pain, but she missed the pain of the wealthy. She specialized. "Not being able to give is a cop out," she had said. I had to be careful not to feel guilty. I could be easily overshadowed by her.

\* \* \*

The Hierophant was more natural than the Empress though her entertaining spirit sometimes bordered on scatterbrained. She was a tall, gray-haired, thin woman with rosy chipmunk cheeks. Goodness easily flowed out of her. The Empress, prone to judgment and self-criticism, had to work at it. The Empress wasn't a real person to me, rather a spirit entombed in a body. She constantly philosophized.

"You learn a lot about a person when you work side by side," she said to me.

I learned a lot about myself while working on the barn. I'm terribly embarrassed to make mistakes in front of others. Every day that week at Mandala, I ventured out to practice banging nails on boards before the crew came out to work. Funny, I thought, I always encouraged my students not to be afraid to make mistakes, but I couldn't apply that to myself. For the first time, I was learning skills that I wasn't comfortable with. It made me sympathetic to my students' feelings. I finally knew what it meant to "not get it" in class, since school learning had always come easily to me.

Indiana and I tried building steps to the barn. It wasn't simple and we had to call the Empress for guidance. As she explained the process, I realized it involved figuring out the third side to the triangle. Just practical application to theory! In the end, it was the Empress's common sense that accomplished the task. Although she lacked technical math skills, her common sense and intuition were strong. On the other hand, I had figured out the problem on paper but couldn't make the transference. She must have thought me stupid. I couldn't "see" what she wanted me to do with the wooden boards.

At lunch break, the Empress asked me, "Why are you here and what are you looking for?"

"That's a Twenty-nine-year question!" I exclaimed. We both smiled and searched into each other's eyes. I knew she wanted an answer, so I thought, and said, "Meaning." I got embarrassed after I said it, and she got noticeably quiet.

When I returned to the city, I took the Artist's suggestion and signed up for an art class. I knew it would be a struggle as I had little artistic ability. After class I pigged out. I couldn't satisfy my hunger these days. My ears started ringing again. What was I not listening to? I had felt fine all weekend at Mandala.

The Artist came home at around six, and we went to her parents' house for supper and a bath. It was wonderful to laze erotically in the tub and then sit on the porch sipping a glass of wine while talking to her parents.

"You should do some running," I said to the Artist.

"You're so judgmental," she retorted. "I like to eat."

"But it would be healthier for you to lose some weight."

"You don't understand. Being thin only causes me macho problems with men. I've had too many unpleasant experiences with men when I was thinner. I prefer it this way. When I'm thin, sex is too much an issue. I can do without it. Thank you very much."

"OK," I said, though I didn't really understand. "I love the physical, and I love feeling good about myself."

"You're such a romantic. So passionate! Everything is sooo important to you! You know what you need, you need a built-in psychiatrist, a role I am not willing to play. Quite frankly, I have my own needs, and I don't have time for yours," she went on about me, and frankly I was surprised that she had taken such notice. "You may be blunt but you're not always right. I know how you are. I used to be that way, too. Using that little sexy body to get what you want. Most maneuvers are for sexual purposes anyway."

I supposed she was right, and I could see how a lot of my life was motivated by sex. I had consciously tried to change that by coming to the community. That was the reason for being honest with the Empress in the letter and for being up front with the Artist. No false pretenses anymore. Everything was out in the open. I couldn't erase feelings, but I could stop dreaming up the fantasies and the disappointment when they didn't happen.

I bought the Artist a sugar cookie after my next class. A peace offering. I had no right to try and change her. We should love people for the way they are. The Empress says she accepts everyone. Would she accept me if she knew I found her attractive? I watched her. She would get up quietly. Brush her teeth, blow her nose, go outside. She never would break the silence or the pattern. I wondered if she was praying during these simple rituals. Sometimes her eyes would search mine out. I couldn't believe that our motives were the same. For her, the physical was the lower nature in man. For me, it was the most real. Yet aren't the physical and spiritual both expressions of God?

My indecision angered the Artist. She always proceeded in a determined manner. It was hard for me to watch the Artist at summer school. It reminded me of St. Francis. She intermingled with parents, kids, and teachers so easily. I felt like crying all the time. I just wanted to quietly slip out of existence.

After school, I dropped the Artist off at unemployment and came home. I started reading a book by Marge Piercy about lesbians. The Empress recommended it.

One morning before going to art class. I went to wash at the bathroom down the hall and locked myself out of the apartment! Thank god, I had my pajamas. My hair was wet, and I wrapped a towel on my head and started walking to the Artist's parents' house to get another key. I laughed all the way, thinking, just my luck, I'll get hit by a piece of the Sky Lab!

Class was good. The teacher set up a still life- a small table and objects on top. He told us to paint any view that interested us. I painted from the floor looking up at the underside of the table. I was the only one who chose that view.

The Artist came home, and I showed her the painting. "You are so free like a child. I loved being a child." She described her childhood as "perfect crystal bubbles of past experiences." I cooked while she rambled. I enjoyed listening. That night she worked on her canvas. In the morning, I noticed that she had erased one of the figures, leaving just the couch and two figures. The shapes were less distinct than before.

Every Thursday night there was a classical concert given at the University. I usually attended. When I got back from that night's performance, the Artist was in a weird mood and said the meanest thing to me.

"Are you the devil?" she asked.

"What? Stop it!"

"No really, I mean it. Are you the devil?" she continued teasing me though she could see I was getting upset. I went to bed and got up the next morning, still mad at her. I hadn't done anything to provoke such a statement. All I did was help her when she needed it. Didn't she realize that people with sexual orientations different from the norm always think they are evil? Sex and sin. Good old Catholic upbringing.

The next morning, I told her that I was upset with what she had said. She ignored my feelings and said she was only kidding.

Was I headed for another damn failure with this Hospitality House? The Baptist church that the Empress suggested as a possible location was absurd. The Artist broke into laughter when I mentioned it. She took me to see the building. It was a huge monstrosity and would cost a fortune to heat! The regulations about heating and zoning were totally frustrating. What worked in the woods didn't work in the city. The Empress had no sense of city reality.

The Artist had been depressed lately with her job, next fall's unemployment, the house, herself. She was not as happy as the façade she projected. She tended to escape from her problems, like sex and love. She would rather have been thin but was afraid of it. I needed a break, so I decided to go to the woods over the weekend. I left Friday afternoon.

When I saw Lady, it was as if a plug had been pulled out of me, and all my frustrations about feeling displaced, about the house, about the Artist came pouring out. Lady just listened. That was the hardest part about the secret relationship with Sarah. I couldn't discuss the frustrations with anyone.

Indiana and I spent the morning climbing up Blue Hills Mountain. She told me about her Catholic school upbringing and then her journey to South America, Africa and Bolivia as a Peace Corps nurse.

"It's hard for me to give time to myself without feeling bad about it," she confided. "I never wanted to be like my mother who was totally immersed in serving my father, but then I found myself totally immersed in my career in a similar fashion. No time for myself. No time for another person or for having a child. I've always had feelings of inadequacy, not realizing all my potential. I tried leaving my job once and came to Maine but returned in less than one year. It wasn't enough time. You should stay the whole year in Maine," she said to me. "Give yourself at least that much."

I was disappointed with myself for not telling Indiana I had been involved with a woman, but I was afraid. I didn't want to lose her friendship which I valued so much.

As I was leaving for the city, the Empress noticed me. We were standing outside the octagon house. She walked over to me and stood next to me with her rosy, radiant face. In a momentary attitude of real concern, she said, "You should build a retreat house for yourself out here. Wouldn't that be good?"

"Yes," I responded in a bit of a daze. How would I have the time to visit the community once the Hospitality House started?

I left with a renewed sense that she really cared about me in some small way. The pleasurable treat of being in her thoughts was satisfying enough for me not to care about the reason for it. I lived for the times when she took me into her confidence. It was a shot of energy to get me through the lows.

I wrote in my diary: Eating too much lately. Sign of dissatisfaction. Ears are better, but then my throat hurts. Can't swallow. Can't swallow this? Dual life. Back and forth. Should stabilize somewhere. Need to experience more pain to balance. Want to be a peacemaker. Pray for this. No selfish return. Must read more of the gospel. An older woman said to me "When you change yourself, things start to happen." Internal berserk state right now. Mind tight. Tried running. Running hard. No relief. Why is there no relief?

The Artist was not happy with my Friday note which stated, "needed to get away."

"I want us to work out a spiritual community between us," she said. "You can't keep running back to the woods."

"I don't think I'm ready for that commitment."

"I'm willing to not see my family and friends and change parishes so that we are on the same footing," she responded.

"I don't think that's wise. It would make us totally dependent on one another." I was afraid this was starting to feel a lot like the relationship I just ended. What to do? She needed community and I needed aloneness.

"What about a compromise?" I asked. "I'll stay in community all week with you, but on weekends I want free time to go to the woods."

"No, I want total commitment." I didn't understand her insistence of all or nothing. I thought it better to start small rather than getting in over our heads. I needed the woods.

"You want the best of both worlds," she added. She reminded me of Sarah always complaining when I went home on weekends to see my family. Is it necessary to give up the dearest parts of one's self for a relationship? Shouldn't loving someone free oneself to be who she truly is and satisfy needs? It was too confining here in the city. I needed the different types of people that the woods community provided. I was excited about building the retreat house.

I prayed to the Lord for an answer. "Help me see what to do. I don't want to hurt anyone. But she expects too much. Do I have anything to offer the community? Should I just go live out there?

The Artist and I rested, and then we went to dinner with her sister and brother-in-law. During the meal, the Artist suggested that we go to New York and stay at one of the Hospitality Houses for a few months to gain experience. I thought the idea was great. Maybe too great. My enthusiasm depressed her since this was not exactly what she wanted to do. She wanted a house in her own city. Later she admitted, "That would be lost time for me. Beside I don't have enough money."

"I have enough money to get us through," I responded.

"That only causes problems," she said.

She went to bed early. I apologized upsetting her. In reassuring voice, she said, "Dorothy, I'm not mad at you." I felt relieved.

In the morning, the Artist announced that she had changed her mind. "I decided Chicago would be a better place for me. I have many friends there, and I won't starve." Another rejection! She was the only person I knew and now she was leaving.

She called later that day to say she had lined up a teaching job, "You should come out there with me." she said on the phone. Her instability was driving me crazy. When she returned, I pretended to be asleep. I didn't want to talk to her. She got in bed and then turned on the light. I knew she wanted to talk so I said, "What?"

"I called Chicago and cancelled the job." Her words were not a surprise. I was relieved, but at the same time afraid.

"I hope you are doing the right thing for yourself," I said.

"Chicago has nothing to do with what I want."

"I wasn't going to go out there with you if you did."

"Let's go to Mandala for a visit, "she replied to my surprise.

We journeyed down for the weekly community picnic. We stopped to visit Lady, and after a few glasses of wine walked down the hill to the lake house. Weird vibes filled the room when we walked in. The Artist jokingly, but defensively, announced, "All the things Dorothy said about me are not true."

"Are you feeling guilty?" I asked her and teasingly shimmied up to her as if we were involved.

"Are you staying for the weekend?" interjected the Empress looking directly at me. I shook my head. "No."

"Why not?" she persisted, leaning closer to me.

"I don't know why," I said as I looked at the Artist and implied that there was some force holding me, which wasn't true at all. The Artist certainly didn't care if I stayed or not. Maybe I was seeking sympathy. Maybe I was trying to set up a jealous triangle. I left with her.

I interpreted the response of the Empress to mean that there was some interest on her part.

Saturday, the Artist left early. I noticed that she had done some work on her canvas. There was a shape that remotely resembled a couch and only one figure left. It encouraged me to work on my still life. I added a red striped tablecloth to my painting. I blotted out all the objects on top and just kept it simple. After working on a color exercise, I went to the Artist's parents' house, sat with her dad for a while, then showered, ate, and relaxed. It was wonderful, no tenseness.

Later I met the Artist at city hall. No progress. We went to see a lawyer, a young Republican who was overly concerned with his position in the town. He made a point of telling us what boards he served on but avoided the issue of the Hospitality House.

I got very tense at the meeting. It bothered me that the Artist knew more than the lawyer, and yet, she had to play his political game. She defended herself by saying, "We have to go through him to get to city hall. I don't mind playing the game if I get what I want. He will be an ally."

The Artist was now in love with two priests! Two unlikely choices. Safe choices. If she didn't get either one, it wouldn't be because of her but because they are priests!

I went to Mandala the following weekend and slept in Indiana's empty tent.

After supper, I walked back to the campsite in the pitch black using Bear's flashlight. The first half-hour was the worst. I could hear every noise. I kept praying "Are you sleeping with me Jesus? No bears, please." I didn't move, once I settled into the sleeping bag. I stayed the entire night and was proud of myself for doing so.

In the morning, the Empress and I talked. I poured out all my frustrations about the house.

"How is the Artist?" she asked. She was more worried about the Artist's insecurity than mine.

"She goes back and forth. It drives me crazy. I don't feel like I'm doing anything concrete toward this house except offering her support."

"You two have a lot to work through. Friendship. Community. The house. And the house is the least of your worries."

"It is?" I asked.

"Yes, I could get you the house right away, but are you two ready?" she queried. Confused, I thought, 'What is she talking about? It's like she planned this painful time and thinks it's necessary.'

"I would have to say 'No'," I responded honestly, remembering how the Artist had gone back and forth about the Chicago issue. I laughed in frustration, lowered my head, and cried, "What am I going through?" She reached out and touched my hand. I looked at her in surprise. She can be so gentle at times. Why does that mean so much to me?

Maybe the painful time was necessary. The inner longing kept me humble. I was too peaceful out at the community. I could so easily slip into egotistical self-contentment. Base desires kept me from self-righteousness.

After having a wonderful bran-blueberry muffin, I went to help Ma Kettle. Later, I ran and then snuck down by the lake and walked around the rocks. I saw TinMan, one of the male members, who was drunk and making angry comments. I think he wanted to sleep with me, but I wasn't interested. I rushed back to the lake house.

Lady came to visit, and she asked about the Artist. I related the incidents of the week to her.

"It's understandable that you are affected by her actions," said Lady. "You recently left one unsteady relationship, and now you are involved in another very unstable one. There is a bond between you, whether is it spoken or not."

She was right. Women form natural bonds. Love on some level. Whether it becomes physical is another matter- a serious and conscious decision, not made lightly. I learned that with Sarah.

I returned to the city and had to do a lot of errands for the Artist as her moped had been stolen. During Mass, I noticed the Artist remained sitting just as I always boldly do. I hate all that jumping up and down. The Artist went to play racquetball, and I went back to the studio apartment to work on my still life. She had done more work on her canvas. The background had become quite simple with dull colors. A figure was now standing next to a bed. The scene was starting to get interesting.

She came home exhausted. We ate and then talked for a while in bed.

"I never feel like I understand what is happening to me when I am going through an experience," I said.

"It's always easier to look back, like with your experience with the Queen," she said. Then she made a strange comment to me, "You know what's going on now." I had to think. Maybe I did, but I wasn't so sure.

Art class was frustrating. We had to paint outside. Too distracting—bugs, wind, no easel. I chatted with an ex-drug addict who had almost died in a car accident and then rediscovered life. He renewed my faith in the need for a hospitality house.

I returned to the studio and heard the Artist and another voice coming up the stairs. She brought home a very good-looking man. Blonde California type.

"You're high priority this weekend," she said as she snuggled up to him, playing the femme fatale. She didn't even introduce me till I said something about it. It weirded me out. I gathered my clothes and left to get a hot fudge sundae. I had a hard time when women catered to men. They had asked me to join them for dinner, but I refused. It reminded me of the night Sarah brought a man to stay over. She was trying to make me jealous. I had dated men during our first year together. I wouldn't have minded her dating either if she had taken him somewhere else, but right in our own apartment . . . that was too much!

I'm too moody, I thought, as I sat eating my ice cream even though I wasn't hungry.

Where did I belong? With a gay group? At Mandala? Were they really like me or was I just imagining? Did we all have hidden desires? Did the Empress? I wished she would just be a person to me. All we talked about was the house. Did anyone exist who could understand me? If I were beautiful, I would probably be the most dramatic, emotional person around. I was secure in career, but in relationships, not so much. It was easier to live in fantasy. There I could say and experience anything I wanted.

I took a young fellow who had had a nervous breakdown to the concert with me. My companion was a very gentle, frightened person. He painted till the breakdown. He felt badly for the lost time. When I brought him home, he gave me a small sketch he had done. I was honored.

His companionship diverted my repeating frustrating thoughts, but when I got home, they started all over again . . . Were we approaching this house all wrong? Maybe we could just start feeding people and forget all this legal rigmarole. Who cared how the city defined us? We were not a business. What were we waiting for? A whole month had gone by!

The Artist wanted to do everything right in the parish's eyes. I didn't care about the parish. Back and forth between the Artist and the Empress. I trusted the Empress, but she never talked to me. I didn't know what was going on in her mind. I hated this limbo state!

I went to the campus and just sat listening to music. I longed for something but couldn't put my finger on it. I decided to go home and paint what I was feeling.

\* \* \*

I welcomed the release of my feminine creative side, not used very much in the past. While painting, I thought about how the Empress, Bear and the Hierophant had given up their femininity to survive their lifestyle. Lady was the only one who maintained her feminine side, but she was on the outs with the others. A strong woman should be able to live this simple self-sufficient life without sacrificing her womanness, without becoming an imitation man.

On the weekends, I usually returned to the woods. Ma Kettle invited me to join her. We went to pick up a seventy-year-old looking man who was being discharged from the hospital. He was unshaven and so emaciated, that he could hardly breathe, let alone talk. His chest looked as if it had collapsed. I couldn't look at him. Ma Kettle jumped on the bed, hugged him and introduced me, "This is my cousin Dorothy. Dorothy come and shake PaPa's hand." God, I admired her natural South American approach. She had a way of making everyone feel at ease even in the most awkward situation.

"Did you miss my lovin'?" she teased. "You been cheating on me with all these pretty nurses?" Her affection made him smile and he responded in a cry-talk, "Yeah, get me outta here. I need a cigarette."

"OK. That's what I came for. Let me get the nurse to get you out of bed, and we'll get you dressed. Start taking your clothes off." Then Ma Kettle walked out, and I followed right behind. If he was going to start undressing, I wasn't going to hang around for the performance! Ma Kettle sensed my uneasiness and said, "Dorothy, go check at the desk about his discharge."

Getting him in the car was another chore for which I was little help. I drove so that Ma Kettle was free to tend to his needs. She gave him a cigarette. I questioned her later about doing so, but she reasoned, "Dorothy, that man is gonna die any day now. We might as well let him die happy. He's only in his fifties, but he's determined to end his life. All he lives on is his liquor and his cigarettes. I'll fill his refrigerator when we get him home, but he won't touch a thing."

This was my first experience with outreach work and Ma Kettle.

I knew our similar Mediterranean temperaments would bind us into a lasting friendship and that I could learn a lot from her.

After supper, Lucky Luke and I took the kids to the local tavern to hear the guitar player. Lucky Luke was a frequent visitor to the community. A James Taylor look alike, he always stayed at the Kettles.

Because of the poor progress we were making with the Hospitality House, I began thinking about asking the Empress if I could move to Mandala for the remainder of the year. The Artist and I were not spending much time together anyway. We seemed more and more to be going our own ways, and it wasn't the same path. One night she said to me, "I wonder about someone who feels a need to help disturbed people." She was referring to my work with the mentally disturbed artist.

"They have as much right to existence and caring as anyone else," I replied in defense.

"You can't save the world, Dorothy."

"True, but you can try and help a need when you see it as long as it doesn't consume you."

"That's what I worry about," she responded.

I loved being at Ma and Pa Kettle's. They were so good at reaching out and helping other people. Their support for one another was apparent. They shared all they had and just asked that everyone pitch in to help in whatever way he/she could. I always washed the dishes when I ate there. There were plenty of chores to go around, whether it was picking peas, or milking the cows, but I was picky about which chores I would do. They teased me about being such a city girl.

"We'll have to teach Dorothy how to do chickens, "said Pa Kettle as he put a big grin on his unshaven face and squeezed his hands like he was wringing a neck.

"Not me. No way. I draw the line."

The Kettles were totally self-sufficient. They grew all their food and raised animals for slaughter. They bartered for whatever else they needed. A wood stove fueled by tree cuttings on their property got them through the cold winters.

The dwelling was no palace, but there was always plenty of food. The main house was a two-story building with red clapboard hanging every which way. There was no special design to the windows, and most were probably just dump throwaways. Attached to the house was a smaller shed. This provided the main entrance and a place to hang coats and store boots. The wood on this part of the dwelling was naturally weathered, and the roof need some repair. There was always a dog tied just outside the door. Bicycles lay haphazardly in the path leading up to the house along with large pieces of wood that needed to be split.

The back yard was an even sorrier sight. There were a few small barns or sheds that needed repair. The grass was high and uneven and looked more like straw. Wood and hay and junk metal were thrown all about. Chickens ran wild. Pigs were confined in a wood pen. Cows roamed down in the back.

The inside of the house was also unkempt. Piles of clothes lay everywhere. The downstairs had separate rooms, but upstairs was unfinished. Ma Kettle had hung big sheets strung over long roping to separate the boys' space from the girls' space. With nine kids of varying ages, Ma had to devise some method of privacy. The furniture was basic, extremely basic, but all the kids were dressed in the latest mod fashion. They had all the newest gadgets. Rock music blasted from the bedrooms. These kids were not deprived of anything and just as hip as any city kid.

A spacious bathroom downstairs contained a big tub for relaxing. Ma would come home after a stressful day of social work, sit in the tub, and yell for Pa to bring her Southern Comfort and tea. This was her quiet time, and no one dared bother her.

Pa Kettle told me how the Empress had spent a year tenting on their property before she got the land for building Mandala. She had had a disagreement with the Carmelite community. She and two other nuns left. The Empress desired country living, so she bought the property by the lake and started Mandala. It had only existed for the past 2.5 years.

The next morning, I stopped at Duffy's Restaurant for a delicious home-made muffin, and while feasting, I decided to enjoy this month of August. I didn't want any responsibility. I just wanted to have fun. There would be enough time for work in September. I decided to accept the math teaching position at the Learning Center of the Co-op. It was against my better judgement, but at least it would be a way of becoming part of the Co-op community.

I worked all day Saturday on the barn. The Empress and I were up on the roof. We were facing each other straddling the middle beam while hooking in the rafters. It took all my courage, but I managed to ask, "Would you consider my staying out at Mandala for the year?"

"That would be fine," she said. "You could live in the barn with Tin Man and Gene. They have decided to stay the year as well."

"Great," I said thinking how hysterical this would be.

"How do you think I should deal with Tin Man's drinking problem?" she asked.

"I think you should talk to him about it."

"Yes, you're probably right. Do you know why you're here yet?" she asked as if there were some predestined answer. I thought for a moment and said, "I was happiest when I worked in the small community of St. Francis. It got me through the bad times." She nodded understandingly. Staring into her face reminded me that there were certainly other reasons but not ones that I wanted to mention.

The possibility of living with men was exciting. Tin Man was a comedian, despite his drinking, and Gene was so gentle and quiet. I liked them both and thought that we would get along fine. When the Empress announced the new living arrangements, the Hierophant protested. She was not wild about the co-ed living.

"What will people think?" she shouted at the Empress. "They already think badly about us. I insist on two separate living spaces for men and women." The Empress didn't respond. She usually didn't publicly voice an opinion contradictory to what the Hierophant wanted but did what she wanted in the end. I laughed to myself thinking there would be nothing to worry about with me being gay!

After community supper, Indiana and I paddled the canoe almost the entire length of the lake. So peaceful. There was a large rock island in the middle and secluded houses further down on either side of the lake. We joked about my living with Tin Man and Gene. She suggested I build my own house. She made me feel so normal. I did so want to tell her I was gay. The trip back took all our energy.

During the night I woke up thinking about a conversation I had with the Empress. We were down by the lake and talking about women writers. She made a comment about Doris Lessing, and I started talking about Virginia Woolf's *A Room of One's Own*. I was making a point about the part regarding Shakespeare's sister when I noticed that the Empress was glancing around as if she wasn't paying attention to what I was saying. I wondered if I bored her or whether she knew what I was referring to. I just assumed that she had read the book. I never thought to ask if she did. I would have expected her to admit that she wasn't familiar with the work. I certainly have shown my ignorance many times to her.

Instead, she ignored my comment, got up and said, "I'm going inside to escape the mosquitoes." Thank God, I was stronger than when I first came. That rejection would have devastated me. With all her talk of the gospels, didn't she realize how unwelcome she made people feel at times?

I attended my first fiddle concert on Sunday with Indiana, Tin

Man and Scarecrow. Scarecrow, who was playing in the competition, had been living in Mandala for a few months. He had a separate, single-room house in the woods by the barn. A funny sort of lanky fellow with a light-colored, reddish, long beard, he had lost most of his hair although he was only in his twenties. His clothes hung loose on his body, as he slowly moved with long steps in a Rip Van Winkle way.

The concert was good, but it didn't take long for me to have my fill of fiddles! Indiana and I took a break and meandered through the grounds making our way to the makeshift bathrooms at the top of the hill. On the way, she told me about a friend of hers who was involved with two other women. "I find this very exciting," she said to my surprise.

"What about the jealously issue?" I asked.

"Well, women are supposed to be jealous, but I don't think this was the case in this relationship."

"I was involved in a seven-year relationship with a woman," I admitted. This was as good a time as ever to tell her.

"Oh," she commented. "How did that go?"

"Great in the beginning. Then I needed out. It was my first serious relationship." We walked quietly for a while, and I was worried that she might be uncomfortable with me till she asked, "Do you want to go see the sweatshirts with me?" Then I knew it did not matter to her.

On the way, we met a few gay women who were friends of hers. I liked them immediately. One woman was so relaxed and open in talking about herself.

"Come and visit me," she said. "I'll fix you up with whatever kind of woman you want!" Well, this would be interesting, I thought.

I returned to the city on Monday after working on the barn, having breakfast with Gene and taking a nude swim by myself. It was so wonderful and sensuous to feel the lake water on every part of my body. I lay in the sun before departing.

What a surprise when I walked into the studio. The changes on the canvas were incredible! The Artist had obviously spent a lot of time on it. I knew at once that it was finally finished. The couch was gone, and it was replaced with a bed. An abstract figure stood to the left of the bed. The bed and room were basically white with dark shading, and the figure was a combination of reds and violets mashed in a twirling sensation. Though the bed and room gave a sense of being immovable solids, the figure seemed to jump out at the viewer. I could not wait to tell the Artist how much I liked it. I tried working on my own painting but got too discouraged. I decided to skip art class. Instead,

I rushed over to her parents' house to wait for her. Her grandfather and I had a few gin and tonics and then feasted on wine, cheese, and pretzels. I was feeling no pain when she finally arrived. She took me to the mall for a yogurt sundae. "I really like your painting," I said. "I knew it was done the moment I saw it."

"Thanks. It sort of evolved this weekend."

"It's nice to tell you about something I do like for a change. I'm really upset with my own painting."

"I'm sorry you got so discouraged with your painting but that's why there are so few artists. It's hard to stick with the hard work involved in painting."

The next morning, I got up and decided to try again at the landscape. I shouldn't run from hard work. I had to follow through on this project to the end. I had focused on doing one tree which became a Christ image to me, and I ignored everything else around it. I decided to redo the piece as a more realistic drawing. Something I could handle.

I received a letter from Sarah. Her tone didn't project any anger. She told me that Catholic High had left messages for me to call. In the letter, she included a clipping from the newspaper announcing the opening of a VP position at Catholic High? Had the Queen of Swords left?

The Artist and I had breakfast at the Bagel Shop located in the heart of the city. It was my favorite spot, and I enjoyed many hours there just sitting and reading. No one ever bothered me. It was owned by a young Jewish couple and was very European in style with small crowded tables. The bagels were as good, if not better than NY bagels. I tried hinting to the Artist about my decision to join the community at Mandala. I was trying to get a feel for how upset it was going to make her. Instead of discussing the issue, she ignored my hints and said, "I have to go make some phone calls at my mother's," and she rushed me out. I tried to talk to her in between the calls. I provoked her saying, "I make you mad, don't I?" That was enough to get her going.

"You left the house cause. Yes, I am mad at you. I have a right to be mad at you." I didn't say anything. I just wanted to cry but smiled. I knew she would never stand for my tears.

"You should have told me a long time ago that you were thinking of moving there."

"Well, you told me to do what's best for me."

"Well, I would have been happier if you just came out and told me, but I still have a right to be mad."

"I always feel caught in the middle."

"Everyone feels that way."

I left feeling really depressed and went to art class. Did my painting using very dull colors. This time I painted a tree reaching for survival between two other trees, one rather massive and the other dark, straight, and tall. I edged them all in violet. I was in an off-the-wall mood. After class, I decided to go back and try to explain my decision. I found the Artist at Mass. I stayed till Communion, then waited in the car for her. She came out and got in.

"I'm so aggravated!" I said, which she loved hearing. She was rolling with laughter. "Our philosophies are so different!" I went into this big whole life history to explain my actions and ended by saying, "You're just too strong a character for me."

"We're both strong characters. We could work at a relationship."

"It won't work, and I'm still going."

"And I'm still mad, but I'll get over it." With that we went back to the studio apartment. She painted, and I read.

In the morning I ran, stopped at the Bagel shop and began reading my book. I couldn't put it down. The Empress had suggested a book written by Marge Piercy entitled, *Woman at the Edge of Time*. It was about a woman in an insane asylum who was visited by a person from a future society . . . *Three personalities . . . insanity . . . nonsexist language . . . receivers . . . was there more to this story? Sr. Emmaus said I brought Christ to people because of myself, not in spite of myself . . . what did it mean? There seemed to be a dark figure ahead of me . . . I felt as if I was following footsteps . . . as if someone were ahead of me . . . sometimes I would look in the mirror just to see that person inside of me . . . I was so frightened now . . . I felt neurotic . . . had to understand myself . . . truth was what I came for . . . The Queen of Swords said, "You can't save the world" Judas, I felt sorry for Judas . . . a victim of fate . . . opposite sides of the same person . . .*

Somehow the Queen of Swords had gotten my phone number and called. She wanted to know if I would be returning in September.

"I haven't gotten the contract yet," I said. "I was waiting to receive it to respond."

"They are going out late."

"I don't think I will be returning, but I will make a formal response when I get the contract."

"I encourage you to do so. I hope you are enjoying your time in Maine."

"I am. You should visit. You would love the quiet."

"I'd love to. I want to keep in touch with you," she responded as if we were the best of friends!

I received the contract ten days later. I sent it back with a letter stating, "after difficult and serious deliberation, I have decided not to return to my teaching position in September."

And I thought to myself, now who am I?

\* \* \*

I packed the car and left for the woods the afternoon of August 1st. A good day for a new beginning. When the Empress found me swimming alone in the lake that afternoon, she said, "You seem happier."

"I'm happy because I'm making decisions," I answered.

"That's good. Finally, out of limbo. Just keep praying."

"I do pray," I said. She looked at me out of the side of her eye with a sarcastic smile. "No, really, I do. Don't make fun of me," I added.

"I'm not making fun of you. I know what goes on in your mind."

"Really? Then what am I thinking now?" I looked at her with adoring eyes and a big smile on my face.

"Never mind. I have chores to do and so do you. Too much play is not good."

"No play is not good either."

"All right. All right. Play is good but chopping wood is better! You need to get going on winter wood or you will never make it through. You have a lot to learn."

"Are you going to teach me?"

"I'll teach you all I know."

"Oohh. That should be interesting," I said in my best sexy voice.

"Hey watch it. Be a good girl" she said smirking and started walking toward the cottage.

"I am good, very good, that's the problem," I said as I splashed water at her. She started running and shouted, "I bet you are!"

I lay back in the water. I loved her when she was this free and easy spirit. She did not show this side very often. I felt blessed.

That night at supper a woman spiritualist attended the meal. She was a psychic who did open readings. I was afraid of what would come out in my reading, so I left before she got to me. I went for a walk by myself in the woods and thought about the Empress's words "to keep praying". I was trying but it was hard. I decided simple was best and kept repeating, "Lord make me a channel of your peace." Words of strength.

My first night in Mandala was quite upsetting. I woke up trying to scream the word "mother," but could not. Only some muttered noise came out. If I had been able to scream it out, I think it would have been loud enough to wake the entire community!

I decided to start each day with meditative time by the lake. I still felt awkward with the Empress except when she was in a playful mood. I was so aware of her. Did she sense this awareness? I was afraid to call it love. I didn't even know her. Or did I? Talking with Bear, I learned that the Empress and I had the same belief that personal weaknesses keep us humble. The Empress had called it *poverty*. I had a hard time expressing my spiritual ideas with her. We didn't talk the same language. We named things differently. She rejected me constantly. Maybe she wanted me to find my own strength. Indiana said that the Empress needed a spiritual confident and that I should be it. I wished!

On Monday I met with the previous math teacher from the Learning Center. His disorganization frustrated me. I got as much as I could but realized I was on my own. In the afternoon, I went to a meeting about the Co-op calendar. I volunteered to help organize the project- setting deadlines and lining up a printer. All at once, I found myself involved in a wealth of new creative responsibilities!

Even though I was happy, I was having restless nights. I would wake up, and my mind would rehash conversations from the day . . . " I think one could be a total woman and live out the gospels," said the Empress.

"Have you achieved this?" I asked.

"No," she responded. "I'm trying to achieve this."

"What are you weak in?" I asked. She smiled and didn't respond. My imaginary mind answered . . . "sexuality? Isn't that it? The Hierophant is a good friend, but she doesn't fulfill all your needs. You are a very sensual woman. Some people give more when they are loved. I need to grow spiritually. We could help each other. The love between Ma and Pa Kettle doesn't stop them from giving to others. We're alike. Both intense. We could have a true partnership. The Hierophant is primary in your life right now. That's ok. I don't need you now. I need to learn other things like building and praying and being independent. I wish I could hug you . . .

I sensed a new tenseness between Bear and Lady. It had started when Cleme arrived. Cleme and Bear were long-time friends. They had been novices in the convent together. Cleme had left the convent years ago. Bear confided in Cleme her problems with Lady, who could be demanding and overbearing at times. Having a flamboyant artist temperament, Lady bossed Bear around. Bear hated confrontation so she usually gave in.

I prayed in my own simple words . . . Lord, I know you are with me. The forest reflects your presence. I hear you in the stillness of the pines, in the air and the song of the birds. I feel at one with you who is so strong yet gentle. Make me a channel of your peace.

Saturday brought insight. It was the weekend of the Co-op Fair. I didn't really have any part in the activities, so I decided to drive to the town of Hope to visit the lesbian community. I got halfway there and decided to turn around. I had to stop dividing my energies.

At the Co-op, I bumped into Ted, the acting manager, who for some reason started telling me about the Co-op, and I began to realize the burdens of the Empress. Ted complained about the disorganization of the Co-op: "It needs a strong leader to pull it together. People can't deal with the solitary manner of the Empress. She exists in her abstract ideas."

I sympathized with the Empress. She was a futuristic woman who had to contend with the realistic problems of those who were not philosophically on a par with her. The Empress had a vision. Getting people to realize the vision was another story. The Co-op provided a total community experience for the poor and elderly. The energy required was tremendous! After listening to all his complaining, I left feeling very weighty with some sense of her internal pain. I went to lie down in my car.

The Empress walked by but did not notice me. She wore her green khaki pants, long jacket and black beret covering her hair. Her sleeves were rolled up. I watched as she roamed around the fairgrounds, stopping to chat briefly with all the people, but always maintaining her separate, dark solitary self. She put her arm around each one, shook her head, and kept her eyes looking to the ground as she listened to their problems. From one to the next. All their burdens piling onto her. I wanted to be a help to her, not an added burden. I prayed that God would show me how to do it. I hoped she'd stop and talk but she continued on. Instead, I met up with Lady and ranted to her. She understood me.

That night I read from John about the part where Jesus kicks out the money lenders and says, "Destroy this temple and I will rebuild it in three days." My experience at Catholic High destroyed me. Yet, in three days I moved out and found Mandala. The Lord showed me direction. I was in the process of rebuilding.

Sunday morning, I had planned on spending alone time, lying in the sun, when Bear came and said, "The Empress asked if you would work on the house with her."

"I would consider it," I said and we both laughed.

The Empress and I worked all morning. She taught me how to frame windows. Then we took a break and talked for a long time. I swam and she sat at the edge of the lake. I realized she was not the person I imagined she was, but I did love her.

"I'm very much at peace," she said. "I can sit and pray for hours."

"Not me. How can that satisfy you? What about your sexuality? I'm full of contradictions."

"I don't believe in the gay lifestyle although I do have the same contradictions in myself. I don't like the jealousies aroused by such a relationship. These types of relationships require much time and effort. I believe in community. That's worth the effort. I need to stay in one direction."

"The relationship between John and Christ seemed to be one of love," I responded. "I don't think there is anything wrong with gay relationships. The only problem with my last relationship was my immaturity." We talked more about Christ and community and I felt young compared to her. I was glad we could be honest with one another.

We continued building all afternoon. The Empress drank and got a little tipsy in the hot sun. Her eyes were cast away, and she was lost in her quiet thoughts. Mostly we were silent. At times she would turn and stare at me. I asked, "Are you thinking or just tired?"

"Thinking," she responded.

About what, I wondered. I watched as her strong masculine hands with long fingers carefully held the thick shaft of the hammer and pounded each nail into place. Over her red turtleneck, she wore an over-sized, white, short-sleeved shirt that hung loosely over her green khaki pants. A green felt hat covered her hair. The brim was pulled down over her ears. I could still see her face and noticed a raised mole on the right side of her cheek. It didn't detract from her beauty. I loved the way she called me "woman," at times, like she owned me. It happened when she was trying to explain her carpentry methods. I would interrupt and contradict her. It would aggravate her, she would laugh and yell, "Be quiet, woman! Do you want to learn or mouth off?!"

I enjoyed making her laugh.

"You need a personal secretary," I said after she kept bossing me around. "I want to apply."

"You're hired! But you need to get rid of all that jewelry. You're such a city slicker," she said.

"Hey, all that jewelry means something," I responded in defense. "This necklace was a gift from my sister and this ring from my Aunt."

I extended my hand in her direction. She grabbed my hand and pulled it toward her to get a closer look. I flushed at her touch.

"Well, it doesn't go with your carpenter outfit. If you hit your finger, you'll never get them off."

"Okay," I said, pulling back my hand in self-protection. "Point made."

I played gofer all day getting her beers and tools. Later, I had to force her to finish the job we started. The drinking made her lazy. It was difficult being so close to her. I was so attracted to her. She would die if she knew my fantasies of making love to her ... violent physical lovemaking ... passion turning into pain ... kissing ... groping ... slapping ... giving myself totally to her ... loving her body ... feeling those long fingers inside me ... letting down the hair ... her hands all over me ... her body wrapped around me ... melting inside me ...

"Hey, where are you, woman? Daydreaming again? Hold this board for me. Then we can quit. You need to eat."

"Day fantasy."

"We fantasize when we can't cope with the world," she said.

"I'm not meant for this world."

"None of us were," she responded.

The next morning, I worked on the roof by myself. I was ecstatically happy. It wasn't work at all. I cut off the overhanging ends of the rafters and finished the side. I felt like a queen on that roof. From that vantage point, I could see forever. The world was mine. The Empress was supposed to come and help, but she never made it. I knew she wouldn't!

I went for a swim and then bought some beers to bring to the lake house. I tried to give the Empress money for supplies, but she wouldn't take it. "Talk it over with the Hierophant. She keeps the books."

After dinner, we all walked up to the barn to watch the Empress harness the horse who lived in the fenced in yard surrounding the barn. On the way up the hill, she caught up to me and in a gentle voice said, "I'm sorry I didn't come and work today." I smiled, understandingly.

I was starting to get a sense of how things worked in the community- who had the power. A dump truck incident was very telling. Bear oversaw this vehicle. She had planned on using it to hay one of the local fields, but she came back in a huff that morning and said, "I can't believe she told them to take the truck!"

"Who?" I asked.

"The Hierophant. She told the group from Mass that they could take my truck to Bar Harbor for the day. I need it for haying."

"Go tell the Empress," I suggested.

"Yeah, you're right." Later she came back up with a confused look on her face.

"Did you get it settled?" I asked as we walked toward the truck.

Before she could answer, the Empress came up and in front of everyone questioned Bear, "Is there any reason why they can't take the truck?" Bear was kind in her response. She didn't want to get into a confrontation in front of all of the kids.

"Well, I thought I would get that haying done, but if you really need it, I suppose I could do it tomorrow."

The kids took the truck, the Empress left, and Bear went home upset. The Empress always defended what the Hierophant wanted. Right or wrong.

Tuesday morning, I lay in my bed and cried softly. It was painful to love. The Empress left for work on her motorcycle and I left for the city. The Artist and I had lunch, a farewell meal.

"It's not the right time for this house," she said. "I may go out to Arizona."

"I'm happy in the woods," I said. "I feel like I fit in at the Co-op. I think I can be an organizer."

We parted as friends, and I was appreciative of how she had taught me to express my desires.

I slept in the studio apartment by myself that night. I could not get the Empress out of my mind. Indiana said her boyfriend had seen a white light around the Empress when he met her. Maybe she was a spiritual being living in a human body. I didn't see it. I just felt love for her. The Empress had said that the Co-op needed good people like me, but she doesn't know all of me.

That night a phone rang continuously upstairs from 2:30 am till 6:30. It was so aggravating. I kept thinking of the man who said he had killed twelve people. I imagined that he had found out where I lived and was calling to aggravate me. I fell asleep and woke up startled as I felt something scratching on the side of my bed. I fell back to sleep and again woke up hearing a voice say, "Dorothy, he knows where you are." That really scared me. I finally fell asleep when the phone stopped.

Sarah always told me I wasn't serious about anything. The thing I was most serious about was learning about myself, so I began a journal. I was trying to see patterns. I found it fascinating to watch myself. I was so absent-minded. The other morning, I dressed, and as I went to go out the door, I saw my bra hanging on the chair. I wondered what I had put on. Bear and Lady caught my bewilderment. We all laughed.

Later Bear saw me carrying a piece of wood. "Why are you carrying around that piece of wood," she asked.

"I was up on the roof and had a thought. There was no paper, so I wrote it on the wood." She shook her head.

How I amused myself!

On Wednesday morning, I returned to the Co-op and met Ma Kettle. She ran up to me and hugged me in the parking lot. She was so free with her affection.

"Come on Mama. We gotta go pick up some kids," she said as she jumped in her car. I did the same, as the Empress walked by, looked at us, but made no comment.

It was always a whirlwind being with Ma Kettle. Before we finished one project, she was halfway to the next. She dropped me back off at the Co-op. At that point, Lady came out from the office and yelled to me, "The Empress was looking for you. She left you this note." She handed me a folded piece of paper which read "Come and help me at the barn." I felt like a child with a new toy. I ran as fast as I could to the car and sped out.

I found the Empress chain sawing trees in the woods. She stopped working, and we had a beer at the round house and talked. I was still slightly uncomfortable with her. We talked mostly about family.

"My sister was supposed to come out today, but she called and couldn't make it," she said. I sensed her disappointment.

"Do you have any other siblings?" I asked.

"Yes, two other sisters who live in heaven. I've tried to be a mother to my nephew Shawn since his mother died. He was so young at the time. It's been difficult for him."

"I have a younger brother, John, and he's coming next week to visit."

"Really? So is my other nephew, Skids." Then her mood switched, and she said, "Let's get some work done." She got quiet and seemed preoccupied as we worked. Concerned, I questioned, "Is anything wrong?"

"I don't want to talk about it," she responded and kept working. I wondered if it had to do with the fact that yesterday the tractor had fallen over when Bear was riding it. Luckily, Bear had enough time to jump out of its way. It could have been a terrible disaster.

Volunteers came out later in the day to work on the barn. "Let's get some beer," said the Empress when they arrived.

Back up on the barn roof, we started into one of our usual, petty, puppy-love arguments.

"I think we should cut this section," I said.

"Why? No one will see it. Just leave it!" she responded.

"No, I can't"

"Just leave it, woman"

"Do you think you're always right?" I asked in a frustrated tone.

"I don't want to be right. I only want to get the roof done!" she looked at me with those deep dark eyes twinkling from the alcohol.

"So Lucky Luke is living with a girl now," she changed the subject. "I want him to stay at Mandala, but I'm afraid people will talk."

"What do you care that people talk? Aren't we above that here?"

"Well, I agree, but the Hierophant thinks it will be a problem."

My green monster reared its head. "It's always what the Hierophant thinks. Why does she matter so much? Who's in charge here?"

"Watch it," she yelled.

Bear and Cleme came up on the roof, and we got five of the trusses tied in. It was hard work. But it was so gratifying to watch them go up and be part of the making. When it was done, we were all good and tired and went to rest. Bear invited me to come over. While we sat drinking our beverages, The Hierophant came up looking for her little dog, Chico. He was a small nippy Chihuahua who barked at everyone. He thought he was a big German Shepherd! I was too tired and sore to deal with her, so I went outside. Lady followed me out and said, "You're putting yourself in a frustrating position. I've seen the Empress do this before. A piece of her is dead, and you are asking for something that is not possible."

"I don't believe that. Are my feelings that visible?"

"Yes, to me anyway. I'm worried about you."

"Don't worry. My eyes are open. I realize I risk rejection, but I can't stop my dreams."

"You're deeply passionate. Maybe you ought not show so much of yourself."

"You're right but it's hard for me not to."

"There is a strong bond between the Empress and the Hierophant. The Empress got real upset when the Hierophant was in the hospital with cancer. The Empress felt she wasn't giving enough of herself to the Hierophant and was afraid of losing her. The Hierophant is a ground for her. She is the only person the Empress has been able to live with for such a long period of time."

"I didn't mean to fall in love," I said, realizing this was a more complicated situation than I thought.

"I know. You just came out of a painful relationship. I don't want to see you get hurt again. Believe me, I know about unconsummated love."

"Thanks for your concern. You are a true friend. Either way is painful."

I went to bed early and woke up during the middle of the night. My thoughts were so confusing . . . I woke up thinking I wanted to have her baby . . . I never wanted to have a baby . . . I must love her . . . she makes me feel so womanly . . . I just want to serve her . . . I could see the full moon through the trees lighting up the entire sky. It was so beautiful. I went outside and sat in the "garden of agony." I prayed for guidance and help.

At 5:15 am, I packed the car for my weekend trip to Connecticut. Lady needed a ride to her brother's. She read me sections from one of May Sarton's book on the drive down. I identified with the passages. Lady was so perceptive. She genuinely cared about me. I learned that her childhood had been difficult. Her mother was extremely sick and dying when she was only eight. Maids raised her, but because she and her brother were alone a lot, she became a substitute mother. Her father remarried but divorced when her brother was still young. Lady became her father's confidant. Her outward cold, honest shell was developed as a protection against her emotional youth. She hated dishonesty.

"I don't know how long I will be able to stand the physical requirements of Mandala," she said. "I need a lot of alone time and it's impossible to get it here. The work ethic is so strong." This was a major point of contention between her and the Empress. I realized she had given up on any possible relationship between her and Bear. Their relationship was not physical.

"It's hard to change another's way of being," she warned.

"I think the Empress is more sensual than Bear."

"People don't always admit these kinds of needs to themselves," she responded.

"The Empress admitted to me she has those needs," I said.

The car engine started to hesitate on the way down, but I didn't stop. As soon as we crossed the Hartford line, I could really feel the rise in the pollution level. My throat and nose bothered me, and I felt sick. I missed Mandala already. My glands swelled up that night.

I was like a teenager with my sister.

"How do you know when you are in love?" I asked her. "Am I attractive, Mar?"

"You sound like you're in love," she said. I didn't tell her who it was. "We both need to be loved," she added. "You're a simple person. It's better not to seek love, but to let it find you."

I overate all weekend. My sinuses acted up, and I felt awful. Mar rubbed my back. She sensed my tightness. Dad offered building hints, and Mom said to me, "You need a job in chemistry and a person to love, and then you will be happy."

"Was I always quiet as a child?" I asked her.

"Yes, and secretive. I'm worried about you living in Maine. The cold is going to get to you. You're prone to sickness of the throat."

Enough of the protective concern, I visited my teacher friend Amy. She and her friends were smoking pot and drinking when I arrived. They couldn't believe that I was living without electricity and running water in the woods.

"We love our conveniences and although we get bored at times with our lives, we wouldn't change anything." I blanked them out. I no longer could justify this lifestyle. At least I was feeling life-the stillness of the night-the emotion of George Sand sitting under the piano while Chopin played-the frustration of Vita's loving Virginia from a distance.

Later, I went to visit Wolf. She was in a bad mood. "I'm disgusted with my friends. No one is around when I need them." I wondered if she included me in this list. It didn't bother me if she did. I had tried enough with her. I didn't feel guilty anymore.

My brother, John accompanied Lady and me back to Maine. As soon as we arrived, Lady got into an argument with Cleme. She came over and screamed her frustrations to me.

"You're the only person I can yell to," she cried. I wondered how long she would last in that situation.

The Hierophant had left for a three-week trip. Skids was staying with the Empress, but he was leaving to visit a friend. The Empress ignored me in her usual manner that morning. Then later, she came up and told me to watch Skids till he got picked up. She didn't even ask politely.

I stayed at the Hermit's house since he was away. I spent a lot of time just watching the waves and reading. The book about lesbians proclaimed that when one lesbian wanted another, she treated her as an object. Was that true?

On Tuesday, the Empress had a change in mood, and invited me to stay at her house. "You can sleep up in the loft bedroom," she offered.

That afternoon, Skids and I went canoeing on the lake. As I lay stretched out in the sun at the end of the boat, with my hand dancing in the water, I imagined myself a wealthy Italian baronessa . . . A wide-brimmed red hat shaded my eyes as I read *The House of Lions*, a book about the Bloomsbury group. Skids serenaded on the guitar.

After our sailing jaunt, Skids and I prepared a McDonald's special supper–Italian French fries and hamburgers. Later we watched the news while the Empress played her dulcimer. Life was wonderful!

I asked the Empress, "Do you see a contradiction in that the Father doesn't judge but the Son does?"

"No," she said, "I see Christ as a mirror and therefore causes self-judgement. Community can help us overcome our failings."

"It appears to me with all the petty internal bickering in community life, spiritual growth is actually hampered," I responded.

"The community is young," she responded. "Only three years old. We are still children. We need time to get to know one another. We each need to find our place."

"If there are problems to begin with, I can't foresee them getting better. It's harder to correct bad patterns once they are formed. It's easier to stop them before they start."

"You have to learn patience. It takes time. All good things take time. Pray. You must pray constantly."

"Life seems to be full of triangles. Don't you think?"

"No. I don't experience them. I feel free. Do you see triangles here?"

"I'm not ready to discuss them," I said. I didn't feel comfortable talking about the triangles I saw between her/the Hierophant/me and Bear/Lady/Cleme.

"Let's do something fun, she said. "Let me analyze your handwriting."

"You analyze handwriting?" I asked in a surprised tone.

"Yes. Here, write your full name," she said as she handed me a piece of paper. "Ok. Let's see. Overall, the handwriting is simple, yet creative. You are intuitive, have a poor self-ego and need approval. You must change the way you write your name. Make it more affirmative. Make the D stronger and cross your t's. And why are you still wearing so much jewelry?" she asked, taking hold of my hands. "Can't get away from meaningless physical things? You like the finer things in life, like going to restaurants," she continued.

"What's wrong with going to restaurants?" I asked. "You do it. I gave up a lot coming here."

"You're right. It's easy for me to get into the restaurant syndrome too."

She was deeply spiritual and had a great sense of the gospels. I must have seemed a silly novice to her.

In the morning, I read the gospel where Jesus walked on water to the disciples. I didn't understand the significance except that Jesus appeared when the situation was difficult, in *"rough water."* The disciples recognized him, but he did not get in the boat. *"Do not be afraid. It is I"*- such comforting words. I had switched to the *House of Lions* when the Empress came over and told me to choose gospel readings for the day's Mass.

"We are not liberated enough to use something from the *House of Lions*." She laughed picking up my book. "You will be responsible for picking readings for the week. You must learn."

"I am new at this," I responded.

"You will learn." She smiled.

\* \* \*

The Empress had to appear in court that day and left wearing a dress. Not exactly her style!

When the Empress returned, we worked on the barn. I realized how forgetful she was. Yesterday she had told me to forego the 24" settings and just put them over the studs. Today, she told me to change the settings. I was puzzled! I figured she had a lot on her mind as she shared with me the details about her day in court. She was defending a woman who was trying to get custody of her children. The woman was a bad wife, and her new boyfriend had shot the husband. The husband was the victim in this case.

"What will you do? How can you defend that?" I asked, bewildered by the circumstance.

"I see a difference between being a good wife and a good mother. I will be a character witness for her. If you want to understand poor people, spend some time in court," she said to me. "It's a horrible situation for these people. There were no chairs. The Sheriff was offensive. People were handcuffed. They tried to look presentable, but their clothes were soiled. On the opposite end are the lawyers in their three-piece suits."

I realized the contrast was the driving force for her. This increased my admiration for her. I loved her gentleness with the poor.

Friday night the Empress and I dropped Skids off at the Kettles' and then we went to pick up lumber. I drove her to get the truck. She opened my glove compartment and searched through the envelopes. I commented, "Good thing there is nothing personal in there."

"Come on now. There is nothing in here that would shock me."

"Probably not. Do you even consider yourself a nun?" I asked.

"More or less. I believe in commitment to the gospels and the vow of chastity. Abstinence gives me tremendous amounts of energy."

"Not me." I laughed. "Are you happy then?"

"Yes, I think so," she said hesitantly. It was a difficult question for her.

"Tell me about your past. Were you poor?"

"I did ok," she responded, but did not go into much detail. We stopped to see her mother whom she calls "Gram." She warned me before we entered the house that there would be feuding.

Her mother was a large, domineering woman who sat in the middle of the room and spouted orders constantly to anyone in hearing range. I could well imagine that she controlled the lives of her two sons who lived with her on the big farm.

"Are you coming to spy?" she asked her daughter. The Empress shook her head and smiled as she stood by the wall near the door. There was safety in distance.

"Come and sit down," ordered Gram.

"I'm ok standing," the Empress responded.

"You," she said pointing her cane at me, "sit down in this chair in front of me." I did as I was told but glanced toward the direction of the Empress. "Don't worry about her," she said pointing now to her daughter. "She's not social. She doesn't care about us. There are a lot of problems out here. You wouldn't know, living out there in the woods. I just make the best decisions I can. Thank God I have this girl living with me. She's so helpful. Does my chores and helps me get around. You know I have a hard time getting around." She looked at me and raised her cane. "Bad legs and back." Then she turned to the Empress, "And your brother is no help. . . ." She went on and on about the farm problems. I felt bad for the Empress.

"Do you want some supper?" she finally asked after her complaining.

"No, Gram, we have to get back," replied the Empress.

"And who is she?" she asked pointing to me.

"Dorothy helps us at Mandala."

"Oh, they brainwashed you into going out there. You need to get out in the real world. Don't stay there too long. Find a man to take care of you."

"Right, that's what I need." I laughed but didn't dare contradict her.

"Let's have some tea and cake before you leave."

"I don't want any, Gram," said the Empress.

Gram just ignored her and said to me, "You'll have some. Won't you? I made some nice cake this morning." I didn't say anything but knew I would have to eat it. She called the girl to bring us some tea and cake. The Empress didn't budge and remained by the wall.

After about an hour, we left and stopped for supper at a diner on the way home.

"You seem uncomfortable," I said to the Empress watching her fidgeting in her seat. Her eyes kept glancing around the room like someone would see us together. She was wearing her green army jacket and black tam. I was in green fatigues. We looked like we had just returned from an army drill.

She laughed and looked at me. "It was a hard day." She didn't explain, but I knew it had to do with seeing her mother. The experience wiped me out so I could imagine what it did to her.

"Just relax. I'm not going to attack you," I said. "Your mother is certainly a handful!" I said sympathetically.

"She's all right. She comes from good stock. You don't find women like her anymore. We kids weren't easy to bring up."

"So, do you usually have dinner with beautiful women?" I asked as a diversion.

"Yeah. Good thing no one knows me here. I'd end up with a reputation."

"It would be worth it."

"Watch it. Give me the bread."

"Can't you say 'please'?" I teased and held the basket back.

"Pass the bread, Woman, before I knock you down."

"Oooh. I'd like that. Are we feeling feisty tonight?"

We continued teasing each other during dinner like we were lovers. I felt close to her and I thought she felt the same about me.

On the trip home, she said to me, "I'm glad we stopped to eat." I took it as an apology for her tense behavior in the restaurant. "I only had salad today. I need to eat better." Her big white husky dog Argus was being unruly in the truck. "Sit in the middle and let him hang out the window. That will calm him," she said. So, I moved into the middle. I loved sitting so close to her. Her strong hands shifting the gears. I couldn't take my eyes off of them imaging what they could do. I rested against her strong shoulder as Argus kept pushing me in her direction. I melted in my seat. I didn't dare move for fear I would attack her. Being so close was difficult for me.

We got to her house, and she made us tea. She turned on the

battery radio and the TV, which ran off a small generator. It was the only house in the community with any electric power. The TV was only used for special programs that the Empress wanted the members to see. We sat on the floor together in the pitch black.

"Wow. This is special, TV," I commented.

"Yeah. You city folks can't be in the quiet too long," she teased.

"Hey. That's not fair. I'm doing pretty well," I said and nudged her in the side.

"Watch it. Stay on your own side. Or I'll have to get tough with you."

"Is that a promise?"

"Never mind. Be good."

"I am being good. You don't know how good I'm being." I said and sat quietly drinking my tea. We were still close together on the floor. I could feel her body twitching and moving about like she didn't know what to do with herself.

"You're fidgeting again," I said.

"No, I'm not," she said as she tried to calm herself. I felt we were on the verge of something, but I wasn't sure. She got off the floor and sat in the chair. A frightened look registered on her face. I think she was afraid of what I might do. She had given me the impression she desired me, but with that look on her face I knew she wasn't ready to face that part of herself, and I would never force myself on her. It would have to be her move.

"It's so nice," I said trying to encourage her.

"What is?" she asked. I didn't respond. I was afraid I was projecting. I caught her staring into the distance as if she were pondering something serious, something troubling her. I wished I had the courage to ask what it was, but here I was a nobody. I didn't ask. Finally, I said,

"You drive me crazy. You never say what is on your mind."

"I always say what is on my mind," she responded.

"Did you ever love anyone?" I asked.

"Yes many. I still love them." Then calling my bluff she said, "If you have something to say, you better say it." I wanted her so badly, but I didn't have the courage to tell her how I felt. It was awkward. Later, I wondered if I had said the right things, would the night have ended differently? Shortly, she announced she was tired. She went to bed. I remained in front of the TV and watched her close the door to her room. I was a wreck. I couldn't sleep knowing she was so close. I wanted to shout her name. I got up and went to the bathroom to let her know I was still up, but she didn't come out.

I had a dream that night that I was pregnant and carrying the second Christ. I was chosen, and the Empress knew it, and she was waiting for me to tell her. I almost screamed out in the dream. I awoke unable to distinguish reality from fantasy. I was so sure it was true. I knew she was appointed to help me through this endeavor and that after the child was born, we would go off together. What a sick mind! I ran and prayed in the morning. I read from John, *"What I have to offer is of the spirit, the flesh is of no avail"* and I knew what she was offering me was not of the body, but only growth in spirit.

The next morning after my run, I found the Empress in a good mood. Rock music was playing on the radio and she was friendly and playful.

"Good morning. Did you enjoy your run? Would you like some pancakes? I'm cooking," she asked as she rubbed my shoulders.

"Ok. Yeah. Sure. What got into you?"

"What do you mean?"

"You're in such a good mood."

"I'm always in a good mood," she said handing me a plate of wheat pancakes. "Here, you eat your breakfast while I go change. I want you to come with me today. I'm marrying a young couple."

"Ok," I answered, wondering where this new friendly person came from. I decided I'd better talk to her as it was getting bad for me. I needed to get my feelings out in the open. She came back into the kitchen all dressed up in a long dark skirt, flowered top, and fancy headscarf. It was a character I wasn't familiar with.

"Wow. A dress and fancy scarf! That's new."

"Don't get smart. I do dress occasionally," she replied.

We started up the hill to the car. I was in my tight jeans with tailored shirt and the clunky, thick, heeled shoes I wore when I dressed. My hair was cut short, masculine style, and covered by a red, white, and blue bandanna. I was still very thin and quite muscular from all the building and carrying. I was comfortable with the way I looked.

About halfway up I got the courage to say, "I'd like to talk to you about something that has been bothering me."

"Sure," she said glancing in my direction.

"I feel like such a child. I don't know how to say this. I had no intention of getting involved with another person, but I feel like there is something between us. It's not your problem. It's mine. But I need to know. Is there anything between us?" I was embarrassed the moment the words left my mouth. I must have sensed what was coming.

"No. I don't feel that way. And it's not good for you to feel that way."

"Yes, I know. But repression is bad for me. I have to face my problems, so I thought if I talked to you about it, I could resolve it."

"I understand. Feelings like that usually come out of a poor relationship with one's mother. I don't have that problem with my mother," she said calmly as if she believed it to be true. The comment raised my eyebrows as I knew otherwise.

"You need to become a giver. At some point, your mother becomes a sister, and you see her needs and weaknesses and then you can start giving to others. You need to laugh at yourself more. Do you ever laugh at yourself?"

"I'm trying. Now more than ever. But you're right. I do take myself too seriously."

"I kid with you at times to make you feel comfortable, but that's the only reason."

We reached the top of the hill. The sun beamed through the dew drops on the trees. It was a gorgeous site, but I felt childlike. My head was cast down. If she had a dual personality, I had just told the wrong person how I felt. She implied it was entirely my problem and that she had no part in the making. Tomorrow, she would be the quiet self who ignored me. I had come close to the real Empress, but my honesty was threatening enough that it would take a long time for her to reveal herself again. If she ever would again. I had acted impatiently.

She did not talk much on the long ride. The dwelling turned out to be a small trailer, located deep in the woods. In the front yard, family members stood around waiting for the festivity to begin. There was excitement amid true poverty.

The cake, wine, and maid of honor never showed up. The Empress asked me be maid of honor. Out of necessity, I agreed. But first, I had to be hairdresser. There was no one else to help her. I was sharing in one of the most important days of her life, and I had never even spoke to this person before. I knew how difficult her life would be. How difficult her life must already be! She was as nervous as one would expect a jittery bride to be.

"Does my hair look all right? This piece keeps falling out," she said as she pushed a strand of hair back under the veil.

"You are a beautiful bride," I commented, trying to erase her insecurity. The woman was young, yet two small children clung to her legs during the marriage ceremony. She and her groom looked lovingly at each other. There would be no honeymoon.

Dressed in blue jeans and bouquet in hand, I walked down the aisle next to the bride. We stood in front of the Empress-turned- priestess. The severity of the situation was overwhelming. The Empress and I looked at each other with empathic communication.

We did not speak much on the ride home. I was glad to be alone afterwards and walked down to the lake. The Empress went right to her room. I wrote in my journal to the sound of the water slapping on the rocks.

The next day I got my period. I had skipped a month, and my system was off. I wondered if my need to talk about my feelings to the Empress was instigated by the PMS. Whatever, I couldn't change what had transpired between us. My intuition overshadowed my rational mind, and my emotions got the best of me. If I had waited a day, I might have been ok with the feelings.

The Empress only came out of her room for Sunday Mass. She ignored me as I had anticipated she would. Her eyes did not meet mine during the service. She was quiet and heavy with emotion. I talked with the others after Mass even though I knew she wanted to just go back to bed. I joked about making "going away muffins" for Cleme as she was leaving the next day. We discussed predicting the future, and the Empress remained silent and pained. When everyone left, she headed for her room.

"I'm going to Ma and Pa Kettle's," I said as she was closing the door.

"I don't care what you do," she responded. "I'm staying in bed."

I felt so badly for what had and had not happened. If I could relive that morning, I would not have mentioned anything about my feelings. I just wanted to know what direction we were going in. Friends or lovers? Why had it bothered her so much? Did she see parts of herself in me? If she didn't care for me, then what difference did it make to her how I felt? For me, the pain I had obviously caused her was worse than my frustration of sleepless nights. I wanted to get back to just being her friend.

That night I went to bed terribly upset. I didn't want to wake up. I welcomed the thought of death. I kept repeating to myself in bed, "Lord, have mercy on me," as I envisioned throwing myself out the window.

Argus, the Empress's dog, came up the hill later in the morning when I was working on the barn and rubbed against me. I hugged him even thought I didn't really like dogs. I felt like she was sending her familiar to say, "It's ok," because she couldn't do it herself. At work, I prayed, "Make me a channel of your peace," and I started feeling an inner comfort.

Before bed, I read from John V: 25 "*I have not come of myself.*" I remembered I had said something similar to the Empress. I was bound for Boston but because of Sr. Lidia's message I ended up in Maine. Maybe there truly was a reason why I was here. The passage mentioned Jerusalem, and the other night for some reason during our conversation, the Empress referred to the passage where Christ said, "*Oh Jerusalem, how I would love you.*"

I saw her as the female Christ. Would there be a Judas? Who? I told the Empress if she wanted disciples, she had to teach. Was I part of some great plan? It was slowly making sense to me, and yet I hardly believed it could be true. Were my dreams of having the Empress's baby symbolic of giving birth to her spirit? Was I crazy? Yet I felt saner than ever.

I was reading a lot of Carl Jung. The meaning of dreams and the unconscious had aroused my interest. Jung grew up near a large river and was affected by the water. I understood this. When I was younger, I would sit for hours watching the waves. I always knew I would live by a lake. It was a feminine force that calmed me.

A few days passed and the Empress got over her rejection of me. She started treating me normally again.

* * *

One evening, Lady invited me to visit. She started ranting about how upset she was that the Empress did not call her when Bear went to the hospital after her accident with the vehicle.

"Have you figured the Empress out yet?" I asked Lady. "I think she is schizo."

"She's not there at times," Lady responded. "That's for sure."

"You see it too?" I commented.

Skids was with me, and he wanted to go down to the lake house. I told Lady I had to leave. I could tell that she wanted me to stay longer so she could continue to vent about the Empress.

"Stay and have some wine. We just opened a new bottle of California Merlo," Lady suggested. She knew I enjoyed wine and that her invitation would tempt me to stay, but I left with him.

The next day, the Empress took me to a small farm meeting in Harbor Port at the home of Helen and Scott Nearing. The couple had built the house when they were in their nineties. The garden was an artistic creation. On the ride to the meeting, the Empress confided to me about the situation with Lady. She felt the situation was getting worse.

"Lady is a manipulator," she said. "It's getting difficult for Bear. In a Christian sense, we must help her. Bear thinks that since you are close to Lady, you could be the mediator."

"I understand what you mean about her being a manipulator," I responded and proceeded to tell her about my experience with Skids and Lady the other night. However, I felt like a Judas talking about Lady to the Empress. Lady had been such a good friend to me. How could I talk to her about the problem with Bear without hurting her?

After the meeting, the Empress asked, "Do you think Helen likes me?"

"Of course," I responded and thought, 'How could she think someone would not like her?' I told her how proud I was of her when she spoke for women's rights in the all-male meeting and stood her ground when they opposed her. Her insecurity came as a surprise.

The Empress was whacked out at work on Thursday morning. She was trying to write an article for the paper, but she was restless and cranky. At one point, she carried on about some missing chicken. Weird! I got the impression she had eaten it but had forgotten. I suggested that we go for a muffin as she needed to eat. We got Skids and went to Duffy's. She went on about people worrying about winter coming and not having enough food. She was in such low spirits and preoccupied. I tried to lift her out of the depths but couldn't. She went back into her office and closed the door. I helped in bookkeeping and then went out to Mandala to work on the barn with her nephew, Shawn, and my brother John.

John said to me, "You look tired and mad."

"Really?" I said, not knowing why I would be. There was no reason. Maybe the Empress had drained my energy.

She came out much later in the afternoon wearing her green hat with the brim pulled down over her head. I knew she would be in a good mood. This seemed to be the case every time she wore this hat. And sure enough, she was her happy-go-lucky self. I accused her of drinking, but she denied it. She stared out into space as we worked. Finally, she got it together and did some work. At dinner, we had a few beers. She ate well and even had dessert. Her transitions were difficult to watch. I never knew which personality would appear. After dinner, she went out to chop wood and then visited Bear. When she came back, she said to me, "Are you in a bad mood?"

"Me? In a bad mood? No! What about you? I can't stand to watch you destroy yourself. You were so spacey today. It's like you have a dual personality. Sometimes you're fine, but sometimes, you just space out like you have no control."

"I was concerned about Skids and Shawn and the dynamics between them," she said in defense. "They both vie for my attention, and I feel torn. I feel like a mother to both." This made no sense to me as both boys seemed strong and independent.

"You were drinking, too. Weren't you?" I asked.

"So were you."

"Yes, but you repeat yourself and say dishonest things when you are drinking," I added.

"Don't you do that too?" she responded defensively. "No one is honest with themselves. There are probably five people within me."

"Can you tap into someone's energy?" I asked out of frustration. I was wondering how she had gotten out of the early morning foul mood.

"No. Why? Do you think I can?"

"I don't know what you can do. But I do know that you have not faced an aggressive part of your nature, and it comes out when you drink. Something is bothering you. You're not happy."

"That is probably true," she responded. "But basically, I am happy, and people are worth my energy even if it spaces me out. When you give, you can't expect return. I don't think you understand that. I don't know what you expect. Van Gogh says, 'we sow seeds, but the crop is elsewhere.' Do you believe that?"

"Yes," I said weakly, not sure what I believed.

"Someday you will have to commit to something," she advised.

"If I did commit to something, it would be a serious choice," I answered.

"What do you want to be committed to?" she asked.

"I don't know but it would be serious." I laughed.

"What about a hospitality house?"

"I don't know. I need time."

"How much time does one need?" she asked.

The conversation was going in circles. I gave up, went to bed, and cried. Then I went out to get the bag that I had left on the kitchen table. She was sitting on the couch and asked, "Are you all right?"

"Yes, fine," I responded sharply and went back into the room. I didn't feel like I was getting anywhere with her, and I didn't have the energy to continue.

The next day I spoke to Lady. "I've given up on the Empress," I told her. "There is nothing between us. I'm only interested in community now."

"I understand, and that's a good attitude for you to take."

"There is something else I want to talk to you about," I said, thinking this was a good time to bring up the subject the Empress had suggested. "The other night when you offered me wine, and Skids wanted to leave, I felt like you were trying to manipulate me."

"Manipulate! That's a strong word for it," she said expressing hurt on her face. I realized I had said it all wrong. We had some further small chat, and I hoped I hadn't lost her friendship.

My brother left on Saturday morning and I cried. I really cried. I felt as if a part of me was gone. I ended up taking Skids into town. He had put me in an awkward situation with the Empress by telling her that I said I would take him when I hadn't said that. She was happy that I was spending time with him and I didn't want to disappoint her. Later, I told her that we had to teach Skids responsibility since he was a trickster who would try to get away with whatever he could. She did not see this.

The Hermit left right after Mass and wouldn't stay to eat. Supper was weird. Scarecrow started coughing up some pig's feet. I had this shocked, disgusted look on my face. The Empress looked at me and shook her head. We both laughed. The Lady flamed on about opera. The conversation drove the Empress crazy though she maintained an outward calm. I knew Lady did it on purpose to aggravate the Empress. She was such a good actress. I felt caught in the middle, as I knew how each felt.

After everyone left, the Empress went out and sat alone on the porch. I went to bed. I felt tight and couldn't sleep. My mind rambled on about the Empress. She proclaimed that people are fragmented. Is it because she was fragmented? I could see different personalities in her based on her dress. I started to make a list of her different personalities.

1. Dressed up. This woman is spiritual, quiet, in control and feminine.

2. Green hat and sunglasses. This woman is fun! She drinks, kids about lesbianism and is masculine.

3. Hair down. Very sensual woman. Natural and free.

4. Bandana with hair out. Very spaced out. Quiet. Pensive. Ugly.

5. Beret hat. Happy, confident self. Social. Able to laugh at herself.

6. Full bandana. Work person. Normal.

The Empress had said we speak in symbols. Were the hats then indicative of a different self? I decided that the American myth like the German myth that allowed Jung and others to predict a Hitler, was tied up with movies, music, and books. The American culture was being swamped consciously with evil material and so it will move in that direction and become destructive. The next "war" will be a mind take over. A spiritual breakdown of the world. How could we get back to simplicity and move in the direction that Teilhard de Chardin suggested?

Whether the Empress was a divided self or not didn't matter. But what did matter was that her contradictions were driving me crazy. She would say one thing and then do another. The other night I had asked if I should buy some wine for supper.

"No. I want to play down the use of wine," she responded. That night Tinman brought wine. She was thrilled and drank two glasses.

*       *       *

Sunday mornings were rest and quiet time for the Empress. I took the canoe out on the lake. After a few hours, the sky became overcast, and the wind started blowing. It took all my energy to get back into shore. I had to rest before joining the Empress who was already working on the barn. She showed me how to lay down the floor. After that, we cleaned the open space under the barn. We didn't talk very much. Later, she and Skids took out the canoe. I decided to go to Duffy's.

As I was sitting alone and reading, the Artist and a few of her friends came in. They invited me to join them.

"Why don't you come back with me to Bangor?" asked the Artist. "We can talk and catch up on what's been happening."

"That sounds very good right now."

Later that night we sat at the kitchen table sipping coffee.

"I seem to be getting in the middle of the Empress, Bear and Lady," I said and told her about the manipulation incident.

"You shouldn't take on that problem. Be strong and stay out of it. It's not your problem," she warned. "You seem to have a need to straighten out other people's messes."

"But aren't we our brother's keeper?" I said, thinking, 'Where does one draw the line?'

"It's not your problem," she insisted. "It will only get you into trouble. They are big girls and can handle it themselves."

"I just get so mad. I listen to their complaining about one another, and no work gets done. We have so many projects going. I don't see how we can even finish one. Even the Empress gets into petty bickering. She loses track of what we are doing and goes off into her own world."

"You know Dorothy, you think you are Dorothy Super Worker. Work and accomplishment are high on your priority list. Then you get mad at others for not doing the same. You have no right to demand of others what you demand of yourself. People give and do what they need to do. You must let everyone be themselves. Your life will go smoother when you realize this."

"You're right. I can't expect everyone else to keep pace. And I put the Empress on such a pedestal. She can't possibly live up to my expectation. I've been thinking of her as the female Christ. Now isn't that a great image to live up to!"

"It comes from your need to find Christ within yourself."

"You're right. She needs to be who she is, and I need to be who I am. It's strange, but she seems to have different personalities. Real different. Like one doesn't know what the other is doing. I think something happened to her, and it's buried deep within."

"If there is something buried within her, it's probably best to leave it alone," she responded vehemently.

I returned to Mandala just after Monday morning Mass. There I met Tinman walking back to his living space.

"So, you stayed out all night?" he asked with a smile on his face. I didn't respond and just smiled, thinking to myself, 'How did he know?' Later, I realized that the Empress must have told him. When she saw me, she said with the Cheshire cat grin, "Didn't come home last night? What were you doing?"

"Wouldn't you like to know?" I teased back, slinking up next to her. She laughed and affectionately hit me on the back.

I went to the office and was busy with paperwork when Skids came in and sat on the edge of my desk.

"So did my Aunt holler at you?" he asked.

"No. Why?" I responded.

"She said she was going to holler at you for staying out all night and then chain you to the bed."

"Really?" I responded in disbelief. Why had she acted like it didn't bother her? I was thrilled that she thought enough about me to want to keep me "chained in," maybe I should go off more often and stir up her dander!

I worked outside on the barn all afternoon while the Empress stayed in and cooked for our evening guests- Skid's friend and Lucky Luke and his date. The evening was quite enjoyable. The Empress seemed sad, but friendly and talkative. She brought up the subject of money, and I learned that the Co-op was in debt.

Skids and his friend disappeared up into the loft while the adults had coffee. When I retired to my bedroom, I could smell the remains of cigarette smoke and my personal possessions were in disarray as if the boys were looking for something. I wondered if they found my books on lesbianism. Skids had been acting strange during dinner. His request to the Empress that she, "Wake him up for Mass" was so out of character. This kid had street smarts and knew how to schmooze to get what he wanted.

Every day was so full. I worked in the office in the mornings then went out to work on the barn in the afternoons. A good balance of mental and physical work. During lunch with the Lady, the psychic joined us. I shared my concerns regarding the Empress's mental state.

"I agree with you," said the psychic. "There is a deep unhappiness inside her. And anger. She is a very fragmented person and needs to control. When I did a reading for her, I saw a huge castle, gray and dark and empty with no furniture. I think she is spiritually empty. I'm not even sure she was a nun. She depends a lot on the Hierophant for her spirituality. I feel sorry for her. I must warn you not to try and get too close. The defenses are high, and she will back away. I don't see you staying out there too long. There are things there that you need right now, but they will pass."

"You know I keep having dreams of the Empress and sometimes I'm having her baby and other times it's a violent scene."

"That's because you see the Empress as a man. Would you like me to do a reading for you?"

"Yes, please."

"I see an elephant which refuses to be led," she said. "I see the color red. That is a good color. I see only happiness for you. No danger. I see a wedding." For whom? My sister? Me?

Her take on the Empress was disturbing.

Skids and his friend came back to Mandala with me. They were going to stake a tent. On the drive over, I confronted them. "Were you guys smoking up in the loft the other night."

"No. Why do you say that?" asked Skids.

"I smelled smoke up there."

"No. You must have smelled the wood stove."

"You better not smoke up there," I said, raising my voice. "And why were my things thrown around? Were you looking through my stuff?"

"Oh, we were wrestling, and things got knocked around."

"Well, you better stay out of my stuff," I said sternly.

After working on the barn, I went down by the lake to treat myself to a pampering bath. At least once a week, I needed to just dote on myself. The Empress had a late meeting allowing me alone time. I ate cheese, apples, and drank wine, while I read. Simple pleasures. I was finding happiness in the simple. Such a difference from the woman who lived in the city and rushed around.

I read till the Empress returned. We made small talk and she seemed in good spirits. She mentioned that she missed the Hierophant. Probably to make me jealous. One time our eyes met, and then she quickly went to bed without saying goodnight

When the Hierophant came home, the Empress changed dramatically! Suddenly she was talking and acting in a caring manner. She hugged the Hierophant and I believed that the psychic was right about her being the Empress's strength. The Hierophant flamed on about her meetings and about poverty, communication, and other such issues. The Empress hung on her every word. I went to bed.

We didn't experience poverty at Mandala. Not in the true sense of the word and I'm not sure that we had to. We were living very well in this peaceful environment. We had everything we needed.

After a wacko night, I spent the next day alone. Had breakfast at Duffy's, shopped, and then did bookkeeping till around 1:00 pm. I felt terribly frustrated. The psychic saw me and asked, "Why are you so gloomy?"

"I'm frustrated," I responded.

"I felt the same way after my divorce for about a year," she replied. Someone told me masturbation can be addictive, but I don't believe it. It got me through." She left with Lady.

I went home and worked off the frustration by doing carpentry and singing out of the windows of the barn. No one could hear me. I swam and took a bath. Then I cooked and felt somewhat happy.

Everyone came home for supper. The High Priestess came with her husband and two children and another male friend. They were all weird. No one seemed real, except the husband. While talking about religion, I learned The High Priestess was a Quaker and did not believe in Christ. She was caught up in the suffering and injustices of life, but mainly talked about birds, not people. Her husband, who devoutly believed in Christ, appeared more stable. Her son was into other religious experiences, talked incessantly, and was confusing.

The male friend immediately announced, "Okay, everyone identify yourself and tell us what you do." This turned me off, but I didn't want to be antisocial. He told us how he published books in Boston, and all the people he knew and everything he does and what he likes to eat and how he exercises every day for an hour, and where he shops and where he vacations. It made me want to puck. To my surprise, the Empress seemed impressed. The Hierophant was her usual flaky self after one glass of wine. She tended to joke about people and liked to build herself up by talking about her simplistic religion. The Lady came in all dolled up in fancy clothes and jewelry—trying to get the Empress's goat. She talked all night about buying new clothes. The Hermit sent over some reading material to discuss and never showed up himself

Later, I shared my impressions with the Empress, "I feel bad for the High Priestess. She seems out of touch with reality. Her husband acts as a balance. The male friend seems to be on an ego trip."

"Really? I liked him. I didn't think he was on an ego trip," she responded.

"You didn't? That's interesting." And with that comment I went to bed. I didn't want to deal with contradiction.

The Empress was eating again now that the Hierophant was back. In high spirits, she was probably so glad to have the Hierophant back after living with me for two weeks. The Hierophant was a much simpler woman than I.

The Empress put on country music and starting singing, "Lay your head against my pillow . . . " I loved her voice. It made me melt. I had to leave.

I learned about the shadow from Jung's book. The shadow is projected on to others and must be taken back for one to be whole. I had to learn how to do this. Jung says man is poor in spirit because he no longer lives a symbolic life. As Jung grew older, he became lonely in a human sense, but discovered a kinship with nature. The Empress seems to do this with her animals, Argus the dog and all her cats and while she is working in the woods.

I asked the Empress if she wanted to work together on the barn.

"I can do it for a while, then some relatives are coming," she responded. Without much help from the Empress, I finished the floor. I kept asking her to cut me some pieces of wood with her chain saw but she didn't. She forgot, or she was ignoring me. I wasn't sure which.

At one point, she was leaning out the open window space, and I asked her to move. She wouldn't, so I pulled at her shirt.

"Hey watch it. There's sensitive merchandise under there," she teased and laughed. She sent me to buy more tar paper. When I got back, the Hierophant had joined in the work. She seemed weak. As I was lying on the floor listening to my radio, the Empress walked by and said, "Well, do you want to get this house done, or do you want to daydream? I can't get it done by myself."

What a lot of nerve, I thought! My only break for the entire day!

After I quit working, I took a swim, then dressed, and took off for Bar Harbor. I had volunteered to work in the Co-op extension store for the weekend. Shortly after arriving in town, I ran into the Artist and her mother in a bookstore. They were vacationing for the weekend, so I treated them for supper. I kept spending money like I was rich, but my supply was running out. I was in a weird mood and couldn't satisfy my hunger.

"Let's get some candy," suggested the Artist after dinner. At the candy shop, I loaded up. We went to see Star Wars and I fell asleep during the show.

Coincidentally, later, I met Scarecrow, who had been working in the store for the past few weeks. He was out walking in the streets and gave me the key to the store so I could sleep there. Things have a way of falling into place here.

I was totally happy in Bar Harbor. I decided to just be who I was. To talk to myself in a positive way. A rebirth! And, I didn't feel hunger all day.

I returned Monday night just in time for supper. The Empress avoided me. Scarecrow, Lady, the Hierophant and I talked about the Pope.

"He's an anachronism," I spouted. "All his bishops are too. They don't have a sense of reality. And they spout off directions to the person living in the real world. Do you know my mother thinks she is going to hell because she uses birth control? What do they know about having a family? What right do they have to make good people feel guilty? My mother never hurt a soul. She won't even take communion because she feels she is sinning."

"You should be the female Pope," said the Hierophant hysterical at my emotional outburst.

"That's the last thing I want to be!" I shouted. This loud comment caught the Empress's attention.

"The pope should be talking more like Castro," she commented. "And where were you this weekend?"

"I went to work at the Bar Harbor store," I responded.

"Next time leave a note saying when you are leaving and returning," she said as she walked away. I was shocked that she even noticed I was gone. I tried to continue my conversation with the Hierophant, but by this time, she was on to another topic.

"Do you know how much the truck cost to fix?" she said in disgust. "It was supposed to be only $800 but when the Empress went to pick it up, they charged her $1300."

"Did you pay it?" I asked turning to the Empress.

"Yes," she responded.

"Why didn't you fight it?" I continued.

"I don't know. I don't know about these things. The Hierophant pays the bills of Mandala," she said in defense. These women play at being businesswomen, I thought. Five hundred dollars more and she didn't even question!

On Wednesday two nuns, Doctor and Painter, from New Jersey came to visit Mandala. The Doctor had an established practice but was looking to move up north. Painter was joining her to set up an extended spiritual community in the Co-op area. Both were women I could identify with.

Community supper was a first for true "communing." Tinman shared his frustration with his drinking problem and his need to be loved. At least Scarecrow and I could identify with him. The psychic suggested that we all hug Tinman. I realized he was basically a nice guy.

Scarecrow and the Hierophant got into an argument over rent money.

"You should be giving $50 a month to the community," she told him.

"I'm already giving my time," he answered. "Do you know how much that is worth? Besides when I discussed volunteering with the Empress, she didn't say anything about paying rent."

"I'm sure she did. She told me she did," retorted the Hierophant.

"She didn't tell me I had to pay anything," chimed in Tinman. Apparently, the Empress told these men one thing and told the Hierophant another. There were comments expressed about the Co-op being run the same way- inconsistently. The potter was leaving because he felt he was not doing what his VISA grant required. People were upset with the Empress's way of doing business. She could be unfair or dishonest at times. Her faith was great, but her sense of realism was lacking.

"I don't like the way decisions are made," added Scarecrow. "Instead of community vote, the Empress just makes them."

"But you don't know all the pressures she is under," said the Hierophant.

"She pays a lot of the bills out of her own pocket, and her grant is running out. We have to find ways to pay the mortgage."

The conversation turned to Mass. Tinman and Scarecrow felt it was more of a ritual and did it for community sake. Tinman admitted he had remnants of belief but felt he was not worthy to take communion.

"We speak the words, but we don't carry them out," he said regarding our stab at Christianity. Then he bravely commented on the Hermit's relationship to the community. "He does his own thing. Says mass and leaves. Doesn't get involved in anyone's problems. His life is clean," declared Scarecrow.

It was hard to contradict his description.

\*   \*   \*

With all my weight gain, I knew I needed a break. Eating was an addiction for me. I would eat to the point of not feeling good, but instead of stopping, I would eat more. The Empress didn't realize the effect she had on me. I left for home and the Empress left to visit Indiana in Boston. The Empress had been so withdrawn lately and I hoped Indiana would help her out of her funk.

I visited Wolf. She seemed contented. She had accepted her situation. "Our relationship is much better, almost perfect," she professed, though I had a hard time believing her

On my way to see Doris, I stopped in Stop and Shop and bumped into Sarah.

I had feared this meeting, but it went ok. I asked her to come with me to see Doris, but she declined saying she would be in the way. She invited me for supper, and I accepted. We talked like old friends, no tension. I felt bad that after all the years together, there was nothing emotional left between us.

I saw Adele the next day. We discussed Sarah and the fact that she was detaching herself from people in our shared past. She probably felt they were more my friends than hers. She confided in Adele that the apartment felt empty without me.

I drove back to Maine Monday night in the moonlight and mine was the only car on the road. It was spectacular.

The next day, the Empress didn't speak to me. I sensed she was upset with me, and after a few glasses of wine at dinner that night, she said, "People are coming and going as they feel like it. They stay out all night. How can we maintain community?" I didn't say anything. Then she continued, "When you work on the barn tomorrow, do as I instruct you. Don't worry about what other people tell you." This was in retaliation to a conversation with Scarecrow, contradicting her style of carpentry.

She didn't love me. Why did I have to take the brunt of her ravings?

I had been helping in bookkeeping and realized what a mess the finances were. Funds were all mixed up. The Empress's sense of justice was twisted. No wonder she wanted to know what I thought about the ending in *Woman at the Edge of Time*. Did I agree with using unjust means for a certain end? Did the ends justify the means? I wasn't so sure.

They made me treasurer of Mandala. My name was now on the checks. I wasn't sure that this was a good idea.

Prayer was harder these days. Thankfully, I was sleeping better, but I seemed to be in a cold, aloof, independent state. Tinman and Lady had been hanging out together a lot. A power struggle between the Hermit and the Hierophant existed. And now the Empress brought Cowardly Lion, a young fellow, back with her after her last trip to the city to live in the community. Apparently, his mother was overbearing and divorcing his father. Tall and thin with longish, jet-black hair, Cowardly Lion was super quiet and stayed to himself a lot. I didn't feel comfortable with him. Right away, he had assumed the bandana uniform. I began to question if I wanted the community lifestyle. Did I really want to live in this poverty? Was it self-punishment? I talked to Ma Kettle about my uncertainty of living out in the woods. She reassured me that I was good for the group and could help them build community spirit.

"You bring a fresh outlook," she said. "They need that. Don't give up." I decided I'd keep trying.

Thursday's meeting at the Learning Center was depressing. The instructors complained about how hard it was to keep the student's attention. I was tired of trying to entice students in material that I found naturally interesting. Teaching shouldn't be so difficult. Knowledge is a gift.

I drove home and found the Empress sitting on the back porch. She had been crying. I knew it was about money. After I confided in her about the Learning Center meeting, she opened up to me: "I've decided that everyone will have to give a percentage of their earnings to the community. This is non-negotiable."

"That seems reasonable," I answered. "Just tell everyone."

"You think it's ok then?"

"Yes, definitely. Don't worry about it. Let's go do some building to get us out of these foul moods."

"Let's have a glass of wine first," she suggested.

I agreed, as wine always put her in a better mood. And it did. She kidded me while we worked. Cowardly Lion got a charge out of our interaction. Later, he said to me, "She gives you a hard time. More than the others. But you give people a hard time, too. Only kidding," and then added to ease the blow, "But they can take it."

The more I was with Cowardly Lion, the more I liked him. He was very perceptive. He was also considerate and helpful. As we were talking, the Empress came over and said to me, "So are you going to leave your tools around as usual?"

"What are you talking about?" I said. "I'm the only one who picks them up. You never do," I added.

"Hey, watch it," she smiled and climbed down.

Bandit, the Empress's cat slept on my head all night. That morning, I substituted for the Secretary at the Co-op since she had some personal business. I bossed everyone around like she did. Secretary was a tyrant. Even the Empress was afraid of her.

Later, I bought tarpaper for the outside walls of the barn and Cowardly Lion helped me tack it up. The Empress came home and said she would come back to help us, but she never did. Instead, she stayed at the lake house with the Hierophant. That night, I had a wonderful dinner at Ma and Pa Kettle's. Veal parmigiana and eggplant. Of course, I ate and drank too much. It was disgusting. Then I went to a meeting. Bear and the Empress came.

When we left, a hurricane was rolling through the valley. I waited at the turnoff for a ride on the truck since I didn't want to drive my car in the mud. Bear drove in with her vehicle and I jumped into the other truck with the Empress.

"Too chicken to walk in yourself?" she teased. I felt bad for waiting, and I think she felt uncomfortable driving alone with me for the eighth of a mile. There was no moon out, and it was dark and windy and wet. We started walking down the path to the lake house. I tried to keep up with the Empress, but she was too fast. I was afraid of falling on the slippery rocks, so I hung behind.

When we got close to the porch stairs, I said to her, "Empress, I can't see." She yelled back some instructions, went inside, and closed the door. With my books and pocketbook in hand, I started up the steps that had no railing, missed the edge, and fell hard onto my ass and side. It was a three-foot fall. I was in such pain and couldn't get up. I called to the Empress and then just sat there stunned, hurt, embarrassed. Finally, she opened the door and saw me down in the dirt. She went back to get a flashlight. I handed up my things and slowly got up. My hand was bleeding, and my side was sore. I didn't want her to know how bad I felt so I laughed and said, "What a jerk." I started washing the blood off.

She stood near the sink and said, "I have to go to bed. I have to get up for an early trip with the Hierophant."

"Sure. No problem. I can do this alone." She disappeared in her room. I got stomach sick wiping the blood and digging out the pieces of rock imbedded in my palm. I rested a bit before pulling myself up the ladder to the loft. When I got up there, I took off my wet clothes and just put on a robe. I could not put on pajamas. I was in too much pain. I lay down carefully.

The next morning, I noticed a huge black and blue on the side of my thigh. It emphasized how ugly my body was becoming from overeating.

In the morning I wrote my first poem—about the fall. It was sappy and emotional, but an initial attempt at creative writing. A red booklet became my "poem notebook" to distinguish it from the black and white speckled composition pads used for the journal. I liked using these notebooks because the pages were so tightly bound. I felt secure I would never lose any of my writings, and at this point my journal was my most important companion.

Maine had awakened new talents within me. Before that, I had always hated writing, especially those "what I did this summer" exercises in English class.

Saturday and Sunday, I worked. Oh, so carefully. Bending was painful. Cowardly Lion helped me finish one side of the barn. We were beginning to feel comfortable with one another and even cracked jokes. I ate at the Kettle's on Sunday, pigged out again and felt awful after it. Ma Kettle was concerned about my fall.

I still didn't feel well all Monday but did manage to clean up the barn and then took a bath in the tub in the Empress's bedroom. It was the only one in the community and a bitch to fill by hand. But it was worth it. So soothing to sit in the hot water.

I taught my first math class in the afternoon. There were seven in the group and most of them were weak in the basics, except for the High Priestess. It was geared for using math in real life situations like finances and carpentry. I was taken aback when they called me by my first name since I was used to students calling me Ms. D . . .There were three men who really needed to learn this stuff for their jobs, two young mothers, and one older woman besides the High Priestess. The class dragged at times, but for the most part went well. I was impressed at how they took the practice exercises so seriously.

Following class, I went to do my laundry. I met Tinman in the market while I was getting some juice. He was drunk, and the tire on his car was demolished. He needed a ride out to Mandala, but I had promised the High Priestess that I would help with the newspaper. It was an unchristian decision not to help him, but I was afraid of him when he was inebriated.

The High Priestess was editor for the social justice newspaper called *Wonder Time*, with a mailing of about four thousand. It was a fundraiser as well as a means of getting the word out about the Co-op.

Tuesday night we watched the movie, *Coming Home*. God, did I want to put my arms around the Empress! Of all the people to love, why did I have to fall in love with her? She didn't even appreciate the movie. I had to wake her when it was over. I could see that only person she was concerned about was the Hierophant. The closeness I felt the week we spent alone was just in my imagination. It provoked streams of poetry about unconsummated love. None of it good!

Wednesday community supper was my chore, so I cooked chili. I felt honored that even the Hermit came. The Empress said to me, "That was a meal like my mother would cook." I took this as a compliment though I know she had mixed feelings about her mother. I didn't overeat. Thank God. I had been feeling short of breath and I think it had to do with the flea powder on all the animals. Fleas were a major problem. There were so many animals. Bear, Hierophant and the Empress each had a dog. And the Empress had four cats.

Overall, the week was productive. I still had depressing moments, but I was managing to tolerate them. I got my period- probably why I had been eating so much. Added to the loneliness that I was trying to fill. Ma Kettle and Cowardly Lion were the only two people that I could confide in at this point.

On Thursday, I met Tweedledee, an elderly, short, stout woman who lived about five miles from town and one of the Co-op's outreach clients. She needed to go to the Medical Center and then shopping. Lucky Luke had warned me that she would insist on bringing sacks of her things with us as she suffered from paranoia.

"Why do we have to bring these bags with us?" I asked when I saw the three filled bags on her front porch.

"Because he comes and destructs my things when I'm away," she replied readily.

"Who comes?" I asked.

"Him."

"Who's him?"

"The villain across the street. Come here and look," she answered in an anxious tone, as she led me into the house. She went over to a side window and very carefully pulled back a piece of the curtain so that we could look out without being seen.

"See he's sitting in his window now just waiting for me to go," she said in a whisper. I really didn't see anyone in the window, but I said, "Oh yeah, I see." Lucky Luke had advised me to just go along with whatever she said since it was impossible to convince her otherwise.

"He eats my peanut butter, spills milk on the floor, and rips my clothes when I'm not here," she continued. "It's awful. Just god damn awful. Men like that should be shot. Just dragged outside and shot. A woman has to worry about goin shopping. Can't leave her things for a moment. Got to worry about that villain coming and doing those things." The lines in her face deepened when she referred to the villain.

"Really? Wow. I guess we should take them then." So, I put the bags (and they were heavy bags) into the trunk and we left for the store.

Watching her shop was an experience. She would pick up an item, examine it for ten minutes, and put it in the cart. She'd add in the cost in her little price clicker, which also took a considerable amount of time as her fingers were gnarled with arthritis. Going down the next aisle, she would pick up the last item and say to me, "I don't really need this." And she'd go put it back on the shelf and unclick the price. She repeated this process every time I took her shopping, and after hours of mulling around, she always ended up with the same five or six items.

In the afternoon, I went to Ma Kettle's for a bath and learned how to make apple sauce and cook green tomatoes. The Kettles farm had electricity and running water which for me were luxuries. The tub was raised up on a platform, and I felt like the Queen of Sheba lazing in it. Later, I rested in one of the makeshift bedrooms with my thick, heeled shoes lying by the side of the bed. I was exhausted and fell asleep. When I awoke, I heard Ma saying to Pa,

"Those shoes have got to go!"

The next day Tweedledee called for a ride back to the Medical Center and since I had some free time, I volunteered to take her. When I got to her house, I found her dressed in her sleeping gown and robe.

"You can't go to your appointment in your night clothes," I said to her.

"I'm not leaving this house," she replied adamantly. "I'm too upset. I'm not giving that mother-fucker any more opportunities to steal from me."

"It will be ok," I responded reassuringly. "He won't come. There isn't enough time. Your appointment won't take long. Why don't you get dressed?"

"Are you sure? I don't know. You don't know how sneaky he can be."

"I'm sure. Go get dressed." With encouragement she got ready. When she came out, she said to me, "I need a favor. Will you help me next week?"

"Sure," I said trying to appease her. "Anything you need, I'll help you with."

"Good," she responded relieved. "I want you to help me catch that villain!"

My face dropped and I cringed thinking about what I had just agreed to. Catch the villain! Oh God! She got in the car after I put the bags in the trunk and was very agitated all the way to the center. She rambled and repeated. I tried changing the subject, but it didn't work. We met Lucky Luke at the center, and he was able to calm her down, though he didn't do much but read his paper and once in a while say a word to her. Luke seemed to have the knack for handling her.

At lunchtime, I met Ma Kettle at Duffy's Restaurant and we joined the Empress, the Hierophant, the Hermit, and Lucky Luke who were already there. The conversation ranged from religion to politics.

"I think Kennedy should run," said the Empress.

"Really, I think his chances are slim," retorted the Hermit.

"Me, too," said Lucky Luke.

"What do you think about the recent news that four PR prisoners tried to kill Truman?" asked the Empress of Ma Kettle.

"Well," said Ma. "They will probably try to continue to overthrow the US government when they get out. I don't agree with them, but I sympathize with the PR people. I am American, but the Americans did some awful things to the PR people."

I worked in bookkeeping after lunch. Karen and Alley ran the department. Karen, who had been hired by the Hermit, was relatively new, but very competent. Alley had been working there for four years. Since Karen used modern systems and Alley was from the old school, there was friction between them.

It rained hard after supper. Bear, Hierophant, Empress and I relaxed on the parlor chairs and listened to the sounds from the lake.

"I think we need to come up with some basic requirements to build community on," said the Empress. "We need a list that we can give to potential new members to read before they join."

"I agree," I said responding to her suggestion.

"It wouldn't matter if you didn't agree!" she retorted.

"You're such a hard woman!" I said looking at her. How did she think that made me feel?

"Hey, watch it," she said. "I'm not hard, just principled. Speaking of principles, I spent the day with Molly. I love that woman. She and her husband have great concern for one another even after all these years. They're both in their eighties, and yet they won't allow each other to do certain things which would be harmful to their health. Isn't that cute?"

"Yeah," I said thinking the Empress wants this kind of relationship with the Hierophant. I wished it were me.

She continued, "Molly thinks people are sick because of the air. She said to me today, 'look at where the planes come in over Bangor. The trees are all dying. What do you think that stuff does to people?'"

In between conversation, there was a comfortable silence. The Hierophant fell asleep on the chair. She said mean things about people, but basically, she was a good person.

On Saturday, I made apple pancakes for everyone, and then we worked all day. Everyone, except Scarecrow, who went to a fair. The Kettles came out for supper. Mass was noisier than usual as the kids were acting silly. I could see that the Hermit was having a hard time maintaining his composure. He had wanted to start before everyone arrived, but I asked him to wait, which he did. It upset his routine.

Sunday morning, Cowardly Lion and I tried to bake bread, but we used yeast packs instead of yeast cakes, and the bread didn't rise too well. After that, we worked all day on the barn and then went to supper at the Kettles. They served roast beef, a welcomed treat from the usual rice and beans!

Elaine, one of the Kettle's teenage daughters, had a crush on the Cowardly Lion. She sat near him, gazing into his eyes. "Can I live in the barn?" she asked Empress.

"That's a good idea," I teased trying to get the Empress's goat. "She can sleep with me."

"None of that at Mandala," laughed the Empress.

"I don't mean anything bad. I always get blamed for things I don't do."

"It's the things you'd like to do that bothers me," she retorted, still smiling.

I woke up the next day in an awful mood. I wanted to just be alone, so I waited till everyone left and then I drove to work myself. I called my parents.

Class was good. The High Priestess and I pondered infinities while the rest of the class was doing fractions! Some of the students hung around at the end, and we discussed pregnancy. I'm not sure how we got on the topic except the two younger women had had children early in life. I was still playing with toys at the age they had their children!

I went home and ate supper. My body was full of anger. Later I went to Duffy's for pumpkin pie with cream and sat and read Jung. I wasn't sure why I felt this way. I had had a good weekend. I even felt a little thinner. Sometimes I thought about suicide, but I knew it was not something I could do. I wouldn't be upset, though, if I found out that I was dying of a disease.

The next day, I did the food thing again. Had pumpkin pie, strawberry muffin, blueberry pie, and one chocolate candy. Why was I doing this to myself? What need was I trying to satisfy? Why couldn't I be happy with good friends and people that cared about me? Why did I have to have someone special in my life? What happened to the rebirth? The Empress kept looking at me after dinner.

I was so depressed and tired the next day that I pulled over and took a nap in the car. I just could not continue. I ate too much at lunch. Later, I picked up the Cowardly Lion, and we went to chop wood.

My spirits were uplifted by a visit from Brother David, a Benedictine monk from Redding, Connecticut. He was a peaceful, soft spoken, sincere man. After reading a small book by St. Benedict, he had decided he wanted to live the simple life. Although he searched, he couldn't find it in the outside world. He and four other monks started a new community. They shared meals, worked together each morning, and then would spend alone time in the afternoons. After supper, he shared some of his ideas about developing a sense of community. One idea tickled me.

"In your community do you dance?" he asked. I had to laugh.

"No, I don't think people here are into dancing," I responded.

"Well, ideas cannot be forced. There is no need to imitate what another community does."

\* \* \*

Today was the day to "catch the villain." Tweedledee had two bags filled with the usual- tea, cat food, powder, and other assorted items.

"Take those bags, and I'll show you where to go," she said. This time she was all dressed and ready. I loaded the car and started down the road. About two miles up the hill, she said, "Okay, stop here, and park on the side." Before she got out of the car, she took off her coat and said, "This is so the old woman across the street doesn't recognize me and tell him I was watching.

"Maybe you should wear my red hat that will really disguise you," I said, joining the fantasy.

"That's good," she said and put on the hat. She got out of the front seat of the car, got in the back, and crouched down. "Okay, I'm ready. Now drive back down past my house to the top of the hill and park. We can watch my house from there. And when he goes inside, we'll go down and catch him." I did as instructed. "I'm afraid my niece will see me. She lives in the house next to him," she added in a low voice.

"I can drive a little farther away," I responded.

"Good. Let's do that."

We waited about twenty minutes. At one point a car looked like it was turning into her driveway, I almost dropped my teeth and thought 'could this be true?' But the car turned into a dirt road a bit farther up.

"Tweedledee, I don't think he's coming. Maybe he knows we're watching."

"You don't want to wait a little longer?" she responded convincingly. "He's sure to go over there."

"No, I think we've waited enough. Maybe another day."

"Okay. Then take me shopping. I need flour, baking powder and corned beef."

On the way home, she talked about old times. "There was a theatre in town. My husband and I would go every Saturday. Loretta Young and Gary Cooper were our favorite actors. I miss doing things like that. And now I can't afford it any way. When you have to start watching your pennies and scrimping on food, they ought to just take you out and shoot you," she said. I felt bad and responded, "Everyone goes through bad times."

"That's true. I shouldn't complain. My cats are well fed, and I eat what I want.

"I'll take you to lunch on Monday," I said.

"That would be fine," she smiled.

After I left her, I wondered what would happen if she were confronted with the truth that there was no villain. I noticed she talked more about him whenever I was getting ready to leave. Maybe loneliness triggered her paranoia. If there were someone coming to her house, she would never really be alone.

The High Priestess was the only student to show up for the next math class, so we had a concentrated session. Teaching was more exhausting than physical labor.

When I go home, the Empress and the Cowardly Lion were watching TV.

"My mother is coming for the weekend," she announced excitedly. "She can teach you and the Cowardly Lion how to bake bread. She makes good bread."

"That would be good after our last two failed attempts," I said as Cowardly Lion nodded in agreement and laughed. I couldn't understand her excitement based on our last visit to her mother's. The Empress didn't feel comfortable being in the same room with her for a few hours. How was she going to stand a whole weekend of her mother? And how was her mother going to get to the house at the bottom of the hill? She had a hard-enough time just walking on flat ground.

Discussing community, The Cowardly Lion said, "There is a split between Scarecrow, Tinman, Lady and the rest of us. I don't feel comfortable talking with them, but I feel good talking to you."

"I think you are right," chimed the Empress.

"Unfortunately, I agree," I said.

"What can we do to overcome this problem?" asked the Empress.

"I don't know," said the Cowardly Lion in his youthful innocent manner. "It's the people. We all are honest with each other. Well, there are some things we don't tell. Everyone has secrets." Then feeling defensive about the criticism, he looked at the Empress and clarified, "I mean, I don't have any secrets, but if I did, I would tell you. After all, if you can't tell a nun, who can you tell?"

I burst out laughing and said, 'What we do to the children of America!" The Empress looked at me and kidded, "Watch what you're teaching them." I threw a ball of Reynolds Wrap at her.

"I want you two to write down your ideas of community for future people," ended the Empress. "That will be a start."

"And we need to start doing more of the outreach work," said the Hierophant.

"Ma Kettle can't do it all herself. Lucky Luke is here sporadically. We need to devise a network of people we can call on to help."

"We need to do more of the outreach ourselves," I retorted. "We can't expect other people to do it if we can't do it."

"Maybe the Hierophant is right," said the Empress. I wasn't surprised she agreed with her cohort.

"I heard today that Ted has accepted the EDA grant sponsorship. That will be good for him, said the Hierophant.

"Yes, I heard," said the Empress.

"He may live with one of the women in the community to keep his costs down," added the Hierophant. I laughed and the Empress smiled.

"Why are you laughing?" asked the Hierophant who missed the hidden meaning. The Empress and I had a conversation earlier that Ted and this woman would make a good couple.

"People may talk," said the Empress in defense.

"Oh, you mean about the two of them being together. That could be a problem," said the Hierophant.

"Who cares what people think?" I said.

"Well, the Co-op doesn't need any more gossip," said the Hierophant.

"Well, I can understand people not sleeping together at the Co-op, but in private, who cares what they do?" I commented.

Manipulation from the Empress again. She asked if I would go to Ellsworth with her to pick up some materials. I agreed. Later when I went to pick her up, there was a note telling me to go myself since she had to take care of another issue.

On Friday when I got back from Ellsworth, the Cowardly Lion told me that there was a big meeting that afternoon with the Empress, the Hierophant and Bear. The Empress called Bear into her bedroom to talk privately. Then she spoke with Hierophant. "I think it must be about Lady," he commented. "Lady and Tinman have been going out each night together and leaving the grounds.

To me the Empress said, 'Don't be surprised if two people leave the community. It will be a good thing as the rest of us will be of one spirit.'"

After hearing that, I understood why Thursday community supper had seemed so strange. I arrived at the end of Mass and heard Bear say, "Let's all pray for support for Lady." I didn't think much of it and nothing further was said. But I sensed uneasiness in the air all during supper. Tinman and Lady left together, and Lady had a humble look on her face.

I questioned Bear and found out that Lady was leaving Mandala. She and Tinman, who was attending AA, were involved in a relationship. Lady was moving to a friend's house temporarily. They packed and Bear helped them move.

It had been such an emotional weekend. Luckily, I was staying in the cabin between the houses of the Empress and the Hermit. For me, it was like being on retreat and provided the relief I needed. I had the whole space right on the lakeshore to myself. I began a mini-fast eating only chicken, salad, and water.

Besides the Lady and Tinman fiasco, there was another "catastrophe". One of the Hermit's Siamese cats fell off the Empress's back porch and couldn't move its back legs. She told Hermit when he got back from his trip.

Hermit's two Siamese cats had been attacking the Empress's kittens, Archie and Bandit. We had been joking about things to do to them like shooting them with a vinegar water pistol or BB gun. Cowardly Lion threw one in the lake one day, but it got out ok. So now something tragic had happened to one of the cats. I wondered why, as cats usually land on their feet.

The Empress looked worn out at Saturday supper. I wished I could have given her some comfort. Lady came to Saturday night Mass and requested two songs. One of them really affected Bear, and she got up and left during the mass. At the end, Lady herself got up and left without saying a word to anyone.

Scarecrow announced, "I think what is between Lady and Tinman is good. We didn't provide what Tinman needed. Lady was the only one who reached out to him in the way he needed. Tinman is a new man because of her. Not many of us show our pain, especially the Empress."

"That's true," commented the Empress and added, "Bear has been in pain for the last six months. I also want to emphasize the need for celibacy in a community such as ours. We can't function properly without that basic rule. People can do what they want outside of the community, but here there must be rules. I'm going to invite Peter Berrigan to Mandala. I visit their house when I am in Washington. I'm sure he'll return the favor, and it will be good for us. A shot in the arm.

"What about Philip and Elizabeth McAllister?" I asked.

"I'm not impressed with his brother Philip and his partner Elizabeth," she responded. "They have copped out on their vows. And they rally around issues too much. Their main concern is to tear down the Pentagon. They are not living the Christian lifestyle. I'm only asking Peter."

We were all relieved to have this day end. On the way out,

Scarecrow came over to me and warned, "You're living with a bunch of nuns, and there is so much life in you. You should reconsider. I really like you and want the best for you. Get out more."

"Thanks for your concern," I responded. "I appreciate your honesty. I'm not sure what is going to happen to me just yet, but I'll figure it out."

"The Empress is a driven woman," he continued. "People do things for her. I was always impressed with her speaking ability. I felt proud to be part of her work when she spoke at the no-nuke meetings. The Empress can get to people. But she is not inspiring like Brother David in her personal life. The potential is there, but she lacks something. She doesn't see herself as others do. And the Hierophant is a bad influence. I admit that I have an antagonistic relationship with her. I won't pay into the community because of her. When she goes away, the other guys and I get along fine with the Empress. She is easy to talk to. But when the Hierophant is around, she gets uptight and unapproachable. She's a fake. The Empress is just neurotic. A puzzle."

I wished I could solve the puzzle.

When I returned to the cabin, I found Bandit inside. I wasn't quite sure how he managed to do so, as the door was closed. In reading from the gospels of John, I noted at least four places where John talked about "the disciple that Christ loved". Who was it? John himself? In the last reference Christ spoke of this disciple staying behind till he comes. Peter appeared to be jealous and Christ reprimanded him, saying, "What does it matter to you? You are to follow me." It certainly gave a human twist to the whole story.

It was Scarecrow who finally taught me how to make bread. He was such a self-sufficient guy and his comments kept me in stitches.

"Did you hear what the Empress said to Tom about his surgery?" asked Scarecrow.

"No, what did she say?" I asked.

"Well, Tom announced that he had to take time off because he needed to have surgery. Had to have his prostate scrapped. The Empress said, 'You don't need that surgery'."

"Tom said, 'Like hell I don't. I'll use that till I die'." I couldn't stop laughing. "You should have seen the color of the Empress's face! Purple, red, then back to purple," he added. "Tom loves to get her goat. Speaking of purple. Did you know that the lesbian community thinks that the Empress is gay? They've adopted her as some sort of hero."

"Really. She'd die if she knew that." I laughed. "Imagine, the Empress, leader of the lesbians!"

Lady's friend, the psychic, came out to visit, and Bear avoided her.

During a week lunch with Tweedledee, our conversation was almost normal, even though she did bring up the villain a few times. We made plans for her to teach me how to make muffins. "I like you," she said while we were eating. "I feel comfortable with you. I don't feel comfortable with everyone. I don't even feel comfortable with that Ma Kettle. At least you call when you say you will. Not like her. She makes me wait."

"Well Ma Kettle is busier than I am."

"I don't care. It's not nice to leave people waiting. Do you want to meet my cats?"

"Yes of course." She brought me into her bedroom and lying on the metal posted bed were two humongous cats. They must have weighed 35 pounds each! When they stood up, their stomachs hung down and dragged on the mattress.

"Wow. Those are big cats," I exclaimed.

"They're my babies. Aren't you?" she said rubbing her face into the dark tiger cat with the big white bib. The other cat was white with a few big black spots.

"Yes, you are. You are my babies. And Mommy loves you. Now don't get up. You need your rest. I'll feed you later. Some nice turkey. You like turkey, don't you? I only give them the best," she said as she walked me out to the car. I realized I was growing fond of her even if she did drive me crazy at times.

"Would you like to come out to community for Thanksgiving?" I asked. "I'll pick you up. We're having an open dinner for the Co-op members."

"Oh no. I don't like to eat in front of people."

"You ate in front of me. Please come."

"No. I don't think so. It's too far."

"Well, I'll ask you again. I want you to come."

\*   \*   \*

Teaching was a great diversion for me, but I was concerned about Star, one of the young mothers. She constantly bit her nails in class and was really uptight. The other young woman, Deb, was a Baptist who believed that because she smoked and drank, she wasn't going to heaven. She married at sixteen and had her daughter at nineteen. She was now twenty-two and trying to get her GED. So was Star, who had one son. In contrast, the men in the class joked and kept the class light.

After class, I attended a planning meeting to discuss a community learning workshop in November. Ellen, the principal, went out of her way to explain how everything functioned in the Learning Center. I felt closer to her than her husband, Andy, who shared in the managing responsibility. It was probably just my thing with men. I felt the same about Scarecrow and Tinman, backing away when they tried to get close. I felt better with Cowardly Lion, perhaps because he was young and feminine. Pa Kettle made me feel at ease too, especially when he expressed his feelings. And with Ted, I could talk philosophy.

I extended my involvement in the Learning Center and agreed to do a night class as well.

An interesting feud began. The Kettles were having a big get together on Friday night, but The Hermit had decided not to officiate the mass. Pa Kettle wrote the following sarcastic note to him about what it means to be a Christian and sent a copy to everyone:

Re: Mass at Kettles
    In the beginning there was God
    And God created people and loved them and guided them.
    And the people formed organized religions to worship their God.
    And they put one person in charge of the rituals
    And as time went on the rituals became routines, chores to be performed much like sloppin
        the hogs with as much meaning.
    And the people forgot the purpose of the rituals- to pay homage to their God- and the rituals
        became God to them.
    And some of the people said the rituals have no meaning, let us then find another way to
        pay homage to our God.
    And they did. They loved one another, helped one another, and by their lives they worshiped
        and paid homage to God.
    October fifth we will pay homage to God by gathering together, sharing our love, sharing
        what we have and hope that God will have the time to join us.

Hermit wrote the following sarcastic note back and put copies in all our mailboxes:

Pa,

I am not God; I am a human being entitled to love like anyone else. After your note to me, which is thoroughly disgusting, your get together October 5 in the name of love is sheer hypocrisy. God does not bless self-righteous people. You have no monopoly on love.

Hermit

The Hermit was a bit immature and unrealistic about his ministry.

Lucky Luke approached me about doing social work. Jokingly, but with a serious undertone he said, "Don't you want to work with Ma Kettle on the outreach program? You'd be great at it."

"I don't have any experience," I answered.

"You don't need experience. Ma Kettle will teach you all you need to know. Think about it."

"I'll think about it."

"Outreach needs caring people," he continued. "We can't keep up with all the work. There's so much going around here and not enough people to do all the projects. But that's what happens when you're running a "shoestring" operation. Something has to give somewhere."

My relationship with the Hierophant had improved due to our work on the Co-op calendar. A genuine caring woman, she always hugged me when I returned from Connecticut. Sometimes she drank too much, but I think it was to escape her physical suffering. In contrast, the Empress and I constantly butted heads. She commented on my love of deep conversation . . . "Talk is cheap. Words have no meaning. Conversation is shallow. Silence and work are the true modes of expression. People spend too much time writing." Referring to me?

Though I enjoyed my time with the Empress, it reminded me of how much I wanted her. I was better off alone.

I wasn't sleeping well and dreaming a lot. I had a dream about Lady: *I went to visit Lady at a huge, old-fashioned house. Her father let me in. Later he tried to seduce me. Her mother, a beautiful woman, came, sat me in a chair and with some kind of psychedelic instrument, started showing me my insides, my guts. I got grossed out and asked her to stop. I moved close to her and started caressing her face.*

In a second dream, a gorilla who had on a mask was chasing me. When the mask came off, I saw my older cousin Vinnie.

. . . Vinnie introduced me to erotica. Every summer I spent two weeks in New York visiting him and my cousin, Nancy. Sometimes I would sneak into Vinnie's room. He had a whole drawer full of dirty books. I read the erotic parts. Vinnie never tried anything with me, but we joked about sex. One time during a scrabble game, we only used sexual words to describe our thoughts. Vinnie was big and rough, but I knew he would protect me always.

I spent most of the time with my cousin Nancy. By the end of the second week, we couldn't stand each other. I used to go across the street and play with a girl who lived with her grandparents. I thought she was rich because she had a croquet game. No one I knew had one.

One day, Nancy and I got into a physical fight. She tried to kick me. Nancy was a foot taller and much bigger, but I was faster. I grabbed her leg on one of the kicks, and she fell back to the floor. She lay there stunned and quiet, and I thought she was going to kill me, but instead, she started laughing. Then I laughed. We forgot our anger. She got her playfulness from her father, my Uncle Charlie. A big gruff man. He would tell us scary stories. One night sitting in the yard, he told us the story of the golden arm about a man who lost his arm and came back as a ghost to find it. My Uncle played the ghost, repeating, "Who stole my golden arm, who stole my golden arm. Louder and louder each time and on the final, who stole my golden arm!" He grabbed my arm and shouted, "You did!" I screamed my brains out. And every time he did it, someone screamed their brains out. It didn't matter that we knew the ending . . .

\* \* \*

Tim, the horse, had become a problem. Scarecrow usually ended up taking care of him. Tim broke through the electrified fence around the barn and ruined the cement base of the chimney. He was so big that when he banged into objects, he left a dent. And it was expensive to feed him.

I met a young girl, Louisa, at the gas station who noticed my CT plates. She had come from Connecticut as well. She appeared to have a mental problem but seemed to be doing well. She lived in a newly-started spiritual community for the mentally ill, run by a Father Carter, whom I had met during the summer at one of our community suppers. I couldn't wait to tell Ma Kettle about meeting Louisa.

On Friday, I baked three cakes at the Learning Center for

community supper at the Kettles. Ma Kettle arrived and called to me, "Mama, I want to talk to you. Come on take a ride with me. I got to go pick up some fellow at the health center in town." I jumped in the car with her and off we went.

"I met Louisa who lives at Father Carter's community," I said. "I'm going to go visit them. The place sounds interesting."

"Yeah, I know about them," she responded. "I visited them, too, and invited Louisa for tonight's supper. Can you pick her up?"

"Sure."

"Good. I talked with the Empress and she's so happy you are making meals for everyone. She wants you to continue"

"Really? I never get that impression from her. I always feel like she wants to be alone rather than eating with the rest of us."

"No, no. She wants community to work."

"Why doesn't she tell me?" I asked, surprised at the revelation. I didn't understand why we needed Ma Kettle as the go-between.

"She's shy," she replied.

"Shy? How can she be shy?"

"She doesn't like dealing with people problems."

"She has to. We live in community!"

"Just keep doing what you are doing. You are good for them."

"I don't think so."

"Yes. Yes. You are," she affirmed.

"Well, I don't get it," I said, a bit upset. I just wanted to go back to the Co-op. She dropped me off and I took off for Mandala to work on the barn. I finished the floor with Cowardly Lion's help. Afterwards, he came with me to pick up Louisa. She was surprised to see me and didn't know about the supper. Either Ma Kettle never asked her, or she forgot. What-ever. She was excited about coming.

A lot of people came to the Kettles. Before supper, the Empress said a prayer, and then Pa Kettle talked about Christ. "Well, it's too bad the Hermit was too busy to do mass, but you know when Christ was gathered with his friends at a Passover meal, he took some bread, broke it and passed it around. And now I'm going to do the same. So, if anyone wants to join me, please do so." And with that comment, he broke some bread and passed it around. He did the same with a paper cup of wine. It was a revolutionary experience. It was one of those moments where you felt something special was happening. Here was a lay person expressing the true meaning of Christ. He had a bag of peanuts by his side, and I felt for sure that he was going to pass them around, too! He didn't. Later, we all sat around and played guitars and sang. The Empress took off to buy a bottle of wine that she and Bear drank. The Hierophant came late with some of her nun friends.

* * *

I moved into the little cabin house attached to the barn. It was about five feet wide by ten feet long and had one door and three windows. It was supposed to function as the community kitchen but since I didn't have a space, the Empress suggested I live there. I relished having a space to myself even if it was tiny. I had a small cot, a wood stove, a table and chair and some shelves. That was all that would fit. Unfortunately, the cabin bordered the horse yard. The electric fence noise drove me crazy at night.

During the afternoon, I directed the crew of four men in working on the upstairs barn. The Empress was sick from the night before, so she never came up. We got all the insulation tacked up, finished the wood siding, and boarded in some of the windows. The Hierophant cooked a wonderful ham supper, a treat after a hard day's work! At Mass, the conversation centered on relationships and divorce.

"We have to realize that God has joined two people together for some reason. That's why the church frowns upon divorce. That's the key," said Bear.

"I think it's between the two people and not the church," I retorted, and Scarecrow agreed.

"She's right," he added. "No law can rule over such an intimate experience."

Even Hermit agreed," I know I feel foolish giving advice to a married couple when I have no experience of it."

I drank too much wine that night and had trouble sleeping. Tim, the horse, got out of his pen and started banging the cabin. I shut off the electrical fence to stop the buzzing. Sunday, I ate all day trying to replenish my electrolytes.

On the property was a stream winding between the dense thick forest of trees. We spent time a lot of time clearing out the area. Cutting trees was hard work but the Empress loved buzzing her chain saw. I did more of the grunt work carrying the cut pieces to the road and trimming off the small branches.

For lunch, I went to Tweedledee's. She ran around so much in the house that I was worried she would have a heart attack! She made me take the leftovers, which I knew was a bad idea. I ate them as I watched the snow fall.

Hermit lent me his recorder so I could play music. I was looking forward to solitude upstairs in the barn, but Cowardly Lion didn't go to class. I carried my things to Bear's hoping to be alone there, but she came home early. I retreated back to my small space and lay under the covers.

The next morning, I apologized to Cowardly Lion for being so moody. I chopped wood while he made breakfast. I think the original plan of living with two normal men, Tinman and Gene, had been more appealing than living with a seventeen-year- old. I really didn't want to be a mother.

Scarecrow and Gretel, the resident potter, began spending time together. They took me to Belfast to the big Cooperative Store. Gretel was liberal minded and interested in women's issues. She reprimanded Scarecrow when he made the following comment about Holly Near: "I used to like her music before she became a lesbian."

They gave me good recipes on cooking with bulgur and millet.

Lucky Luke and I went to see *Clockwork Orange* and the next morning, the Empress and Bear asked, "Did you have a good time?" How did they know? Nothing was sacred in community.

At the lobster dinner for the Hierophant's birthday, the topic of the housing project came up. The Co-op was involved in building houses for poor families.

"The educated liberals are running everything, and nothing is getting done," said the Empress. "Before, if you wanted to do something, you just did it. Now everyone is worried about legalisms. I'm sorry we got involved in this subdivision nonsense. We should have just bought separate property and built."

"That was the problem with the Hospitality House," I said. "We got so caught up in the city legal requirements and forgot what we were trying to do for the people."

The Empress looked at me in an understanding way and said, "We'll do a hospitality house here." I think she meant it.

The Empress was nicer over the weekend because the Hierophant had gone away on a short trip. She even put her arm around me when Scarecrow said, "You two look alike. You could pass as sisters."

"We are sisters in a sense," she replied pulling me toward her. She was always in a better mood when she was alone.

We were getting another horse! Ugh. Now there would be two to bang around the cabin! I said to the Empress, "You should keep them near your house. You like horses so much." She responded with one of her fake whacks. I wasn't kidding though. Then, she rooked me into doing a task for her. After Mass, she came up to me with those sad brown eyes, "Can you help me out?"

"Sure."

"I need you to do some typing."

"When do you need it by?" I asked.

"This weekend," she responded.

It turned out to be a whole contract that took all morning. Then I wrote an article for the newspaper on practical math. I had to cancel my visit with Tweedledee.

Two kittens, a brother and sister, named Fearless and Monkey were left at the Co-op. I adopted them and renamed them Narcissus and Goldmund. Narcissus, the bigger of the two, had long furry gray hair with black streaks and sparking green eyes. Goldmund, the thin, nervous female, had short gray hair with brown lines and a small weird face.

I was finally making use of my math skills! Karen, in bookkeeping, needed a formula for total taxable sales. Then I had to figure the amount of bricks needed to fill the space under the wood stove. Bear and Cowardly Lion didn't believe the number I came up with, but it was right.

I was hard pressed to finish pending projects before going to the educational workshop. I didn't know how I was going to keep up with the wood chopping and my classes. I planned on driving back and forth. Then I got a call from Adele. She had the following dream about me and said, "Dorothy, it was more like a vision than a dream." . . . You were getting married. You had planned the wedding yourself. The man stood off to the side. He was insignificant, a nice figure, but not of great importance. Then you came down the aisle. I felt you were carrying a heavy burden, and sure enough, you were carrying the cake . . . The scene shifted to St. Francis. You were pulling down a slide screen to give a lecture. Two soldiers were fighting, and one pulled the other's face off. There was blood. I felt you were teaching that if people don't get to caring about one another, the earth will be destroyed.

She had picked up on my mood. I discussed my plight with the Hierophant. "Dorothy," she said. "Forget the wood, cancel your classes, and stay at the workshop hotel. Don't worry, we'll survive without you." I took her advice. The Learning Center got a substitute for my classes. Now I only had to make a surprise visit home for my mother's fiftieth birthday.

I left for Connecticut later that week. Cowardly Lion agreed to take care of the kittens. On the drive down, I stopped to see Doris who frowned upon my new lifestyle. "Do you wear those fatigues every day? What are you, in the army?" she asked.

"No. It's just easier to dress like this," I defended. "We're working with poor people, and so we don't want clothing to be issue. Besides it's more comfortable especially, when you're working in the woods."

"Woods?" she exclaimed in surprise. "I thought you were teaching."

"I am teaching but it's just one of my many jobs. We do everything by ourselves. Chop wood. Build houses. Say Mass."

"What are you taking about? she asked as her tone got louder. "You can't say mass! You're not a priest!"

"Who says you have to be a priest? It's just celebrating the memory of Christ. It makes more sense for the common person to do it. Women should be celebrating Mass."

"I'm against women priests," she shouted. "Now you're going too far!"

We disagreed on every topic.

My mother was surprised to see me. Both she and my Dad cried. We had a wonderful meal, and then the rest of the family came to visit. Later, my mother said, "I only see you doing this for about a year, and then you'll get back to a real life."

"Mom, I was never meant to follow the normal path nor would I be happy doing so." I loved my mother, but I couldn't live up to her expectations.

Mar and I talked till late that night. "I sense your relationship with the Empress has changed," she said.

"Yes, we're not as close as before. I have been doing my own thing. It's creating some problems."

"You must do what you want, and not worry what the others think. Don't try to please them."

"You're right. I'm trying."

"Also, Dorothy, what are you doing to your body? You've gained so much weight. You're not eating right."

"No. I'm not. Eating too much junk food. I gained a lot of weight. I've got to stop doing this to myself." I could count on Mar being honest. Painful or not.

After a great weekend, I drove back and found the small cabin in such disarray. My flashlight, lamp, and radio were gone. Things were pulled out from under my bed. Dirty dishes were piled in the sink, and in general everything was a mess. I had left it so neat. I was so disgusted. Thankfully, I was leaving in the morning for the educational workshop.

Most of the attendees at the conference were involved in alternative education. The retreat center, a huge white house facing a large lake in the middle of the village, was surrounded by green rolling hills.

Each room was comfortably decorated and had a private bath. The food was excellent. I was glad to be temporarily immersed in such luxury.

During one of the exercises, I realized how negative I had become. We had to write things about our self and share them with the group. I hated doing it. I sat with a disgusted look on my face while listening to people go on and on about themselves. When it was my turn, I just read off a few words.

Why had I reacted so violently to the exercise? Why didn't I just make the best of it and try to get to know people better? Where was the attitude coming from? I realized I had assimilated the attitude of the Empress. She hated this "educated class" of people. Was I projecting her prejudice? I decided to relax and enjoy. Who knows? I might learn something that I might need some day.

I managed to get through the week of workshops, sometimes enjoying the participation and sometimes not. On the last day, we worked on goals and objectives, but the intellectual jargon drove me crazy.

When I got back to Mandala, I built shelves and binged all weekend on food and wine. While we were working, the Hierophant ran over Cowardly Lion's puppy. Instead of just saying she was sorry she tried to excuse her absentmindedness. "I thought Dorothy was getting him," she declared as Cowardly Lion held the limp body in his arms. I was nowhere near the puppy. I was so glad to visit Tweedledee on Monday. She was the one person here who just liked being with me.

On Tuesday, I worked in bookkeeping. Alley had been out sick, and Karen was at her wits' end trying to keep up with the work. Ma Kettle came in the office and asked me to take a child to Bangor Hospital for some tests. Karen needed me. Ma Kettle needed me. I didn't know what to do. I complained to Secretary, and soon the Empress came to talk to me.

"Empress, I feel torn. No one can depend on me. I keep getting shifted back and forth between jobs."

"It's because you do things well that everyone wants you."

"But I feel so scattered."

"I know the feeling. We must do the best we can. Go to Bangor. The child needs those tests. The numbers can wait."

I began to worry that something was physically wrong with me. Every morning at around 11:00 am, I got weak. I had to leave whatever I was doing and eat raisins, peanuts, bananas . . . or whatever I could find. Mentally, I felt very distant.

I finally got my period, a week late. I used to be so regular. It was a terrible experience. I woke up and had bled through my pajamas. What a fiasco trying to clean with no running water! Too cold to go outside, so I used a pee pan at night.

I had been listening to "The Best of Judy Collins". It reminded me of past times with Wolf when we would sit and listen without having to talk. Just be. It was hard to sort out my feelings now . . . Sarah, Queen of Swords, the Empress. It was too confusing. This year was worse than last, and that was a bad year!

In *Man and his Symbols*, Jung says we go through quiet embarrassment when we realize things in our subconscious. I think my experience with the Empress forced me to re-examine myself. "Instant intimacy" is what the Empress called it. The place mat at Duffy's read, "Geminis have superficial emotional involvement."

The Empress asked, "Is this true? You're a Gemini."

I said, "I hope not."

Could the Empress and I represent each other's shadow?

The Doctor and the Artist joined the group for community supper. We read an article called "Hope for a Second Reformation." The Empress started the discussion, and it was as if she had planned out the whole conversation. It was very pointed, but I wasn't sure to whom. Maybe all of us.

"I've been speaking to a Jungian philosopher who said we are on the verge of change. There will be a new era of scarcity. The gospel will have to become a reality. People by necessity will have to become responsible for their brothers. The gospels have never really been lived. Colleges are at fault. They have never taught self-sufficiency. Students are dependent on their parents and then, as adults become dependent on welfare. There is no difference between children of the poor and children of the middle class. The older generation is made of better stock." She spoke with a mocking tone about the college educated, my generation.

My dream that night: *Adele and I visited a very distinguished older man. He was well dressed and wore a scarf. He had a huge house, which looked like a castle, but more modern. I woke up in the house and had a red rash on my face but a woman (muse?) said, "It was all right."*

*Adele, the man and I were walking. He fell and passed out cold. When he came to, he said, "I passed through hell, but I'm all right. I'm using my experience for a book." Then he mentioned something about Sebago Lake.*

\*　\*　\*

My mind was expanding in this new life in the woods. The classroom was all around me. Dreaming was a new language to understand. I started making a conscious effort to remember and record my dreams.

Reading *Man and his Symbols*, I learned that communication was possible through symbols. Animals were part of this communication; they reflected our feelings. Four was an important number, the number of the self. The fourth person of the Trinity was female, a possible dark and evil force. There were no coincidences; and every event was meaningful. I accepted these truths and a whole new area-the unconscious was revealed. I was no longer interested in trying to please others, but in understanding and accepting myself.

I started to analyze all the animals in the community and their owners as a means of understanding the people better. I wrote the following list in my journal:

| | | |
|---|---|---|
| The Empress (castle) | Gloria (cat) | has fear, runs away, affectionate, uncertain |
| | Argus (dog) | lazy, lovable, strong, beautiful, watch dog, gentle but can be aggressive |
| | Bandit | playful, affectionate, sneaky |
| | Archie | clever |
| The Hierophant | Chico (dog) | horny, bitty, sick, barks |
| Bear | Shannon (dog) | playful, not confident, bites hands, coming into her own |
| Dorothy (elephant, red) | Narcissus | playful, beautiful, sexy, affectionate |
| | Goldmund | scrawny, aggravating, nervous, needy |
| Cowardly Lion | Puppy | young, simple, cute |

That morning at Mass, Gloria was sitting on my lap. Bandit jumped on. I was petting the two of them when Gloria snapped at Bandit.

The Hierophant brought wine to the rice and beans dinner, and after drinking a glass or two she became her usual biting self.

"Dorothy, you're fat," she said. "We're going to have to call you Mama Dorothy." It was in jest but hurt. I had to laugh. I was fat.

I had gained about thirty pounds once again. The Empress sensed my sadness and changed the topic.

"I want us to be self-sufficient," said the Empress. "We should have things like an auto repair shop and a cheese shop in the community."

"You mean like the Shakers?" I asked. "They phased themselves out because they were celibate. There were no younger members to carry on their work."

"How does that apply to us?" asked the Empress.

"Celibacy is a denial of self. It's a stupid vow," I said. "The road to the self is the confrontation of all parts."

"That's not true," retorted Bear. "I consciously made a choice. I could have loved a person, but I chose universal love."

"Yeah. It's just another part to choose," agreed the Hierophant.

"What if I decided not to develop my spiritual part?" I responded. "Wouldn't that make me less human?" The Empress responded, "What am I doing that is less human? How am I acting? Maybe the problem is your needs. What can this group give you?"

"Well, community would help," I answered. "We say we want to build community, but we cancel dinners all the time. We're all too busy for community."

"Okay, then how about one person staying home each day to fix supper for the rest of us?" suggested the Empress.

"There's so much to do at the Co-op though. Can we afford to keep one-person home?" asked the Hierophant.

"Talking about community," said Scarecrow. "I don't know how much longer I'm going to stay."

"I don't know how much longer I'm going to stay either," said the Hierophant joking.

"Well, that leaves me, Cowardly Lion, and Bear, said the Empress as she nudged the Hierophant.

"You left me out!" I shouted.

"Well, so do you want to learn how to milk the goat?" she teased.

"No," I responded.

"Ride the horse?" she added.

"Yes," I said. She missed my point.

I changed the conversation to a less offensive topic. "I have been reading Jung and I believe there will be a new language," I said.

"I agree," said the Empress. "And it will be simple."

"Simple, but the method may be complex like in dreams, animals, or symbols," I said. "Maybe the language of imagination."

I was doing more and more outreach work in between my other jobs. At least it got me away from the Co-op. Friday, I drove Terry, a divorced mother, home and discovered she was only thirty-one years old! My age! She looked about fifty. I guess it was from having two kids. Also, she had a lot of family problems. Her parents were divorced, and her stepfather was having relations with her sisters. When I walked into her house, I had to hold my breath. Dirty dishes and clothes were scattered everywhere. I decided I would raise money for a car and teach her to drive so she could gain some independence.

Lasagna ingredients cost me twenty dollars, but I had come to believe that God would provide if I did his will, not mine. That afternoon in the mail I got a $52.00 insurance refund check and a $50.00 check from Sarah. My prayers were answered!

I delighted in primitive living, cooking on the wood stove, and peeing in a pan like the Greeks. My clothes came from the donation box. I found a great powder blue work shirt and green army jacket. This offset my $42.00 dentist bill. God only knew why he had to take an X-ray.

Karen in bookkeeping filled me in on the Co-op politics. Local people were upset with the Co-op because taxes had not been paid for the past few years.

"There was also a lot of charging done with no intention of paying," said Karen. "A good way to make enemies," she continued. "I have been trying to remedy this by paying a little on each of the bills. I keep money hidden from the Empress so I can do this. If she knew about the money, she'd spend it on new projects and forget about the past obligations."

"I think you are a wise woman to do so," I commented.

"About two years ago," she said, "the Co-op asked the Empress to step down as president. They got a new manager who was firmer, but he had run-ins with the staff who were still loyal to the Empress. He would fire people and the Empress would rehire them. He couldn't take it and quit. Fortunately, the Learning Center runs independent of the Co-op and is in the black. But the administration supported the resignation of the Empress, so she has never forgiven them. Thus, there is a split. Like with Grace who was fired after she took in Lady, Tinman, and Ted. After the Empress hired Grace back, she accused Grace of spending more time on her own real estate side job than doing the contracts she was supposed to be doing. They had an argument and neither one ever got over the hard feelings. The Empress only sees immediate needs and can't plan ahead," she continued. "The Hierophant tries to make up for this, but she doesn't always handle situations well either. The Empress won't let her. The Hierophant oversees volunteers. The Empress needs good people around her to continue this work. You know in the beginning I thought you were sent to bookkeeping as a spy for the Empress, but I know now that that's not true. You're just trying to do what is right. Your concern is genuine, and I appreciate your help."

"Thanks for saying that," I said. "I'm not a spy. The Empress and I clash a lot. I don't always agree with her ways either, but her heart is in the right place. She wants to help people."

"That's why we all stay isn't it?" she added.

\*   \*   \*

The Empress responded to current needs. That's why she spent time with me when first I arrived. I was so whacked out and needy. I mistook her concern for sexual interest. She was just satisfying her own needs. She was doing the same thing now with Cowardly Lion. He had become her latest interest.

My guess was that Scarecrow would be the next to leave the community as he had been clashing with the Hierophant and confiding in people outside Mandala. That was a definite no-no. The Empress could not tolerate opposition unless she was totally secure with the person's loyalty.

After the lasagna dinner, the Empress complimented me profusely on my cooking. "I want to apologize for being negative at times", I responded to her kind words. "There are personal things I have to work out."

"I understand," she said. "It takes time to get over a relationship, even one you wanted to leave. Besides, you have gone through many changes in a short time. Be easy on yourself."

"You're right. I can be somewhat self-destructive."

"You're not alone. We're both complicated people. I do the same thing."

"It's depressing isn't it?" I added.

"Yes," said the Empress. "You need to pray constantly. That's what I do. It helps. Keep at it. It gets easier. Keep writing, too. It's a good way to clean out your system."

On Saturday we were to go to Boston for the weekend to visit a shelter for the poor. The Empress was talking, and we were going as support. The Empress pulled one of her "cute" tactics on me. She came up in the morning with her hair flowing down and asked, "Can we use your car as there will be four going?"

"Sure," I responded, thinking she probably didn't want to drive. When it was time to go, the Empress got in the Hierophant's car while Bear and Cowardly Lion came with me.

On the way, we had lunch with the Empress's mother and brother. Her brother was very perceptive. He had the same beautiful eyes as the Empress. He shook my hand and said, "Oh, a city girl. What are you doing out in the woods? Looking for a man?"

"No looking for myself," I said.

"You'd be better off finding a man," he continued. "Men and women are not complete without each other. You can't develop to the fullest alone. Men and women are different. You can't be a man."

"I don't want to be a man," I responded. "They've made enough of a mess of things."

"Like what?" he questioned.

"Like the world situation. Women could do a better job. We'd probably have less wars."

"I agree that men and women are equal, but men are better suited to ruling the world. Women like to take care of their own families." he said.

"That's why the world is in the great shape it is! Men's rule."

"You're very opinionated, aren't you? You'd look much prettier in a dress."

"Yes, and that's what I need to wear to chop wood. Right?"

"That's what you need a man for," he retorted.

"I don't need a man," I said. The Empress smiled but didn't get involved in the conversation. Even Cowardly Lion kept quiet.

"You take everything in, don't you?" the brother said to Cowardly Lion. You'll only stay out here for a short while," he said to Cowardly Lion as if he intuitively knew.

The Empress talked that evening in the shelter. She began by explaining about the Co-op and its projects. Then, she went into her criticism of education and spouted her usual, "The middle class feeds off the poor with all its social service jobs."

The Pine Street Inn was a depressing place. Rows and rows of cot beds with very little walking space in between. The blankets were multicolored, but the room had a dark gloomy tint, reminding me of the living quarters at Dachau. Men checked in all hours of the night. I had a hard time sleeping. It inspired me to write an article entitled, "*What's wrong with America*?" for the Co-op newspaper.

On the way home, we stopped again at the Empress's mother's house. Her brother started in on me again. "You are trying to prove something," he said. "You're always fighting. No one listens to you."

"You're right on that one. But someday I'll find someone who listens," I responded. "I'm tired of fighting. I'm battled scared."

"You give evasive answers to avoid criticism. What's your aura like?" he asked.

"Intense!" I said.

"What's your aura like, Brother?" asked the Empress who suddenly took an interest in the conversation.

"Multicolored," he responded.

"I see red in you," she snapped. "Internal conflict."

The psychic had seen red colors in my future. The conversation exhausted me, so Bear drove the rest of the way home. Cowardly Lion rubbed my shoulders.

When we got back, I went to visit Tweedledee, who sensing my weariness, gave me a big hug. It was her birthday.

At 12:00 midnight in my little cabin, I woke up feeling angry. Goldmund was sleeping on me, and I pushed her off. I wanted to hurt someone. Cold ran through my blood. I felt afraid and had to light the kerosene lamp. Evil thoughts ran through my brain. I looked at my hands and they appeared not to be mine. I wanted to call to the Cowardly Lion to come and stay with me, but I didn't. I felt the Empress was with me and that I was a lost soul roaming the night air. I was shaking inside. I thought about Lake Sebago and the dream I had had. Was this my shadow side? I felt like I was going to do something mean. I asked God to help me.

Dogs were barking. The water in the black kettle was boiling hard. Narcissus kept jumping on and off the bed. The night was restless. I thought about the dream that I had had about the Empress where we fought. Was I to help her face her animus? Her aggressive part? What was my destiny? Did I want to love her or fight her? I remembered the night I sat on the parlor floor, and she ran into her bedroom with that look of fear on her face.

I picked up my journal and couldn't stop writing about everything that had happened during the past few days.

At around 4:00 am it got calm. The dogs stopped barking. The water in the kettle stopped boiling. The cold left my body. Narcissus was sleeping calmly at the end of the bed next to Goldmund, and I was finally able to get to sleep.

I felt drained in the morning. I was still aggravated by Narcissus's presence. No one else had heard the dogs barking. My off mood continued, and I left Mass crying. The first reading was about not worrying about those who kill the body. The second reading was about death, faith, and being brokenhearted. It struck too close to home. Too much death. I ran out and up to the tent pitched in the wooden area where we always chopped wood. I screamed into the air for an answer.

"Why am I here?" Silence answered me. I started laughing, as I felt very foolish.

\*   \*   \*

I returned to the dentist for a refilling of two teeth. It was very painful. I thought the dentist was trying to retaliate for my nasty comments about his bill. I sat in the chair with tears running down my cheeks, and he asked sarcastically, "Well, when was the last time you went to the dentist?" Dumb question to ask while someone is crying and has her mouth full.

On the drive back to Mandala with Bear, I continued crying, and it was for more than just the tooth pain. I thought about Sarah, my changing moods, and the things I had written in my journal.

I agreed to take Lucky Luke's social work job, but I was worried about my attitude. The people I would be servicing had enough negativity in their lives, they didn't need mine. Both Ma Kettle and Lucky Luke thought I would be good at the job, and so their confidence encouraged me to accept. Now they just had to get the Empress's blessing, but I was afraid she might think I was pushing Luke out.

I felt gonzo that evening and ate peanuts, carrots, and sunflower seeds. My body was freezing. I decided not to go the Empress's house for supper, but Scarecrow and Cowardly Lion were determined to get out of my bad mood.

"Look," said Scarecrow as he held one of the cats right to his sniffling nose and tearing eyes, "I'm a physical wreck, asthma and allergies." We all laughed at his sorry sight. I felt normal again. The three of us bopped down to the Empress's house skipping arm in arm down the hill, just like a scene from the movie, *The Wizard of OZ*.

At dinner, the Empress prayed about my doing a good job in the Outreach position. She seemed pleased that I had accepted it.

Bear told us her dream that the Empress was in the woods and got shot. She felt she should warn the Empress since the dream was so upsetting. I told Bear that I was worried about the Empress's spirit that I felt a restlessness about it.

"Don't take it to heart," she said. "The Empress has a way of making people uncomfortable."

The next morning on my run back to the cabin, I heard gun shots.

I dropped to the ground thinking hunting season must have started. Here I was dressed in gray sweats of all things! I surely could have passed for some animal to a hunter. I was scared to death, so I crawled all the way back, singing at the top of my lungs, "I'm not an animal. I'm a person and I'm running in the woods."

I changed into work clothes and started off to the wood area. Cowardly Lion, Bear, and the Empress passed by me in the truck. She didn't stop to offer me a ride up the hill. When I arrived, my facial expression conveyed my annoyance as she asked, "Woods life is hard, no?"

"No. Woods life isn't hard, just the people living in it, "I responded.

Nuns make me laugh. Regarding taxes, Bear said, "I don't support war, so I don't pay any taxes." The Empress agreed, "Neither do I."

"You don't have to, you are nuns!" I said. "It would be more of a statement if you weren't nuns."

I never knew what to expect in the classroom. When I arrived at class, Ethan, was sitting in his chair breathing heavily. I worried that he was going to pass out. He wouldn't do any of the exercises. During the break he shouted, "I hate life. I just want to die. Fuck the world. Fuck everyone in it. I have to sit in this Goddamn class to get my social security check. I can't get a job because I need a diploma."

"Then why don't you make the best of it and get the diploma?" I asked.

"Or why don't you just kill yourself. Suicide is an ok option," instigated one of the other male students.

"Big help you are," I yelled.

"Yeah. Stop feeling sorry for yourself," said Deb. "I'm supporting a small child at home and going to school. Be glad you just have yourself to take care of. You should be glad you're not starving like those Cambodian children."

"I am starving," said Ethan.

"Be glad you have a place to come to and complain and that you are getting money," I said, in support of Deb.

"You're right. I'm just lonely," he responded.

"Why don't you come out to Thanksgiving dinner and help us out at the farm," I asked.

"We had a farm but lost it when my Dad died. I like family get-togethers," he said. "Okay, I'll come out. That would be nice." Suddenly, his physical appearance changed. A big smile broke out on his face, and you could see he was excited. He became beautiful to me.

"You'll have to cook or bake something," I added.

"I can do peanut butter cookies," he responded.

"That would be great," I said. I realized I was doing a different kind of teaching up here- outreach. We all had the power to be the wounded healer. We just had to feel another's pain.

I still had a lump on my backside from the fall. I was worried about it and hoped it wasn't serious. I had faith that God would take care of me as there was so much of his work that I had to do.

At night I rested peacefully by the table with the kerosene lantern my father had given me. He had had it from his days in Hawaii when he was in the Navy. I sat in the chair under a warm blanket by the wood stove. The door was open so I could see the flames from the fire. "Suzanne" by Judy Collins was playing on the tape recorder. Life was beautiful and I was content.

I fell asleep and then woke up around 1:00 am with Tweedledee's molasses baked beans turning in my stomach. They were so heavy and, along with the tea and peanuts, upset my stomach. I had to sit on the pot while I wrote in my journal.

I attended a meeting in Augusta on obtaining state funds. What a fiasco! They spoke in a language that even I couldn't understand. The leader rambled on and on but didn't say much. I kept interrupting him, asking questions to try to bring him back to reality. I could see that he was getting aggravated with me.

The next day at a seminar, his whole style changed. He spoke clearly and made sense. After the talk, I went up to tell him so. I apologized for having given him a hard time the previous day.

"Well, Dorothy," (I was surprised he knew my name) consider it the law of karma," he said. "I've done a lot of barking in my days!"

This meeting inspired an article about government systems. My everyday life was fueling my creativity.

I finally went to see the doctor and he suggested that I take a hypoglycemia test. During the test, I noticed a change in my handwriting after the first hour. I felt weak, heavy and had little control of my hands. My brain was clogged and there was a slight shake within my body. I kept yawning. After two hours, I felt a little jittery, but clear-headed. My body felt cold and my arms ached. The results confirmed that I had a borderline case of hypoglycemia. The doctor said not to worry and suggested that I eat smaller meals and more often avoiding high sugar foods.

Lately, the Empress had been wearing her confused outfit, the bandanna with her hair sticking out. The Hierophant had gone for the holiday. Why was I afraid the Empress would commit suicide? Maybe it was just myself I was worried about. Loneliness played havoc with my mind. I wished that Christ were enough, but he wasn't. I needed a more physical relationship.

I stopped to see the Artist. Her painting was framed and entitled, "Agony in the Garden." Appropriate!

\* \* \*

Thanksgiving dinner was a success. Many of the town's people came with their children. Ethan slept over on Wednesday night; and later during the day he fell into depression. I had to tease him back to normalcy. I took him to my favorite spot in the woods, a place deep off the path lined with tall trees in a semi-circle that when the light shone down through, it created a sacred space in the middle. When I sat in the center, it seemed as though I was being touched by God.

I watched the Empress trying to impress the town's people. She talked about making a pond and raising horses. I think she wanted to be like her brothers. I started seeing her for what she really was—her quietness, her anger, her insecurity, her gentleness, her defensiveness. She was not an honest woman, but she tried to make up for her deficiencies.

The mornings were the best time to be in the woods. It was still and a mist hung over the treetops. The dew sparkled on the grass. I felt closest to God. Life was meant to be lived in beauty, not in war and hatred.

One night, the Empress announced that she wasn't feeling well. "Maybe I have arthritis. I get weak fast. I think I'll see a doctor," she said. She didn't need a doctor to tell her what was wrong. It was obvious that she just didn't take care of her body. Last night, she had eaten two pieces of pie, then had a beer. Her eyes started tearing, and she was sneezing. She admitted that she was allergic to all alcohol. That didn't stop the Hierophant from buying it, however. They both drank constantly. What kind of a friend was she? We had to keep ourselves strong to serve.

Sr. Jane Frances appeared in my dreams. Was she representative of authority? In last night's dream: *I was teaching and wanted to go to a talk. I asked Sr. Jane Frances if it was ok. She just looked at me. I left a book for her.*

Cowardly Lion was becoming so totally withdrawn these days. He clung to the Empress, hanging on her every word. He needed to be with people his own age. On the way to visiting clients with the Empress, we talked about his situation. "I'm worried about him," I said. "He's too quiet and can play the servant role."

"I love him and would do anything for him," she responded.

"I love him too, but I think he needs some counseling," I retorted.

"I think he's all right," she said. "He just needs time and he'll come out of his shell."

"He voices your opinions you know," I warned. "The other day I heard him talking about the Hermit and he sounded like you."

Startled she retorted, "I never criticize the Hermit in front of Cowardly Lion."

"Yes, you do," I responded thinking how contradictory she was. She told the High Priestess that she was in favor of "an eye for an eye." Then, the next night, I heard her proclaiming that "turning the other cheek" was the only way to proceed in this world. Who could figure her out? I couldn't.

At supper, Bear noticed cuts on the Empress's arms. I joked, 'You're not into flogging yourself, are you?" Her eyes looked down askance as if she didn't want to answer. Could she be into self-punishment?

That night I had the following dream: *I was on a farm and lying on a bed. A black heavy object was hanging over me. I tried to scream but couldn't and woke up.*

Lucky Luke introduced me to a new client, Tweedledum, an elderly, chubby woman with gray hair, who lived in an apartment in town. She always dressed in black. She was diabetic with leg pain, so she shuffled when she walked. Her laugh was addictive, and her deep-set eyes twinkled. She reminded me of my own Grandmother.

We took Debra, a middle-aged divorced mother with three boys to the doctor. Luke confided that he feared incest. When we returned to the Co-op, I went into bookkeeping to talk to Karen. Ma Kettle walked by the office and called me to come with her.

"Watch what you say to Karen," she said. "She's in a church that many of your clients attend." I hated all these warnings. "Watch this one. Watch that one."

I liked Karen!

Sometimes I didn't even trust Ma Kettle. I needed to learn to keep everything to myself. My emphasis was on helping people.

I replaced the plastic covering acting as a door to the outhouse with a wooden one. Now it looked more presentable.

The Empress's Brother, dragging the kids and Gram, came on the weekend to give lessons on dealing with workhorses. Teddy and Timmy had become a handful, and the Empress was the only one who could control them. From the interaction with his kids, it was obvious her brother was a disciplinarian. The Empress said he became angry and harsh when his wife left him.

The Hierophant came to watch the training. She again commented on my shape. The Empress's brother joined her and enjoyed watching me lose my temper. I jumped when he tried to push me next to the horses.

"You're so untouchable. You stay there, and I'll stay here. You're too much of a sissy to learn to ride these wild beasts," he laughed. To prove him wrong, I got on one of the horses, though I was scared to death. I clung my hands into the sides of the horse's neck.

At lunch, Gram praised my string bean casserole with cheese and nuts. "This is good," she kept repeating. "Brother isn't this good?" "She's a good cook and has a good singing voice, too. Will make a good wife. Don't you think so, Brother?"

"Yeah, and she's so submissive, too." He chuckled. To avoid the potential conflict, Bear chimed in, "I especially like the almonds you put in the casserole. They must have cost a lot."

"Where is your money tree? You always buy good food," asked the Empress. I ignored the entire conversation.

After supper we sat around the table and chatted, Brother stayed by himself and watched TV. I went over to talk to him.

"Anything good?" I asked.

"No, I don't really watch it. TV just stops me from thinking. How do you get your release?" he questioned.

"Working in the woods, I guess." It was the first civil exchange between us.

My dream that night: *The Empress sat on my lap wearing only a loose shirt. I said, "I love you." She dashed off, saying, "Well there's some advantage to that and maybe that's the way it must be. . . . In water, three animals were floating. A lion, a horse and the other I couldn't make out. They were huge and stuffed. They remined me of the shit floating in my pee pan!*

The Empress and the Hierophant drove by my cabin. I was worried they would stop in and see my pee pan on the floor. I still hadn't emptied it. The natural functions had always been a source of embarrassment. I could never pee in a public bathroom if someone else was in it.

. . . In nursery school, I had to go to the bathroom. The nun sent an older girl to accompany me to the basement lavatories. She stood in front of the bathroom door and kept opening it, saying, "Are you finished yet?" Finished? I never even took down my pants. Every time

I tried, she opened the door. I pulled them back up. There was only one solution. I shit in my pants. I stayed like that for the rest of the school day. It was uncomfortable and required tricky maneuvering pretending to sit on the chair. My mother came to pick me up and as we walked back home, she said, "What do I smell?" She knew it was coming from me. I confessed. At first, she was upset. "Dorothy, how could you?" Then she started laughing. She made me walk three feet behind her. She cleaned me in the tub. I was so embarrassed . . .

\* \* \*

Ma Kettle was sick, so I picked up all her appointments as well as my own. I brought wood to Tweedledum who had made my favorite pastina chicken soup. She needed to go shopping and we picked up another elderly woman. Mistake! Both were vying for my attention! Like two children!

I stopped to meet Toni, a pregnant woman with two children. The trailer smelled of urine, and there was no gas in the stove. I was concerned because her moods shifted instantaneously. When I first looked at her, she was smiling, but when I appeared to look away, a deep pain registered on her face as if she were holding back tears. She was very agitated, and I was afraid that she would hurt one of the children unintentionally.

After work, I returned and spent the entire afternoon with her. She became more relaxed with talking. I watched the kids while she showered. She told me her husband was moving out that night. Doing social work gave me an understanding of what my sister must have gone through with her divorce. Her husband left just before the birth of her second child. I thought about the fact that I was giving more to strangers than to my own family.

After the stressful day, I went to the Kettles for supper. As we ate, Pa Kettle said, "I eat every meal like it's the last supper."

"Really, that's ominous," I said. "Are you that concerned?"

"I guess I know something that you don't know."

"What?" I asked but he didn't respond. Lucky Luke came and sang to us. I slept well that night.

Every day was the same routine. I took Tweedledee shopping and had to wait an hour for her food voucher. Halfway back to her house, she announced that she had forgotten cat food, so I had to turn around and take her back.

I went to pick up an elderly gentleman for a doctor's appointment. He was in his underwear on the couch, drunk as a skunk. He used crutches to walk, and I couldn't get him up. Thank God, the neighbor gave me a hand. One of the other passengers fed him cookies and that kept him happy.

Sharon, one of my outreach clients, confided that Dawn was stealing her things. After she called Dawn a slut, they had a fight. Sharon asked me to be her big sister and pick her up for the prayer meeting.

Cowardly Lion mouthed off at breakfast about wanting to talk to Scarecrow regarding his lack of interest in the community. I didn't like it. It sounded too much like the Empress. She had him doing her dirty work. We all became servants of the Empress. Bear kowtowed to the Empress because she realized how quickly the Empress could turn against a member and she didn't want to lose her living place. My respect for Bear was diminishing. In addition to all her work, she drove to Ellsworth to get the Empress's nephew a license.

Argus had been in a foul mood lately. He was attacking Shannon, Bear's dog.

Saturday morning, I got up early to work on a grant proposal. The Co-op was trying to get government funding for a building project. The Empress had asked that I complete the application form, which was quite extensive, almost like a mini book. I'd never done anything like it before.

Luke told me that Sharon had run away. I thought I had been making some headway with her, but apparently not. We went over the Kettle's for dinner. I went straight to Ma Kettle to ask her advice about Sharon. She sat me down and said, "Here, have a glass of wine. Relax. Mama you can't save the world. Kids do these things. She'll come back when she's ready."

"But I was really trying to be a friend to her," I said.

"I know. It doesn't matter what you do. Something probably set her off."

"What are we going to do? What if something bad happens to her?" I asked in an upset tone. The Empress walked over to me and said, "Calm down woman." I got quiet and pigged out. Pa Kettle wanted me to stay the night, but I left early.

A letter sent to the Co-op said, "the nuns at Mandala are elitist and do like the Church, inviting all, but not really allowing entry." Admittedly it was difficult for people to get to Mandala. I didn't know how much longer I could justify living there. When I was out at Mandala none of my clients could reach me. I thought about moving into town, but I did love the separateness this life afforded me.

Ted and the Hierophant were buying the Empress a water pump for $259 and wanted us to contribute. I had no money.

I told Bear that I was worried about seeing Sr. Lidia over the holidays.

"Why?" she asked. "Sr. Lidia was supportive of you at Catholic High."

"It still bothers me to see anyone from the past," I admitted. "I feel like I ran away. I still consider what I did as a failure."

"She doesn't see it that way," assured Bear. "Don't let those hypocrites break your spirit."

The weekend was so upsetting because of Sharon running away. I never dealt with this kind of work before, and it was hard not to take it to heart.

The idea of completeness by necessity giving rise to inconsistency mulled around in my brain. The number ten was the number of completeness and I realized that the Empress, Bear, Ma Kettle, and AB, who ran the farm program all had ten letters in their given names. All women connected with the Co-op, all complete but inconsistent. I wanted to share my discovery with someone but didn't dare. Bad enough, I said too much to the Empress about my ideas regarding Christ.

"Don't you think each one of us is really Christ?" I asked her while we were working on Saturday.

"I'm not God," she said and looked down with a humble glance.

"No, I guess I fall short of that too," I responded. "You know, Empress, we're not accessible to people out here at Mandala. I'm not sure that I can justify our very cushioned existence."

"I know what you mean, and I agree that we live a good life, but we all need a break from work. We need a place where we can escape and refresh our spirits. If not, we wouldn't be able to give. Trust me on this one."

"Maybe you're right," I responded. "Did you ever think we might be parts of each other's shadow?" Spiritual and Sensual?

"I'm not a shadow," she responded. "And where do you come up with these weird ideas? You think too much! You need to do more work with your hands."

"Yeah. I do come up with some beauties. Don't I? Thinking stops me from feeling."

"When do you feel?" she asked. I really couldn't answer this because I wasn't feeling these days. I only felt when I was eating or drinking too much, and it was usually a bad feeling.

"I don't feel," I said.

"That's not true. Your feelings are apparent the moment you walk into a room," she said.

"I guess I carry emotions from day to day, and it shows on my face."

"You've got to learn to let go. When I go to bed at night, I wake up with no thoughts."

"I wish I could do that."

"You can. Keep praying," she advised.

\* \* \*

Saturday night was the feast of the Immaculate Conception. The Empress chose two readings from the Book of Wisdom. One was in praise of wisdom, and the other spoke of love of Mary. The Empress commented on Mary's submission, her "yes" to God. "Her submission seemed too one sided to me," I retorted. The Empress just gave one of her "look downs" which said without saying, "it's not worth commenting on." Instead, she put on a Joan Baez album.

I woke up in the middle of the night and started writing thoughts. Narcissus jumped on me. I started thinking . . . '*You've become me. I've become you . . . sexual, narcissistic side . . . footsteps ahead of me . . . part of a book . . . the female Narcissus and Goldmund . . . Maine . . . escaping the killer . . . the Empress's eyes . . . our relationship . . . the animals . . . dreams . . . my clients . . . how will it end?* . . . I was totally exhausted after this, but I still couldn't sleep. Was this a creative outlet? I knew then I would write a book. The Empress would be the Muse. Animals would be involved. This was the meaning of my dream with the animals that looked like shit. Shitting is symbolic of the creative process. I got the idea of the book from Narcissus, but I didn't want it to end like Hesse's. Females should act differently. More compassionate. I talked to the Empress about my dream and the importance of animals. "Animals in a dream represent our instincts," she said. That made sense to me, sort of our base feelings. "People in our dreams are just parts of ourselves," she continued.

My cats just wanted to eat and get affection, just like me.

On Sunday morning, I walked outside and saw Bear and Shannon.

"You know, Bear, you are the most spiritual of all of us. You just do your work and don't complain or get involved in gossip," I explained and just as I said that, Argus came running up the path, baring his teeth and attacked Shannon. I screamed. Bear went after them, kicked both, and finally got them apart. The Empress came, picked up Argus and threw him but he continued to jump at Shannon. Shannon stood his ground. Bear got upset. The Empress said, "Maybe eventually they will have to fight it out, and one will submit." I thought about my animal theory but didn't say anything.

Bear and I left in the truck with Shannon riding on the back. I said, "Maybe Shannon would overpower Argus in an all-out fight."

"It would be out of character for him," she responded. "Argus is more in tune with aggression while Shannon is more playful."

Later, I saw the Empress holding a choke chain. She was obviously worried that Argus would hurt Shannon or someone else. "That's really going to make him happy," I said pointing to the chain.

"Stop. It's just a collar," she said.

"Not a collar I would want on." I felt sorry for Argus. He was such big beautiful free spirit.

"What are you talking about, Woman. You wear a tight collar. When are you going to let me in?" That remark threw me for a loop! Didn't she know I let her in a long time ago?

She took me to visit a priest who was living in a huge mansion. When I walked through the rooms, I said, "Maybe you could sell some of this furniture and raise money for the poor." He got defensive and said, "I get a lot of guests here. I need all this furniture. It's a big house. Besides, it's not all mine, I just use it."

Later, I mentioned his defensiveness to the Empress: "It's not what you say that makes people defensive, it's your lifestyle. We must be radically Christ. That speaks more than words."

"Oh, I went easy on him," I responded. "I could have said worse, but I didn't want to embarrass you."

"Oh goodie," she said, teasing me. That was her favorite phrase these days, and then she added, "The material is easy to let go. It's the attitude that's difficult."

One of the town's couples was going to watch Toni's kids for a while to give her time to get her husband back. She was not into her kids and I couldn't imagine that she could get her husband to stay. Even if he did, he'd go berserk. I dropped the kids off. The poor couple never had children and they welcomed their visit. Unfortunately, Toni didn't give them much in terms of clothes, diapers, or other supplies.

On the way home, I stopped to see Tweedledee. She gave me the guilt trip, "No one was around to get my mail and groceries when I was sick." I stayed till I couldn't take the complaining anymore. It was late at night when I started back for Mandala. I saw the Empress and Bear up ahead of me. They turned into the Co-op, and I continued up the road to our community. I wanted the Empress to know that I was working late since she was always criticizing that I didn't work hard enough, but I would be home before they saw me. I turned into the driveway and started up the hill. The car rolled back and caught onto a huge boulder in the road. I couldn't get the car off it, so I had to wait. Soon the Empress came and pushed my car over the boulder with her truck. I wondered if my thoughts willed that to happen.

Narcissus fell into the bucket of water! Crazy cat!

I wrote in my journal in a handwriting that was foreign to my normal script . . .

> . . . *There is an evil person within. She's critical. She hates herself. I'm afraid of her. She's extreme. How can I control her? Her thoughts are powerful. Evil must be loved to be overcome. There is a witch within all females. Eve caused Adam to eat. Fool. She wanted knowledge and sacrificed naivete for it. He was willing to stay naïve. Mary was born sinless. But then she never had to choose. How can I identify with someone who had no evil part pulling at her? I keep having dreams and thoughts of the Empress killing herself. Why? Is there a part of me that wants to hurt her? For rejecting me? Like when I was a child and a part broke off and I thought I killed my parents. I was so young. .I can't say the word. Yes, you can. Say it. I tried to forget but I couldn't. I relived it every night. Every time I closed my eyes. Over and over again. But this time a part within found the solution. The broken off part. I pulled out a gun and shot everyone. Tell me, Dorothy. Tell me. Why are you evil? I can't tell. Yes, you can. Tell me or you'll have to tell a doctor. No doctor. I'll tell you. Oh God! Oh God! I shot them! I shot my parents. I'm so evil. You didn't shoot them. It was a dream. Only a dream . . .*

I shared Bear my thoughts with Bear. "I'm worried, Bear, and frightened by the possibility that the psychic life is real. I think we can influence matter."

"Don't get carried away with the imagination," she replied. "My brother went through the same kind of thing. He had a break down after my father died. He had wished him dead the week before he died, and so he felt responsible. My brother tried to commit suicide a few times. Luckily, he hasn't succeeded. We're all over-extended at the Co-op. It's a form of self-violence. We all try to do more than we realistically can do. We feel responsible for all these less fortunate people."

The Empress interrupted our conversation to introduce a photographer who wanted to compliment Bear on her photographs for the newspaper. Bear said, "I'm not that good. I'm not that productive either."

"You can't accept compliments, can you?" I said to her after the Empress had left.

"No. It's the Irish background. Makes one humble."

"Not Italians. We think we're great and to hell with everyone else's opinion!" I said.

"That seems healthier." She laughed.

The Empress asked if I wanted to stay at her house for the weekend since she would be traveling. I jumped at having a bigger space.

I had one final dental visit. I dreaded it. His attitude changed after I told him I was doing outreach work. I didn't have enough money to pay the bill and he said, "Don't worry, it's Christmas." I went to the bank and paid the bill anyway.

I walked to Duffy's after dropping off my car for new brakes. It was cold and my hands were freezing. In five days, it would be Christmas. The Empress, on her return, stopped for breakfast. "Cowardly Lion and Scarecrow are lonely," she said.

"They don't have the in on loneliness," I retorted.

When I returned to the cabin, I found that Cowardly Lion had kept my wood stove going. Thank God. It was so cold that I could see my breath while I was practicing the guitar that night. Narcissus, Goldmund, and Archie slept under the covers with me. I still hadn't gotten the hang of keeping the stove lit all night.

The next morning, I awoke to find that all my can goods had frozen!

\*    \*    \*

Narcissus was a beautiful cat with thick fur. In the mornings, he would follow me to the car, winding in and out of my legs as I walked. I loved him dearly. He was so affectionate. Goldmund, on the other hand, was quiet and aloof. She hadn't grown very big and was still quite fearful.

The Hierophant's mother had died while she was home visiting. I knew this would make the Empress even more sympathetic to her wishes.

The Empress was the master manipulator. At supper, she talked about people growing through their mistakes.

"You had to break fingers to learn about the power of mechanical tools," she said to Bear. "And you, Scarecrow, your temper gets the best of you." She didn't mention anything about me. Rejection worked better on me.

Subconsciously, we all knew how to deal with one another. I came to believe that evil comes in the conscious use of power over another to cause a result.

I left for home on December 21st, the Friday before Christmas. The Hermit hitched a ride to New Hampshire. In route, we started talking about Hesse.

"Do you like the book *Narcissus and Goldmund*?" I asked.

"Very much," he responded. "But I don't think the Empress likes it."

"Really?" I said wondering why the Empress pretended she liked Hesse when we talked about the writer. "How did you get involved with the Co-op, anyway?" I asked.

"I was the Chaplain in the monastery when the nuns kicked the Empress out. I wrote to the Bishop in her defense. She was the only one serving the needs of the people. The rest just wanted to stay in their private worlds. The Empress went out to the community, breaking the vow of cloister. The Empress is impulsive when she does things, but she is usually right. My background forces me into a more conservative approach, but secretly I admire her courage."

So, this was the reason the Hermit provided the "nuts and bolts" to help the Empress in her projects. Secretly, he cared very much about her. Maybe this caused tension between him and the Hierophant.

On the way home, I stopped to see Doris. I felt like crying the whole time I was there. She couldn't look into my eyes, and therefore, I kept mine down. She had bought a new car but was uncomfortable when telling me. She hated Kennedy and the welfare system. My ideas were too out there for her, and so I didn't dare discuss them. Then she talked about the kids in her classroom and the Doris I remembered emerged. She was so dedicated to bringing out the best in each student. Before I left, she off-handedly asked, "So what are you doing?" I told her, and she responded, "Oh."

I spent the night at Adele's and shared all my ideas about animals reflecting our different selves, synchronicity, how the book emerged, and the evil thought patterns. She understood and related two similar experiences, "There was a time in my life, I could have killed Jerry. I was house bound with the two children, and I watched him escape every morning. At least that's how I interpreted it. I wanted to beat him when he couldn't understand why I didn't get any work done during "the free hours of the day." Then when I was a small child, I wished my grandmother dead. I repressed that thought, and when she did die, I felt responsible. It wasn't till I was an adult that the subconscious feelings resurfaced. It took a long time for me to accept that I had nothing to do with it."

We discussed the cake dream, and I got the impression that the "wedding" in the dream was not a wedding in the normal sense. The burden of this spiritual marriage was "heavy."

Adele and Jerry were fighting in the morning about who should wash the kitchen floor as Jerry's family was coming for dinner. I decided it was time for me to leave.

It was good to finally be home. Hot showers, oil heat, mechanical conveniences. After primping, I sat down for coffee with my mother. "I have had a great sense of Nonnie lately," I said to her.

"You were her pride and joy. She called you, *'Cuore di Nonna'*. One day when you were around eleven months, she called you over and you just got up and walked to her. You had never taken a step before."

"I must have been drawn to her power."

"Another time I scolded you, and she hit me. When she was dying, she only regretted leaving you. 'Why do I have to leave her,' she said."

"She looked like such a strong woman from her pictures."

"Oh, she was strong, but also gentle. She helped everyone in need. She came over from Italy with her mother. They ran a little sandwich shop and lived with relatives. A year later she married your grandfather. She had two brothers and one of them didn't get along with your grandfather. The brother was a big man and a drinker. One evening Nonno and he got into an argument. The brother threatened to strangle your Grandfather and proceeded to squeeze his neck in jest, but he wouldn't let go. It was your grandmother who pulled him away."

"It's funny that I don't consciously remember her, but unconsciously I do. I will meet her someday," I said confidently. We both cried and hugged each other.

Then my mother lamented, "It's not the fact that you live in Maine. It's just the way you live. You're used to so much more. How can you give up so much? How can you survive with so little? No electricity. No running water."

"I live very richly Mom," I said. "Don't worry about me. I'm living a spiritual life."

"Your grandmother was spiritual. She loved Mary. She was very sick just before she died. The breast cancer had spread into her bones and she couldn't move. On her last day she raised herself up into a sitting position, arms lifted toward a picture of Mary hanging on the wall and said, "She's here. She's coming to get me! And with those words, she lay back down, closed her eyes and died peacefully with a smile on her face."

"I think she really saw her," I said.

"I think so, too," my mother replied.

My dream on Christmas morning: *The Empress and I were not together. She had a heart operation. I called her. It was a serious operation. I was worried. I scolded her for not telling me about it. I told her I loved her and cried on the phone. I asked if that made a difference to her. She remained quiet.*

If the Empress is right about people in our dreams being part of ourselves, what was this dream saying? Parts of myself were not in tune? Did I need to undergo a massive surgery on part of myself? Then could I love myself?

No one made a big deal about all the weight I had gained. There were a lot of hints dropped about my family longing for my return though, "You're coming home next year . . . Don't sell your antiques. You will want them when you come back."

I had a date to see Wolf the Sunday before Christmas but when I rang the doorbell, no one answered. She never called to explain why she wasn't there. And I didn't call to see if she was all right. What had happened to our relationship?

Ever since the reading at Mass from Zephaniah, "Jerusalem, your judgement is over," the Empress had been civil to me and our friendship had returned to normal. When I got back from Christmas vacation on Thursday, she took me to dinner at the home of an outreach client. Later that night, we practiced guitar together.

"Thanks for practicing with me. I can't sing alone," she confided.

"Why not? You have a nice voice."

"Maybe, but I can't carry a tune."

"Are you tone deaf?" I asked, concerned.

"Could be. I never really thought about it. I love playing and singing, but I don't feel I'm good at it."

"It doesn't matter how good we are. Only that we enjoy it." I said, trying to be positive. My love for her was stronger than ever. But I had accepted that it would remain on a friendship level. I vowed that I would never take advantage of her or betray her in public.

The Empress and Bear had another argument over the dogs. The two animals had been fighting again, and the Empress grabbed Argus and yelled, "Someone grab Shannon." Scarecrow started kicking Shannon, and Bear got so upset and screamed, "There are too many bosses around here!" Everyone went silent. Bear was normally a calm person. She took Shannon into the house, and when she returned, she questioned the Empress, "I thought we had decided to let them fight it out by themselves?" The Empress didn't say anything. She obviously knew she was wrong.

That night the Empress and I drank wine and watched TV together. We sat close. I wanted so much to reach out and put my arm around her but didn't dare. She was her usual distant self. Gloria came in limping. We nearly bumped heads trying to see what was wrong. Then Argus came in and sprawled on top of us. We laughed as we pet him.

After watching a program on homeless children, I went back to my cabin. I sensed she wanted me to stay, but I didn't want to do anything that might ruin the relationship we had built up again. The Hierophant was to return soon, and I would have to again retreat into the background. It was a frustrating situation for me, but there was nowhere else I wanted to be.

Sunday night we went to the Kettles. They had saved me some of Ma Kettle's special Christmas home brew. I drank the whole glass and then had tea with Southern Comfort. While Ma Kettle and the Empress went to pick up the kids, I went off into one of the bedrooms and played the guitar. I had taught myself the chords and could do a few songs from memory. I started singing my favorite, "Snowbird" by Ann Murray. When the Empress returned, Skids dragged her in to listen to me sing it. I was so embarrassed. When I got to the part which said, "The thing I want the most in life is the thing that I can't win", I stopped and couldn't go on. My voice got weak. Sensing my unease, the Empress left. Later, I excused myself to her by saying, "I didn't know the words well enough."

I spent one of the most painful and frustrating, yet totally beautiful, days of my life the New Year's Eve day of 1980. After Mass, I carried water to the cabin, cut wood, and then with Skids and the Empress, helped the Hermit with his garbage. It was neatly piled under his house. He was the only person I knew with neat garbage! Skids and I had potatoes and eggs for breakfast. We sang our way to the Co-op. He made me playful.

I made my visiting rounds. Grand Pa, Molly's husband, was in the hospital again with cancer. She was so down. I couldn't lift her spirits. She just sat on the rocker and looked out the window, just waiting and knowing and having to accept.

Then I stopped at Toni's. The kids were back. Debbie, the fifteen-year-old, was pregnant. Toni's feelings for her husband had turned into hate. She followed him the other night and saw him hugging his girlfriend in the car, "Get away from my husband!" she demanded. When the girl refused, Toni pulled her out of the car to fight her. Luckily, no one got too hurt.

Toni was still aggravated. I felt she was capable of serious violence. And unfortunately, she had stopped going to counseling.

By the time I returned to the Co-op for lunch, I was depressed. I finished the day with a visit to Tweedledee and listened to her yakking for over an hour. I had to turn off my mind to keep my sanity. Her repetitions drove me crazy.

For relief, I went to Tweedledum's to get cheered up. Her mind was sharp, and she had a good sense of humor. "*Come on a my house,*" she sang when she saw me, and her eyes twinkled. "Dorothy, you've got to start watching your weight," she said.

"You're right. I need to lose weight. It's my New Year's resolution," I promised her.

My last visit was to Star who was down to earth and real. If Christ were around, he would pick Star be the second Mary Magdalene! She was dating John, an alcoholic, who was separated from his wife. She didn't pick good partners, but she was a good mother.

When I got back to the Co-op, AB, the woman who ran the farm program, was there with a bottle of Bacardi 151 and hot chocolate. The Empress started spouting about the problem of over population in the world. Scarecrow said,

"What we need are more nuns and homosexuals!"

"That's what we have here!" I commented.

*　　*　　*

Both the Empress and the High Priestess were Cancers. Hard to believe as they were so different. The High Priestess and I had more in common. We talked about journal writing. She admitted, "There's a part of me that I couldn't even bear to write about even in my journal."

"That would be the most beautiful part of you," I replied. She smiled, embarrassed. Later, I confided to the Empress, "The High Priestess is so fragile. She reminds me of one of the animals in the Glass Menagerie, hard yet easily shattered." The Empress commented, "If I had more time, I would spend it with the High Priestess."

I confided about Toni. "Her husband probably loves having two women fight over him. He's such a namby-pamby not making a decision one way or the other. He should either leave Toni for good or stay and try to make the marriage work. I can't understand that attitude. What kind of person would do that?" I asked.

"Someone like us!" The Empress responded and we both laughed. "Someone who keeps coming back for more," she added.

We drank milk and coffee brandy at the Kettles that night and watched the hostages on TV. It was so depressing. Sloane Coffin and a few other religious leaders did a special Christmas service. The captors let the hostages be seen on TV. They acted jovial. Everyone knew it was fake.

I swerved only once on the drive home. I got the fire going, and as I looked into the flames, I thought about committing suicide. I envisioned pushing a knife into my heart. I cried myself to sleep. The damn batteries in the tape recorder ran out so I had no music to drown out the tears!

The Empress and I had one of our usual disagreements. Ma Kettle started commenting about the people we worked with, "People don't have enough food."

"But it's their own fault," I retorted. "They mismanage their funds. Look at what some of them buy! Instead of getting good cheap staples like beans or lentils, they buy junk food like chips, cigarettes, candy. And then they waste money on partying . . . "

"You're so analytical," said the Empress. "I hate listening to people being analyzed!"

"Well, it's true," I said back. "Come and have dinner with me, and we can continue talking about it." Amazingly, she agreed to come. We talked about diet and the need to eat correctly. "Eating satisfies an oral need," she commented.

"I didn't think you had any oral needs," I teased.

"Watch it!" she said, hitting me on the shoulder.

At supper, the Empress and Scarecrow discussed building. The Empress beamed when she talked wood and carpentry. Even the Scarecrow admired her knowledge. Then the discussion switched to religion. The Empress commented, "There are two rabbis in Israel who believe the Messiah is coming to save us from nuclear destruction."

"She's coming this time," I emphasized.

"Do you understand what following Christ means?" she asked, giving me that disgusted looked.

"I don't think I'm at that point of knowledge yet," I answered.

"You think a lot about it. I feel a great energy in you, but you get to a certain point, and you stop."

My body went cold, and I started shaking. At first, I couldn't speak. Then I said, "I think accepting one another is the true message of Christ. The more I learn about myself, the more I see parts of myself in others and they in me. It helps me to understand. Yesterday when

I couldn't go into a hospital room to visit a dying man, I realized how Ma Kettle must feel, and yet she goes in."

"You're right that Christ felt compassion," the Empress said and lowered her eyes.

My spiritual part was a very deep, hidden, almost embarrassing part of myself.

Tweedledum said that I have a fat ass!

I could feel myself again. In the morning I ran with Shannon. I jumped for joy. There is no Christ where there is no joy! Lydia, my prior student, had come to visit. She brought me joy. She hated school and wanted to come and live in Maine. I took her with me to visit clients. Star nonchalantly blurted out that she thought she might be pregnant, "Wasn't I mad at him!" was her comment. Didn't she think she had something to do with it, I thought.

Friday night we all went to a horse auction with AB and her husband, Bad. Cowardly Lion, Lydia, and I sat behind the seat of the truck, all cold and squished. In the show, Cowardly Lion and Lydia sat up on the top bleacher, and I sat with the Empress. On the way home, we got a flat tire. The Empress and Bad knelt down together to change the tire. Someone had fingered out the word "fuck" in the dirt on the glass.

"Such an appropriate word," I teased. "Someone might drive by and wonder what you two are doing."

"Where is your mind woman?" retorted the Empress. "Someone will get the wrong idea. I'll take care of you later," she said smiling.

"I wish you would." I laughed.

Lydia said I brought out the humorous side of the Empress. "You're good for her," she commented.

\* \* \*

We finally found a place for the Hospitality House. It was an abandoned building, with three floors and plenty of rooms, in the center of town. It just needed some major work. On Saturday, Scarecrow fixed all the pipes, and I worked on the insulation.

Sunday, Cowardly Lion treated us to breakfast at Duffy's, and then we took Toni's kids skating on a small frozen pond. Lydia and I danced on the ice. We all sang and pushed each other around and acted like kids.

The next afternoon, the Empress invited me to go for drinks. We both had a few, and she was in the self that liked me.

"Susan is our song. Isn't it?" she asked. WHAT? That threw me for a loop.

"Yes, I guess so," I replied.

"So, did you have a good time with Lydia?" she questioned.

"Yes. I did. She makes me carefree," I said while thinking, 'but I love you.'

"Good. You need to be more carefree. You're too much into the self and psychology."

"Yes, I can be intense," I replied.

"Speaking of intense. Can you help me with the review of my part of the proposal?" she asked. "I need someone to read, correct, and type it.

"Yes, of course. This has to be done right. We don't want to break any rules and go to jail."

"Jail would be a rest for me," she said.

As we talked and drank, I realized she needed me to do more of the original writing than she had originally implied. She didn't do a lot of the work she was supposed to do. I couldn't trust her when she was under the influence of liquor. Sensing my anger, she said, "If we get this grant it will provide jobs for people in the Hospitality House."

"Don't try and bribe me," I said. "I do things because they are important. The grant is important, you don't have to justify."

"Also, can you take me to the airport tomorrow?" she added.

"Yes, I'll take you to the airport. Anything else?"

"Take me home."

I woke up in the morning feeling like Judas. Gloria rubbed up against me as "Susan" played.

Later that morning, Bear came up to tell me that the Hierophant had returned, and she would be taking the Empress to the airport. I didn't have to do it. I wasn't surprised.

After Mass, I went down to the lake for skating. I sat for the longest time at the edge, afraid of falling through a weak part of the ice. Finally, I got up enough nerve to skate near the shore. I proceeded with caution moving from one rock to the next then, I got daring and ventured out further, skating figure eights and doing turns. I felt a wonderful sense of freedom. All alone on that spacious white expansive body. The barren tall trees painting the faded, gray-clouded sky. Cold licking my face. I wanted so badly to skate to the middle but held back.

*       *       *

Tweedledee couldn't decide whether to wear a scarf or hat. She kept trying each one on. First the scarf. Then the hat. Back to the scarf. The scarf kept slipping so she finally opted for the hat. A wise choice.

It was a relief to get back to the office until the Hermit called me in his office to discuss the fact that "people were talking about each other." I was shocked that he would approach such a topic. He never got involved in personal problems. I wondered where the motivation had come from. It wasn't hard to guess when he didn't object to my response, "I don't think this is an issue you should get involved in."

The wood crew drove their truck into the Co-op with a flat tire. I was flabbergasted that they would risk ruining the wheel by not changing the tire. I rushed into Ted's office and complained. "What were they thinking? Who is in charge here?" I asked.

"Well, the Empress is in charge of them," he said. "But they don't listen to her. It's an ego thing. Grown men taking orders from a woman doesn't cut it. If she were a man, she could tell them off,"

"Why does she have to be a man to do so?" I responded.

"That's just the way it is up here," he responded.

The Doctor accompanied me on my rounds so she could become acquainted with the people aided by the Co-op. She got a charge out of Tweedledum referring to me as "fat ass."

"Does that bother you?" she asked.

"No. She really likes me. It's her way of showing affection. I know she really thinks I'm cute."

"That's a healthy attitude," she responded.

"You have to have a healthy attitude to do this work. If I took all the criticisms seriously, I'd be a basket case." I asked her how the Painter had been doing since her sickness?"

"Much better since we moved here. I felt it was necessary to get her away so she could do her work in peace without distractions. She's a sensitive woman and a capable artist."

"I can see that." I said. "She's lucky to have you to take care of her."

"She takes care of me, too."

I started writing the first section of my book.

I spent all my free time at the Hospitality House. Annie, one of the more colorful but spacey tenants, confided that she was a psychic. "I'm really good with people," she said. "I know how to handle men." She told me about the time she hitched a ride from some guy she met in a restaurant. He drove down a dirt road and parked. When he started to try to kiss her, she said, "Oh good, this is how I planned to die. After you rape me, I'm going to kill myself, and everyone saw us together at the restaurant so they will think you killed me." He immediately drove her back to the main road.

"I can tell you how to get a man," she continued.

"How?" I asked, playing along.

"You lie on a bed with your legs spread apart and feet together. You use pillows as a reading table and read this passage from the Christian Science book and the spirit will enter through the vagina, 'God is all, there is no space and time; therefore, God is everywhere and fills all. If God is all time and I am a child of God and made in his image, then time is not, and I am a baby again, pure and virgin.' This closes the vagina and makes you attractive to men."

"That's quite a method," I commented. "I never tried that one."

Morning Mass was hysterical. At one point all the dogs and cats came running through the room chasing one another. The Hierophant read the wrong line and got giddy. Chico, her dog, was licking her nose so she couldn't see the page. "This is a funny Mass," I spurted out. The Empress couldn't hold back her laughter and went outside to blow her nose. The Hermit kept a straight face through it all. I didn't know how he kept his composure. I was sure he was fuming inside!

I beeped for Tweedledee to come out to the car as I was running late. Rushed, she left her pocketbook with the key locked in the house. She panicked and uttered, "This must be the doings of the villain. He's always trying to confuse me. What are we going to do now? He'll get my things."

"I'll get inside," I said as I climbed up the bathroom window. The window pushed down a bit and I was able to squeeze through and roll in headfirst. I had visions of hitting my head on the tub, but I managed to hold on while I got my legs around.

"Now I'll have to lock that window," she said. "He probably unlocked it last time he was here. That must be the way he gets in. I always wondered how he managed to get in. Now I'll fool him. God damn him! Next time he comes, he won't find that window open. God damn. God damn him."

\*   \*   \*

I'd been dreaming about the Empress again. I woke up feeling her arms around me. It was so real. Like a healing. We talked last night after supper. "I want to know what you think I should do?" she asked.

"Why? You wouldn't believe me if I told you," I responded.

"Stop it. I respect your opinion. I've been invited to the World Council of Churches meeting in Paris. I'm not sure I should go."

"Of course, you should go! Paris! It's my favorite city. So romantic. I can be your guide," I said, thinking I would love to be in Paris with her.

"I'm not going for the romance. It's business, and I'm not sure I can afford the time or money."

"Aren't they going to pay for your expenses?" I asked.

"Well, the room and board are paid for, but I will have to pay for the flight."

"You can get an inexpensive flight. Book ahead. What an opportunity!"

"Yes, it is exciting, and I can't believe they asked me."

"Why shouldn't they ask you? You're famous."

"Not as famous as some of the attendees."

"You'll be great. You'll bring the female input."

"How about the spiritual input?"

"That, too."

"So how are you doing with the social work job?" she asked.

"It's difficult," I said. "I had to deal with another runaway. I don't approve of all the drugs these doctors put the teenagers on. They prescribe them so easily. It doesn't solve the problem. It just band aids the wound."

"It is difficult trying to solve people's problems," she sympathized.

"Yes. It's hard doing that work all day and then coming home to no one. I find community lonely."

"I get lonely at times, too."

"It's impossible to do this work without support. Ma Kettle is lucky to have Pa at home. He replenishes her. There's nothing here to do that. I need to be loved."

"Love comes in many forms."

"I need physical love."

"You switch from your mind to your heart so quickly. You get too wrapped up in yourself."

"How can I talk out of any other place but myself?"

"You're speaking from your own experience, and the work we do requires that you live in Christ's experience. You have to lose yourself."

"I try. I try to get my mind and heart in line, but it's not easy."

"Keep praying. The road to individuality is lonely."

"You're an individual. Does that bring you happiness?"

"I'm happy."

"I'm glad for you."

"You need to face your dark side."

"I face it every night."

The Artist came to visit and stayed for the community meeting. What a scene! A great painting. We sat around the kitchen table. The Empress had her arm around the Cowardly Lion. The Hierophant played with Chico throughout the meeting. Ma Kettle sat at the head of the table trying to get everyone's attention while she tried to juggle the kids pulling at her skirt. The Artist and I sat off to the side. Nothing got accomplished.

The Artist bribed me to return to Bangor with her and spend the night at her mother's house with promises of a hot bath. I jumped at the chance!

When I walked into the Co-op office the next day, the Secretary and Ma Kettle were talking. "Don't you think Dorothy's too moody these days?" asked the Secretary in a loud enough voice so I could hear.

"Yes," said Ma Kettle. "She shouldn't be living at Mandala. There's too much unexpressed emotion out there. It's not good. The existence is too separate."

"I agree," said Secretary. "She needs more social life. She needs to do something besides work and community."

"Well, I guess you two have solved my problems," I responded.

"We have. Now you have to," said Ma Kettle. Just then the Empress came out of her office. "Don't you think Dorothy needs to get out more?" asked Ma Kettle.

"I think she gets out too much," exclaimed the Empress. "She needs to calm down. Build a house out in the community. Put down some roots. Hang around with stable people."

"Be nice," I said.

"I'm being judged," she said.

"No, you're judging," I responded. She looked at me with that funny look.

"Come on, Mama. We got work to do," said Ma Kettle as she grabbed my arm and dragged me out the door.

January 23rd was the first major snowfall. It was so beautiful, seeing all the white on the trees. The horses loved it and ran around the yard biting each other playfully. Despite the snow, I faced a busy week with plenty of appointments.

While I was hiding in my office, the Empress stopped by and asked me to fill out a government form.

"Wouldn't the Hermit do a better job at this?" I asked.

"I can't trust that he will get it done," she said.

"Why not? What's wrong? I asked.

"Everything and nothing," she answered as she handed me the form. The next day, I started working on it and the Hermit saw me.

"Would you like me to fill that out? I do them all the time," he said.

"Sure, that would be great," I said. Why didn't she ask him?

Something was wrong. I saw the Hermit being mean to the new little dog the Empress and Hierophant had gotten. Was it pay back for his cat?

The Hierophant complained that someone was "visiting" their house and smoking upstairs, leaving ashes, eating bologna, and leaving papers in the fireplace. Could it be one of the Empress's other selves?

The days went by so quickly. There were so many tasks. Pressures came from all sides. Each day brought a new set of problems. Scarecrow and I worked on the chimney at the Hospitality House in the morning before I did my outreach work. I was late getting Tweedledum, so I had to spend extra time with her, and then I didn't have time to cut wood. Then I was late for Tweedledee. Ma Kettle called to tell me that the elderly gentleman in the hospital with cancer had died. It was the typical all-around bad day. I walked the mile and half into Mandala and wasn't too afraid. I sat alone drinking in the cabin that night. A half-empty gallon of wine was sitting on the floor next to me when the Empress came up and took my glass away: "I have the same problem with Molly that you have with Tweedledee and Tweedledum, but I don't drink over it."

"Well, that's how I get over it," I said, feeling no pain.

"This doesn't get you over it," she said raising the wine bottle. "You need to go to bed. I didn't object.

On Monday, I took a woman living at the Hospitality House to Bangor. She had a speech problem and couldn't hold a job. "I'm a full-fledged parasite," she said. As soon as we got to the mall, she dashed out of the car and announced, "I'm in my element now." She was nowhere in sight by the time I got to the lobby. I searched but couldn't find her. I had to go back without her.

I stopped to see Star and complained about the woman who ran away. Star was having her own problems. She had called her old boyfriend who came over and they slept together. "Now I'm all confused," she said. "Do you think he still loves me?" I wanted to scream at her, but I had no right. Star mistakes sex for love, as I do.

*     *     *

Despite all the time and hard work filling out the endless pages, the federal housing grant didn't get funded on the first go round. This was hard to understand since Maine was one of the poorest states in the union and certainly well deserving of a low-income housing grant. I went to visit Pa Kettle to discuss the reasons for not getting the funding. He explained that the local towns were not backing the housing grant. The federal government wouldn't give money to a community if there was no local support.

"The Co-op has done nothing to try and cajole these people into supporting the grant," he continued. "So, when asked, they just answer no to all the questions. These people don't want low income housing in their backyards. They have been against it from the start."

"From the start!" I exclaimed. "How come no one told me?"

"You know how the Co-op works," he answered. "No one deals with reality. I've been telling the Empress that she needs to deal with these people and scratch their backs."

"Maybe we should reapply and this time I'll try to get some positive support."

"You can go ahead and try, but it's not easy, "he warned. "I've been at this for a while, and it's an uphill battle with the federal government as well."

I had to decide if I was going to go to Paris. I was having my usual day. I had fallen on my ankle that morning, and later in the day, the car broke down while I was driving clients to Bangor. I left Tweedledee's house without taking her shopping since I couldn't take any more pressure. Moreover, it was cold and strenuous living at Mandala.

The Hierophant saw me sitting depressed in my office. "You need to get away," she said. "This outreach work is stressful. I have a friend, Lorraine, who lives in Portland. I go there periodically to recoup. She likes the company and has an extra room. I'm going to call her. I want you to take the weekend and go relax."

I cancelled all Friday appointments and drove to Lorraine's house. She was away for the day but had left a key outside.

A whole house to myself! Electricity, hot water, and heat that didn't require so much work! This was heaven. I took a long hot bath, ate a normal dinner, lay on the couch, and listened to soft classical music. It was just what I needed to counter my internal turmoil. When I was in my animus stage, I would ignore feelings and bury them.

Lorraine was easy to talk to. She was an ex-nun. She left me alone Saturday to do some shopping. By evening, I was ready for company and we went to do laundry together.

"I had a hard time with community," she said. "It's demanding. A lot of different people with a lot of different needs. I'm much happier living alone."

"I always admired the Transcendentalists and their simple life at Brooke Farm. I guess this is my attempt at a Brooke Farm," I admitted. "I always thought community was the most Christian form of existence"

"You're right. In true community, people bring out the Christ in one another. But it can't be forced."

"I thought it could work," I said sadly.

"I don't think Brooke Farm worked either," she said. "But take courage. Help comes from places you least expect it. It never comes from those you expect. And then sometimes you have to throw in the towel."

"I'm not ready to give up yet," I said.

"Keep trying but if you need to get away, you're always welcome here."

By Sunday, I felt great. I took a ride around the region and found an area called Lake Sebago just like in my dream. I was worried that something would happen, but nothing did. I realized that I was living too much in the subconscious. Also, that I had limits. I decided that when I got back to Mandala, I would move upstairs in the barn. It had a larger wood stove, and it was easier to keep warm. Cowardly Lion would be a welcomed living companion.

Though I felt obligated to get back to work, I forced myself to stay through Monday. I wrote in my journal . . . I'm Alice in Wonderland rushing to a destination I never know. I meet the cast of characters and look into the looking glass to see myself. I fall into dark holes and change sizes. I get battered around on the game field of life. I never know who I will be. I'm Dorothy searching for my dream world, fighting witches along the way, helped by lions, scarecrows, and bears. Alice returned to reality. Dorothy's destination was home. Cowardly Lion is the sincerest. Bear is the most spiritual with humility and self-criticism. Scarecrow is able to let go and enjoy. The Hierophant makes me laugh. The Empress is the most difficult. Lucy in the sky with diamonds, the Great Oz, the visionary, the dreamer, the magician, the magus, the unity of opposites, the secretive crab, the simple yet profound. . . .

I returned late in the afternoon to discover that the Empress had been sick all weekend. She went for an X-ray. Cowardly Lion and I waited at her house to make sure she was all right, but it was getting late. I had to leave to go move my things up into the barn.

After reviewing finances, I decided I couldn't afford Paris. Just paying twelve dollars to fix my car was a struggle! When I finally told the Empress my decision, she said, almost in defense, "Well, I must go. I can't let my niece down. She's all excited about going."

It was difficult to return to work on Tuesday. I didn't schedule many appointments and had lunch with the Hermit and the Empress regarding our future strategy on the grant. Both agreed with my suggestion that we should reapply. Later, I visited Tweedledee who played the sympathy sick routine. I gave in and was nice to her. We were friends again.

I decided to see if my passport was still good. The thought of being in Paris again was so appealing. And it would be a great opportunity to be part of the Empress's entourage! I decided to go, regardless of the motive.

The Empress and I walked to the stream to get water. The snow sparkled a prism of diamond colors in the morning sun light. The Empress confided that she was disgusted with all the animals. Bandit was fighting with the Hermit's cat, Mark.

Star's birthday fell on Valentine's Day. I invited her to come to supper. She was thrilled to spend time with Cowardly Lion.

"Don't you just love him?" she said, hugging Cowardly Lion from behind. "I know he's too young and irresponsible, but isn't he so cute and shy," she continued and then turned her attention on me. "You should get married, Dorothy. You won't be young forever."

"It will never fly, Orville," commented Bear. "As I opened my mouth to respond, the Empress said, "There's no need to expound on that comment. And Cowardly Lion is not ready for commitment either. There's too much work to do around here to worry about relationships."

Later, Cowardly Lion and I went to Star's mother's house for birthday cake. I laughed when she opened her aunt's present. "Oh, another night gown," she said leaving no doubt how she felt about the gift. Luckily, the $22 she made from her other cards seemed to please her. It was a hefty amount.

Cleme came to visit Bear. After Mass, Bear invited me to the round house.

"Bear, you live in two worlds, here and your community in Connecticut," I said, on our walk up the hill.

"Not really. I'm just into one thing, dedicating my life to Christ. It doesn't matter where I do it or where I live. I might make a difference to the convent in Connecticut by doing this work here. They could use some challenging ideas."

We sat by the windows with coffee. Cleme took my hand and said, "Let me read your palm."

"Sure," I responded. "Anything to figure out the puzzle."

"You rule your fate," she began. "You are led by your will. Before, you were influenced by your parents, and it blocked you. You need to be in a place where your talents are recognized. You have writing ability, and you lean toward the arts. Do you believe in reincarnation?" she asked.

"Yes," I responded.

"You are an old soul," she continued. "You have experienced different lives. You're independent on the outside, but really dependent. You're self-influenced, sensitive, and healthy. At age 35 or so, a drastic change will occur in your life and you will assume a leadership position."

This all seemed very positive to me.

At breakfast the next morning, Star told me she needed to get away from her old boyfriend. She asked if she could stay with Cowardly Lion and myself. I knew Cowardly Lion wouldn't object, and I certainly would love having her, but I suspected the Empress would not be thrilled. I was right.

"Is she dating?" questioned the Empress when I brought up the topic later that morning.

"She dated a guy for three years, but they split up and she needs time to decide what she wants," I responded.

"I just don't want any men coming out her to see her. Maybe she should stay in the Hospitality House," suggested the Empress.

"She won't bring anyone out here. She just wants time to think," I responded. Just then, the Hierophant came rushing into the kitchen.

"Someone has been throwing my clothes around the room. And there's a wet sock on my bed," she announced all flustered.

"Maybe it's a playful ghost!" I exclaimed. "Who would come out here and not take the TV or other expensive tools and only throw your clothes around?"

"I don't know, but it's getting me upset," she said. The Empress and I looked at each other and laughed.

"Speaking of ghosts. Here read this short story by Tolstoy," the Empress said as she threw me a small paperback book.

I went back up to the barn. Cowardly Lion fed the horses while Star and I got wood for the stove. On my way to the spring to get water for cooking, Narcissus followed me. During dinner, a potentially dangerous event occurred. We had been using the picnic table in the barn as our dinner table. Star and I were sitting opposite Cowardly Lion. When Cowardly Lion got up, the equal balance was lost, the table tipped over, and the kerosene lantern fell to the wooden floor. Luckily, Cowardly Lion was quick in putting out the fire. I shuddered to think what could have happened with all the dry wood around.

Before bed, Star and I talked about our loves. "The Empress had no right to do what she did to me," I said. "She pursued me when

I was at the edge and vulnerable. When I confronted her about us, she made it seem like it was all my doing."

"You can't trust nuns," Star said. "They don't know about feelings. You need a regular person. And I need a real man. Do you think there are any real men left?"

"I don't know. They are hard to find. So are good women!" I added. "We're better off alone."

"Yeah. You're right," she agreed. "Who needs the aggravation? I get enough of that from my son!"

I read the short story by Tolstoy that night. It was about a fallen angel who had three lessons to learn—what men are made of, what they don't know, and what they live by. I wondered who the fallen angel was. What was the message here? Why did the Empress want me to read this book?

In the middle of the night, I woke up thinking about evil. I had a dream of walking down the path with the Empress and throwing snow at her . . .

*"I love you," I said to her.*

*"Why?" she asked.*

*"Because you are evil and beautiful at the same time."*

*"That's what I wanted to hear. I want to be loved in spite of my evilness."*

Who was I really talking about? Myself?

\* \* \*

I met Sherry, the Empress's niece who was coming to Paris. From her light, fun loving spirit, I knew she would loosen the Empress up.

At a meeting about the grant, I was honest about the things we had done wrong, especially about alienating the town's decision-makers. "We made a big mistake in not approaching the town leaders and trying to get their support. We need to do some fence mending."

"I'm not kowtowing to these self-righteous men," responded the Empress.

"What we are trying to do for the poor is right!"

"It may be right, but we can't get it without their help," I warned. "We need to be nice to them. We need to kiss some ass. We need to change our ways."

"We shouldn't have to change our ways to get what is right," she said unwavering.

I knew the Empress was upset with me. "You're a demanding woman," she said as we walked out of the meeting.

"How else are we going to get this approved?" I answered. "We have to play the game. What's important is getting the funding. I don't care if you like it or not. I want to get this money." She ignored me for the rest of the day.

I was depressed and vented to Star. "I feel like I'm always fighting to get the others to understand my position."

Star told the Empress. The next morning, I went to Mass early so that I would have time to look at the lake and found the Empress leaning against her door. We both were wearing green army jackets.

"Why are you upset?" she asked.

"You've been ignoring me. Your actions changed toward me after I was honest at that meeting."

"That's a projection. Don't lay that trip on me."

"Well, why were you ignoring me?"

"I was just weary from all the stresses around here."

"Okay. So, I guess I took it too personally."

"You take everything personally," she criticized.

"Empress I'm Italian! Italians take everything personally! It's our nature. We love opera."

"Opera is for the stage," she exclaimed.

"Aren't we all on stage here? Aren't we just acting out parts to some universal play?"

"You may be playing, but I'm not. I don't have time," she answered.

"We all have time, Empress. We all have time. Maybe that's all we have."

"Then use yours wisely!" she advised.

Star asked again about moving to Mandala. We discussed it after Mass, and everyone agreed it wasn't a good idea. It would be an added stress for Cowardly Lion and myself. Of course, no one wanted to tell her, so I had to explain and take the brunt of her pain. She got mad at me, but by Friday night, she was glad to see me again. She realized that it would be difficult being out there with a young child.

I finally got Maine plates! Now I was official.

The Empress and I were on the outs all weekend. I missed Saturday morning work (as did Cowardly Lion) because I had to go change my tires and have the plates put on the car. Star and I picked up her son. It was a quiet dinner. The Empress listened to Joan Baez tapes, and I amused Star's little boy.

On Sunday, I had breakfast with Tweedledum and spent the rest of the day primping. When I went to get my chain saw that evening, I saw that a screw was missing. The Empress had borrowed it for Saturday chores. She was always telling me to tighten the screws, yet she used my saw without doing so. I wasted an hour trying to fix it.

The Empress drove over to the Kettles on the snowmobile. She was such a wild woman!

In the morning, Argus, her dog, was lying on the ice acting cold and distant. The Empress commented to me that the "chain saw was working perfectly: I just looked at her and didn't respond. At Mass, I gave a reading about lying, judging, and spreading ill feelings. I said it like it was meant for the Empress. I walked out after Mass and prayed not to have these feelings. Argus followed me out. He ran past me and lay down. He waited till I got near him, and then he would run on ahead again and repeat the game. He jumped in the car with me when we got to the top of the hill.

At my office, I opened a letter from Sarah and found a $3000 check for some shared bank account she closed out. That improved my mood.

I went to visit the High Priestess and she threw the following Tarot reading for me:

Covering me: Magician- unconscious into consciousness; ability to take power from above and direct it through desire into manifestation

Crossing me: Queen of Pentacles- the Empress's significator; creative animus; fertile work

Beneath me: Ace of Cups- in past; new beginning already started; fertility; flowering of creative principle

Behind me: Lovers- friendship, close harmony; material and spiritual

Crowns me: Three of Cups- emotion; happiness; success; good luck

Before me: The Star-inspiration from above; hope, good health; spiritual love

Fears: Wheel of Fortune- seeker; good luck; large forces at work

Family opinion: Eight of Cups- frustration

Hopes: Six of Wands-hard work; burden to conclusion

Final outcome: High Priestess- companion to Magician; hidden influences at work; subconscious

I felt that this reading was incredibly positive and forces beyond myself were at work.

*   *   *

The little Datsun was getting a lot of mileage with all the driving between Ellsworth, Bangor, and Orland. Every so often it would rebel and break down. This afternoon, it was a flat tire. Ma Kettle, the Hierophant, and Secretary left for Duffy's while I stayed and tried to change the tire. After getting the tire bolts off, I found the jack was worthless. Luckily, the woodmen saw me and stopped to help.

At lunch, Star was the topic of discussion. "People are talking about Star," said Ma Kettle. "She may be involved with drug use."

"That's just hearsay," I responded adamantly. "She's come a long way with school and her self-concept."

"Well, I'm just telling you to be careful about your associations. It reflects on the Co-op," she replied.

"I don't care how it reflects," I stated emotionally. Star was my friend, and I could see that she was really making headway in her goal for independence. She hadn't missed any school and still managed to be a good mother.

At community supper Ma Kettle shared her ability to sense things before they happen. "I had a dream about a boy falling off a boat. Three days later two boys drowned in the lake," she said. "I get premonitions. So does the Empress. You know, I wanted to tell you the Empress has changed since you arrived. She used to come here and sit quietly. Now she's singing and playing the guitar. It's because of you."

"Yeah, well, I'm glad I had some positive effect on her. Most of my effect has been negative," I answered.

"No, Mama. She loves you."

"Yeah, like a sore thumb."

One of the visitors told me that he enjoyed reading my article entitled, "*Who's Religious?*" from the Co-op newspaper. Bear overheard him and questioned sarcastically, "I meant to ask you, are you using that term as a noun or adjective?"

"Definitely an adjective. Do you know anyone who qualifies?" I retorted.

"Maybe my dog, Shannon! He is religious about tearing up my slippers. I can't keep a good pair in the house. No matter where I hide them, he finds them. Good thing I love him to death."

"He wants to keep you on your toes, Bear," I joked

"Yeah, well, he's doing a good job."

"Have he and Argus made up yet?" I asked.

"Yeah, they pretty much stay out of each other's way. It works better that way."

"Bear, are you going to come on the Paris trip?" I asked.

"Negative," she responded. "Too much to do here." The Empress walked over. "Who's negative?" she asked, catching the tail end of the conversation.

"Everyone's negative," I responded. "I have been watching my thought patterns and noticed I always see the negative first. Why is that? Why do we say <u>no</u> before <u>yes</u>?"

"It's a learned pattern," answered the Empress. "Watch mothers with their children. They don't say 'Yes, go ahead and pull down those things off the table. Yes, go ahead and fall down the stairs. It's always 'No, don't do that. No, don't go there. No, don't touch that."

"So how do we overcome that?" I asked.

"Change thought patterns," she responded.

"Not easy!" I exclaimed. "I can't even change my own."

Besides her bags, Tweedledee had four small trash pails to bring shopping. I picked up another woman who was going to her son's, and she had bags. I thought Tweedledee was going to die when she saw the other packages entering the car. She feared that some of the bags might get mixed up.

At breakfast, Cowardly Lion said to me, "You always get the last word in with the Empress. You don't back down from her like everyone else does. You're strong."

"You think so?" I asked surprised at his observation.

"Yes, definitely. It's good for her."

"We usually don't agree on things."

"That's cause you are opposites."

"That's for sure."

"Opposites attract." He smiled.

I had grown so fond of Cowardly Lion that I missed him when he left for a few days. He was such a gentle soul. I had to defend him when the Empress complained, "He's not always working in the leather shop when he is supposed to."

"Talk to him," I suggested. Of course, she didn't.

My dream that night: *Wolf was rubbing some black material off a metal sheet and the sheet was getting hot. Her fingers started burning. I wanted to stop her, but someone stopped me and said, "Let her do it. She's reliving the Christ experience."*

\* \* \*

Cowardly Lion and I invited the Empress and Hierophant to dinner. The chicken with onions made the barn smell wonderful. The Empress came in with that weary look.

"What's wrong with you?" I asked.

"Someone left the glass door open, and the wood stove went out," she said giving an accusing look to the Hierophant.

"I didn't do that," responded the Hierophant. "And who left the barn door open this morning?"

"I did," admitted the Empress. "But I thought you were behind me."

"I wasn't behind you. I left early with Bear. I told you I was leaving early."

The Empress just lowered her eyes. Living with the Hierophant was not easy.

"So, did you get your passport?" I asked the Empress.

"No, they returned my application because they didn't like my "head gear." I had my bandana on in the picture."

"I told her to take it off," announced the Hierophant. "But you know the Empress. She does what she wants. So then, I had to write like I was Mother Superior of the order and clarify that it was part of our dress code."

"They accepted that!" I exclaimed laughing.

"Well, it got her the passport," answered the Hierophant.

The Empress hated conversations about herself. As a diversion, she asked about the author Dostoevsky. "So, what do you think about his women characters?"

"I don't think they were complete women," I responded. "They were either perfect angels or whores."

"I see them as Christ figures, especially Sonya," she responded.

"What about Camus and Hesse? Which author do you like better?" I asked.

"Camus touched on things Hesse didn't begin to see," she answered.

"Really? I see it the other way around. Hesse was a step further than Camus."

"It may be different ways of looking at the same thing," she commented and continued, "Speaking of different. You seem more settled these days. Are you?"

"Yes. I'm trying to just do my work these days and not get hung up on all the other garbage," I responded.

"Hmm. You could do this work in another place. So why are you here?" She asked. "Do you know yet?"

"To live out the will of God for me," I said rather confidently.

"Well-chosen words." She laughed.

After coffee, the Empress and the Hierophant left, and Cowardly Lion sat listening to me play the guitar.

"She plays games. Doesn't she?" he said to me.

"I think she does, but I'm not sure she is aware of it."

"If you ever want to spill your guts, I here for you," he offered sincerely.

"Thanks. I'm not sure I want to."

"I've learned a lot taking care of the horses," he continued. "They're very different. Tim is always trying to get out of the fence. He teases and looks at you with that 'try and catch me look.' Teddy just stays quiet. He's not happy. Maybe because he's not worked enough. He's a strong horse. He was bred for hauling."

"You're very perceptive when it comes to animals," I commented.

"I like animals more than people," he confided. "Look at the dogs here. I feel sorry for Shannon. Argus comes up and takes my dog, Puppy, away to play. Shannon goes and kicks the dirt, like he's saying, 'I'm lonely.' Shannon doesn't mess with Argus. Argus is both beautiful and dangerous."

"Yes, I always feel Argus could turn on you. It's in his eyes. He's part wolf. I wouldn't want to get in his way," I responded.

I went home for my Dad's birthday at the end of February. It wasn't a great visit. My sister went skating with Charles, her new beau, while my parents watched the kids. Aaron broke a plate and Mom got all upset. My brothers complained about all the noise the kids were making. Dad complained to me about my younger brother, who was not good with money.

I felt badly but I had to ask him for a loan. The Vista payment was late in coming, and I needed some work done on the car. He gave it to me without a second thought. After Sunday dinner of homemade pasta, I left for Maine. I arrived around 10:00 pm, parked at the bottom of the hill and walked into Mandala. The moon was full. The sky was so bright, I could see every rock on the path. I wasn't afraid at all.

Monday morning, I helped a woman move out of a trailer into a town apartment. I returned to pick up a clock that she had forgotten and drove right past the trailer. In turning the car around, I got stuck in a snowbank. Unfortunately, I didn't have a shovel and the more I tried to maneuver the car out, the more embedded it became. Three women in a jeep drove by. They came back and pushed the car back on the road.

The next few days were stressful rewriting the grant. The process was so complicated. Star was upset as her boyfriend left again, and her grandfather had died.

On Thursday night, we met with the Orland town selectmen to explain the family farms project seeking the grant money. Bear did most of the talking, as she's good at mediating. We needed a letter of support for the grant to be approved. Judging from the comments at the meeting, there was some hope.

"It's not that we have anything against the poor; they got to live somewhere, but we can't let our property values go down. You know what happens when people don't keep up with their property. Everything around them goes down, too," said one of the leaders.

"You're assuming that these people will not take care of their property," I said.

"Well, I've seen it happen before. They go into this nice shiny place and in two weeks, it looks like a pig's sty. I know some are clean, but we can't take that chance. It happened in one of the houses they built already."

"That was an unusual situation," explained Pa Kettle. "The people who went into that house were not ready for the responsibility. We didn't have a choice. The demands of that funding were strict. We have more control on this grant. We have good, hard-working families ready to occupy the houses."

"It's true that you can't judge everyone based on one bad seed," said Walter, one of the more reasonable town leaders. "We'll have to discuss this at our meeting."

Though I didn't feel totally positive about the meeting, I thought maybe with a little prodding, Walter could be convinced to write a letter of support. I decided that it might help to get letters of support from state government officials who tended not to be as prejudiced as the local officials.

I vented to Pa Kettle my frustrations. I knew I was over my head in this project. He explained, "Listen, I know what you're going through. I've written grants for the Empress before. It's not easy. The wording is complicated even for the educated. They ask a lot of stupid unnecessary questions. Most groups can't handle the application as it requires a huge amount of work. Thus, fewer applications. It's the way the federal government works. Don't get hung up. Make up answers. Pursue the support of state leaders. Just do the best you can and give it back to her."

The following Monday night, Bear, the Hierophant, and I faced the Hancock County Commission to defend the proposal. This group acted as a clearinghouse for federal funds. They polled officials in the towns where the proposal would be located. The grant involved the towns of Bucksport, Orland, and Penobscot. The three-year project involved the purchase of three woodlots, the building of 15 family farms, and the development of small industries to process and sell forest and farm products. Part of the money for the proposal was to come from a HUD neighborhood self-help development fund.

At the meeting, the committee raised three issues: 1. Whether the project would decrease local tax revenue while increasing town services; 2. The economic feasibility of building homes for the amount of money allocated; 3. How the project would be affected by local ordinances. Again, Bear led the rebuttal. She was an excellent speaker, inspiring, clear, and logical. Her basic argument was that the Co-op was merely trying to help people.

"As for the tax question," she stated, "I can assure the committee that the houses would not be tax free. The success of the Co-op has depended on volunteer labor and we intend to continue in this vein. Of course, we will hire professional workers to do the bulk of the labor, but volunteer help will defray a lot of the cost. As for local ordinances, we intend on following them and work closely with town leaders. We have been meeting with them to explain the project and keep them informed of our progress."

Her words fell on deaf ears. There was much criticism and attack from the floor, but she held her ground and never lost her composure. Finally, the Executive Director got up and surprisingly took an opposing position.

"Why not have federal money pumped into Maine? It's better than footing the bill for the Chrysler Corporation. Why not allow us to create jobs here in Maine?" And then as if the words were sent by heaven, and he was the messenger angel, he said, "And besides this project is consistent with your growth management goals and objects as stated in the Hancock Booklet." I wanted to cry. Someone finally understood and supported us!

He continued, "I motion that the proposal goes to HUD without coming back to this committee." To which a conservative member jumped up and responded, "I would like to see it come back revised first before we give our seal of approval." The vote was 13-2 in favor of tabling support for the proposal until a scaled-down application was submitted.

I woke up at 4:00 am still on a high from the meeting. At least they had not thrown it out. There was a possibility of support for a revised proposal. Of course, this meant more work. I wondered why the Empress hadn't shown up for the meeting.

The next few days were insane. Besides the responsibility of the grant revision, I attended a Governor's Council Meeting on the family. The whole time, I wanted to punch holes in the walls. I hated the Empress for getting me involved in the grant project. It was such an important one and I hated failure.

I was reading a book by Serrano about the friendship of Jung and Hesse. The part about the mystical marriage impressed me and reminded me of the tarot reading the High Priestess had done for me. I asked her to read the part and see if it meant anything to her. She didn't understand it and said, "Jung is illogical."

The tarot reading started with the Magician and ended with the High Priestess. Wasn't that a mystical marriage of sorts? In between were the Ace of Cups, the Lovers, the Star, and the Wheel of Fortune. All cards promoting such a union. The Queen of Pentacles was in the ruling position.

I cut wood all Sunday morning. Got my period. Weekend was a wipe out. I had been crying a lot and working till late at night on the proposal, trying to meet the deadline. In addition, I wrote my article for the newspaper.

On Monday morning, I met with Bear and the Empress to go over issues in the grant.

"Empress, have you finished the revised budget numbers?" I asked.

"Not yet," she said.

"Empress! I need those numbers," I exclaimed. "We have to get this done before the Paris trip."

"I'll work on it today," she promised.

They fooled around for the rest of the meeting, avoiding my questions. Nothing got done.

Ma Kettle took care of my appointments so I could work on the grant. The Hermit went to a "stress class" and came back to find the office machine not working. He remained calm, though, and after fixing the machine, he helped with some of the grant application sections.

I didn't know anything anymore. I seemed to be more consciously neurotic. I didn't care. I was eating again for energy. Sometimes I felt insignificant out at Mandala. Then there were times I believed I was making a difference.

I overheard the Empress say to the High Priestess, "I don't want to be Sister with a capital S, just small s." I wondered if my article on titles had affected her.

Bear said I had the Empress doodling. We were all under pressure over this grant. The battle was not over. We would have to go to the towns' boards and then back to the Hancock Planning Board. Three articles appeared in the local newspapers about the grant. Prejudice was 'alive and well' against low-income families!

*    *    *

Seeking a more suitable environment for his allergies and asthma, Scarecrow moved out of Mandala. Also, Bandit the cat disappeared. Cowardly Lion was upset, and I shared with him my theory on animals. He concurred. As we were talking, Puppy, Narcissus, and Goldmund jumped up together on the chair, reflective of the way our minds were in sync.

I finished writing the grant on Friday, March 14th, and on Sunday, I was on the plane to Paris. It snowed all day Friday, so all my appointments got cancelled. The Empress had worked till the last minute on the budget numbers.

The World Council of Churches meeting was held in a massive old brick monastery in the city of Paris. An extensive stone wall enclosed the grounds, and once inside, it was impossible to know that one was in Paris. Inside the building were many dark long hallways and weathered stone staircases. The religious inhabitants lived in an older section quite remote from the conference area, which had been remodeled to accommodate groups used to more modern conveniences. Our bedrooms were small, but quite comfortable.

From the reception the Empress got from each participant, I knew that her work was well respected here. More so than in the states. The Hermit and I made up the Empress's entourage. We dressed differently, then the others attending the meeting. They wore normal street clothes, but we wore headbands and work clothes.

Each day, we listened to a speaker on a relevant topic. The meeting room was well equipped with headphones to translate into each language. Later, we broke into smaller groups to discuss the ways in which the talk related to our individual work.

The participants were so fascinating. The German was deeply knowledgeable and well read. The Sicilian was compassionate, humble, and quiet, with a concern for understanding. The radical woman was French. The leader was a joker with an underlying seriousness. Everything was so important to the Frenchman and needed discussion. Bill, the happy American, enjoyed life and all its connections. His wife, Margaret, was amiable and friendly. The Swiss had deep eyes and an intense facial expression, giving the impression he wanted to say something, although he never did. The Englishwoman was outspoken but made good sense every time she spoke. The Englishman was absentminded. He forgot his camera and lost his ticket to one of the dinners. The Jesuit had to be right. After all, he had studied for forty years, and therefore, had to know something. The Hermit was critical and uptight. The Empress was her usual self and maybe a bit more confident. She immediately opposed the first speaker whose topic was "manipulation by language" and exclaimed, "Intellectuals don't see reality. Only the poor do. They want to work. The intellectuals don't."

Later, in private, I took issue with the Empress's comment. "The poor don't see the inconsistencies," I said. "The intellectuals do."

"That doesn't make them right," she said.

"Yes, but how can I follow you if you are inconsistent?" I asked.

"Deal with your own inconsistencies, and leave mine alone," she replied. "We can't always live up to our ideals. We just do the best we can."

That evening after supper, a group of us went to a café for drinks. "So, what do you think about having women priests?" I asked.

"I think we need the female influence in the Church," said the German. "She completes the triangle. Women priests are necessary."

"We don't need female priests," said the Jesuit. "Women have a role already in the church."

"I agree with you," said the Englishman.

"The women's role has been downplayed in the church. A subservient role. It is a male-dominated society and unchristian," I retorted.

"You just don't understand the importance of the woman's role," said the Jesuit.

"Easy for you to say when you're on the power end," I replied. His face became flustered, and he turned to discuss the issue with the Englishman, as he couldn't be bothered talking to an "ignorant" American woman.

"Washington had a vision of a woman, a Mary, saving America. It was someone from across the ocean. Maybe it's the feminist movement," added the Empress. Her support surprised me.

Many left early, but a core of us stayed further to discuss theory. The next morning at breakfast, Bill, the happy American looked at me and announced, "So I heard you stayed till 4:00 am in the morning! How can you be up so early?"

The Empress looked at me with that pained look of disapproval. Bill didn't notice and continued asking about our lifestyle, "So are you people really living in the woods without running water and electricity?"

"Yes. We are trying to live a simple life. It gives us more time to spend just doing our work, as things don't get in the way. We can focus on what is important," said the Empress.

"Yeah," I said. "One morning I was so desperate for a Kleenex that I tore up a shirt into little squares!" Everyone laughed.

"It's not that bad," said the Empress hitting me on the shoulder. "Don't give them the wrong impression."

"I'm just kidding. Really, it's nice not being bombarded with things," I said.

"I know what you mean," replied Bill. "Your lifestyle is amazing in today's world, especially in America. Can we "package" this new lifestyle and spread it around? Is it enough that it is happening in your small environment?"

"I think it's very influential to know that there are people living that way," replied the Englishwoman. "One doesn't always have to "package" everything. Isn't that typically American to want to do so rather than just appreciate something?"

"You two are so typical of the different approaches of male and female," I said. "Males always want to 'do' while females can just 'appreciate.' "

"Yes. We do have different approaches. Don't we?" added the Englishwoman. "Today, the speaker relied so heavily on complicated diagrams to explain his theory. I couldn't understand the points he was trying to make with them."

With that comment the Jesuit got up as if to dominate the Englishwoman and myself with his height and said, "Our teachers always use diagrams to teach. I understand the speaker's problem. Using diagrams is a more technical and therefore, more intellectual way to speak."

"I don't agree with that," I said. "Just because something is technical doesn't mean it's more intellectual. As a matter of fact, if the speaker is unable to make himself understood by the audience, how intelligent is that? Intelligence means something different to me than to you."

"You are obviously missing the point here," he retorted dismissing my criticism.

"I agree that technical diagrams are a more male approach, but so much of this meeting is male dominated anyway," piped in the Empress.

"Speaking of male domination, what do you people think of

Khomeini?" asked the Hermit. "It was reported that Khomeini said international communism is as bad as capitalism."

"Oh good," said Margaret, the happy American's wife. "Now that we are on the same level together, we can both fight Iran."

During the meetings, the Empress and I got along fine. We were considerate of serving one another, but outside of meetings, she ignored me in her usual style.

Although the Empress spent most of the time with her niece, we spent Saturday together shopping and ended up in a flower market in the middle of the Isle de France. I strolled away from her and bought a red rose. I gave it to her as we crossed the street, and by the look on her face, I could tell she was uncomfortable with my gesture.

"It's for you to leave at Chartres tomorrow for your mother," I said to relieve her uneasiness.

"Oh, she'll like that," she responded and took the rose.

At Chartres, my aloneness was overwhelming. I found myself staring at a huge rock that sat in the middle of the garden. I felt like the rock. I wrote a poem as I watched the Empress and others walking around, touching the rock.

At supper, the Empress's eyes were more spiritual than ever. I found it even harder being so close to her all the time. My pain was deep. I knew she would never love me.

Throughout most of the meeting, I found myself in constant opposition to the Jesuit. His didactic style alienated me. He sent the Hermit and me a message to make sure that we kept to his way of thinking in the small group he was leading on theology and technology.

On Sunday, he gave the Mass and talked about Martha and Mary, the two women closest to Christ. He said Martha was action and Mary was contemplation, and that both sides were necessary. I saw this theory actualized later when we were in Boston on our way home. There was an older woman carrying two heavy suitcases. The Empress looked at the woman. I read her mind and went over and helped her with her bags.

At the end of the meeting, plans were presented for the next yearly meeting which was to be held in Africa. The Jesuit and the Frenchman were chosen to attend. The Hermit got up and spoke very strongly in support of women being represented at that meeting. The German agreed and said, "The meeting should be balanced, I nominate that the Empress be a participant." The leader noted that only two from this group could attend and that either the Jesuit or the Empress could go. He would be in touch with a decision.

That night, Bill, the happy American, and his wife took the Empress and me to a French restaurant for dinner. At the end of the meal, the Empress turned to me and said, "Time for you to go back to Narcissus and Goldmund." I wondered if she knew the deeper implications of that statement.

We returned home late Sunday night. I dragged the next day and came home early to rest before supper. The Empress had been drinking with the Hierophant, and when I walked into her house, I said, "Well, nothing has changed,"

The Empress yelled from the back porch, "Keep your thoughts to yourself!" The Hierophant was flaming and accused the Empress of being a mother figure after the Empress criticized her for not eating right while she was gone.

I looked at the Empress and said, "So is that what you are?"

"Now you know better," she replied smiling.

"So how was your trip?" asked the Hierophant.

"She stayed out late every night and went off by herself," replied the Empress.

"That's not true, I responded. "I was exceptionally good. And the trip was great. Particularly challenging and stimulating. The participants were impressive. They really liked the Empress. They want her to attend the next meeting."

"Really?" said the Hierophant. "You didn't tell me that."

"Well, I don't think they are going to ask me. I'm sure they will pick the Jesuit."

"That would be a mistake," I chanted. "You really should go."

"We'll see," she replied. "I'm not sure they are ready for the female influence yet."

\*   \*   \*

A new volunteer, Jill, from Philadelphia had been staying at Mandala all week. Bear and the Empress sang the Empress's favorite song repeatedly, "*You picked a fine time to leave me, Lucille.*" I was bored and sat in the corner with a headache.

At work the next day, the High Priestess announced that the Empress was thinking of asking me to be the next editor of *Wonder Time*, the Co-op newspaper. "You will be good because you can combine outreach with your writing," said the High Priestess. "I understand you're still out of it from the trip," she said. "Think about it. I would like to leave the newspaper with someone I can trust."

I took a client to Bangor hospital and slept in the car. The next day

I was sick with a head cold. The Empress said, "Looks like the world traveler is not feeling well."

"C'est la vie," I said.

"You must be getting old," she retorted, and she and Bear laughed. I was too sick to respond. I just wanted to sleep. Resting at home, I wrote a letter to my sister. I told her to always hug her daughter, as it is impossible to make up for this lack of love. I grew up watching the contrast between my mother and my aunt. My mother stayed home and raised the kids. My aunt was a career woman always fighting for a cause. I put a value judgement on the two different lifestyles but came to realize neither was better. Even though my life appeared glamourous as a teacher and world traveler, I had much pain and aloneness.

During the week, we watched a Jesuit speaker on TV who talked about the concept of love. He said that we never express what we feel. After the program, the Hierophant said, "I love all of you." This embarrassed Bear, and I teased her as we were going out the door: "Yes, and now we're going to make love." She just about ran. The Empress laughed. Later, Argus followed Cowardly Lion and me up to the barn and followed us in. He never did that before. Then he nudged me to pet him.

My dream that night showed a major shift. Four people were involved. Four is the self number . . . the squaring of the circle . . . the archetype of wholeness . . . *Two gay women were talking to me and another older woman. They felt unjustly accused of assaulting women just because they were gay. They knew Wolf and took me to a little house where Wolf was doing black and white sketches. One sketch was of a person, but ingeniously, Wolf had used animal parts, a dog's head and forearms, to create the figure.*

I talked to Ma Kettle about the newspaper job. She marched me into the Empress's office to discuss it. The Empress's response confused me.

"I am considering two other people as well. I want to give preference to the low-income community with jobs at the Co-op," she explained.

Secretary came in, dropped off the monthly schedule, and said, "You should be teaching another math class." She quickly left. I looked at Ma Kettle, "What was that supposed to mean?" The Hierophant came in, and I questioned why the Secretary said I should be teaching another class.

"Well, you know you have to put in the lost time for the Paris trip," she responded.

"Are you serious?" I screamed. "After all I do? You're worried about the week I took off to attend that meeting." She got flustered and was almost in tears and said, "Well, the Secretary has to account for the paperwork of accrued time on grant money."

"I don't give a damn about paperwork," I said. "Nor about the little money I make. I'm hurt that you two think I am cheating on time." I took the schedule and put myself down for another teaching class and walked out.

Pa Kettle got the same treatment at the next staff meeting. He offered to plan the program for the summer fair and the Secretary said, "You only do things for a price." Bear also gave him a hard time. The Empress and Hermit were silent.

Pa Kettle took his offer back, and I didn't blame him. I wasn't sure where this new attitude was coming from, but I was sure someone had provoked it.

On a beautiful Sunday in March, Cowardly Lion, and I worked on the farm pond clearing trees. The Empress made a big pot of barley soup for supper. A new person, Kate, from Searsport joined us. The Empress got on her usual soapbox about "The poor have no group to identify with, as do the Blacks and the Puerto Ricans. Everyone should work in the factories for five years, and then they will realize how hard it is. The middle class lives off the poor in their government-funded jobs." We all knew the routine since we had heard it so many times before. Bear commented under her breath, "We always wash our dirty laundry in front of guests."

"Let's sing songs," I said picking up my guitar. The Empress got her guitar and we all sang. I did a rendition of "El Paso" and tried to imitate Pa Kettle. It brought some laugher.

"Remember when we sang Clementine in Paris and everyone loved it?" reminisced the Empress.

"Yes, that was fun. Everyone thought you were a bona fide Country Western singer," I said. She must have enjoyed our escapade that night more than she let on. "Don't tease me," she said, embarrassed, remembering how loose she was that night.

The Hierophant and I walked into Mandala late Thursday night. We took the lower rock path, which was close to the bears' den. This route was shorter, but more difficult as it required climbing through brush, and in between large rocks. The full moon helped but it was difficult keeping on the unmarked path. We seemed to be going in circles. Thankfully, Archie, the cat, came and met us. He led the way to the houses.

It was Holy weekend and everyone in community spent this time in meditation. It rained all day on Good Friday. I wanted to go home and pray, but I had to drive a client to the hospital in Bangor. The entire week was busy with appointments. And Tweedledum insisted that I come for lunch every afternoon.

I wasn't as productive as when I first had arrived. I tired easily. The other day, when the Empress and I had walked in, I was carrying a heavy package. The added weight made it difficult for me to keep up with her. I got short of breath. She noticed I was struggling, so she took the package from me. I wanted to cry, but just kept going.

God had provided again. I received a $27 check from Catholic High for an overcharge on taxes, a $30.00 check from Sarah for a refund on tickets, and I found $40.00 in my wallet. I was wealthy!

Easter morning service was held at the Hospitality House. We played guitars, and everyone sang. Indiana came for the event and commented on how well we harmonized. She didn't realize how difficult it was getting the Empress to do even that much!

Hierophant and the Empress worked on the retreat house behind their dwelling. It had been vacant for a while, and they intended on using it for guests. Cowardly Lion and I hauled water, cut wood for fire, and worked on the middle bedroom. Later, Narcissus followed me over to Bear's for a visit. Bear read, and I played the guitar. Narcissus rolled around on the floor begging me to pet him. Then he climbed all over the cabinets trying to get my attention. Finally, he jumped onto my lap. I had to stop playing. I pet him, and we both fell asleep for an hour. When I woke up, I told Bear I had been dreaming.

"You know I had a strange dream last night and I don't usually dream," she said.

"Tell me about it," I responded.

"Well, I was in my house sitting at a round table. There was a ferocious animal at the door. It looked like a golden retriever, and then it turned into a huge bear. The animal pushed its way in and put his paws on the table and started eating. I was worried, but the Hermit and the Empress said to be still, and he would go away. The Hierophant took off. I got up and went into another room and closed the door. The bear broke the door down. I stood there looking scared and offered him some food I had in the room. He took it and went away.

Was she afraid of her own feelings? They found their way in, and the only way to get rid of them was to "feed" them. Interestingly, her dog Shannon was a golden retriever, and the golden retriever turned into the bear, an animus figure.

Later that night, I went to visit the High Priestess. Scarecrow was there. The High Priestess proclaimed she was upset with the Abraham reading on Holy Saturday night. Stoned during the Mass, she believed she had a religious experience during the reading. She said, "As I listened to the words, I thought, 'that wasn't the way it should be.' At that moment, I felt a direct line of communication open to God. He spoke to me and said, 'you're right. That's not the way it should be.'"

The way she described the experience, I couldn't help but believe that it had really happened. She spoke of these otherworldly experiences as if they were natural occurrences for her. Her ethereal being and connection to the subconscious intrigued me. I was mesmerized in her presence.

Chico, the Hierophant's dog, was on his last legs. He could hardly walk. Even though I hated that dog, I felt sorry for him. It was sad to see him going downhill so quickly. I broke down and petted him this morning.

On Wednesday, I had to go to the airport to pick up Jack, a city slicker from California and a volunteer for the summer. He was an actor with big, beautiful, blue eyes, but he didn't impress me. From his facial expression, I knew I didn't impress him either!

I was dressed in my green army fatigues, red bandana, and heavy boots. Jack had slick hair and was wearing a flimsy silk shirt and lightweight pants. I thought 'this guy doesn't have a clue as to what he is getting himself into.'

The drive back was long and quiet through the rolling hills of Maine. Just as we were on the down slope of one of the steeper hills, the song "*Bolero*" came on the radio. I had seen the movie *Ten* with the famous love scene. Obviously, Jack had seen it, too. He turned and looked at me, and we both cracked up laughing.

"You saw the movie too!" he exclaimed. "I know what you're thinking."

"Of course, I can think of nothing else when that song plays," I said shaking my head. Tears were coming out of my eyes from laughing so hard.

We became immediate friends from that point on.

The High Priestess invited me for dinner during the week. Our conversations were always intense, and this one was about anger.

"Maybe women are angry with themselves for not being who we are as women," she said.

"You mean for all the time we accept the male attitude about the world as correct," I added.

"For all the times women don't stand up and say 'no' and accept the consequence of that <u>no</u>. We're a passive being. We don't like confrontation. We're good at camouflaging internal strife and accepting things we can't change."

"And we get mad at each other for doing it," I responded. "But it's really ourselves we should be mad at."

"Exactly," she said.

I woke up in the middle of the night thinking about my conversation with the High Priestess . . . As women, do we not confront each other enough? Can women scream at each other and come away as friends? Men do it all the time. We don't have the same trust . . . maybe anger originally stems from being angry with our mothers for not supporting us at times . . . I never felt that my mother appreciated who I was. When my article was published, I sent it to my aunt. My mother wanted me to be successful in another way . . . through marriage . . . but that was her means of finding happiness, not mine . . . I never screamed at my mother . . . Could I still be angry for that incident that happened as a child? Maybe I felt that my mother should have "saved" me from it. She allowed me to experience it after I admitted the truth . . . I was obsessed with sex from the early age of four. The earliest thing I remember was sitting on the back steps of our brick apartment building by myself, masturbating. It took years for me to say that word. I must have known it was something I wasn't supposed to be doing. When a neighbor stood on her porch watching me, I immediately stopped.

I did it when I was alone. I would hide behind the parlor chair and partake in my little pleasure. Sometimes, my mother caught me. One time she got out a knife and said she would cut my hands off if she caught me doing it again. That stopped me, for a while.

My obsession continued into kindergarten. I had a lot of free time as I always finished the class work right away. My comrades played in the big cardboard playhouse with furniture, but this didn't appeal to me for some reason. I sat in my chair and engaged in the activity I found much more pleasurable. Until one day. At the end of class, the teacher called me up and gave me a note to give to my mother. I cried the whole way home, sensing that the note was not good. My mother, seeing my despair, tried to comfort me by saying, "The principal wants to see me. Maybe this is something good about you." I just shook my head. I knew better.

We had an appointment the next day. My mother met with the principal first, then a call came for me to go to the office. The teacher escorted me. The principal sat in a chair behind a big desk and told me to sit in the seat in front of her desk. My mother sat off to the side. The principal did all the talking. My mother was probably too embarrassed.

"You're touching yourself in class," she said. "Why do you do it? Are you in pain? Do you have a terrible itch?" she asked.

I was embarrassed beyond belief. Imagine a kindergarten child having to speak about such a topic to a principal. Mustering all my courage while fighting back tears, I responded truthfully, "I do it because it feels good". From the look on her face, I knew this was not the right answer, but I would admit to no other.

The meeting ended shortly after that, and my mother told me that my dad had gone to get the car. We were going to the doctor's office. Gosh, this was too much for a five-year-old to handle. It turned out to be too much for a twenty-year old to handle. I said little from that point on. It was out of my hands. I merely had to put up with it all somehow. The "somehow" later caused a lot of problems for me.

I still remember the doctor's name. I still remember what he looked like. I hated his looks. We went down the cement steps of a brick office building to a small examination room. Everything seemed dark to me. My Mother helped me undress. The doctor came in and made me lie down on the examination table. He looked around inside my vagina and then called my father to come and look. I remembered him saying there was nothing physically wrong with me. I didn't remember seeing my mother at this point. I didn't remember if I was crying, but I don't think so. I didn't remember feeling anything at all. I remembered cold. It was like I wasn't there. Even now I sweat when I think about this experience. I get this awful feeling from the waist down. It was not an experience one could easily forget.

My mother then dressed me, and we went into the outer office. The doctor sat at his desk, looked at me, and said, "If you continue to do this, next time I will have to give you needles. Do you understand?" I shook my head yes.

"I want you to promise that you will never do it again," he added. I readily agreed. The thought of needles was not too appealing

We went home and that was the end of the problem for my parents, but it was only the beginning of problems for me. I relived that experience repeatedly every night. Reliving the feeling of embarrassment. Only in a deeper hidden part of my brain was I able to resolve it. Unknown to my conscious mind, my subconscious mind thought up a favorable protective ending. An ending I didn't discover till I was twenty and in college, thanks to the watchful concern of a friend. It was my junior year in college. I had broken up with the boy who wanted to marry me, and then gained forty lbs. My grades dropped from A's to C's except in my major. Every time I would get drunk, I would start crying that I was evil. One night, a classmate pulled me into a dark room. She threw me on the floor and sat on me.

"Why are you evil, Dorothy? Tell me why," she said forcefully while pulling on my shirt collar.

"I can't say," I cried continually.

"If you don't tell me, you're going to have to tell a doctor," she yelled and slapped me lightly on the face. The word doctor terrified me.

"No. No. No doctor."

"Then tell me," she ordered. I no choice but to comply. . . .

"I used to play with myself."

" You masturbated."

"Yes. Yes," I cried.

"Say the word, masturbation. Every kid does it."

"Okay, masturbation." Then I told her the story about going to the doctor's office. Every night, I relived it. Over and over again. The pain. The embarrassment. . . .and then, and then, eehhh. Oh my God! Oh my God!"

"What? What happened?" she asked. I was in a daze at this point. I didn't even know where the words that came out of my mouth were coming from. It was a part, a well-hidden part, that made itself known.

"I shot them! eeehhh. I shot them!" I screamed.

"Shot who?" she asked.

"My parents! My parents! I took out a gun and shot them!"

"You shot them in your dreams. Not in real life. Only in a dream," she repeated.

"I didn't shoot them?" I asked crying from the depths.

"No, you didn't. You're not evil," she assured me.

"Not evil?"

"No. Dorothy. You were only five years old."

If I had screamed at my mother would it have helped? Would it have saved me from years of psychological hell?

I screamed at Bear in a discussion we were having before our strategy meeting with the Empress and Hierophant for the Hancock Planning Commission meeting.

"Bear, the Empress and Hierophant don't realize they can't go into this meeting cold. The Planning Commission is ready for us now. They are going to want answers. We need to present a united front and project that we know what we are doing. I'm sick and tired of playing games. At every meeting they beat around the bush, and we get nowhere. And you don't help either. You get right into their avoidance mode. I'm sick of you, too." After I said that to her, I was afraid she was going to hate me. "I'm sorry," I said.

"No, it's all right to vent at me. It's good to say what you really feel. It's the only way we can move ahead. I know your motive is to get this grant passed."

I felt so relieved. It allowed me to say what I thought at the strategy meeting with the Empress and the Hierophant. I took control and gathered all the materials we needed for the council forum. I reviewed them and came up with a plan for responding to the committee.

"At the planning meeting, I want to speak first and read the letters of support we received from the state officials. Then I want the Empress to answer any questions from the floor. She's good at this, and she speaks from the heart, especially about this project. It should convince people of its necessity. Are we in agreement?" I asked. Everyone responded affirmatively. They dared not contradict me as my presentation was strong.

"We should support each other no matter what is said," added the Empress.

"I agree," I said. "But we should know what we are going to say beforehand."

"I agree with Dorothy," supported Bear." We need to project the image that we know what we are doing." She gave me a side glance, and I knew she was referring to our earlier discussion.

"Thanks Bear," I said and then added, "The only problem we are going to have is that they won't understand our approach. It's not the typical approach."

"Well, I can fudge and make up some answer to them," said the Empress.

"No, "I yelled. "Just say the truth. Our approach is different. It's new. It's female. And what's wrong with that?"

The four of us attended the meeting the next night in Ellsworth. The hall was packed, and there was a table set up in the front for us to sit at. Bright lights were directed at us. It prevented me from seeing all the people when I got up to talk. This was a good thing as I was nervous as hell. But I managed to get through reading the letters of support from the governor and US senator of Maine and from leaders of various state departments. My voice was a little shaky, and I wasn't as confident as I wanted to be, but I got my points across.

The Empress fielded questions. She was calm. She actually used my line about us having a different approach when responding to a comment from a commission member.

"I mentioned this proposal to a group of farmers," he said. "They laughed at the idea and didn't think it will be profitable."

"This is not your typical business approach," said the Empress. "The farming aspect of the project is not meant to provide families with their main income. It is only a chance for them to gain self-respect and some economic autonomy."

At the end of the meeting, a vote was taken. To our surprise, the commissioners approved the revised project by a 12-6 margin. This approval meant that the grant could now be submitted to HUD for consideration since it had the blessing of the Planning and Program Review Committee, the group charged with commenting on area projects involving federal funding.

When we walked out of the meeting, the Empress and I literally jumped for joy. I wanted so much to hug and kiss her. Instead, we danced in a circle, our arms entwined in the air and chanted like children, "We won! We won!" Our spirits were joined, and none of our past personal problems seemed significant. Both of us knew how difficult it was to get to this point, and it was such a relief to have a bit of success. Even if it was only momentary. The only problem now was that we needed letters of support from the two remaining local towns. Without these letters, the grant would be doomed for failure.

Conscious of my stress, The High Priestess invited me for dinner. We drank wine. I talked as she prepared the berries and cheese appetizers. I could tell her anything. The wine usually made me melancholy, talking about my past relationship with Sarah. As we were talking, some of her friends came over. We couldn't continue.

After dinner, we went to a Chris Williamson concert at a local hall. I sat next to the High Priestess and could smell her intoxicating scent. It melted me.

The High Priestess was enjoying the experience. "I love seeing women supporting women," she said laughing and clapping her hands. She was obviously comfortable floating amid this sea of feminine vibrations. She looked at me lovingly and kept moving closer to me. I wanted so badly to put my hand under her shirt and rub her back and brush my face up against hers.

Unfortunately, her husband had also come to the concert, and during our earlier conversation, she had mentioned about her loyalty to him so I wasn't sure how she would accept any forward gesture on my part. I was terribly afraid of rejection, especially after the Empress incident. The only reason I even considered some deeper interaction was a comment she made when I was telling her about my gay relationship: "I'm not gay or don't think I'm gay, but I am open to all possibilities."

Nothing happened but after that night I knew, given the right set of circumstances, something could happen between us.

I fell asleep quickly that night after drinking all the wine. In the middle of the night, I woke up with thoughts racing through my brain . . . Why can't women support each other? Women always think they are going to fail. My student said to me she would fail the test before she even saw the question. The High Priestess says she was always a failure. Having her son was the first real thing she had done successfully. The High Priestess supports me. She encourages me to write and I can do so. I have said some of the meanest things to women and they have said some of the meanest things to me. When St. Francis closed, I walked up for communion. The principal was giving out the hosts. She looked at me and said, "May the Lord be with you." I looked her straight in the eye and sarcastically said, "I pray the same thing for you, Sister." . . . " emotional cripple" . . . "liar" . . . "negative" . . . "for a price" . . . "did you have a good time?" . . .

In the morning I thought, 'maybe constructive creativity comes through when we awaken our animus.' The Empress can't learn the guitar because she can't concentrate or focus. She can't tap into her animus. What would ever happen if our two animuses were working together at the same time? What could we accomplish?

\* \* \*

The vote in support of the farm grant made the front page of the Bangor Daily News. In addition to the Empress, my name was splattered throughout the article. I was quoted as if I were some celebrity," Dorothy says . . . "

I couldn't stay at the Co-op. I was in a weird mood. I didn't know why, but I felt depressed. The Empress saw me on my way out and said, "Well, you made it, Dorothy. Are you on a high?"

"No, quite the contrary. I'm on a low."

The Tarot cards had come true. The High Priestess said she hated the card of the high priestess who lets the person impregnate herself.

The Empress asked Jack to write a grant on student funding. She didn't dare ask me.

Ma Kettle needed money to fix her car, so I brought it up at our weekly meeting. "We don't get funding till June," said the Hierophant.

"How do you expect her to function till June?" I raved. Everyone got upset.

On Friday, I spent a whirlwind day with Ma Kettle. We went to

Toni's house. She needed a washing machine. We went to Annie's house. Her son barricaded the door. He didn't want to move into the Hospitality House. Ma Kettle talked him out. We started moving her things out. Puerto Rican style.

"Just take these sheets, lay them on the floor, put the small stuff on top and wrap it up," said Ma Kettle. I looked at her like she was crazy. But she already had two sheets filled and tied up before I could say anything. "Now I just have to find a washer and dryer for her," Ma mumbled to herself as she continued packing. When we were leaving the house, Ma Kettle started running to the street, waving her hands, and yelling, "Stop, stop," to the truck passing by. "Is that a washing machine?" she asked, as she pointed to the appliance in the back of the truck.

"Yeah," said the guy.

"Does it still work?" she asked.

"It still works," he responded.

"Where are you taking it?" she asked.

"To the dump."

"Oh good. Can we have it?"

"Sure, lady. It's not the greatest, but you can have it."

"Good. Can you bring it to this address?" she asked and didn't wait for an answer. She gave him a piece of paper with the address. "This woman Toni needs a washing machine. Thank you. God loves you, and I love you too!" She reached in the car window, pulled his face to her, and gave him a big kiss on the cheek

"I guess so. That place is right near the dump," he replied. And so, she got a washing machine for Toni. But she wasn't finished with this poor guy.

"Oh, if you're going by the dump, can you drop off these bags of garbage?" She again didn't wait for a response but motioned for me to help throw some bags into the truck. "Here Mama. Help me get these into the truck." The poor guy couldn't say no even though his vehicle was already loaded. He left quickly since he was afraid of what she would ask for next.

"Well, that was easy," I commented. "Toni will be surprised."

"Mama, you just have to ask, and you shall receive," she said as she hugged me, and we both laughed.

The Empress came up that night to chitchat, and I was in no mood for talking. I had gotten home late after an emotional day with clients. I had to bring the Doctor to see a woman who was going crazy because her husband had left her.

I started venting, "There is no support here. You give mixed messages. I don't trust you. You asked Jack to do part of the grant writing without telling me what was going on."

"I can never fulfill your expectations," she responded. "What do you want from me? Tell me. Then I'll tell you what I can give."

"I want you to be up front with me. Tell me what's going on. I want to be part of the communication."

"I tell you what's going on."

"Empress, you don't tell me anything. I learn things through other people all the time. It's so aggravating."

"You're not my conscience," she stated.

"No. You don't have one."

"And you do? Always taking off. Staying out all night."

"Is this about the celibacy thing again?" I asked. "I'm not doing anything, but I'm not into celibacy either."

"Don't you see it as part of the gospel?" she asked.

"No. I need a personal relationship."

"Well, you're not going to find it here."

"I know that," I responded.

"So, don't take your frustrations out on me," she said and left. I sat there thinking 'why did we always end up fighting?' Was it masking a deeper set of feelings?'

The next day I worked hard in the woods with a group of kids. In the process, I managed to hit myself in the face with the shovel and ended up with a black eye. It was painful.

"Into self-punishment?" asked the Empress when she saw me.

"Yeah, it feels good," I responded.

"Take a break. Let's go visit my niece," she suggested.

"Ok," I said, thrilled to get away with her for a while.

We spent some time with her niece Sherry and her husband. When we left, I said, "Her husband is so insecure. He's so critical of your niece."

"They do the best they can. They help people without taking money or being on a Vista grant." I knew I had hit a sore point and so did she.

My dream that night: *Narcissus and Goldmund died. I was walking down a road and saw their carcasses. Actually, I only saw their heads, skulls and blood.*

Jill volunteered to work for a year as the Hospitality House manager. With her counseling background, she would be a desirable addition.

I got a letter from the HUD representative saying that he never received the grant application. Where could it have gone? More work. With all the stress and by watching what I ate, I had lost five pounds.

The Empress commented, "You seem to be having a hard time keeping it together."

"I'm trying to stay sane, Empress," I responded.

"Nothing can throw me," she added. "I have a deep relationship with God. Do you?" she asked. I didn't know how to answer her. At least Virginia Woolf flipped out after writing a novel. What was I flipping out for?

I decided to take on the responsibility of editor of *Wonder Time.* I was truly out of my mind! We had our monthly Co-op meeting during which the High Priestess made it clear that she hoped I would take the job. All the people from the Learning Center voiced their support of me, except Bear, who in a nervous voice said, "I hope the newspaper sticks to the philosophy of the Co-op and does not include 'reactionary' (as she termed it) articles." She didn't look at me, but I knew her comment was directed at my choice of article topics, which were off beat and sometimes beyond the scope of the Co-op. I had a hard time toning down the article on the religious, but the High Priestess helped, and she was going to include it in the next edition of the paper. I was glad because I wouldn't have to put it in myself.

"Do you mind hurting people's feelings?" she had asked.

"Yes, I do," I responded. "But I would do so if it was the truth."

"That's good," she responded. She always supported me. She had taught me so much about writing and the editing process.

When the article finally came out, no one in the community said anything to me. The article questioned labeling people as religious or homosexual or professional or drug addicted- terms improperly used as nouns limiting the understanding of people. One senior woman in the craft store said, "I really liked your article and agree with your ideas about labeling." Surprised, I shared this comment with the High Priestess who said, "I respect that woman's opinion so you should consider it a high compliment."

At community supper, the Empress commented on the Hermit's article and how much she liked it. Pa Kettle made a point of praising my article right after that as a means of getting her goat. No comment from the Empress.

The Cowardly Lion had been in his glory working with a group of schoolgirls last week. People his own age was good therapy. Now that they had left, his attitude had changed. The Empress commented about his depression.

"Yes, I think it has to do with the girls leaving," I responded.

"It's more than that. I heard him complaining about Jack doing the grant for youths when he can't get money for his leather shop. That sounds like your influence. You are conveying a feeling of resentment toward Jack."

"I have no ill feelings for Jack," I exclaimed. "We are good friends. What bothered me was that you didn't consult with me about the issues of that grant."

"Cowardly Lion is also telling people I am hard to work with," she added.

"Blame yourself for that one! Not me," I answered.

I walked away, thinking our relationship was still so strained. I didn't have the energy to work on fixing it anymore. I could make it alone, and I had to be true to myself whatever the price. Truth and integrity were priorities. All I ever wanted to do was help her. To let her know she was precious to me, but it never came out that way. We got into each other's hair all the time. It might be time to cut it short.

The Hierophant got her cancer test results back and they were not good. The Empress was upset.

Singing at the Hospitality House prayer meeting, Jill had a great voice along with being such a stunning-looking woman. She was in her fifties, but her body was that of a thirty- year-old. She had long, grey-blonde hair. Having left her minister husband, she was floundering around trying to find out who she was now that she wasn't a wife anymore.

The Empress asked Jack to forge signatures on letters for the grant. I warned him against doing this.

I went to a Maypole party with Gretel and the High Priestess. The High Priestess always had an entourage of interesting people surrounding her. We had exotic food and drank too much wine. That night I gave the High Priestess her first chemistry lesson. She was such a good student that we were able to get through chapter one and two in the first lesson.

# Part Three

*The ascent or way out*

## The Lioness

The lion is the symbol of the sun and of gold. Females are
the best hunters. The lion does not fight for the sake of
fighting. It avoids confrontation and will leave the scene of
danger if possible. Lions hunt primarily by stealth, and the
most common method of killing is strangulation. Females
do most of the work. A lion denotes the rising of feminine
energies. When a lion shows up, there will be opportunity
to awaken to a new sun. Trust your feminine energies-
creativity, intuition and imagination.

(excerpts from *Animal-Speak by Ted Andrews*)

ON SATURDAY, MAY 3rd, 1980 I met the woman who would have the greatest effect on the rest of my life. The Lioness arrived with three other male Harvard students, who came to volunteer a week at the Co-op in exchange for living arrangements and food. The Lioness was very academic and immediately engaged me in conversations on power, women, religion, and the difficulty of integrating one's personal philosophy in the real world. I welcomed the intellectual challenge having been shut off in the back-wood's community for so long.

Things were changing that weekend at Mandala. Jack and Jill went to the Kettle's on Saturday night, and Jack didn't return to the community. The Hierophant left to visit a friend who was dying. Bandit the cat was in a weird mood and jumped all over me that night at the lake cottage. The Empress said he was lonely. Chico was worse and hardly moved off his bed. He wasn't the only sick animal. Teddy the horse had lost a lot of weight and was coughing.

Goldmund was pregnant and very fat. So much so, that Cowardly Lion had nicknamed her "Prego". When she finally delivered the litter of three kittens, she wouldn't feed them. One died right away, and Cowardly Lion tried to feed the others, but they wouldn't eat. Goldmund stared at us, begging to relieve her of her motherly duty. When Cowardly Lion told the Empress what had happened, she said, "I always thought there was something wrong with that cat!"

One of our primary tasks was to insulate the Hospitality House, not an easy job in a tall and spacious dwelling. Scarecrow and Jack were supposed to help, but they didn't stroll in until 11:30 am and then sat down to eat. I was furious and screamed at them. It didn't stop them from eating.

During my venting, Ann, one of the former residents of the Hospitality House stopped to visit. She was moving her family to another city. She said to me, "Dorothy, you won't find what you want in the community. There, you have to follow, like in the army," she warned. "You're too sensitive for this place. And you seem depressed," she added. "I think you need to move elsewhere."

My ears were echoing all week. Jack had gotten on my nerves. His grant was due on the 16th, and even though it was already the 13,th he was just meeting with the Empress and the Hermit. I told him a long time ago to get this done, but he let it go. Besides letting his responsibilities slide, he had also left the community and was living at the Hospitality House. Knowing him quite well, I sensed that he was hiding something. At the weekly meeting, The Empress asked him his initial impressions about the Co-op. He responded with a deep, pensive look and said, "Gee, that's a difficult question as I'm just starting to get a clue of how things work. There's so much going on I'll have to think about."

When we were outside alone, I looked at him and started laughing.

"Well, I didn't think I had fooled everyone!" he exclaimed. "I'm going to live in the house between the Empress and the Hermit this winter," he confided.

"Right," I said giving him that I-don't-think-so-look. The Empress would never allow that.

Sometimes the Doctor would accompany me on client visits. I enjoyed her witty responses to my difficulties regarding the social work.

"Tweedledee always gives me a hard time," I said. "Then one day I went to her house very depressed, and she was nice to me."

"Why don't you always go there depressed!" she suggested.

Completing the layout of my first paper gave me a great sense of accomplishment. I loved the process and the seclusion required to complete it. It was like fitting pieces of a puzzle together - rearranging the articles and pictures on the blank pages. I was happy doing the task.

However, my good mood was short lived when I received a letter of rejection for the HUD grant. It was missing the local government support letter. HUD advised we could reapply but only with that letter.

The signature of Walter Adams, the town selectman was required. But at this late date, even if we got the letter, our chances of actual approval were slim. HUD already knew that there was controversy over the project and was not likely to give money when success was questionable. And most of the money had already been distributed.

Fortunately, the letter did not have to guarantee wider local support. It just required Walter's personal support. Everyone disagreed on to get it. That night, I went privately to see Walter and humbled myself. I tried to appeal to his common sense, "Walter, this money is going to be given to some community in the US, why not ours?" He acknowledged the validity of my reasoning, but it didn't overly convince him to lend support to the low-income housing project.

I spent the next week living and working at the Hospitality House and found out why Jack had moved there. He was enthralled with Jill, and she with him. Though she was uncomfortable with the age difference, she was flattered to be pursued by such a good-looking young male.

A religious woman, Jill never did anything out of line. Even when she got mad at Jack, the worse name she could call him was "secularist." No swear words in her vocabulary! Little things upset her, like the fact that we had Mass daily with or without a priest. Jill's opinion on priests differed from mine and we argued about their role, but then one day, she was scolded by the local priest for being late to Mass. At that point, she threw up her arms and said, "I agree with you, Dorothy."

Periodically, the Empress visited the Hospitality House, but she wasn't impressed with the way we were running it. "This is run like a college dorm!" she declared.

It didn't stop our fun. While we were working, Jack, Jill, Cowardly Lion and I would play Hollywood by acting out a different character. I didn't realize the Empress was aware of our antics, but then one day when we were teasing each other, I suggested that she invite Hollywood to come out and make a movie at Mandala.

"I thought Hollywood was already here," she replied.

The Empress complained a lot. If she wasn't complaining about the Hospitality House, then she was complaining about the barn or Cowardly Lion and me. "You two rascals don't listen to me," she said. "I have no control over you."

"Well, why should you have control over me? I'm not becoming a nun," was my response. This didn't endear me to her.

Cowardly Lion agreed to feed my cats while I was away for the weekend. When I returned, the Empress came up and hollered about leaving the cats all week. I couldn't understand her making such an issue about the cats. When Cowardly Lion came back into the barn, she stopped talking. I continued on, "I can't live very long in a place where I'm not supported." She left and I turned to Cowardly Lion and asked, "Did you mind feeding the cats?"

"No not at all," he replied.

Manipulation. She tried to get people mad at each other. Division gave her more power. My independence made me immune to her antics.

I shared my concerns with Gretel, the potter, and she agreed that there was negative energy at the community. "Don't you feel like you're taking on the Russian army!?" she asked. "I think everyone out there is weird, and it's due to the water!"

"I feel like I'm in the second act of a play," I said to Gretel.

"Let's write the ending and see if we're right," she suggested in jest.

"I must be crazy," I said.

"No, it's not you. It's them," she countered.

\* \* \*

At the farm meeting, Pa Kettle, the only sensible person in the group, told the Bear to use two different colors of paint for the lines on the properties where we were currently building houses to distinguish between the funded and non-funded properties. According to the ordinances, the properties were supposed to be separate. He didn't want trouble with the town; They could argue we weren't following directions.

"Let's hear it for icing on the cake," chimed in the Bear, obviously disgusted with Pa Kettle's comment of appeasement. I knew Pa Kettle was right. We agreed to reapply for the HUD grant. Pa Kettle suggested removing the local town as a possibility for the housing site, but I knew the Co-op members weren't going to listen to him. They never listened to reason.

Star kicked her boyfriend out and enrolled in an education program. I hoped she was serious this time as he was a leech and could be violent. She also applied to Job Corps. In filling out the application, she had to answer 'yes' to questions about a history of mental illness. The facilitator told her that it would take time to get the doctor's response, and thus the application would be delayed.

"My face dropped to the floor when he said that," said Star. "And you can't imagine what happened next! He tore up the application, got out a new one, and told me to check 'no' to all the questions!"

That redeemed my faith in the system. Some people managed to stay human despite the rules of the system.

Walter stopped in to discuss the grant, and he seemed more positive about signing the letter. He had some questions for Pa Kettle and me. After he left, I asked Pa Kettle why the community wasn't trying harder to get on Walter's good side. Pa Kettle explained that a large chunk of the Co-op's funding came from a private group that supported projects which were trying to get the government to do what they say they do. It was to the Co-op's advantage not to have the government support the grant. "This is just the situation the funding group likes to dig its teeth into," said Pa Kettle. So, I was damned from the beginning. Frustration registered on my face. Pa

Kettle responded, "Dorothy, you'll learn. In this group, if you're not part of the solution, then you're part of the problem. Don't take it to serious."

I saw Walter Adams later in the week, and he told me he was working on the letter! Was there still hope?

Gretel and I went away to Bar Harbor. She played flute while I lay on the blanket sunning. She told me she didn't get any funding money for the pottery kiln. "They want another potter," she said.

"Why? You do such good work," I replied.

"I'm too independent for this group. They don't like my free lifestyle."

Later we were walking in town and met Jack, Jill and Cowardly Lion. Jack told me the fire alarm had gone off in the Hospitality House earlier in the week. The firemen came and complained about the furnace.

"Ma Kettle hasn't done anything about it yet. I'm going to tell the Empress," he declared.

"Talk to Ma Kettle first," I didn't want to give the Empress an edge on Ma Kettle.

I found the wooden cross of Christ that Sarah had given me lying on the floor. Its arm had broken. Narcissus probably made it fall when he jumped up on the sink counter.

On Friday, I saw the Artist in Bangor. She asked, "Are you really doing anything out there I the woods?"

"We're changing the collective unconscious," I responded. "It will make a difference."

"To whom?" she asked.

My dream: *The Empress and I were making love. We liked each other's hands. She said, "You're sicker than I am."*

\*   \*   \*

June 1st was my birthday—the big thirty. I spent most of it alone but that night there was a party. Jack wrote a poem for me entitled "Bella, Bella, Bella".

Bella, Bella, Bella!
You've reached the big
THREE – 0!
Bella, Bella, Bella!
How you got there is
an anthropological secret
Bella, Bella, Bella!

With your big red hat
your knapsack and guitar,
Carrying ballads and songs
to be sung by all –
in various degrees of harmony.
Bella, Bella, Bella!
With your snatches of laughter
Infectious, communicative, appreciated!
Your essence- purely Italian
Knee-jerk emotion
Fresh-perked passions.
(at the drop of a good Chianti)
to me, you'll never be
half baked,
I like to watch you
Simmer over a low fire
You're a good recipe,
And when you're fully cooked
I'll sit at your table anytime.

It was one of the best birthday presents I had ever received. I liked being called beautiful, especially since I didn't consider myself such.

During the day I had to go to a meeting with the Hermit. The car ran out of gas and we had to wait for a refill. After about ten minutes, Hermit got really edgy and screamed, "I can't wait all day."

"Why don't you walk to the restaurant and have coffee while I wait for the help?" I suggested. In a childlike manner, he said "no!" very emphatically. At the brink of tears, he paced back and forth, while I sat quietly, but concerned, that this grown man was obviously so upset.

Finally, he left, and I feared for his sanity. I found out later that the Empress was going to be away for the week which meant that the Hermit had to manage the community. This wasn't his forte. So sensitive, he hated being in charge. But he had his redeeming qualities especially regarding women. In a discussion about Mary Daly's writings, I commented that Daly was very angry.

"Many women don't even realize they should be angry," he responded.

That night after supper, we were singing the lemon tree song and at the part which says, "and the fruit is impossible to eat," the Empress, who had been drinking, turned to me and said, "except the Hierophant." Now what was that supposed to mean?

I missed having my confidant, Jack, around. He was on the outs with the community and wasn't allowed on the property. He was just too Californian for them. Gretel had hooked up with a new beau, Hansel, so I didn't see her much either.

My daily schedule was outreach work two days a week and carpentry three days. The newspaper I managed in between. Weekends were just as hectic. This one, I drove Star to graduation, worked on the barn, and then typed my article. In addition, I stopped at Hospitality House and found Jill all upset. Some of the dwellers had gotten poison ivy, and one of the in-laws staying at the house was beating on the kids. Always issues!

The Lioness returned to do some extra volunteering. This time she brought her guitar, so we went out in the yard to practice singing. I liked having a partner, but our rendition of *Thunder and Lightening* was pretty bad!

"'Georgia' is my favorite song," she said, after a few verses.

"Mine is *Joan d'Arc* by Leonard Cohen. I listen to the tape all the time in my car. I'm totally fascinated with her."

"I was named after Joan d'Arc," she responded.

"Really?" I said and thought, 'Did I lure her to this place?' "So why are you back?"

"I have some free time," she replied. "And I want to be a carpenter."

"A Harvard graduate carpenter," I said teasingly. "That's a good one."

"It makes more sense than what I'm learning," she replied as she ran back in the house to help Jill.

Hansel and Gretel were now living together.

I woke in the morning wishing I were dumb so I could just enjoy the simple things. After all, the more we are given, the more we must give back. Just a few months of social work, made me realize it took a lot of love to be successful. I didn't think I was making headway with any of my clients except Star, and that was only because we had become friends. I wasn't just a counselor to her. She knew my faults and that I had bad days just like she did. I was proud that Star beat the odds and made something of herself, despite her difficulties. After graduation, she got accepted into a nursing program.

From Tuesday till Thursday, I had a VISTA meeting in Bangor. When I got home, I was exhausted and slept on the dock jutting into the lake. Later, at the barn, I found Cowardly Lion and the Lioness. She had moved into the community while I was gone.

The Empress came up the hill and asked us to help move a wood hauler. The Lioness and I ran out to the field. The hauler was sitting in the middle of the dirt path.

"Stand on the back for weight," the Empress said to me.

"Hey, don't get nasty," I replied as I jumped up on the back and the front lifted.

The Empress was at the front end pulling. The Lioness and the Hierophant were at the wheels with the Lioness directing the Hierophant. I waved my hands in the air like a gladiator with a whip on a chariot. "This is the way it should be," I shouted.

"You like being on top? Don't you?" chuckled the Empress with that deep smile that I loved.

"You bet I do!" I exclaimed. The Lioness laughed and her blue eyes glistened in the sun.

I took a swim the next morning at 4:30 am. The lake was beautiful at this time, so quiet and calm. After haying that day, I moved down to the Empress's house. I was going to stay in the loft for a short time. Later, the Lioness and I went out on the rowboat. Cowardly Lion asked, watching us paddle, "Are you rowing to Greece?"

"Maybe! Don't worry if we don't come back," the Lioness shouted. We left the shore happily singing Judy Collins songs.

\*    \*    \*

My Seventy-two-year-old "boyfriend", Mr. C, an Outreach client invited me to dinner. The Lioness asked if she could come. I was happy to have her company. So did Mr. C. He gave her a big kiss. On the way back, I stopped at the office to check my mail. There was a letter from Walter Adams giving his support to the grant. I read it to the Lioness. She knew how important this letter was to me. We flung our arms up and screamed.

The next day, the Lioness while riding Teddy in the fenced in yard was thrown off. Her back was sore, so she spent the rest of the day sitting in hot water in the big metal tub in the barn. She would get quiet at times and lost in her aloneness. I sensed some fear, of what, I wasn't sure. I decided not to bother her and went off instead to a concert with friends.

The next morning, she confessed, "There's something here that makes me resentful and angry. I smell it. Is it my insecurity?" she asked.

I was afraid to answer. I didn't want to influence her one way or the other. I wanted her to draw her own conclusions about this group.

"It's different here. Just watch and don't get involved," I said. "Enjoy and learn."

"That's a big order," she responded. "What do you think about these nuns? Are they real? One of the freshmen at Harvard who went to a Catholic high school told me ex-nuns are dykes. But I don't think that's true about these women."

"How do you know?" I asked.

"I don't feel any sexual vibrations coming from them," she answered. I wondered what she felt coming from me?

The Hermit had to travel for a few days and asked me to baby sit his house and watch his two cats. Weird cats, I might add! I jumped at the offer, loving the idea of being so close to the lake.

The first night, the Lioness came down to visit as I had hoped she would. Looking at her, I noticed how beautiful she was. She had that classic goddess beauty of fair skin, long blonde hair, and blue eyes. Not too tall, her body was tight, and pleasing to the eye when she dressed in her usual tee shirt and green jeans.

Remarkably, I hadn't noticed how beautiful she was when I first met her. Physical beauty didn't impress me until intellectual beauty was evident.

Apprehensively, she sat down. "So, what did you do before you came here?" she asked.

"I was a teacher and lived with another woman for eight years."

"Really? Eight years. Was loving another woman good?"

"Yes. Very good. The lifestyle has its problems, but overall, it was good. Because we were teachers, we had to keep our homosexuality secret. We even bought twin beds since the apartment only had one bedroom. Imagine for eight years sleeping on one twin bed together! The first few years were heaven, but then I wanted to experience other lovers. She was my first gay love experience."

"So how did you get out of it?" she asked.

"Well, I told Sarah I wanted to leave, but she got so upset that I stayed another five years. Then I lost my job. I really needed to get away, so I came to Maine for a two-week vacation and never went back."

"That must have been difficult for you both," she said.

"It was," I replied. "It doesn't matter whether you are the leaver or the leavee. It's still emotionally hard."

"You must miss her?"

"I do. I miss the closeness of another woman."

"I've never been involved with a woman, but I understand the attraction," she revealed. "My first roommate at college was a beautiful Indian woman. I was so attracted to her. We spent a lot of time together. She teased me and led me to believe that she was interested in me. When I finally got the courage to do something, she rejected me."

"That must have been painful for you," I responded.

"Yes, very painful. I tried dating men, but I could never go all the way with them. It didn't feel right."

"I know what you mean."

We sat talking out by the lake till dark. I asked her to stay. We went into the house, and it became awkward since neither one of us knew what to do. Hints were dropped about sleeping together, but I wasn't entirely sure she wanted me. Finally, I told her to go to bed. I made her sit on the floor first. I hugged her and said, "I didn't want it to end without us acknowledging each other. I wouldn't do anything to hurt you."

"I feel so stupid," she said. "I don't know anything compared to you." I laughed thinking how young and naïve she was. She turned away embarrassed.

"I didn't mean to laugh at you," I said as I pulled her back.

"I know," she said.

"I never want to do anything to hurt you." She looked at me with those soft blue eyes, and I kissed her check very lightly. It was difficult not kissing her lips, but I was afraid of my own feelings.

"Now go to bed," I said. "Here, take this sheet." I tossed her the sheet from the chair. She wrapped herself in it like a squaw and ran into the small bedroom.

The night was difficult for me. I kept thinking of her body so close to mine. I wanted so badly to kiss her. To feel those soft lips on mine. To feel her warm cheeks rubbing mine. To run my fingers through her long mane. Throughout the night, I wanted to call to her. But I didn't.

The next day was awkward as well. We kept our distance from one another. But later, during supper at the barn we became close again. I had a beer and kept looking into her eyes. She looked back and would rub her body against mine every time she crossed the room. Then she sang "Try to See It My Way" to me. I knew we would be sleeping together that night. When I started to leave, she came and stood close to me in the doorway, blocking my exit. I closed my eyes and breathed in her scent.

I was just about to ask her to stay with me at the Hermit's when Jill arrived. "I've decided to spend the night at Mandala. Bear says there is an extra room at the Hermit's house. Can I use it?"

"Sure. Yeah. No problem," I said in a disappointed voice. Thinking, 'Well, that put an end to any plans I had.'

"Great. I'll leave my stuff down there and then I'm going to Bear's. I'll be back later."

The Lioness and I strolled down to the lake. It was a warm, still night and she said, "Let's take a dip," as she pulled off her shirt and pants. She was naked underneath. I followed suit and took off my clothes and got in the water. We floated around. It was fairly dark, but I could still see the outline of her breasts and her hard, curved ass. It was so hard not to reach out and touch her. But I knew Jill was coming down soon, and I didn't want to start anything I couldn't finish.

The air started to cool. I got out and put on my bathing suit. Then I sat on the lounge chair sipping wine and watched her play. I waited patiently. Soon she got out and put on her suit. She sat on the big rock about ten feet in front of me. She lay, head back, stretching her whole body to the form of the rock. Her arm hung down the side. The other pillowed her hair. The moon was orange and she cast a beautiful shadow in its light. Her nipples were hard and pointing upward. My heart was beating fast.

"You look like the Little Mermaid," I said. "Do you know the statue I'm referring to?"

"Yes. But I've never seen it. Was it worth seeing?" she asked.

"Yes. Do you want to be alone? Why are you sitting so far away?" I responded.

She didn't say a word but came and sat at the edge of my chair. I sat up and rubbed her back. The touch of her sent tingles down my spine. I wanted to pounce. I started to move closer to her.

Just then Jill came running down the hill behind the house. I pulled my hand away. In a distraught tone, Jill announced, "Bear's friend Pam had a heart attack."

Pam had been visiting Bear all week. She left that morning. Pam was Bear's oldest and dearest friend. She was not doing very well- a lot of medical problems. I knew something was wrong when Pam had left for the bus station and had shared my premonition with the Lioness, "I don't think we will see Pam again." I wasn't sure why I said it.

"Bear's going to drive to the hospital. I hate to let her go alone at this late hour," said Jill.

"Why don't you go with her and keep her company," I said. "Take my car."

"Really? That's a good idea. Are you sure you don't mind us using your car? I don't think Bear's truck will make it."

"No. Take it."

"Thanks," she said as I got the keys out of my pants pocket and threw them to her. As an afterthought, she said, "Lioness, you can use my nightgown if you stay. I left it on the chair in the front room. Use anything you need." We looked at each other and didn't say a word.

As soon as Jill left, I hugged the Lioness. She responded. I needed her. I needed her comfort. I felt very badly that I had the premonition.

"I feel so terrible," I said in an upset voice. "Sometimes I dream things and they happen. "Do you believe me?"

"Yes," she said. Then she laid her body on mine. I hugged her and kissed her head. We whispered as we talked. I could feel her heart pounding against my chest.

"Are you afraid?" I asked.

"Yes, but I want to be here," she responded.

"Let's go inside."

We went inside the house. She was still wet. She started shaking.

"Take off your wet suit," I said. She did. And I took off mine. We put on underwear and lay together on the Hermit's bed. I thought, if he ever knew! Two women making love on a priest's bed!!!

We didn't rush. First, we just brushed our lips against each other's cheeks. Then we started kissing, lightly then deeper and harder. She tasted sweet.

"This is a celebration of Walter's letter," she said.

"To Walter Adams," I shouted and held her face between my hands, kissing her lips.

"It drives me crazy when the light hits your hair," I said. She smiled and kissed me back.

"I love you," I said without hesitation.

"I love you, too," she said, but from her puzzled look I was afraid it was just a romance for her.

"You're free to go at any time," I said to ease her fear. "I will be strong."

"Locked doors being opened," she responded.

She was so nervous. We wrapped our arms around each other. I slid off my bra and then hers. The touching of bare skin made her sigh. She was so soft. I loved her smell. Neither one of us could breath. We kissed for a long time and fondled each other's breasts. Then I brought my hand down and rubbed the inside of her legs, moving slowly up to the lava spot between her legs. When I touched her inside, her whole body shuddered, and she jumped. I pulled my hand away. Slowly. Not too much in one night. She wasn't ready. It didn't matter to me. I came just being next to her.

"I'm sorry," she said. "I, I can't. . . .

"It's ok," I said putting my hand over her mouth to quiet her apology.

"We can take it slow. There's no rush. When you're ready."

We feel asleep in each other's arms. I woke up in the middle of the night screaming.

"What's wrong, Dorothy?" she asked, hugging me.

"I had an awful dream," I said. "The world ended, and I couldn't be with you." I was shaking. I held on to her tightly. She hugged back and said," It won't happen." She was so gentle and understanding. I lay back assured that she was right. That moment I knew I really loved her and would love her forever, no matter what.

In the morning I awoke thinking I had just had one of the most sensual love making experiences ever with a woman, and yet we never took off our underwear!

*     *     *

Jill came down later in the morning and didn't say a word, but she knew something had occurred. There was the unused nightgown on the chair where she had left it the night before. The Lioness was still in bed, and I was bathing nude in the lake. I didn't care that she saw me naked.

"How is Pam doing?" I asked.

"She's holding her own. Bear stayed with her at the hospital. I came back, but it was too late to walk down to the Hermit's house, so I slept up at Bear's." Good thing, I thought!

I dressed and left for work. On the way to my office, I dropped the signed grant letter from Walter into the Empress's mailbox, and then I did some paperwork. In the afternoon, Jack and Jill and I proofread the next edition of the newspaper. I was on such a high–the Lioness, the letter, and a successful paper!

I couldn't imagine life being any better.

The Lioness spent the day with the Empress, the Hierophant, and the Bear. I wanted so badly to see her. I had shared so much of myself with her the past few days, I was scared. I didn't how she was going to react after our night together, especially since I was getting emotionally involved.

After a late Mass, the Lioness and I left the group. When we got near the Hermit's cottage, she hugged and kissed me. We both looked at the boat in the water.

"Want to take a night ride?" I asked.

"Sure," she replied. "Mandala is beginning to feel good to me," she added and smiled lovingly.

Back at the cottage, we rushed into the bedroom, removed all our clothes and got into the bed. She lay her body on top of mine and stretched out my arms. Her blonde hair hung down on me. She kissed me deep on the mouth inserting her tongue. Then she kissed my neck. I rolled her over to the side. We held one another in a tight embrace. I couldn't hold back any longer. I wanted all of her. I rubbed down the side of her body to the inside of her legs and parted the lips between her thighs. I slowly circled my fingers over the soft flesh, pushing closer to her tight opening. She was so wet and hot. I inserted my finger deep inside her, and she whimpered. Tears from the overpowering emotion filled my eyes. She ran her hand down my body and pushed her fingers inside me. We were one body. We shook and held onto each other tightly. Our tongues searched each other's mouth. Our thumbs rubbed each other's hard clit. We both came very easily. We kissed and kissed and kissed and fell asleep in each other's arms. When we awoke, I took off the gold cross that my aunt had given to me as a child and put it in her hand.

"This necklace is very precious to me. You are precious to me. I want you to wear it." She smiled as she hooked the chain around her neck.

"I feel like a freshly picked grape," she said.

"I feel like the reincarnation of Vita Sackville-West," I replied. "And I can tell you she's at peace."

The Lioness became the focus of my attention. Sometimes, she was so childlike, and sometimes, so womanly. I loved when she got mad and yelled, "Fuck" or "No one is going to tell me what to do." I loved her laugh. It had such an evil tone. For some strange reason, I felt we were meant to be. She reminded me of the Wolf whom I loved in college. She had the same striking blue eyes, and soft blonde hair. Our level of intellectual conversation was similar. Quickly, she revealed all her insecurities.

"I'm such a social failure," she confided. "I have no people skills. I tend to take over when I'm in a group. It really bothers me that I need to do that."

The hard part was that I couldn't show my affection for her in public. And, I was already thinking about what I was going to do when she left for school. It made me cry. I wondered if that would be the end? I was sure I was going fall apart when she left, but I couldn't let her know, especially since I had said that I would be strong.

The next night, the Lioness and I drove around looking for a place to sleep. The Hermit had come back, and there was a Group of fifteen kids sleeping in the barn so the cottage next to the barn was off limits. We ended up parking on the road to Mandala. We just sat and talked for hours. We finally ended up at the Bear's, sleeping in separate beds. In the morning, I went to work, and the Lioness slept late. Later, with Jack and Jill, we went to visit Ee, a gay guy whom Jack had met from a neighboring town.

Ee took us to a bar where we met the Sea Captain and Tim. The Lioness and I were obvious about our relationship. We didn't care about the rest of the world. We slow danced among the 'het' couples.

"You too are great," said the Sea Captain. "I love that you have no shame about your love. I want you to come to my place. I have a house on a lake. You'll love it."

"Sounds fun," said Jack. Everyone jumped into the car and we followed as his car raced through winding roads in the dark woods. After a while, we turned into a secluded driveway leading up to a huge mansion set deep in the woods.

"Follow me," he yelled as he led us through the house and out the glass doors in the back which opened onto a deck with steps leading down to a sandy beach on a lake.

The Lioness and I immediately took off our clothes and went nude bathing.

Jack and Jill got into a canoe and paddled off. The Sea Captain lived with his ninety-year old mother who was sitting in the middle of the yard sipping on champagne. People roamed around the yard, eating and drinking. All different types. We felt right at home.

After our swim, the Lioness and I ended up on the couch, kissing. Then we went to the Sea Captain's bedroom. He had told us to use it. But what he didn't tell us was that he was going to use it, too. In the middle of the night, after too many martinis, he flung himself on the side of the bed.

"I've never done things like this before," he declared as he snored himself into oblivion. The Lioness had been sleeping in the middle, so I placed myself between her and him as I knew she was not comfortable with this sleeping arrangement. The Sea Captain was harmless, so I said, "Let's just stay here. It's late, and there's nowhere else to sleep anyway. I'll watch him. You sleep."

Reluctantly, she closed her eyes and nestled into my arm. The house was wall-to-wall people since everyone was too drunk to drive home. They bedded down anywhere they could find a spot. I covered the Lioness's ears trying to protect her from the loud snoring blasting out of him. Neither one of us slept very well that night.

In the morning I swam nude. A little boy came up to me and said, "You need a towel." He handed me a towel and added, "My mother said I couldn't swim because I didn't have a bathing suit."

"That never stopped me," I declared and couldn't believe my arrogance.

Later, the Sea Captain took us to a picnic where there was a bunch of wild, angry gay men. Ironically, there was no food. The Lioness and I went into the woods. She wasn't thrilled about the potential lack of privacy, but I wanted her. We made love in the leaves. As we lay there holding each other, we could hear music coming from the house.

"That's the same song that my parents used as their wedding song," exclaimed the Lioness. Good sign, I thought.

We slept in the barn that night. She wrote "FPG loves VSW (but you need clean sheets)" on a paper and gave it to me. Our lovemaking was always incredible, as often as possible, and anywhere we could manage it. The cats were usually in bed with us. I felt closest to her when I looked at her with that look of longing, and she returned the same desire. I never felt so loved.

"I'm so happy to have a whole woman to myself," she declared. "I love being around you. I love watching you work. I love watching how you rush around. When you're working on the newspaper, you're awesome." I couldn't believe that she loved me so much. Could it be true?

"Do you know what you are saying?" I asked.

"No, but will you help me to learn?" she responded.

We had various names for each other. Venus on a half shell, Alice in Wonderland, and Cheshire cat were a few she called me. She also told me I looked like a Rubens' woman. "I love your beautiful dark eyes," she declared. Once I called her a wolf to which she replied, "I'm only a jackal." Then she told me about a dream she had had. In the dream, she was a harness with no horse. The harness turned into sand. There was laughter, and she got mad at herself.

"I think the dream had something to do with the Indian woman from college," she surmised. "I'm not a fighter but more like my mother—gentle."

"You're precious," I whispered.

One afternoon, I took her for a palm reading. The reader said she was stubborn, intelligent, and would take one major trip in her life. Later, she would choose to be alone and, in her solitude, become a creative writer. I hoped that didn't exclude me.

A new group of volunteers arrived, and I brought them over to the Hospitality House. Lisa, a tall, attractive, light-haired woman with large breasts, joined the house building crew. Immediately, she became friends with the Lioness and me.

During the week, I finished the layout for the paper, and then Jack and Jill and I went to the printers. Jack and I talked about the Empress and how difficult it was to work with her. Jill said to me, "You see things too much in a psychological way. You are beyond the natural level." I wasn't sure what she meant.

"We just have to love the Empress for what she is," she continued. "And stop trying to analyze her." Jill was kinder than both Jack and me.

When we got home, the Lioness and Lisa were upset with the interaction of the Empress and Bear with Cowardly Lion. At lunch, they hollered at him in the restaurant about his relationship with another man. That night, I drove Cowardly Lion over to the Hospitality house to give him a break from them.

I had told the Empress that I would take care of her house for the weekend while she was away. When I got down there, I found her nephew. That upset me. I needed to get out. The Lioness had a way of calming me.

"Come on, let me treat you to a beer to celebrate the finalization of the next issue of the paper," said the Lioness.

Now that I was having an affair with the Lioness, I didn't think I could survive living in the community anymore. I went to talk with the Bear.

"I'm concerned that the Lioness is a temporary relationship for you," she said.

"You're making a major decision to leave the community based on this fleeting situation," she said. "She's awfully young to be making a lifetime commitment. I'm afraid you're going to get hurt."

"It doesn't matter," I said. "I know what I want. She doesn't know yet. I'm not asking for a commitment. What I have now with her is precious. I can't live dishonestly anyway. It's probably better if I leave."

"I wish Pam were here to talk to you. She's a wise old woman. Maybe she could talk some sense into you," she replied. I had to laugh remembering it was because of Pam that we got involved!

I took the next day off and The Lioness and I went to visit the High Priestess at an open house for the local newspaper. After meeting the Lioness, the High Priestess invited us for Sunday dinner. At the reception, we talked to a doctor who knew Anne Sexton, the writer.

"She was a mess from the beginning," he said about the artist. "Worse after the stroke. Talked a lot about God. Sometimes she loved him, but most of the time she hated him." His own wife had died six days after they were married. After the reception, he took us to the museum in town. Then the Lioness and I walked arm and arm on the beach.

That night I went to a lecture, and the Lioness stayed at the community and talked with Cowardly Lion. She was upset when I got home.

"He's really hurting. He needs counseling, but he won't go. I know he won't," she said sadly. I made a fire and tried to make her laugh.

I helped move a woman into the Hospitality House the next morning. We used plastic bags. "This is the Italian way. Puerto Ricans use sheets!" I exclaimed. The Lioness and Lisa came to help. The Lioness had learned that Bear's friend Pam was going into a good convalescent home. This put her in a better mood.

The Lioness and I left for Bar Harbor on the fourth of July. In the car, she revealed, "My father gave me two pictures of people for my name sake– one of Joan d'Arc and one of Rupert Brooke, an English poet during WWII who wrote for Churchill. He did some not-so-good propaganda. He was gay and foolish. I love horses, and there is a picture in my parent's house of four horses. I always thought it represented my three siblings and me. My grandparents live on the Cape in a wealthy neighborhood. My grandmother had a break down, but my grandfather was also weird. One night he came out nude to get a skunk out of the kitchen."

As she talked, I drove around looking for a hotel, but there were so many "no vacancy" signs out. It was a holiday weekend. I turned into a hotel on the main drag with small cute little red cottages. The woman wasn't going to give it to us till she realized we were lovers and desperate.

"Please, please. Just for one night?" I pleaded.

"Ok, for one night," she agreed as she smiled at the Lioness who sat in the car wearing my big red straw hat.

We bought wine, cheese, crackers, and oranges for the room. I took the Lioness to my secret beach on the ocean. We lay on the rocks and hugged and kissed. People could see us, but it didn't matter.

The ocean was freezing but that didn't stop the Lioness from jumping in. I stayed on the rocks watching her. I loved her sense of adventure. Later we walked through town and had tea. We returned to our little red cottage, took showers and made love. The Lioness surprised me when she took her fingers out of me and put them in my mouth, letting me taste myself. It was so erotic. It made me go wild. I went down on her. She tasted so sweet. I could lick her forever. She went down on me, but I could tell she wasn't into it as much as I was. It didn't matter. I could spend the rest of my life just making love to her. We slept after tiring ourselves and later went into town for a Greek dinner. We walked on the beach and the Lioness's mood changed. Almost morosely she uttered, "I don't know what you want."

"I want you to be yourself and to be happy," I responded. "That is real," I added.

"I'm not ready for anything. I've already given you too much," she said.

"I know you're just starting out," I replied. "I know you need freedom. Maybe we can get together at times."

"I will be proud to have you visit me," she said. I cried soft tears, and we returned home. I gave her my Adrienne Rich book, *Dream of a Common_Language*. I read some of the poems to her, and we fell asleep. In the night, she woke me up. Her fingers were inside of me, but she fell back to sleep. I loved her so much. In the morning I left her sleeping and did my run. I sat on the porch and wrote in my journal-Life is beautiful despite all its sadness . . . I can't help but be content."

On Saturday, we met some friends at the ocean and picked mussels. We drove back to Mandala excited about our seawater treat. After a good night's sleep in the barn, I got up early and did my run. I wrote in my journal and then got back into bed with the Lioness. She awoke in that same depressive mood as the other night and told me that she was worried about her father and what he would think about her if he found out. This was not her only concern.

"I'm afraid you're getting too serious," she said. "What are you going to do when I leave? I'm afraid for you."

"Don't worry about me. You don't give me enough credit," I said. "I have other options too."

"I might get involved with Gaye, the black woman at school."

"Go ahead," I said, which surprised her. "Try it. See if you're comfortable with another woman. See if it fits." I thought 'this is more in her head than reality.'

"And what if I get involved with the Empress?" I added.

"That would be ok," she replied realizing that I was open to different relationships as well and not as confined to her as she thought. We talked about love. Then we made love and had blueberry pancakes for breakfast.

Conscious that the Lioness needed some free time, I spent the day roaming around. She appreciated that. We met later at Mass. The gospel was about inhospitality being the worse sin, even worse than the sins of Sodom and Gomorrah. On the way to the lake, the Lioness asked me what my impression was of the community.

"Conscious confusion," I responded.

"I think you've hit on something," she said. "But why?"

"I don't know. There seems to be a fear of success here. Sometimes I feel like a Judas. I don't understand their motives or goals. Like with this government grant. I'm not sure they could handle the funds if they got them. Jack and I have discussed the fact that they don't really want the money."

The Lioness and I watched Lisa get out of the water. Her shirt was wet and clinging to her large, beautiful breasts. We looked at each other and gave that sneaky laugh that you use when someone is thinking the same thing you are. At Mass, Lisa had given a reading about Jerusalem having comfort at the breast.

"I could get a lot of comfort on those breasts," I whispered to her. The Lioness cracked up.

The Lioness confided that she wanted to pursue her psychic talents. Maybe she was my high priestess, companion to the magician. I memorized every bit of information. Her sun sign was Aries, and she liked Pierre della Francesca.

Every day, I woke up and wondered how she would respond. But each day, I felt assured of her love. She confided her inner most thoughts, regarding her relationship with the Indian woman, she admitted, "There is still bitterness and some feelings."

"You still care and that's good. We should never harden or not care," I warned her.

"Being with you makes me want to give more to others," she said.

That night, we went to the High Priestess's house for dinner. Her husband had left to pick up his mother. While the High Priestess and her daughter were cooking, the Lioness and I listed to cello music. It was like being in a Greek temple. There were blue glass figurines sitting on the tables and old glass bottles in the windows filled with herbs and dried flowers. The High Priestess floated silently around with a smile on her face as she cleaned the strawberries. The Lioness and I sat on the couch and touched lightly at times. We tried not to be too obvious.

The mother-in-law arrived, along with other friends, and we talked about the apocalypse. I suggested that there could be another way, but the Lioness believed in the apocalypse theory. Hoping to get the Lioness away from the depressive conversation, I asked the High Priestess to do a Tarot reading for each of us. The Lioness's cards revealed she was optimistic, scholarly, and spiritual and that she was the Queen of Wands holding on to the past. My reading was:

No. 1 Covering card: 8 of Wands—Great haste, too rapid advancement

No. 2 Crossing card: 6 of Pentacles—generosity, sharing beliefs

No. 3 Beneath card: Knight of Pentacles—exploration, study

No. 4 Behind card: 3 of Wands—beginning of enterprise, work

No. 5 Crowing card: 9 of Swords—sorrow, loss, worry

No. 6 Before card: The Star—spiritual strength, insight (High Priestess said this was a powerful counter card to the 9 of Swords

No. 7 Fears: 4 of Cups—discontent with present joys

No. 8 Family/Friends: Strength—mastery of animal nature by spiritual

No. 9 Hopes: Queen of Pentacles—anima figure, earth mother, fertility

No. 10 Final Outcome: King of Pentacles—animus, master of creativity

Half of the cards were major Arcana, which meant a lot was out of my control. Overall a positive reading with some strong outside influences.

The next day I needed that strength. The Empress asked the Lioness to meet her at the barn at one o'clock. I was distraught. I knew she was going to confront the Lioness about her relationship with me. It was obvious that we were involved and in direct opposition to the community's rule of celibacy. I vented to Jack, who suggested that I talk with the Empress right away. I found the Hierophant.

"I want to have a meeting with the group," I told her.

"We want to speak with you, too," she replied.

We made an appointment to meet at ten o'clock. I found the Bear and asked her to attend. She was sympathetic to my situation.

"Isn't there some condition we could make so you could stay on at the community?" she asked.

"I don't think so," I responded, knowing it was way overdue to leave.

Ten o'clock came, and I walked into the local restaurant. I didn't see anyone at first, but then I noticed that the Empress had chosen a quiet table in the back. Bear, Cowardly Lion, and the Hierophant sat with her and I joined them. It was awkward, and I started shaking. Tears were rising in my throat, but I managed to hold them back. As I calmed myself down, I started talking.

"I really value my life here in Mandala. But I can't stay any longer. There are things that I can't condone anymore. Issues are not dealt with by the group. Instead, they are handled roundabout and not always in a kind way."

"What do you mean?" asked the Hierophant.

"Well, like last week when you spoke to the Lioness and Lisa about Cowardly Lion. Cowardly Lion got all upset and so did they. And speaking of the Lioness, I'm sure you know that we are involved."

The Empress turned to the Hierophant and asked, "Does the Cowardly Lion have anything to say?"

"Please deal with my concerns and leave Cowardly Lion alone," I asked.

"Why do you want him here then?" questioned the Empress.

"Because he's part of the community, and he deserves to hear what I have to say," I countered, angrily. Sensing my frustration, Cowardly Lion responded, "I have nothing to say."

From then the conversation developed into a personal confrontation between the Empress and me.

"You're very negative and not honest," said the Empress to me. "You say different things to different people."

"You're really talking about yourself," I replied.

"Empress, she is honest," supported the Hierophant in direct objection. Totally ignoring her comment, the Empress went off on an obtuse angle.

"So, what is your ideal community?" asked the Empress.

"One that would allow for different lifestyles," I retorted. "Your community can't exist unless it liberalizes. You're too matriarchal."

"So, what is your ideal?" she questioned again. "You know there are things I can't stand either, like the uncleanliness of the place," she added.

I gave up at this point. Then she said, "I don't even like asking for your help because of your attitude."

"My attitude!" I shouted. "I've done a lot of things for you."

"Don't give me that," she responded. "You shouldn't be doing it for me but for yourself. You can quit the paper if that's how you feel. There are three other people who want to take it over."

I should have called her bluff at that point, but I retracted my statement. The paper was not an easy job to fill. It finally ended with the Empress saying that she thought the Lioness and I could remain on the grounds. She said she was growing very fond of Cowardly Lion and me and so she wanted to make an exception.

"I don't want to be the exception," I said.

"You're right. There can be no exceptions. Empress, this has to remain a celibate community," emphasized the Hierophant.

"I would have to leave if it wasn't," added the Bear. I knew the Empress could not afford to lose Bear since she had been a great support for her.

"You won't have to leave since I'm moving out," I said calmly. "I just need a few days to get myself organized." The meeting ended shortly after that, and the Empress never went out to Mandala to talk to the Lioness.

The next morning the Empress came up to the barn and worked. At Mass she was quiet and detached. Maybe it had to do with the fact that the Hierophant had left that morning on a trip. Funny, last summer I would have died for the Empress, and now I was leaving her.

I had to travel to Bangor to do some work that day. When I returned, I went to Bear's. The Lioness was there, and she ran out to see me.

"I missed you," she said, hugging me.

"I really missed you, too!" I said. After a nude dip in the lake as boats rode by, we went for dinner at Joseph and Mary's house. They lived with their four-year old daughter Angelica in one of the houses built by the Co-op. They always teased me about being a" liberated woman" and usually, I teased back, but I felt a little uncomfortable that night. I wasn't in the mood. The Lioness sensed my feelings and left me alone. Instead, she played with Angelica the whole time.

Later, we visited the Bear. She had been haying all day and was too tired to talk so we left her house and walked down to the lake. There, we lay on the ground for a long time, not really talking much. I was wiped out from the emotion of the day.

"Let's go up to bed," she said. "You need to sleep."

As we climbed the hill, she walked close to me. Just before the top, she stopped me and put her arms around me. We hugged for a long time.

"You're beautiful," she said.

"You think so?" I questioned.

"You're fine," she said in a soft, tender voice.

The next day, after my chores and supper at the Doctor's house, I picked up the Lioness from the Hospitality House. I wanted her so badly that I stopped the car right in the middle of the path into Mandala. I moved over to her and started kissing her. I kissed her hard. She didn't respond. I could tell she didn't want to be in the car. Frustrated, I got back on my side and started the car.

The next evening, we went to the Hospitality House and had supper with a Vietnamese family. They were so calm and humble.

The Cowardly Lion had decided to move out of the community as well. He rented a small house and the Lioness and I slept in a twin bed at his place. I woke up in the middle of the night and had this terrible loathing of being touched. Maybe it was because the bed was so small. I felt cramped.

I spent all afternoon in the sun by the lake. The Lioness came down and we took the small boat out. While I rested, she rowed to a calm spot at the tip of a small island in the lake. She landed the boat on a huge rock jutting out of the water. We lay quiet on the rock. She wrote. I took a swim. Afterwards, I got out and stretched my body onto the surface of the rock so I could feel the warmth of the sun everywhere. The Lioness started gently touching me. I kept my eyes closed and kept myself still. Her touching turned into deep caressing. She took the top of my bathing suit down. She rubbed my exposed breasts till the nipples were hard. Then she moved her hand down my stomach to between my legs. She slipped her fingers under the tight bathing suit and inserted them inside me. I was so excited but kept my body stiff on the rock. My calmness excited her. She went in deeper, rubbing my clit with the palm of her hand. I came. I told her that my time with her was a glimpse of true peace.

"Do you know what you are doing?" I asked.

"What I'm doing this summer is you," she announced.

"Did I upset you the other night in the car?" I asked. "I can be a bit overpowering. My needs are great. How deep is your love for me?" She remained quiet. "I guess that's not a fair question," I added.

"It's a good question," she responded as she lifted her body to a sitting position, "but the answer is . . . " Before finishing the sentence, she jumped into the water as if she were chasing something. And she was. She had apparently knocked my sunglasses into the water when she got up. She tried to stop them from falling too deep but couldn't. She was very upset when she climbed back on the rock dripping wet. I just laughed and hugged her. Later when the water settled, we could see the glasses sitting on a protruding ledge of the rock. She was able to carefully maneuver with her foot and retrieve them. We left shortly and she rowed back. Even though the wind was blowing against us, she didn't want any help from me. Her stubborn nature welcomed the challenge. I enjoyed the ride.

The Lioness and I spent a lot of time at the Hospitality House and once Jill almost caught us making love. It was a bad scene. The Lioness had spent the day with Star while I was with Jack who was upset, but too mad to discuss it. Apparently, he had a flare up with the Empress.

After working on the paper, I went to House to pick up Jill to go to Bangor. The Lioness was there but Jill had gone shopping. The Lioness and I went up to Jill's room in the attic and lay on the bed kissing. Jill returned, walked into the room, and saw us. She immediately ran out, upset. We felt bad. Even though she knew about our lesbian relationship, it was another thing to be literally faced with it.

Jill decided to stay home with the Vietnamese family, and so the Lioness accompanied me to Bangor. We went to my favorite Jewish bagel shop, located down a short flight of stairs in a building in the center of town. We sat for a long time talking. Then we walked to the park and lay on the grass.

"I want you to be with me forever," I said to the Lioness.

"At this point, I would have to say no," she responded. I wasn't surprised. One thing about our relationship was that it was honest, bluntly honest, even if it hurt to the core.

"You love truly," she said. "I could never give what you have to offer." I thought to myself, 'in time you will to the right person.'

We returned and I found Jack ready to talk about his confrontation with the Empress.

"She accused me of spying and ease dropping," he said. "Do you believe that? Then she said the gossip had doubled since I arrived. Then she lied to me about one of the workers. I can't deal with her anymore," he said in disgust.

That night, the Lioness and I left for Belfast and got a motel. It was storming outside. The Lioness's stomach was upset so we went for some food. That calmed her down. I soon found out what was upsetting her. Her parents were coming to visit. I knew she was concerned about balancing everyone's needs.

"I want to do right by all of us," she announced. I had this sinking feeling she was going to leave with them.

In the morning, I ran, and when I got back, we made love. We had breakfast with a woman who had lost her husband ten years ago.

"We never lost our desire for one another," she announced.

Tomorrow would be her sixty-sixth birthday. She played the song on the jukebox, "I wish I were eighteen again." I asked the Lioness that we always be compassionate with one another.

"I'm not sure I know what that means," she replied. "But I'll try in my own way."

On the way back, we bought some honey for Jill as a make-up present for upsetting her.

An open house at Hardclimb Hill, a woman's retreat center, proved to be very interesting. It was the total opposite of Mandala. Rooted in self-awareness and sensuality, the community built beautiful dwellings. I learned that one of the founding women had been in the same cloister order as the Empress. They both had left the order and gone their separate ways, creating very different living environments for themselves and others.

Meanwhile, the Lioness spent the day with her parents. They dropped her off at the retreat center at the end of the day, and I met them. I could see that the Lioness had gotten her arrogant, analytical, stubborn, self-willed personality from her father. Her mother, on the other hand, had a gentle nature. She was concerned with me having to drive the Lioness around all the time. Her father asked me innocently, "So what's been going on?" I didn't really think he suspected anything, but the question hit a nerve for the Lioness. We didn't sleep together that night.

\* \* \*

On Monday morning, July 14th, 1980, just about 1 year after I had moved into Mandala, I moved my stuff out into a cabin at a local motel just about one-half mile down the road from the community. During the year, I had written a newspaper article promoting local business with this motel as a featured spot, so I knew the owners. We worked out a deal in which I would clean cabins in exchange for rent. It would save me money and get work done for them. The owners lived by the main road in a big white house with rental rooms. Down the hill were individual small cottages for rent. This was a seasonal motel as none of the cottages had heat.

The location was ideal, only steps down to the lake. The cottage was surrounded by tall pine trees providing shade and privacy from the other residences. White with green trim, it included a big open deck on the back facing the water. The deck was held up by thin solid pine logs, so the house looked like it was walking on stilts. The shade of the pine trees kept the ground damp. Fallen pine needles covered the ground giving it a red hue. The interior consisted of one large room with bed and kitchen and a small bath with shower. Finally, a built-in shower! This saved me from trips to the Learning Center for a fifty-cent shower. I was happy as a pig in shit to be there.

To my pleasant surprise, the Lioness didn't go home with her parents. That night we had supper at the barn with the rest of the group. I didn't want anyone to think I was mad at the community. I wasn't. I just wanted to be free to live my own lifestyle. Lisa cooked ratatouille as a special treat, sort of a "last supper" for us. The Empress was not thrilled with the menu selection. She always hated "health food," which she called "wealth food." The Lioness got mad when she learned that a family with two children were going to be staying at the barn.

"I can't stand it," she blurted.

"Well, it's good then you're leaving," chimed in the Bear, who had overheard her comment.

Our first night in the cabin was wonderful. Finally, we got to sleep on a big bed! We had breakfast on the porch in the rocking chairs and felt like queens. I spent some of my day painting a wagon at Mandala. Then I had to bring a pick tool to the building site. Jack had quit the community job and was looking for employment in Castine. That evening, we had supper at the Hospitality House and then returned to the cottage. The Lioness lay on the bed and started rubbing her arm and chest. It got me so excited that I jumped on her, kissing and tickling her body all over. She rolled over laughing. We were so happy and carefree.

Lying on the bed that night, I thought, my life has been absurd—painting wagons, running from place to place, dealing with crazy people—except for the Lioness, she made everything worthwhile.

The cats loved their new home especially since they didn't have to deal with any other animals. The Lioness nicknamed Narcissus "Nar cass" with a Spanish accent. He loved when she pet him. Whenever I wrote in my journal, he jumped up and had to sit on my lap. More of a loner, Goldmund preferred sitting on the porch rocker and watching the waves.

Star came to visit one evening after the Lioness and I had spent a lazy day drinking rum and wine coolers. We fell asleep early on the bed together, and Star caught us. The questions multiplied.

"So, when did you two start liking each other? Are you going to stay together? I'm ashamed of you, Dorothy. I like you, and I accept you, but I don't approve of what you are doing," said Star. She had brought her son and boyfriend, who had fewer problems with our relationship than Star. I knew my friendship with her would outweigh her initial reaction. "I'm gonna pray double for you, Dorothy," she announced as she left.

"Good, I need it," I said, and the Lioness and I chuckled and ran back onto the bed.

It had only been a few days yet the family with two children living at the barn were already looking to get out! They inquired about staying at the Hospitality House. I talked to Jill who was in a tizzy. The Empress had threatened not to support the house if the "wild parties continued."

"What wild parties?" I asked. Jack was not allowed there anymore, and Jill threatened to move out. If she left, I would have to move in since I was on a VISTA grant requiring more social work, and additionally, it would be lonely when the Lioness went back to school.

My outreach work continued its hectic pace. One day I had to chase down a woman who had left the Hospitality House. She had begun to wander around and ended up in a motel. After she ran out of money, the motel called for someone to pick her up. When I got there, she made up some story that she had been kidnapped. It reminded me of Tweedledee's imaginary story about the villain.

\* \* \*

I discovered that the Lioness loved the Cape and every summer she and her dad would go sailing there. She was very close to her father and thought her parents would accept this lesbian relationship. I thought otherwise.

"My parents are liberal," she said.

"It's easy to be liberal when it's not your own," I responded.

My parents and aunt came to visit the next weekend. They stayed in the motel at the main house. It was the first time they had ever traveled to see me. I was so thrilled, but they were not.

"Dorothy, how can you live like this?" declared my aunt.

"This is a palace compared to where I lived in the community," I responded. "At least now I have electricity, running water, and a real toilet."

"That's more than I had as a child," piped in my Dad who was more understanding. He grew up in Italy on the island of Ponza. The family house was built over a cave in the wall of a mountain. Food was scarce-pigeons and fish and vegetables from a small garden. After living in America, he never wanted to return to the poverty he left behind.

That Saturday, I took them to Mass at Mandala. The Hierophant was friendly, but not the Empress. Despite her aloofness, my father went over to talk to her. We returned to the cabin for supper, mussels and snails over spaghetti, a favorite meal of my father. They left the following morning after visiting the Hospitality House.

Back at home, the Lioness and I talked on the porch. I was depressed, probably due to my family's leaving and I started crying about the community, "Things should have never happened this way. It's not my way. People keep missing each other and hurting each other." Then I rambled on about our relationship. "I will love you no matter where you are. You will never have to doubt my love." She started crying, "I want to be with you if you ever want or need to cry." Then she second guessed herself and added, "But I guess it only matters what one does, not what they want to do."

"You can't always do what you want," I said.

"You're appeasing me," she smirked.

"I've left people from my past and that was hard and cold on my part. You have a lot to learn about love. If you do all the things you want, then you will learn. Why do you want to be with me when I need to cry?" I questioned.

"For my ego," she responded. "And I have a big ego."

"I don't need your ego," I said as an overwhelming veil of sadness fell upon me. I masked my depression by going off on an unrelated philosophical tangent. "Sometimes I'm not sure if my basic feeling for God is love or anger. There is so much beauty yet so much pain. How is one to feel in such a world? Despite all the sadness, I love the world. I choose yes instead of no. How do you feel?" I asked her.

"I feel like a caterpillar with green guts," she responded.

"Caterpillars get squashed."

"I don't think I'll get squashed."

"I don't think you have green guts."

We sat in silent for a while. I calmed down and stated, "I don't know whether I helped the Empress or not. Maybe I set her back even more. Do you know the story of the red rose?"

"No," she replied.

"The red rose talks to a little boy and tells the boy, one must water me every day consistently, and then I will start to rely on you and trust you and know I am loved. I'm not sure I did that. Maybe that's what the Bear is doing. She stays by the Empress's side even when she disagrees with her. I'm not as steadfast. What about you?"

"I may be the Jack of Hearts," she responded.

"Is that a good or bad card?" I asked.

"It doesn't matter if it's a good or bad card. The Jack of Hearts is the thief."

"You can't steal something that is yours to begin with," I assured her.

"It shouldn't be mine," she said sadly. "I don't deserve it."

"No one needs to deserve that. Love is freely given." To which she shook her head and with a deep pensive look, she said, "You're a bird."

"A bird is a symbol of transcendence," I responded. "Why am I a bird? Because I fly?"

"Yes," she said.

"Then I'm not bound to the earth, and I will create my own nest, apart from reality. Do you know what you want?" I asked.

"I want to be as in the time when the Indian woman at school threw a knife at me and for a split second, I didn't know what would happen. It missed, but it didn't matter which way it went."

I didn't have an immediate response for this one. Much later, I declared, "You're such an enigma. Sometimes I think you do what you think you should be doing, rather than what you want to be doing. You pursue causes rather than people."

"It's not causes for me as much as a direction. Heart and mind in tune, working together," she retorted her voice getting louder.

"I used to be that way," I said, "but I revised my priorities. It must be the law of karma. I'm getting back my own medicine." With that, she started hugging me and sucking on my breasts.

" Did you ever see the Bergman film *Cries and Whispers*? I asked.

"No, why?" she replied.

"It was the simple housekeeper who comforted the dying sister by placing her head between her naked breasts. She simply gave her body. The other real sisters couldn't face their feelings. The servant girl was the most compassionate figure in the movie. To take a sick dying girl in your arms, that's true compassion. I always want to be that way. Meaning must come through one's individual life pattern, not through the place one works. I will make it my goal this winter. Last winter I was learning how to survive. Now I will search for meaning."

"Good luck. Right now, I'm just searching for pleasure," she said as she continued to fondle my breasts.

\*   \*   \*

The Paul Winter Consort was performing locally so the Lioness, an entourage of young people, and I went to hear them. As we walked into the concert, I felt so eccentric, dressed in my army fatigues and bandana. The Lioness and I held hands, and sometimes I would lean over and kiss her. She liked all the attention. I liked being able to express my feelings. I reveled in the masculine. I was so proud that she was with me. That night at the cabin we had a wild night of lovemaking, and it continued in the morning after crying and talking.

The next night, we had a dinner party at the cabin. Jack and Jill, Hansel and Gretel, Cowardly Lion, Star, the Vietnamese family, and a few others came. We feasted, drank, and laughed. But Lisa never came, so later the Lioness and I went to see her. It wasn't like her not to show up. We found her sitting in the barn kitchen with a new volunteer. She was upset by a conversation about Cowardly Lion she had had with the Empress who implied Cowardly Lion was on his way out as far as she was concerned. He was still working in the leather shop even though he didn't live in community anymore. The volunteer had told the Empress about a line from a letter that Cowardly Lion had received from his father. It revealed the Cowardly Lion's gayness. The letter was lying open in the leather shop. I got furious.

"You had no right to read the letter, let alone tell someone else about it!" I screamed. The volunteer screamed back. It got nasty. I left and he started banging things around the kitchen. I went back to calm him. I hugged him and said it wasn't his fault and that he was caught in the middle. I was really mad at the Empress.

Lisa told us that the Lioness and I were no longer allowed at Mandala except for community supper. I didn't care anymore.

The Lioness and I made love in the morning. She was wet and soft. The moisture was dripping down her ass. I loved it. I was addicted to her. She had come to realize her potential to attract women. She confessed that she wanted to explore this talent and was even interested in Lisa. I was afraid of that, but her admission didn't stop our intense relationship. Sometimes we were just quiet, but our desire for each other was very apparent. We needed to be physically close to each other. I loved fondling her in public places. I was the first woman she had ever made love to. Actually, I was the first person she had ever made love to. I knew from experience this was not in my favor.

That night while I talked with Cowardly Lion, Lisa and the Lioness were having an analytical conversation. As I watched them out of the corner of my eye, I felt my age. It would be hell for me when she left, but not so for her, she'd forget me easily. Even though she missed me during the day, loved seeing me at night, and expressed how much our kisses meant so much, I knew it was only for the moment.

I started working in the woodshop making wooden breadboards.

The instructor kept telling me my shapes were uneven. I decided I didn't want them even, so I continued making them curved and unsymmetrical. I drew my inspiration from the Lioness's body.

One morning the Lioness had a dream that her mother said something to her about her evading her sister. She woke up crying. Then she remembered something about buffalo all cut up as if to be eaten. She jumped up and got dressed and wanted to leave. When she met me in the shop that afternoon, she was quiet. That evening, we were supposed to have dinner with the Bear and Pam, but Bear told Lisa and the Lioness that Pam was too tired to be with people, so she canceled dinner. Later, we found out that they went to the local restaurant. Lisa and the Lioness were so upset. I tried to make them laugh when I got home, but the Lioness took it to heart and cried. I told her that she had to be detached.

"I can't love if I am detached," she said. Her tears were more than just about the canceled dinner. Maybe she needed to see her parents or talk to other gay women.

The next day I rushed home to ask the Lioness if she wanted to go to Boston to see her folks. She was worried about money and how she would feel coming back, she cried again.

"You shouldn't have to deal with my insecurities," she said.

I tried to comfort her, saying, "You couldn't possibly know what is going on in your head. This is overwhelming for you. Loving a woman. Dealing with your family. Being out here in the woods."

We talked for a long time, and I told her I thought she was missing her friends and family. A little later, Hansel and Gretel came over. We all went swimming. The Lioness took a shower, and then Hansel and Gretel gave the Lioness and me a foot and head massage. Just what we both needed. After supper at the Café, we went to a bar and danced together—all four of us slow dancing, hugging each other. Then Hansel and Gretel took us to see the caboose they want to live in. They left us alone in there.

I felt strong in the morning and decided that I would put the paper off till the second week in September. I planned on going to the Cape the third week of August. I could move into the Hospitality house till September. However, I needed to save money to buy tires before I could go to the Cape. I looked forward to being alone this winter. I planned on writing, reading, playing guitar, making new friends, learning carpentry and photography, and healing. All this would keep me busy. I would not back out on the commitment to my job regardless of what the Lioness did. I needed to learn perseverance, and I was determined to survive on my own.

That night, I had a dream that *I was in an apartment with the Empress and the Hierophant. I went into my own room and closed the door. I lay on the bed. There was a face on the wall (like a stick-up). I pulled it down onto the bed. The Empress tried to come in, but I wouldn't let her. She was smiling.*

*       *       *

The Hospitality house stressed Jill. There was no money or support. The Empress had kicked Cowardly Lion out. Furious, I went to Mass at Mandala, spouting off about the readings. One was about Sodom and Gomorrah and Abraham asking the Lord to save the community even if it were for forty, thirty, or twenty innocent people. I said quite forcefully how the real sin was the sin of inhospitality. The Bear prayed for some dead woman. I prayed for Jill's work with the Vietnamese. Then I got up to leave. The Empress, who didn't look at me for the whole mass, asked, "Are you staying for supper?"

"No," I replied, then added as an aside to the Lioness, "it would be hypocritical to stay and eat here."

The next morning, Lioness and I drove over to Castine and walked on the beach. It was beautiful—quiet, foggy. We dug our feet in the sand. We stood touching bodies for a while in the sea. Then we lay face up on the sand. "The earth protects and rejuvenates us," I said. Then I turned to her and said quietly, "You are so elegant. You should never settle for anyone who makes you feel less than that."

"That's makes me feel good," she said. "You always make me feel so beautiful." We were quiet after that. Returned home on "e" on the gas gauge. When we got into bed, she made love to me. I came over and over again. I never felt like this before. "I love when your body trembles," she said. I tried to make her come, but she couldn't. "It doesn't matter," she said. I fell asleep thoroughly exhausted.

I woke up just before dawn. She woke me up. She was hard and rubbing against my leg. I rubbed her with my fingers. She was so excited. Then I went down on her and she came. "I don't think I could do it as long as you can," she said.

"I love licking you," I responded. "I could do it forever."

She was restless. I rubbed her head and said, "I love you."

"Thank you."

"I will miss you."

"I will miss you, too," she said and fell asleep before I did. Both of us were lying on our backs. I turned my head toward her and stared. The light spread over her face making shadows. Her blond hair spread over the pillow. I smelled it. I melted. I turned my head so she couldn't see my face. One tear fell down my cheek onto the pillow. Then a stream followed. If she wanted me, it had to be for desire, not out of pity for me. I knew she needed to be away from me. Tomorrow she would come with me to Bar Harbor, and then the next night there would be a going away party for her departure to the Cape.

Her last day was very emotional. Even in bed the night before, we were both spaced. The gang came over for supper that evening, and never wanted to leave. One of the guys suggested the Lioness stay an extra day. To my pleasant surprise, she agreed. We spent the day together at Winter Harbor. Had supper at a little dive. Sat for hours on a rock watching the sun set and boats coming in. We drove to the tip. It was windy, and the waves were wild.

That night we made passionate love. In the morning on the breakfast table was a rose with a note that said, "dear transcendent stormy petrel . . . this rose to celebrate one month of passion, learning, and love." As we were leaving the cabin, she slipped her silver chain with the woman's symbol into my pocket and said, "keep this till I return." I took off my green army jacket that she loved and put it on her. I drove her to the station. It was the first of August. I watched the bus drive off.

I missed her as soon as I got into my car. That night I received the following message, "Home safe. Will come back. Happy, scared, excited. Love, L."

\* \* \*

After the Lioness left, my energy dropped. Creativity was at a low. My daily calendar had heavy, deep, dark pen doodlings. I missed her terribly. I left her a phone message and later received one from her. Finally, a day later, we connected and talked. I kept touching the silver chain around my neck. As I held on to it, I could feel her vibration.

The back of my legs hurt. I couldn't sleep. I thought about the paper. The next edition was due to go to press. At this point, I wasn't getting much support, so I decided to do it alone and fuck them all. I planned out my next articles.

After another bad night, my throat hurt, and my glands were swollen. I was eating more than usual again. Jack saw me moping in my office.

"Not doing too well, are you?" he asked.

"Not really. I miss her very much."

"Here this will cheer you up. I picked up the mail. You got a letter."

I ripped it open. It was from the Lioness. It read: i was happy to be home and somewhat shocked-part of me fits right back into the old patterns and part is disoriented - and i was missing you constantly at my side. i kept wanting to tell everyone about my homosexuality . . . i awoke with a wonderful dream taste in my brain. Something convoluted involving Mother Teresa being asked to give sanctuary to someone amidst the cool tiled halls, atriums with fountains and pools as i have always imagined Babylonian temples and baths to be (where Alexander the Great died of fever; his Persian boy lover at his side). M Theresa was potentially devious in the dream, but outside the sea was rolling against the marble quays, and there were young women dressed in light flowing robes lining the stone walls. Whatever danger lurked in the intrigues of the temple, i was in none, i felt a sense of "at-home-ness" and dove out into the delicious heaving water. I met two women, one i think at the edge of the quay, one later far out in the water, over our heads. They were nameless in the dream, without history, but i must have known them for i went to them without hesitation. I laid my head on the first and it was like being in the circuit of a powerful current. She disappeared, and then I dove into the sparkling blue water and found the other. I embraced her from the back, my hands around her breasts, with that same feeling of ecstatic electricity and woke.

i sit now at this dining table, looking at the cove. Later, Dad and I will go for a jaunt in the boat so I can touch the sand and feel the spray of the Outer Beach. I wonder what kind of a time you are having today. Must be a mad house. At dinner, i played the juke box and missed you . . . i am less confident about telling my parents. They ask me where did you get the jacket? Where did you get the cross? Who are you writing to, and I tell them not only are you coming to the Cape, but I may go visit your parents in CT.

I think about you and feel incomplete that you are not here with me, that we are not off on jaunts together, that we do not begin and end the days. I think I miss you more than I had expected . . . I'll be back up in Maine on Friday, August 8 and then we can go to the Cape, if you would like? I am impatient to be with you again . . . Till love, L

I couldn't wait to see her. My spirit had been rejuvenated by her words. It was muggy outside, so I worked on two wooden spice racks to take my mind off her.

At a poetry reading on Thursday night in Blue Hills, I bought the Lioness an expensive, handed-printed poetry book on Italian paper. When I left, I felt itchy and started scratching. A rash spread over my entire body. I went to the Doctor's house, and she gave me a prescription.

"Maybe you're allergic to being alone," she teased.

"I don't know if I'm allergic, but I certainly don't like it," I responded.

The Lioness arrived around 4:45 pm, one week from the day she had left. The bus was late. I waited in the car. When door opened, she ran off and jumped into the car. She was wearing the blue work shirt I had given her and a headband. We hugged. She kissed me.

"It's so good to be back," she kept saying. I drove home. I had taken the pill for the rash, and it made me drowsy, but that didn't stop me from making love to her. Amazon woman was born that day.

She worked on Saturday while I shopped and did some outreach work. I gave her a unicorn book and an army jacket (she left hers on the bus) that I was saving for Christmas. We spent Sunday together. The night was beautiful. I made love to her, and then we both fell asleep. I woke her up in the middle of the night by rubbing my hand up and down her smooth torso. I was so excited and wanted her fingers inside me. She did so without me asking.

Monday morning after a muffin at Duffy's, we took off for Boston and then to the Cape. In the car we talked about all kinds of things—selfishness, guilt, mental versus real feelings . . . We never ran out of topics. We stopped to see her father and brought flowers to her mother. I met some of her college women friends, then we saw the Judy Chicago exhibit, "the Dinner Party." It was good to be surrounded by the energy of such important woman, my favorites - Susan B Anthony, and Virginia Woolf. We shared the sound tape so we could be close.

Later, we stopped to see Harold, my professor from college who had been supportive of me when I was leaving Sarah and my teaching job. Impressed with her intelligence, he commented, "A Harvard student, not bad Dorothy. This one will keep you hopping."

We had dinner at her parents' house. Her father made me a martini; I did not think he liked me. He wasn't very impressed with Mandala either. "The Empress looks like she knows she failed," he said. "Bear has pledged her loyalty so she's not leaving. I don't really see why she stays; she seems to have more on the ball."

I didn't say anything and hated myself for letting him get away with that statement. I didn't appreciate his attitude. The Empress had accomplished a lot, but not according to male standards.

Overall, her father made me nervous, and I made some stupid comments during dinner. The worse was asking what he thought about the Kennedys, knowing full well that he was working in the present Republican administration

The Lioness and I slept in a room with bunk beds. We hugged for a while. Then she got into the top bunk. Feeling the martini, I flamed on in my arrogant way, "I am more woman than the rest of your woman friends. I won't play second fiddle. You love me, and you're here because you want to be with me." She didn't say anything. She knew it was the liquor talking.

In the morning, I jogged and prayed. It was a beautiful sunny day. I sang out, "God is everywhere." Then, I showered and woke the Lioness with kisses.

During the entire visit, her mother seemed overprotective. I wondered if she suspected something. She was uncomfortable with me and I didn't know what to say to her.

The Lioness always stood about ten feet away from me. She needed time to decide what was important to her. What lifestyle she wanted to live. I was secure in my love for her, and I knew she loved me, but she wasn't ready to face the opposition.

We had breakfast with one of her friends Kim. "I really like you," she said. "But then again, I would like you anyway because you are with the Lioness. You two look good together," she continued. "I like how you act toward one another."

When we left Kim's, we got to the car just in time before it was going to be towed!

On Tuesday, we drove down to the Cape. We stayed in a cute bunkhouse on her grandparents' property and spent the day at the beach. Then we visited Pam before going dancing in P town. I loved leading the Lioness around on the dance floor. We fit together so well. She was a little taller than I but not by much.

The next morning, I was walking around nude in the bunkhouse. Without warning, her grandmother appeared at the side door. "Quick. Jump in the shower!" said Lioness. It was a close call. I was out of breath and shaking. Her grandmother had wanted to show her friend the bunkhouse and she kept talking and talking. We laughed hysterically when they finally left.

"I thought I was going to turn into a prune," I said. "I didn't have any clothes so I couldn't come out of the shower."

Thursday, we were back at the beach before going to Ciro and Sal's in P-town. Laying on the sand, we talked about things are bigger than ourselves.

"You're a clearer channel," she said.

"Maybe, but parts are fuzzy, I responded. "Some people seem to be playing the same parts. I can't distinguish who is who."

"It's like the Christ story," she said. "I read somewhere that Mary

Magdalene was a wandering ascetic after JC died. John was in a whole different camp and yet recognized Christ for what he was. John came looking for someone who was the voice. Who are you?" asked the Lioness.

"Another voice," I responded, but I wasn't sure why I said that.

Friday, the Lioness went back to Boston and I left for my parents' house in Connecticut. On the way, I stopped to see Adele. She told me she was having premonitory dreams. She would have momentary feelings of doom. Usually, she told her husband, and he believed her. One day, she was in the car and had a feeling that something was happening to someone in the family. Her husband's father ended up in critical condition. Then she dreamt of a nuclear explosion in a town starting with New. She later read how something similar had happened in New Jersey. She thought maybe she had the power to see the future, especially the negative events.

When I left her house, I had a visualization as I was walking to my car. I pictured Adele, her daughter and I walking down the street. A car came around the corner heading straight for us. Adele pulled her daughter into the bush. I stayed but wasn't afraid. Later, I called her to tell her about this premonition, and she said, "Something happening to my daughter is my biggest fear. You must have picked up on that."

On the way back to Maine, I visited the Lioness and we stopped at a Friendly's. It was hard sitting across from her. I wanted to kiss her. She sat with crossed legs in the car. I drove around looking for a place where we could talk. It was terrible. Finally, we ended up on the Regis campus. I kissed her. She admitted negative feelings but added that they were probably projections. Her parents questioned our friendship. "They are beginning to suspect something is going on between us. It would be easier for them to accept a woman from Harvard or one more my own age."

The pain shot through my whole body, from feet to head and back down again. All I could do was raise my eyes up to the ceiling and cry. "All I have to give is myself and that is all I could ever give. I can't do anything about those things. I will never be a Harvard graduate. Nor do I want to be a Harvard graduate! It's so contrary to my philosophy. And I cannot change my age."

"I don't want to feel that way," she said, probably in defense of my reaction.

"Are we playing games, Lioness?"

"I don't think so," she responded meekly.

I kissed her and I could feel her trying to catch her breath.

"Does that mean anything to you?!?" I asked.

"Yes," she replied softly. I thought to myself . . . I'm not sure what's happening. She is not strong enough to fit . . . I mean . . . fight her father . . . though fit is a better word. He has such control over her. Our values are different. Arguing is in vain. We just have to respect each other for what we are . . . the Lioness says my concept of loyalty and his are the same . . . maybe she is right.

After I cried, we got back together. "Don't give up on me yet," she pleaded.

"You would rather love someone like Lisa, right?" I asked.

"No!" she replied and laughed quietly. I wasn't sure why she was laughing.

"To me, people are equal," I said. "It doesn't matter what school they go to. Sometimes I feel more intelligent than other people, but I don't base my judgement of them on that."

A cop came by the car and so we left. I brought her back to her dorm.

The next night was bad. I was brooding over the Lioness. I drank too much wine, ate too much, and went to bed early.

The Empress left me a message that her mother wanted me to come for dinner. The Hierophant was away. I felt weird being there alone with the Empress and her mother and said something about "not having a boring life" in response to a question her mother asked me. The Empress thought I was talking about her life.

"I don't live a boring life," She chimed.

"I didn't mean yours," I responded.

Later, she mentioned that one of the cats was being difficult, "like some people." I assumed I was one. Then the Bear came down and they started talking about the medical profession. I wasn't into it. As I was leaving, the Empress looked into my eyes. Why, I'll never know.

I spent time with my cats. Narcissus was so glad to see me. He looked skinny. There was no letter from the Lioness. I knew that was a bad sign.

The Lioness phoned on Friday, but I missed the call. Even though it was still August, the temperature was cooling, and vacation season was ending. Not many people were staying at the motel so there was little for me to clean. It was time to move on.

I heard about a small vacant A-frame cabin in a neighboring town. A Co-op worker gave me the name of the owners and said that they might be willing to rent it. When I contacted them, they suggested that I see it before deciding, so, I went to check it out. It was located on a dirt road off an isolated main road. I had to walk about ¼ mile into the woods to get to the cabin. The area was gorgeous. Tall white pine trees surrounded the cabin. It was quiet and desolate, but I loved it.

The cabin itself was ridiculously small and primitive. It measured about 8 x 10 with a tiny screened in porch, 8 x 3. The door was locked so I could only look through the one front window. It was dark and dusty. On the rear side, a metal chimney stuck out from the roof-exhaust for the wood stove.

As my VISTA grant income was $50 per week, I wasn't in a position to be too choosy. I couldn't imagine that the rent would be very high. I told the owners I wanted to rent the A-frame. The woman chuckled when I asked how much for rent. "As long as you leave the place in better condition than you found it, you can stay there for free. We're not using it."

"Thanks," I said, quite pleased with this deal.

"By the way, there's no woodstove. You'll have to bring your own. And you'll have to supply the wood. There may be some left over from the last occupant, but I doubt there's much. If you still want it, you can pick up the key." Which I did on Saturday and spent the entire day cleaning it out. The A-frame had a loft that was big enough only for a small twin mattress. As no one had lived there for a while, it was pretty gross. Some chopped wood lay around on the ground and an old double mattress was leaning on one of the trees. I felt brave considering such a solitary environment. Having survived one winter already, I felt confident about the skills I had acquired.

The next few days, I worked on an article for the newspaper and taught class. I also caught up on my visits to clients in anticipation for a trip on Thursday to Boston to see the Lioness. My life was busy, but all I could think about was seeing her again.

I picked up the Lioness late Thursday after her last class. We had dinner with Harold and Ralph and slept at their house. The Lioness was quiet and distant the whole time, but once we got in bed, she loosened up. We made love while Betty, the cat, lay at the foot of the bed. I woke up in the middle of the night with negative thoughts about her not loving me anymore, but in the morning, she was fine, and I knew she loved me.

After touring Boston on Friday, we headed for Connecticut so the Lioness could meet my family. All the women in my family joined us at a Greek restaurant for dinner. The Lioness was in good spirits. We slept at my aunt's in her spare bedroom. When we started making love, the Lioness was so noisy, I grabbed the pillow and pushed it over her face. We both got hysterical. It didn't stop us, and before she came, she whispered loudly, "Suck". It drove me wild.

Sunday, I took her to meet the Wolf. The Wolf and her lover were on the outs, so it was a bit uncomfortable. The Wolf and I strolled into the kitchen for a private conversation.

"What a knockout," she said, glancing at the Lioness.

"I love her," I said.

"Yeah, tell me about it!" she responded sarcastically. She wasn't too obvious about what she thought about our age difference. "Well, I have to go to the old blonde and make up. I love her, but I don't like her. She hits me." Surprised at her admission, I questioned, "Why do you let her?"

"Maybe I deserve it," she responded.

"You don't deserve it. No one does," I retorted strongly.

We slept at their house, and the Lioness was in a quiet mood.

"You don't feel the same, do you?" I questioned.

"No," she stated bluntly, and then added, "My mother thinks you're dependent on me."

I knew her parents were a strong influence on her, and no matter what I said, I was doomed. "I'm not dependent on you. I'm living alone up in Maine. I'm doing ok. But I enjoy seeing you."

"I enjoy seeing you, too, but . . .

"Look, you're back at school, and I won't be seeing you as much anyway. Don't shut me off now. I'm afraid I'll start detaching if you start rejecting me. Let's just enjoy. Maybe the distance will be good for you, and hopefully, for us."

"Maybe, maybe not," she responded.

When I drove her home the next day, the song "Sailing" came on as soon as I turned in the driveway. This had been "our song" all summer. I looked to see if it had any effect on her. But she was still distant. She got out, and I was left with my thoughts on the ride back. Was she just someone passing through my life? A summer love? Some loves are forever, and I knew, for me, this was one of those.

Back in Maine, I went to see two gay women friends and cried my guts out. I told them what the Lioness had said. One offered to write to the Lioness that all lesbians have family problems. Her lover knew about her gayness before she did and gave her a lot of time. "Maybe she just needs time," she consoled.

I received a long letter from the Lioness two days later.

9/2/80 Dear Sackville,

I'm sitting in a restaurant after visiting with Janie, the one who wants to live with me. Janie doesn't know but if she'd asked the right question, I would've told her about you. She was afraid to express her feelings for me in a letter and then had been happy she'd done so. I wanted to say something special but decided that "I'm not hot for your bod, but I love you anyway," wouldn't quite do . . .

Getting together with a friend, biochemist whose bod is almost enough to make me wish I were straight . . . "Sailing" on Fl 105!

Indian woman called. I was nice . . . I think I can be her friend and not get wound up in revenge. We'll see . . .

I feel like I'm coming into my own. I want to cut all my old ties at the college, to be alone, independent, free, to cut a swath of a different color, to be accountable to no one at school. Sort of anti-social, not to mention snobby. I want an expanded image. One that cannot be labeled "lesbian," but one that is spontaneously, natural, unselfconsciously sensual. I want to turn men on without trying and to make converts of "latent" heterosexual women without trying to seduce them. Ain't I a bad, arrogant-bitch, purple girl? I'll let you know when the balloon pops. It's going to pop when I realize that no one loves my scent but you. You banana.

Thanks for the weekend. Stay safe and well and strong. I think about you. Love the Lioness

9/6 God I wish you were here. I have to tell you the diamond popped off the cross. There is a slight chance it will be found . . . funny how I had said to you earlier when you were wearing it that I liked the plain side better. It always gives me such a chill in my soul when I lose something that has been given.

I'm waiting to hear from you and see you on the weekend of the 20th if that's still good for you. Love, L

PS Got a great letter from Lisa.

I sympathized with her problems, but I had my own. Winter was on the way and I had to get ready. That weekend, I went to the craft store, and there was a wood stove sitting outside with a sign, "take me." So, I did. It was a perfect size for the cabin. I had some trouble but managed to hook it up.

Each morning, I chopped wood. The cats were happy with their newfound, freedom and we played together in the leaves. I kept a big ax by my bed just in case. There were bears in the woods! I had no lock on the inside door, and at night it got pitch black. Where was this courage coming from?!

The pictures to go with my article got lost so the Hierophant redid them. She was the only one giving me support.

Sandy, a gay woman from the Co-op, told me that the Empress and Red, a woman from Hardclimb Hill had been lovers. She added that Red left the Empress for another woman and that the Empress got everyone to alienate Red and her lover. The Empress, Sandy said, had been seen later at parties very drunk and would sleep with women but the next day would ignore them. This really hurt. The Empress had been playing games with me. I was right in my thinking that there could be something between us. It was a bad night for me. I called the Lioness and told her. I was so spaced on the phone that she said she would call me back that night. When she did, we had a good conversation about us. I asked why she never said she loved me when we were together, but she wrote it in her letters. She couldn't explain why.

I had a dream that *I was at a party. A dog started biting me. I got on a chair. The Lioness came. I went into the bathroom, closed the door, put on a French hat and went back out to make the Lioness laugh. She had water in her mouth and spit it out at me. We both laughed.*

\* \* \*

Bear helped with the layout for the next paper. Gretel helped with the proofing. I asked the Empress to change a line in her article as I felt her choice of words was unnecessarily violent. She had written, "Use love as our weapon." I suggested that she use the word "tool" instead of "weapon." She wouldn't change it. The Bear defended her and said, "Sometimes love is violent."

On the weekend, I attended a workshop at Hardclimb Hill and visited with Red and her lover. Twice, Red scolded her lover for interrupting her. Then she adamantly demanded that she make a decision about breakfast. It made me uncomfortable. I would have told Red to go fuck herself. Yet, the woman played into this dominance. I found it hard to believe that the Empress could have loved such a woman. Maybe that was my problem, I wasn't bossy or obnoxious enough for her. Maybe she liked being put down. Maybe her low self-image needed reinforcement.

When the paper was done and sent off to the printers, I called the Lioness to firm up the weekend visit. Her father was not thrilled about my coming to Boston. I had dinner with Gretel to catch up on the Co-op news. Cowardly Lion was having a hard time finding a place to live and Star was sick of her boyfriend—the usual. Gretel told me that Hansel was paranoid about her going out without him. She had to call him when we were at the restaurant. I told her I wished I had her problem.

Waiting for paper to be delivered the next day. I started thinking . . .

*What's keeping me here? The creativity? The importance of my job? Being an editor even if it was for so small a place? A revolutionary place? Is that why I stayed? Could love of the Lioness pull me away? I wasn't sure.*

*Usually, I was the lover, the pursuer. If I stopped pursuing her, what would happen? Would that be the end? What were the Lioness's true feelings? How long could I exist in this limbo state of not knowing? On the phone, she would say that she loved me and then in person she would never say it. Was it easier to lie on the phone?*

The Lioness knew me well. She knew I was upset when she told me about her father's questioning my visit to Boston. I told her how I had been influenced by my parents and feared that she would be too.

I hadn't been sleeping well. I was frustrated and missed her lovemaking.

Then I received this letter from the Lioness. I called it the Vita letter since she wrote Vita Sackville-West on the inside envelope. My fears were laid aside.

9/15 (after phone call in room) Dear Lieutenant,

I just reread your letters and wanted to respond . . . maybe it is easier for me to write than say it. Something gets in the way of my feelings, freezes them so that I do not know them, I cannot touch them . . . Then my intellect starts to think, what should I be saying . . . I am so stupid on the phone with you.

Dear Lieutenant, you are like the tree now outside my window. It is given and bright and it fills my small low window and reaches out its branches to me- I can almost touch them. And the tree trusts me, or is strong enough itself to give freely, and does not expect a price or a bargain, but simply offers and waits, and is true . . . Now I am getting mushy.

I am in awe that you know who I am . . . people like the Indian woman don't understand what I'm all about. They miss parts of me . . . you feel what I am trying to be. You love me for what I would want to be loved. I am more myself when I am with you. God, I am arrogant. . . . Arrogance that's dark. But there are also lights that flow when I'm with you . . . I am <u>truer</u> when I am with you. There is more spontaneity and joy in the moment. You make me feel as if I could do anything . . . you make me feel closer to being who I truly am . . . more totally than anyone else has ever made me feel about myself. It may be egocentric, but that is precious to me.

Maybe I just have to face up to the fact that I am terribly egocentric.

I want to make love with you, L

Her words touched deep inside me.

The Lioness said how she always got surprised at my height. "You have a tall presence even though you are short." Cowardly Lion said one of the carpenter workers knew the Lioness and I were involved. He could tell by the way I protected her.

The silver chain that the Lioness had given me with the woman's symbol broke today as I was taking it off. I was so upset. I wanted to fix it right away.

\* \* \*

Cowardly Lion and I worked till 9:00 pm Wednesday night to get the paper mailed out. The next morning, I took him to his parents' home in Massachusetts before heading on to Boston. I got there early in the afternoon, and the Lioness was still in class, but I managed to get into the common room. She shared a living space with four sophomores, even though she was a junior. She actually slept in a single bedroom downstairs from the big common room. There had been some question as to who was going to occupy the private room, but when the Lioness told her father about the dilemma, he decided his daughter was not going to put up with any sophomore demands.

"We're going in there tonight," he huffed. So, they packed her stuff, drove to the dorm and deposited her things in the single room, assuring the Lioness a private space. "He was dressed in a sloppy shirt and torn shorts with a big stogy in his mouth. He freaked the security guard out when he presented his own Harvard ID," commented the Lioness. Secretly, I think she liked it that her father had defended her.

I climbed up on the ledge in the common room and posted myself there, hoping to surprise the Lioness when she came in. Instead, I scared one of the poor sophomores when she arrived home to get some books. She came in, looked up, and saw a strange woman in army fatigues hanging off the ledge! She screamed. I calmed her down and told her I was waiting for the Lioness.

The Lioness finally arrived home but must have seen my car parked outside. She ran into the room looking for me and was surprised when she didn't see me.

"And who are you?" I called down in a Cheshire cat accent. She doubled over with laughter. In her arms was a sack full of gifts for me—a grape candle, the record "Sailing" and a poem book by Tess Gallagher entitled *Under Stars*. Inside the front cover where it said "For Ciaran, for moja, the Lioness added. "For 3 months, Love L". She was so happy to see me, and I was thrilled that she had thought so much about me to buy the gifts. We hugged and kissed, but suddenly she became morose and upset.

"What's wrong?" I asked.

"I just went to the GYN. My syphilis test came back positive last week, and so I had to take a retest."

"Syphilis? Where would you have gotten syphilis?" I couldn't imagine where she would have gotten this. I certainly didn't have it.

"The doctor says it could be a false positive. I'll get the results on Monday."

We went to the Women's Center on campus. The Lioness liked showing me off. When we came back to the room, she said, "I felt like I acted stupid. It's different having you here on campus. I'm sorry."

"Don't worry about it. You acted ok," I assured her.

We took a shower together. It was exciting sneaking around the common bathroom. Then we went into her bed and kissed. Before it got too hot and heavy, I got up and put the "Sailing" record on. Then I stood at the end of the bed and danced nude in a slow, sexy manner over her body. She watched. By the end of the song, I lay on top of her, rubbing her shoulders and moving my pelvis to the beat in between the verses. Her breathing was deep. We met somewhere in wonderland and made love.

Friday, she had class, so I walked around and spent some time in the library. She met me later for coffee, and one of her roommates joined us. We went to see the movie *Fame*. The film upset the Lioness because there was a homosexual boy in it. She held me tighter. When we got back, we made love again, and she was so into it. We stayed in bed all Saturday morning making love. She lay with her clit touching mine. It drove me wild. All this lovemaking exhausted her, but she wanted to join me for a walk down by the river. We just lazed in the grass taking in the sun and sights. When we went back to the room, she slept, and I read.

She woke up in the middle of the night screaming "Mother." I just held her. I think she was upset over the syphilis test, and the fact that she hadn't told her mother about her gayness. She had always been honest with her parents. The stress of the secrecy was too much for her.

The next night, we met one of her male friends for dinner and then saw two flicks, *Simone de Beauvoir* and *Colette*. The war scenes upset me because I had visited the concentration camp in Dachau when I spent the summer in Europe with Sarah. I remembered that the area around Dachau was so beautiful with trees and flowers and blue skies. The buildings were impressive, red brick with fancy woodwork. Inside were the ovens. I could never get rid of that yucky feeling I experienced when I looked into the ovens. I felt so detached after the movies and told her so. I also admitted that I felt like this after masturbation. I had never revealed that to anyone. She held me tight all night.

The next morning, she woke up with swollen glands. At breakfast, she told me I should leave Maine: "You shouldn't let yourself be manipulated by them." I loved that she was so concerned about me. She put on a dress to go to a shower with her mother. What a knockout she was! It was hard to leave her, but I had to get back to work.

Driving back, I thought about her struggle. She had to deal with so many "grown-up issues" yet she just wanted to be the child and have her mother tell her what to do. I refused to make any decisions for her. She tended to listen to others and ran to people who didn't really care about her. I hated seeing her in pain. I wished I could take it away, but that would be too easy. She had to face life. I told her I was going to tell my mother that I loved a woman. That would be honest, and maybe then my mother could understand better than my just saying I was gay.

Further up on Route 1 in Maine, I saw a truck pulled over on the side of the road in front of a cop car. The truck looked familiar and sure enough it was the Empress, the Bear and the Hierophant. The cop stopped them for a burned-out head light.

The next day Argus, the Empress's dog, greeted me. I was still upset over leaving the Lioness. He peered down from the truck window and gave me an empathetic look. Then I went to visit Gretel and told her about the "syphilis weekend."

"It's like a curse," she said.

*   *   *

Jack had decided to go back to his California job. Jill would return to New Jersey. "How will you two survive without one another?" I asked.

"It will only be a temporary separation if I have my way," answered Jack.

Back to work on Monday, the Bear and I dug out a cesspool. She told me that the other day the tractor had rolled backwards down a hill when she was on it. She had to jump off. She was overworking herself again.

Nuns from the Doctor's convent were visiting. "Oh, you're the newspaper editor," said one of them when I was introduced. "I read it at breakfast. The paper is excellent, and your writing is good," she added.

"Thank you, thank you very much," I responded. It was encouraging to get positive feedback especially since I heard more of the opposite.

A new woman volunteer, Carrington, boldly stepped out of the Craft store when she saw me and waved me over, calling out my last name like she knew me. She was of average height, with short dark hair and a masculine, but attractive face. I sensed that we were going to be good friends. She had a medium-sized black dog, named Molly, by her side. And her cat Sam was in her car.

That night, the Lioness called. She still hadn't gotten the results of the syphilis tests. She had to go talk to the doctor tomorrow. "I wish you could be with me when I get the result," she said. "I love you," she added, but her words didn't convince me. She was still unsure about her gayness. I wished she would tell her mother.

On Tuesday, the Lioness called back. The test came back negative. Thank god! She invited me down for the weekend.

That day, I spent some time with Carrington. "I want you to introduce me to the Doctor," she said in a determined voice. "I'm worried about my mother. She has cancer. I want to discuss her problem with the Doctor."

She started crying as she was telling me the story, but I had to leave to do my outreach work. Next time I saw her, we were both wearing blue jeans with a red top. "We are psychically in tune today," I said to her.

"I guess I picked up your vibration," she responded.

Narcissus hadn't been around much. He had been roaming in the woods and Goldmund had been scratching herself all the time. I kept throwing her off me. Wasn't writing much. The silver chain broke again when I came out of the shower at the Learning Center.

The week was busy, and all I could think about was seeing the Lioness. I rushed around doing chores on Friday and then left for Massachusetts. At around 7:00 pm, I got to the dorm. The Lioness was sleeping and didn't answer the bell, so I sat upstairs and ate my supper. I watched the Tower clock. Then I heard someone say "shit" in that typical Lioness-aggravated style, but the voice was unfamiliar. It was the Lioness, but her glands were still swollen. She was glad to see me. After I gave her a unicorn book, she said, "Funny. I was thinking of unicorns in relationship to you."

We embraced and then went to a woman's bar called "*Somewhere.*" Downstairs in the bar were three vocalists singing female music. Upstairs was the dance floor with a revolving silver ball, glittering the space with stars. It was still early, and not many people were dancing, but we liked having the space to ourselves. The Lioness had on a Chinese silk shirt. It was so sexy to touch! We chatted with a group of four older women. One was heavy set and wore a red shirt with black pants. Her hair was pulled up under a jazzy black hat. She projected sophistication. She and her partner were good dancers, and the Lioness and I enjoyed watching them.

"We love you two, especially your hat!" the Lioness shouted.

On Saturday, I bopped around while the Lioness worked in the library. We met for lunch in the park. The Lioness introduced me to hot and sour soup and Chinese dumplings. It was cheap but so good. We tried to get into a Yo-Yo Ma concert, but it was too crowded. Back at the room, the Lioness put on Bach guitar. We made wild and passionate love.

"You're such an Amazon woman when we make love," I said to her.

"And you become so innocent," she replied.

Talking in bed, she seemed calmer and more secure. I asked, "Did you notice that I didn't have on the silver chain?"

"Yes," I did," she responded.

"It broke after I took a shower the other morning,"

"Well, maybe you're not meant to wear it."

"I just need a stronger chain. I didn't realize my strength when I was taking it off."

The Lioness asked, "Are you happy in Maine or are you just biding time?"

I started crying. "I can't get into the real world. I have been there and don't fit in. If I leave the Co-op, I'll do a menial job. I won't go back to teaching. Maybe I'll be a cleaning lady."

"That would be all right," she said. "What do you want? What do you need?"

"I don't know," I said. "I'm confused. I'm not sure where I am going. Here I am thirty and don't know what the fuck I am doing. It's such a mess."

She disagreed and said, "They are fucked up, not you."

"In one world the motives are bad; in the other the motives are good, but the relationships are bad. I'm tired of fighting."

"The battle is one sided," she said. "They're not even aware of it. Most people quit sooner than you."

"The Bear says the Co-op survives by people like me staying. I told the Doctor I couldn't justify what happened to my friends, but she said, 'it happens everywhere, so why not just stay here?'"

"I don't think the Co-op is good for you," she responded.

"It gets too confusing, and I stop thinking."

"Do you feel?"

"No." Then I got quiet and said, "It always ends where I know I need to be loved. That's the most important thing. I can't help it. I need to share. I need to go home to someone to share ideas with."

"That's a good start."

"When I was in Europe with the Empress, I loved it, but I was alone, and it didn't mean as much. Experiences are better when shared with someone." I cried a lot. She rubbed my back. She cried as well.

"I know more now about what I want," she said. "I want to be a poet and then a great lover."

"You are a great lover already," I said.

"I need time to play the field. This Thursday I am meeting with my mother and telling her about my being gay."

"I hope that goes well for you."

"Me, too."

On Monday, Carrington and I went to check out a rental house. We contemplated sharing a space for the winter but then she decided to take a small cabin by herself. It wouldn't be ready for a week, so I invited her to stay at the A-frame. It was terribly small for two people, but I felt we could manage for that short time.

That evening, there was a note that the Lioness had called and left her number. I was in a state of shock. It was not like her to call so soon. We had been together all weekend. Was she just feeling sorry for me because I had said that I needed to be loved?

The next day I told Carrington about the call. "Are you sure of your feelings for her?" she asked.

"Yes, I'm sure," I said without hesitation.

"Well, I was glad to see you Monday morning." I worried as Carrington was staying at my place till Sunday. What did she mean by that statement? What would the Lioness think if I slept with another woman?

I received the following letter from the Lioness:

9/29 Dear D

I miss you terribly and right now . . . Sunday night was so dismal. I feel as if there is an empty hole that you've just left hollow . . .

Dear Sackville, thank you for your tears. Sometimes I think I must not have cried enough. I cannot cry by myself; it feels too much like indulgent self-pity; it feels horrible and dirty. But my tears, when I allow them to come out, they are the truest experience I have of my own feelings . . . and it is precious to me that you also cry with me, it seems to be the meeting of the true self with the true sadness of life . . .

I am strangely but truly so happy that you have opened doors so that I could release some of these things and weep with you. I feel so much closer to you, I feel that we've shared something from the depths of those "under-the bedrock" wells in us. . . .

Hopefully, I will see you this weekend. Love L

Carrington confided that she was suicidal last year. The guy that she had been dating for the past five years just got up and left her. She loved him enough to marry him, even though she was also seeing a woman.

Her stay at the cabin forced me to build a ladder to get to the loft and a compost toilet. I had been using the woods, but with company I decided I needed to be a little more modern. The screened in porch became the perfect place for a toilet. Peet moss eliminated all the smell.

On Wednesday, she brought Molly and Sam out to the A-frame. We had dinner at the Doctor's and took showers. I cooked eggplant with yogurt, and we watched *Playing for Time* with Vanessa Redgrave about Jewish women in the concentration camps who managed to survive by playing in an orchestra. It was a depressing movie, especially since I learned *Madame Butterfly* was Mengele's favorite opera.

When we got back to the A frame, it was comical managing

all the animals. Molly slept on the porch. Sam was in the loft with Carrington, and Narcissus and Goldmund slept on the main floor with me. No privacy at all!

During the night Carrington cried out. I called up to her, "I really like you and feel very close to you." I was hoping that would make her feel better. We started singing. She had a great voice and we sang "Suzanne" (my favorite song) together. She seemed ok after that. We talked and I told Carrington that I had no direction at this point in my life. There was nothing I wanted to do except write a book. Maybe if I quit the paper, I could do it. Just get a menial job, the Lioness didn't care.

Could I really write about people who were still alive?

I called the Lioness the next day as I was really missing her. She was missing me too, and we firmed up plans for my coming to Boston on the weekend. "You're not shacking up with Carrington, are you?" she asked with a hint of jealousy in her voice

I got to Boston late Friday night. The Lioness said she felt like Mary Magdalene and had visions of getting stoned. We talked for a long time, but she was distant and tired, so I went to bed discouraged.

After breakfast, we left for the shore looking for a hotel. We ended up in a Howard Johnson at Horseshoe Beach. I had wanted a small B & B by the ocean but couldn't find one available. We had a Chinese dinner and then went back to the room to dance. I had brought my stereo and records. We made love. In the morning, I understood her distance the night before, when she asked, "did you ever think about why you were gay? My mother thinks I am afraid of men. She thinks you are negative and that you don't like men."

"I don't hate men," I said in defense. "I just don't love them. There is a difference."

"My parents said I have to decide how to approach the gayness matter both publicly and privately and semi-privately. i.e. with grandparents, with friends, with school . . . "

"I don't think you have to make such a decision so soon. That's a lot to decide when you first discover you are gay. Most people keep it private for a long time till they are sure."

"My mother says your situation is different. You live in a small community and have been at it longer. I have to worry about a job."

Economics, I thought, really who cares about the economics? She was upset now.

"Living with someone will not be easy," I said. To which she quickly replied, "I'm not living with you all my life." After that comment, I walked into the bathroom to brush my teeth. She followed me in and kissed me forcing her tongue in my mouth. That wasn't fair. What did she want from me anyway?

We left for breakfast and I asked, "How are you?"

"Awful," she said.

"I'm ok."

"How can you be?" she said and started crying. We went to the beach. She cried out about the world situation and that she thought the end was near. I realized that she was projecting her own fears about the end of childhood and entrance into adulthood. Her safe reality was coming to an end.

"You won't be able to sleep at the dorm anymore because I have to keep this quiet," she said.

"I may not tolerate that," I responded.

Later in the room, she confessed she was insecure about her feelings toward me. "I want to be in a relationship. That makes me feel good and confident."

"That's good," I commented. "Do you still want to see me?"

"Yes. Even if it's for a purely selfish reason. I don't want to not feel good again about myself. I like that you want to hold me and that you love me." She started to cry and asked, "How can you stand hearing that?"

"It's honest."

"I can't stay with you tonight because I have to meet with my father to talk about my gayness."

"Do you want me to come back after your discussion with him?"

"No."

"What about next weekend?"

"I'm going to the Cape."

"Okay."

We checked out of the hotel. I wouldn't let her pay and that upset her. She hated being economically dependent on me. She started acting like a child.

"I'm glad you are older and know what you want. At least I don't have to deal with your instability, only mine," she voiced sarcastically.

I drove her back to Cambridge and got so lost coming out of the city. Circling three times, I followed 28S to a dead end and into a tough section. I was so spaced. To find my way to the turnpike, I had to go back to Boston.

I spent the night at a beach house in Cohasset. It was owned by the Doctor's order, and she offered the Lioness and me a room for the night . . . *Lioness, I thought, you're such a turkey. You could be here now with me, sitting by the fireplace, listening to classical music in this*

*huge mansion. But instead, you are with your Dad talking analytically
about your gayness. You're missing out on such splendor. I miss you.
I know you like my kisses, and my touching drives you wild. But what
will happen to our relationship now? Will you let the fringes destroy
the inner beauty?*

I was quiet the next day. My emotions were so confused. I listened
to Chris Williamson instead of mingling with the other people in the
house.

I read about the Lioness's sign in *Medicine Wheel*. It fit her to a
tee. Budding Trees Moon (Red Hawk)- their color is yellow; fire opal
is their mineral; dandelion, their plant; red hawk, their animal; They
like sun and warmth. They like to be in active situations which utilize
their intense mental, physical, and emotional energy. Like their stone,
they are porous, and their spirits can be easily stained . . . They are
usually willing to listen to new ideas or philosophies, and sometimes
they accept things that later prove harmful for them . . . in wrong
situations or under too much strain, they can fracture.

Red hawk people are often the symbol of hope for any struggling
new idea. Their connection to the moon, or their emotions, is more
difficult for them to deal with, but very essential if they are going to be
successful in learning to use their own energies well. They move fast.
They favor things that appear clear and fear the complexities of their
own and other people's emotions. . . .

When I returned home, I visited the Cowardly Lion and he looked
healthier and happier.

Carrington encouraged me to spend the rest of the week at her
cabin. "You need a break from the woods especially after your
experience with the Lioness," she said emphatically. I decided she
was right.

In the morning, while she made breakfast, I sat on the couch
playing with Sam and Molly. "I've lost Sam and Molly to you," she
said. "They like having you around."

"Whaat?" I said in a spaced-out voice, as I was lost in my thoughts
about the Lioness's meeting with her Dad.

"Listen, go call her," she ordered. "I know you're worried about
what happened. I'll clean up. Take Molly with you." So off I went to
the Co-op to call. The Lioness answered the phone.

"So how did it go?" I asked.

"Well," she said, not thrilled to hear my voice. "We had a good
talk. He warned me about closing options i.e. with men. That people
would only see me as gay. I understand what he means."

I didn't respond.

"He's only trying to be helpful," she continued. "He's thinking about my future. He said there were three issues to think about: career, gayness and us."

My silence continued. I knew what he thought about us, and it wasn't good. I attempted at some small talk, but it was difficult. She was distant. I was distant. When we hung up, I thought about words of Adrienne Rich, "It is the lesbian in us who is creative, for the dutiful daughter of the fathers in us is only a hack.

I knew this was a fight I could not win. Nor did I intend to. She would do what she wanted, or should I say, what he wanted. The more I thought about it, the madder I got at the Lioness for not standing for anything. This whole thing about not cutting off her relationships with men made that the higher priority. I didn't need to hear that. Love was not to be experienced in a vacuum. Neither was sexuality. I loved the Lioness and that made me gay- not the other way around.

I had a friend do the I-Ching for me and it confirmed my path of inactivity, patience, and waiting for obstacles to be removed.

The next day at the co-op proved frustrating. The grant was not approved. The governmental agency tore it apart. It didn't help that we had so much trouble getting local support. The Empress tried to alleviate my disappointment. "Don't worry about it. This happens all the time. Trying to do things for the poor is not easy," she reassured.

When I got to Carrington's that night a young man was there. They both had been drinking. I felt like the third wheel. They were drinking the bottle of wine I had left for her in the morning with a note suggesting we share it at dinner. She obviously had a better offer and I certainly knew how good it felt to be in his shoes. When I was with the Lioness and one of her male friends, it made me happy to know that I, rather than he, would be the one sleeping with her . . . I remembered back to high school experience. I was on the yearbook executive staff and we were attending a meeting in New York. There were five of us at the same hotel. Merai and I shared one room, and the guys were in the adjoining room with the chaperone. Merai was a beautiful, tall, thin girl with an unforgettable singing voice. She was the lead singer in all the high school plays, and I had a crush on her. No one knew I was gay and even I didn't think it was possible, so I dated boys. Anyway, it was late at night, and Rob, one of the guys, snuck into our room. He couldn't stand the chaperone anymore so he decided he would sleep with us. He got into one twin, and we got into the other. I loved being next to her but kept myself turned away from her. Rob whispered to her from the other bed and she went into his bed. I was destroyed. Such pain. I wanted her just as much as he did. Merai was a lot smarter than him. He wasn't in her social group of friends. I was . . .

I couldn't stand the situation with Carrington and her beau, so I went to bed.

The next day I sat by the lake thinking about the Lioness. It was hard for me to do anything else. When I left that weekend, she had said she would be in touch by letter. When it finally came, she told me how she had spent the weekend at the Cape, and it rained the whole time. In jest, Carrington asked, "Did you wish it on the Lioness?"

"No," I said, but secretly I was glad. In the morning, I woke up calling her a fucker.

Carrington told me to read *Women in Love*, a sensuous store about two men in love. She explained that one man tries to save the other man who is being destroyed by his woman; she's too intelligent for him and he can't keep up with her. I assumed there was some deep meaning for me.

Carrington got bad news in a letter from her mom. Her mom needed another operation. She got so upset and decided she had to leave. "Just when I was settling in. Well, now you can rent the cabin at least it has electricity." I agreed. It would give me time to write in a comfortable place alone. "If all goes well, I'll return in January," she added, and asked if Sam could stay with me.

We went to a prayer meeting and supper with the community that night and sang songs like old times. When we got up to leave, Bear said, "Stay and sing 'Irene.'"

"No," I replied. "We have to go. Carrington has to call her mother." The Empress turned to the Bear and said, "You can do it, Bear." All the while, the Hierophant's attention was consumed with a nun visiting from her order. The new nun thanked me for playing. Then one of the guys carried my guitar to the car.

"People are reaching out to you," said Carrington in the car.

"I don't want it," I said.

"Did you want the Empress to love you?" she asked.

"Yes," I said, and it was a painful admission.

"You're acting out of pain now," she said. "I want to come back and figure the Empress out."

"That was my goal. Good luck!"

Carrington asked me to read her some of Adrienne Rich's poetry, which I did, and she fell asleep. She cried out a few times in the middle of the night.

The next night we stopped at the Doctor's who invited us to stay and eat. Carrington demanded that we leave. She screamed at me in the car, "I don't like to impose." I just laughed. I understood her Italian temper, and knew it was masking her real concerns.

"What's really bothering you?" I asked.

"It's difficult for me to go home because my father is abusive, "she confessed. "He almost choked me last year. My mother always intervenes."

"You won't stay with him now that your mother is in the hospital? Will you?" I asked.

"No. I'll find another place," she said as she sat in the chair smoking her pipe.

Carrington spend Sunday afternoon at Mandala and told me that Bandit, the cat had returned, but had lost an eye and broken his leg. After a discussion about how Argus, the Empress's dog, had a mean side, she said, "Molly would never turn on you. I'm leaving most of my things," she said, "and I will return to save you from yourself."

On Monday, October 13, Carrington jumped up and ran out to the car. I followed her and we shook hands. She had been a hard character to understand. Sometimes so caring and other times so distant.

I sat in the car listening to opera when she was gone. I read from the book, *Last Unicorn* by Peter Beagle that unicorns live alone. They have a pleasant smell and are immortal but are also vain. Nothing happens to a unicorn that doesn't happen to their person. They are not meant to make choices, and though they are the wildest of beasts, they sleep sound. It reminded me of the Lioness.

That afternoon, one of my friends, Sandy, came and said she was following her intuition and felt that I would be upset when Carrington left. I told her how difficult the departure was. She said, "I thought Carrington would be a hard person to live with."

Although I was leery about calling, I talked with the Lioness later that day. She was glad I phoned. "I'm sorry I missed your call the other day," she said. "The Cape was not all I expected it to be. I'm tired of not having a home base. I hate going back to the dorm."

She told me she was spending a lot of time with her parents talking about her gayness. They were still trying to figure out the "method of approach". I laughed. Even she could laugh about it at this point. "My mother told my father that she was a good mother. That made me feel good. My father makes my mother feel bad at times. I'm glad my mother knows in her heart she is a good mother." I detected a bit of guilt in her voice. At the end of the conversation, she surprised me by saying she had decided to come up for the weekend.

I called my mother. She said she was thinking of me. I told her that I had moved. That made her day. I told her how the Lioness was coming up to visit.

"That's good because I hate to think about you being alone in the woods," she replied. It felt good to be open with her about the Lioness.

I broke the goddamn chain again! I just put my hand on my neck, and it caught the chain and it broke. Third time!

I saw Bandit at Mandala. He didn't look so bad. I was going to take him to my place, but I couldn't find him when it was time to leave. I spoke with the Lioness and realized I was at the bottom of her priorities now. She was arriving late on Friday. I shared the plans for the weekend which included a visit to a woman's community.

"A real lesbian weekend," she said sarcastically. I got mad, maybe hurt, at her response.

"You're between two very different philosophies. You have to decide which one is more important to you," I said.

It was getting hard to please her. Was she was coming up here to balance the fact that she was spending so much time with her parents? She didn't write all week. I wasn't sure I could handle the change. Two weeks of not seeing her was too much for me.

The Lioness had said, "You should keep calling me names." Did she want me to get so disgusted with her that I would stop loving her? I tried the same tactic with Sarah.

The ending pages of my notebook were filled with major doodling in red, black, green, and blue ink, all around the Lioness's address and directions to her parent's house. I listed the things that the Lioness liked: unicorns, Pierre Della Francesca, della Robbia, malamutes, Labradors, Constant Comment tea, Indian things, lion, Silver Maiden, blue and red coral, turquoise, and mother of pearl. On the final page I taped the "FPG loves VSW (but you need clean sheets)" note.

\* \* \*

"We know what you want," the Lioness had said to me. The words hurt as I reflected about the past weekend visit. Maybe I deserved it. I had been obnoxious.

When I picked the Lioness up at the station late Friday afternoon, she had on a red hat and at first, I didn't even recognize her. We hugged and then went to see my friends, Beth and Teresa.

During cocktails, the topic of being gay came up.

"I love the words lesbian and dike," said Beth. "They are so graphic like the N word. It grabs you by the horns."

"I was gay since I was five," declared Teresa.

"Really?" questioned the Lioness. "What about you, Beth?"

"I didn't know I was gay," stated Beth. "I still wouldn't know if you didn't tell me," she said as she hugged Teresa.

"I can't believe you. You jerk." Laughed Teresa. "Why do you think you were always calling me right after you'd drop me off from baseball practice? And coming over my house every day. And carrying my books. And . . . "

"OKAY! OKAY! Let's not get carried away. I just didn't know!"

"How could you not know?" I exclaimed in disbelief. "I knew from high school, but I didn't think I could act upon it."

"I understand what she's saying," said the Lioness. "I didn't know either."

"You know now," I said kissing her ear. She rolled her head and threw her hair back." Boy, do you know now," I said as I melted into her smell. She gave that devilish laugh and kissed me hard on the mouth.

"Time to go eat," I exclaimed.

"Eat what?" said Beth, evoking laughter.

Obviously, the Lioness enjoyed being with them. We made love that night and again in the morning and both times, she was the aggressor. I knew she loved me, but then again, maybe she was still trying me on for size.

We were supposed to have breakfast at the Doctor's, but the sex was so hot that we couldn't tear ourselves apart and ended up being an hour late. Instead, we had brunch!

Later we went to a women's community in East Blue Hills. It was a great place! The women had built their own houses. It was raining outside, drenching us, but we visited each one. I was hoping the place would have a favorable impression on the Lioness. I wanted her to see that women could live together in a meaningful way.

After dinner, the Lioness was tired, so we just went home. She fell asleep. I woke her up in the middle of the night with kisses. I went down on her. She got firm but couldn't come. "I'm too relaxed," she said as an excuse. We fell asleep in each other's arms.

I got up first and made coffee. When she awoke, she offered to help me wash my hair at the basin and nearly burnt my head. There was no running water in the cabin, so we had to heat water on the wood stove for washing. She let the water get too hot. In her detached, childish, arrogant, analytical mood, she paid no attention to what she was doing.

"I may give in and be co-opted," she said. "I think I want to have a family. I want people of all ages around me. I don't want to be only with women."

"Do you want to do this with a man?" I asked in a state of shock.

"That is possible," she replied.

"I would be happy for you, but I couldn't stand to watch it. I would be too jealous.

Her announcement put me in a weird mood. I jumped up on the bed, got silly and started bossing her around, trying to break through the heavy cloud between us. Her childlike attitude made me strong and domineering.

As she lay there curled up, soft and laughing, I looked at her, and the feeling of desire surfaced strong.

"We know what you want," said the Lioness said as she locked her legs.

Frustrated, I got up and walked outside to go to the outhouse. Yes, it was obvious what I wanted. I couldn't help it. It was cultural. I was Italian and a lover. I returned and said, "OK, let's get dressed and go to Pearl's for lunch.

I drove her back to the bus station. We were early so we sat in the restaurant waiting for the bus.

"I think you should leave the Co-op," she advised.

"I can't just yet. I want to finish out my VISTA grant. I don't want to leave the Co-op like I left Catholic High. I want to be able to come back here. I want to feel I could walk in the front door. She nodded in understanding. Then she got teary eyed.

"I wish I could leave knowing that I loved you," she cried to me. "I feel like I'm leaving you the wrong way."

"What would be the right way?" I asked. She grasped my hand but couldn't respond. I spoke for her, "It's not something one intellectualizes about. Love is either there, or it's not." I said the words with such strength that I amazed myself. She cried the whole time she was boarding the bus. I didn't cry until she was out of sight. I didn't want to lay that trip on her. I went home and began writing.

I noticed the two roses in the vase on my reading table. The red rose was in full bloom. It was strong, beautiful, open, looking upward with some of its petal turned down. It was proud but grounded. The pink rose (which Sammy munched on in the morning) was stained, opal color and looking downward, sad and shriveled.

The weekend together was full of ups and downs, which depressed my mood. I called her on Tuesday to ask if she wanted to go to New York with the Doctor and me to see an opera during the weekend of

November 15th. In a shy voice, as if she anticipated flack, she told me her sister was coming for the weekend.

"That's ok," I said. "You need to spend time with her." Then we chatted for a while about frivolous issues. Then she dropped a bomb. She had a dream about Lisa, and in it, Lisa had asked her to call or write. That was too much for me to handle. Always afraid that the Lioness would get involved with Lisa, I couldn't hide my jealousy and so I ended the conversation.

When Sandy saw me the next day, she said I looked pale and that I had lost weight. I immersed myself in work and spent all day on the catalogue, then I went home feeling tired and shaky. It was a full moon, and I sat on the porch listening to the "Moon Light Sonata." At bedtime, I grabbed *Delta of Venus* by Nin and read all of the parts where women made love to women, fantasizing all the time about the Lioness, her sweetness, her soft thin body, her eyes of blue green.

The next morning, I realized I had locked my keys in the car. I walked and found the Bear. She had a tool to open the door. Argus jumped in the truck with us. I called him to my side, but he hesitated and went to Bear.

"Well, that's a better way to go, Argus," I said.

Nothing was going right. I went to see a movie entitled *How I won the war*. It was so awful that I walked out. I was missing the Lioness badly, but I couldn't do anything about it. I hoped she'd get over her insecurity. She was certainly worth the wait. I decided to act lovingly. I could act no other way.

Things materialized when I needed them. I found a pair of black pants and shirt in the free clothes bag at the Co-op that I could wear to the opera.

In the afternoon, I helped the Empress build a porch entrance to a trailer owned by an elderly woman. The Empress went on with her usual pet peeve about professional people buying up property and displacing the poor. At least she agreed with me that buying houses for low-income people was not going to solve the problem. They had to be able to afford them.

The Empress put down the cinder blocks in front of the trailer.

"Don't you think we should even off the ground first?" I asked.

"No, we'll just build on top of the blocks," she responded. Her methods didn't seem logical to me, but she was the boss. We both laughed as we watched one of the guys trying to get the base platform off the truck. The truck tilted and almost fell over! We had to call for help. It took ten people to place it on the blocks, and the elderly woman sat and bossed everyone around. I wondered how we ever accomplished anything.

It was a weird day and a weirder night—stormy, rainy and windy. The door to my cabin was open when I got home. I just went to bed.

Beth and Teresa came to visit. They were so theatrical. Everything to them was repressed lesbianism, which they felt was the natural way.

"The Lioness is too analytical," said Teresa. "She questions too much."

"It's obvious she is emotionally drawn to you," added Beth. "She's just not ready to accept her gayness."

"It may take a while," said Teresa. "Remember how you pulled back at one point in our relationship, Beth?

"Yeah, then one month later, things happened," she said looking lovingly at Teresa. They both laughed.

"I'm giving the Lioness till December," I declared.

"That's the spirit. Women need to support each other and never mind about trying to explain to men or the rest of the world," responded Beth. "We'll be here for you."

I couldn't sleep. God damn it. I was supposed to go with the others to see the Empress's mother who was in the hospital. I decided not to. Instead, I took Tweedledee for a sandwich. On the way back, we stopped at my cabin. She loved the cats and gave them the left-over beef from her sandwich. After bringing her home, I got out a picture of the Lioness and kissed it passionately while "Send in the Clowns" played on the stereo. Then I went to bed.

In the middle of the night, I awoke. My head was off. The only thing that brought me back was making love. Kind of hard to do alone in the woods.

> *. . . I wanted her here now. I wanted her to rub her body on mine. I wanted her to pull my hair. I wanted her kisses. I wanted to look deep into those blue eyes. I wanted to entangle our bodies, to straddle her and open my cunt on her backside, . . . moisture running between us . . . her arms outstretched on the pillow, her hair softly strung out on the pillow . . . I wanted to hear her cat purring . . . the movement of our bodies, rocking, capturing each other's rhythm . . . turning her over . . . kissing her . . . fingers in each other's hair . . . rubbing between our legs . . . hot, moist, . . . fingers sliding in, up, up as far as they will go, touching soft spots, touching hard spots further in, way up . . . lost in the overpowering sensations . . . feeling*

*it come out of your mouth... tongues touching,*
*licking, teasing, circling... breathing heavy, tension*
*mounting... riding the waves... reaching the crest and*
*falling back down... back into each other's arms... soft*
*skin upon soft skin, eyes closing, breath slowing down,*
*sleep, sleep, sleep... drained... heavy sleep...*

All the cats were finally back with me. They were mature now and didn't claw the way they used to. Bandit had joined Sam, Nar and Goldmund. So far so good. No fights. Everyone sat in respective corners cleaning themselves.

"We are family. I have all my cats with me," I sang as I cleaned.

Sandy came over. She was upset about leaving and, more so, that she and her lover were fighting. She cried, and I didn't know what to do for her. Trying to lighten the mood, I said, "Sandy, I so gonzo last night that I ended up writing pornography." That cracked her up! She left in better spirits.

The next song Christopher Cross did was one about breaking up. How appropriate!

Someone left bags of live chickens outside the Co-op office door. So cruel! The group went to lunch but didn't ask me, so I did laundry and shopping, stopping home afterwards. Bandit greeted me at the door and as I pet him, I felt his many scars. He was limping from a bad leg and his eye was swollen. I wasn't sure he could see out of it. Thankfully, he had given up his wandering nature. He loved my affection, seeking it time and time again. But he still had bad habits. Often, he would jump on the table, knocking things over. Narcissus was jealous of him and I had to put Bandit outside when Narcissus wanted his share of my affection.

I listened to Leontyne Price while the cats relaxed. Goldmund and Narcissus sat with me and Sam was on the bed. A cute fellow, he kept his distance. Well mannered, he didn't run after food like the others. This was one of my favorite times being alone with the cats while enjoying my opera. Sandy believed that women were bringing back the Renaissance. I will miss her dearly to use a Lioness word.

"A woman should be living with cats," she had said. So here I am with four of them. The number of the self.

The paper seemed to be coming along even though I had no ambition to work. My spirit was dampened. I dozed and had a dream that a girl from the restaurant was making love to the Lioness. It was so vivid. I got up and rushed to the Co-op to find that I had missed a phone call from the Lioness. I called her back. She answered, and I sensed a hint of her missing me in her voice.

"Dorothy, how are you? Good to hear your voice."

"Good to hear yours," I said.

"The Cowardly Lion called me," she continued. "He wants to return to the community. Things are bad for him. I told my father and asked him to help. He made me feel stupid for asking. He said, 'these things take time and I have a lot to do.'"

"Don't feel bad," I said, sensing her depression. "Patriarchy." It angered me that his opinion meant so much to her.

"I'm applying for a summer teaching job in my hometown," she said.

I thought what a good way for her parents to kept her under control.

"I talked to my father about it and told him I wasn't sure I wanted to do it. Maybe it's too much for me. He got upset that I didn't want to do it."

"I'm not surprised," I said.

"Then I got upset," she said.

"You sound down," she asked.

"I'm ok."

I felt worse after the phone call even though she told me she planned possibly to come up the next weekend. I cried myself to sleep that night.

At night, my ideas always surfaced for the book. While writing, I thought about Bear's advice that I would have to leave the Co-op to find out who I was. What was that supposed to mean? I decided to leave the Co-op in the summer. That would give me time to train the next editor.

Sandy and I had breakfast on her last day. I gave her the book, *Dream of a Common_Language*, we talked, and I told her about the phone conversation.

"The Lioness is a mixed-up child," she said. "You can see the confusion in her face. She is always thinking."

The next letter from the Lioness didn't make me any happier. The letter had no greeting. It just read:

It has been sort of a weird weekend, though basically good. Saw a lot of people, mostly men friends whom I'd like to know better . . . I was thinking of the Cowardly lion. He called me, hoping to catch a ride back to Maine. He couldn't really talk on the phone . . .

Cleaned up my room today (!) and found something you must have left accidently, a note from the Bear reading "D, I have a piece of refrigerator backing about 2.5 × 3 that might cover that lady's cesspool . . . " I'm keeping it, it's too good, too perfect. I think of you at points and wonder what you're up to. Hey, I didn't mean to shit on your putting my poems in the paper. I mean, it's really flattering, . . . the encouragement, support, and criticism you've given me about my writing . . . I'm sorry I was so pissy about it. I think also of that cute little house, Sam, the Egyptian, the cats . . . I think you've got it all straight, about spending time alone . . .

I went to the campus gay dance with Carrie. It felt good to be in a gay environment, being able to express my sexual preference . . . I love women, I love their bodies, our bodies, I like to think of kissing women, caressing them, knowing their beauty . . .

Carrie and I danced, I felt good because I felt like she was getting something she'd been wanting for a long time- to dance openly with a woman she was attracted to . . . she said I could spend the night in her waterbed . . . I said that I'd sleep sounder in my own bed. . . . I just didn't know how hot or cold she was that night, how "turned on," and how much tension there would've been between us because of what she might have wanted, even if she didn't ask me for it. . . . .

. . . Write when you've got a chance and say what you're up to. I'm really looking forward to our trip to NY. I think about you. Love, L

PS Your green jacket is a great comfort, I wear it constantly and it has become warm and comfortable like an old friend.

Three pages were written on both sides and at the very last line she said, "I think about you." That was it regarding our relationship. I couldn't do any work for the rest of the day.

During the week, the Lioness and I postmarked cards on the same day. The one I sent pictured a childlike woman with blonde braided hair wrapped in a shawl standing in a field. Her back faced the front, and her head was turned to the side allowing only part of her face to be seen. The one she sent was a deer's face clutching a rose in its mouth.

I felt anger last night upon rereading the letter of the Lioness, and I was glad I was alone. She shouldn't have played games as she did with Carrie. Going back to her room. "Not knowing how hot or cold." Carrie probably wanted her. It was mean only going part way. She should have remembered how she felt with the Indian woman. Why didn't she stay?

I tried to call the Lioness over the weekend, but her roommate said she was sleeping. I returned home to Connecticut to visit family. Talking about politics, war, and social security with my uncles at Sunday dinner gave me a headache so I went over my sister's to sleep. She was on a date, and when she came back, we talked about old times and present relationships. I really loved my sister. Having fun was important to us both. Could the Lioness and I still have fun together? Maybe she could come up next weekend, and we could just enjoy each other and forget all the crap. Maybe if we didn't discuss family, men, or love.

Invited for breakfast at the Wolf's, I walked into WWIII. While they took their fighting into the bedroom, I made coffee and waited in the kitchen. When Wolf finally came out, she wasn't in a talking mood. Her only comment was, "I get irrationally jealous when she talks to other women on the phone."

"Do you want to discuss it?" I asked.

I'm too mad to discuss it," she responded. I left soon after.

Just my luck, I missed the Lioness on my way back to Maine Sunday night. I tried to surprise her at school, but I took the wrong exit and got lost. I called from a Howard Johnson, but her roommate told me that she had just left. When I got back to the Co-op, there was a message from the Doctor. The opera plans were a bust. The Met wouldn't open till the end of month, and the Doctor couldn't make it that weekend. She suggested we still got to NY and stay at the convent.

I cried myself to sleep. Tears came easily. A conversation with the Lioness was strained. I felt like I had to hold back now. She had decided she would go to the Cape with a friend for the weekend. I thought she was coming to visit me. I tried to act like there was nothing wrong. She sensed disappointment in my voice. I sent her a long letter, but I didn't feel comfortable sharing any feelings with her.

Back at the cabin, with Narc on my lap, I listened to Maria Callas. Bandit had disappeared all weekend according to my kitty sitter, but he came home when he heard the music. Sammy jumped up on my lap for affection and Goldmund was nowhere to be found.

That night I dreamt about having a baby. Well, I had nine months till the VISTA grant would run out. Was the book my baby? I wrote a poem in the middle of the night about the Lioness and called it

Amazon Woman ... *those magical mysterious blue eyes ... the sea beams out from them ... they were blue ... they were green ...*

A funny thing happened during the middle of the night. Bandit cried to go out, so I got up and let him out. In the morning when I woke up, he was back inside! I didn't know how he got in.

On the national scene, Reagan won the election. What would the next four years be like? Carter lost very badly, but his outgoing speech was brave. Hansel, who was distraught over the republicans winning, tried to make light of the situation by cracking jokes. He wanted us all to move to Canada. Every time I saw him, he would be singing, "Bomb, bomb, bomb Iran ..."

\* \* \*

Dreams were very important to me. Carlos, from the educational center, was someone with whom I could discuss such ideas. I took his class on charting sun signs.

"People only dream on an individual level," he said.

"I disagree," I said. "Women are more aware of the subconscious level and many of their dreams are about the world situation."

"If that were true, it would be a big change in the theory of dreaming."

"Our dreams reflect the collective level," I continued. "Maybe because women are coming into their own, they are more in touch with the collective unconscious. Helen Caldicott is a good example. Here is a woman who gave up her career to talk against nuclear energy. She's asking women to stop having babies till all the craziness is stopped. What will happen now with Reagan?"

"God only knows," he responded.

The next day, I had to bring my car to the garage for repair. The sky was overcast. I started walking back to the Co-op and realized that I must be quite a sight with my big red nap-sack, white scarf, green jacket, and black hat. Sort of like an overloaded munchkin! As I started singing," Make me a channel of your peace," the sun broke overhead, and I felt so wonderful and peaceful. I got my bike out of my office and rode down the hill. What a good feeling riding with the wind in my face and tears in my eyes. I wrote the Lioness a more stable letter that night about my feelings.

It was dawn and the light beamed through the window of the cottage. The prism dangling from the wood beam cast a circle of colored flames. Goldmund lay on the pillow in the center of the circle, and Narcissus lay beside me. We were on the small twin bed nestled in the corner covered by a quilt with big flowers ... I drifted ...

I thought about Mary, the cleaning woman at St. Francis, who was in the hospital dying. I went to visit but couldn't bring myself to go in the room. Her breathing was so heavy. I looked at her through the window . . . " *Dorothy, here's the key to the old locker in the teachers' room. Go empty out my books after school,"* she had said to me on the day she was leaving for surgery. "Why don't we go get them now?" I asked. "No. I can't. I'm not supposed to be in that room."

In the locker, I found a carton of cigarettes and a pile of dirty books! Now here she was a tough, thick-skinned woman who swore and laughed despite the hard knocks dealt to her by life, lying helplessly on the bed. . . . tubes coming out of her mouth. I had to leave. I felt badly that I never went in to hold her hand. I cried. Then I relived the meeting the day after the big meeting with the Board of Trustees of the school, the Administration, and the parents. The bosses had said that the school would remain closed. That day I just sat in the big chair and sobbed. Doris's words came back to me," You still hoped something would happen? Didn't you?" The pain was so deep that all I could do was lower my head and sob even more . . .

Goldmund strolled over and licked Narcissus's face. Narcissus pulled her down on top of him, and they started kitty fighting while "La Divina" played in the background.

I sensed that Carrington was back. I stripped the bed and washed the sheets. I meant to call her but decided against it since I didn't want to ruin the surprise. One of the local teenagers had asked me to join her for dinner. She was a typical Mainer, fidgety, overweight yet exuding self-consciousness. We didn't have a lot in common to talk about, but I liked her. I wondered how she would feel if she knew I was gay. She came back to my cabin for tea. We were sitting and resting when she said, "I hear a car door." Sure enough, it was Carrington. We hugged. She was her usual wound up self. She had to unpack right away. After coffee and Amaretto, we went to the Co-op so she could call her parents. That night we talked. The last few weeks had been hard for her.

"My mom won't tell my dad that she is in pain. He's tired of seeing her sick and she doesn't want to add to his aggravation. I'm so disgusted with him." She admitted that she hated him.

She called a friend to see if she could stay with her, but the friend was studying so she decided to remain with me. I told her about the Lioness. At one point, Goldmund jumped on the chair that Sam was sleeping on and lay right on top of him.

"My mother needs another surgery," she confided, and I could see the news was tearing her apart. "I'll hang around till May, then go back home to one of my lovers."

Later that night, I talked with the Lioness. She cancelled her trip to the Cape because she couldn't afford it. I offered to pay for her to come to Maine, but she said she was going to see her cousin who was going through some bad times.

In the morning, Carrington was still visibly upset. I went to shower at the Co-op and remembered that it was her birthday. I drove all the way back to wish her a happy day. She was appreciative.

Later in the day, I saw the Empress. She didn't look healthy— stumbling around, a pale color to her skin and down a few pounds. I asked, "You don't feel well, do you?" She smiled and responded, "Fair to middling."

"You liar," I said knowing she would never admit to being weak. Using that low, quiet, "we need help voice," she asked me to come work at Mandala on Sunday. I told her I would try but couldn't promise.

As I lay on the bed that night, my thoughts centered around the Empress. Narcissus jumped down on the floor a little distance from Bandit or Blackie, as Carrington had nicknamed him, who was sensuously spread out. Little by little, stretch by stretch, Narc got over to where Bandit was. Their paws touched. It was a sight of wonder. Two beautiful cats. Meanwhile, Goldmund sat on my head the whole time.

The following day, I received a letter from the Lioness:

Dear D

I received your letter today and wanted to tell you that though I can't do justice to a full reply now, I appreciate the letter very much.

Please do not be sorry, or at least, do not be sorry for being sorry.

It's not a crappy letter. I know you are writing from the heart. I hope I did not hurt you too much by my last letter. Your letter helps me to ask questions and understand myself and you . . .

Please do not expect too much from yourself, trying to understand, trying to "see" more. You are trying to see a lot, for you, for me. You are helping me to see.

Please do not be sorry that "mercy does get strained." Remember what Adrienne Rich says about gentleness, when mercy is no longer a shielding but discovery, though sometimes painful:

Thank you for your honesty
love, L

That night Carrington and I went to dinner. I bought her yellow roses and candy for her thirtieth birthday. On the way home, we stopped to see Gretel's kiln. The fire burned brightly through the bricks.

Carrington said she had to make a decision. "What is that?" I asked.

"No, no decisions tonight," she replied. I wondered what she meant.

It rained on Saturday. Carrington was not in a good mood. I asked if she would answer a question honestly.

"I might," she said.

"Would you rather I get my own place so you can be here alone?" I asked sensing my presence bothered her.

"Fine. Where?" she quickly replied.

"I could probably get a room at the Jed Prouty's."

"That's a bad idea," she replied. "I just need time to get used to living with someone else. I'm still tired from the trip."

"That's not the point. You shouldn't have to get used to it. You need to be aware of your needs. I will be fine no matter where I live." Company came, thought, so we never resolved the issue.

I spent the entire day on Sunday working on my writing as Carrington read. She was back to treating me badly.

I decided to drive to Boston on Tuesday afternoon and surprise the Lioness. It was to be a visit from the "French Embassy." I tried to call her but couldn't get through. In the morning, I saw Carrington who had a black eye from walking into a car door. Still not in a good mood, she lit into me for not having the chain saw. I went back to get it for her. As we worked together, I felt like I had to walk on eggs, trying not to upset her. Finally, I told her how I was feeling.

"I'm not allowed my moods?" she replied.

"Do you treat the others like this?" I asked.

"Let's drop it," she said. I left and went to Hansel and Gretel's. I confessed my situation with Carrington and how she was trying to drive me out of the cottage. They suggested that I move in with them.

That night Carrington was in a better mood. In fact, she acted motherly toward me when I told her I felt like I was coming down with a cold. She must have felt sorry for me. While in our respective beds, she said, "One of the women asked if we were lovers."

"Guilt by association," I responded.

From the time I moved into the cottage, the cats and I had established a routine. I was the pied piper. The cats would hang around my bed waiting to be fed. Then they would follow me into the kitchen, meowing in unison before eating. All the time, Molly waited patiently for me at the door to do a run. This morning was the first morning Molly did not come to the door.

When I returned, Carrington got up and started yelling, "Did you close the door on purpose so Molly couldn't get out? All the banging she made trying to get out woke me up." I couldn't believe Carrington woke up complaining about me.

"No," I said. "I closed it so you couldn't hear me outside."

I gathered my things and rushed to the Co-op. I left a message at the dorm telling the Lioness I would be there late in the afternoon. My intuition had been sharp lately. When the Lioness returned to her room, I was standing on the inside of the doorway dressed in the costume of a French lieutenant. Black mustache, green jacket, and black beret! I couldn't wait to surprise her. But she didn't find humor in my get-up instead she just hugged me long and tight.

"What's wrong?" I asked sensing something was amiss.

"My grandfather died today at 2:00 pm. I was going to go home, as I have to go to the Cape tomorrow with my family, but I stayed because you were coming. I tried to call you, but you had already left."

"Let me take you home," I responded.

"It's too late now, but tomorrow you could do so." Later, while talking to her mother, I heard her say, "The first thing Dorothy said when she heard about grandfather was that she would take me home." I was glad I had said the right thing. Her grandfather's death was the first important death she had had to deal with. I was glad I was there for her. And she was too after I got the "ashes" off my face!

She looked exhausted. Her grandfather had a heart attack on Friday, and she was depressed all weekend. She almost came to see me. I must have picked up on her vibrations —that's why I felt so strongly about visiting in the middle of the week, not my usual time to visit. That night, we drifted to sleep with our shirts on. A good thing we did because I would have gone crazy sleeping next to her nude body and I knew she wasn't in the mood for sex. She was restless all night. At one point she jolted up and said, "Oh Jesus!" Then she ripped off her shirt. In the morning I couldn't help myself and started rubbing her back. She rubbed mine back. I began kissing her and rubbing between her legs. We made love.

We lay in bed in the morning just holding each other. I told her I wanted to have the same image as the Empress.

"What's that," she asked.

"The mother image," I replied. "I hate the institution image."

She asked how living with Carrington was going and I told her.

"Carrington will not be honest with her feelings," she warned. "The cats are a problem, so many living in one space. You need to move out."

I let the Lioness read what I had written so far on the book. To my surprise, she saw deeper implications to some of the images. That made me feel good.

When I dropped the Lioness off at her parents' house, I wanted to see her mother and express my condolences. Her sister ran up to the car and said, "Mom is in the shower. She said, 'thank you' for bringing the Lioness home." I thought to myself, 'She doesn't want to see me'. The Lioness turned to me and said, "What?" (as if she heard my thoughts). I left without answering.

On the highway, I could still smell her on my hands.

Carrington was in her usual bitchy mood. She accused me of hiding a can of Molly's dog food. "Why would I do that, C?" I replied. She mellowed when she realized she had put it up on the radio where the cat food was stored.

"I thought about it, and I think you should move out," she announced.

"I agree," I said.

The rest of the conversation was distant. She kept apologizing for not having thought about it long enough before asking me to move in. I left. I didn't feel comfortable staying. I went to Hansel and Gretel's.

Hansel commented on her negative energy and said, "We must be strong, or else we become sponges to the negative energy. If we are strong, it goes back to the sender." That made sense to me.

I went back home, spaced but calm. I lay on the bed. Carrington was in a nicer mood and said, "I acted too quickly. Let's try living together again. I want to learn to share."

"I don't think that's wise. I could understand trying if you didn't want to be alone, but for any other reason it doesn't make sense."

My spirit was starting to break. My mind drifted back the words of the Lioness, "You're like a loyal dog."

"Maybe a loyal cat," I had answered.

"Cats can't be loyal," she responded.

"I think they can. Look at Narcissus and Goldmund."

Then she confided that she felt pressured from both sides.

"I've felt squeezed between the middle for a while now. By the way I can't go to New York with you because I can't get a ride with my aunt.

"It's all right if you don't go," I said knowing this was just an excuse. I would always take her shit and later it would make me feel terrible. I did everything for her, and this is what I had to hear. Next time, I'll tell her to fuck off.

During the week, I went to a psychic. She was an older woman in a wheelchair. Rubbing a piece of my jewelry in her hand, she said, "You're more like your father's side. There is a baby living in heaven giving you courage. You have crossed the ocean and you will do so again. This has to do with your future life, an obligation, 1-1 ½ years maybe. You see things in the future, and that saves you. Go with it. I see you doing therapy, not physical, a psychologist or psychiatrist. Something to do with the mind. Others will be looking in. Keep writing, definitely, don't stop. It's your life work."

When I asked her about the Lioness, she said, "stomach sick, knots, throwing-up, turmoil for one or two more years." I asked if there were negative powers around me to which she replied, "No, things are spiritual. God's plan. Not personal manipulation. You're too strong for that." She continued, "I see a head tumor, someone in the family, dead. Why do I want to jump out of a plane with you? Parachuting? Marriage, later, man with three pensions, definitely married lady; ten years maybe." When I asked if I should leave Maine, she said, "Yes, definitely. You are going abroad. Maybe later you can come back here to retire."

\* \* \*

I went to New York with the Doctor as planned. The Lioness had called the Doctor and from the conversation, the Doctor felt it was wise that she didn't come. I was a little depressed at breakfast, not having her by my side, but I decided to enjoy the moment and started chatting with a nun who worked on an Indian reservation in Arizona. She had worked in Brazil and talked about the extreme poverty. "People literally live in garbage. No self-concept. There are huge multi-corporations with no humanism. Little children pull people around in carts. I saw a black man nearly naked lying in the street, and I will never forget him."

Then Taiwanese nun did a palm reading for me. "Your emotions are deep and strong," she said. "You can do things, but you stop yourself. You're not forceful. Too considerate. You're too serious. Will have one-on-one relationships and connection to groups. Rich. Money comes, but you spend it. Not always that way. Conditions change. You try to be good; it doesn't come naturally. You can have meaning. Your work does not bring money but meaning. Don't worry so much. There is something you want to do but you must think about it first. You must persevere and not give up. Your hands are small, and you want to do something big. You are blocked. It's hard for you to express yourself. Work hard. If you want to do something, you must do it."

That night, we saw the play *Children of a lesser god*. Sign language was a much better way to communicate. It was so emotional. Later, I spent more time with the Taiwanese sisters. They were such happy, wise women. Very affectionate. The Doctor said, "They don't accept the crucified Christ as we do. They go immediately to the risen Christ. They don't get halted on the cross."

We joked about starting a Taiwanese restaurant in Maine to do spiritual work. After I heard that the pot, they use in a Taiwanese restaurant hadn't been cleaned for eighty years to preserve flavor, I said, "Why make them come to Maine, let's go to Taiwan." They all cheered.

The next day, we saw the Viking exhibit at the Met, but I enjoyed people- watching more. One woman reminded me of the Lioness. At the Cloisters housing the unicorn tapestries, I bought the Lioness a poster, a book and a picture of the tapestries. I discovered that the unicorn was a symbol of returning to a previously better life through destruction. The lion was tied up in the destruction. I couldn't get the vision of the Lioness with her blonde mane rustled upon the pillow, her cream-colored skin, and blue eyes out of my thoughts.

When I got back to the cabin in Maine, Carrington was off the wall. She was in an irrational violent state, banging things around, being short with the animals and then talking calm to me. She even kicked Molly. I was leery about being alone with her. Hansel and Gretel came over, and Molly kept growling at them. Unusual behavior for this dog. Gretel said, "Maybe she's picking up on my dislike of dogs." Hansel said, "Maybe it's because of the invasion of her small space." Maybe she was picking up on Carrington's psyche I thought.

After they left, I listened to Maria Callas and wondered what was next.

\* \* \*

My life was so unsettled. I was a woman without a homeland. Contrasted with living in the same apartment with Sarah for seven years, I had now lived in five different places over the last year.

Tuesday, November 18th, brought the first big snowstorm of the season. It was beautiful. White everywhere. I pulled my car out of the driveway and right back in again when I realized how deep the covering was. Instead, I walked to the Co-op.

All along the road, school buses were stuck in the snowbanks. The Hierophant said, "God sent the snow to prevent us from going today to Augusta for the Governor's VISTA meeting!" I thought she was right. The Bear was to receive an award at this meeting despite all the criticism of VISTA expressed by her and the Empress. In one article, the Empress had downed CAP (Client Assistance Program), and it was after the organization had given money to the Hospitality House!

After working on the newspaper, I joined Hansel and Gretel's playing guitar and spent the night. Tired from all the walking, I retired early. The next day I headed back home to dig my car out. Despite shoveling for three hours, I was nowhere near getting it out, so I called some friends to come and help.

Carrington came home with a guy. Hansel and Gretel again invited me to stay with them. As the Lioness was coming for the weekend, and I knew we couldn't stay with Carrington, I decided to take them up on their offer.

I picked up the chain I had broken from the jewelry shop. The jeweler had soldered it but said it was stretched and could break again easily.

While I was there, I asked if he could design a special piece of jewelry. I wanted a silver hawk with an opal in the middle. He said he could and that it would cost about $50.

The Lioness arrived Friday night. We made love till around 2:00 in the morning and then slept on blue satin sheets. In the morning she said that she had come up this weekend with plans to break up with me.

"It's too much for me," she stated.

"I know at this point you are only doing things out of obligation," I said. "I knew last weekend that's why you wanted to come up."

"I have real negative feelings about you," she said.

"Then I agree. It's time for us to be apart," I replied.

"Try not to please me," she said. "It only makes it harder."

I started crying. This upset her, and I could see she was worried about me.

"Don't mind my crying. It's a relief for me," I said. "I do feel weak when I'm crying though."

"I think you're strongest when you are crying," she said in a way that made me feel good about myself.

"I don't think I'm healthy so I'm going to see a counselor," she said. "Everyone knows what they think but me. Someone asked about my work at the jail and how I would change things. I couldn't respond. I never thought about how to make it better." She was obviously upset with herself.

"Maybe you see too many sides. Maybe these questions are not easy to answer. It's ok that you couldn't answer. Answers can sometimes be superficial," I said. We fell asleep totally mentally exhausted.

Hours later, we woke up to the sounds of a chain saw. Neither one of us had much to say. I worked on the paper. She read. After a nap, we went to the sandwich shop for dinner. She didn't want a whole sandwich, so I said I'd eat whatever she left. She loaded the sandwich with mayonnaise and mustard and then ate it all giving herself a stomachache. On the drive home, she kept the window wide open. I was shaking with cold.

She held me like a little kid that night in bed.

"I feel like I make people uncomfortable," I said to her.

"How?" she asked.

"I'm not sure how. Just my person maybe."

"Who?"

"The Empress, the Bear, Carrington, The Wicked Witch of the South."

"They haven't faced things in themselves yet," she replied. "You don't make me feel uncomfortable."

On Sunday morning we tried to make love, but she couldn't come. I didn't want her to leave that way, but she was too exhausted. Jumping in and out of two different worlds was taking its toll.

She told me that she wanted to be "possessed" by her family rather than breaking away from her them. She wanted to stay a child since there was no reason to do otherwise.

Then she tried to make me pee in the bed. I had to go, and she started touching me between my legs. I kidded her, "This is turning you on. Isn't it?"

She laughed and said, "I tried to make love to Carrie. Last week I slept in her bed. I told her I wanted to kiss her."

"How did she respond?" I asked.

"Well, when I touched her, she returned the stroking, and I could see that she was turned on. But something wasn't right. It wasn't the way it's supposed to feel, she said.

"Maybe she isn't right for you."

"Maybe. I'm glad it felt good with you on Friday night. I like you, Dorothy."

"I like you too, Lioness."

"I think we can still be friends," she said softly.

"I'm not going to wear the chain anymore," I said. Then I became pensive and asked, "Do our kisses still mean anything to you?"

"Yes. They make me float."

The she told me how she resented her friends getting too close. "I don't like the obligation friendship carries," she confided.

"Do you want to be known? I asked.

"Yes, some day."

"It's something I want to work toward," I responded. "We keep so much hidden. So many thoughts and ideas that no one ever knows. What makes you happy Lioness?"

"Jerking off," she responded without a second thought.

I cracked up and thought she's right. When it comes right down to it, lovemaking is the only thing that makes me happy, too. Exposing one's core. It takes a lot to give yourself to someone.

"Why do we value a doctor's work more than a cleaning woman's?" I asked her.

"Why do we reward those who are given more to begin with? It's not fair. The change of consciousness must come from those on top. They have the intellect to see, and it's hard to pretend one doesn't notice."

"They've managed so far to turn away," she responded.

"Good point." And then I thought is that why she wants to be possessed by her family? Because what they stand for is valued? What I am, is not. As the High Priestess had once said to me, "The bride didn't have enough money."

I took her back to the station later that morning. We met Carrington on the way.

"How was your weekend," I asked.

"It was bad. Those cats," she said at the point of tears. I ignored her as I had enough of my own problems.

Well, I didn't do what Sarah did to me. I let the Lioness go rather easily. No threats. No pleading. I guess I truly loved her and wanted only her happiness. I did get weak once and said, "I think what we had was special. But you can't have the beauty of the rose if you tear off the petals." We tried to have our usual breakfast at the bagel shop but had to leave before the kippers came out since the bus came in early. I bought cookies and a bagel for her to take along.

"Are you considering leaving early?" she asked as we walked to the station.

"No, I want to learn perseverance."

Her last words to me as she neared the steps to the bus were, "What will you do with your life now?"

I thought 'end it' but said, "Live it." Then I continued, "I'm in a rest period now. The obligation you feel is your own hang up. There is no commitment between us. You are free to do as you please. You can be involved with whomever you want. You're beautiful enough and now you're experienced."

I stood and watched her get on the bus. I felt cold and shocked knowing that I was alive and yet not feeling alive. The warm creative blood had been drained out of me. The Muse had left the Magician. Who would she impregnate next with her power of inspiration?

\* \* \*

All in all, I was happy with the next edition of the paper. It was my baby given I had written about ¼ of it myself. In it I printed one of the Lioness's poems. Although she had said the poem was about hope, I felt it dealt with confusion.

It was hard to accept the fact that she didn't want me. That night I had angry thoughts again. I wanted to become thin again. Maybe this would make her want me. Then I would be mean to her. Why were my thoughts so contrary? I could never be mean to her. I reread the Vita letter, and it made me cry.

Meanwhile Sammy was fighting with Bandit, who was crouching down in the corner. Nar kept his distance.

That night I had a dream that *I was following a woman on a bike. She rode ahead. She turned the corner, and I couldn't see her. I went into a house, but she wasn't there. I rode around another corner and went into a different house. There were people there. I asked about her. She came out on the porch all fancily dressed. We laughed and got ready to go again.*

The jeweler left a message that the necklace was done. I was so excited till I saw it. It was awful! It was a waste of money and cost $57. A lot of money when you are living on a VISTA grant! It didn't look anything like a hawk and the opal was not a fire one like I had asked for. The jeweler kept saying, "It looks real Indian." Right! I just paid for it and left. I had no intention of giving it to the Lioness. I took it as a loss.

It was Thanksgiving weekend, and I went home to Connecticut and spent quiet time at my parents. I had decided not to shave anymore or use deodorant. It reminded me of the Lioness's smell. The first night I had fears that something would happen to her. I got down on the floor and prayed to Jesus and Mary to protect her. I realized that the bad feelings were just my own insecurities. I wondered if I would see her at Christmas.

Upon returning to Maine, I moved into the extra bedroom at Hansel and Gretel's place. Hansel was a gentle soul with an even gentler voice. Tall and thin with wild gray hair, he was a masseuse and a dreamer. Gretel was Jewish, of average height, and always wore a bandanna to cover her long thick dark hair. She was the more practical of the two. Hansel's son, from his previous marriage, lived with them. Little Hansel was about fourteen years old, quite precocious and full of trickery.

The first night I slept there I was awakened at 2:00 am by sounds of chopping wood. On my way to the outhouse, I saw Little Hansel standing out in the thunderstorm with his ax and I thought, 'He's weird and is going to get electrocuted!' I continued toward the shed making enough noise in case anyone was already using it. No one responded. But when I opened the door, there sat Hansel with his head down. He popped his head up and said, "Join the party." He was just as weird as his son.

I fell back to sleep reading Freud's *Interpretation of Dreams* only to be awoken by the light tapping sounds of mice feet running across the kitchen floor. The running feet continued throughout the day, but they were so fast, they appeared liked little gray streak marks.

The next day, health conscious Hansel suggested we fast to purify our systems. We decided to appease him until little Hansel made popcorn. Little Hansel sat on the couch eating each piece like it was manna from heaven. It didn't take long to break us.

"Let's go to the café, "I suggested, and Gretel agreed. As I drove, Hansel and Gretel smooched in the back seat of my car. Little Hansel pigged out on ice cream before supper, ate supper, and then ate two pieces of pie. How he kept so thin was a mystery. Looking around the restaurant, Little Hansel said, "There's all wierdos in here, and we're the worst." I perked up and stopped to buy bananas and milk for breakfast. Couldn't eliminate the eating pleasure for too long!

Every day at their house was a happening. One morning, I went out to warm my car, and when I came back into the house, I saw Little Hansel crouched between the 2' × 4's holding up the wood pile. He was hanging 2' off the ground. It was dark, so I didn't see him till I was right beside him, and he scared me.

"What are you doing?" I shouted.

"Now I know what the wood feels like," he said seriously. "I'm not putting any more choppings between here," he declared.

I added the Lioness's dream to my dream journal. In rereading her dream, I noticed that she had made a point about the Persian boy who was a lover of Alexander the Great. One afternoon, when I was in the bookstore buying a card, I found a book by Mary Renault called *The Persian Boy,* so I bought it.

I felt so depressed and violent, but my exterior remained calm. One morning, I woke up on Beth and Theresa's floor. We had gone to see the *Killing of Sister George,* and I fell asleep during the last act from drinking too much wine during dinner. They wouldn't let me drive home.

Before going to Beth and Theresa's, I had stopped at a jewelry store in Bangor to look at fire opals. It was not a good thing to do as now I wanted to buy one.

When I woke up, I thought, I will do so. I will live the passionate life of the romantic, loving without being loved in return . . . Someday I'd be famous and the Lioness would want me and I would ignore her at first . . . and then I'd take her back . . . What was I thinking? . . . I couldn't buy the opal . . . How could I buy her such an expensive gift? . . . I might never see her again and then I'd be penniless and in debt because of this useless fire opal . . . so what! . . . I would buy it and live only to write and be poor. It was a symbol of hope . . . Even though I was low on money . . . phone bill, book bill, MasterCard bill, and if Hansel and Gretel went away I'll be strapped with the house bills. No, I couldn't afford this stone . . .

I tried to call the Lioness the next morning, but she wasn't home. Her roommate said she had a paper due. I did my outreach work—a near disaster. I had dropped Tweedledee at the 5 & 10 store and went back to my car to get some bags.

Meanwhile, Tweedledum was walking by my car and said, "The Lord must have sent you. I have a cold and need a ride home. First, I have to get some tomato soup. They are only 5/$.89. Isn't that great? You can come for some hot lunch."

Of course, I couldn't say "no" so I took her home and had lunch, knowing Tweedledee would be finished and upset when she couldn't find me.

When I returned, I saw Tweedledee walking out of the bakery. "Where were you?" she asked.

"I went to put my car in a better space," I said.

"Oh, I must have missed you when I went to the bakery." Thank god she blamed herself for my not being there. I brought her home and decided to drive back up to Bangor to buy the fire opal.

With tax included, the stone came to $262.50. I put down $40 which left me with $10 in my pocket till my next pay. I agreed to pay $50 per month COD. The saleswoman gave me a payment booklet, and I was pleased with myself.

"You were sold last night," she said. "You picked out the best one with lots of deep fire streaks."

I couldn't afford a setting for the stone, but I hoped that someday I would. Right now, only buying the opal was important.

I went home beaming over this romantic gesture! I was so excited that I went to the pottery shop to tell Randi, the other artisan. Hansel and Gretel came shortly after, and I told them. We all jumped and danced around singing, "Romantics, all of us!"

I slept peacefully that night knowing that the fire opal was waiting for me. Such a beautiful stone.

I went to the mall the next day in a state of internal bliss and contentment and bought a little magnet plaque designed with painted grapes and the letters FPG. There was no doubt that I was crazy! And I wouldn't have wanted to be any other way. Passion and love motivated me.

Continuing in my wild mood, I put up purple drapes in my office at the Co-op. The secretary went nuts! Too way out for her!

Tweedledum called for me to take her shopping. She bought me a pair of gloves. She was trying to buy affection. I liked her better when she was miserable.

After work, I went into the Empress's office to tell her that I had decided to leave in July. She got a bit upset and I was choked up while telling her.

"Well, let's see who is interested in taking over the paper," she said. The Hermit who was ok with my decision. That day at the staff meeting I felt like I didn't belong there anymore. Everyone was arguing about a Kentucky craft group calling the Co-op a welfare system. I couldn't get into the discussion. I left the meeting and called for tickets to see Helen Caldicott who was to be in Boston the next week. I wanted to do an article about her.

\* \* \*

Gretel's grandmother had died so she and Hansel left for the weekend. I sat in front of the fire. Not knowing if she would even respond, I left a message for the Lioness. Then I went to the small house, rounded up the cats and brought them back to Hansel and Gretel's. Narcissus was being such a bastard to Goldmund. He kept biting her on the neck and trying to mate with her. He was so horny.

My night was filled with dreams of the Lioness. Not pleasant ones. In them, she was not interested. I kept my head under the covers to get warm. I woke up hearing the Lioness's voice so clear and distinct. "Good morning, Dorothy," she said. It left me with a warm feeling.

Little Hansel was good company. He wanted to go to the market, but I was too tired. He hummed around for a while and then left while I was on the phone. I felt bad thinking something might happen to him on this cold night. One hour later, he returned looking like a frozen icicle.

"Did you calm your munchies?" I asked.

"No, it was too cold. I only got to the pottery shop, and my hands turned orange, so I came back."

"Are you still open to going? I'll take you," I said.

He meekly nodded his head like a little kid, "Sure." So, we went, and he got his Devil Dogs, Twinkies and chocolate pudding.

Nar and Goldmund were wild that night. It must have been the mice. We watched a fat chubby one pop out from behind the kitchen closet during our breakfast.

I typed all morning and Little Hansel watched me. I found an old speaker's top to a stereo that made a great desk. I put it on top of a blue milk carton crate which was sitting on a plastic box where we kept the peat moss for the compost toilet.

That night, Little Hansel made us popcorn. I put on some music and started dancing.

"You could enter a midget-disco contest," he said and continued, "No really, I'm serious." I threw a couch pillow at him. The Lioness had not called. Later Little Hansel came and massaged my neck. "I want to get my fingers in shape," he announced.

"For what?" I asked.

"Climbing trees. Did you ever get high in a tree?" he asked.

"No," I answered shaking my head.

"It's a real buzz on."

Little Hansel was such a character. He did the most bizarre things, like frying peanuts in oil, or chopping wood on the parlor rug, or falling asleep with his headphones on. Today he cut up his jacket with the excuse that he always wanted "sleeves." He got a charge out of teasing me.

Saturday was my day for primping. I told Little Hansel if he left me alone all day, I would treat him to a grinch burger for supper. He was thrilled, and so was I.

While he zonked out on herbal cigarettes, I took a bath in the tub. The tub was small but the hot water soothing. After tweezing my eyebrows, I went to do laundry.

When I got back from laundry, he was so out of it, but he still wanted to go for burgers. He ate two devil dogs and a crème puff before we even got to the restaurant. After supper he went into the drug store, and I visited a friend. When he got back into the car, he was more spaced.

Missing the Empress and my friends, I walked down to Mandala the next Saturday evening for dinner. The Empress had been drinking wine and offered me some. She sat off to the side behind the stove in a protective manner. We talked for a while about dreams and Jung.

"I don't think one should get lost in the subconscious," she said. Then she came over to me to show me what she meant using the circle of my glass to represent the self. Her fingers pointed out the conscious and unconscious part by touching my hand. I was surprised that she came so close.

"Do you ever have dreams that predict the future?" I asked but she did not answer, and instead asked me, "How do you incorporate the unconscious into the self?" I had to think for a moment.

"You know psychotics live in the unconscious," she said before I could respond.

Later, we walked up the hill together to Bear's cottage. The Bear said, "It's not time for you to be with a group. What will you do in July?" I couldn't answer that one with any certainty.

"I will go home," I finally responded and added, "My mother will like that."

"Would she?" asked the Empress in a concerned voice.

I slept at the community and went to mass in the morning. Nothing ever changed except the cast of characters. The Hermit started Mass with half the people missing. He still didn't care. One of the cats got sick and puked. Kate started laughing. That made the person doing the second reading crack up. Then Steve asked the Hermit about some mountain in Greece where women are not allowed during the Mass. I thought, here the lion and lamb roam together.

We spent the day roller-skating in an indoor rink. On the news that night, we heard that Soviet troops were building up along the Polish border, and that Syria and Jordan were hot spots. Four nuns were killed in El Salvador, and Khomeini believed that both the East and West were his enemies!

The new calendar was on my desk first thing Monday morning. On the front page was a picture of Ma Kettle and Lucky Luke doing outreach work. I guess it didn't matter that I worked with Ma Kettle all year.

Everything got me upset. Checks were held back because VISTA allocation was still uncertain. Figured! After I bought the stone. The palm reader was right. My money situation was changing constantly. The Empress commented on how I was in a bad mood today but that yesterday I was in a good one.

"That's just how life is," I retorted.

Later, she showed me a letter in praise of her article. It emphasized about her being a nun. Reassurance?

News flash—John Lennon had been murdered! Was there no end to the madness?

I saw a yellow van turned over on the road to Castine. It was the High Priestess. After I found out she was ok, I asked her about the Caldicott article.

"Don't fool around with the local papers. Submit it to Bangor. They may appreciate it, "she said. "Where are you living these days," she asked.

"I'm living at the house with Hansel and Gretel," I said.

"Good. Everyone lives there," she responded but I wasn't sure what she meant by that.

I went for coffee at a local pub and wrote in my journal, "like Vita, I am losing Virginia." When I got back to the office, there was a message from the Lioness. She had left it simultaneous to my writing about her in the pub. I was too afraid to call her back. Last time I picked up the phone to call her, I had gotten butterflies in my stomach.

I held a meeting for the next edition of newspaper, but nobody showed up. Later I saw Bear who said apologetically, "Oh, Dorothy, I tried to make that meeting."

"It's ok," I responded. "There was no meeting. We'll have to get together with the Hierophant for the lead article." Just then the Empress walked by and as I greeted her, she ignored me and started talking to a worker. I just chuckled to myself.

Tweedledee was in rare form at our next appointment. She wanted to go shopping, but I told her I had to leave for Boston so she couldn't take a long time. When I returned for her, she went on about how she only managed to get in the post office and didn't have time for all her shopping. I started teasing her and she said, "I can't imagine you coming from your parents! They are so nice. What happened to you?"

Back at the office I got a call from Bangor Daily News. The publishers were possibly interested in article on Caldicott. Yes! I left for Boston with Kate from Mandala who wanted to attend the talk. Previously, we had had a good discussion about dreams. Her method of resolving conflicts in dreams was to repeat the dream and then ask the person to name their highest symbol of power and love. I had tried it with a Lioness dream, and I saw a flower.

We arrived around 6:00 pm, and I called the Lioness, but her roommate told me she was in the café. I walked to it. When she saw me, she stood up. She was wearing her grandfather's cap.

"Oh my God. What are you doing here?" she asked surprised to see me. I hugged her though I knew it made her feel awkward.

"I'm going to see Caldicott," I said. The Lioness was obviously upset.

"I'm not doing so good," she said with her head down. "I'm going to leave Harvard."

Shocked, I asked, "Where are you going?"

"I don't know, but I need to figure things out." I don't want you to see me this way," she said at one point trying to avoid my eyes.

"Do you want to come to Maine?" I asked.

"No," she responded very quickly. By this time Kate had come into the café and we couldn't continue the discussion. While I tried to get directions to the church where Caldicott was speaking, some guy walked by and the Lioness got all excited. Right in front of me, she made a date to see him on Sunday. I felt stupid. Kate and I left. I had asked the Lioness to come with us, but she had a tutorial. I said I would call back to see if she wanted to join us for coffee.

I was so depressed driving to Arlington Church, and felt uncomfortable with the Bostonians at the meeting. After Caldicott spoke, they played songs and people danced in the hallways. I couldn't get into it. The meeting broke up around 12:00 so I didn't call the Lioness, instead, we left for Kate's parents' house. Not arriving till 2:30 am, I slept late and woke up thinking about ideas for an article. I didn't dare think of the Lioness and our interaction.

After breakfast, we drove back to Maine. Kate told me it was much easier for her when I was at Mandala. "You raise their consciousness," she said.

There was a message from the Lioness that she was on the phone all night and hoped I didn't spend too much time trying to hook up for coffee. I called her back and told her about the talk. She wasn't very interested in it.

"I told my family around Thanksgiving time that I was very unhappy at the Harvard dorm. They said I could leave."

So now I knew it was their idea, not hers.

She added, "I've been spending a lot of time at June's. June is a family friend. I prefer being in her house. I cried to her the other night. She says I could stay at her house."

When we hung up, I didn't feel too good about the call. She was very distant. We weren't really talking to each other. I sent a card with a little girl with short brown hair looking into a pond with lily pads and purple flowers.

On Sunday, I wrote my article in the Bagel Shop, and at night went to a woman's dance. It was crowded, but I didn't find anyone that was worth pursuing. I hung in the corner till Beth and Theresa arrived and encouraged me to get up and dance. It was fun being with them, but I missed the Lioness. These types of places made me miss her even more. I didn't drink much but driving home I kept falling asleep and almost veered off the road. That finally woke me up.

When I got home, I found Goldmund sick. She was weak and foaming at the mouth. I was afraid she might have gotten rabies from a squirrel bite. I rushed her to a vet in Bangor the next day and he kept her overnight. Narcissus became restless. He missed his sister. He even peed in my bed, which was unusual.

For some reason, I felt less upset over the Lioness. I had faith in my symbol of hope and thought that someday we might be happy again together.

I went to visit Star to vent about the Lioness. She updated me on her new loves, and I told her about the Lioness. Just like old times.

I prayed Goldmund was well enough to come home soon.

*       *       *

It was December and I was so tired of problems! Today, the car wouldn't start. The house was freezing. It was hard to do anything in the cold. Nar, Goldmund and I huddled around the wood stove. Little Hansel was trying to kill a mouse with some sort of blowgun. Goldmund had not been doing well since I brought her home from the vet. The laceration in her mouth prevented her from eating. From her listlessness I knew she was in a lot of pain. I kept petting and holding her, hoping the affection would aid in her recovery. Sometimes she would lie on Nar. He didn't appreciate it as her breath was so foul. He was depressed and not eating much.

Little Hansel was in one of his freak-out cessions. "This metal doorknob is a source of energy loss. My solution would be to make plastic knobs," he said. He was always spouting off his ideas. His father had told him if he wanted to live upstairs, he had to buy his own cord of wood. I knew he felt like a burden to them. Intelligent but strange, he reminded me of the Cowardly Lion. I tried to deter him from his nasty pot smoking habit by stating that I liked him better when he was straight, but it didn't work.

The house was as weird as all of us living in it! The tub and compost toilet were in the living room partially hidden behind a huge rubber plant and a make-shift curtain. A big spider plant stretched over the tub. My head would get caught inside the sprawling plant leaves when I dried my hair. A piece of copper tubing served as the towel rack. There was a "touch and go" toaster in the kitchen that mostly never went, and a loud water pump clicked on every time the water faucet was turned on. The long sill of the kitchen window made up of smaller square panes housed Gretel's hydroponic plants. The window, which opened up to the woods, was so pretty in the winter when it was covered with frost. A big braided rug hung outside for decoration. Hansel and Gretel slept up in the loft. I slept in a side room off the living room, and God knows where Little Hansel slept. If he slept!

I called my sister as I was upset over Goldmund. She had a dream that I had come home, lived with her, got skinny, grew my hair long and that we went out together. Sounded good! As soon as the Empress could find someone to take over the editor job, I would be out! It was so good to talk to someone who cared for me.

I lay in bed Wednesday morning. It had snowed for the past two days. I thought about the Lioness. Her mother had said to her she might be in love by Christmas. With whom I wondered. Certainly not me. I was resolved to the fact that I couldn't bother her anymore. When I looked around at my material situation, I realized that it was really sad. My bed was on the floor. It smelled and was cold, not very attractive for a lover. Especially someone used to so much better.

I had a unicorn pillow made for the Lioness. It was white satin on purple, and the detail in the unicorn body was so delicate. One of the women in the craft shop had created it for me. Actually, I had quite a few Christmas gifts for her—a book, the pillow, a chain, and pictures. I wasn't sure whether or not to send them. I decided to wait and see what happened.

Goldmund who always slept by me went outside in the morning and didn't come back all day. She had either gone to die or heal herself. I called her all night, but she wouldn't come.

Hansel's wish to leave his job came true when he got fired. With only a half a month of severance pay, he thought they could survive on the money Gretel made from her pottery. She wasn't as sure. He told her to be positive. We would see. Money or lack of it can ruin a relationship.

Hansel was contradictory. I think he pushed Narcissus off the loft ladder the other night. I saw Nar fall on his side, not a usual happening for a cat to lose his footing. Nar runs scared whenever the ladder comes down. Hansel was not very compassionate when it came to animals and kids. Yet he had his good side. "One must maintain one's spirit in the face of adversity," he would sing. "Tomorrow we are getting a Christmas tree although money is tight."

I wanted to leave Maine. It was so difficult with the Lioness gone. In an attempt to keep a positive spirit, I dressed in colorfully–blue pants, green shirt, red over shirt, white scarf, purple pocket scarf and gave up the military Mandala dress, which turned people off.

Hansel proposed that we make and sell compost toilets to help with our money problems. Sounded good to me. A necessity should sell!

Goldmund had come back! Over the past few days, she seemed better though she was still having trouble eating. I managed to get some medicine and nutrition paste into her. She was feisty and kept jumping up on the counter. I kept putting her down for fear Hansel would see her. He went bonkers when he saw Goldmund trying to get some water into her mouth from the leaking faucet in the kitchen sink.

"It may be brutal, but I would rather she stay off the counter," he said to me.

"She'll probably die for sure. It's the only way she can get water into her mouth," I said.

"I don't care," he responded. That upset me—that patriarchal attitude that allows war and decides which people live or die. No compassion. I ignored him for the rest of the day. He tried to talk to me later, but I wasn't interested. I went to bed and cried. It was probably a release for the Lioness pain as well, as I hadn't been able to cry lately. That night, I pulled Goldmund under the covers with me. She stayed but, in the morning, jumped down. I waited for the battle. And sure enough a scream from the kitchen, "Get down," and the door slamming. She was so stubborn. And so was he.

Still no word from the Lioness. I had a dream about her. *We were walking, and she got in a plastic boat. She was doing everything to avoid me. I got angry and told her how she was acting. She started crying and said she loved the way I hugged her and how I made a big deal of her, but she couldn't stand the family situation. We kept walking, and two little boys came and were playing in the water.*

It was the week before Christmas, and I had only one dollar. It had been snowing and didn't look like it would stop. I detoured and walked through the cemetery on the way to work. I saw deer running. It was so quiet and peaceful.

That morning, I sat in my office with my feet on the desk and just stared out the window. I thought about the Wolfe . . . I remembered the day Wolfe and I walked in the nun cemetery. There was snow on the ground. She wore a long camel hair coat, hands in her pocket. Her blonde hair was short. Quietly, we read the inscriptions on each gravestone. Then we went back to our rooms, to our shelters of loneliness. She told me later that she was ready for a relationship. I never thought she found me attractive. Being older, I never pursued. Yet, I longed for her. Sometimes we would sit on opposite sides of the room listening to Judy Collins or the Moody Blues. Neither speaking. Occasionally, she would let me into her inner thoughts.

"I don't think of myself as beautiful," she said. "It's a curse to have to look at this face." I should have told her how beautiful she was. Too beautiful for this face . . .

Carrington came in the office and broke the spell.

"You look awful, let's go to breakfast," she said throwing me my backpack. I told her about Goldmund and Hansel and the Lioness. It relieved some of the anger.

"Let me take Goldmund till she gets better," she said. "People have no respect for animals. There is a company that is hiring natives to kill elephants for their tusks. Imagine killing a beautiful being for its tusks!"

"I can't. It's too depressing. This Christmas is depressing."

"There doesn't seem to be any joyous spirit here at the Co-op," she said.

"That's typical," I said.

Later that day I got such a boost. My article was published in the *Bangor Daily News*! I almost missed it because the editors had changed the title. I was so excited and ran to tell everyone. Then I called my mother and went out to buy more issues. Hansel and Gretel invited me to come home for pea soup and squash dessert. It was their way of healing the tension between us.

That evening, I wrapped the Lioness's Christmas presents in newspaper and then lay under covers in the living room. Goldmund had begun eating and cleaning herself again. The nutrient paste really made the difference.

It was like being in a comedy show every night at the cottage. Last evening, Gretel was vacuuming. Hansel was farting. Little Hansel was laughing because the vacuum kept opening and Gretel was getting aggravated. She told him to "Go take a shit." Then I started laughing and Little Hansel came over and put his head on my chest to listen to my heart. Hansel brought me a cup of coffee with a brown paper bag on his head like he was a chef. Little Hansel decided to take a bath and sat in the tub with his jacket over his head. Then Hansel picked up the pumpkin that was sitting in the window and carried it around the room a few times.

"Why are you doing that?" I asked.

"Walking it around because it never goes anywhere," he replied. Then he sat it in the middle of the parlor floor, and we named it the "invalid pumpkin."

\* \* \*

On December 19th it was below 30 degrees and the pipes froze so we had no water. Nar slept by my head all night to keep warm. I woke up to fantasies about the Empress ... *getting drunk* ... *our eyes meeting* ... *kissing* ... *coming home* ... *her passing out* ... *me lying next to her after undressing her*. ... .*her waking up to my naked body* ... well, the thoughts kept me warm anyway.

I got a call from my mother. My father' ticket was picked in a lottery drawing and he was therefore eligible to win up to $250,000. With a guaranteed minimum of $1000, Jan 2nd would be the date of the drawing in Hartford.

Not a day went by that I didn't think about the Lioness. Did she think of me or was I a distant memory by now?

We chopped wood Sunday morning. Then had breakfast together. We were like a family though we were so different. Little Hansel gave me a back rub after chopping, and Hansel had been doing nice things for me. I had lost fifteen pounds so far.

On Monday, the temperature was 20 degrees, and my car wouldn't start. I had to cancel all outreach appointments till Tuesday. That day, Tweedledee and I stopped for lunch in a popular downtown restaurant. I happened to glance to my left and noticed the man who was always reading in the library was sitting at a table across from us. He worked at the town hotel as a dishwasher and ordinarily wore a white uniform with a brown trench coat and orange hat. Always smiling, he appeared to be a gentle soul, but one from another reality. As I watched him, I saw that he was looking across the table as if another person were sitting with him having lunch. His lips moved, but no sound came out. His facial expressions changed in reaction to the imaginary conversation. Once he even laughed and gave that, "Oh yes, how could I have been so silly" expression. I felt as if for a few minutes I had entered his other worldly reality. Then I lost the connection and even though I tried to get back in I was unsuccessful. He started reading some junk mail and ended the "conversation." After dessert, he got up to leave and I noticed that he was wearing a shorter, classier trench coat than his usual one. He must have dressed up to meet this "person" for lunch. Wrapping his reading material under his arm, he headed for the door. As he exited, I saw that his coat was torn down the lower back. I was so into loneliness that I could see it in others.

One of my clients told me about tying a yellow ribbon around a tree to bring someone home. She said it was for the hostages, but I decided in my romantic frame of mind that I would do it to bring the Lioness home. I tied a bow on the tree outside the house.

By Tuesday afternoon, the pipes had thawed. Thank God! I saw Ma Kettle at the Co-op.

"I had a present for you, but it's gone," she said.

"What was it?" I asked.

"A purple scarf," she replied.

"I already took it." We laughed as I pulled the scarf out of my jacket. She hugged me.

I decided to treat myself to a real bed. In a secondhand store, I found an old bed frame, which I cleaned and polished. It sat about 2 feet off the floor, and I felt like a queen sleeping in it. The cats loved it too. I added a red candle for Christmas to brighten up the bedroom.

No Christmas card from the Lioness. How could she have loved me so much this summer and now, not even a card? I had a dream about her early on Christmas Eve morning: *My gay gym teacher was there. We talked but didn't mention about being gay. Then we went to a gay meeting. The Lioness was there. We kissed. I said, "There's still something between us." She agreed and kissed me again. I said, "Let's meet on Saturday."*

I got to the office at around 9:30 am on Christmas Eve and there was a message that the Lioness had called. She would call me back. Ten minutes later she called again.

"I'm at my father's office so we don't have to worry about the cost." Her voice sounded happier. We talked for a long time. I even detected that same little bit of "missing me" in her voice.

"I'm so busy and not wild about the materialism of Christmas," she said. "We're visiting my mother's parents and then going to the Cape for a few days to see my grandmother."

"Would you like to come up here for a few days?" I asked.

"I can't. I have things to do. I can't enjoy myself when I have things pressing on me," she said. "I'm still thinking about taking a semester off and getting a job. School has no meaning for me."

"I have presents for you, but I don't want to send them. I want to see you." She said that was good but didn't commit to any definite plans.

After the conversation, I went around delivering gifts and then stopped at the Co-op before heading out to Ma and Pa Kettles' house for Christmas Eve dinner. There was a card on my desk with a note inside that said, "All you who enter here, leave hate behind." It wasn't signed.

At the Kettles, coquito, a Spanish Christmas drink, was served. We toasted whenever someone new arrived. Later, Ma Kettle and I had Southern Comfort in tea. Boy did that warm the insides. The Empress and the Bear arrived, and Pa Kettle and I challenged them to a Christmas carol contest.

That night, I went home to an empty house as Hansel, Gretel, and Little Hansel had gone to visit family. Due to the bad weather, I had decided not to go home. Besides, I wanted to spend the weekend writing. It was time to get serious about the book that had been going around in my head since leaving teaching and coming to Maine. I knew it would be quiet, and I could get a lot done. I moved my stuff up into the loft as it would be warmer up there.

On Christmas morning, I awoke and said "Merry Christmas" to myself. Nar had stayed out all night and came in meowing. I had to go down and pet him. He was such a baby. Finally, he came up to the loft with Goldmund and I and he started cleaning her. This was the first Christmas I had ever spent alone. I was proud of myself. I wasn't wild or overeating. I was calm. I wore my purple scarf in bed. Ave Maria was playing on the radio and that made me cry. Then I read Anne Sexton's last letter to her daughter and that made me cry more. It was addressed to her daughter at age forty since Anne knew she would never make it till then.

I tried to start the car to no avail. It was −30 degrees out. Everyone was stuck. Then I made a few phone calls to friends. When I called my family, they told me that they missed me. I stayed in bed all day with the cats and wrote.

By 5:30 pm, I had finished Chapter Three and felt so drained. It was hard being creative and alone. There was nothing to replenish the lost energy. I could only do about seven pages per sitting. In between, I cooked oatmeal, lit my red candle, and ate in bed. In my true romantic mentality, I had the notebooks and pen lying on the bed with the pages I had written. Soft music played. I fantasized about the Lioness, cried, and fell asleep.

The next day the temperature was no better. It was 20 degrees in the kitchen, and the pipes were frozen again. As the wood was damp, it was hard to keep the stove going. I could see my breath in the house. Ironically, a radio announcer said that in the South there were record warm temperatures. I kept drinking coffee to keep warm. I kept my sweater and scarf on while under the covers. I typed all day in bed. With Goldmund under the covers giving me inspiration and Nar staying outside for experience, I was contented. But if anyone ever saw me like this, I would be committed!

The Doctor and Painter came over later in the day and gave me a big notebook with a black felt pen and a note saying, "for chapters 6,7,8." They invited me to dinner for the next night. Then Star came by and jumped under the covers with me. We drank coffee and brandy. The milk poured with ice floating in it.

I woke up on Saturday morning at 3:00 am to the sounds of running water. I was excited at the thought that the pipes had thawed, and the faucet must be on. Well, they had thawed all right, but they also had burst. Water was flowing all over the kitchen floor. I panicked and didn't know what to do. I called Hansel.

"Unplug the pump and heater," he said.

"Of course," I shouted. "Why didn't I think of that? The water stopped shooting out.

Despite the mess, I felt good. I had accomplished a lot. I had been telling myself all week that I would be in a writing mood and I was.

Soon the temperature started rising—4 degrees which could go up to 22 degrees. 'A real heat wave,' I thought!

My Saturday morning dream: *I went to see the Lioness in some café-like place. She came in and told me that she had moved into another room. She wasn't happy.*

Loving from afar had its advantages. A certain peace to it though lacking the physical pleasure.

Goldmund was so much better. It must have been from healing hands holding her under the covers (along with the medication and nutrient paste!). I loved her nose. She had been lying right on my neck the past few days. She loved to be close.

Saturday afternoon, I went to the Hospitality House to see if I could get someone to fix the pipes, but no one was available. I was so spaced from all the writing that I couldn't focus on such a practical issue as fixing the pipe. Chicken soup at Tweedledum's helped, but when I got home, I broke a mirror—seven years of bad luck!

In that afternoon's mail, I received a letter from my Uncle and Aunt E, my mother's eldest sister. It was addressed to "Sweetheart." If they only knew how much that meant to me. I did more writing and later, had supper at the Doctor's and got to take a much-needed bath in a normal bathroom.

On Sunday morning, my car still wouldn't start. I walked to Duffy's for breakfast. In route, I met the Empress's nephew walking the other way. He warned me about walking too far in the street.

"It's dangerous. You'll get hit. With all this snow, trucks will never see you." I took his warning seriously. When I got to the restaurant, I met Tee, the woman living across the street from Hansel and Gretel's, coming out of the restaurant.

"I'll come back and pick you up later," she said. That was a relief.

I spent the rest of the morning chopping wood till Star came. The song "Sailing" played in the background and we reminisced about the past.

"I ran away at age fourteen," she said. "I was hitchhiking and got picked up by a man going to a New Hampshire army base. He told me that he knew someone who owned a house on a lake and that I could stay there. This person gave shelter to runaways. When we got to New Hampshire, he said it was too late to go to the shelter so I would have to sleep in his car. Then we stopped at a restaurant and he put something in my drink. It put me to sleep. I remember getting out of the car and going to sleep again on a bed. He left and came back later in the afternoon and started rubbing my leg. I jumped up and edged against the window.

"'Are you scared?' he asked me. 'Think I'm gonna rape and kill you?' I ran to the door to get out and he threatened, 'There are dogs all over outside. If you step out, they will attack you.' So, Dorothy, I thought, it's him or the dogs. I preferred the dogs!"

I burst out laughing, admiring her courage. She continued her story and told me that when she ran out, a truck was going by. She hailed it down and told the driver she was a runaway and needed help. The man in the truck took her to a military police station and the officer put her in solitary confinement. She called her mother at 5:00 am in the morning to come and get her. When her mother arrived, she said, "Star, one hand wants to love you and the other wants to beat you!"

But the fiasco didn't end there. She told me that she had dreams of that man attacking her in the car, raping her, and killing her with a knife. The dreams continued for a long while.

When she was six, she recalled, she and her cousin would go into the outhouse and look at each other's bodies. One day they saw an eye looking at them through a crack in the door. This reminded her of her favorite white cat. He always came to her when she called, but one day he didn't. Star went up on the fire escape of the house and saw the cat all rolled up with its eye hanging out. She had repetitious dreams of a cat with one eye looking at her through the window. "I could never have a white cat again," she said.

"I always wanted to tell that Lioness, 'does she realize what she is doing to you D?' She better get her shit together." I appreciated her concern for me, but said, "Maybe it's a good thing you never spoke to her about it."

*　*　*

During the week, I visited Tee and Em, two heavyset women, who shared the house across the street. Tee was in her usual jeans and plaid work shirt, while Em wore a Chinese silk shirt and long black skirt. The typical odd couple! Their house was a mess and they were always apologizing for the mess. I didn't care.

They met in boarding school. Tee sent Em birthday cards after they graduated and then went to visit her seven years later. They were supposed to move to Colorado, but as Tee put it, she was "in her insecure state" so she moved into Em's apartment in New Jersey. I didn't totally understand their relationship, but Tee would tell the dogs to "Go get Mommy," referring to Em. Tee made a point of saying that she slept with the cats, and Em slept with the dogs. But even at 1:00 pm in the afternoon, they were still in pajamas watching the soaps.

Living off trust funds, Tee had never worked. She was especially nice to me, offering a shower any time I wanted and lending me magazines. I sensed, though, an underlying anger or uptightness. Her eyes were always gazing downward, and she giggled when she was unsure of herself. Only thirty-one years old, she acted like she was fifty.

On the other hand, Em, the "prima donna" ruled. A real femme fatale, she dressed to the nines and was always primping as if she were living in New York City and preparing to walk her dogs on 5$^{th}$ Avenue.

On the walk home I kept hoping that the Lioness would surprise me and show up at my door. But I knew she wouldn't do anything that irrational. It would have been so romantic to be together this weekend when I had the house to myself. I went so far as to put her gifts under the stained-glass tree Christmas Eve like I expected her.

It was snowing again, and the writing was going badly. I was stuck on a transitional part and needed diversion. Still no call and almost New Year's Eve. I rationalized it would only be a token gesture before a holiday if she did call. And if I wasn't important all the time, then what was the point of being important around holidays.

Both Tweedledee and Tweedledum called for rides. They were driving me crazy. I couldn't face the bags, so I took Tweedledum shopping. Tweedledee called back. I phoned her and said that I would take her tomorrow.

"No, I have to go today. The roast is bad," she said.

"Okay," I said, "but no bags."

"Okay," she agreed.

Then Tweedledum called again, "I need to go back for soup and pie, huh, Pet?"

"I can't Tweedledum," I replied. "I can't."

It was always worse in the evening. I was so spaced out, drinking wine, eating popcorn and string beans. Star came over and smoked a joint. When she called her boyfriend, he accused her of being gay. She told him "to fuck off." I asked if she would like to come to Connecticut to meet my family on New Year's Day. She agreed.

On the last day of 1980, I slept late. I sent a letter to the Lioness with a copy of my article and the excuse of wanting to wish her a happy early Joan d'Arc Day. I hoped I didn't appear too sappy.

\*   \*   \*

Star invited me for lunch at her Mom's house. When I got home, Hansel and Gretel were back a day earlier than planned. That freed me up. I called Star.

"You're not changing your mind about going to Connecticut, are ya?" she asked.

"No. But how about going today instead of waiting till tomorrow morning?"

"Okay, I'll just have to leave wash in the machine," she replied.

Her mom made us a thermos of coffee, tuna sandwiches, and

cookies for the ride. By 4:00 pm we were on the road and by 11:30 pm we were at my mother's. Just as I walked in the door, the phone rang. Mom picked it up and said, "It's for you." It was the Lioness.

"Just wanted to tell you that 'Sailing' was number 13 song of the year," she said.

I was so glad to hear her voice, but it was so difficult. I got nervous and jittery, and my dad said, "You look faint, are you ok?"

She told me her parents had gone to the Cape, but she had stayed in Cambridge.

"How are you?" she kept asking.

"You know us manic-depressives manage to show the good side. I'll let you read my diary one day. So, what are you doing tonight?"

"I'm going to see June," she answered.

"You're pretty tight with her," I stated.

"No, not really."

"I miss you," I said. "I haven't been able to write. I guess I need diversion."

"I don't know what I need," she responded in a sad voice.

"You've given me a lot," I said trying to cheer her up.

"What does that mean?" she said sarcastically.

"Don't you know?"

"Christmas was awful," she said before I could answer her.

"It was awful for me too," I responded. "I spent it in bed writing. I got to Chapter Five."

"I admire you," she said.

"Skip it or play with it," she suggested regarding my block.

"I can't skip it and I can't play with it. I can only write truth. I thought you'd have a date tonight."

"No date. Just did the family thing, but it wasn't satisfying like before." I was surprised to hear her admit this.

"Maybe I could see you at the end of January?" I asked her.

"That would be good. Maybe I can handle it by then."

"It is a really nice surprise to hear from you."

"Good, I'm glad. I'll probably flunk all my exams."

"You won't flunk," I assured her. Then we hung up. I was an emotional wreck. I ran into the bathroom, crying. Mom asked Star why I was crying. She made up some excuse about work being stressful.

I couldn't sleep that night. I woke up thinking about her . . . *a fantasy . . . both of us on the bed nude . . . looking at her beautiful body . . . her hands were holding my breasts . . .* I fell asleep and then got up to have coffee and cereal.

The family support helped me overcome the call from the Lioness. During dinner, my mother said to me, "I want you to get married. That would make me so happy."

"Mom, you should want me to be happy, not necessarily married."

Later, my father commented on my sister's beautiful blouse. Then he looked at me, and said, "The farmer."

I wanted to tell my mother about the Lioness. My sister told my father first about her and Paul, her black boyfriend, as she knew it would hurt my mother more. I think my gayness would hurt my father more though. As I loved my whole family, it would be hard to tell them.

Lying in bed, I asked Star if she thought the Lioness was beautiful.

"No, not really," she responded. "I mean she's all right but no raving beauty."

Funny, I found the Lioness so beautiful . . . too beautiful for me . . . Then Star said,

"You can get better." I laughed hysterical.

"I think the Empress is more beautiful than the Lioness," she added.

I heard my father walk into the parlor and turn on the light. My brother was sleeping. He threatened to scream if Dad didn't turn off the light. It was so nice to be home . . . familiar scenes.

The next day, my sister told me how my brother asked one day, "Why is D always writing about women?" My mother defended me by saying, "Because she believes in the woman's movement." My sister said she thought, but didn't say, "It's because she's gay!"

"That's not entirely true either," I said. "I do believe in the woman's movement."

"Yeah, but many women are gay because of politics."

"That's not my reason," I said.

"Maybe you haven't found the right man," chimed in Star.

Men didn't have any effect on me. Though I found them attractive, I never could love them. I never wanted to get that close. Women stirred such emotion in me, both great love and great pain. I found it more acceptable to give my will over to a woman. I couldn't seem to let the guard down and show weakness to a man. I certainly was weak with the Lioness. Even though I had had sex with men and enjoyed it, that's all it was . . . sex. The less I knew about them, the better it was. In fact, in the past, I had picked up men in bars for the sole purpose of having sex. Sort of what one expected men to do to women.

January 2$^{nd}$ was the big lotto drawing day for my father. Though he had high hopes of winning the full amount, he ended up winning only $2500.

One of the local priests, Fr. Nadumerly was at the lottery site filming a commercial. He asked the big winner to give half to the church. The commercial was about "praying for a parental change in attitude on the priesthood." I asked, "Should we pray for female as well as male priests?" He didn't appreciate my comments.

Star was home sick already. Later, Mom caught me crying and I lied and said, "I hate going back."

We left early the next morning for Maine loaded with food, typical Italian style. On the way, we stopped to see Cowardly Lion who decided to come back with us. Star got bitchy as she expected the Cowardly Lion would be all over her, but he wasn't. In his last letter to her, he had indicated that he might want to try a platonic relationship with her. That wasn't enough for Star. I sympathized.

He told us that everyone was calling him "gay" and that some guy tried to pick him up. He didn't go. Star was quick to respond, "Well, if you didn't act so faggy!" That comment really hurt the Cowardly Lion, and I got mad at Star.

"You have no right to say that," I said. "People are what they are. You can't escape your fate." The Cowardly Lion, who was an artist, suffered all his life from the teasing of ignorant people.

On the political front, Iran was still holding the hostages. They wanted 24 billion. Reagan called them "barbarians" and "kidnappers." Things looked bad.

The temperature was −34 degrees outside last night and 30 degrees in the house. I couldn't get my feet warm even under the covers. Nar slept on my stomach, and Goldmund, on the side of my head. They were so hungry when I got home. Tee told me they were outside the whole time I was gone. She wasn't happy about that. She and Em were very compassionate to their animals.

I was finding it difficult living in the little house. The place was always a mess, and I was paying for a room I couldn't always use because of the cold. I had to visit friends to get some warmth.

Soon after, I got a letter from Jack. Jill was supposedly going to meet him in January, and they were to get married. And no surprise, she was still uncomfortable about the age thing.

I called the Lioness on January 6th. She had no classes but was studying. She was depressed.

"That's cause you miss me," I said, kidding.

"It's junior slump," she corrected me. "Everyone goes through it."

"Of course," I said.

"My father says I should stay at school as I haven't found an interesting job." I didn't respond but thought, 'insecurity trap'.

"He makes me feel like it's my fault," she continued. "I'm not making the most of Harvard."

"You need to do other things besides school. Like having a social life," I advised. "Speaking of my social life. I feel like I'm up in the air. You left me hanging. I don't know what you want to see me or not."

"We should talk about it," she commented. When? I thought. We didn't write anymore.

"I don't know who you are anymore," I said.

"I don't either," she replied.

This conversation didn't help me any.

That day, I worked on the newspaper and then visited with Carlos, the teacher. His girlfriend, who was quite a bit younger than he, had moved out.

My life was full of blessings for the rest of the week --a letter from a friend on the Cape, a bath, a homemade meal from Tweedledum, coffee and bread pudding with rum sauce at Macloud's Restaurant- I was in 7$^{th}$ heaven.

Articles were coming in for the next edition and I couldn't wait to do the layout. It was the one thing I could do without anyone interfering. I took Tweedledee shopping and brought Cowardly Lion back to Bangor. While there, I visited Ruth, a classy, fun, sophisticated woman. Ruth had been recording her dreams for the past three years. I asked if she enjoyed her dreams.

"I love to go to sleep to dream," she said. "But I hate to dream about my grandson because every time I do, something happens to him."

I thought about Adele's dream of my getting married and holding the cake. Powerful symbols. Did it have something to do with the mystical marriage and the burden of creativity?

\* \* \*

It's sad that the only living creature I could expect physical affection from was a cat!

The Cowardly Lion came with me to pick up Little Hansel at the Bangor bus station. The last time I was there, I was with the Lioness.

"You miss her, don't you?" he asked.

"Yes, very much," I replied. "But some things just don't work out. Know what I mean?"

"Yes, I do. More than you know," he replied, and then told me that Star and he were not working out as housemates. I felt badly for him.

It was difficult being in an uncomfortable living situation. When I dropped him off at Star's house the first thing she said was, "Doesn't he drive you crazy?"

"No," I said and thought that maybe he and I should get a place together. We had lived amicably together at Mandala.

That night I escaped to a party for Painter at Ma and Pa Kettle's. Hansel and Gretel had been fighting all afternoon. Hansel couldn't take it anymore. He cried for hours. Little Hansel and I tried to be inconspicuous, but it was difficult in the small dwelling. I was relieved to finally leave. Later, Hansel came to the festivities by himself. Already a little tipsy, he started spouting off about celibacy with the Empress and the Bear. Ma Kettle threw a piece of cake at him. But it didn't stop him. He merely winked at me, and then encouraged Pa Kettle to give his opinion, which of course, was supportive.

"I think it's time we left," I said looking at the faces Ma Kettle was making at her husband.

"A very good idea," agreed Ma. We left, laughing.

"Hansel, you are a beautiful man," I said getting in the car. He just smiled and passed out in the back seat.

Cabin fever was getting to everyone. Star and the Cowardly Lion were fighting. Star didn't think he was doing enough to find a job. She needed more time alone. Cowardly Lion said he would start looking for another place to stay.

After supper, Star put on an Abba album. Wrapping my long purple scarf around my neck, I started dancing and jumping from chair to chair. This amused her. Then I mistakenly started talking about the triangle in *No Exit* by Sartre. Star thought I was implying that there was a triangle among the three of us. We tried to convince her that there wasn't. But Star was smoking and drinking so there was no convincing her.

Since I wasn't writing much, I started reading *Androgyny* by Singer. My masculine side was definitely stronger now. I looked different to myself. Rather hard looking. Detached. I was trying to digest all the book had to say . . . the Greek myths . . . woman goddesses . . . I think they reflected our own development as individuals and as a society. All of these stages were inherent in us and would come to pass in the world. Individuals were able to predict the future. We were a reflection of the cosmos and vice versa.

On Monday, my car wouldn't start again. A neighbor jumped it, but then the car got stuck in the driveway because of the left-over snow. Tee and Em helped push the car out. Tired, I went to the café and wrote the Lioness a letter. Later, when I tried to start the car again, the battery was dead. I had left my lights on. I didn't admit this to the maintenance man.

I managed to drop off the paper for proofing just before it started snowing again. Winter was not easy in Maine!

Goldmund had been acting strange. Detached. She wasn't coming up to the loft but would sleep on the wood pile. Little Hansel said she tried to jump on the wood stove. He had blocked her but thinks she might have done it. Narcissus had been sleeping with me but wasn't eating much.

My horoscope said that I was procrastinating with work, so I tried writing again in the morning. I was thinking I could write better if I was warm and had a room of my own. Meanwhile, Narcissus rested on the notebook the Doctor had given me for chapters 6,7,8.

Finally, that afternoon, the Lioness called! She sounded nervous. She was glad I was coming to Boston next Thursday and wanted me to sleep over. That put me on such a high. It would be like the first time again since it had been so long. She was under a lot of pressure and might pull an all-nighter to finish a paper that was overdue. I told her I had lost some weight and would dress differently—"no army boots."

"I love your boots," she said sympathetically. "I know what it's like to change styles. I had to go to court and so I put on a dress. Everyone did a double take. I felt like a transvestite!" she said.

"Lioness, you are a woman, you know." What a woman, I thought. Her beauty was untouchable. Her words could be harsh and turn people off, but I kept coming back. Maybe that impressed her. I just hoped she wouldn't carry it so far that I would lose the drive.

I told her I was writing again. She got excited and said, "I want to read about your family relationships, happenings, etc." When I hung up, I realized that the work wasn't in a readable form, so I worked on it all night.

The next morning, I got everybody up early. I had such energy again. We cleaned.

I had to laugh at myself. I had $39 to my name. I needed new brakes. I was typing on cardboard boxes, but I was happy. All I needed was a long hot shower!

My successor as editor was Pa Kettle. I felt good about turning the reigns over to him.

On Saturday night, I finished chapters 6 and 7. It was such a relief, but it left me so empty. I needed to be held. I tried to sleep but couldn't. My mind kept thinking of ideas though I was too tired to write. I masturbated hoping it would put me to sleep. It didn't. I go up and made a pot of coffee and ate oatmeal with honey and fruit. The cats were restless as well.

That Sunday, I worked on the paper layout. Carlos, one of the gentlest men I had ever met, invited me out to his house. He spoke in a quiet tone. I loved watching him smoke his pipe. He made mackerel dip while we listened to Greek and Spanish music. Then, we sat and talked about the gospels. I felt that they should be intuitively understood. He agreed and suggested that Christ chose symbols that would be understood by a particular group. Perhaps, the symbols were universal from the collective unconscious. Were Christ's symbols any different than those used by other cultures like the Greeks or Romans? Carlos thought symbols were a flow of infusion with the spirit, more dominant in some cultures than others.

It would be easier to love a man.

*    *    *

On Monday night the Lioness called. I was in bed.

"Sorry I woke you," she said.

"That's ok," I replied.

"Just wanted to check as to when you would be leaving Boston as I'm making plans to go to the Cape with a friend to see my grandmother. We're leaving on Saturday and I wanted to know your plans and if this makes any difference for you."

"No. I'll work around your schedule. It will be nice for you to see your Grandmother."

"Yes, I need to see the water. I'll call to see if I can bring a friend."

"I'm sure she will be glad to see you."

"Well, she may be booked. Mom and Dad wanted to go last weekend, and she had too many people out there already."

"Are you taking the bus?" I asked.

"Yes. We'll leave around noon."

"I'm going down to New Haven after I see you."

"You don't have to stay over if you don't want to," she said hesitantly.

"I want to sleep with you," I assured her.

"Okay then. See you then. Go back to sleep."

"Guess, we're even, huh?"

"About what?"

"Waking each other up."

"Yeah," she said and hung up. I came up to the loft and got that queasy feeling in the pit of my stomach. "You don't have to stay."

"Going with a friend." The call to let me know how unimportant I was to her. Why couldn't she leave well enough alone? I asked her what she had done that day and mulling over her response I knew why she called.

"Jerked off," she said. "I shouldn't use that phrase. I went to a concert with my parents. I didn't want to go but it was fun, and they were glad I went. I had a dream that night about *freight-colored bathrooms and a flying saucer. I chose to stay in the bathroom.* Anyway, the moral of the dream was that I could have gone on the saucer, but I chose to stay behind. "

She must feel guilty about seeing me. I cried but not as badly as usual.

I had a terrible headache in the morning. I went back to bed. Star called and said, "I know you. If things go well with the Lioness, you'll stay down there."

"Fat chance!" I thought. The unicorn brings change through destruction but can't escape his own. Betrayal by the virgin.

Nar caught and ate a squirrel yesterday. It was awful. I made him go outside. He was upset with me for putting him out and ignored me for the rest of the day.

The hostages were coming home. This was upstaging the million-dollar inauguration of our new president.

At 5:00 am in the morning, I wrote an article on the math ability of women, in reaction to an article in *TIME* magazine. I stopped at the *Daily News* to drop it off. It was going to be a full moon and I planned on staying home.

January 23rd, 1981 marked the end of 444 days of the hostage crisis (and eight men dead). The captives were taken to Wiesbaden, Germany where Carter had flown to meet them. The announcement came ½ hour after Reagan had become president, and already he promised to fix the economy starting by signing a hiring freeze.

The visit with the Lioness went well. I got into Boston at about 7:00 pm and waited till 7:15 to call her. One of her friends saw me and offered to get her, but I wanted to call. I waited outside, and finally she came out donning a new hat. We walked to a Chinese restaurant. The bill came to $6.50! I was nervous the whole time while eating, not knowing how to act. We talked about things in general and then went to the bar, Prelude. We danced. I had on my purple scarf. She let her hair down. We sat on the floor. She started kissing me. I rested my head in her lap and said, "It's been such a hard time. So cold."

"You keep it all inside. Don't you?" she said softly.

We danced again and then caressed each other.

"I think we should leave," I said.

"I agree," she responded.

Back at her dorm, we showered together, got into bed, and made love. We slept close all night. In the morning we played around and chatted. She talked a lot about June which didn't sit well with me.

"It's time for you to read Chapter 7," I said, trying to change the topic. She did while I lay close to her. She thought it was the best chapter I had written so far.

"There is a different voice. Like a child. Maybe you have to be a child to write," she said. "There is no sense of separate time or space in reading this part."

"Maybe that's because for me that's how I see all these happenings as connected. Time is not linear," I responded.

"Do you want to meet a friend of mine? She wants to meet you. She's twenty-nine and discouraged with Harvard. She was a high school dropout but now a very solid person." Then she hesitated. "I want you to myself, but she's had a hard life."

"Let's meet with her," I said. So, we joined her for breakfast at a greasy spoon restaurant. I didn't think she was as solid a person as the Lioness had described.

The Lioness had stopped visiting her parents, a reaction to getting so wrapped up in what they thought. Her father lit into her for her not doing anything, but not wanting to go back to Harvard. Later, he called to apologize. She was relieved but then got mad at herself for being so affected by what he thought. She had decided to keep her distance from them.

"You know it's your problem. You are allowing them control over you," I said to her. "You're resolving it in a child-like manner –shutting out what you can't deal with. It's not fair to them. If you know how it affects you, then redirect your reaction."

"You're right," she agreed.

We went back to her room and just hugged. We talked, and it was comfortable again. She spoke about wanting to be a saint, and I responded, "If that's what you want, then you have to experience all things and consciously give them up. There can be no trace of secret desire because someone will see through. Selflessness must be real. You don't want to be like the Empress!"

She laughed. I gave her the Christmas gifts, which she loved, especially the unicorn cup and pillow. Ironically, her mother had also given her a white stuffed unicorn with a yellow horn. She placed the cup near the stuffed unicorn. "Have you introduced these two? Are they getting to know each other?" I joked.

"I hadn't thought about it yet," she responded.

"Do you think we could see each other once in a while?" I asked. She hesitated with a response.

"I don't know," she said. "I don't want it to be a have-to thing. I don't want to feel like it's time to see Dorothy again."

"I don't mean that. I don't want have-tos either. I just thought it would be nice to see each other occasionally." She changed the subject.

"Speaking of have-tos, I don't want to feel responsible for people," she answered readily.

"Most of your friends have problems. No wonder you don't want to feel responsible. Like that girl this morning. She flunked two exams even after you spent a lot of time studying with her."

"You're right. I should choose my friends wiser." I hated coming across like an ogre.

The Lioness took a nap. Watching her sleep, I noticed the cross was fastened around her neck. She wasn't wearing it when I first arrived.

Later, when she awoke, she said, "It's nice to be able to be sexy for a while. You make me feel beautiful."

"You are beautiful," I responded.

I left around 4:00 pm but took a wrong turn so didn't get to my mother's till around 7:00 pm. I was exhausted and went right to bed after eating.

On Sunday, I sat in front of the fireplace at my parents. It reminded me of Maine.

"See D, you don't have to go way up there to have a fire," said my mother.

\* \* \*

Well, what I always feared finally happened. Narcissus got hit by a car and Tee called at noon to tell me. She didn't want me to come back and find out. She asked what to do with his little body. I asked her to please bury him. Mom told me to cry, and a few tears came, but not much. Then we went for a walk. I talked about the book. My mother responded, "I know you're going to Europe. You're going to get a call. I read your horoscope every day. I'm resigned to the fact that you will live in Europe someday."

I spent the entire week at home visiting with family and friends. I gave my niece and my nephew stick horses. My niece named hers Rosa because there were roses on the ribbon tied around the neck. My nephew named his George for no reason! They were going to join me in a visit to Adele and her children on Tuesday.

I tried to drop hints about my gayness to my Mother and Aunt.

"No matter how many hints you drop or how much you intellectualize, it won't matter until you come out and say it," advised my sister. "Aunt thinks something's up, but not Mommy. Mommy gets mad when Aunt implies that you and Sarah were involved. She keeps saying two women could live together without being that way. You threw them off the track when you dated men a few times."

I stopped to see Mrs. HD, my high school chemistry teacher and a great mentor to me. When I was trying to decide on colleges, she took me up to her alma mater and introduced me to all the professors. When I moved on campus, I felt as if I was seeing old friends. My parents were not college graduates, so they didn't know how to help me.

Mrs. HD had gained weight and looked like a principal. She had spent the last year in charge of an alternate school which she loved but she did so well, the administration brought her into the large high school. She seemed to be having some of the same problems I was.

"D, the more you do, the more threatening you are. There are thirty-seven administrators and only five are women. It's very difficult for women." As I left the building, I looked at the faces of the present students. They looked hard, lost, and disinterested. I didn't think I could go back to teaching.

The visit with Adele didn't go as smoothly as expected. My niece and nephew were playing in Adele's daughter's toy room. When the daughter saw the foreign children on her turf, she marched in, screamed, and chased them out.

"She won't let us play with her toys," said my niece. Adele tried to encourage sharing. "Daughter show the children how to play the game." That helped. Adele was pregnant with the second child and had already gained eighteen pounds. Her husband had to build another bathroom outside the upstairs bedroom as Adele had a history of "having to go quickly" . . . I remembered the time we were waiting outside in a theatre line and Adele had to go. She was eight months pregnant with her first child and big. Uncomfortably big!

"Let's just go ahead of the line, Adele. I'll explain you're pregnant," I said, starting to move up to the front.

"Too late, D. I'm not gonna make it," said Adele, and with that she pulled her coat and dress away from her body, squatted right on the sidewalk and peed. I looked at her, and we both cracked up. Later, her husband needed to talk to her and called the theatre box office.

He described Adele to an usher. It didn't take long for the usher to
find her.

"D, how did she know it was me?" asked Adele with a puzzled
look on her face. I looked at her with that "Adele, you're about 'fifty
pounds overweight and pregnant and short' look."

"What did he say to her that she picked me out so easily?" she
continued getting angrier and angrier. "Did he say I was fat?" . . .

I went to see the Wolf on Wednesday. We listened to Joni Mitchell
in the car and stopped at a New Haven bar for a drink. We talked
about the time I had called her from the gay bar in New Haven when
I was so drunk. It wasn't a fun conversation for me.

"I'm on the edge," she admitted.

"That's because you're bottling up your creativity and wasting in
a bad relationship," I said. The Wolf had written some good poetry
in college.

"You're right," she agreed. We went back to her house and she
wanted me to stay for supper, but I declined. I was beginning not to
enjoy being with her as much.

I almost told my mother during this visit that I was gay. I didn't
know what was holding me back. She asked if I saw Sarah anymore
and whether I would be invited to her wedding.

"No," I responded.

"Why not?" she asked, not understanding why I wouldn't. I made
a lame excuse, but should have said, "Mom, we were involved, and I
left her. She hates me." Instead, I chickened out.

My sister put makeup on me, but I had to wash if off. I couldn't
stand it. It made me feel like a "sell-out".

Saturday, I lazed around since it was my last day in Connecticut.
I dreaded going back. I kept getting flashes of Narcissus. I couldn't
believe that he was really dead.

When I got back, Tee told me she had to bring Nar's body to the
dump. The ground was too frozen to dig. I couldn't stand the thought!
I wish she hadn't told me.

Hansel said Goldmund was stronger than Nar since she got
through that awful sickness. I slept late that morning with Goldmund
near me. Both of us were missing Nar. Carrington said that she might
move back home at the end of this month, and then I could move
back into the little house.

I sent a more extensive article on women and mathematics to *New
Directions for Women*. Besides writing, my time was split between
teaching a chemistry class and taking an astrology class taught by
Carlos. At one point in the class I didn't agree with Carlos's math. He

thought he was right, but I stood my ground and then he admitted, "Stand corrected."

The next morning, the newspaper meeting was . . . POW . . . POW . . . BANG . . . the Bear came, then the Hierophant, then Pa Kettle, then the Empress and a few others. What a switch now that Pa Kettle was taking over. I commented, "Gee, at the last two meetings I was the only one in attendance!" Ignoring me, the Empress raised her hand, saying, "Can I bring up two issues?"

"Go ahead," I said.

"Well, because of finances we may have to reduce to four issues per year."

Immediately, the Bear and Hierophant objected, pointing out that the paper was a good fundraiser.

"And the second issue is the purpose of the paper," she continued. "We have to think about the constituency that we serve."

"Please explain in simple language," I said. At this point, Pa Kettle took over and said, "The paper should show what the Co-op is doing."

"Well, you need writers to do that," I answered. "During the last two meetings, I was the only person in attendance."

Then the Empress addressed Bear and said, "Wasn't the last issue supposed to be about the Family Farms? We need more substance to our articles."

"I'm the editor, Empress, not Bear," I answered. "Why don't you ask me? I've now completed four issues, and no one offered any suggestions or guidance."

The Bear and Hierophant tried to calm things down. Pa Kettle chimed in and said, "The Empress wants the paper to be a sort of advertising for the Co-op."

"That could get icky," I said. The Empress started going on about the poor people.

"Empress, you have lost writers and haven't replaced them with new ones," I said. "It's hard to do this with a staff of one."

"This is no criticism of your work," said the Empress in defense.

"It certainly is," I retorted. The Empress tried to leave, but the Bear wouldn't let her.

"Empress stay and let's hash this out," she said. The Empress sat back down. After much discussion, we agreed that the next issue would have a four-page spread just on the Family Farms and that Bear would submit a photo essay. The Hierophant and I would write the lead article on the effect of the Reagan administration on energy in Maine. To my surprise, the Hierophant defended me throughout the meeting and later said to me, "I know what you have been going through."

It was a "hot" meeting. I could see that Pa Kettle would have a calmer effect than I. After this issue, he was to take over. He planned on doing much of the work from his house. Good idea, I thought.

The Empress was the first to get up to leave. She made some patronizing comment about how she met someone in the bank who liked my article. I just looked at her with a" don't patronize me, it's not becoming" look, as I was too mad to say anything.

I retreated to my familiar bagel shop. My mind was tired. I felt so low. While sipping my coffee, I overheard some of the conversation of three macho guys sitting at the next table.

"What the fuck is sodomy anyway? Putting it in the ear, or nose?" said one.

"Ah, it's some strange piece," answered another.

"Forget that. What about my problem?" asked another who was obviously feeling guilty that he was cheating on his wife.

"Look, just get your lover an apartment. Get your wife a car, and she'll be happy."

"But I'm in love," said the cheater.

"Bullshit, you're in love! That's the difference between an American and a European guy. The European keeps a mistress. He goes and bangs her and when he gets tired, he goes home. The American feels guilty and thinks he has to divorce his wife."

I just stared at this guy with dagger eyes. I hated his attitude. He stared back and I knew he got my message.

On Saturday morning, Gretel told me that Randi, the other potter, was looking for someone to watch her house for a month or two since she was planning to go away.

"Are you interested?" she asked.

"Yes, yes," I said and thought I need a solitary place to write.

The Doctor, Painter and I spend the day at Bangor library. We were going to celebrate Chinese New Year by going to a Chinese restaurant. It was the same restaurant where the Lioness and I had eaten. The Doctor tried to distract me saying, "Do you know that in the East there is a lack of sexualism? Asians don't talk in terms of male or female. They don't even have pronouns to distinguish. Sex cannot be exploited in advertisements." I shared the conversation I had overheard at the Bagel shop. Then she told me what happened to one of her female doctor friends.

"She put on her lab coat and when she put her hand in the pocket, she found a penis in it that someone obviously put there as a joke.

The perpetrators had thought it would throw her off since she was teaching a class. On the contrary, she registered no reaction, except to take it out, and throw it on the table, saying, "Does this belong to one of you, Gentlemen?"

On Sunday I stopped at the Hospitality House and found out that today's supper was to be a fare well meal for Bill and his family.

"Aren't you running the house? I asked.

"Well, we were, up until today. It's a bit of a sabotage. Ma Kettle asked us to leave. She didn't want to renew our six-month commitment. You know my wife is pregnant, so we have to have a doctor. I'm taking the family to Boston, then I'll come back to work." I was shocked. The saga continued.

"I asked Ma Kettle if there was anything we could do to resolve the problem," he continued. "'Yes, get out,' she replied."

While I was doing my laundry, the owner of the laundromat said to me, "Well, I saw your picture in *MS* magazine."

"What?" I asked.

"Didn't you see?" she said. "Your picture was in *MS* magazine along with the Empress and a young boy. It was an article about battered women."

"Well, I guess I'm getting to be quite a celebrity," I replied. "Maybe I'm leaving at the wrong time." No sooner did I say that then the phone rang.

"It's for you, Miss *MS* celebrity," the owner announced sarcastically. We both got hysterical.

"I'm writing a book about the Co-op," I said to her after the phone call.

"Really? I'd love to read it," she replied. "It would be a best seller in Maine. Everyone wants to hear the dirt on that group. Everyone is disgusted with them. You know, a few years ago, the Co-op crew came and asked me the names of houses where people needed winterizing. I gave them three of four names. They weren't down-and-out people, but elderly who could use the help. Well, they never got the help even though I know the Co-op got the grant. I went to the Co-op later and asked why they never got help. I was told 'they didn't get to them.' After a while, you don't believe anything they say out there. People come in gung-ho and go out disillusioned."

Ella Grasso, the first women governor of Connecticut, was buried today on February 9. General Haig attended the funeral. She had been a great lady and probably could have gone on to be President or at least Vice-President of the country. Everyone loved her. Her motto was "Bloom where you are planted." She got us through the ice storm of '74 when she declared a state of emergency. What a week! It had been impossible to travel anywhere. Lines were down, and snow, piled high all over. I was teaching junior high at the time and had to bring all the animals to my house. My cat went nuts. I had snakes, guinea pigs, and gerbils all in the middle of the parlor floor in cages.

\* \* \*

My car died!!! The owner of Carter's garage showed me that the head had cracked through again.

"Are you a gambling woman?" he asked. "I can try and fix it. A new head will cost you $190. I can fix the old one for $75 but there is no guarantee."

"I'm a gambling woman," I replied.

After chemistry class the High Priestess said to me, "People say the paper is getting much better."

"That's funny," I confided in her, "at the last meeting they told me the articles were not substantial enough."

"If they think your paper is not substantial, what had they thought of mine?" she questioned.

"I really don't know. I can't figure them out," I responded. Her husband came early to pick her up, but she stayed a bit longer to talk to me.

Since my car was out of commission, I womaned the phones in the office. It turned out to be a blessing. The secretary's mother died, and she had to leave.

I was feeling down till the Hermit came in and said, "Your article on the 'Gender Factor' was printed in the Editorial page of the *Bangor Daily*. Wow!!

In between calls, I started working on an article entitled, "Women at the CO-OP." which described how the Co-op was different from other organizations being that it was female run. I liked the way it was progressing. I decided to use it as the lead article for the last paper I would edit.

Goldmund had been acting strange and bleeding. Kittens again?

I signed up for a sign language class. I was learning to live without the Lioness by keeping myself occupied.

It was Friday the 13th, and everything was going wrong. The battery in the green truck was stolen. My car was still not fixed and might not be for another week. The Empress's nephew's car came in with a broken windshield. I didn't know how I would get to Bangor. Tomorrow was Star's birthday and I wanted to treat her.

But everything turned out ok. Ma Kettle had to go Bangor, so she dropped me off at Star's house. We watched the soaps, had dinner at our favorite restaurant, Mama Bellducci's, and then went to see the movie *Nine to Five*. What a treat!

I woke up fantasizing about making love to the Lioness. I worried about her living in June's house. Being an artist would she ask the Lioness to pose nude for her sculpture?

Star, her son, and I watched cartoons even though the Road runner gave me a headache. People kept coming and going. A quiet, older, gay woman came over and said to Star, "So you were out with your gay friend." Her ex was bisexual and violent, not the kind of woman you would expect this nice woman to be with. Apparently, she loved to talk about sex and started telling us what she liked. I got embarrassed. As Star listened, her eyes opened wider and wider. It wasn't an appropriate conversation for a birthday party.

* * *

Goldmund had her kittens. I found blood and a tiny head in the bed. She had been running around crying. It was time to get her fixed. I don't want her or me to go through this again.

I had a dream of the Lioness: *I went to see her at school, and it turned out to be a grammar school. She was sitting in a chair among other students. She was not glad to see me. Then I was taking sleep off a cat's eye. It was a very heavy covering and hard to get off. I kept rubbing the area. The cat was not thrilled.*

* * *

A sophomore from Harvard came to work at the Co-op for a semester. She said that for every semester she was in school, she had to take one off, because Harvard was too bureaucratic and conservative. How did the Lioness stand it, I wondered?

Murphy's law. The car could not be fixed. I gave Mr. Carter $250 from my savings and that was only a down payment.

My laundromat friend suggested I investigate running the Bar Harbor Craft Store for the spring and summer. This shop was a spin off from the main Craft Shop at the Co-op. The Empress was agreeable and told me to check with the manager of the Craft Shop at the Co-op. The store sold handcrafted goods made by local people.

I worked out a deal with Randi for staying at her house. What a relief! Little Hansel had a contagious staph infection, so I suggested that he use separate utensils. Gretel readily agreed, but Hansel made a comment about cat germs, referring to when Goldmund was sick. He added that Goldmund had knocked over a vase and broken it. I was glad to be getting out!

The car cost $341.00. I asked if I could pay the rest in two weeks as I only had $25 left in the bank. Mom called just before I left for class. She and my father wanted to send me money, but I said no. I finished my article on the Tuesday spinners, a group of women who had been meeting for the past two years to spin and weave.

Finally, I saw the article in *MS* magazine. The picture was of the Empress and I wearing our head bandannas sitting at the kitchen table. I was looking admiringly at her as she spooned out food from a big pot.

The Empress told me she was reading a book by Thompson called *Falling into_Grace* and that the new concept of Christ would be a combination of John the Apostle and Mary Magdalene. That made me feel peaceful. John's gospel was the gospel of love.

\* \* \*

Star was in love. She had met a tall blonde Texan named Bart. He wanted us to meet him at a bar called *Nashville North.* Star got a babysitter, and we went. The bar had red and black lights and women in cowboy hats. We sat and watched the weird patrons and at 10:30, we decided to leave as Bart never showed.

On our way out, we bumped into him. He was good looking with a deep dimple in his chin. We sat at a table and he bought us drinks. I really didn't want one, but he insisted. I watched Star play up to him. From one side of her, she was saying, "I'm not that kind of girl," but from the other, she was already in bed with him.

He was considerate and told her not to expose her feelings so quickly. "You'll get hurt that way," he said and then looked at me, "Are you really that bored?"

I was.

"You know," he said, "If you just relax, you'd have so many men after you. You'd need a baseball bat to keep them away."

I didn't say anything for Star's sake. Star made him promise to call. We left around 12:15, and Star talked for another hour. I couldn't keep my eyes open, but she was so excited. I listened to Star all morning asking, "D, do you think he will call? D, do you think he will call?"

Gretel came into my office today, sat down and asked, "Dorothy, do you ever feel psychic?"

"Yes. Why?"

"I was in the Ellsworth unemployment office, and who was standing right behind me but Lucky Luke. I remembered that you said the other night, 'Well, it's time for Lucky Luke to be bopping in.' When you said that, I thought you were crazy since I couldn't imagine why he would be back."

Star called. She was down on Bart. He hadn't called. She wondered if he was just a good bullshit artist. Duh!!!!

My dream of the Lioness was not pleasant. *She wrote that some other woman was number one. "There I said it." She was going on vacation with her. I cried and crumbled the letter.*

Finally, a letter from the Lioness. It was dated 2/17 and in green and blue color ink.

Dear D,

I see you've hit the big time! Photographed in MS magazine! When I found the article, I couldn't help exclaiming aloud— "My god," several times. I was absolutely tickled. The Empress in MS. Perfect, perfect! . . . If they only knew . . . thought of you always faithfully telling me to be happy and wanted to say Happy Valentine's Day, too, three days after the fact . . .

I am writing and that makes me feel euphoric. Plus, I've been living in June's house while she's been in Florida . . .

I feel good about my parents, the immediate tension w/ in myself towards them has disappeared. Our relationship is supportive again . . .

Just been at the Cape for the weekend. My sister came. She's got her first real boyfriend . . . mum and dad advised her not to sleep with men before marriage (every so often I think how I must have really blown their minds, bluntly telling them about my relationship w/you) . . .

Wonder how you are doing . . . If you're planning a spin down to your folks and you'd like to stop for the night let me know. That was a good time we had. Love L

PS a lesbian friend of mine says she worries about me that all the people around me here are basically unsupportive of my gayness and that I'm afraid to be gay? I guess. So Valentine's Day I went out and bought myself $15 worth of books --all homosexual literature. One you have got to read, better than *Choices*, a story of a lesbian romance during the Depression, but a recent book called *All True Lovers* by Sarah Aldridge. Want to know what you think.

I was thrilled that she wasn't involved with anyone and that she suggested that I stop for the night. At least she wasn't shutting me out. She didn't say anything about her feelings for me, but I wasn't surprised.

I had lunch that afternoon with the Mandala crew. The Empress thought my article about women at the Co-op was beautifully written. Pa Kettle told me there was a letter in the *Daily* in reaction to my article on the Berdow/Stanley research and women in mathematics. I loved it. The guy was so off base, writing . . . *"The feminist movement couldn't possibly have found a poorer spokesman than D . . . Whether D and her ilk like it or not, the evidence is conclusive. Women have tested substantially lower than men in mathematical ability, and blacks and Hispanics have done significantly poorer than whites in the testing of cognitive abilities . . . "* I noticed that he didn't capitalize Blacks. This guy was a prejudiced son of a bee. My ilk. I liked that phrase. Implying I had a following. I was already working on a response.

* * *

A reunion! Indiana, Armond and Lucky Luke had all come back for a visit. Armond brought clams and beer and we had a feast. The beer, however, made me more depressed, and I made the mistake of calling the Lioness. She was so analytical on the phone. No feelings for me at all. She was still at June's and sooo happy in her work. "June is an artist. She's responsible for my writing. It's all because of her. She encourages me. She understands me."

"That's nice," I said, wondering if she knew her effect on me.

"I saw Adrienne Rich," she continued, "and she's not so good at readings. She doesn't do to me what Dylan Thomas does. She's such a small woman."

"She may be small, but she has a power effect," I replied. She ignored my comment and continued on her own tangent.

"I'm surprised at how fast the mail is. Now you'll have to wait four weeks for my next letter. You respond so quickly. I don't have the time."

"Take your time." Not sure why, but I asked if I could visit. She was on vacation and agreed to see me. Even so, I felt worse after this call.

The car needed a ring job, and Datsun wanted $250 to do it. Having used up all my resources, I was really at a loss of what to do, and I didn't want to ask my parents for help.

During the week, uplifting letters came from my father and Doris.

I decided to go home for a few days, and as one of the Co-op workers was driving to New York, I managed to hook up a lift to Connecticut.

I arrived home late Saturday night, obviously upset, so I decided to be honest with my mother. After a hot bath, I walked into the kitchen and said, "Mom, are you a happy woman?"

"Well, I have my good and bad days," she responded. "What do you mean?"

I tried talking but I started to cry, "Mom, we've never talked woman to woman, and I want to talk to you."

"What's the matter, D? Are you sick?" she asked in a concerned voice.

"No"

"Something is on your mind?"

"Yes"

"What is it, D?"

"It's not easy to tell you, and I'm at the bottom Mom. I need your support and I can't deal with your pain."

"What D? What is it?"

"Mom, we're quite different. I've chosen a much different lifestyle than you, and I've suffered enough for it. I can't suffer any more. I'm gay, Mom." Her back was toward me since she was going to the cabinet to get cups for our coffee. Her hands went up to her head.

"Oh, no," she said in a distraught tone.

"Ma, I was involved with Sarah for seven years."

"I knew it. That's why I hated her."

"I know. That's why I hated bringing her here."

"Why didn't you tell me sooner?"

"I couldn't. I wasn't sure. Why? Would it have made any difference?"

"Yes. I could have helped you," she responded.

"This summer I was involved with the Lioness, and then she told her parents about us. That made her stop seeing me."

"See, they stopped it. It's wrong."

"Well, she's being what they tell her to be, but that doesn't mean they've stopped it or it's wrong."

"Do you want to change?" she asked.

"No. I don't think so."

"Then you're telling me there is no possibility?"

"Ma, I don't know what I'll be five, ten years from now. I'm telling you what I am now."

"I don't feel comfortable talking about it," she motioned that my brother and father were in the other room.

"We don't have to talk about it anymore."

"This will kill your father."

"I know. I'm not sure I'm ready to tell him."

"What did I do wrong?" she said on the verge of tears. "Your sister and her breakdown and now this?"

"Ma, it's not a matter of doing something wrong. I don't see it that way."

"Dorothy, you're too intelligent for this. What about your future? You had everything."

"Ma, what did I have? A job? I have more of a future now. I can really do something. The book is a psychological study. I think it has potential."

She was obviously upset, and I felt that I had said enough for one night. We went into the parlor to watch TV. I noticed that she cried softly sitting in the chair. I went to bed and wondered how she would feel tomorrow.

The next morning, we didn't say anything about the conversation, and both of us acted like nothing had transpired between us. I escaped to Adele's for the day. Adele was going to take the next year off from teaching to take care of her two children. She was close to delivery time and huge. I confided my conversation with my mother.

"Don't worry D, she will come around. Mothers always do. Take it from me," she advised.

On the trip back to Maine, three of us were squished in the front seat of the truck, with a ram, a sheep and a one-hundred-and-fifty-gallon fish tank packed on the back! I returned in time for my Chemistry class, after which the High Priestess gave me an unexpected gift, an eight-sided prism. It was beautiful, and I hung it in the window. While I was gone, she had moved out of her house and was living in a hotel.

"I have no money," she said. "But I needed space from my husband. The children are upset, and both he and I are depressed, but I stop home every night to see them." I was upset for her.

Wednesday, I proofed the paper at the Bagel Shop. Pa Kettle said that was the reason I liked proofing, so I could eat at the Bagel Shop! He was right! Pa Kettle was such a character with his straw hat, gray-streaked beard, and pieces of straw hanging out of his mouth. He said that this issue of the paper was my best. He loved the lead article, although both he and the Hierophant disagreed with the picture I wanted to use. A parody of the Sistine Chapel, it showed a black woman touching fingers with a white woman and the caption said, "And God created woman in her own image."

They were so opposed that I agreed not to use it. Instead we were going to use a picture of the Bear on a tractor bailing hay.

There was a letter written in my defense by a woman who was a Phi Beta Kappa in Mathematics from UMO in the *Bangor Daily News*. It refuted the letter written by the guy who opposed me. Right on.

Despite my preoccupation with the paper, I kept thinking about my mother. All in all, I was happy that I had finally come out to her. But I was afraid that she had hopes of my changing. When I left on Tuesday she said, "We'll talk again." I knew what she meant.

\* \* \*

VISTA was being cut by 40%. That would put a damper on Co-op projects. I hoped that I could survive till the summer. Reagan favored raises for the senators and thought El Salvador could become another Viet Nam.

I moved into Randi's house on March 12, the day before Friday the 13th. I was to share the dwelling with her cat, "Cat-Face." It was a comfortable dwelling and the most normal one I'd lived in over the past two years. A real bedroom and bathroom, running water, and electricity.

Pa Kettle and I worked together on the paper layout. I had been giving him instructions on how the process worked. The Bear joined us for coffee.

"Why don't you consider staying in the area and getting a job at a local newspaper?" she suggested.

"It's nice of you to want me to stay close, but I don't think I can do that. I need to go home for a while," I responded, pleased at her concern.

"Do you prefer the city or country?" she asked.

"It doesn't really matter as much where I live as much as who I live with. There's no one up here I feel really close to. I need more." She understood and said, "Yeah, I know. I can't really live with the nuns in my community and that's why I came here."

"I understand. You function better alone."

"Yes. But the winter was hard for me, too."

"I've been working on a novel and want to spend next year doing so," I said. She looked at me strangely like she intuitively knew it had something to do with Mandala. We got along so much better when the Empress was not around. Bear was so controlled by her. The other day we had gone for a beer and when we returned, the Empress had walked by us and gave Bear a nasty look. The Bear glanced back at me as if to say, "Eek, I've done something wrong."

Star really socked it to me the other night after I complained to her about my phone call to the Lioness. "

"Dorothy, the Lioness is not interested in you, and you still call her. You have to give yourself the same advice you give us women about our men," she scolded. And I knew she was right. It was hard to accept. Maybe I shouldn't visit the Lioness at the end of the month.

I was getting behind in my bills. The jeweler kept sending me notices. My phone bill to the Co-op was $80. Then there were Penny's, Master Card, Amoco, and my car insurance. When you're poor, it just keeps getting worse because you have to charge to survive.

My dream of the Lioness: *I went to see her at school. We were walking, and she went up to meet a boy. I continued reaching out to other hands, familiar faces. One man said to me, "The way is to start at the bottom, find the way to the top and then out."*

It snowed all day Saturday, and I just stayed in bed all day missing the Lioness. I brought Goldmund to the house, and she and Cat Face were getting along. Cat-Face was a very loveable animal in contrast to Goldmund, moody and always crying. I put her out for most of the day. I couldn't stand her when she was like that. At night she was better and played while I worked. It was still windy and cold out. I spent a lot of time under the wool blanket.

What was I going to do at the Co-op now? Without the paper? It took up so much of my time. I still thought of the Empress at times, but I didn't have any feelings for her anymore. I was not sure about visiting the Lioness. Star's statement had cut deep. I was always waiting for that special thing to happen. Not even sure what it was. But it never did.

Goldmund had been gone a few days. Where was she?

I had "abdicated" the throne. Pa Kettle and I picked up the finished paper. I got depressed thinking that it was my last. He brought a bottle of wine to celebrate and wore me out talking about woman's liberation!

Still no VISA check. Thank God my income tax return had arrived. I still couldn't pay all my bills.

The Bear made a big show this morning at the Co-op about how she loved my article on women at home. She said that it had come from my guts. I was embarrassed. The Empress said she was proud of me. I thought that was weird. I worked the rest of the day on bundling the paper to mail.

Goldmund came home at the witching hour last night.

Today, I went to the bank and paid all the bills I could. I would starve over that fire opal. I was crazy to buy it, and the romantic has been driven out of me by her lack of response.

The Empress was worried about an elderly woman who was not answering her phone. She asked that I visit with her. We talked on the way over.

"You might be back in a month after city living," she suggested.

"One month won't do it," I said.

"I like my gardening," she said ignoring my response. "Next year I want to plant flowers, maybe roses and strawberries."

"That's a good life."

"Yes, very good," she responded, and right then I knew there could never be anything between us. We were each too set in our different ways and had an established pattern of dealing with one another.

When I ran into Carlos, from Learning Center, he told me he liked my article, but he thought I went easy on the Empress and her crew.

"They don't deserve such praise after all their backbiting," he said.

"You're right," I answered. "But I didn't want to go out on a bad note. Besides it got me so much praise."

Goldmund and Cat-Face were fighting. I had a tricky time keeping them apart, so I threw them both out. I had lost two more pounds and my check finally had come!

My next project was the craft catalogue. At a meeting I found out that the cost of the catalogue wasn't covered by the sales. The Hermit couldn't explain why. He just kept saying, "We'll have to talk about that. You'll have to explain that to me," while shoving the jobs onto us.

After the meeting, I mailed a letter to the Lioness. The Empress asked me to go to Bar Harbor with her to see a storefront. She wanted to rent a secondhand shop as the current one had closed, and the women had lost their jobs.

"It's class conflict," she explained. "The poor always get treated that way."

I was too depressed about leaving the paper to worry about the poor. Then she started badgering me about celibacy. "You probably find it much easier not living in the community," she said.

"Yes. I had to be realistic about my needs."

"Love surpasses all physical attraction and infatuation," she continued. "Real love goes beyond that."

"You're right, but I can't deny my needs."

"Real relationships with close friends mean more, and celibacy is necessary. It's more than just being with people you get along with. If you ever change your mind, I want you to feel welcome to come back. I can't guarantee that we won't fail you again. But it might be better now."

"Thank you. But I don't belong out there. I have to find my own place.'

"Sometimes we see people as photographs and miss that they've changed. I was going through some personal trials when you were living out there."

"Yes, I surmised. The first time I came back to visit Mandala after moving out, it was difficult for me, but I didn't want to leave with bad feelings."

"Things were not going well. There were so many people living out there, it was difficult."

"You have to be realistic about who lives out there. I believe more in neighborhoods. I can't live in community. Too many people. Too many rules."

"Well, it's about universal love," she replied.

"Yes, but even in community, one is limited to how much time and love one can give. There is a choice as to who you give it to."

"I could never be involved in a primary relationship," she said. "I am happy being celibate. It has made me grow. Christ gives the invitation but not all can accept."

"For me the energy needed in community is not worth the personal reward. I need support from an individual to be the best person I can be."

"Look at you," she added. "You're depressed, and I'm happy. We'll have to see where you end up and if you're happy. I guess our backgrounds are different. At nine I was doing the work of a 20- year-old."

"You're a strong woman," I concurred.

"I realize your generation is used to more things," she said. I knew she was trying to understand me in her own way, and that despite all the differences, she still wanted me to move back out there. I was touched.

We got in the car and I said, "Look, it's a full moon." She responded, "Someday I may come and say I need you." This was after two Tequila Sunrises, so I didn't take it seriously.

"Empress, you'd never admit that. You won't let someone else take care of you. You can't be dependent."

"I'm ready to die thought," she said. "I don't think I will live a long life. I have seen some of the other life, and I would like it there. Actually, I like it better."

"You deny existence," I said. "I like this existence."

"No, you don't. That's why you're having problems."

"Maybe you're right. I both love and hate it. Where is this all coming from?" I asked.

"I've been under the weather, maybe flu," she responded.

"It's more romantic to blame it on the full moon. I will miss you." Then in my confident, kidding mood I said, "Well, Empress, you could have had me, but you didn't want me. It was your choice." She laughed.

"I guess you need to go?" she asked again with those beautiful brown eyes looking right into my face.

"Yes, I need some family love. You've got Bear and the Hierophant you can rely on. I don't feel like I belong out there."

"Not really," she retorted. "They still send money to their communities. Everyone does what they need to, but I think everyone grows from living in Mandala."

"That's for sure." I laughed. "One way or another!"

"Someday we'll have to take a trip together and just have fun." Then she told me how she had gotten a letter from Jaques Blanck from the church meeting and that he was in a hospital in Paris.

"He really liked you Empress," I said.

"I liked him too. I have to go back to Paris and make better plans this time and stay longer." She talked about me taking care of her dog, Argus. I was not sure why. I blamed the drinks.

I felt like we had really communicated for a change, but I was worried about all the death talk. Much had been unsaid, but we made some headway. I wasn't sure she was totally in touch with reality. The Empress was a series of boxes, one inside the other. She was tucked away deep in the innermost box. So difficult to get to. So much covering. And some of the boxes were made of stone. Could anyone penetrate? I wished she could learn to have more fun. She was so driven, such a complicated person, so many defenses. What was truth to her? Confusion dominated our conversation. I couldn't think clearly when I was with her. My mind was cluttered for a long time after. I just came home and sat.

\* \* \*

Tee and Em came over and brought me yellow daffodils. I fell asleep in the chair under the blanket looking at the flowers with Goldmund on my lap. My pooke woman mug that reminded me of the Lioness was in front of the vase. I had bought it from Randi. It was a white cup with a powder blue rim. The handle was a woman's body with her belly and pink round nipples sticking out. The windblown hair was yellow, long, and wild, flowing back on the mug. The hands were paw-like and attached to the side of the cup. Each had three red nails. The mouth was big and red and out of proportion to the rest of the body. It was the part that made it look pooke. I had my morning coffee every day from the mug and felt like I was drinking from the Lioness.

The world news was depressing. Pakistan was getting aid and its leaders had the nuclear bomb. India was in a state of upset. People were fleeing El Salvador as the situation had gotten worse. Poland had had a major strike. There were 22 killings in Atlanta; people were arming themselves. The US was criticizing those of our allies who didn't believe in a heightened nuclear build up against the Soviet Union.

On Sunday, I went to a Blue Hills Concert. Every time I saw a blonde woman from the back, I thought of the Lioness and a sadness came over me. As I was looking over the balcony at the crowd below, I realized that these people were wealthy, and I could never be a part of this class. One had to be born into it. It was worse for the middle class since we sensed the difference and knew we could never be a part of the elite. The poor class didn't even think about being a part of it.

The Lioness called that night. Our conversation was better than the last one. March 24th would be her twenty-first birthday. I planned to see her on Saturday. I wanted our relationship to be authentic whether it was for a minute, a day, a week or a lifetime.

When the weather got warmer, I went to Bar Harbor with Vera to check out spaces for a craft shop. Vera ran the Craft Shop at the Co-op. Her husband had started a ministry career late in life on one of the local islands. They moved there, and Vera had studied with him although she never enrolled or got credit for it. Then he met a younger woman and got involved with her. He had the balls to move her to a tent in the backyard of their house! Vera told the woman to leave. It became a legal battle over the land. Vera won, but her husband bought property across the street from her. Then he moved to Connecticut. The court had awarded her $40/month alimony, but when he moved to Connecticut, the court lowered it to $15/month. She offered to waive it if he gave her the property across the street, but instead, he had sold it to his sister who was building a house. Since then he refused to talk to her because she refused to talk to the girl friend. It had been four years. She was lonely and would take him back. "He's a good man and the island people love him. They held the position open for two months hoping he would come to his senses."

We roamed through the town. Vera was not confident that we

would get a store this year. She was frustrated about the Co-op finances. She wanted the Craft shop money to be separate from the rest of the business. She wanted the nuns to come out more and meet the community and to finish one project before they started the next. She loved working at the store. One time a man came from Washington to interview her, and he implied she was working in a welfare system.

"I'm working under a visionary," she said. He backed down and said, "I know what you mean because I met her."

My mother had called and left a message. She was babysitting for my sister's children but wanted me to know she was thinking about me. I sensed not only a nervousness in her voice but real concern.

All my dreams were sexual. I knew I was frustrated but I didn't know what to do.

I wondered if the Lioness thought having sex with a woman was gross now because of her parents' attitude. Women kept society together. Pa Kettle talked about women holding the family together. Maybe we could extend that concept into the world. If we saw nations as children of one family, then we could change the course of the world. No wars. Mothers don't shoot their children.

I discussed my writing with the High Priestess. She liked the idea of fairytales and symbolic names, but she thought it would be hard to do.

"Writing requires a lot of focus," she said.

"I'm not sure how to do that yet," I said.

"Don't worry about that yet," she said as if she knew something.

"How is it going with your husband?" I asked.

"I tried talking to him, but we don't listen to one another."

"Do you want to work on the relationship?" I asked.

"Yes, but it must change."

"Does your husband want to work on changing?"

"He says "yes," but he doesn't do anything to make it happen."

I was worried about the High Priestess. She was an extremely sensitive being. This relationship problem with her husband would take its toll on her. She was prone to drinking a lot, and she told me she cried herself to sleep many nights. I loved when she shared her inner most secrets with me. I was a mortal getting a glimpse of an ethereal goddess.

Tired with the writing career, she confided, "I want to be a nurse. But I'm not really sure why I want to do so. Or for how long. All jobs lose their hold once the routine becomes easy or mastered. People roam about looking for the perfect job. But all jobs have a certain amount of routine. Maybe we're just too idealistic." She stopped as if she were listening to herself.

"That's a very mature attitude to have come to and accepted," I responded.

"I haven't accepted it," she replied honestly.

\* \* \*

Uranus moved out of my 5th house on Saturday the 21st and Sunday was my first good day in a while. Many of the planets would be in Aries this weekend. This would be interesting since I was seeing the Lioness, an Aries.

On Friday, after breakfast with Star at the Bagel shop, I left in a snowstorm, five inches of snow on the ground, but when I got into Massachusetts it was sunny.

I stopped to see Indiana, at her house, Mill Pond, in one of the surroundings towns near Boston. It was a beautiful old home on a large piece of land with ducks and woods all around. That night we attended a showing of *Eight Minutes to_Midnight_*about Dr. Helen Caldicott, and in the morning, she gave me the grand tour of her abode.

I was late getting into to Cambridge to meet the Lioness and proud of it. "Sailing" was playing as I pulled into the parking space. But she out did me and was a half-hour later than I. We spent the day in Rockport just walking around the shops. I had gotten tickets for the opera "Semele" by Handel. I had always wanted to take the Lioness to an opera. This one was about an unfortunate woman loved by Zeus. She insisted on seeing him as a God. When her wish was granted, she died from all the brilliance. Hera had tricked her into asking for such a self-destructive wish. Zeus saved their child, Bacchus, who was born in fire and nursed by rain. It was a long opera, three hours, and the Lioness kept saying she was tired. I took that as a hint that she didn't want to make love, but, boy, was I wrong. It was one of our better love making jaunts, which continued in the morning.

On Sunday, before I dropped her at her parents' house, we talked.

"I'm hurt that you seem to be going out of your way to let me know I'm not important to you anymore. Your mixed messages confuse me. I'm not sure any more how to respond. I'm kept hidden in a secret part of your life," I said. "I'm the lover that you visit in the deep dark dungeon. I'm living in a fairy tale. I'm the woman who licks your cunt, but god forbid that someone should find out about me. After our last time together, I didn't want to see you again."

My bluntness upset her, and she responded, "I guess it's like having my cake and eating it, too. I never expected what happened this summer to carry into the rest of my life, my future. It was an isolated incident." I stopped the car and yelled, "An isolated incident?! Is that what I am to you? You don't face your feelings," I said to her.

"You're right," she responded and told me how she felt she had shut down since South Dakota when she was doing outreach work with the Indians. Tears began to roll down her cheeks, but I remained strong.

"Why aren't you crying?" she asked.

"I don't know. I don't know why I'm being strong. I'm sorry," I said. "No, I'm not. I want to feel sorry but I'm not. Why should I be sorry? I'm the one with real feelings."

"I don't want you to be sorry," she said with a childlike voice and added, "truth and love."

"You've taught me to be independent," I said. "If this relationship doesn't cause you to grow then there is no sense in continuing."

After all my honesty, I expected her to run even further from me. But I felt good saying what I had said. It settled me and gave me some peace. If she did shut me out, I thought, it would be ok since I wouldn't be losing something I didn't really have.

On the drive back to Maine, I tried to make sense out of her words. She had told me that on her birthday she had met with one of her guy friends who was interested in her. He was surprised to hear that I was coming down. "Thought 'that' was over," he had said to her. She told me this was her best birthday ever, but I got the impression that she was just saying that to convince herself. She spent a lot of time with her family and wanted them to be the most important thing in her life. She reminisced about her father reading to her and her siblings as they were growing up. I got the impression she wanted to crawl back into that safe environment, to stay there always and not to have to face life. Yet her writing expressed an angry negative side—the horse with trapped legs that started killing itself; the rabbit caught in the well who couldn't get out. The talk about shutting down in South Dakota really worried me. She couldn't deal with the reality of suffering, pain, and injustice. The fact that she was in the upper class and never wanted for physical comforts made her feel guilty about other people's misfortune.

She was going through some sort of sexual crisis. She read aloud sexual poetry when we were in bed. The passage was about having sex with a man's organ. The woman described it as "minnows in her mouth." I wondered how much the Lioness fantasized about the penis. She was the most sexual she had ever been with me this weekend. I felt like she wanted more, but I didn't think it was just me she was making love to. She got so excited when I got so aroused by her.

"I love watching my body give you such pleasure," she had said. Her climax was huge and her screams louder than usual. And then making love again in the morning. Even just kissing her ear made her wild. She came over and over again. At least we parted on a positive sexual note despite the conversation in the car, which she said, "was the most important conversation we have ever had."

Try as I might to get her out of my system, I had to admit, I loved her more now than ever.

Star was proud of me for being honest with the Lioness. It was because of her that I had gotten the strength to do so. So many times, I had told Star to be strong with her men, and now I had to apply it to myself. She played the song "Still" for me and joked, "We should be lovers."

"That would be bad for our friendship," I said. "I don't think you could make love to a woman anyway."

"You're right, and if I did, I would deny it to the end!" she laughed.

That night I watched the Reagan episode at Beth and Teresa's. I didn't want to be alone while it was going on. The jellybean president --what an image! Beth was glad I was honest with the Lioness. "You've been hurting so it's better to get it out," she said and gave me a much-needed hug.

Later in the week, when AB saw me, she said I looked different but good.

"I'm dressed up," I answered. "No more heavy shirts."

"Don't you love how the sun feels on your skin," she asked.

"Yes. Spring. Time for love," I said.

"Yes, maybe that's why I have been playing rock music!" Just then the Empress walked out with three shirts on.

"How can you wear three shirts?" I asked playfully. "It's spring and time for love and skin."

"Then I better put more shirts on." She laughed.

It was raining and I sat by the fire drinking hot coffee out of my pookey mug. The Lioness body cup. I played with it and rubbed it as if I were rubbing her body. It reminded me of what it was like to touch her. Now Chopin, raindrops, and coffee gave me happiness! Even though the Lioness had said I was more classic than romantic, I felt romantic.

Before going to a concert, Carlos prepared supper for me on

Saturday night. Salami, cheese, a Spanish rice dish and wine. After the concert, we drank more wine at his house and listened to Chopin and Beethoven. We drank too much. Carlos confided that his daughter was gay.

"I don't understand this kind of relationship," he said. "I think one needs opposites to grow." Then he added, "You remind me of my daughter."

I went home and was crazed. I needed sex. I was cold and put my head under the covers. I wished the Lioness were here. Damn the Lioness. Damn mother-fucker. I hated being alone. I needed to be loved. Carlos could be someone I could love, but the emotional attraction was just not there. He was sensitive, compassionate and intelligent. Why didn't I feel anything for him?

Bear came into my office on Monday and asked, "Did it ever cross your mind for an instant to apply for the director job at the Learning Center?"

I smiled and said, "No, Bear, not even for that long a time," as I snapped my fingers.

"Oh," she said. "It didn't huh?"

"No, I have other work to do and can't split myself."

"Yes, I know what you mean," she replied and never asked me again.

A week later, Bear told me that she decided to take the Learning Center job. For "six months, not two years." She tried to convince me it was her own decision with no pressure from the Empress. Right. I just listened to her.

Soon Randi returned, and I had to move out again. I managed to rent the cabin that Carrington had stayed in. It was a bright and sunny there now that spring had arrived.

I spent the day with the Hierophant taking pictures for the catalogue. We went to McCloud's for dessert—apple brown betty with buttered rum sauce. Nothing better to raise one's spirit! She admitted to me how discouraged she was living at Mandala. "I've been wanting to leave for over a year now. It doesn't feel good out there to me anymore." She told me she was bringing another nun from her order to live out there, and she doesn't know what effect that will have.

"Everyone is psychotic out there," she continued. "Bear is threatened by me. She does everything to please the Empress just to get her approval. The Hermit drives me crazy with his childish ways, and the Empress defends him. He locks himself up in that cabin and only comes for Mass. And then he doesn't allow any questions during Mass. Can you imagine?"

What a crew, I thought! Thank God I was out of there.

I had a dream about the Lioness. *We met to talk things over at a baseball game. We sat down and she went to get food. She brought back a small child, a boy. I was uncomfortable and got up to leave and said, "I don't know why I see you." She came running after me. "I can't stand it anymore," I said. "You know I don't feel comfortable with kids. Why did you bring a child if we have to talk?"*

This was the first dream in which I was leaving her and wouldn't deal with her childishness.

*       *       *

I sent off a $25 check for the opal. I had been in a weird mood all week, eating too much. Sitting in my office and looking at my lavender curtains, Carlos asked if I slept in lavender sheets as well. I laughed and said, "No, but maybe that's my problem. I have no sheets." Hansel offered a set of white sheets to which Gretel added, "you could dye them like you do everything else."

The High Priestess said I focused her when we did chemistry class together. She couldn't do the math problems when she was alone. Did I need a woman around to focus me?

*New Directions* was interested in my article. The editors wanted me to incorporate a few other articles about math and women into my article. I could do that. I worked on it all Saturday. I decided to approach *MS* magazine next about doing an article.

I was back to living primitive again in Carrington's cabin. Using a pail for a toilet. On Sunday morning I was like the Degas bather, standing nude by the wood stove, washing myself in a small basin of water. I remembered how the Lioness used to get so excited to see me. She would run off the bus. Her eyes would look into mine. We couldn't keep our hands off each other. We just wanted to get into bed and hold each other. I was the ugliest I had ever been, heavy, with short hair, and yet she loved me. Now everything was different. No exciting feelings. Now we were drowning in reality --Boston, family, society, images. I had asked her if things would be better if I moved closer.

"No," she said. "It would be worse."

The last morning together, I asked her if she ever thought of me. She shook her head "yes," but I wasn't convinced. I thought she was just appeasing me. She didn't want to deal with the true answer.

Goldmund had caught a mouse in the kitchen. Actually, two mice. I flung them outside to her disappointment. I left a milk carton on the porch overnight and in the morning, it was gone. Must have been a big animal.

I was happy with my thoughts. I was happy with Goldmund on my lap, happy in my cottage with the sun, birds, and quiet. When I was lost in my world of writing and ideas, I would forget my aloneness and needs. Nothing else existed. Just my thoughts and the words on the paper. I could go for hours, revising and rewording. I had finished the article for New Directions and got all spaced. I had lunch with AB but even her humorous take on life didn't bring me back. "You should have seen the look on the postal clerk's face," she announced. "I put my hand in my pocket and pulled out two quarters as well as some pubic hair."

* * *

My VISTA would run out June 13$^{th}$. The Bar Harbor store had been arranged and there would be living facilities up over the store. I would be working as a salesperson in the craft shop.

On Holy Thursday, I decided to fast till after Easter. I wanted to experience the pain of Christ. I was wearing red today and purple on Friday for the Passion.

I sent off a letter to *MS* magazine. I felt crazy to think that the publishers would accept my proposal—an extended version of the *Women at the Co-op* article.

I took Tweedledee shopping on Good Friday. "God damn it! It's his Friday to come (referring to the garbage man) and I don't like anything to bother me when I have to go to Doug's." She was tying up the garbage bags when I arrived. I noticed she hid the mustard, ketchup, and sugar in the wood stove. Just another day in looney tunes.

Kate, the gay professor at UMO, called to see if I wanted to go to Washington for a protest march on the war. We were to meet in Cambridge the first weekend in May. I wrote to the Lioness to see if she wanted to get together.

Secretary at the Co-op gave me a purple pen!

That night, I was doing dishes. Goldmund jumped up on a pile of wood under the kitchen window and surprised me. I always wanted to be surprised by life.

The night before Easter Sunday the moon was full and everyone at Mandala got drunk. Totally out of character, we sang and danced. The Hierophant retired early. Later, I jumped on her bed, and Chico barked wildly at me. The Empress watched from her chair. Bear tripped over my guitar, which she thought was a wild animal.

On Easter Sunday morning, I had breakfast with Tweedledee. She told me she would cry when I left. "We've had our spats, but I like you," she said. Then I went over Tweedledum's and sat on the floor listening to her stories. She was relaxing in her rocker, looking out the window with her big, beautiful blue eyes. Her gray hair was pulled back in a ponytail on top of her head and she was dressed in black pants and a loose-fitting smock shirt. Her voice trailed off getting softer and softer, but she kept talking and talking.

Sometimes she looked into my eyes, and I wondered what she was looking for. As I looked into her eyes, I knew that I was looking for my grandmother. That day I stayed longer than usual.

"You have good people D. You can't talk to them when they're dead. It's good you're going home. When I was in the nursing home, there was an old Italian woman that everyone snubbed, but I was friends with her. I liked her. She was a good woman. She didn't hurt anyone. Just cause she talked different. When her family came to visit, she always said to me, 'You stay.' The Co-op will never find another one like you, D. You teach, you do the paper and outreach."

When I got up to leave, I kissed her forehead and rubbed her back. I felt like Dorothy when she heard her family calling her and decided it was time to go home. It was still hard to leave her friends in Oz.

I called *New Directions for Women*. The junior editor liked the article and was bringing it to the editorial board meeting.

While I was working with Vera on the calendar, the Empress came in mouthing off about something she needed by the end of the day.

"And I write about how different this organization is than other organizations," I said. "What lies! I'm going to burn for this," I teased.

"Stop it." She laughed and hit me with the newspaper in her hand. "You won't find another organization like this across the country."

"That's for sure!" I replied. Swat, she hit me again.

The next Saturday night, I went to a dress-up party at Richard and Frank's, friends of Beth. The house was way up on a hill with a huge barn. It had been owned originally by the playwright Robert Anderson who had written *Tea and Sympathy* and was married to the actress, Teresa Wright. It was a gorgeous house. Every window had a view of the mountains.

I went as Betty Davis, wearing dark sunglasses, baggy olive-green tailored pants and matching sweater, hat, heels and carried a long cigarette holder and an axe.

Doris Day music played in the background. Most of the guests were gay. Later that night I was kneeling next to a blonde woman.

We were alone in the room, reading magazines on the coffee table. I gently placed a kiss by her lip. I wasn't sure why. I felt sort of foolish, yet sort of brave as I knew she was with another woman. She just looked at me. Then someone came into the parlor, so I went back to reading the magazine.

I told the High Priestess about dressing up as Betty Davis and she told me that one of her friends actually knew the actress. The friend went to school with the daughter of Betty Davis. She said Betty was harsh, and very tough. She threw money around showing off.

I was deep into working at my desk when a dirty paper flew onto my desk. I saw Bear walk by, and I screamed for her, "Get the paper off my desk."

"It was the Empress, not me," she responded.

In a rather firm, definitive voice I said, "Empress, you get this off my desk. It is not a garbage pail!" To my surprise, she came right in and got it off. I seemed to have a newfound source of power now that I was leaving.

The Learning Center chose the nun from the Hierophant's order to be director instead of the Bear.

According to the Hierophant, Bear was not happy with the choice and promised, "we'll get them." The Hierophant was spending most of her time with the nun. I could see that interesting forces were lining up. It was a good time to be leaving.

"I feel caught between the Bear and the Learning Center," said the nun. "I really don't want to hurt Bear."

"Don't feel that way," said the Hierophant. "It was fated that you would get the job. Besides, it's nice for me to have some help finally. Things were bad five years ago when I first came. Everything was dispersed with no direction. The personnel manager had nothing to do with hiring, and no one knew what they were doing."

"That's sounds like it is now," I said.

"No, it's much better now," responded the Hierophant.

When I left for Connecticut on Thursday, I hadn't heard from the Lioness, so I assumed the worse. She didn't want to see me at all. When I got home, my mother wanted to talk about my gayness.

"Now, Dorothy, last time you were here we talked about something. I don't know if you want to talk about it, but you weren't serious, were you?"

"Yes Mom, I was serious."

"Oh, D,"

"Mom, I'm very serious. That's why I told you."

"But I just want what's best for you."

"What you want and what I want are two different things. I can't live my life trying to make you happy."

"Yes, I know," she said in an upset tone. It was obvious that we didn't agree so it was probably better to avoid the topic since it was painful for both of us.

After dinner on Friday, I was watching TV and the Lioness called. "Didn't you receive my note?" she asked.

"No," I responded. "What note?"

"That's what I thought. You should have gotten it early in the week. I'm sorry. What did you think?" she asked sincerely.

"Well, I thought you didn't want to meet."

"That's what I was afraid of," she said.

"What did the card say?" I asked.

"It said, 'Let's meet for dinner.'" My immediate thought was—dinner only? But I didn't ask. I didn't want to hear the answer. I was suffering already. My stomach was upset. "I'm coming in tomorrow morning to leave for Washington for the peace march. We could meet Monday or Tuesday on my way back."

"I'm not available either day," she responded.

"What about breakfast tomorrow?" I was running out of options. "I could leave at 6:00 am and be there around 8:30 am."

"Fine," she responded. "I'll see you around 8:30 am in the courtyard."

I was so shaken after this phone call. I went to my sister's to talk about it. I told her how stupid I felt. She told me that she still had feelings for her old boyfriend, Charles, even after he was so rotten to her, so she understood how I felt. "It's not stupid, she said adamantly. "It's normal."

After a restless night, I got up early and left as planned, but didn't get to the university till around 9:45 am due to heavy traffic. When I arrived, the Lioness was not in the courtyard. I managed to get inside the dorm, but she wasn't there either. Then just as I was leaving, I saw this streak come tearing around the gate. It was the Lioness in blue cap and a yellow work shirt her mom had given her. Her face was beet red, and she was on the verge of tears. I hugged her and started to laugh. She started choking.

"Shall we sit down for a while?" I asked.

"No, I'm all right," she said while taking deep breaths. "I got up at 6:00 am and said to myself, 'D is leaving now.' So, I went back to sleep. I got up at 7:00 am and said D is halfway now so I can sleep for a while longer. Then I overslept. When I got up, I ran straight from the bed to the street."

We had a nice calm breakfast. At times, she had tears in her eyes. I didn't ask why. She had been doing a lot of work, and just handed in a paper. June had been in Europe all month showing her work.

"She will be coming back this week," she said relieved.

"Are you worried about her?" I asked.

"Yes," she said and went on to explain about June's exploits in Europe. I listened half-heartedly.

We talked little about us. There was no time. She told me how she got a phone call at 2:00 am from some college boys down in Georgia. They decided to call Harvard. One of the boys had a grandmother with the Lioness's last name so they called information and got her number. She thought it was fun that they did that.

"I like doing crazy things like that," she added. She planned on writing to the guy after he wrote and apologized. I really couldn't get into this conversation. Her childish manner repulsed me, and I didn't feel it was wise for me to see her anymore.

She tagged along to pick up Kate. On the return ride, I caressed her fingers. She seemed to like the affection but didn't offer any plans to meet on my return. After she got out of the car, Kate said to me, "Don't see her anymore. Those straight ladies are a drain on us."

I was open with Kate and told her all about the Empress and myself. She questioned how I knew she was gay too.

"What is the channel for getting information around the Co-op?" she asked.

"There's no channel. I just assumed you were gay. When I started talking about myself, you seemed to understand," I replied.

We arrived in Queens, and her two sons were hanging on the fire escape of the apartment. She decided to buy a hibachi grill to have a barbecue on the small iron porch. As we were cooking, two fire engines arrived, and the firemen looked up at us.

"I guess this was a bad idea," she said. Later that night Kate asked, "Mind sharing a bed with me?"

"No, fine," I said. But all night, I lay facing the other direction without moving. It was difficult for me to sleep next to a woman and do nothing.

We had breakfast at a Friendly's restaurant, and I had a disagreement with the manager about politics. Kate bared her teeth and said fiercely, "and you think you can change the mind of Haig when you can't even change the mind of that Friendly manager?"

I was quite taken aback. She was an overpowering personality. She called herself a Marxist Lesbian. We had a standing battle on our methods of approach—violence versus pacifism. She had been celibate for the past five years. Before that, she had lived in Ireland with a female lover until the lover's husband objected. Kate moved back to Maine and waited two years for her lover to join her. The lover finally agreed to move to the US, but just days before Kate's birthday, the lover called and said she had taken a job and would not be coming over. Kate asked her to come for ten days at least. She refused, and Kate sent a "fuck you" telegram.

"Actually, I had to revise the wording. The office would not send my first version," she said sternly.

Kate liked strong coffee, cigarettes, whiskey, and women. When she dressed up for the trip to Washington, she looked very smart. Attractive salt and pepper hair. Kate was a professor who had been fired from the University when it was reported in the newspaper that she was a lesbian. The reason given was incompetence. Three weeks later she was asked to leave her apartment. The super said she was too noisy.

"If you go against the system, you will be fired," she warned. She had a very masculine facade, but I sensed an insecure side. I thought she could be gentle if she wanted to be.

Overall, the weekend was enjoyable, and the march was a huge success. Before parting, we stopped at a diner in Cambridge, and she told me to get in touch with her before I left Maine.

When I got back, I found the Lioness's letter waiting for me. It was depressing. I was glad I hadn't received it before the trip. She couldn't handle more than dinner, and it would have difficult for me to leave her. It read:

Dear D,

Dinner would be neat for me. Hopefully, I will have just passed in one of my papers . . . I'm afraid I'd like to ask you to find somewhere else to spend the night . . . I'm under a lot of academic pressure right now. I guess I just don't feel up to dealing with "authenticity" over more than dinner. What you said really struck home . . . Please don't come feeling hurt and let me know about anger . . . I've had a funny few weeks. Part of it is being lonely cause June's away. Two nights ago, I just broke down, crying-work pressure, not getting anything done and being scared of failure, and this upwelling of grief . . . I am feeling more and more, a fear of my own very hidden dark side that I'm afraid to let myself see . . .

Your writing projects sound exciting- you're hitting the professional circuit! I keep thinking and being awed that you told your mum . . .

Love L

I was right about thinking she would run scared after my honesty.

\* \* \*

I went into work late on Tuesday, and we all just ignored one another. Then the Empress said rather sarcastically, "Did you go down there and get all your energy out?"

"I didn't go down there with energy," I replied.

"I know. I'm just kidding," she responded and walked into her office and shut the door.

I really didn't like her anymore. I went home to sleep. Goldmund was waiting on the roof. She had been gone for three days per my kitty sitter. She rubbed her face on mine.

When I woke up, I tried to do chemistry but couldn't read. I really thought I was losing it. This thing with the Lioness really affected me. I kept looking in the mirror to make sure I was still there.

By Wednesday, I was a little better and helped Pa Kettle with proofing the next edition of the paper. It looked good. I toyed with the idea of calling Kate to go with me to see a film about *Ulysses*, but I didn't trust my motives. I was still so hung up with the Lioness. I liked Kate and thought we could be friends. I said to myself, 'D, you can't be an operatic woman in the aloneness of your room.' I didn't call. Instead, I went by myself and stopped at Carlos's for a glass of wine with a few other people from the Co-op. He asked me to read a short story he had written about a woman he was involved with. I gave him my thoughts as I was reading, and he said I was reacting and not being critical. Was there a difference? The woman was insane. I told him I got the impression that he didn't feel she was sincere. Funny, on the next page the woman character accused him of the same thing. I told him I didn't feel his emotion in the piece. He said that was what he was trying to evoke. I found that strange.

"What is life to you?" he asked.

"A learning process," I responded.

"For me, it is movement," he said.

"Two nice abstract ideas," I added.

Then, somehow, the conversation focused on suffering. "Suffering is useless. I find it contemptible," I said.

To my surprise, Carlos responded, "D, I never saw anyone who suffered as much as you. Did you know it shows all over you? You're so young, and yet you hit such lows. You're not God, and you are not responsible for the world. What are you going to do with all the suffering?"

I couldn't answer. I just started crying.

"Do you know you brighten up the Learning Center with your infectious laughter?" implored Carlos to lessen the blow. I got up and got my coat.

"I better go," I said. Carlos walked me to my car, and I knew he felt concern for me. I went home, started a fire, and cried. I cried in the morning on the way to Bangor. It probably had something to do with the weekend and the Lioness.

She used to be such a fun part of my life.

\* \* \*

A gay symposium was held at USM in Portland over Mother's Day weekend and Beth encouraged me to attend. My grandmother had died on Mother's Day. A big, strong, full-breasted woman, she towered over my grandfather who delighted in her robustness and bragged, "more to love."

Cooking was her specialty. To this day people still reminisced about the meals they had had in her kitchen. Her veal cutlet was to die for. Her love of opera passed to me. She had her quirks, though. No one could take the wine from the table till she was finished with it. If her daughters lingered a bit too long on the stairs after their dates, my grandmother kept yelling their names from the third-floor porch. Even with a broken leg, she made my Aunt guide her down the street so she could search for my mother who was out a little later than she should have been. In her early 50's, she got hit by a car and landed flat on the hood with her chest. She developed breast cancer a few years later and it metastasized into her bones. My mother and aunts said the accident caused the cancer. Maybe they were right.

The day before she died, she could hardly move. Mom took me to the hospital, though, and miraculously her spirit revived. I was only 11 months old. She held me all day oblivious to all the pain in her body. It must have bonded us because I've always felt her presence in my life though I was really too young to remember her. I only had one year of her. One year to cause a lifetime of longing.

I learned that Mother's Day started as a mothers' protest to war. Later, It was changed to a mother recognition day. I didn't call my mother.

To my surprise, one of the workshops on May Sarton was led by Kate. Apparently, Kate was a personal friend of the writer. After a video of a poetry reading, Kate came over and asked if I had gotten over the Lioness yet.

"Not quite yet," I replied.

"Well, don't waste too much of your time. Look around you. There are plenty of available women. No one is worth that much pining. You'll see that eventually," she said.

I roamed around the campus by myself but found it hard being in the gay environment. I wasn't sure why. I couldn't be natural. I felt like a junior high girl standing by the wall waiting to be asked to dance. Later, I shared with Beth how I felt, and she understood.

"You're not alone," she said. "Everyone feels like that. It's scary putting yourself in a vulnerable position."

Beth invited me to join her friends for supper. We met at one woman's apartment and there was a trunk full of costume clothes. I put on a pair of purple pants and scarf and everyone else followed suit dressing up with scarves, sequin jackets, feathers, etc. It was so eccentric. We made such a scene walking into the gay play that night, and then to the dance, which was fun till the window came crashing down due to the heavy wind and rain. Everyone left for the bar, *Rumors*, a wild place with red lights and drag queens. Despite the mobs of people, I felt very lonely. Shortly after arriving, I told Beth I was leaving, and she begged me to stay at her friend's apartment.

"You can't drive all the way back. You've been drinking. Just stay the night and leave early in the morning," she insisted. But I lied and told her that I had a hotel room.

Instead, I drove to the next town and parked in the lot of a shopping center. I wrapped my sleeping bag around me and slept in the car. It wasn't too bad, just chilly in the morning with no place to brush my teeth.

The next afternoon, after a productive day of work on the catalogue, the Hierophant came and asked me to go to dinner on Wednesday at one of the local's homes.

"I can't. I have a dinner date with the Empress. She wanted to take me to dinner before I leave."

"But she agreed to go with us that night," she replied. I didn't say anything. Later, the Empress came into my office and said, "Our dinner date is Tuesday, right?"

"No, it's Wednesday," I replied.

"You said Tuesday," she insisted.

"No, I didn't. I have class on Tuesday. Wednesday was the night."

"Well then, can you go after class on Tuesday? Is that too late? The Hierophant has plans for me on Wednesday."

"Yes, I can go after class." I wish I had just canceled. This dinner was just a formality anyway. Why did she want to put me through it?

But supper on Tuesday with the Empress was enjoyable even after all my negative thoughts. Not wanting to drink locally, she suggested a Chinese restaurant in Bangor.

"I thought about drinking Tequila sunrises all day," she said sipping her fourth drink while I was on my second.

"The gay lifestyle is not an easy one," she said as if she had some understanding of my difficulties.

"You're right on that one," I said.

"But one should not have such a limited understanding of one's self," she continued. "We are more than our sexual preference."

"I agree," I said. Then she alluded under her breath about herself coming out of a difficult, "violent", situation.

"What do you mean? Explain," I said.

"I'd rather not get into it," she replied.

"How did you and the Hierophant get together?" I asked thinking that the drinks had let down her guard a bit.

"The Hierophant had written to me and asked if she could come and work."

"It must be hard for you with this new nun living out there. You must feel like the third wheel," I said.

"It's different. But you never know. I might surprise her and have another plan," she added but didn't expand on what that plan might be. "I don't think the Hierophant likes me," she said very vulnerably.

"She likes you but not your methods," I responded.

"It's hard overseeing a diverse group. Mandala means a lot to me. It's the first place where I could grow flowers. I'm a socially limited peasant girl, uneducated. God led me to Mandala. But I think now it can take care of itself. Maybe it's time for me to move on."

"You don't mean that," I said. "Mandala needs you." She just nodded and turned down her eyes. She could never leave Mandala. She needed to be needed.

"What was your life like before you entered the convent?" I asked changing the subject.

"I was on the verge of going away with a lover," she stated.

"A woman? Or man?" I asked.

"One of each," she answered. We both laughed.

"What do you want your life to be?" she then asked me.

"Operatic, passionate, not boring," I responded lifting my glass.

She laughed and said, "Your life will never be boring, I can predict that." She asked how things were going now that I had found love.

"I found it and lost it," I replied. "The Lioness told her parents about us and that has made the difference."

"Oh, that's too bad. You must be really hurting. Do you still see her?"

"No, not much. It's too difficult. She's under a lot of strain. They hit her where it matters the most—her career. I don't seem to fit into the pattern. Maybe if I were twenty and a Harvard graduate."

"What do you want to be?" she asked.

"Not twenty and a Harvard graduate! I just want to be the woman I am."

"Well, it depends on where her head is."

"Yeah, life is so much fun."

"Isn't it?"

We left soon after and she dozed in the car, her head drooping toward my side. I suggested that she stay at my place as she was in no shape to drive.

"Just drop me off at the Co-op," she retorted. "I can sleep there."

"I won't attack you. I promise. I'm taking you to my place," I said, as I was afraid she would try to drive home once I dropped her off. Hesitantly, she consented.

She slept on the little bed next to the window in all her clothes. I played the *Moonlight Sonata* for her, but she was asleep before it ended. I turned it off, undressed and got into my bed. I was surprised that I was calm and not bothered by her sleeping so close. I slept well except that Goldmund would periodically dig her nails into the covers.

The next morning, the Empress got up early and announced, "I want to go to Mass."

I laughed.

"Why are you laughing?" she asked.

"I don't know. Nervous reaction." I wasn't sure why, myself. Drinking made everything funnier. I stayed in bed and watched her leave.

Later that day, Tweedledum finally pulled the bare ass trick on me. She walked out on the porch with no pants on. I was afraid she had lost it. But she quickly went back inside and came out with her pants and then spent the next few minutes roaming around the house like a little child. I remained calm.

"What are you doing?" I asked.

"I'm not feeling well," she said. "Sore Suzy."

Even Goldmund was acting nuts lately. She jumped into the stove and came out sneezing from the cold ash. Then she shredded the newspaper. The High Priestess said, "she's not meant to be a mother." I took her to be spayed and hoped that would calm her down. When I went to pick her up, I found out that she had been pregnant with four kittens. The procedure cost me more money than anticipated.

Star came over on the weekend and after dinner, she smoked a joint. Then she started in on the usual, "I would sleep with a woman if it was the right time. But I wouldn't want anyone to know. It wouldn't be for feelings or anything. Someday, I'll do it." This was a little too pushy for me. I told her I wasn't interested in sleeping with any woman especially after the Lioness.

"Oh D, you need a fling." Then she asked me, "Tell me honest. Did you ever think about me that way?"

"Well, in the beginning, I thought you were rather attractive. Those blue eyes drove me crazy. But you were a student, and I don't mess with students." I knew where this was leading, and I thought to myself, why do straight women always want to experiment?

"Oh, D. How flattering."

"But not now. We're good friends. It would not work," I added.

My reasoning didn't seem to convince her. I'm sure the pot had something to do with it. She tried a bit more to pressure me, but I backed off.

"Let's go out," I said. When we came back, she asked, "So do you have a vibrator?"

"Why," I asked.

"I want to use it," she said.

"Oh," I responded.

"Would you rather I use it on you?" she asked.

"No, Star." We went to our respective beds. I turned out the lights and realized she was serious. I felt so awkward listening to the buzzing and so thankful when she turned it off! But shortly the buzzing started again.

"D, do you have two of them?" she asked.

"No, Star."

"Then it must have gone on in the box."

The next morning, she was a bitch. Everything bothered her. It was raining. I asked if she wanted onions in her eggs. She said she didn't care. So, I put them in but then she complained about them.

"You should know when I say, 'I don't care' it means no."

"I didn't know that." This was not going to be easy. A woman scorned!!! When she left, I threw the vibrator out.

\* \* \*

I began reading *Recovery* by Sarton and realized that Kate was mentioned in the book. I felt so foolish spouting off to her like I did. No wonder she didn't pursue a friendship with me. Sarton wrote that Kate had put a prism in her window.

The High Priestess had given me a prism. When I next saw her, she was at her wits' end with her husband. She was reading a book on divorce to protect herself since she knew he would contest her wishes.

"As if legal chains have any effect on our feelings," she said. She was sharing a place with a woman friend, who also had kids. "Living with her has been the most comfortable time of my life," she declared. I wondered if the High Priestess ever thought about the possibility of being in a lesbian relationship.

During my last few days at the Co-op I entertained a new woman, Audrey, who came to volunteer for the summer. I suggested that she apply for one of the Bar Harbor jobs after she poured her heart out to me. She had left the Peace Corp where she had been working with lepers. She couldn't handle the physical nursing work especially since her background had been accounting. She had been roaming since. Later when I told Ma Kettle that Audrey might be applying for the craft store, she said, "Mama, you should know that that woman has a drinking problem and gets violent. She lost her last three jobs. But maybe you can help her."

"I'll do my best," I said, and worried that maybe I had done the wrong thing by suggesting that she come work at the store.

On my last day, I made the final payment of the fire opal and then headed off to the popular tourist spot. Lisa and Audrey had been approved as summer workers. Audrey was going to live in the apartment and Lisa decided she would pitch a tent somewhere in town.

The store was in a great location right across the street from the main square in Bar Harbor. It didn't take long for Goldmuld to adapt to the new environment. She ran out into the big back yard and began playing with the bees. Above the store was an apartment complete with a gas stove and hot water! I was ecstatic! Baths!

In the front, a porch extended over the roof of the store and was perfect for sunbathing. From this height, it was possible to see the ocean, a short four-block walk. I had never worked in a tourist town before, but I felt at home having grown up in a shore town.

The first day, I tried organizing the shelves in the store, but customers kept coming in and I did about $60 worth of business in two hours. Lisa arrived in the late afternoon and relieved me.

It was a beautiful sunny day, so I went down to the ocean rocks –one of the first places I had taken the Lioness last summer. Being by the shore really was good for my psyche. I loved lying in the sun. I relaxed and wrote her a letter.

The next day I built a shelving unit to display goods. Unfortunately, I had to stop work early to drive back to the Co-op to pick up my check. The Lioness called while I was in my office. Our conversation was going fine till she said, "we should talk about things."

"What things?" I asked. "Do you want me to visit?"

"No, not that," she said in an upset tone. "Forget it. I'll write to you," she said and hung up rather quickly.

I ended up with a wicked headache. It was better when we didn't interact.

Later, Lisa asked why I was upset, and I told her about my conversation. She defended the Lioness saying, "Maybe she's not meeting her needs by focusing on one thing."

"She's running away from her needs," I replied. I didn't really want to discuss the Lioness with Lisa. Lisa had lost weight and looked great.

On the weekend, Lisa and Audrey went clamming and I minded the store. The police had discovered Lisa's tent and made her take it down, so she moved into the apartment and bedded down on the parlor floor.

On June 1st, my 31st birthday, everyone from the Co-op came up for a potluck supper. I really didn't want a fuss, but Ma Kettle brought tons of food and a lilac color iced cake. The small apartment was overrun with people. One of the kids put on the faucet to the clogged bathroom sink and water overflowed down to the store. What a mess!

The Empress gave me a pottery mug. The best present, though, was a letter from Jack telling me that Jill and he had finally gotten married. There was no card from the Lioness.

After everyone left, Lisa, Audrey, and I drank a gallon of red wine. Lisa suggested we go to the beach, and Audrey bought another bottle of wine on the way. Bad move. After finishing that bottle, Lisa and I ran around hooting like Indians while Audrey squatted under a tree with the empty bottle in her lap.

"This sucks," said Audrey. Then she called me over and said, "Sit next to me." I did, and she hugged me while slurring, "I love you."

"You love me now," I said.

"I love you every night," she replied. I chalked it up to the wine. She started crying and I couldn't understand any of what she was saying. We went home soon after. While I was kneeling feeding Goldmund, she came over and started rubbing my back.

"I wish Goldmund would come and sleep in my bed," she said. "I'm offended that she doesn't like it when I hold her up in the air."

Then she looked deep into my eyes and moved closer as if she was going to kiss me. I didn't know quite what to do. I needed physical closeness, but I wasn't over the Lioness. It didn't feel right so I got up and went to talk to Lisa. Audrey marched into the bathroom. When I finally went to my room, I prayed that she wouldn't try to come into my bed.

She either forgot me, or was too drunk to do anything, but she went straight into her own bed. Later that night, I heard her in the bathroom, bumping around and drinking water. She put on a Heart album at full blast and got back in bed. I waited for a while, then went into her room and turned down the volume. She was fast asleep.

The next day, Audrey got a call from the local woman's baseball team asking her to substitute for a sick player. She got her bike and headed for the field.

Later, while Lisa and I were preparing supper, a woman knocked on the door and asked if Audrey lived with us.

"Yes, she lives here," I said.

"Well, here's her glove and bike," she replied. "She broke her arm. It was a freak accident. She broke it when she was throwing the ball into the home plate diamond."

That night, Audrey came home very upset about not being able to do anything with a broken arm. We tried to cheer her up, but it was difficult as she was in pain and uncomfortable. She played solitaire, while I read. That night, she didn't sleep, and I heard her get up at least twice. I felt bad that I hadn't hugged her when she was crying the other night.

But by Friday she was doing much better. She asked, "What are you doing tonight?"

"I'm just staying here," I replied.

She kept dropping hints that she wanted to sleep with me. I wasn't sure I could do it, though her body was appealing --very thin, tough, and solid. She was masculine looking with a cute Aquarianlooking face and short blonde hair. Nice to look at and at this point the Lioness seemed unreachable. I had to admit, I was curious about what it would be like to make love to Audrey.

On Saturday morning, Audrey and I watched the store and chatted. In the afternoon, one of the team players took her to the hospital. After a few beers, Lisa and I cooked fish and when Audrey came back, she and I went to watch the girls play softball. The team gave her a card and a small present. It was very touching. On the way home we stopped at the dump so I could pick purple flowers.

On Sunday, Audrey's brother came to visit. I went up to take a nap. On her way out, she stopped in my room. She stood in the doorway for a while and then whispered my name. I pretended that I had just woken up. She came over to the bed and I rolled over and hugged her leg. She returned the caress. It was a bit awkward, but a first attempt.

"I have to go," she said softly.

"I'll see you later," I replied affectionately.

"Maybe sooner than later," she added.

When she came back that night, she was blitzed. A few guys joined her. She announced she had to go get a refill on her medicine. One of them was obviously interested in Audrey. He offered to take her to get her medication.

"No, if anything I'll have D take me," she said rather abruptly.

The guy was shocked by her response. She didn't care one bit. Instead, she pulled me into the bedroom and started kissing me. It was wonderful. Such relief. The guy kept knocking on the door.

"I just want to talk to you, ok?" he shouted.

"It's not ok," she responded and kept opening and closing the door telling the guy to leave her alone. Eventually, we took a break and went back into the kitchen.

Finally, everyone left. Lisa and I danced on the porch in the moonlight. Audrey went to the bedroom. Soon I undressed, went into her bedroom, and closed the door. It was a night of wonderful kissing but a bit frustrating as Audrey's arm was in a sling. She couldn't do much but enough under the circumstances. Her body was great. So trim and smooth. I went down on her. She loved it. We fell asleep and woke up kissing in the middle of the night.

"I should tell you I'm a pest to sleep with, unless you enjoy it," she said.

"I enjoy it," I said.

\*    \*    \*

I went to the Co-op on Monday and found a letter from the Lioness dated June 4<sup>th</sup>:

Dear D,

Thanks for your good letter . . . Talking would be a good idea but may be difficult to arrange. I start work for an elderly couple, living on Cape Cod. The woman has Parkinson's, and I will be her hands. When you finish in Maine, I may be able to meet you somewhere in-between. I am very aware that you have made most of the effort into the relationship. I do not forget your writing to me: "I would like to maintain a connection with you, but I will not be the only one to put energy into it and make decisions about it."

. . . Shit. I guess I should just dive in. What I have been feeling is that I don't want to be involved sexually with you. I do not want to deal with the ambiguities and the ambivalence I feel . . .

I am ambivalent and ignorant about sex . . . I am ambivalent about Lesbianism . . . I am ambivalent and afraid of intimacy . . . This discussion has become too abstract . . . Clearly, I enjoy sex . . . The scanty experiences I had with men were strange and uncomfortable. All that was changed with you . . . you helped the lioness shake out her mane, flex her muscles, give voice and throat to a purr of unabashed delight . . .

I've been ambivalent about our relationship from when I gave you the rose and didn't know if "that is what I meant" . . . I am not willing to devote time and effort to our relationship. Sexual attraction on its own doesn't work for me, and I'm not willing to bank on the possibility that we "have something deeper" between us. . . .

I like you D. I like you best when you are strong and powerful in yourself, when you are standing up for yourself, when you are being honest and forthright and independent, even if that means you are telling me how you think I'm avoiding something or that I am full of shit. Be in touch. I will, too.

Stay safe, L Ppps happy 31<sup>st</sup>

She was right about one thing: "this discussion had become too abstract." She had moved me from her heart to her head—a dangerous place to be.

It was a sad day for me—the day we entered the world of abstraction and the best of what we had was gone. This letter was the final realization that I was really out of her life. I felt like I was holding my heart in my hands and it was wounded and bleeding. I would have to learn to patch it back up and tuck it back into the protective shield of my breastplate. And how was I going to do that?

I slept with Audrey that night, and it was awful. I tried to make her come and I couldn't. I got so frustrated and disgusted with myself. I asked her questions, which she didn't want to answer about drinking and her past. Then I sat up and just listened to the quiet. She looked at me.

"I like the quiet," I responded to her questioning eyes. I tried to cry. I couldn't even do that. Finally, I lay back and fell asleep. We woke up in the middle of the night, and she started kissing me. I couldn't imagine why after the way I had acted.

"I love you," she said.

I couldn't say it back to her. In the morning, I tried to entice her.

"I knew you were a horny one," she said. "But I don't think it's me you want to make love to."

She got up and went to work while I stayed in bed. I was zonked. Audrey confused me. I confused me.

On Wednesday night, I went to my own room to sleep, but then got up and went into Audrey's room. I wasn't sure if she wanted to be with me. She did. We hugged, and she cried. She said it was the Dylan music, but I knew that wasn't the real reason. We talked for a while and then she made love to me with her free hand. It was such a relief.

"Was that good enough," she asked.

"Couldn't you tell?" I smiled. She smiled back.

In the morning I wrote the following letter to the Lioness:

Dear L:

I think communicating by letter is the best we can do right now

Regarding your wish that I had been angry or let you know when I was hurt—I consciously didn't want to do that since that would only cause you to react to my feelings.

I reserve the right to grow. I want to be a centered woman who does not control others. I want to be honest but not manipulative.

I am important to you though you are afraid to admit that for you worry about future implications. I am not concerned with future implications. There are things I must do for my career and self, but unlike you, I do not want to focus only on them. Quite contrary, for the first time in my life, I am finding all sorts of people, women especially, who intrigue me. I want to wade in the water for a while. My confidence is improving. I like my liking women.

I think there is more between us than sex, but it was only after sex that we re-entered our level of communication and became just L and D. . . .

I am not attracted to a person based just on sex. I did not think you were attractive till we started talking in the garden. Remember, I wasn't impressed with the omelets! . . .

There are intense feelings between us whether we ever choose to live them out or not.

I have slept with other women besides you but did not find the intenseness as with you.

I worry about you shying away from intimacy. Growth is painful, and we are not always perfect.

My plans are uncertain. Audrey, the other women, broke her arm, and I may stay till next week. I plan on returning in July. We could wait till then to meet, or we could meet sometime next week.

I do think we need time away from each other to sort out things. I'm not sure how I will react to seeing you. I know you like when I am strong, but part of me is very weak. I'm afraid our relationship has entered the abstract realm.

Take care, good to be in the sun again. Love, D

Shortly after receiving my letter, the Lioness called, and we were to meet on June 22 at the Cape.

\*　\*　\*

There was a lot about Audrey I really liked. Proud with an easy manner, she was more masculine than I. A classy gal who wore a different colored watchband for each outfit! I loved her soft, curly, blonde hair and trim body. She kept me laughing with the bold statements that came out of her mouth.

During the week, I had to take her to the hospital. Her arm was not healing properly, and the surgeon had to rebreak it. After they wheeled her into surgery, I went to pick up the fire opal. Funny, the stone didn't have that overpowering beauty it had when I first picked it out last winter.

I waited outside her room. Soon the door opened, and the nurse motioned me in. Audrey was passed out, lying on the sterile table, arm heavily burdened with a white plaster cast. I wanted to just hug and kiss her. When she awoke, tears ran down her face. She was in pain. I hugged her as much as I could without being too obvious. I was amazed at how my feelings were growing for her. On the way out of the hospital, we stopped to get her pills. I bought her a little doll, which said, "Hug me" on it. While I was in the drug store, I could see her sitting in the car. She couldn't see me. She was crying. I gave her a pain pill right away, and she slept on the way home.

Lisa cooked for us. She and I had tequila sunrises while Audrey rested. When Lisa left to work the store, Audrey got up and came for tea in the kitchen. She joked that I take my shirt off. So I did. This shocked her. I offered to take my pants off, but she didn't think that was a good idea.

"You're always surprising me," she said. "Other woman I have been with were not as sexually free as you." Then she pulled me onto her lap. We made love on the kitchen chair. I came by rubbing myself. I wasn't sure what she thought, but I didn't care. She was almost coming when the phone rang. That broke the mood. It was difficult with her arm. And she was very shy about lovemaking.

In the morning, she told me that she liked it when I went down on her. I did, but she still couldn't come. I told her I didn't always need to come to be satisfied. She said it took her a long time to come. I was at a loss. I had never felt so unsure about how to make a woman come. Her body didn't tell me what she needed. I never would have guessed that she liked oral sex from her reactions. I liked waking up beside her. She was always kissing and caressing me. It was nice to be with someone tender. I told her that she was the most affectionate woman I had ever been with.

On the weekend, we went to a party at Hansel and Gretel's. We had clams in the teepee, crabs by the fire, and beer everywhere. The ride home was tough. Audrey kept slapping me to keep me awake. I sang "Betty Davis Eyes" at the top of my lungs. The next morning, one of the guys asked me if I was going to be Betty Davis all day.

During the night, I woke up. Audrey was kissing me. She said she loved me, but I told her that I had had deep feelings for the Empress and the Lioness and that I wasn't ready to do it again right now.

The Hierophant came up to visit on Sunday. She told us that there was a woman in her 60's who was going to volunteer to work at the Bar Harbor shop and that she was going to live with us.

"I don't think that's a good idea," I said. She disagreed.

The woman showed up on Monday as I was flaming with an

Italian couple, buying out the store. When they left, she said, "I hear it's a full-time job."

"No," I said, "only twenty hours."

"But with living space?"

"No, there are three of us already."

"Oh," she said and left.

I had a dream about the Lioness. *We met and both of us had huge backpacks. We were carrying them around. The Lioness was in sort of a daze.*

Audrey and I went for dinner to all you can eat for $7.95—crabs and shrimp. We tried to make love that night, but it was getting harder and harder. We didn't really love one another. We cared about each other and her feelings were stronger than mine. Anyway, we stopped trying.

On Sunday, Lisa helped me load the car for my journey down south. Audrey and I said goodbye upstairs. She cried. I left and stopped at the Co-op to get my purple curtains. Then I headed for the Cape and arrived at about 8:00 pm I called the Lioness and she offered to meet me at Fishmonger's. I got there first and ordered. She arrived 45 minutes later looking rather anxious and on the verge of tears. She sat, and we chatted. I could tell she wasn't comfortable. She kept splashing cold water on her face, so I suggested we leave.

We dropped off her car and went to the beach. I put my black horse blanket on the sand. We lay down. It was cold and windy. I pulled the bottom half of the blanket over our legs. Our bodies touched slightly. Talk was awkward. We spent most of the time in quiet. It got very dark as few stars were shining.

"I really need a shower," I finally blurt out.

"Okay. Take me home," she responded.

When I parked in the driveway, the conversation really began.

"I'm sleeping with another woman," I said.

"I know. I knew when you referred to Audrey as the "other woman", that you were sleeping with her."

"It's not what you think. It doesn't mean anything. I was just trying to support her when she was in such pain."

"I always had a fantasy of wanting to give my body momentarily to someone in a healing sense," she responded. "I must admit I felt a pit in my stomach when I read that part."

"Really? I'm surprised."

"Me, too," she responded and added, "I felt both jealous and relieved at the same time."

We talked for a long time—honestly and openly. We were both

dying. Finally, she got out of the car, and I left to find a hotel room. The only room I could find cost $28! I told the owner I was a Mainer and not used to such high prices.

I passed out on the bed from exhaustion. I woke up startled in the middle of the night feeling like a stained woman. I felt I had betrayed her. From then it was touch and go, thinking about the Empress, thinking about the Lioness, feeling like I was at the edge, like if I let go I would never come back . . . Weird phenomenon . . . Breaking pieces. . . . Noises with no noise. I got scared. I don't know what held me together that night. But somehow, I got through.

In the morning, I called the Lioness, got a cup of coffee, and picked her up. As it was going to be a cloudy day, she suggested an afternoon matinee show. I agreed.

We went off to buy a paper, but it was Monday and no matinees. We drove to the beach and walked out and lay on the sand, side by side. It showered a bit, and the wind was wild. I rolled over at one point and started crying saying, "Why does it matter so much what some people think?"

"Who? The Empress?" she asked.

"Yes. She sets ideals I can't live by."

"What ideals?"

"Living for others. Overcoming the material. I wish I never had met her. What do you think my relationship with her is?"

"Do you love her?" she asked.

"I don't know," I said and turned away from her and started rambling. "Why does the negative always come first? I want to be famous. I am so egotistical. I hate incompetence. I take myself too seriously. I don't know anyone with more mind problems than me." I turned to look at her, and she was gone. She had run down the shore, crossing in and out of the water.

When she came back, I said, "You should have screamed at me to stop my self-indulgence." Instead, she apologized for leaving. I suggested that we go play our guitars. She added before we left, "I want to make sure you get everything out and ask all the questions you want to. Is there anything else you want to ask me?"

"Do you ever foresee us as a possibility?" I asked.

"No," she said definitively.

"Well, I guess that's bottom line. There are no other questions."

From this point on I felt differently. More animus. Rejection pushed me into another part. I got strong and detached and started joking as we went back to the car. We talked about how it usually takes three days to unwind from a visit between us. I took her home and on the way she said, "When I read the part in the letter about the other woman, all I wanted to do was make love to you."

That brought all feelings back to the surface. The way I felt when we made love. The waves were rising, and I was riding them. She cried and I cried. I reached for her hand.

"It was so mechanical with her," I said. "I couldn't even make her come. I felt like such a failure."

"It takes a long time to know someone's body," she responded.

"Why was it so easy with you?" She didn't answer, and I got the impression that she was glad there was an Audrey.

As we approached her driveway, she pointed and said, "Go that way. There's some place I want to show you." She said it was called The Point. It was a nature trail leading to the shore. We walked quietly arm in arm and then sat and watched the water. It was a beautiful place. We talked more.

"Do you think you'll want to marry and have children some day?" I asked.

"I don't know. I have a fear of being with men sexually."

"That's only a problem if you want children. You could choose a woman."

"You're right, but I don't know what I want at this point."

"If you fall in love with someone else, you should tell me," I said to her.

"You shouldn't wait till I fall in love with another. What if I never do?"

"I can't say what my needs will be at that point. Our feelings are obviously different. You don't have the same feelings I have for you."

"I have a bad taste in my mouth," she said.

"Well, you have feelings for me but not enough to make a difference in your life."

"Maybe that's true," she said. Then she got pensive and said, "I want to see you again."

We parted in good spirits, feeling close to one another. We hugged in the car. I kissed her check. She kissed my lips. It was hard to know what each was feeling from the kiss, so much had built up in defense between us. She got out of the car, and I drove home to Connecticut. I missed her terribly.

I had given her the caterpillar with the pipe, but she liked the seal with the blue eyes.

The next few days were difficult at home. I spent a lot of time with my sister. One night, I went to a gay bar in Westport and fantasized on the drive down about meeting women there and asking them to dance. I hoped to meet my gay gym teacher there. But there were very few women in the bar. The music was so loud it hurt my ears. After watching men dance for about an hour, I left.

I watched a blue jay fall gently from a tree, land on the ground, breathe heavily, and die.

During the week, I got a letter from the High Priestess telling me that Mercury was no longer retrograde. Maybe things would get better. She sent a purple scarf.

Letters from Audrey and the Lioness arrived on the same day. One challenged me intellectually, and other, emotionally.

Audrey called me on the word <u>care</u>. I had said in my letter that I cared about her but that I was still hung up with the Lioness. Her response was angry.

> Dear D,
>
> When you were here, it didn't matter what happened because I had you. I'm starting to feel short on humor and closer to self-destruction. I hate feeling like this . . . I can hardly believe that you are not interested in getting involved with another woman. I guess the Lioness must be "the one" for you. . . . I was pretty taken when I first read your letter. That was a day of tears. I didn't hear anything I was expecting to hear, and I felt almost like I was talking to a stranger. I thought that in fact if you were trying to hurt me, you did a good job. I just want somebody to really love me. As for care. What does that mean? All I ever get is care. My insurance agent "cares," as far as that goes!
>
> I hope I don't sound too bad. I really don't want to. . . . but I am part of this, and I wanted to let you know how I felt.

And from the Lioness:

> Dear D:
>
> . . . It was really good to hear from you. I was out of it for about a day after you left but then normal and am glad to hear you didn't go through the three-day bit. I am happy you feel that I was able to give to you; I want to be "authentic" . . . You are kind about me running to the water . . . if you feel comfortable opening up to me, I would like to try to help you share. . . .
>
> I'm glad you're home and, boy, can I imagine how the Co-op seems like another life. Different rules. I understand

what you say about being back with your family and how you care about them. I am feeling very strongly about my family. They are the thing most sacred in my life; i think i would die for them . . .

I'm doing ok down here . . . I went to a gay cookout on an island. It was <u>nice</u> to spend time with gay women. A totally different current operates . . . Of course, I must keep this secret from the family I am working for.

I am sitting in a little dockside café writing to you . . . June wrote a great letter in which she said, "I think I feel an enormously powerful neuter when I'm in my studio. I care about great art, not male or female. And there is about great art something profoundly impersonal, something almost? Cool? Great art is ruthless." <u>That's</u> what I feel. Particularly about how great art is impersonal . . . <u>That's</u> the way I want to write . . . I want to shatter illusions. . . .

I wonder how you are doing making CT fit you again. Please keep in touch and stay safe. It was good to see you.

Love, L

As I put the letter down, the green-eyed monster raised its head. The Lioness agreed with June. June who "writes a great letter and says great art is impersonal." I couldn't disagree more. My concept of the operatic woman defied the impersonal – rather she lived and died for the personal. The impersonal feeling was a place to escape to – to avoid feeling pain, rejection. I chose to drown myself in the living, in the difficult world of human beings for that is where the true use of the intellect was put to the challenge. The abstract was easy compared to the realm of the human. My writing would be based on this and no other.

I tried writing a response. I tried taking each sentence apart, pointing out the faulty thinking. Her words meant more than mine . . . She had a hold that I wanted to have . . . But I didn't, and a response would not evoke it . . . better to let it cool within myself . . . I had to learn to live without her, with myself, with failure, with rejection . . . The Lioness was into different things and nothing I could say could change that fact. We spoke a different language. I had to let it go. I put the pen down and crumpled the letter.

I spent the day with my niece at the beach. Detached, I sat and watched her playing in the waves. After a while I joined her in the water but stayed close to the shore. I realized that I never ventured far out into the deep. I didn't like when I couldn't "see." Fear of the unknown. It was the same with life. My niece called to me and said, "Aunt D, you're a baby cause you don't swim in the deep." It was almost as if she had picked up on my thoughts.

\*　\*　\*

My father was having back surgery. I was glad to be back in Connecticut. He had already had by-pass surgery and retired. Early on in his career, he had a bad accident on the job. He was drilling on the roof of a hospital building. An electrical pipe was embedded in the floor structure where it should not have been. The drill hit the wire and he was electrocuted. As he was dangling on the verge of death, a fellow worker somehow pushed him and broke the connection. It made the afternoon news. My mother was watching the special bulletin on TV at the time, not realizing it was my father they were talking about on. After that, he had premature heart and back problems. It was difficult for this man who loved work to be so limited by illness.

One afternoon, he asked me to cut the hedges. I grabbed the hand cutter.

"Use the shears," he ordered. "We have electricity down here."

I didn't want to use them, but he insisted. He was watching me as he stepped up the small embankment of the grass and tripped. I was standing right next to him but couldn't prevent his fall. His leg was cut very badly and wouldn't stop bleeding. I wanted to cry. I felt so bad. He was already in enough back pain.

"It's ok," he said sensing my guilt. "I'm used to life."

I continued cutting the hedges and managed to cut the cord. I braced for the screaming, but none came. Rather calmly and quietly, he spliced it back together. I finished the work. We chatted, and I enjoyed being with him for the first time in a long time.

I decided not to write to the Lioness anymore. Her letters threw me into a dither. That afternoon, I went to the beach, fell asleep on the sand, woke up abruptly, and ran into the water. I swam into the deep end, deeper than I had ever been.

That night, I reread the Lioness's letter and did not feel as angry as before. I didn't think she had intentionally tried to hurt me. She was just confused.

Feeling horny, I decided to go back up to Maine for a few weeks. Audrey had called earlier, and from the conversation, I knew she wanted to see me. I had mixed feelings. I needed physical love but was afraid it might be awkward being with her now that my feelings were out in the open.

The next day, I left for Bar Harbor and arrived late in the evening. On the drive, a hawk flew in front of my car. The speedometer and odometer stopped working.

"No mileage on this trip?" I thought.

When I parked the car, I saw Audrey looking out the window. I waved but I she didn't recognize me.

"Forgot who I am already?" I said as I walked in the door.

"It is you, D! I'm so glad to see you," she said and from her tone of voice, I could tell that she had been drinking.

We got into bed and kissed for a long time. It was nice to feel more of her body as the new cast was smaller and only covered her arm. We fell asleep and kept waking up kissing. We didn't talk till early the next morning. I was honest and told her I didn't think there was anything between us. I told her I wasn't good for her. She cried, and I held her, and then we had sex.

Goldmund had gotten fatter. She was glad to see me and had slept at our feet all night. The QE II had arrived overnight, and Audrey and I got up early to see it. It was docked just outside the main part of town. Due of the influx of tourists from the ship, the craft shop was busy all day

That night Lisa and Audrey counted the money. I got very moody and didn't feel like talking. I went to take a bath. When I came back out, I hugged Audrey. We went for a quiet walk and then to bed, but I couldn't do anything.

"Let's just hug," I said.

"That's fine with me," she answered. "I'm happy just to hold you."

The next day I watched the store so that Audrey could have some free time. At dinner, she said, "I'm going to ask one of the baseball players for a date."

"Good. That's good," I responded. She pretended she wasn't bothered by my lack of interest, but I knew her better.

We went to a party together on Sunday night. I stayed in the parlor while Audrey remained in the kitchen. When the music started, we danced. She drank and smoked quite a bit. I made her leave with me just after midnight.

On Tuesday, I called the Empress and asked how she was doing.

"Good," she responded and didn't ask how I was.

"How is the store doing," she asked.

"Good," I responded.

"We need to keep selling. These poor people depend on us. I have to go to a meeting now," she said and hung up the phone. I banged the phone down and said, "Fuck her." I turned and Muriel, a new woman who was volunteering in the store, was standing right behind me.

"I hate that woman," I said.

"Want to talk about it?" Muriel asked.

"It's too long a story to tell," I replied.

"I have all day and a bottle of good French wine. Want to join me?"

"Sure," I said. We sat at the kitchen table getting to know one another. From her makeup and wild clothes, I could tell Muriel was eccentric and free spirited. After polishing off the bottle of wine while munching on cheese, olives, and bread, I said, "I love French wine. I love French women. I love France. Matter of fact, I love everything French."

"Me too," she said. "Paris is my favorite city."

"Mine too," I replied, "I was there in the 70's and would love to go back."

"Me too," she said, then added, "I wish I had a reason to go back. I know. Let's make a date to meet in Paris."

"When?" I asked.

"Let's see. Has to be a good year."

"How about 1984?" I asked. "That will give us both time to prepare."

"Great. How about in May?" she replied. "Paris is beautiful in May."

"Okay. Let's meet in May, on Mother's Day. Whatever Sunday that is. Let's see. Where? Hmm. I got it! Under the Eiffel Tower at 4:00.

"It's a date," she agreed.

"And there is no excuse not to be there, barring death or sickness in the hospital," I added.

"Agreed," she said, as we clicked our glasses to secure the pack. I took the promise seriously.

That night, I had dinner with Lisa. She told me that she could never understand why Audrey and I had gotten involved. Audrey had gone out with some other friends. When she came back, I was sleeping, but she tried making love to me. I tried to stop her without being obnoxious, but she continued so I let her. She satisfied herself, and then we slept.

Audrey and I slept together for the entire stay. I finally learned how to make her come. If I just lay on top of her and rotated my hips, she came. This was different than what I was used to with the Lioness.

I decided to extend my stay till early August. "Extreme moodiness" was the only way I could describe my mental state since coming back to Maine.

On Sunday night after work, I went to Sand beach by myself. It was a wonderful experience. First, I lay between the mountains and the sea. I felt like part of the environment dressed in my navy sweatpants and dark green army shirt. Even my skin matched the sand color. Then I walked barefoot down toward the water. The wind was wild. I started climbing up on the rocks. I wanted to go to the top, but I was afraid since it was getting dark. I forced myself to go on, though, and I was glad I did. The wind was overpowering up there. It howled and whistled. It was dark. I stood at very edge of the peak with the upper half of my body hanging over the ocean below. I opened my arms to the wind. It blew in my face. My body hung suspended and supported by the powerful wind. I wasn't afraid anymore.

A psychic told me that Aries people <u>think</u> what they feel.

One night, I decided to just stay home alone. I lay on the couch. Audrey came in and asked, "Who are you waiting for, Sleeping Beauty?"

I was thinking "the Knight," but I answered, "the mock turtle."

"I make good soup," she replied.

We started talking about our feelings for each other. She had been drinking.

"Why don't you love me?" she asked.

"There are parts of myself that I don't naturally share with you. You need someone who can give you more. You deserve to be loved completely." She seemed to accept my answer. Later, some friends stopped over. I went out on the porch with them. Audrey went to bed fully clothed. After everyone left, I read for a while and decided to sleep in the parlor. I heard her get up in the night. She made some soup for herself, and then stood by the couch eating it.

"What?" I said.

"Thanks, D. You're a real good friend," she said and went to bed.

I went out early the next morning and walked the foggy beach. I tried to write a letter to the Lioness but never finished it. There were dogs barking, and the waves were crashing, and I was distracted. I went back. Audrey was in a friendly mood.

For the next few days, I visited friends at the Co-op. Everyone missed me. When I got back to Bar Harbor late at night, Audrey was still up. We made love. It was good for both of us. We both came, and I enjoyed being next to her body. It was just dealing with her the next day that I had a hard time with.

Do I dare believe all that happened next? The Tarot reading was almost completed. The anima figure I mistakenly thought was the Empress, was the High Priestess. They were both mother figures and Cancers. How could I have known? It would never seem possible what took place.

On Sunday, Lisa, Audrey, and I went to a Blue Hill fair. Lisa ventured off on her own while Audrey and I had lunch in the small restaurant. As we sat there, the High Priestess and her husband came in and sat at the table next to ours. The High Priestess was wearing a feather hat and an owl mask in honor of the festivities. She looked happy enough and I thought maybe things were better between her and her husband. Then I caught a glimpse of her true feelings as I stared. Her eyes looked down and displayed that heavy given up look. When she looked up, she caught me looking at me.

"Can you come for a visit tomorrow and stay for dinner?" she asked.

"Yes, of course. I'd love to," I responded.

On the way home, Lisa and I chatted, but Audrey was quiet. At the apartment, Lisa and I sat at the kitchen table drinking tea, while Audrey went down to the store shouting a sarcastic, "Have a good night", as she slammed the door behind her. I tuned her out and started cleaning blueberries to make pies. When they were done, I brought Audrey a piece. She was still in a mood.

"What's wrong?" I asked.

"Nothing," she responded. I detached myself and went to bed.

She came in later and explained, "I was angry with myself. I feel worthless. You have so many woman friends. I'm jealous."

I ignored her needs. She tried to caress me, but I stiffened. It was not the way I wanted to treat her on my last night in Bar Harbor.

The next morning after reminding Muriel of our date in Paris, I left. Audrey was already out, so I didn't get to see her. I did stop at the Co-op on the way down to see the Empress. I asked if the Bar Harbor store was living up to expectation.

"Well, it's doing better," she said in a non-flattering tone which I dismissed because I knew it was doing the best it ever did.

"How is the new nun who is running the Learning Center?" I asked.

"She's doing wonderfully," she responded. "It's good to have her." Her comment was so in character and fake, but I didn't flinch.

"I hear you are moving," I asked wondering if the rumors I heard were true.

"Oh, yes. I'm moving into the little retreat house next to mine. The Hierophant and the nun will stay at my house."

"Is that good?" I asked.

"Yes. A growing experience for me," she said. I left since I couldn't stand any more dishonesty. She couldn't possibly be happy with this move. She loved her house. I went over to Tee and Em's to see if they would keep Goldmund, but they were going on an extensive trip and had brought their animals to the Vets.

I drove on to Castine stopping at Hardclimb Hill on the way to talk with Rosa. She didn't recognize me, now that my hair was longer, and I was slimmer. She asked how I liked the Co-op and I told her that the place had really psyched me out. She totally understood and confided, "When I finally left the Co-op, I sat on the couch. I decided I wouldn't do anything until I felt motivated to do so. It took three months before I pulled together and wrote my first poem." As I left, we exchanged addressed and she told me to keep in touch.

When I arrived at the High Priestess's house, I found her standing, pensive, in the garden.

"I've done something stupid," she said. "I had an affair. "Strictly physical attraction and lust. My husband found out when he read my diary."

"He read your diary!" I exclaimed. "Aren't you furious about that?"

"Yes, but the worse issue is that things are coming to an end. We can't live together, but he doesn't want to let me go. He got furious when I said I was going away to school." As we walked, Lupin the cat followed. I had left Goldmund in my car with the window a crack open.

As we continued down the wooded path, she asked, "What is it like loving a woman? Is it any easier? My husband and I don't talk the same language." I didn't respond. I could only give a prejudiced view.

After supper, much wine and smoking a joint (my first), she offered to do a Tarot reading for me.

"I just bought a new feminine deck, and I want to try them out," she said. "You'll be a good guinea pig."

The cards were beautiful, colorful with feminine images. They flowed out of her hands easily as if directed by some higher force while her comments emanated from an eternal knowledge source. The Devil card appeared and upset me.

"I feel like a Judas at times, and the Lioness feels like Mary Magdalene," I said. "I really miss her. I love her so much. She is so beautiful. So beautiful," I kept saying, getting more and more depressed.

"What about the Empress?" she asked. "What's her role in this?"

"She's not conscious," I said.

"The Empress is the Magician," she said, "and Joan d'Arc."

"But when I played that song, the Lioness appeared," I said. "She's Joan d'Arc to me."

"The roles keep shifting," she said. "I feel for Judas. It must have been hard to be in such a position. I liked him."

"The Magician is dangerous," I said.

"Passion is dangerous," she said. I started crying at the mention of passion. My head hung down very close to her face.

"I love her. I love her and miss her," I said again and again, crying, as I continued falling into a deep dark hole. I couldn't hold on anymore. I was sinking deep, deep. . . . Then to my surprise, she gently raised my head, drew it to her face, and kissed me. It was a sweet, gentle kiss.

"To answer your question, making love to a woman is gentler," I said.

"There is a small bedroom at the top of the stairs," she replied as she guided me to the hallway steps. "Go up there and wait for me." I did as she instructed. It was dark, but I found the room and got on the bed. Shortly, the door opened, and she entered. She lay on the bed close to me. I started kissing her.

"I love you," she said.

"Do you mean that?" I asked, surprised at her quick admission.

"I don't know. I don't want to hurt you. I don't know how to love you. I don't know how to make you come?"

"Don't worry. I could never image being with you like this. You have given me such a great gift." We undressed, and our bodies melted into one another. "Does this feel foreign to you?" I asked.

"Oh no. I do love you. You're so small," she said as if she were expecting me to be bigger. I started kissing her all over and caressing her back. The Moonlight Sonata played in the background.

"Oh, D," she whispered as she moved her whole arm slowly up between the cheeks of my ass. It aroused a wonderfully sensuous feeling.

"Oh God," I responded never having felt that before. It made me wild. I went down on her and she was so sweet just like the Lioness. I was in ecstasy, lost in her womanness. Her beauty. Her softness. Her skin. Then she surprised me and went down on me. It was too much for me to bear. I came right away, then I pulled her up. I just wanted to kiss her lips. She kept saying, "Oh, D, I love you." Then the unthinkable happened. Her husband came up the stairs, opened the door, and turned on the light. He saw us. The High Priestess pulled the covers over me. I didn't even care. I just wanted him out so we could go on with our lovemaking. I was disgusted with the interruption. She yelled for him to leave as she got up, pushed him out and locked the door.

"How much more must I be subjected to!" he screamed through the door. "I demand to speak with you right now! You have five minutes, and then I am burning this house down."

"I must go," she said to me as I tried to hold her. It was difficult for the two of us to stop our embrace.

"I want to spend the night with you," I pleaded. I was so hungry for her. "Promise you'll come back."

"Yes, I will," she said as she got up and opened the door. "Sleep well," she whispered as she floated out.

Later that night, she snuck back into my room as she had promised and said, "I still have a commitment to him. I can't stay."

I understood though I didn't want her to go. "When you are free, we can be together."

"Yes," she said.

"Will you wake me in the morning?" I asked.

"Yes, yes, I will," she said and left. At first, I couldn't sleep. I went outside to go to the bathroom and wiped myself with the dew on the grass. I called her name into the night sky. I went back to the room and fell asleep.

When I awoke, there was a kitten on my chest and a glass of water sitting on the bed table. I got a faint glimpse of someone running out of the room. I looked out the window and saw green apples hanging from the tree. Looking back in the room, I saw a white blouse hung on the wall chest on the right. There were feathers on the end of the bedpost. A sewing machine sat in the corner. I knew I was in the High Priestess's secret hideout.

I glanced up at the ceiling and saw Pegasus. At least I thought it was Pegasus. But focusing, I realized it was a blonde woman riding a white horse. A hidden self, I thought.

The door opened and The High Priestess entered. "I came to get some clothes from the closet," she said.

"Pegasus?" I asked pointing to the painted figure on the ceiling.

"No. That's Lucy in the sky with diamonds," she responded.

"What time is it? Are you going to work already?" I asked.

"It's 7:00. Not yet."

Just then her husband called her name. She left. I thought to myself, 'Should I just leave? Is that best?' Quickly, I dressed and left my scarf on the pillow as a sign to her. I quietly ran downstairs and went to my car. Goldmund had managed to escape through the small opening of the window. I called her name, but she didn't come. I got in the car. I couldn't spend the time looking for her. I started the engine.

Just as I was putting the car in gear, the High Priestess ran down the driveway, came up to the car and motioned for me to lower the window.

"How is your cat?" she asked.

"She's gone. She managed to slip through the window."

"Oh, no."

"It's just as well," I said. Obviously, she doesn't want to leave Maine."

"I'll take care of her," she said. "She'll come to us."

"She'll be all right. I'm sure," I responded.

"Now you'll have to come back," she said. She opened the door, got in the car and kissed me.

"Please write to me," I said trying very hard to pull myself away.

"I will." She got out and I left.

I was high all day though I had a terrible hangover!

*    *    *

I was so exhausted I pulled over to the side of the road and slept for two-and-a-half-hours. The words of the High Priestess repeated over and over in my mind, and I tried to make sense out of them. But was there any sense? What did it mean . . . roles kept changing? What was the High Priestess picking up on? Why did I feel like John, Judas, and Christ all at the same time? Why was the Magician dangerous? Why was passion dangerous? Was she worried about herself as dangerous? Jung said the mystic was dangerous . . . The High Priestess said the Empress was the Magician. Yet to me, the Empress seemed schizophrenic. Or was she onto something? She always encouraged me to write about women affecting women. Why? Was the Lioness right when she said Jung was a sexist? Maybe he didn't understand woman's language or approach. Or maybe he needed a woman to interpret. The High Priestess said men and women don't speak the same language. Sarton said that women writers and sex don't agree: "They need to invent a new language. The language of sex was masculine." I sent the High Priestess the black paper rose from the Mother's Day poster. I wondered if she thought I was a "stupid thing." She told me her Aunt lived on an island, alone and senile. She could see herself doing just that and losing it. She talked about "staying and dying."

Dying was resigning to a situation. I hoped she found the strength to get out.

At this point, I preferred the High Priestess over the Lioness. She was more considerate. But I knew her cancer crab sign would make her side-step off and not show her true feelings. I remembered the day I caught her sneaking to take a picture of me. She was so embarrassed. She would think herself terrible to be upsetting lives. Her words of passion were just for the one night. The mystical marriage was forbidden love.

At my mother's, I found a letter from the Lioness dated Aug 9th, the day I had slept with the High Priestess. It didn't hurt me as usual. She seemed even more childlike than in the past. She seemed to be going through a religious crisis.

Dear D,

Have been thinking about you. It's August and I am feeling like I've let the summer pass me by . . . Are you rested at all, psychically and physically? And (dare I ask) two months later, how do you feel about two years at the Co-op?

I am ok. Getting tired of this job . . . I've been in the doldrums for two to three weeks and have just come out of it this past week.

Haven't written any more but have the beginnings of another story in my head. The first sentence goes like this "Up on Cat Mousam Road there's a tree that stands as a dead shrike, in a gale." Do you ever remember driving south from Bucksport and seeing that sign on a bridge over the highway? "Cat Mousam Road". I always thought it was a great name.

Sometimes I feel so tender toward the woman I work for, as if she were my baby.

You know, I often think, if I died now, I'd have nothing to say for myself? I want to have something to say for myself . . .

A friend called, and she had me in tears grieving over God, who I guess I would love, if She were there, but whose absence I feel . . . I went down to the water and wept. Took off all my clothes in the silence of the sighing water and went swimming in the bioluminescence, stars above me, stars below whispering "Mother, Mother, O the sea, great killer that she is, great dark wave, in which I am a disoriented molecule, she is my sisters, my lover, my mother.

So, tell me, Kid, do you believe?

Not looking forward to going back to school though I will be living with June . . . I love her. I am afraid of her. I feel like I am helpless to understand who she really is . . . We are mentor and pupil and will stay that way . . .

Every two weeks I go to a potluck and am gay for two hours. Such is the life for this washed-out lavender kid.

How do you cook eggplant?

Love, L

Ps I can't believe these people don't like garlic, and I have to cook for them!

I wanted to call her and suggest we go dancing. But I didn't. Instead, I wrote to the High Priestess. I fantasized about *meeting the High Priestess in the garden with a rose in my mouth . . . walking to the top of the hill and standing there with her at the bottom . . . running to each other . . . embracing and falling on the ground . . . holding the rose to her face . . . rubbing my cheek down the side of her head . . . teasing her with open lips . . . then passionately kissing her on the mouth . . .*

How was I to tell the Lioness about this? Would I tell her of the gray-black-haired lady? And what would I tell her as I wasn't sure myself what happened. She was not just another woman. It was the High Priestess! Knowing the Lioness, she would laugh hysterically when she heard the part about her husband threatening to burn the house down.

I knew the High Priestess wouldn't give up everything for me. I just hoped she didn't feel guilty or ashamed about our interlude. Then I received a letter from her.

Dear D,

I got your letter Friday, and it was a wonderful day . . .

First of all- don't worry about my husband's reaction; he took it better than you might think after his initial freak-out. I'm sorry it was such a scene; if I hadn't been quite so drunk, I might have had more foresight . . . but then, none of it would have happened, and I'm glad it did.

No, I wasn't at all ashamed . . . Surprised, yes. And this is where I get confused . . . I enjoyed our love-making very much; it is so nice to be close to a body that is like my own, but different too; and especially you, whom I love already. But it worries me too--that sex is such a volatile and explosive thing, and I'm afraid it might hurt us as well as give delight. I really like sex . . . But can it just give delight, and not hurt? I value your friendship and your generosity, and everything you've taught me, even beyond the physical contact . . .

But then, you're probably right that I worry too much. I think the next time we get together it should be in a more private place, where someone is less likely to barge in and turn on the light, and rant and rave.(you know, I wasn't really embarrassed either, except for you. The humor in it was pretty great, eh? More like a French farce than the soaps!) Women do handle things better than men. I just do not want either one of us to fall "in love," because it gets into all the miseries of guilt, possession and because I don't know whether I'm non-heterosexual enough for a serious love relationship with a women. Oh, that sounds dumb! I seriously love a lot of women—but you know what I mean, a physical love relationship. . . .

Life is full, and I'm beginning to have fun again. Yesterday I went to a woman's conference. I attended a discussion on sexuality in which I found myself intensely involved. I guess I'm not so abnormal after all, even when I get myself into so much trouble!

O, D, thank god for the loving-kindness of women! I love you dearly . . . Anyway, no guilt, and no shame.

I haven't seen G for 5 or 6 days. She came around and I fed her the first couple of days, but she won't allow herself to be picked up. You're right, very independent.

Write again. Joy to you,
Love, the High Priestess

The letter relieved me. She was ok and moving on. Our lovemaking was good even if it wouldn't be a forever thing.

\* \* \*

I needed a job. Checking the want ads in the paper, I called for an office cashier position with an Electrolux vacuum dealer. He asked me to come in for an interview. As I walked in the office, I heard him repeating the same spiel he gave me on the phone, so I said out loud, "Same old story."

"Who's that girl?" he laughed pointing to me. "I'm hiring her." We hit it off well. Up front, I told him I was a "hard woman."

"Does that mean you won't make coffee?" he asked.

"No, I like coffee."

"What if a salesman calls you sweetie?"

"I'll call him honey."

"Ok, go home and think about it, and I'll call you later to see if you're still interested."

As soon as I got home, I phoned to tell him I wanted the job.

"You just left here!" he exclaimed. "I haven't even made up my mind yet." Then I told him Manpower had called me and that I was going to take their job if he didn't decide soon.

One hour later, he called, "Ready to come to work tomorrow?"

I worked at the Electrolux place for one day, and then the boss gave me the day off. He wanted to try out another woman. He liked both of us. I told him I could only guarantee him a year. He wanted someone with more permanence.

I decided to change my life pattern and not worry about anyone but myself. I started bartending school and decided to get a local job for at least the winter and then decide where I would live.

I liked being back with my family, but I needed a loving relationship.

The Lioness called me during the last weekend in August. She sounded down though she wouldn't admit to any depression. She was on the Cape with her family. I asked if I could come and visit her. She thought it might be wiser to wait till she was through with work the following week, but I convinced her to meet on Sunday night to do a show.

Then I added, "Some weird things have happened that I want to talk to you about."

"You alluded to this in your last letter," she responded. "I want to prepare myself."

Her response surprised me. Why would anything I do bother her since she proclaimed no feelings for me?

When school ended, I applied for a bartending job at a local steak house but didn't get it. My mother said I had changed.

"You're more cynical and blunt," she said.

"I just can't keep my mouth shut anymore. If I think something, I must say it," I explained.

"You seem so unsettled," she continued. "Like you don't know what to do with yourself. I know you want to go back to Maine. You can go back. I just want you to be settled," she said.

That's a switch, I thought!

Just before I left for the Cape to see the Lioness, I got a call from the manager at the steak house.

"We want to offer you the job now. Can you start today?"

"No," I replied.

"Okay. Tomorrow morning, then?"

I took off in cloudy threatening weather, but when I got on the Cape, it cleared. I knew our visit would be good. I drove into the yard with the radio blasting. The Lioness ran over to the car.

"I'm so glad to see you," she said as she hugged me. I was thrilled to see signs of her missing me.

"Had dinner yet?" she asked.

"No."

"Then let's go. I'm treating you."

During dinner, I told her what had happened with the High Priestess. Her response was predictive.

"You creep, you beat me again."

"Does it bother you to hear about my affairs?" I asked. She got flustered but responded, "Oh no, not at all." When we got back into the car, I went to kiss her after saying, "I like you a lot, Lioness."

"Why do you?" she questioned.

"I don't want to intellectualize it," I answered.

My response annoyed her, and she said, "I'm a poet, and the word you mean is rationalize."

Feeling very stupid, I backed off. We were not in a good place.

"Where do you want to go?" she asked.

"Where do you want to go, Lioness?" I turned the question back on her.

"Do you want to go home?"

"I can't go home again."

We went to the beach and lay under the horse blanket from my car. At first it was awkward. I said to her, "I feel like a helpless romantic."

"Why?" she asked.

"I don't know what to do any more."

"You don't have to do anything. I want to make up in a half-hour for all year. Are you getting a room or going home tonight?"

"I'm not getting a room alone," I answered.

"Then you're going home," she said. I didn't know why, but I hugged her. She kept avoiding my kiss.

"Why are you afraid to kiss me?" I asked. "I'm not going to force you into anything hot and heavy."

"I don't know why," she said. "I don't want us to hurt each other again."

"Did you hurt?" I asked, surprised at her response.

"Yes, maybe not." She could never admit that I had some effect on her. She could never admit she had feelings for me. We finally kissed, and all the feelings came back.

"Did you feel anything?" I asked. "Did it feel the same?"

"Yes, I like kissing you," she admitted.

"I wish I could rape you," I said frustrated.

"Don't ever say that!" she got so upset and I felt so bad.

"I won't, not ever again. I promise." And I hugged her tenderly to let her know that I meant it. "I wish we could melt into each other. I would die for that." She looked at me with that surprised look like she couldn't believe what I had said.

"I would die for that," I repeated and meant every word.

"I have so much fear," she said changing the subject. "And that's so contrary for an Aries."

"What are you afraid of?" I asked.

"Afraid of failure," she responded.

"You will never fail."

"What are you going to do about High Priestess?" she asked.

"Talk about fear. I'm afraid of that situation," I said. "I will not instigate anything further as I don't understand it."

"Maybe it's one of those things that only happen once," she advised.

"You're probably right, and it doesn't matter if it never happens again. It was so wonderful."

"Maybe you'll write a hymn to all the women you have loved at the end of your life."

"A song. No. An opera," I added.

"Count me out of that one," she said. What a response for the leading deva!

We continued hugging and kissing under the stars. At one quiet moment, we felt tiny feet crawling on the end of the blanket.

"Did you feel that?" I asked.

"Felt like legs," she replied.

" A message from the sea goddess?" I asked. We both laughed and the tension broke.

"I prefer when we are just Dorothy and Lioness," I said. "I enjoy it when we can be light with one another. No complications." Then I asked something I wish I hadn't. "Have you been kissing anyone this summer?"

"Yes, but you won't believe who."

"Who?" I asked with jealously in my tone. I started naming all the women she had mentioned in her letters.

"None of them. It was a man."

"A man?!?" I yelled.

"A thirty-nine-year-old man," she responded.

"And was that good?" I asked rather shocked.

"Yes, I enjoyed it. It was good for my ego."

"Well, if it were thirty-nine-year-old women, I might agree."

"He says I like kissing him because he's soft like . . ."

"Like a woman," I chorused in. "Does he know about you?" I asked.

"No, I should tell him and blow his mind. But I have feelings for him, and I don't want to hurt his."

"Will you see him through the school year?"

"I hope not." We hugged again, and I could see she was getting sleepy. She had gotten in at 3:00 am the morning before. I didn't dare ask why.

"We should go, "I said.

"I don't want to," she responded.

"Well, we agree on something," I said. But I started the car and drove her back as I had to start work in the morning.

"I feel peaceful," I said.

"I'm glad," she said. We hugged and she got out. I drove away watching her standing in the driveway.

I thought to myself, we are always leaving one another.

Thinking about her kissing a man was too painful. I didn't think she would get pregnant, as I doubted, she would go that far. This weekend I had felt like I was kissing a child. She used to be a woman.

In one of our conversations she told me that her grandparents had spoken against gays saying, "they brought down the moral integrity of the country." I told her that my mother got upset when my sister started dating a black man. I never heard my mother swear, but she swore over that: "what's fucking wrong with her?' It was my mother's problem. "We need to support people like my sister," I told the Lioness.

"Do you support her?" she asked.

"Yes, I do."

When I told the Lioness that Goldmund was still in Maine, she said, "I was never fond of G."

"Why not?" I asked. She said, "Cause I know what animals are." I didn't understand her answer, but I didn't ask her to explain.

\* \* \*

I worked so many hours in the bar, I felt like a robot. I wrote to the Doctor in Maine, "I hate watching businessmen eat. The suits. The attitude. The shifty eyes. There must be a better way. There's no softness in it. Just detachment, money, accomplishment, efficiency. I wish I had money to enter this world and upset it. Imagine a raving romantic in the business scene! Important decisions are made at lunch while sipping one's martini and slushing one's buttered lobster. Food is the vehicle to everything." Later in life I learned golf is a close second!

I had a dream about the Lioness. In the dream she was getting married. I went to the hall dressed in an opera cape, walked up to her, put the fire opal in her hand, pulled the woman's chain off from my neck and left. Then I had an upsetting dream about Carlos. I was lying next to him. Very comfortable. We started kissing, and he took his pants off. I started to go down on him. I noticed blemishes, and just as I was beginning, someone walked in. I stopped. I didn't like dreaming about him.

My horoscope said that I would meet some creative person who would help me realize my potential.

The head bartender, Mack was also Italian. Every other word out of her mouth was "fuck". The first morning I met her, she said, "I'm going to make a good fucking bartender out of you!"

The world of the bar was a soap opera. Each character had a story. It was a world of foul language, complaining, and obnoxious people. I felt I was just killing time. My senses were dulled. I didn't think about the Lioness or the Empress or the High Priestess. I was a nothing here. I did nothing important. Nothing depended on me. No one cared about me. I just went to work, did the job, came home, and forgot about it.

I had the hots for one of the waitresses. She was very attractive, but trouble, and everyone hated her. She walked around so arrogant, telling everyone else where to go. I should have learned from my experience with Audrey the danger of getting involved in a loveless relationship, but I didn't. I loved sex. I loved women. She was slim with short red hair. Very white skin. She wore bright red lipstick and heavy makeup. She usually ignored me till one afternoon after the lunch crowd left and I was singing at the top of my lungs, "and I think I'm going out of my head." She walked by and cracked up. I called her Little Leo. She was playful like a lion cub, but her claws were always open. Someone told me she lived with one of the gay waiters, Gino, and she made him iron her clothes.

One of the other waitresses, Regal, a good friend of Little Leo, nicknamed me dimples. One day, she asked, "Do you take happy pills? You're always smiling."

"No, just manic-depressive pills," I responded.

One morning I went to work and found out that the restaurant had been broken into. Little Leo was called in on her day off. She wasn't too pleased. Amidst all the commotion, she came over to where I was sitting in a booth and shoved her body into me. I yelled, "Hey." She continued walking as if nothing happened, turned back, and laughed. I knew she was playing with me. Was she attracted to me as well?

Mack was an extremely moody person, and soon I found out why. Her lover was in the hospital with a heart attack and a 90% blockage to her main artery. Mack sensed I was gay and warned me about Little Leo. "She's an alcoholic and twenty-eight-years old. Watch out."

When I was picking up food from the kitchen, one of the guys asked, "Where did you get that Ankh?"

"From a woman," I responded.

"Oh, sorry I asked," he responded as his face turned bright red. Regal, who was standing next to me and overheard his comment, chuckled and said, "I like women who are not afraid to be bold." Then Bobby, a young cute male waiter who flirted with all the women, kissed my hand. It was flattering. I could see how older women could get hooked up with younger men.

When I went to get my first paycheck, I made the mistake of getting in the way of the waitress manager, Bertha, who looked and acted like her name. She couldn't find some of the charge slips from yesterday's cash out.

"Did you take them off the clip board," she asked.

"No, maybe one of the waitresses did," I said.

"You bartenders are always blaming the waitresses," she said in a not-so-friendly voice.

"Pardon me," I said as I slipped out to look at the schedule board. Little Leo was there too. She saw the look I gave Bertha then followed me out to the parking lot.

"Why was Bertha in such a foul mood?" I asked her. "Did something happen?"

"No," she said, "just a crazy day. You never know what to expect here. The tensions are high. The moods change."

I was so naïve compared to these people.

The next morning Bertha started in on my vest.

"Here put on this one. You're too big for the one you have on. It looks ugly." I ignored her and kept on the tight vest. Mack was in no better a mood.

"That son of a bitch. She called in sick again," she said, referring to the other full- time bartender, as I was washing the dirty glasses. "Ok. I'm gonna put you on the banquet this afternoon. It's an open bar. You'll either sink or swim."

"Okay, I'll do my best," I responded and tried to keep out of her way.

The next night, the bartender didn't show up again, and I was alone at the bar. At first, I was scared, but then I got to like being the power behind that raised wooden barrier. Customers had to wait till I was ready to take care of them, so they tried to get on my good side. Everyone wanted their next fix right away. It was difficult juggling demands. I was feeling swamped and nervous. Then I felt a pair of eyes staring at me. Turned out to be an old boyfriend from high school. We had a nostalgic conversation, and from then on, I felt relaxed and confident in my new occupation. Good thing, as I got plenty of opportunity. Nightclubs attracted unreliable workers. I was always filling in for someone who didn't show up. I learned fast. The clientele liked me. Mack, my boss, appreciated my ability but at the same time felt threatened.

Sometimes after a shift, we would go out to another bar to unwind. I liked going to Mahogany, a gay woman's bar in New Haven. I was sitting at the counter one night minding my own business when a rather intoxicated woman came and sat next to me.

"You're too quiet," she said. "You'll never make anyone that way. Who do you like? That woman or that woman?" she said pointing to a few single women. "Go talk to them. Please yourself."

"I think I'll just relax for a while. I just got out of work."

"Oh, yeah? What do you do?"

"I bartend."

"I'm involved with an older married woman," she confided. "She likes her security. I only see her on weekends. It's driving me crazy. You know?"

"Yeah, I know." I told her a little about the Lioness living on the Cape.

"Get over her. There are a lot of women right here. You wouldn't believe what I do. I have a different woman every night of the week. That's right. Just one night each. I don't sit around sulking waiting for her."

"Really?" I said. "Aren't you afraid?"

"Afraid of what? You want to come with me tonight?"

"No. I have to work tomorrow." Soon I left. I didn't want to get into something I couldn't handle.

I worked a lot the next month. It got to be rather boring hearing the same stories over and over again. I knew I wouldn't last too long. The only person with whom I could have any semblance of an intellectual conversation was the restaurant manager, a native of Maine. We hit it off, and she confided in me a lot. We ended up sometimes being the only people left at night to close the place. One night she called me aside and said, "I'm being transferred back to Maine."

"Really? Why?"

"Someone called the big boss and told him that I was drinking and having an affair with one of the cooks. I didn't really have an affair with him. I let him sleep at my place one night. He was drunk and couldn't go home."

"Who would do that?" I asked. "Why would they care?"

"Jealousy," she answered. "I was told Mack called him."

"Mack? Is that a rumor? Are you sure it was her?" I couldn't believe Mack would do such a thing.

"I have it from a reliable source," she answered.

"Are you going to fight it?" I asked.

"No, I want to get back to Maine any way. She did me a favor. There are too many cutthroat people working in this restaurant. They have been here for years and don't want any outsiders coming in and telling them what to do. It's been hell since I got here. Watch your back," she warned.

The manager's words were truer than I realized. A few weeks later, I walked into the restaurant and was confronted by Bertha. "Why didn't you tell me a charge slip was missing?"

"What charge slip?" I asked.

"The one from last night's cash out? How can you be so careless about your work?"

"What are you talking about?" I asked. "I am very careful about my work. I don't remember any charge being missing." Just then Mack walked over and said how she had seen me looking through the checks for something after I cashed out.

"I wasn't looking for anything. I had a large bar order charge. I gave the check to the waitress, and then I was worried I didn't add it right, so I went back to re- add it on the machine. I had no idea the charge from this bill was missing."

I was so flustered. Bertha threatened to fire me. Mack looked at me, and I think she felt sorry for me.

"Did you check the garbage pail?" she asked Bertha. "Maybe it fell in there. I'll go look." Then she ran back into the bar and came back waving the charge slip. I was relieved but leery as to how she had found it so easily.

"I found it stuck in with today's checks. It must have been left in the drawer."

"Thank you," I said and tried to erase my suspicions. But they were aroused and confirmed later that evening. The manager called me into her office. "Don't do that again."

"Do what?" I asked.

"Hold a charge slip overnight."

"I didn't hold a charge slip overnight. Didn't Mack find it?"

"She told me you had it."

"I didn't have it."

"Forget it. This is what I was trying to tell you."

"Why would she do this?"

"To make you look bad. She doesn't like you. She did the same thing to another bartender. She left all the bottles out on the bar one night and blamed him for it. Mack is at the edge emotionally."

"I don't need this Peyton Place stuff. This is just a money job for me."

"Just hang in there for a few weeks. At least till I'm gone. Don't confront her; it will only make your life harder." I took her advice but knew one more thing would push me off the edge and I would walk.

The next night Little Leo sat at my bar. "I heard about what happened," she said. "Sick, isn't it? They're all nuts here. Ignore them."

"I'll say they're nuts," I replied.

"Do you want to go for a few drinks after work?" she asked.

"Okay," I said surprised and pleased at her suggestion but a little scared.

We went to the Pub and had a few drinks. Regal joined us. Then we went to Mahogany and had a few more drinks. "I want to go home and change into something more comfortable. Then we can go to a new bar I heard just opened for a few more drinks," said Little Leo.

"I'm going home," said Regal. "I've had enough. I can't keep up with you night owls." We left and Regal went home. Little Leo gave directions to her house. When I pulled into the driveway she said rather flippantly, "So should we go out for a drink or just rush into the house?" I laughed at her forwardness.

"Let's go in," I said.

She put on something more comfortable and then got us a drink and some cheese and crackers. We sat on the couch together. I didn't know what to say. Finally, I said, "Well, should I leave?"

"No," she said. "I think you should stay." I took that as an invitation to do as I pleased. I reached over and started kissing her on the lips. She didn't object. We heard a car door close.

"My roommates," she said.

"I think we should go into your room," I suggested. She got up and took my hand.

When we got into bed, I asked her, "When we met, were you attracted to me?"

"Yes," she said. That was all I needed to hear.

What a night! She certainly lived up to her name. Such a lioness in bed. I couldn't get enough of her. She was so soft and slender. I loved touching her body. Her hips gyrated when I slipped my fingers inside her, and she was so wet. She came fast. I went down on her and she purred like a kitten.

The next morning, we both woke up with hangovers. I met the two gay guys, Gino and Vince, she was living with. She had been Vince's lover before he turned gay, and from her reaction to him, I knew she still was in love with him. He had no interest in her physically but did care about her.

Later she said, "Gino is jealous of me. I don't know why. Vince loves him to death. We don't have sex anymore, haven't for a long time. He has nothing to worry about."

I left for work. Little Leo came in later that day and walked around singing in her monotone voice, "Everyone should eat, drink, and be gay." She cracked me up.

Our affair continued. I wanted her all the time. She was a great lover. I did things to her that I never did with any other woman.

But soon I started to feel like a sleazy lover, slipping out early in the morning before everyone got up. I would kiss Little Leo goodbye as she nestled under the sheets. I had to be in early to clean the bar. I changed outfits in the bathroom of the restaurant, so no one knew that I had stayed out all night. I kept a change of clothes there.

One day she came in to work and was in a bad mood which was so unlike her.

"Did a customer piss you off?" I asked.

"No. It's just me. PMS."

Later I found her crying in the breakroom. "Gino was mean to me." Then she told me about her relationship with Vince. "We were lovers for a long time. I got pregnant but didn't want the baby, so I had an abortion. I used to be a bank teller till one of my friends cashed two bad checks. I was too embarrassed to stay so I became a waitress. I was hired by the Manager, and not Bertha, so of course,

Bertha never liked me. I'll be out of here soon though. I need a more secure job. I don't want to get old and have to eat dog food."

We spent the weekend together, and I realized that this relationship was going nowhere. It was limited. We were too different.

Anwar Sadat had been assassinated, and I was overwhelmed with grief. The world had lost a great friend and lover of humanity. Iran and Libya praised the action.

The next day at work Little Leo sat down at the bar for lunch. She looked morose and tired.

"What's wrong?" I asked.

"Nothing," she replied.

"Something is. You're not you're usually flaming self."

"I don't tell many people this, but I have to have an operation. I have a hole in my heart."

"Surgery? When?"

"When I get around to it," she answered. "I need to save up enough money."

"And you still drink and smoke pot? That's not good for you," I said.

"A lot of things aren't good for me, but I still do them. Like this job."

My heart went out to her. I wanted to hold her. I asked her to have dinner with me and go to a show. She answered, "Maybe."

Maybe I was one of the things not good for her.

After work, she decided to come to dinner. We went to the Mahogany, but she still didn't feel well.

"I just want to crash," she said when I took her home.

"Okay, it's up to you," I said and left.

I went back Mahogany. One of the owners, a wild blonde bombshell, came and sat next to me. She told me that she had been married for five years, and now she lived with a woman, the other owner. All the customers were attracted to her. I was no exception. She flirted with everyone. Her lover, a tall woman with dark hair, was more reserved. She kept a close eye on her partner. I didn't think she trusted her.

During the week, Bertha gave me a hard time about a check from the previous Saturday night. She called me over when I was with a customer. I let her wait. She wasn't too pleased.

"Do you remember the waitress paying you for the bar bill?" she asked.

"No, not really," I responded. She went into a fit. We exchanged a few unpleasant words. I walked away.

I visited Wolf. The last time I had been at her house I had left her the note on the bag. She opened the door, surprised to see me.

"Dorothy, little Dorothy," she said.

"Did you get my note?" I asked.

"Yes."

"Don't you love me anymore? No word from you."

"Just stop. I'm in no mood. I have enough problems these days." She went back to making breakfast. Her lover got up, and they started fighting. A familiar scene.

"Do you want eggs?" she asked her.

"No!"

"What do you want?"

"Doughnuts," she replied disgusted.

"Eat your vitamins. Forget the doughnuts." Then Wolf cracked three eggs into a bowl; the last one was rotten. Her lover looked at her and said, "If you did it like Julia Child recommended, this wouldn't have happened. She cracks her eggs into different bowls."

"Go crack your own eggs," Wolf responded and slammed the door as she went into the bathroom. Her lover grabbed her brief case and left. Same old same old, I thought. Wolf took the phone into the bathroom, so I knew it was going to be a long time before she came out. I started to leave. She opened the door and yelled, "I'm sorry I didn't call. I don't usually call and many of my friends get mad at me."

"Whatever," I said. I didn't like being lumped into the many. I continued out the door.

I spent the fall and winter writing in-between working at the bar and spending time with family. I had taken my typewriter with me from Maine, and many mornings I sat at my parents' kitchen table typing away. No one bothered me so I got a lot done. I still thought about the Lioness and the High Priestess, but I wasn't controlled by the emotion anymore.

One-night, Little Leo was sitting with one of the guys from the kitchen. She was showing off a $4.00 turkey decoration and a gaudy, pearled teapot she had bought for $2.50. I was jealous. I sat next to her and asked if she wanted a ride home. At first, she refused, but then said, "Okay. But I have to do a double shift tomorrow."

I knew she was telling me it wasn't a good night to come in. I took the hint and left. It was definitely over with her.

While shopping I bumped into a nun who had visited Bear. She told me that the Hierophant had moved into a house in town with the nun from her community, and that the Empress was living with

Kate, the woman with whom I had gone to Washington. This was news! Maybe that's why Kate was so friendly to me at first. She wanted the scoop so she could move in. Clever woman. Bear was living alone.

I tried to be calm at the monthly bartending meeting as Mack kept complaining that things weren't being done by the closing bartender. She wouldn't look at me. Good thing as my look would have killed her. The new manager told me I had to work on Thanksgiving. I wasn't too thrilled, but I agreed to do it.

Later during the week, Mack said to me, "The manager said to tell you, he's sick of picking up after you."

"Picking up what?" I asked.

"He didn't say. Just said for me to tell you as I'm head bartender."

"Well, I don't know what you're talking about so I'm going to ask him," I said and then rushed into the kitchen. I questioned the manager about Mack's comments.

"Those weren't exactly my words," he said. "Mack blows things out of proportion."

"She does," I said and thought, I'm ready to quit.

There was a new policy at the restaurant. We were to pool tips. I wasn't too pleased as I had the most to lose in this new arrangement. Night bartenders always made more than day bartenders.

It was quite a while since I had had sex. I decided to try a man. I went to a het bar after work and met a nice guy. He was quiet and lived at home with his mother. He walked me to my car when the bar closed.

"So where do you want to go," he asked.

"Motel?" I asked.

"All right," he responded.

We stopped at a few motels, but they were too expensive. Finally, we found a room in a small place just off the turnpike. It was pretty tacky. I was the aggressor. He came as soon as I started rubbing him. He didn't even get inside me.

"I'm sorry," he said as he couldn't get it up again.

"I guess sex for sex doesn't work?" I commented.

"I guess not," he responded. "My mind says one thing, but my body says another. Do you mind if we leave? I told my mother I would be home."

I was thrilled to get out at this point. I didn't want to wake up to the same fiasco. We dressed. He gave me back my half of the motel room charge. I thought that was gentlemanly.

"You're a nice guy, Bill," I said as I got in my car.

"My name is Bruce," he responded.

"I mean Bruce," I said.

* * *

Little Leo sat at the bar with another woman, and I heard her ask her new friend, "Want to come over for a drink?" I couldn't believe that she made it so obvious.

Sometimes when the restaurant was short of staff, the management put me on the register. I didn't like doing it, and I didn't make any tips. I had a meeting with the manager and told him that Christmas Day was absolutely the last time I would cash. He agreed. But a few weeks after this nice conversation, he reneged on his word. I went into work to check the monthly schedule and saw that he had put me on cashing all week. I saw red. I threw my purple scarf around my neck and rushed into the kitchen to confront the manager.

"I'm quitting," I said.

"Sit down, and we'll talk about it," he said.

"You're taking advantage of me. I said I would cash on Christmas Day, not all week."

"I know. But in the meantime, the cashier quit."

"That's not my problem."

"But it's my problem."

"I didn't go to bartending school to be a cashier," I retorted.

"So, you won't help me out these few weeks?" he asked.

"No!"

"Then, goodnight."

"Good night to you, too." I said, got my things, and punched out. I hugged a few waitresses as I headed for the door.

"That fuck," one of them said to me.

"It's ok," I said. "I can't stand it here anymore." Some of the guys wanted me to have a drink with them at the bar.

"Not tonight, Guys. I'm out of here."

I left for Maine the next day. On the way up, I stopped to see Hansel and Gretel. They were living in Springfield. We bopped around the shops. I introduced Hansel to lupini beans. We got hysterical watching him pop the beans in his mouth. He even popped some into our mouths.

I fell asleep on the couch. Hansel covered me with a blue blanket, rubbed my back and said, "Good night, Beauty."

Hansel's mother wanted to adopt me. "They can go, and you can have their bed," she said. I stayed an extra day.

I stopped at the Co-op and Secretary updated me on the latest scoops. Bear had recently come out of the hospital due to a bout with anemia. The Hierophant and her nun friend had bought the town market and were living in it.

"I call it the Hierophant's folly," said Secretary. "Her nun friend is busy taking people shopping. No mail going in there but her nun friend's personal stuff. Empress is still the Empress. She gets down on the wood crew when they don't produce and sends Bear and me to go tell them they are fired. Then they go out to the job, and the Empress changes the story and says how good they are doing. Lordy, I can't keep up with her. And now everyone is saying what a good job you did with the paper. That's cause they had a falling out with Pa Kettle. We got a layout committee and an editorial committee. We got a committee for everything and nothing gets done."

I drove out to Mandala. Kate was happily living there. The Empress was her usual self. She came and sat with me and suggested some projects I might enjoy working on. I politely declined. Argus came and sat at her feet.

"Do you know where the name Argus comes from?" she asked. I shook my name no. "Argus was a god who saw all, even when he was sleeping. He kept half of his eyes open."

"Really. I miss Goldmund," I said thinking about my old furry friend.

"What happened to her?" she asked.

"She jumped out of my car the night I was at the High Priestess's house on my way home. I'm not sure she is still alive." She looked at me, and I knew she understood my message.

"Bear has a new puppy and two kittens. They are adorable."

"I'll have to stop and see them," I said.

I slept at Mandala on Christmas night. In the morning, I woke up with the string from the sleeping bag wrapped around my neck. I must have had a restless night.

I wanted to call the High Priestess but since I hadn't heard from her in so long, I was leery about doing so. Instead I visited Tweedledee. She was happy to see me and made me lunch. We laughed about how we used to fight.

"And how are those cats of yours?" she asked.

"Narcissus died, and I'm not sure about Goldmund."

"Where is she?" she asked.

"She stayed at the High Priestess's house."

"Well, call her and find out."

So I did. I dialed her number and my heart fluttered. Her husband answered the phone. She got right on and relieved all my fears of calling her.

"I was so happy to get your card," she said. "As a matter of fact, I just got it today.

"The Pegasus card? I sent that a while back. Did you get my second letter?" I asked, remembering that the card was sent way before the letter.

"No. Maybe I forgot to give you my new address last time I wrote. I was wondering why I didn't hear from you anymore." I almost wasn't going to tell her I was in Maine, but I did. Her reaction pleased me.

"You're in town! Come out and see our new house. It's by the river." She gave me directions and I left.

When I pulled in the driveway, she came right out to meet me. She looked good, and I was so nervous. She showed me around the grounds. As we walked in the garden, her cat Lilly rolled around in the grass begging to be petted.

"You're so playful and sensuous, aren't you?" She teased as she bent down and scratched Lilly's neck and belly. "I brought Lilly here to the new house, but she keeps running back to the old house. Goldmund stayed there, too. After you left, she came around for a few days, and I fed her, and then I didn't see her anymore. She could have moved to another house. I don't really know."

"She's a survivor," I said. "I'm sure she's is ok."

We went into the house and up to the cupola atop the roof. We sat next to each other and looked out the glass windows at the county view. I could smell her. Being this close to her but not knowing what was allowed at this point was so difficult for me. I wanted so badly to pull her toward me and kiss her. But I didn't dare. We sat quietly in a suspended moment. Then a car pulled in the driveway.

"My husband," she said as she got up. I followed her downstairs. Her husband was very friendly. He kissed me hello. And to my surprise, he apologized for his behavior the last time I was there. He left to start dinner while the High Priestess and I sat in her bedroom. She worked on a shirt she was sewing for her daughter as we talked.

"Is your husband ok with me being here?" I asked.

"He says he's not jealous, but I know he is. He has been going to EST workshops in hopes of changing. I want a divorce but want to be involved with my husband and my children. He doesn't want to share me. He hasn't been as honest with me about his affair. Apparently, it has been going on for years. Imagine, his lover got upset for him when I had my affair!"

"Are you still seeing your lover?" I asked.

"No. He turned out to be a wimp. He wouldn't take responsibility for our affair when it came out in the open. I was very hurt."

"Hurt? You should be angry! So how are you and your husband getting along now?"

"Well, sexually, we are still very compatible."

"So, what is missing?" I questioned.

"Honestly? Common goals."

"I don't think you will find that in an affair. Do you still feel foolish about our affair? I think it was sincere."

"It was, but I don't really understand my motive."

"I think you were mothering me, the way you protected me when your husband came in."

"I don't really know," she responded. Just then her husband called us for dinner. "You will stay, won't you?"

"Sure," I responded against my better judgement.

There were other people having cocktails when we got downstairs. Her husband called us all to the table and handed out small play booklets of *Twelfth Night*. Each of us was given a part to read. The High Priestess left and came back wearing the purple scarf I had given her over her shoulders. It was hard sitting across the table from her. I was quiet. Before dinner was served, I got up and told the High Priestess that I was expected for dinner at the Doctor's house. She said she understood. I said my good-byes. Her husband walked out with us, and I knew he was afraid to leave us alone. I hugged her and she said,

"Come again."

"Yes," I said, knowing full well I would never go back there without an invitation from her. And that wasn't going to happen.

\* \* \*

The Doctor invited me to stay at her house. It was a good refuge. She and Painter set a cot for me in front of the upstairs A framed window. I spent the afternoon lying on the cot in a bad mood. Painter called me down for tea and to play checkers. She got me to talk, and I felt a little better.

Just as the tea tag predicted, "What we anticipate seldom occurs: what we least expect generally happens," I could never have predicted what happened the next afternoon. I had stopped at the Learning Center and saw Carlos. He invited me out to his house for a drink. He lived on the outskirts of town in a good- sized log cabin. It was neatly kept considering that a man lived in it. His girlfriend had moved out on him.

"I always knew she would leave," he confided. "That's what happens when you date a woman twenty years younger." I certainly could identify with that! His cat lay on the floor, tempting me to pet her.

"That's funny. She's not usually friendly," he said.

He put on opera music and poured us red wine. My glass was never empty. And neither was his. He brought out Italian treats: olives, cheese, bread, roasted peppers. We feasted as it began to snow. The setting was so romantic.

"A man after my own heart," I declared as I raised my wineglass. "Viva. Viva la passion. I think I'll write the book of love." I said, as I lay comfortably stretched on the couch while he sat in the chair.

"Viva," he toasted. "Don't write the book of love, just live it. Viva," he repeated and jumped out of his chair and onto the couch next to me.

He kissed me and said, "You've tempted me to be passionate."

I laughed out loud. We kissed again. I hugged him and found myself liking it. I yawned. He yawned.

"Two tired passionates." He smiled. "Do you realize your effect on men?"

"No. I don't think I have an effect on men," I answered.

"You're a very sensual woman. You're very attractive. I have looked at you lustfully many times at the Co-op."

"Really? I don't see myself that way."

"Does it bother you to be like this with me?"

"No, any man who puts a picture of his anima in his office is alright in my book," I said, referring to the sketch he had drawn of what he thought his anima looked like.

"You remember that picture?" he smiled.

"I do. As for your question, I'm just out of my realm," I responded.

"What is your realm?" he asked.

"I'm usually with a woman. I'm usually the aggressor like you. But I'm tired."

"Two tired aggressives." He smiled. Then he rubbed my back and stomach and came very close to touching my breast.

"I don't usually feel an emotional closeness to a man. But I'm ok with you. I'm afraid of getting pregnant, though."

"I had a vasectomy," he responded. Hearing this, and all the wine, provoked what came out of my mouth next.

"You don't have to keep your hand on top of the sweater," I said.

"No commitment? And we'll still be friends?" he asked.

"Yes," I responded.

He pulled my sweater over my head. I unhooked my bra. He

sucked my breasts. I unbuttoned his shirt, and he took it off. I felt his body next to mine. He wasn't as hairy as I had imagined he would be. We kissed, and I rubbed his head. He kissed between my breasts. I unzipped his pants and slid my hand inside. I rubbed the cheeks of his ass. I teased at going into his front. He started breathing faster and pulled down my pants. He rubbed between my legs. He got up and took off his pants. He held his penis and rubbed it on my cunt. He opened my legs and pushed them back against my torso. He inserted his penis. It hurt at first, but then I relaxed. He was very large. He thrust gently inside me. I felt like he was in my throat. He came very quickly.

"I haven't been with a woman for a while. That was so good," he said. He rested and then tried to make me come by rubbing my clit. I didn't, but it felt good anyway.

"Are we sleeping here?" I asked when it was obvious that we were finished.

"Well, I have to get up early," he responded.

"What's early?"

"4:00 in the morning."

"I'm going," I said.

"No, stay. You're tired and it's snowing. Let's go upstairs and make the bed." I gave in and followed him up the stairs. The ceilings were low. I felt claustrophobic. He changed the sheets.

"There are towels in the closet. I'll probably be gone before you wake up," he said, and he got in bed. I felt sort of weird. I had just had sex with a man I knew, something I didn't usually do, and all he could think about was how early he had to get up. I got a terrible feeling in my stomach like I wanted to throw up. I left.

I drove back to the Doctor's. Luckily, they had left the door open for me. The house was dark. They had already gone to bed. I quietly went to my cot, and lay with my eyes open watching the snow fall as I listened to the "Canon in D." I was glad to be in their house. It took a long time for me to fall asleep.

My dream: *I was in a theatre watching a play. It kept getting interrupted by younger people of high school age. I moved. Someone squeezed air in my face with a toy. I got very upset and said, "Never do that unless I say so."*

The next day I was low key. I helped Painter chop some wood. I thought about the rejection from the High Priestess. I thought about my sexual encounter with Carlos and wasn't sure what lasting effect it would have on me. I only knew that I had no desire to do it again.

I went to visit the Empress's mother. She remembered me.

"You helped them a lot with your writing," she said. "You're a good girl. You could have many boyfriends if you wanted them."

On the way back I met the Hierophant.

"No one is happy with Pa Kettle doing the newspaper," she said. "It's too political. At least yours was more the human-interest line."

"Distance makes the heart grow fonder," I responded.

AB invited me to come to a New Year's Eve party, and Tee and Em offered their upstairs as a possible spring getaway.

I went to Duffy's for a whole-wheat blueberry muffin. Kate and the Empress walked in. The Empress had gained some weight. She invited me to come out for supper, but I told her I wasn't sure I could come as it was supposed to snow heavy later in the day.

"I'm going to head back home before I get stuck up here," I said.

"So, what will you do back home?" asked the Empress.

"Nothing," I said and then added, "family."

Then Kate said to me, "An old friend of yours is coming to a meeting about a book on the Co-op's history."

"Who?" I asked.

"The High Priestess," she responded.

"Say "Hi" for me," I answered.

I left them and went to say goodbye to Hansel and Gretel and Tee and Em. As I pulled into Tee's driveway, the eight-sided prism that the High Priestess had given me came flying off the plastic string holding it to the front mirror. It fell on the dashboard.

I stopped to see the Cowardly Lion on my journey home.

"Let's call the Lioness," he suggested and picked up the phone. I got an unpleasant feeling in the pit of my stomach.

He talked to her and then handed me the phone. After some small talk, I asked, "Do you want to get together? I could stay with you for a few days. That is, if it's not inconvenient for you."

"Better if we wait till after March 15. I have a paper due. I could manage to fit you in for lunch tomorrow, though, if you're interested," she added.

I was a wreck after that phone call. I stayed at Cowardly Lion's apartment and got up to go to the bathroom a few times. I had violent, emotional dreams all night. In the morning Cowardly Lion sensed my fear.

"Don't worry. It will be all right. She loves you," he said.

"Yeah right."

I got into Boston a bit early, so I went to a museum to kill time. As it was, I arrived at June's apartment a half-hour before I was supposed to.

The Lioness greeted me, "You look good," and then she said, "Shit. I have to go copy this paper. Be right back."

She left, and I relaxed listening to opera. I wandered through the house up the beautiful wooden staircase. There was a plush soft white rug on the floor. On the wall was a poster of della Robbia and the cabinet was full of Bach albums. I knew where the Lioness had gotten her favorites. I walked back downstairs and lay on the couch waiting for her.

She came back and started cooking lunch. I watched. She looked the same to me, but I wasn't captured by her beauty as I had been. There was a distance between us. She asked about my bartending job, and I told her all about Mack and what had happened. Then I started to tell her that the phone conversation upset me, but I dropped that topic fast, noting her reaction.

"I've decided to travel next year with a friend. She's the daughter of our minister, and I want to spent time developing a friendship with her."

'Segmentation,' I thought. She segments her life. This was her new thing. She gave me two short stories to read. I wasn't thrilled with either of them and thought, she should stick to poetry. I didn't tell her about Little Leo or Carlos. I didn't feel I had to.

I left when she left for class. We hugged twice. She had that stiff condescending smile on her face. I felt she was holding back tears, but I could have been mistaken. The prism fell down again as I drove off and "Sailing" played twice.

Afterwards, I returned home and got involved in the everyday events of my family. I would be ok until something, a song, a picture, a gesture, would remind me of the past surreal life I had led and the characters in it. I suffered from what I called the "paralysis of frozen beingness. I went through the motions, but the feelings were numb. In my notebook I wrote

> Virginia,
> Why don't you love me anymore? I just can't understand it.
> Vita

I wrote the Lioness a short note and said that if she ever needed me to let me know.

I received a letter from her one-month later

> Dear Dorothy,
> I was very glad to get your note, but I haven't had a breathing space till now . . .

In it she thanked me for my comments on the two short stories. At the end, she asked if I could send her a copy of her dream about the temple and the women floating in the waves.

I rewrote my resume and tried to get a teaching job abroad. It didn't materialize. I wrote her letters that I never sent. I just stapled them to my journal. There was some relief, though, in writing them. The three next journals were just a rehash of feelings for her. Even I couldn't stand rereading them.

She called me on March 25, 1982, the day after her birthday. The sound of her voice made me nervous. She had finished her paper and wanted to see me the following week. I wasn't sure why.

I was supposed to meet her at 7:30 pm, but it poured the entire drive, and I ended up being late.

"For once, I'm late," I said when she opened the door. I carried in a bottle of wine and the first part of the book.

"I'll read this later," she said as she placed the yellow envelope on the desk.

"Let's have a toast," I said as I opened the wine and poured us each a glass. I raised my glass, "to what shall we toast? How about to an unknown future?"

"To the future," she repeated.

"To your paper," I added and sipped the wine. I frowned.

"Not thrilled about the wine? To your book."

"I'll drink to that," I said and sipped again. "Maybe it's the dryness." The Lioness seemed preoccupied. "I feel like eating ravioli," I said getting back to reality.

She picked a restaurant from the phone book, and we headed off. We had trouble finding the restaurant. I panicked when we had to go through a tunnel to make up for a wrong turn. She felt bad.

We finally found it and got a table. The waiter brought over the menu. They only served pizza.

"I'm sorry," she said.

"It's ok," I replied. "I'm not that hungry anymore."

She then suggested that we go home for dessert. She made crepes with coffee ice cream, almonds, and Meyer's rum. We listened to Pachelbel.

"Do you want to go to bed?" I asked, meaning to our separate beds.

"Not yet," she responded. We sat close, and I rubbed her neck.

"Remember the Howard Johnson trip?" I asked.

"Do I?" she laughed.

"Tacky, huh? We even brought in the stereo. Why did we do that?" I asked.

"Did we?'

"Yes, we did. Those were the days we were so hot to trot. We couldn't keep our hands off one another."

"One year ago, we saw *Semele*," she added.

"And we had that fated conversation."

"Which one? We had so many." She laughed.

"Yeah. I try to forget them. The one I took you home crying. We were in a park."

"It wasn't a park," she corrected. "It was the town green."

"Well, it had trees and grass. It seemed like a park to me," I said. My teasing was not doing any good.

"We should go to bed," she said.

"Yeah."

"Celibate celeries," she declared.

"What? Haven't you lost your virginity yet?" I asked.

"No, not ready for that. Have you?"

"Long time ago," I responded.

"I'm into celibacy these days," she said.

"I'm ready to join the club," I said.

I went upstairs and had a hard time falling asleep. Tears ran down my cheeks. Tears for the tacky motel, I thought. I wished we still had the feelings we had had in the days of the tacky motel. One of the cats came up and slept on my bed.

In the morning, she made breakfast and played one of June's favorite songs, *I Never Promised You a Rose Garden*. I hated the song. The cats kept jumping up on the counter, and the Lioness viciously shoved them off.

"I'd rather be with cats than people," I said.

"It depends. Some people are better than cats. June is one." June came up a lot in the conversation. I didn't know this woman, but I hated her. Also, June had taken the coffee beans so there was no coffee.

This was the last time I was in the presence of the Lioness over the next twenty years, but not the last time she had an effect on me. It would be an eternity before I got over her and on some level I never did. To steal a quote from the last letter I received from the High Priestess, "It takes a long time to resolve conflicting feelings about an unresolved relationship, or a badly-ended one."

# Part Four

*The resolution to the self*

TWO MONTHS AFTER coming back to Connecticut, I ventured into a prominent jewelry store in downtown New Haven with the intention of pricing fire opals. To my dismay, I learned that I had paid dearly for the one I had bought. Similar stones were selling in the price range of $60 to $110, not the $250 I had paid.

I inquired about putting the opal into a setting. The jeweler's response was alarming.

"You did everything wrong," he said. "You should never have bought the stone without it being set. Now if you put it in a setting and it breaks, you are responsible. Opals are very delicate stones."

"Yes, I know," I responded quietly.

Winter was rather quiet, mostly alone, mostly writing. When spring arrived, I was ready to move on with my life. It was either go back to Maine permanently or find a reason for staying in the area. I decided to give Connecticut a second try and began attending meetings at the Women's Center in New Haven. There I met J, my reason for staying. We had an affair, fell in love, and stayed together for the next eighteen years. That story is another book.

As for the Lioness, in July of 1982, she sent back my original draft of Part One with penciled-in corrections she had made. She apologized for the time it had taken to return the manuscript. She also criticized my use of flashbacks, a technique I rather liked, and said that my writing was too journalistic. She was right.

To my delight, she complimented my talent for "quickie one-line or phrase characterizations of people and my wrap up or bait-type lines (as she called them) at the end of chapters."

She was working as a personal secretary for a friend and making plans for a trip abroad. She hoped I was well and added that she wanted to read any additional work I had done.

In October of the same year, I received a long letter from Kenya. The Lioness was living among the Kamba tribe, which was known for its traditional healers. She was happy to hear about my relationship with J and touched that I had shared the news with her. She was sorry that she had not been able to find it in her heart to give me the kind of relationship I needed.

In May of 1983, she wrote from Sir Lanka. She had carried my last letter around and had finally gotten time to respond. At that point, she was working on a volunteer project in a small village. Her hope was to begin a two-year BA at Oxford at the end of the year. Her next few letters were postmarked from the UK.

After that, we lost touch and I didn't hear from her till 1991 when I received two postcards sent in separate envelopes. The first was from Oregon where she was en route exploring the South and Northwest part of the country. She wrote, "It doesn't feel right, not to be in touch with you, not to be friends. That may be my problem. But if it feels right to you, I'd like to know where you are. How your life is. Whether you are writing. What you are up to. Watching the surf reminded me of the time we sat on the beach at Nantasket."

Pleased to know she was thinking of me, I wrote her back, and the second postcard came from California. She had taken a six-month job working for the Forest Service calling spotted owls.

Her next letter, dated April, 1991, was rather lengthy. She commented on the twist my life had taken. "Reading your letter over was a kicker. I really enjoyed the delight and laughter I could hear in your descriptions of your career, your entrance into Middle America, your golfing, your work on the house, your cats, your dyeing your hair and wearing heels! Yes, I can see it. I remember you talking about dressing up before you came to Maine."

She described her work with the spotted owls, and I could just imagine her traveling out at night and hooting into the darkness trying to get a glimpse of those well-hidden creatures. She caught me up on all she had done through the years. The dagger struck. She had been having an affair over the past few years with a man she had met at Oxford. I was shocked but not surprised. With all her family pressure this choice was inevitable. Currently, though, she was spending time in women's communities across the US. She and her current male lover planned on taking a trip to Alaska in August and after that there was the possibility that they might split. Apparently, the relationship had only survived at a distance. There was always a continent or ocean separating them, so they spent little time together. She wasn't sure what the next step would be . . . *the future I don't know. I am on a road treading for freedom. Freedom from guilt. Freedom from fear. Freedom to make, create, give voice. Sometimes I'm elated. Sometimes I'm choked with anger. Sometimes I'm whimpering. Sometimes I'm stuck, deaf, dumb, and blind. There's a sound barrier out there I want to bust. Who knows? One step at a time. Drop me a postcard?*

I wrote a long letter updating her about my insurance job, my relationship with J, and what it was like to be living with someone who had a long-term illness. She responded back with a long letter.

Five pages written on both sides. Among other things, she was writing some erotica.

She referred to something I had written about aging and dying, and before either one of us passed over, she wanted to take the opportunity to thank me ... *meeting you and knowing you and making love with you and being close to you were the opportunity for many things, and joy was among them. If there is something I could wish were different, it is that I could have done it all more guiltlessly. I will never forget that night I first lay in your arms, amidst the Hermit's dirty sheets, too excruciatingly ticklish for you hardly to touch me, and feeling, with such amazement and release and joy, that I had come home. That your touch, that my desire for it, was home. Praise that moment, in all its hilarity and ridiculousness and wonder. Praise you, Dorothy. You are one fucking prize. What a ride we had that summer!*

She encouraged me to write anything I wanted about the difficulties of being with someone who was so dependent on me. J had MS. The Lioness would never judge or think me a schmuck. It was hard for me to confide in my close friends about my stresses. It was easier to tell someone who was miles away. She said I sounded resigned, and she was right about that. I was contented with my life, but I had lost zeal.

The next year she sent me a copy of a poem she had written and two short erotic pieces. I wanted desperately to know who the woman was that she was making love to. I wanted desperately to be that woman. All the feelings I had bottled up for her flowed back up to the surface. I remembered again how intense our lovemaking had been. I wanted to hold her again. My present life was far from happy, I had been with J for ten years, and we were struggling. Hanging by a string, any sharp turn could easily break the bond.

The Lioness had broken off with her male lover. She was broke, heavily in debt, and had no job. She had decided to settle in New Mexico and live with a woman, "twice her age." She couldn't explain the connection, but she had never been so confident of a choice. I had never been so hurt by one. I had always rationalized in my brain that I was too old for her. And now she was choosing a woman older than I. Twenty years older. I envisioned this lover to be a beautiful older woman with salt and pepper hair, an artist, a wealthy woman who could care for the Lioness and her needs. Of course, she also had a better body than mine.

I decided to make the best of my life. I didn't leave J, but rather threw myself into my work and got all the insurance degrees I needed to make up for the years of experience I lacked. I was successful. And in many ways, our life was good. We never wanted for anything . . . anything except passion.

Then in May of 1995, I was sitting in my Stamford, CT office and the phone rang. I answered in my usual business-woman voice, "Hello, this is Dorothy. How can I help you?"

"It's me," said the familiar voice. My heart stopped and then started beating so fast I could hardly talk.

"Lioness?" I said in disbelief.

"Yes, how are you?" she asked.

"I'm fine. Where are you?"

"I'm in Grand Central Station on my way to Boston," she responded.

"Grand Central! You're so close. I'm so surprised to hear your voice."

"I just thought I would call and say hello," she said in a monotone voice. "My train is leaving in a half hour."

"Oh. So, how are you? Are you ok? You sound down." I could always sense her emotional state.

"I'm not ok," she responded. "Something has happened. My lover died."

"She died? Are you all right? What happened?"

"She had an aneurysm," she explained.

"Oh, my God. How awful. You must be distraught."

"I'm ok now. Just a little numb."

"I wish I could see you but . . . "

"I'm ok," she interrupted me. "I'm sort of booked with family. I only have a few days, then I go back to New Mexico. Still have a lot to do to get her affairs in order."

"Yes. I'm sure. I feel terrible," I said.

"Don't. I'm ok."

"Give me your address. Can I write or call you sometime?" I asked.

"Sure," she said and gave me the details. Then added, "I have to go now."

"It was so nice to hear from you," I said.

"It was nice to hear your voice too," she answered.

I hung up the phone and was numb. Paralyzed. I couldn't do anything but sit back in my chair and stare. Just then Callas, the Administrative Secretary, walked by my door. She and I were casual friends, but she came back and looked in.

"What's wrong with you? You look like you just saw a ghost," she said.

"I did or at least just talked to one," I said as tears welled up in my eyes. With that she closed the door and pulled up a chair.

"Okay. I'm not leaving till you give me the whole scoop."

Then I told her about my relationship with the Lioness. "I've never told anyone about her. J doesn't know she corresponds with me periodically. She would be jealous."

"Tell me about it," she said in an understanding voice. "I was involved in an intensely emotional relationship with a guy before my husband. He left me. After I married Buddy, my ex came back and wanted me to leave Buddy and go back with him. I never told Buddy. Believe me it was difficult. I know what you are going through."

"Thanks for listening," I said.

"I always knew there was more to you than meets the eye," she smiled. "I knew you had a story and weren't boring like the rest of the crew here. It's always the quiet ones that have more bubbling underneath."

Two months later, I had to go to Omaha, Nebraska to do an audit on a client. I took a group out for dinner and we had a lot to drink. When I got back to my hotel room, I called the Lioness.

"I'm in a big queen-size bed with no one to share it. Want to fly up to Nebraska? I'm as horny as hell." She laughed and then in a sexy voice said, "I bet you're alone."

"I am, really."

"Right."

It was just like old times. Of course, being a little buzzed gave me a lot of courage. I asked how she was doing. We talked for a long time, and I dropped some sexual innuendoes. She played along. It was safe; she was miles away.

The next day, she wrote me a post card and sent it along with poems she had written about love and death. I knew they were about Carol, her deceased lover.

The years went by, and whenever I was on a business trip or inebriated, I would call her. I never told anyone. Only one day, I was walking with my sister, and she asked if something was bothering me. Though embarrassed, I divulged my interactions with the Lioness and swore her to secrecy.

"My feelings for this woman are so deep and strong even though I haven't seen her for many years," I admitted. "I don't understand it." The secret brought us closer. My sister realized that I wasn't the robot-work alcoholic I portrayed to the rest of the world.

Eventually, I took a job in New York City which involved a lot of travel. I got serious about my golf game and started spending time on my own. J sensed my detachment and tried harder to pull me back in. As she became more dependent. I ran even harder. A vicious circle: the more I detached, the more she acted helpless. It got to the point where I couldn't take it any longer, and at the end of 1998, I left her. It was a long, difficult decision to make. An eighteen-year decision and as the breakup was messy, I ended up a wreck. I sought counseling knowing I had a lot of "self" work to do. Suffice it to say, I knew that there were ghosts in my past that I had to deal with before I could lead a genuine existence and be able to offer anyone my love- all my love.

I reread all of the Lioness's letters and realized that she had contacted me first— "It doesn't feel right not being in touch with you." It wasn't I. I wrote a letter to the Lioness telling her that I had left J and that the reason I could never commit to my relationship with J or make her feel secure, was because she (Lioness) was always in my head. I told her it was my problem, not hers, but I needed to say it, and I needed to say it to her, the Lioness. I didn't tell anyone about this letter, not even my therapist.

She quickly answered with a response I named "the scarlet letter." It was written in red ink, and although didactic, it was empathetic of the turmoil I was going through. She was sad to hear about the breakup, especially since J and I had cared for each other for so long. She was also concerned about my wellbeing and hoped that I was in a supportive environment. Then she commented on my feelings for her. "You wrote not to take any of your letter personally. I would always rather be your friend than not if it is workable for us both. When you wrote 'You (me) have always been in the way of my total commitment to J,' you must be referring to a symbolic "Lioness". An idea of me or an imagined attachment different from the one you experience with J. I don't know what this is, but it is about you. In my desire to be friends with you, I have no intention of coming between you and J."

My heart broke. There still was no possibility of a relationship with her. And now there were no excuses. Before, I could chalk up her rejection to being young, being influenced by her parents. But now we were older and both free. She still didn't want me. I knew it was time to grow up and stop clinging to the past. Besides I had enough to worry about with the problems going on in the rest of my life. I didn't respond to her letter.

Around February, I asked for a sign to let me know that I was ok. I was so guilty about leaving J. The Lioness called that very day.

"I was concerned because you didn't call after you received my letter," she said.

"I was trying to break pattern," I said.

"Are you all right?" she asked.

"I'm fine," I responded.

"I knew you would be."

"Thanks for calling."

I hung up and thought one small fantasy had come true. She called me. She thought about me. I wrote her a letter describing some of the fiascos of my therapy.

The next morning, I made my coffee and drank from the pooke mug as I had done every morning for the past eighteen years. No wonder I could never get over her. Every morning I was reminded of her. With a satisfied smile on my face, I toasted the Lioness saying out loud, "I drink from your sweet juices every morning."

Meanwhile, I spent a lot of time alone, reading the journals, writing, and enjoying life in my beach condo. I walked and meditated every morning along the shore. Having lost weight, I felt good about the way I looked. I had come a long way with therapy. It had not been easy, but I was happy with the progression I had made. Despite pursuing occasional dead ends and many rejections, I regained a new sense of self. For the first time, I knew what was important in life, and I knew what I wanted to do with my life. My work was different than my job. I just had to find the means. One thing was for sure, I wanted true love.

In August, I registered to attend a business meeting in Colorado Springs in the fall. My friends, Peggy and Lenny, also attending, called and asked if I would be interested in taking a few extra days to drive to Santa Fe. I had worked with Peggy at another insurance company and we got along well. I also liked her husband Lenny, so I thought the additional trip would be fun. That night, I called the Lioness and left her a message asking if she would like to get together as friends. Even if she said no, I wanted to experience this artistic part of the country.

I woke up in the middle of the night with my heart beating fast. I couldn't sleep. I kept wondering whether and how the Lioness would respond.

Three nights later, as I was having drinks with my cousin and the phone rang. It was the Lioness.

"I'd love to see you," she said in a happy voice.

"Great!" I said. "So, what do you look like? I look great. I've lost a lot of weight since you saw me. And my hair is reddish."

"I'm a mess, a wreck," she replied.

"I figured that," I kidded. As we talked, I heard her shouting to a person in the background.

"Who's that?" I asked.

"Oh, my friend, Kayla," she responded.

A lover? I wondered.

"I can't talk right now," she giggled as she shouted to Kayla, "Hey, stop that."

"Neither can I," I said. "I'll call you Sunday night to discuss it further."

"Great. Good-bye."

When I hung up the phone, I was ok. I hadn't sensed that she had any feelings for me, but it didn't matter. But what was Kayla to her?

The next night, I wasn't as secure. I realized that seeing her would break the fantasy. How would I react to her not loving me again? What if I still felt the same?

I called her on Sunday night. At first, she sounded detached, and I felt like I was interrupting.

"Is this a bad time? I can call you later," I said.

"No. No. It's ok. I'm just tired."

Her attitude changed, and the conversation went more smoothly. She was alone. We made tentative plans, and I was to call her closer to the actual trip date.

Just before she hung up, she said in a soft, sweet voice, "I'm really looking forward to seeing you."

This took me by surprise. I felt myself melting.

The next day, I called the airlines to make reservations. In a good mood, I kidded with the saleswoman.

"Let me give you the reservation number," she said. "Q as in queen."

"That's me," I said.

"And where is the king?" she laughed.

"I don't know, I'm still looking."

"You'll find him in Santa Fe," she responded.

"I hope so," I said, thinking of the Lioness. Was she my king? Last time I was the masculine and she the femme. Had the tables turned? Now that I had lost so much weight, I was into wearing silky, feminine clothes. I wondered if she was fat or thin. Was she with someone and just not telling me?

The next morning, a warning sign. I got up as usual and went to into the kitchen to make my coffee. I grabbed the glass pot to fill with water as I always did, but the pot stuck to the hot plate it was resting on. The plate pulled loose and fell, hitting the pooke mug on the way. They both crashed to the floor. I didn't see what had happened. I only heard the bang. Caught in some suspended time zone, I was blinded for a few moments. When I finally looked down, the pieces of the mug were scattered all over. I picked up the broken-off blonde head, the outstretched arms, what was left of the mug, and some small broken pieces. I tried to glue it back together, but there was a tiny hole I couldn't mend. I couldn't use it for drinking any more. I put it on the antique bureau with my other precious pieces.

I woke up at 3:00 am and couldn't sleep. It was starting all over again. And I wasn't going to see her for another month. I told Callas about going to visit the Lioness. "You fall in love so easily," she said. "You wear your emotions on your sleeve."

Maybe so, but I didn't know how else to be.

One thing was concerning. The Lioness had said she was still working on a project for class and wasn't sure how much time she could spare me. What a strange response! We hadn't seen each other in twenty years, and I was traveling thousands of miles to see her. I chalked it up to natural Lioness. We settled on her picking me up on Friday morning. I was to sleep at her house for one night, and then she would take me back to the hotel. I asked her what she thought about the Saint Francis Hotel.

"I've always wanted to stay there," I said. "They do high tea in the afternoon."

"Hoity- toity, big bucks," she replied and continued teasing. "She's rich now and wants to pick up babes."

"Maybe," I replied.

"I'm not into that plush stuff. I'd recommend a bed and breakfast near the O'Keefe Museum. I've never stayed there but my friends tell me it's nice."

"Well, give me the name and I'll give them a call," I answered. Without delay, I called the B & B. "I need a room for October first."

"For one night?" the owner asked.

"No till October sixth."

"I don't think I have anything for that long. I could give you the one night in Room 6 with a queen bed."

"That's good because I'm staying at a friend's the next night. I'll stay at your place one night and get another hotel for the rest of the stay."

"Oh, I have rooms available starting on Saturday—one tiny room or a twin bedroom, Room 5."

"I'll take the twin, Room 5. No double-bedded room?"

"No," she replied.

I hung up the phone thinking that maybe I should have called the Saint Francis.

My dream that night: *I was going to a gyn with a friend. I found out that the gyn was a former boyfriend, Walter. "I'm not doing it," I said. "I am," said my friend. When it was my turn, Walter came out, recognized me and said, "Let's go into another room to talk. I'm not going to examine you." He wasn't as good looking as I remembered.*

I titled the dream, "Not as I remembered."

I decided to enlarge one of my beach photographs as a gift for the Lioness. I knew she liked the ocean, and I chose the best sunrise shot. The sun hung like a red ball in the sky. It was a muted overcast shot but had a dream-like quality. In the package I also added a beach scene truer to color that I knew she would like better and a picture of my favorite tree. The tree reminded me of the letter in which she described me as the tree outside her dorm window—trusting and strong. I wondered if she would get the symbolism.

Three weeks later, I received a second distressing omen. We had a hurricane- like storm. The next morning, I walked as usual until I reached the place where my tree had stood overlooking the rocky terrain. The tree had been pulled up by its roots. It just hung over on its side. The next morning, it was cut to a stump.

I called her two nights before I was to leave for Colorado Springs. She sounded annoyed and distant, and again I felt like I was interrupting something.

"Is this a bad time?" I asked.

"No, why?" she asked.

"You always sound like I'm a bother."

"No, no. I'm just tired. I was on the phone with a suicidal friend and I talked to her for a long time. I was in bed."

"I'll call back tomorrow," I said in an apologetic voice.

"No. I'm ok." Then she changed her tone and was friendly. She told me that she had two cats and a dog and that her sister lived in the next town.

"We call the dog Ziggy," she said.

'We' I thought. Who's we? She said she wasn't seeing any women. Was she seeing a man? I was having second thoughts about this visit. My therapist had warned me, "You may get out there and find that you don't want to be there. You're always concerned about what others want. Concentrate on what you want."

My dream: *A woman with dark hair had fallen off the edge of a*

*chair. I moved near her and said, "You can stay. I'll take you home,
whenever you like." "I'd like to stay," she said. "I'd like you to stay as
well," I replied. She came closer and said, "I'm really a fanny farmer
inside." I replied, "I'm pretty basic inside, too." We smiled knowing we
were interested in each other.*

During a morning meeting, I thought about the twin bed situation
I was going to have to deal with in Santa Fe. I called the B & B and
spoke with the owner, Leeann.

"Leeann. This is Dorothy. I'm arriving at your hotel on Thursday
of next week. I'm in Room 6 for one night, then on Saturday, I have
to move to Room 5 with twin beds. Has any room with a double bed
become available?"

"Let me look," she answered. "Actually, I had a cancellation on
Room 6 with a queen for the weekend only. But you'll have to move
out on Sunday. That's a lot of moving. Do you want to just stay where
you are?"

"I guess that would be a lot of moving. I'll just stay in Room 5.
Thanks anyway." I hung up disappointed and unsettled about my
decision. Then I thought, so what I had to move. I called her right
back.

"Leeann, it's Dorothy again. Put me in Room 6 for the weekend. I
don't care if I have to move."

I felt so much better. Now I only had to sleep Monday and Tuesday
night in Room 5. I went back to the meeting contented, worked till
around 2:00 pm, and then went shopping for souvenirs. I needed to
keep myself busy.

On the final meeting day, I packed and then waited in the parking
lot for what seemed like forever.

"Peggy doesn't move fast," apologized Lenny when they finally
pulled around the corner.

It didn't matter. We had the whole day. I wasn't going to meet the
Lioness till the next morning anyway.

We took the scenic route to Santa Fe. The landscape wasn't
anything that I was used to. Miles and miles of desert. Flat brown
land. No green. Just sage and tumbleweeds and distant mountains. It
was like driving in a surreal painting.

Passing through a dry, desolate area, we drove by a large sign on
the side of the road that said "Lake Front Lots" with a big fish on it.

"Lake side property?!" shouted Lenny. "Where the hell is the
lake?" He stopped the car dead in its tracks, and exclaimed, "We have
to go back."

Before Peggy and I could catch our breath, he sped the car

backwards all the way to the sign and pulled over. A cloud of dirt engulfed the car.

"Are you trying to kill us?" yelled Peggy.

"No one will believe this," said Lenny. "We have to take pictures."

We took turns posing in front of the sign. Then Lenny said, "Let's go find the lake."

"Forget it," said Peggy. But Lenny insisted, and he was driving. I learned quickly that Lenny was the kind of guy who had to carry through on his thoughts. He made us drive for miles down some dirt road. There was no lake in sight but only a crossroad sign that said "Major Gillpin and Somerset Avenues."

"Avenue?" I said. "Are they nuts? This isn't even a road, let alone an avenue!"

"Lenny don't waste any more of our time," insisted Peggy. "Turn this car around or this is not going to be a fun trip for you."

Reluctantly, he complied.

We had lunch in Toas at the restaurant Orlando per my suggestion as the name reminded me of Vita. Then we split up and shopped. An hour later, we met at the car.

"Buy anything?" I asked.

"Nothing much," replied Lenny. "Only two ninety-two-inch totem poles!"

"Totem poles? What are you going to do with them?" I asked.

"Who knows?" said Lenny. "Peggy had to have them. Maybe by the time they arrive at our home, she'll figure out what to do with them."

Just outside of Santa Fe, Lenny had taken the wrong exit and had to retrack back to the highway. We were tired and hungry. Tempers were running high.

"Look on the map! Can't you tell which exit to take?" yelled Lenny. "Dorothy, don't you know where the B & B is located?"

He had lost his patience by this time, and I was having a hard time reading the map. It was dark outside, and the map was small. The few options I suggested turned out to be dead ends. It was now 6:30 pm.

"Calm down Lenny," advised Peggy. "We'll get there. Just be patient."

"But we have dinner reservations at 7:30 pm, and it's a twenty minute ride after we drop D off."

"I'm sure they will accommodate you whenever you get there," I said. "Aren't you eating at your hotel?"

"She's right Lenny," agreed Peggy. "Chill out. Let's try this next exit." Luckily, it was the right one and we got to the hotel forty-five minutes later. Just as we walked in the office, the telephone at the desk rang. I heard the woman say, "No, she hasn't arrived yet." I knew it was the Lioness, so I shouted out my last name.

The woman heard me and spoke into the phone, "Just a moment. Here she is. She just walked in. It's for you," then handed me the receiver. Tired and aggravated over what had happened in the car, I was in no mood for talking.

"Hi. I'm here. Just got in. Do you want to join me for breakfast?" I asked. "The breakfast is supposed to be very good here."

"Well, my is schedule crazy," replied the Lioness. "The repair man was supposed to come today to fix the heater, but he didn't show so he's coming tomorrow morning between 8 and 9. I can't come to pick you up till after he's done."

I thought to myself of all times to make an appointment for the heater, the day I'm coming. What was wrong with her? I had just arrived and already I was getting upset.

"Okay. Do you want to have dinner with me Saturday night? You have to bring me back anyway, and I can make arrangements while I'm here." Silence." or Sunday night with my friends, Peggy and Lenny?" Silence." Okay, forget about dinner. We can talk about it when you pick me up. Call me when you're ready to come and get me. I have to go. I just got in, didn't even unpack yet. Maybe I'll call you later." I hung up, experiencing that icky feeling that I used to get when we were breaking up years ago.

"This is a mistake," I said to Peggy after hanging up the phone.

"Maybe you should just get a room for tomorrow night and not stay at her place," suggested Peggy. "You can stay in our room if you can't get anything."

How considerate, I thought. She doesn't even know me that well, yet she would go out of her way to save me from this awkward situation.

"I'll be ok, but thanks anyway," I replied.

They left, and I went to my room and took a shower. I didn't even go out for supper. I was too tired. Room 6 was lovely, with bright colors, and a comfortable queen- sized bed. A stuffed red heart cushion hung on the door. I liked the number six. It was the number for the lovers' card in the Tarot. A good sign, I thought. I decided not to call her back. I couldn't deal with it. Not tonight. I felt so awful. Coming all this way to see her. I would have sent flowers for her arrival or met her at the B & B, but here I was being put off for the repairman! Why did I keep thinking that she wasn't telling me something? I was tired of her rejection.

I got into bed and tried to read, but I couldn't concentrate. Instead, I kept thinking about our past lovemaking. I was afraid of tomorrow. Was she afraid?

At 1:25 am, I was awakened by loud rowdy music from a local bar. Thoughts of the Lioness surfaced. Those big blue gorgeous eyes I used to love. What did she look like? Had she gotten heavy? Had she been seeing someone and hadn't told me? Maybe she had a child. Maybe she was seeing a man. Why was she so hesitant to see me? Did she even want to be with me? Crazy thoughts went through my brain. Nonsense. This was nonsense. I had to stop doing this. I just had to let it go. Tomorrow I would find out.

I looked around the room. It was loaded with rabbits and bunnies. Not my usual choice for décor. A beautiful print of a large praying Indian woman hung on the left wall near the bed.

After my morning run, at breakfast in the dining room-more rabbits. A whole cabinet full of them. All sizes and shapes.

To take the edge off, I chatted with some of the guests. I predicted the Lioness wouldn't arrive till noon. And sure enough, she called during breakfast to say she wouldn't be arriving till 11:00. I decided to go to the Georgia O'Keefe museum. That would take my mind off her.

The museum was great. I took my time, renting a tour phone set and spending lots of time at each painting. I wasn't going to rush. If I was late, I was late. Let her wait. I loved the flower paintings, the colors, the sensuous female-looking shapes. My favorite was one called Blue Flower. I wanted to buy the print, but the shop didn't have that one, so I got White Rose instead. When I was checking out, I said to the curator, "I'm surprised more people don't rent these headsets."

"Well about half do," she responded.

"Really? It seemed like only one-quarter. It was really great."

"Did you recognize the voice?" she asked.

"No," I replied, thinking it must be someone famous, an actress.

"It was my voice," said the curator.

I got hysterical and said, "How was I supposed to know that?"

She laughed.

"Well, you do look like a famous actress," I said, observing her beautiful, rounded, soft face and blond hair. "Has anyone ever mistaken you for Meryl Streep?"

"Actually, yes. I have been in restaurants where people came up and asked me for my autograph."

"Well, you look just like her and just as beautiful. I like looking at you."

"Well thank you," she responded. I left feeling good. I was

beginning to enjoy myself no matter where I was. I felt a lightness I hadn't felt before. It was fun to play.

I went back to the hotel at about 11:15. No sign of the Lioness. The phone rang at the desk, and I said to the attendant, "That's for me. It's got to be the Lioness, and she's stuck in traffic." I was partially right. "So, are you stuck in traffic?" I said trying to beat her to the punch. "No. I'm stuck at the bank in Estrada. I'll be there in a half hour." "Take your time. I'll be here." I went and sat on the veranda. It was such a beautiful day. I read my book and wrote in my journal. About 45 minutes later, a white car pulled into the parking lot. It was she. I watched her hurried walk to the front door.

"I'm over here," I said calmly as she headed toward the front desk. Seated in my chair, I took a deep breath. She nervously approached.

I got up and with a smile said, "I spend half my time waiting for beautiful women and the other half rushing to them."

I wasn't sure she heard me. I hugged her and then looked into her face. There were those blue eyes. There was the smile. Her hair was cut short, darker than I remembered. It was wild. It looked like someone had taken a knife and just chopped. There was no style. It was messy, but adorable. I noticed that her teeth were crooked. I had forgotten about that. She had on dark shorts, a tee shirt, and hiking boots. Very masculine, she was thin and more muscular than I remembered. Her skin was tanned and weathered. She had aged.

"You cut your hair? That long beautiful hair. How are you?" I asked. I had to hold myself back. I pretended I was calm even though I was shaking within.

"You could call it a cut. I did it myself. It's easier to take care of this way. I'm fine. And you?"

"Fine."

"You look good," I said.

"You do too," she said looking away from me.

I looked for some sign that she still had some feelings for me, but I didn't see any. She wouldn't look into my eyes.

"Well, let's get your things," she said as she picked up my luggage and carried it to the car. I followed behind. I liked being the femme fatale. There was a medium- sized black dog in the back seat.

"Is he friendly?" I asked. "What's his name?"

"Zig. Short for Zigfried. He's friendly. Aren't you, boy?" she said roughing his face between her hands. "He came with that name. Didn't you? He's a good boy.

She put my luggage in the trunk. "I thought we would stop on the way and get some stuff for pizza tonight. "I have these frozen pizza crusts we could doctor up. We could also buy lunch to take on a hike. You said you like doing outdoorsy things. If that's ok with you?"

"That's fine," I replied. "I'd love to take a hike. I have been in meetings all week. It will be nice to be outside for a change." We got in the car and started off.

"We'll stop at my house first and drop off your stuff," she added.

The store was not far down the road. She parked at the edge of the lot.

"Come on, Zig. You need a walk. Want to join us?" she asked.

"Sure." We crossed the busy street and started walking along the path by a river. When Zig was done, she put him back in the car. Then we went into the store. I felt sort of weird, but I felt like I still knew her. She was acting weird also. I thought to myself 'Well, we haven't seen each other for seventeen years. I guess it's normal to feel weird.' I tried standing close to her whenever I could, making small talk.

We ordered lunch sandwiches, and while we were waiting for them to be made, she said, "I gotta go outside."

She immediately rushed out. I wasn't sure why. Did she not feel comfortable with me? Was I bothering her? Sexually? I really didn't know. She came back about ten minutes later and said something about the dog needing water. Maybe that was it. Nothing else.

We finally got to her trailer. It was a little shocking to see. Very messy. Piles of stuff all around. She had two cats, Ajax and Bandit. Ajax was initially friendly, but when I petted him, he started hissing. I backed off. Bandit stayed on top of the refrigerator, crying. I petted him. Then Ajax returned and rolled around the floor enticing me to pet him. I did, and he attacked. I knew then to keep my distance. The Lioness carried in my luggage.

"I put you in the back room so you'll have privacy," she said making sure I knew we would not be sleeping together. She had obviously already made up her mind. Okay, I had to just take this for what it was. Two friends seeing each other again.

She hooked the dog onto the outdoor chain. There was a little puppy with two different-colored eyes roaming around. He belonged to the people in the other trailer.

"He keeps Zig company. I worry about them though. Last week one of the neighbor's dogs was shot."

"Shot? What kind of a place is this?" I asked.

"It's usually ok. Antics of one of the kids. Are you ready?"

We left for Chimney Rock. It was a great site, and I was determined to make it to the top. Even though I was in shape, I wasn't sure if the altitude would affect me. It didn't. I was thrilled when I got to the summit. I asked her to take a picture of me at the top with Chimney Rock in the background. Ironically, I had run out of film and didn't have any backup.

"Well, a lesson. I don't have to prove to anyone I've been up here. I know I was."

We lay on one of the rocks and talked about a lot of things.

"I hit you once," she announced.

"Really?" I said. "I don't remember."

"I'm sorry," she added in such a sincere tone as if she wanted to make up for all past sins.

"Why did you do it?" I asked.

"You bit my breast."

"Hard? I guess I was into sex."

I talked more than she did, especially about the breakup with J.

"Do you miss J?" she asked.

"Not as a lover," I admitted. "I feel terrible about that. Seventeen years and not feeling anything."

Why do you feel bad about that?" she asked.

"How do you think she would feel about that?" I responded." It's a difficult topic for me, but you asked." I got quiet. She respected my mood. We just lay there for a while without speaking. Then a fabulous thing happened. There were terns flying high overhead. And like beach terns, they started dive-bombing over us. Dive bombing into the air like they do into the water. I could hear the swish of their wings moving the air.

"What are they doing?" I asked.

"They are catching prey, bugs flying below them," she responded.

"Did you see the movie *Better than Chocolate*?" I asked. "Great body painting scenes."

"No," she responded.

"How about *Desert Heart*? It's one of my favorites."

"Yes. That movie could have had a better ending," she added.

It was getting late, and we decided to start climbing down before it got too dark. On the way to her trailer, she asked, "Do you mind stopping to see a friend of mine? I want her to meet you. Her name is Jen"

"No. Of course not," I responded.

We stopped at a gas station on the way.

"I have to get something," she said as she jumped out of the car. She came back with an ice cream bar. "Jen bought Zig an ice cream the other day, and I want to return the gesture," she said.

Soon, we turned into a trailer camp, and she knocked on the door of one of the trailers. A tall, light-haired, motherly looking woman answered. I could tell by the way the Lioness looked at her that Jen was more than a friend, or at least the Lioness wanted her to be more than a friend. I hung in the background. After a while, the Lioness introduced us.

"This is Dorothy. Remember I told you she was coming to visit?" Jen shook her head no.

"Is this your cousin?" she asked.

"Yeah, we look so much alike, don't we?" I teased. "No. We're just friends."

"Dorothy is the friend I told you was visiting," added the Lioness. Jen just looked confused. She wasn't overly friendly. Didn't invite us in. She stood on the top of the steps.

The Lioness climbed up the steps. "I bought this for you," she said handing her the bar. Jen wouldn't take it.

"I can't eat ice cream anymore. I found out that I have an allergy to it," she said.

"Oh really? I didn't know. I'm so sorry," replied the Lioness with a disappointed look on her face. I felt bad for her. She was like a child offering a mother candy and the mother refusing it. It was embarrassing. I kept thinking to myself, 'Just take the god-damn ice cream and don't eat it.' Why make such a big fuss over it? The Lioness asked Jen to join us for dinner. I thought this was a little strange since we hadn't seen each other for years and had a lot to talk about. She doesn't want to be alone with me, I assumed. She's letting me know this woman means something to her.

Jen refused, saying that she had to get up early for work. We left and went back to her trailer. On the way, I said to the Lioness," Why didn't she just take the ice cream? I was embarrassed for you."

"Oh, really. It didn't bother me," she responded.

'Really,' I thought.

When we got back, she took Zig out for a long walk. I was relieved to be alone for a while and listened to music. When she came back, she started preparing the pizzas. Meanwhile, I paced back and forth in the living room. The wild animal in me had returned, and there was nowhere to run. I wanted to escape.

We ate and then sat in the parlor. I gave her the presents.

"*Tu presenti quele cosa del mare,*" I said trying to impress her with my Italian. It didn't. She opened it. I had matted the sunrise shot in powder blue and framed it in an Australian wood frame. I signed the card, "not a Della Robbia, but a Dorothy."

Just as I thought, she liked the small blue-toned picture better, but she didn't get the symbolism of the tree. I thought about the words she had written about the oak outside her dorm window . . . *"something gets in the way of my feelings, freezes them away from me so that I do not know them, I cannot touch them, left in some sort of void. Then my intellect starts to think, what should I be saying, and how preposterous that is, to think "shoulds." Dear lieutenant, you are like the tree now outside my window. It is green and bright, and it fills my small, low window and reaches out its branches to me—I can almost touch them. And the tree trusts me, or is strong enough itself to give freely, and does not expect a price or a bargain, but simply offers, and waits, and is true."*

Her feelings were frozen still. I had hoped the tree picture would revive some feelings for her, but it didn't. I started talking about something else.

"Do you want to see the many faces of Eve?" I asked while taking out the pictures of myself at various stages in my life and pictures of my family and J.

"Yes, I'd like that," she answered. As we studied the photos, I realized how feminine I had become compared to our earlier times. Roles had reversed. This time she was the dyke, and I was the fem. She wasn't as beautiful as I remembered.

I also realized how stressed out I had been the last year with J. Pictures of myself were ugly with deep facial lines and sad, deep sad eyes. We talked about old times in Maine. I showed her old pictures of herself.

"You were the only one who published me," she said, referring to one of her poems I printed in the newspaper.

"Maybe 'cause I'm the only one who knows you should be published. You know I've been doing some of my own writing. I realize writing has to become my lover if I am to accomplish anything. Signs are pointing to my being alone," I said, hoping she would know I understood her choice.

"That must be hard for you, seeing how much you like sex."

"Yes, very hard. But I feel compelled."

We didn't talk too much longer.

"You look tired," I said.

"I'm always tired," she said.

"Not enough sex," I retorted.

"Don't project," she quickly retorted.

"It's my way." I said, thinking, 'That hurt. She must be involved with someone.'

I retired to my room in the back, got into bed and looked around.

The bureau was full of pictures of Carol, her ex, and various other objects. This was the "we" she was referring to. How ironic, I thought, I was sleeping in the room with the shrine to Carol. That weirded me out. As I lay in bed, I thought about the day. I knew the moment we met nothing had changed. I was not the kind of woman she could love. Jen was more her type. But I was ok with it. I surprised myself. Normally, I would be going crazy with her lying in the other room. I wasn't. I remembered my therapist's words about not staying in a situation if I didn't want to.

"You're always worried about the other person loving you. What about whether you love them?" She was right. I needed to get out of this. I decided that after my run in the morning, I would ask the Lioness to take me back to the hotel, rather than prolonging the agony. There was nothing here for me.

That night, the arm pain with numbness came back. It hadn't happened for long time. I didn't sleep well. Finally, I got up and drew the bureau scene in my sketch pad. I thought about the Lioness's living situation. At this point in my life, I was unaccustomed to living in such poverty and disarray. I wasn't even sure where the Lioness could put the framed picture I had given as a gift. It didn't fit in this house. It was the most expensive object in the tiny trailer.

I got up early the next morning and lay in bed for a long while. I wasn't sure whether or not the Lioness was up, but then I heard her go into the bathroom. I put on my sweats and ran into the kitchen. She was leaning on the refrigerator looking sleepy.

"I'm going for my run," I said as I whizzed by her.

I started running down the hill hoping to find O'Keefe's house. O'Keefe used to walk the desert and pick up bones, and other objects. I walked the beach picking up fish bones, lost objects, feathers, and sea glass. I felt a kinship with her. O'Keefe said it was her favorite past time, and it certainly was mine.

Two dogs starting barking and running toward me, but I remained calm. I stopped running and continued walking like they weren't bothering me. They dropped off. I went pretty far but couldn't find the O'Keefe house. I turned around, walked and then danced my way back. I felt strong again. I had taken my camera with me and when I got back to the camp, I took pictures of her trailer. The number 8 hung on the door. The Tarot number for strength.

I entered the trailer. She was standing in the kitchen and I was all set to tell her that I wanted to go back to the hotel. Before I could get the words out of my mouth, she said, "Boy, you ran a long time.

I thought we might go do another day trip. I really want to spend the day with you. That is, if you want to spend it with me?"

Not what I expected to hear. She had that sympathetic sort of tone in her voice, and I couldn't bring myself to tell her I really didn't want to spend the day with her. I could never hurt her.

Instead, I said, "Sure. Where should we go?"

We decided to go to a place called Bandelier National Monument with cave dwellings and then head for Jemez Springs for a hot springs bath.

At breakfast, I told said to her, "I'm feeling out of breath," I don't think it's the altitude, though, because I was fine while running. Last night I also had arm pain." I explained that when I had started counselling, I kept getting left arm pain and numbness. It felt like an impending heart attack, but all my tests came back negative.

"It must be the effect I'm having on you," she responded quite concerned.

"I've always wanted someone who takes my breath away. Is that what you are doing to me?" I asked.

"I don't think I have that power," she said.

"No, but I do. I'm very ruled by the psyche. One night in bed I had a sensation that a woman reached into my heart and put a string around it. She was a person distinct from me and I was afraid of what would happen when she decided to pull on it."

"Maybe she never will," she said.

"I hope not. I was a little nervous about coming out here to see you. Fear of rejection. I've had a lot of rejection this year! I wasn't sure how I would react to seeing you again," I said. Then I shared with her about the cup-breaking incident.

"I was a little scared too," she said. "But then when we were together yesterday in the store and everything went ok, I said to myself, 'Well, that was easy.'"

"It has been a little weird though," I added. "Last night I felt like a caged animal. I paced back and forth across the floor. Maybe it's because I'm not in my own house." I added. "I need a lot of alone time."

"Where was I?" she asked as if she never noticed.

"You were cooking the pizzas," I answered.

We finished breakfast, cleaned up and got into the car. It was a long drive. I made her stop along the way so I could take more pictures. I read aloud each of the numbered signs at the cave dwellings. She took a picture of me climbing into one of the caves. Then we walked through the woods and left for Jemez. We had lunch at a roadside restaurant talking and laughing about old times. Eventually, I told her I was working on a book about my journey to myself.

"Because so many synchronistic things happened to me, this material became the focus for my draft," I explained.

"Do you want to make money with the book?" she asked.

"No, I'll never make money with this book, but it might get me out of insurance. I had a dream about Sr. Jane Frances, a nun I had taught with. In the dream, I created a display of Christmas trees. It wasn't a big money success. Another nun asked Sr. Jane, 'Do you think they will make her explain the loss?' Sr. Jane replied, 'No, it was beautiful.' I knew from this dream that I wouldn't make money, but I would do something significant."

"Then you will," she said.

"I don't know. Trying to put into words what the heart feels is so difficult."

"Why?" she asked.

"Because it's putting a feeling into words. They are two different mediums."

"Who believes in your work?" she asked.

"Adele and my therapist. I even stabbed at doing poetry. One was entitled "Amazon Woman. You were the inspiration."

"I don't think I quite live up to that expectation," she responded.

After lunch, we crossed the street to the bathhouse. No rooms were available, so we roamed in the back yard of the spring house. I felt the hot water coming out of one of the ground holes. There was a stream. We lay by it. The sun was strong and felt good.

"You don't shave?" I asked.

"What? You mean this," she answered, pulling the long hair on her chin.

"No, your legs," I said while rubbing my hand down her leg. "That's hair we call a status symbol. You don't shave that."

"Right," she said.

"You know we are a lot alike," I said.

"How's that?"

"We're both independent, analytical, and lustful. Our work is important. We need space and time alone. We say what we want to each other."

"Did I ever get paralyzed in a situation with you?" she asked.

"What do you mean?" I asked

"Sometimes with Carol I just couldn't do anything. I was frozen. Couldn't decide one way or another so I just froze."

"Not that I remember. You were indecisive at times. But I wouldn't say paralyzed."

"Maybe it's different with you. I always feel I can be myself with you. Making love with you was like coming home," she responded.

"J had said the same thing to me," I answered. I wondered what I represented to these two women. Why did they both say the same thing?

"Maybe we're meant to help each other do our work," I said. "I think it will be a very productive winter for both of us. Come and visit. I have two desks. We could both write. I have some frequent flyer miles if you want to use them." She just looked at me with that smirk and didn't answer.

"You were right about projection," I continued.

"What do you mean?" she asked.

"When you said yesterday that I projected my sexual needs onto you—you were right. It was me who needed sex. Not you. It's been since November. I was embarrassed to tell you that I needed sex."

"Why?" she asked.

"It's so mundane—so base," I responded.

"Don't ever feel embarrassed to tell me anything," she said. "But you came here for more than sex. Didn't you? So why did you come here? What did you expect? You don't think you still love me? Do you?"

Truth time I realized.

"Yes, I still love you. I never stopped loving you. I just buried the feelings. When I saw you, all the feelings came back, but I could see it wasn't the same for you. You don't love me. I don't really know what's between us. There is something. But a good relationship takes time to develop and I'm not moving to Santa Fe, and you're not moving to Connecticut."

"You wanted more from this relationship?" she asked.

"Yes. I wanted more. It's funny. I kept thinking that there was something you weren't telling me, but I guess it was me not telling you something. I needed to see whether there was anything between us. For the last seventeen years, you have been in the back of my mind. I could never totally commit to J. I don't want to get involved in another relationship like that. I want to be totally present to the next person. I want to totally love someone."

"That's good," she said. "Do you think you'll find that love?"

"Yes. I'm capable of great love, and I believe it exists." I started crying softly because I knew she didn't love me. "I need to love. I need to be sexually involved. It's been such a long time. Almost a year. Nothing has worked so far." Then I told her about rejections I had experienced after leaving J. "I always pick the difficult ones. I'm attracted to the non-gay woman. I'm the unicorn who wants to lay its head in the lap of the Virgin and waits for the suffering to begin."

"Don't include me as one of the virgins!" she exclaimed.

"Why not? I was your first female love!" Then I asked boldly, "So are you seeing Jen?"

"No," she answered rather abruptly. "Why do you think that?"

"I could tell by the way you were looking at her that you were interested."

"No, but that's funny, Carol used to say the same thing." And I thought to myself, funny, both Carol and I had the same take on it. Maybe we're seeing something she won't admit.

"Carol never got it," she said in a melancholy voice. "But I think at the end she did. She told one of our friends just before she died that she felt I would never leave her. So much we didn't do. Promises not kept."

"Lioness you did what you were meant to do. You probably gave her more than you know. I hope some thirty-year-old wants me when I'm sixty." But my words fell on deaf ears, she was deep into her own guilt by this point.

"My therapist said after Carol died 'no matter what I had wished, I hadn't gotten to do it, that is, work through to a successful, healthy relationship with Carol and that I would have to do it with someone else. We had our problems. I had brought a lot of shit into the relationship."

"We all do, Lioness," I said empathetically.

"I'm attracted to the person who needs to be saved—that sets off my buttons."

"I don't want to be saved," I said, "but I'm subject to the same pull. I did it with J. I wanted to make her life easier, but in the end, it became more difficult. That's one of the reasons I left."

"I think I lost something way back," she continued. "Maybe with my mother. Watching someone in pain and not being able to do anything."

"Maybe a regression will bring it out," I suggested.

"I tried that, but in the regression, I say this and maybe that, and that . . . "

"You think too much. *Non pensare!* What happened the day Carol died? Were you with her?" I knew this was a painful topic, but she started telling me about it. She never cried, though, not one tear.

"Well, I was in one of my childish, pissed-off moods that morning, and we had an argument. It was awful. We didn't resolve anything and both of us were mad. She left for work, and I was supposed to meet her later that day, but I never saw her conscious again. She collapsed at work. Had a massive hemorrhage. She was rushed to the hospital and never regained consciousness. My therapist was there and came in with me. Carol was hooked up to a support system, and the hospital staff called her daughter. They took her off that night, and she died soon after. I never got to say good-bye."

I felt so bad for her.

"Then I had to go through all her stuff and get things in order. She didn't leave a will, so I had to buy the trailer from her daughter. I finally decided to make this my home. The animals were hers."

"So, she didn't die of breast cancer?" I asked thinking back to her nude picture on the bureau showing her without breasts.

"No, the double mastectomy was prophylactic."

"Wow. I couldn't have done that."

"Carol was afraid. Her family had a strong history of breast cancer. She thought it a small price to pay."

"She was rather masculine, wasn't she?"

"Yes. That always bothered her. She would go into a Woman's Room, and the women freaked thinking that she was a guy."

"You know I really admire you. I saw the nude picture of her on the bureau. Her body was quite aged and with the double mastectomy. Wow. I don't know how you did it. I'm too into physical looks."

"You don't know. It was good. Physical looks don't matter to me. Kayla, my last lover, was a very heavy woman. It doesn't matter to me. I'm into flesh."

God, I thought. She picked this aged, dyke woman. I always thought Carol was one of those beautiful, greyed-haired, striking women or an accomplished artist, but she was neither and now she was telling me that Kayla, the woman she was involved with for some seven or eight months, was fat. I felt awful. Why didn't she ever choose me? I was more attractive than I had ever been. I was smart. I had done some important things in my career, and yet she preferred to be alone rather than be with me.

Well, I had enough pain. I looked at her and said, "Time to go? You still have to take me back to the hotel."

"Yeah," she got up, sort of out of it. Emotional conversations were not her cup of tea.

"I haven't talked about that for a long time," she said. "I used to talk about it all the time when it happened."

We walked back to the car silently. I felt closer to her. I tried to get us back into lighter conversation.

"I live in fantasy worlds since the real world is too boring to me. I want my life to be operatic," I said.

To which she replied, "You are already operatic!"

"You're right. I set the scene. Once I scared some straight woman half to death when I sent her roses and a cryptic love note."

A loud spontaneous laugher came from deep within her wild side. I loved hearing her laugh. It reminded me of the old Lioness. I wanted to touch her so badly. I leaned closer to her, so I could smell her scent.

"I really like being close to you," I said, closing my eyes in pleasure.

"I like that, too," she responded.

We looked at each other. Some spark of memory was lit.

When we got to the hotel it was dark. She was having trouble with the lights in the car, and I went to borrow a flashlight. She carried all my luggage all at once up the stairs into my room. I just looked on in amazement. I didn't remember her being so strong.

"God, you are such a dyke!" I said standing at the top of the stairs as she came up, arms loaded. "But I do deserve to be waited on!" Femme fatal! She smirked at my kidding, raising the lids on those beautiful blue eyes.

We didn't stay long in the room, and I followed her back to the car to fix her lights. She was sitting in the driver's seat, and I leaned in the driver's window to help. We were very close. The lights went back on.

"Well, I guess I'll spend tomorrow doing museums," I said, ready to go back to the room.

"Come and sit with me for a while," she said. I smiled and started pulling my head out of the window. I was going to go sit in the passenger seat, but she stopped me.

"No, sit here with me," she said holding my arm. "Face me." I got in the seat with her. I spread my legs over her lap. I couldn't contain myself anymore. I leaned closer and hugged her. She hugged me back. I rubbed my lips against her neck. It felt so good to be holding her. The breathing got heavy.

"Can I kiss you?" she asked softly.

"Yes," I whispered. "Yes ... "

We kissed. God. It was heaven. I was kissing her face all over now.

"I'd give you anything, Lioness," I whispered softly.

"Anything?" she smiled.

"Well, not anything, but a lot." Her next words were a total turn on.

"I want to fuck you!!" she exclaimed to my surprise.

"I want you to fuck me!" I responded.

Then she had second thoughts. "I don't think it's a good idea if we sleep together," she said, turning her head as if she didn't know what to do. She wanted to make love, but her brain was analyzing. I thought 'don't go into thought land, stay with this feeling.'

"Lioness don't leave me like this. Think about it. I want to."

"Okay, I'll think about it," she said, but I was afraid once she left, she wouldn't give me another thought. Out of sight, out of mind, with her. Just as we were heavy into this conversation, I saw a car pull up in the parking lot. A woman got out. It was Peggy! What bad timing! The worst! I didn't say anything but let Peggy go into the B & B, giving me more time to convince the Lioness that we should sleep together.

"I love your eyes," I said to her.

"I remember how your eyes look in the sunlight when you awake," she said. "I love looking at them. The skin under them becomes pink."

"Think about it . . . There's my friend Peggy," I said as I quickly got out of the car. Peggy was back out now. The Lioness was stunned. I called to Peggy, "I'm over here in the car." Peggy walked to the car.

"This is the Lioness," I said, and she jumped out of the car and shook Peggy's hand.

"Hello, nice to meet you," said Peggy. "Dorothy has talked so much about you. We're going for dinner, would you two like to join us?" I looked at the Lioness.

"No," she said. "I have to go home and feed the animals. My dog has been in all day." She got back in the car. I knew at this point she was not going to stay with me tonight even if I didn't go to dinner. And I didn't want to be left with these feelings and no one to talk to. I thought it best to go with Peggy and Lenny.

"I'd like to go with you," I said to Peggy. "Just give me five minutes to say good-bye."

"Okay," said Peggy. "I'll go wait in the car for you."

I got back into the Lioness's car and started kissing her again.

"To bed or not to bed, that is the question. Please think about it," I said and got back out of the car. She started the motor and left as I stood and watched.

I went to Peggy and Lenny's car and told them what had just transpired and what a critical moment they had arrived at.

"I figured you were sent to save me, so I cut it short with the Lioness. I took it as a sign. Maybe it was better that I let her go. There was a reason. Maybe it made me look less needy."

We walked to a restaurant. I really couldn't eat much so I told them my history with the Lioness. Peggy said, "She's very beautiful."

Maybe I had made a mistake in letting her go. There was so much more I wanted to say to her. I had a sinking feeling she wouldn't deal with her feelings now that there was space between us. By the time we left the restaurant, I was totally spaced.

I woke up at 1:24 am and wrote a poem entitled "Dyke Woman." Then I wrote in my journal, 'The Muse has returned. Now the play begins, Lioness. Do you want the leading role?' This was the reason we weren't supposed to stay together last night. We needed time for the passion and creativity to develop. Besides my therapist always said, "You draw to yourself what you project." I wanted to project a whole independent self. A survivor. I didn't want to appear too needy.

I prayed to Carol, "Please help me! If you love the Lioness, let me help her. What can I say to her that will make her say 'yes'? You can't have her, let me have her. You know I truly love her." I sobbed into my pillow. I knew she didn't love me, though, and that hurt.

With me, the Lioness was her strong, sexual, animus self, not the sweet, weak, childlike person, she was with people like Jen. I didn't want the child. I wanted the lover.

The rest of the night was wild, creative but wild! Thoughts and words spun through my brain. I wrote continuously. I thought about what it would be like to lick her again. This tired me out, and I fell asleep.

In the morning I awoke and thought, 'Will she call me? Shall I call her? Should I email her the poem? Maybe that was a way of getting to her. It might impress her. I really didn't know what to do. Our night had ended in such a fiasco.'

I asked the front desk if I could use their computer to send an email. The clerk suggested a place in town to do so. I called but I would have had to set up an account. It was too complicated for me!

If I left it for her to call, she might wait till it was time for me to leave. If I called, she might think I was too anxious. Such decisions. I went to take my shower before dealing with it.

While I was in the stall, I realized that I had left my shampoo and crème rinse at the Lioness's house. I only used one special brand that I bought from my hairdresser, and the thought of not having my beauty aids for the next few days was not appealing. When I got back to the room, I called her.

"Did I forget my shampoo and crème rinse in your bathroom?" I asked and she went to look.

"Yes, you did. What else did you forget?"

"Nothing else. But now you are going to have to see me again. I need my shampoo and crème rinse. How about coming for dinner?"

"No, not dinner," she replied. "I was thinking, something earlier, if you want to see me."

"I want to see you. I'd love to see you." I was surprised that she wanted to get together again so soon.

"Let me call you back in an hour. I haven't gotten my shit together," she said.

"Do you want to do brunch?" I asked.

"And do it on a full stomach?" she laughed. "That's not logical."

"Oh, right," I said calmly, but my insides were exploding realizing that she wanted to have sex. "You're so logical. I wouldn't expect you to be any other way."

"I'm not always logical," she ended. I got dressed, and she called just about one hour later.

"So, what time can I expect you?" I asked.

"I was thinking around 11:30. Is that ok?"

"That's fine." I got off the phone and danced around the room "Yes! Yes! Yes! I went for breakfast. I didn't eat much and saved the homemade breads and a piece of salmon for her in case she was hungry later.

Desiring to create a romantic scene. I ran down to one of the stores where I had seen candles and bought two. On my way back, I roamed through an outdoor art show and bought a print called "La Regina" of a lioness lying contently in a colorful bed of flowers. I placed the candles on the trunk at the end of the bed and put the "La Regina" print and the O'Keefe "White Rose" print out on display. Then I had about an hour to kill so I went back out. When I returned, she was waiting in the parlor.

"Can we take a walk?" she asked.

"Sure," I said. "Let's drop your bag in my room first."

We walked around. It was a beautiful, sunny day. We strolled aimlessly. It was awkward and conversation was strained. She was nervous, but I wasn't. I was impatient. We strolled through the art show again. While I stood by quietly, The Lioness talked to one of the female artists who had done landscapes of Santa Fe and surrounding areas. Next, we went to the top of the La Fonda and gazed out at the city skyline.

"This reminds me of a trip to San Francisco I took with J," I said. "We met P and H, two elderly gay gentlemen at the lounge at the top of the Sir Francis Drake for martinis. It was dusk. Thirty's music was playing. It was so romantic. P had been a lover of Rachmaninoff."

"Let me show you the St. Francis hotel," she suggested. "You'll like it."

She was right. I loved the hotel. It was my kind of place. I was sorry that I didn't act on my intuition.

"I can see why my therapist stayed here," I said, "It's such a classy hotel, and my therapist is a classy woman. I think I'll come here for high tea tomorrow."

"It's not my style," she responded. "Carol and I frequented the restaurant across the street. It was our place." She took me to see it- a down-home-type restaurant. I certainly wouldn't go there, especially since it was "their place."

Finally, she said, "Let's go back to your hotel."

When we got to the room, she grabbed her bag and said, "I have to take a shower." She opened the closet door assuming the shower was in there and walked inside. I burst out laughing.

"Going back into the closet?" I kidded. "The shower is out in the hallway."

"Right" she smiled, a bit embarrassed.

I undressed to my pink silky underwear. I decided not to put on the Victoria Secrets nightie I had bought to wear, thinking it might be too much. I put on the mauve purple silk robe instead and got into the bed. I sat back against the pillows, propped up on the headboard. She came back wearing a loose-fitting, masculine, grey robe with blue stripes.

"Nice touch," she said looking at the lit candles.

"I'm a romantic woman," I said. She sat next to me on the bed. I wasn't at all nervous and put my arms around her hugging her tightly.

"If this doesn't work, it's ok," she nervously warned me. I wasn't sure what was going on in her head.

"What do you mean?" I asked. "How can it not work?"

"Well, if I don't come it's ok. I masturbated twice this morning."

"You did? Why did you do that? I haven't masturbated for 2 months."

"You anticipated that long?" she asked.

"I anticipated longer," I responded.

"It's better if I don't have to worry about coming," she said.

Okay, I thought. Don't worry, I'll make you come. I never had any problem before. You always came easily. It was always me who took longer.

I flung my leg over her thighs and sat ever so lightly on top of her. I moved my face closer to hers. I opened my lips slightly. Very close but barely touching, I brushed my lips from one end of her cheek, across her lips to the other cheek. Tantalizing and teasing her. She could feel my breath, and I could feel hers. She smiled. Then she kissed me full on the lips. We embraced. It was wonderful having my arms around the person I loved so much. I remembered all that we had shared before. This time it was even better since I felt good about myself. I was thinner and more attractive. Our bodies fit well together.

"I wrote a poem for you last night. Would you like to hear it?" I asked.

"Sure, if you want to read it," she said. I read the poem entitled "Dyke Woman." At the end, I asked, "Are you man enough for the leading role?"

"No," she responded.

"No?" I questioned. "I'm sure you are."

Then I sat up over her and flung my hair back. "I want to be a diva when I grow up."

"You are a diva," she responded. I stood up and placed my bare feet on either side of her. My robe dangled above her.

"Unsash me," I whispered romantically.

"Unsash yourself," she responded. I was dumbfounded. This was not the answer I anticipated.

"Unsash myself? Do I have to do everything?" I asked as I undid the sash myself and took off the robe, exposing my pink silk underwear.

"Nice color," she remarked. We hugged and kissed. I took off her robe. She was nude. I took off my underwear. Finally, all our skin was touching.

"Do you find me attractive?" I asked.

"Yes, of course. Why do you think I want to be with you?"

"I need to know that to be free. You'll have to come to my place to meet the lioness."

"Isn't she here?" she asked.

"Yes, I guess she is, and she's hungry. She's not innocent anymore," I said referring to the way she had described me when we first made love. But she didn't remember so I reminded her, "Don't you remember saying that I was innocent."

"You were never innocent," she said as she pulled me closer and the fantasy came true.... the hugging ... the kissing ... the touching ... rediscovering each other's body. Softly caressing. Pressing against each other. Letting our breasts and nipples touch. This went on for a long time, then I dragged my breasts along her chest to her stomach, lightly over her crotch down her legs to her feet. I started licking her toes. She shuddered and pulled back as if it were too much or too ticklish for her. I stopped and rubbed further up her legs. I felt the hair on her legs but that didn't bother me. Nothing bothered me about her. I continued rubbing up her thighs nearing her cunt. I was so excited now and couldn't wait any longer. I put my tongue near her opening and started licking. There was hair in my mouth, but I didn't care. It always bothered me with J but not with the Lioness. I loved it. I loved the hair in my mouth. I got to her clit. I remembered how her clit was large and outside, not small and hidden inside like mine. She asked me to bring my legs up to her. I did and she placed my cunt over her face and started licking me. I couldn't stand it. It was so satisfying. We licked each other for such a long time. It seemed forever. I didn't even think about coming. All my questions of whether I was still gay vanished. I was enjoying it so much. She was enjoying it. It was such a surprise for me since the last time we had made love, she wasn't into oral sex. It was nice to know she had come to appreciate woman's taste. Then, as if she read my mind, she said, "You taste so much better than me."

She put her fingers inside me. It made me gasp. She gasped. I was so wet and soft and excited. I entered her. Then she simultaneously put her other finger in my other opening. I was in ecstasy. She filled everything. She filled it so well. I was wild. I couldn't concentrate any more on satisfying her. I just got into my own gratification. She slid in and out of me. Her fingers moving strongly. I felt so complete and full. Her wet tongue on me. I felt sensation everywhere.

Oh God," I kept repeating. "Oh God, Oh God." Then I came over and over again. Not the ultimate come that makes you stop but the smaller ones that keep you going and going. Finally, I had had enough and pulled away.

"I want you to come," I said and started licking her again. I licked for a long time, but she couldn't get it. I wasn't giving up. I would have licked her till the next day, the next week, the next year . . .

"Let me try," she said out of frustration, and she started rubbing herself with her hand. "Just keep your fingers inside." She rubbed for a while, but it was obvious she couldn't. She finally gave up.

"It's ok," she said. "I don't need to come. It's because of what I did this morning."

We lay in each other's arms, lightly running our hands down each other's body. I grabbed her hair with both hands and pulled up. She whimpered. I liked when she whimpered. It let me know she had some feelings. I kissed her nose and licked around the openings of her nostrils. She laughed and said, "I was going to do that to you, but I didn't think you could handle it."

"I could handle it. I've waited such a long time for this."

"For what?" she asked.

"To hold you again," I responded. She looked at me like she really didn't understand.

"I like being honest like when we were at the river," she said.

"No expectations, just supportive to each other," I added.

"I thought about going somewhere where there is water to make love, but then I thought someone might see us. Someone always walks in on us." I wasn't exactly sure what she meant by this. There were a few times in the past that we were interrupted, but I didn't think it was significant. What did she mean by "us"? Was there an "us"? We lay side by side at the end of the bed looking at the La Regina print.

"You are so beautiful," she said.

"You gave me such stress release," I said.

"I wanted you to get enough or more than enough. I should have put you at the edge of the bed. Did you ever have someone make love to you like that?"

"No. But I'm sure it would be wonderful and wild."

Then she asked such an unromantic question in her analytically way, "Did I spend enough time on your asshole?"

"Yes, plenty," I responded. "I loved it. I told you I was base. I'm just a simple woman with simple needs. I feel like that lioness," I said, pointing to the print.

"You're so histrionic, she said.

"What's histrionic? I asked.

"Dramatic."

"Well shouldn't an operatic woman be dramatic? You know I thought you would wait till my last day here to call me."

"Well, I thought about 'when can I do this?' Weekdays are bad for me. Weekends are better."

Hum, I thought, she fit me in, so it was convenient to her schedule. Oh well. Whatever. She seemed real in our love making. If this never happens again, I'm ok with it. I got up to get some water.

"You are thin," she said, looking at my naked body. Then she got up to get ready to leave and said, "You didn't get rejected this time." I nodded in agreement smiling the Cheshire cat grin which I wore the rest of the day.

*   *   *

Later that evening Peggy and Lenny came to get me for dinner. We walked to the restaurant in the hotel where they were staying.

"We have to stop at our room and show you Pontius Pig," announced Peggy.

"Who's Pontius Pig? I asked fully aware of their eccentric buying habits "What did you buy now?"

"He's a big wooden pig. He's lovely. You have to meet him," said Peggy while Lenny laughed hysterically in the background.

"Just how big is he?" I said remembering the ninety-two-inch totem poles.

"Oh, not too big, but we'll need to get an extra seat on the plane for him! Only kidding!" said Lenny when he saw the expression on my face.

"This sounds like something you really needed!" I laughed.

Their suite was quite lovely with a sitting room entrance and huge bedroom in the back. Pontius Pig sat proudly on the coffee table. He was as big as a medium-sized dog. Peggy picked him up, exclaiming, "Isn't he cute? Aren't you so cute," as she cuddled and kissed this big, wooden, inanimate object.

"He's adorable. Dumb but adorable," I said, watching this grown woman who was normally so serious making such a fuss over a wooden pig.

"Let's go eat." Said Lenny. "Before I throw that pig on the fire. I'm hungry."

"Do I look like the Cheshire cat?" I asked them as we sat down at our table. "I had enough sex this afternoon to get me through the winter."

"So, she came back?" said Peggy. "That was fast. I guess she changed her mine."

"Yeah. It surprised me too. It certainly gives a new meaning to 'doing the museums.'" I exclaimed.

"How was it?" asked Peggy.

"Oh God, Oh God, that's all I've been saying all day. Oh God."

"I don't think I need to hear more," laughed Peggy. "We get the picture!"

Later, in a more pensive moment, I asked, "What do you think love is?" I hoped on some level that the Lioness loved me. "I'm not sure anymore."

"Love is knowing what buttons to push on somebody and not using them," responded Peggy. Her answer was so quick, I knew it had to have some truth.

The definition made complete sense. Did I push the Lioness's buttons when I said I needed sex? Was that the real reason she made love to me?' I didn't want to think any further.

The meal was delicious, and I insisted on paying since they had done so much for me. On the way out, I grabbed the unfinished bottle of wine and a bunch of orange tiger lilies from the vase by the door.

"Dorothy! What are you doing?" exclaimed an embarrassed Peggy. It didn't make matters any better when I tried to pour the left-over wine from my glass into the bottle. I didn't care what anyone else thought. Lenny was amused. He walked me back to the hotel. Peggy was too embarrassed, too tired, and missing her pig.

I went right to bed. As I lay there, I thanked Carol for whatever help she had given. I felt that the Lioness had given me such a wonderful gift. Herself. In the middle of the night I awoke and stared at the tiger lilies sitting in a paper cup on the nightstand by the bed. There were two flowers and two buds. One flower was large, wide, and open, and the other was smaller and tilted away. I got out my drawing pad and sketched the flowers. I thought I might like to paint this arrangement later, so I got my camera. I took a picture from a distance then I tried to get a close up, but the camera would not flash. That's funny, I thought. Why can't I get a close up? I tried several times, but it just wouldn't work.

Then guilt trip. Maybe I hadn't spent enough time making love to the Lioness. I was so into my own pleasure. I remembered her response after I told her about the cup breaking incident. "The cup was not me. The cup was you."

No, I thought, the cup is you, and obviously there is a hole in you that I can't mend; I hope someone can. I fell back to sleep.

At breakfast the next morning, I sat in a tall, regal chair in the corner by the window at a table for one.

"I'm sitting in the Queen's chair," I said to Leeann as she came to take my order. She laughed. I was sure that by now she considered me a strange woman with all that had happened with the Lioness and the phone calls. She brought my breakfast and I began eating. Tears started swelling up in my eyes. Emotional release? I had been so strong when the Lioness said she didn't love me. Delayed reaction? The fact that she could make such physical love to me and not emotionally love me was hard to understand. I hurried to my room and thought I would call her on Tuesday night, my last night here, to say goodbye. I wouldn't make contact before that. Maybe she would call me, which was highly unlikely, knowing her.

I packed my stuff since I had to move to Room 5. I felt sad about moving out of Room 6, the lovers' number. I'd have to tell Leeann that Room 6 had a new name, "The Lovers." She'd get a charge out of that. One for the books, "Two great lovers made wild passionate love in the Grant Corner Inn in Room 6."

When I moved into Room 5, it was exactly as I anticipated—dull, boring, dark, with twin beds. An ugly picture of a girl holding a doll hung on the wall. I left the room quickly and walked to Canyon Road to do some art gazing. It was a beautiful sunny day, but I was so depressed. Tears kept rolling down my cheeks. I couldn't control it. I saw a sculpture of a huge lioness crawling down a small tree stump with her claws dug in the bark entitled "Hanging On," and that's exactly how I felt. Hanging on! But not by much.

I could only do so many shops, and then I was exhausted so, I went back to the room to take a nap. Later, I showered and went out to have high tea at the St. Francis. In a lovely room, I sat in a high back chair, writing in my journal, wishing I had a lover to share this wonderful experience.

I couldn't understand the Lioness's choices- her life of poverty and down-and-out woman. My lifestyle was the very thing she was trying to escape. Ironically, the Lioness had inherited money from her family. Never pursing an important job, she continued going to school for her second, third, and fourth master. Yet, she said she wouldn't feel comfortable having high tea. Why did she deprive herself? She grew up with this. I was sipping my port and eating finger sandwiches while she was out in the trailer eating leftovers and frozen food.

After high tea, I stopped in a jewelry store looking for a lioness ring but there were none. The saleswoman wished me luck finding it. "I'll keep looking. I'm sure she's out there," I responded. I went back to my dull room and cried. I called my sister to tell her what had happened. She had a bad weekend also. Her lover didn't show up on the weekend. I told her my story and decided I would stay in. My eyes were puffy, and I really didn't feel like socializing.

"Should I call her and tell her how upset I am?" I asked.

"No, I don't think you should," she replied.

"You're probably right."

We talked for over an hour and I hated to hang up the phone. To pass the time, I got some veggies, chips and wine from downstairs and just sat on the bed watching TV. About an hour later, there was a knock on the door. I couldn't imagine who it could be. I knew it couldn't be the Lioness. I quickly put on clothes and answered the door. It was some guy from the next room, Room 6.

"Can you turn your TV voice down. We're trying to take a nap," he said.

I looked at him like he was crazy. It was only 7:17 pm.

"Sure," I responded, not wanting to get into a fight. I thought, you're in a B & B, get a life. Room 6 is being wasted on these two! Still there was no call from the Lioness. I'd call her in the morning. It would be my last day here. I decided to do museums. Right, do museums! I hated this room. I fell asleep crying and woke up about one hour later, jolted up in bed, and said out loud, "That should be it!"

Where did that come from? I went back to sleep. Woke up again one hour later this time, screaming. Screaming very loudly. I was sure the people next door heard me. I called the Lioness right away. I was so upset and shaking. I needed to talk to someone, and it was too late to call my sister. She answered and I said, "I need to talk to someone. I just woke up screaming."

I told her how I was teary all day and how it was probably a reaction to all the emotion.

"Right," she said. "You've been experiencing a lot of heavy emotional things."

We chatted a bit, nothing major.

"So tomorrow, museums?" she asked.

"Yeah, museums."

She was tired from working out. I told her about the knock on the door when I was resting and watching TV.

"Good thing these jerk people were not in the hotel when I was screaming during our love making. I'm sure they wouldn't have appreciated it," I said.

"I thought about that," she responded. "People could probably hear us making love."

"Probably. These walls are paper thin, but most people were out. It was afternoon," I answered.

"With the way we were going, I was thinking they could probably hear us in the street!" she exclaimed.

"Probably," I said. "But who cares? I did high tea today."

"How does the bathroom rate?" The Lioness had a thing about rating restaurant bathrooms.

"I don't know I didn't use it. I'm not like you, going all the time. Well, go to sleep . . . see you again some time."

"Yeah, well," she started to say something but didn't finish. After she hung up, I thought she probably was going to say, "D, don't you realize that was the final fuck?" We hung up. I couldn't sleep. I hated everything. Room. TV. Then the weirdos next door came back, and they were noisy!

That night, I fell asleep and woke up at about 2:00 am thinking about the Lioness. Her saying she wanted to "fuck me" was such a masculine thing to say. Where did that come from? Instead of saying, "I want to make love to you." She said, "I want to fuck you." When I asked her to unsash me, her response was so unaffectionate. She told me her emotional response is delayed for at least a day. Did she think about what happened between us? Was I someone she didn't want to love rather than someone she didn't love? The Lioness had gotten involved with Carol after Carol told her she was attracted to the Lioness. Was the Lioness actually attracted to Carol? Why were they having problems? The Lioness had said to me during the day, "If Carol didn't die, I wouldn't have gotten to know the cat." What kind of a statement was that? It sounded like their relationship had been a struggle. They were only together a short time, and yet they were in therapy. The Lioness had kept saying that Carol was going to leave her if she didn't change.

I knew she would call me in the morning. I guaranteed it. I said the magic words, "I need to talk to you." My need set off a response in her. She would call just after 8:00 am. I pushed her buttons. Did I then really love her?

I did my run at 6:45 am. When I was going around the Plaza park, I broke into a fast sprint then slowed down into a dance. There was a young black male selling newspapers in the street. He had on a colorful outfit of orange and yellow. As I danced by, he started dancing in the street with me. It was good to be so free. I made sure I got back to the room before 8:00 am, and sure enough she called by 8:15 am.

"I didn't want you to think I was cutting you off short last night. I realized that that call might have been your good-bye call. I thought you had something else to say," she began.

"I thought you were tired, so I didn't want to keep you on too long." I said, feeling out of breath. I told her about my dancing in the street with the paper seller.

"We need to talk," I said. "I'm trying to zero in on what's happened."

"Don't look too close," she warned.

I told her I felt like I was in a triangle when she brought me to visit Jen. She said she wasn't sure why she had done so. "Maybe I wanted to show you off."

"Show me off? Then why did I feel like the outsider?" I asked.

"I wanted you to meet my friends, see my life."

"I would do the same if you came to the East. Meet my friends, my brother, my . . . "

"That's why I'm not coming," she responded fiercely.

"Really?" I said, bewildered by her negativity.

"I emailed Jen this morning. She didn't remember who you were. That's why she was standoffish. She thought you were my cousin or my graduate counselor."

"No, just your writing consultant," I said sarcastically. I thought, how much could she have said to Jen about me if she didn't even know who I was. I guess the Lioness didn't make a big deal about me.

"She did say she felt the sexual tension between us."

"Well, I felt like the third person," I said.

"Well, there are others," she said.

"Well, there are others for me, too!" I said. "I don't care that you are with other women. I just couldn't stand to see you with a man."

"Why? Does it make you feel inadequate?" she asked.

"Yes, maybe," I responded. "Men are non-existent for me. Probably because my father was such a non-person to me when I was growing up. I'm working on this issue with my brother and other male friends."

"When you deal with your father, you'll resolve the male issue," she said.

"Stop analyzing me. I think what you did was a farewell fuck. It made me cry all day thinking about that."

"You're releasing," she said.

"How could you do it so well if it was just a farewell fuck?" I asked.

"I do it best at the end," she replied.

"Why? Because you don't have to do it again?"

"Yes," she answered. "No further expectations. There are feelings. I couldn't make love to you if there were no feelings. You were so beautiful. I love how you were so open to me."

"You set the scene for failure, jerking off and then saying it's ok if it doesn't work."

"It's better that I jerked off. There wasn't the question in my head of will I come or not?

"That poem exposed my needs to you. It said more about me than you. I wasn't really surprised at your no response at the end. But what were you thinking when I asked you to unsash me and you said 'unsash yourself?' Where did that come from?"

"It put me in a role that I didn't want to play," she answered.

"It was meant to be enticing, sensual," I responded sadly.

"I almost told you to take off the makeup, but I figured it was your thing."

"Really?" I said and thought, I don't wear that much, just blush and lipstick. "I feel dull without it."

"Oh, D, do you know how beautiful you were at the end? I loved it. The things I find attractive in you, you probably wouldn't."

"So that makes me think 'why not me?' I don't know. I can't say what I'm thinking."

"Tell me," she encouraged.

"Well, you gave yourself to a man and then to Carol who was so old."

"I was attracted to her," she corrected.

"And then you tell me Kayla is a very large woman."

"I'm into flesh," said the Lioness. "Look I have to come into Santa Fe today to do some errands and have my counseling session."

"Do you want to meet me for dinner?" I asked.

"No, I have a writing group tonight but maybe I can go to it a little late. I'll have to call you and leave a message. Maybe we could get together for a while this afternoon."

"OK, leave me a message at the desk. I'm going to go do the museums."

We hung up the phone, and I thought 'if I didn't call, I would never know she was going to be in Santa Fe today. She was going to be in the same town and hadn't even planned to ask me for lunch or anything.' That made me feel so awful. She really seemed cruel. I wouldn't have done that to a friend

I got dressed and decided to enjoy my last day here and make the most of the museums. As I was walking past the reception desk, the phone rang. "It's for you D," said Louise. She had done it again. Caught me just as I was leaving.

"I pushed back my writing group till later so I can meet you around 4:00 pm but I have to leave by 6:30 pm."

"Okay, meet you here."

She always put restrictions on our meetings.

The sun was shining, and I was determined to enjoy the day. I walked to the Museum of Fine Arts in the center of town. I laughed openly in front of a painting called 'The Last Barbecue,' a Southwestern-take-off on the Last Supper. An extremely colorful and gay scene, Christ and the apostles were wearing large Mexican hats and eating barbecued food. A couple came up to me and said they wanted to laugh when they saw it but were too shy.

Upstairs was a special exhibit called "A Journey through Bui-Bui." As I walked into a darkish room, I gasped. There was a woman, dressed in black veil and burka, lying on the floor. I ran out I was so frightened, but when I looked back in from the doorway, I realized it was a sculpture of a woman. Her white hands were extended in front of her, and she was holding something. I forced myself to go back in. I noticed two other women in various poses- one reaching toward the window-another crawling toward the corner of the room. The bodies exuded suffering. Their hands held a different colored light. There were two more rooms, and I walked through trying hard to listen to what these women were saying. The message was so powerful.

As I was paying for some souvenirs, I said to the saleswoman, "God, isn't that exhibit powerful?"

"Yes," she said. "And do you know these women with no light actually live shorter life spans than other women. It has to do with the fact that they don't get sunlight and their whole being is a sort of 'shutting' out, reflective of their dress. I was in Italy not too long ago sitting on a bus. One of these Mid-Eastern men got on and spit at me."

"For what reason?" I asked.

"He wanted my seat and thought he should have it. I was a lowly woman."

"Even in Italy? Not his own country? Did you hit him?"

"I wanted to, but I thought it best to ignore him. Then I went home and took it out on my boyfriend!"

During lunch at the Coyote Café. I sat on a ledge seat on the second floor overlooking the shops. Next to me sat a tall, distinguished woman. Soon, the waiter came to take my order of soup and salad. I asked him for plain oil for my salad.

"You mean olive oil?" he asked.

"Yes, plain olive oil," I responded.

"We only keep that in the kitchen in the other building. I would have to cross over to the other side to get it. Do you want me to do that?" he asked in a disgusted tone.

"Yes," I insisted, and he left shaking his head. I turned to the woman sitting next to me and said, "What a great view."

"Yes, isn't it? I overheard your conversation with the waiter, and I was glad you demanded what you wanted. Good for you! I've been doing some shopping," she said as she showed me some special gift soaps that she bought for her friends back home in Texas. I learned she was traveling with a camping and hiking group. She told me she was in her 60's, but she looked younger.

"Would you believe I had a stroke?" she said to me.

"No! At your age? You're in such great shape."

"I am in great shape now," she explained. "I work out every day yet I'm having a hard time getting health insurance when they see the stroke history. They don't care that my doctor says I'm in perfect health now and that I do fifty minutes on the treadmill every day."

"That's awful. But I know what you mean. I work in insurance, and it's difficult to get them to change their way of thinking. I did some research on MS and now on CAD in the elderly, and I'm always trying to convince them they have to update their rates to be reflective of what is currently in the literature. But it's a big conglomerate and it doesn't move quickly. I feel like I'm on the wrong side. I sympathize with the insureds, not the insurance company. The companies are just out to make money. It's always the bottom line. And the CEO's and top managers get big bonus for using the little guys who do the work. Something is wrong with this picture."

"Did you smoke?" I added.

"No, never smoked. But I used to be a workaholic. That's why I had the stroke. Stress at work. I got out after that and you know what? The money came. So, D get out, the money will come. Enjoy yourself. That's the best advice I can give to you."

With that she got up to leave and I felt that I had been given a special message from a wise woman.

Before leaving, I ordered a meal to go for the Lioness. After all her chores, she probably didn't take time to eat. It was almost time for her to arrive, so I walked back to my room and freshened up. On my way out, I asked Leeann if there was a quiet park in the area where one could talk. I sat down at one of the white wrought-iron tables in the corner facing the parking lot and waited. She arrived exactly at 4:00 pm and hugged me.

"Have you eaten?" I asked. "I brought you a meal." She sat down and picked on the burrito. I told her that the gay waiter had said to tell her, "It was sent with love from the Coyote Café." Then I told her about the park, but she already knew about it. It was the same place she had taken Zig for a walk the first day we were together.

We started walking. Conversation was slow. I thought to myself 'this was a bad idea. I don't know what to say.' As we passed by a church, Our Lady of Guadeloupe, she asked, "Do you want to go in? "She's the Madonna of Mexico.

"Sure," thinking this would be a diversion. But all the doors were locked so we couldn't enter. We continued to the park and once we reached it, we lay down on the grass by the side of the dry riverbed. How ironic the place we started. We had come a full circle.

I began talking. I knew I had to. This was my last chance. "I need to know where we stand." There was that word again—<u>need</u>. "You need to slap me a bit, so I get it."

She wasted no time. It wasn't difficult for her. "Well, I loved being with you physically. But I don't want to be your girlfriend. I don't want to be your partner. I don't want to move to Connecticut and live your lifestyle. I may have sex with you again but it's not something I will pursue." So, there it was. She was blunt and direct and left no room for the imagination.

"Well, I guess that's clear enough. That's what I needed to hear because I don't want to spend another seventeen years, hoping you will come back to me. You told me after we broke up in Maine that there would never be any possibility for us in the future, but I didn't believe you. You were a child and very influenced by your parents. Now you're free to choose."

I was upset and cried a little but nothing tremendous. "I know I said Jen was a mother figure for you, but I guess in a way you're a mother figure for me. The unattainable woman."

"I may not want to be with anyone ever again. I may stay alone," she added.

"Well, that's what the palm reader said about you when we were in Maine. That later in life, you would be alone. Why did you choose such a distance state such as New Mexico?"

"I wanted to be in a place where the environment and land dominated me, not society," she explained.

Then we talked about our writing techniques, a less emotional topic. She told me that she gets together with other writers and they try to stimulate each other. Sometimes, they cut out words from magazines and throw them into the air and pick up a bunch and write a poem using those words.

"I can't imagine doing that," I said. "Writing is such a personal experience for me. Sometimes at night I wake up and start writing something that happened during the day, maybe prompted by objects around me in the room. I can only write what is real."

"Whatever works," she replied. Soon we got up and started walking back to my room. Two guys were behind us, and I noticed that she kept looking back at them as if she were worried. I wasn't, though. I wondered why she was. Only stray dogs bother me.

"Isn't this the drabbest room? I told Leeann she has to redecorate it," I said to her when we returned to Room 5.

"It's downright putrid!" she added. I sat on the bed.

"Weird pictures," I said looking around the room.

"This one's ok," she said, pointing to the picture on the wall. I got up and looked closely at it, and thought, funny, the artist's name was Jen.

"Can I kiss you?" she asked as I walked back to the middle of the room.

"Yes, of course," I replied, surprised at her desire. My heart melted. She lay next to me on the bed and we kissed. Neither one of us did anything to send the other one over the edge. I did not want to have rushed sex. I wanted to leave her with the thought of our great sex from the other day. From the depth came the next words, "If you ever need me, please call even if I'm with someone. I'll always be there for you. That's a promise." She looked at me with those blue eyes and smiled.

"Will you tell me if you find that person?' she asked.

"Why not? I tell you everything." And I thought to myself, 'why not, you don't care.' "I need a new cup," I said.

"What does the cup represent to you?" she asked.

"A new love," I responded.

"I told my therapist about what happened between us," she explained. "He asked if I would make love to you again. I told him I didn't know. He asked, "Why not?"

Both of us knew there would be no intense lovemaking today.

"Last feels," I said trying to take the edge off. I looked at the clock, and it was 6:30.

"I'm glad you came to see me," she said.

"I'm glad too," I said and started crying softly. Always me crying. Always soft tears. "Crying is good," I added. "We ended badly last time in Maine. This is better. I can accept it more."

"Should I call you in the morning?" she asked.

"If you'd like," I said.

"I'll call you," she responded.

"Do you want me to leave the parking sticker at the front desk?" she asked.

"No. I'll walk you out," I said.

"I just thought you might want to stay here."

"Maybe I should." But then I regained my composure. "I'm ok. I'll walk out with you." I got up and hugged her, "Good-bye Hon," trying to keep it light. "I love you."

"I love you, too, on some level," she answered in a childlike way.

"I know you do."

I washed my face. She grabbed my hand as we climbed down the steps and walked through the B & B. Everyone watched us. I was so proud she wasn't ashamed of our love. As we passed by the guest book, I said, "Someday when you're a famous poetess and I'm a famous writer, they will know that Dorothy and the Lioness slept in Room 6 and everyone heard them!"

"I hope I'm not famous till I die. I don't think I'll be famous anyway."

"You will be. I know it," I said with confidence.

"Take care of yourself," she said

"Oh, I will. I don't believe in poverty!" I retorted.

"I mean spiritually."

"That too. *Ciao.*"

And she got into her car. I walked back onto the porch and leaned over the rail. She pulled out of the parking lot and as she drove by, she yelled out the window, "*Ciao Bella.*"

"*Si, grazie,*" I responded and sat back in the chair. I stared at the empty chair where she had sat. An empty chair now filled only with great memories.

The evening was a calm and peaceful. I didn't go out for dinner. I stayed in my room and got ready for the trip home. I went to bed early and woke up at about 11:00 pm to noises. I wished the Lioness was with me. It was still hard for me to understand. I knew I would never get over her, never stop loving her, and never stop wanting her. How could a new lover understand her effect on me?

\* \* \*

I woke up early the next morning and ran through the main streets of the city. As I looked up at one of the buildings, I saw a raven, then a second, and third fly off the roof.

"Where's the fourth?" I yelled up. And sure enough, the fourth flew off. Four, the number of self. I laughed and cried happy tears. What a great sign! The sky was red with sunrise.

It was time to go home. I felt ready to write again and get some serious work done. The fantasy was over. The Lioness didn't call in the morning. Maybe that was better.

The airport was tiny, very tiny. In fact, the ticket person was also the person who checked luggage through the x-ray machine, collected tickets before boarding, taxied the luggage to the plane, and loaded it!

The plane was late. I walked over to the window, perched my knees on the couch and looked out at the runway. . . . This is the part where *Desert Heart* could have had a better ending. . . . the Lioness realizes she loves me, gets in her car and rushes to the airport to stop me from leaving.

I had always wanted to be the second woman in her dream.

I stared out the window at the runway, not looking back, giving her ample opportunity to surprise and embrace me from behind.

But alas, *Desert Heart* didn't get a better ending. I watched the plane land. It looked like a mini plane! If there was any turbulence in the air, we were going to feel it! We boarded shortly. One of the pilots was also the flight attendant. With no overhead luggage space and only one seat on either side, passengers could see the pilots as there was no door to the cockpit. As I leaned over to the guy sitting across from me, I said, "Hang on. It's going to be a bumpy ride." He was too young to appreciate my Betty Davis humor.

I tried to relax. I was not going to die in a plane accident. "Deep breaths. Take deep breaths." The letters <u>Zia</u> were written across the front wall. A good sign. <u>Zia</u> means aunt in Italian and my aunt always protected me. And after we took off, I actually enjoyed the flight. It was smooth and watching the landing at front view was exciting.

That night, I didn't get home till late. It was good to be in my own bed again. In my soft, purple, satin sheets. I woke up thinking about her and our wild sex. Maybe we could have phone sex, I thought. Before I had gone to bed, I emailed her about the trip home and give a description of the Number 8 card of the Tarot--<u>Strength</u>. I shared that I had read from a magazine on the plane about some literary prize award Adrienne Rich had won from a Santa Fe group. The association also gave money to aspiring writers. I told her to apply.

The next day, I saw my sister. I told her how I thought the Lioness was a mother figure and maybe that's why I couldn't let go.

"She's more like a father figure," she said. "She's detached, cold, selfish. The male who is never there for us. Such a dyke. She's like a man. They can have sex with no feelings."

Maybe she was right.

When I sat down at my computer, I saw that the Lioness had responded to my email. She knew about the literary group and had attended an interview featuring Rich the night before I arrived. Why hadn't she told me about this lecture beforehand? She knew Rich was one of my favorite writers. As a matter of fact, I had introduced her to Rich when I gave her my copy of *Dream of a Common Language*. I would have arrived earlier if I had known about the lecture. How could she be so thoughtless?

That night I headed out for a women's golf league lobster dinner. As I was driving down I-95, I thought about what I was going to say to Justine, my friend, when she asked, "So are you moving to Santa Fe?"

"No, it was just a final fuck. Final fuck," I said out loud. And then

I rolled down the window of the car and screamed, "Final fuck! How many of you know what the final fuck is? Come on. Raise your hands. I'm sure you know what the final fuck is!"

And then I thought, what a great title for a poem; get a pencil; hurry before I lose the lines. All I had was the yellow sheet with the directions to the dinner. So, I grabbed a pen from under the dashboard, put the paper in front of me on the steering wheel, and tried writing in between the lines of the mailing. It was difficult balancing the paper, writing, and trying not to hit the two cars on either side of me. This was creativity. Not the child's play of throwing words in the air. This was real feeling and pain coming through in words.

Not sure how, but I made it to the dinner without getting into an accident. The event was BYOB, so I had to go back out to get a bottle of wine.

The chairwoman saw me and asked, "Leaving so soon?"

"No, I have to get some wine." When I returned, I found out that Justine was sick and wasn't coming to the dinner. No one to vent to. I sat at a table. I drank a lot. I entertained the women with my rantings of the final fuck. When I told them my Lioness story, one of them exclaimed, "She sounds like a guy. They do that kind of stuff."

Did the Lioness take on the persona of Carol?

As I sat there, Lonnie came over and gave me a beer. "Here have a Michelob," she said. And she walked back to her table. I saw the bottle was unopened. I followed her and said, "Lonnie, how am I supposed to drink this beer?" She grabbed the bottle out of my hand and bit off the top.

"God what a dyke you are!" I exclaimed.

"Yes, I am," she replied.

I looked at her. She had just admitted that she was gay. I had always thought she was gay, but she had recently married. That threw me off the track even though I knew some gay woman made the choice to marry. They wanted children or they had been hurt badly by some woman or the gay lifestyle was just too hard to live.

"So, then Gerry is your lover?" I asked.

"Right, but don't tell anyone. We have to protect her children."

"Sure, I won't say anything." Just then the chairwoman came up to me and let me in on the secret of who her female lover was. Wow, this was getting interesting! These women were married but had female lovers. This put a whole new perspective on life. I spent a lot of time talking with one of the women, Cara, and would have liked to go home with her, but I didn't dare ask. It was hard to tell who was gay, who was not, and who was bi!

By the time, the dinner was over, I was as drunk as a skunk. I stopped at Calas's house. Her husband answered the door holding their baby. When he saw what shape I was in, he announced, "I'll take the baby upstairs and leave you two alone."

We sat at the table. I put my head on her leg and told her the whole story about the Lioness. I was sobbing and my nose was running. She gave me a dinner napkin to clean my face.

"I still love her. How can she do it, Calas? How can she say she doesn't love me? How can she do it so well?"

"She loves you," she said. "You have to know that. She's running away big time."

That night I got up a few times and hugged the porcelain goddess. The next morning, I saw a trail of my clothes from the door to my bed. Soon after, my brother called, and I asked him, "Did you hear the bells ringing this weekend?" It was a joke we had about how the bells would go off when I finally had sex as it had been so long.

"No. Why?" he asked.

"I had sex. Boy, did I have sex. It was beautiful but now it's painful. I drank a whole bottle of wine last night at the dinner."

"You needed to do that," he said.

I was at my sister's the next day listening to her on the phone complaining about her boyfriend: "The more he rejects me, the more I want him."

Wasn't that the truth?

*     *     *

The next few weeks were tough. I cried for no reason. Everything was fresh in my head, not a memory from seventeen years ago. I couldn't get the lovemaking out of my mind. It was better than ever. I was writing poems late at night on some weird high. I told Adele about it.

"It's a gift," she said.

"Yes. It's called insanity!" We both laughed.

I went to visit J and told her about the Lioness.

"I think there is some connection between you two and it will always be there," she advised. "She is your Muse. You will continue through this life journey like waves on the shore, crashing in and then gently flowing back out."

Maybe she was right. I realized that I was the same age when I met the Lioness that the Lioness was when she met Carol. Impressionable thirties!

One morning, I emailed the Lioness and suggested that we might have another encounter in the future: "Let's do a next time. I don't need you all the time, just some of the time. I'm much more creative after being with you. I like this long- distance thing."

That afternoon I received a book in the mail from her on creative writing. An unexpected but nice surprise. I sent her a thank-you letter addressed to "My lover and nothing more." In it I expressed my sadness at not being able to "hand her again." I wrote "You are the cup. There is a hole in you I wish desperately to mend," and signed the card, "Butterfly with a Lou-ling base."

"What's a Lou-ling base?" she asked in her next email. She was heavy into her schoolwork and had sent a poem about a doe. I commented that the poem was tight, hard for the reader to get in. I didn't sense any feeling except awe. I asked her to send some poems that expressed more feeling.

I explained that in the opera *Turandot*, Loul-ing was the angry spirit inside the princess. "Every time I'm at a meeting and say something that alienates everyone, I attribute it to Lou-ling."

She wrote back that she heard the aria "Nessun Dorma" while she was driving by the river where we had had our talk.

"Isn't that song from Turandot," she asked. "I told my sister about your visit. She thought it was great."

Every return email from her gave me that sinking feeling in my stomach just before opening it. I feared it would say nothing about us. And it never did.

I mentioned in one email that I had another business trip to Arizona coming up in January. I offered to stop on the way home and spend a few days with her. She nixed this as she was going to be out of state. Regarding any future interlude, she wrote, "Next time is a possibility but one that I'm not willing to make any commitment to until some months have passed. If a definite opportunity becomes available and I'm in the same mood I was ten days ago and you're still interested, then maybe . . . "

She complained about her writing . . . " Felt like hard work . . . kind of slogging away . . . No new stuff . . . there wasn't anything interesting readily available to make a poem from three weeks of daily writing practice."

Nothing interesting in the past three weeks! What was I—a dull encounter?

I got my pictures back from Santa Fe. They were all distant and clouded, not like the ocean and sunrise shots. I put the ones of the Lioness on my bureau.

I had one picture of her from our Maine tryst. She was standing on rocks with the ocean water flowing toward her, and her head tilted to the right. One of the new pictures was similar. In this one, she was sitting on rocks with a stream flowing away from her, her head titled in the same way.

I took the fire opal out of the safe and put it in front of Aunt Sophie, a handcrafted figure who sat on my bureau. I had bought her at a craft store in Mystic. Her tag said, "Aunt Sophie grants the wishes that help you succeed at your endeavors." I had sensed her calling to me when I entered the store, so I had bought her. The saleswomen had said, "These dolls pick you out." Maybe Aunt Sophie could do something. I put the repaired pooke cup in front of her, too.

That week, the Lioness emailed some poems which I obsessed over for days trying to interpret. I looked up words in the dictionary. I searched topics on the computer. I woke up at night analyzing them, hoping they would provide some insight into her. Two were done from postcards. One was of an obscure Klee painting and the other a place in Prague. She had used them for inspiration. I went to the bookstore and library to try and find them but couldn't. I thought these might have some connection with Carol but found out later in one of her emails that they were just postcards some woman had brought to her writing group.

One poem made me question whether she loved Carol or wanted to love her. The Lioness didn't deny or object to what I had said. I sent a few long interpretations of her poems and the effect they evoked in me. There was no response. I thought I had offended her. I knew what it was like to have one's work criticized. I sent an email apologizing for my bluntness and then another which was going to be my final. I was losing hope. I was losing interest. The cryptic email said, "I forgot to tell you the prince's name in *Turandot* was Love, and that's the final word of the opera."

A few days later she emailed and apologized for her silence. It was inadvertent. She was so busy with other things, schoolwork, hiking with women friends. She responded to my poem critique and added that she appreciated my time and energy. Then she expressed a sadness at not being given enough time to resolve her relationship with Carol. Her writing, she felt, could not resolve it since it lacked Carol's voice.

That morning while walking on the beach and thinking of the Lioness and Carol, I found a baby's sucking nipple with penguins painted on the rim. I looked up penguin in my *Animal Speak* book: "The penguin is capable of lucid dreaming an astral projection . . . it can jump out of water." I wrote to her that she had the ability to communicate with Carol but not in the traditional way. She would have to start dreaming and jumping. She sent me back a poem comparing art and the male penguin's protective holding of the egg on his foot.

Her response to my emails started dwindling, and I was getting bored with her analytical rantings and questions. I needed more. I was obsessed with someone who didn't want me. All my journal entries were about my feelings for her. This was not healthy. Everyone warned me to stay away from her.

"Looks like she can hurt you deeply," said Calas.

The arm pain came back, and I started eating more to fill the emptiness. I knew what this could lead to. It had happened before where I gained about Twenty to thirty pounds after a rejection. I didn't want this to occur again. I liked the way I looked. It was time to give her up and just accept her as a writing friend.

Then came the last straw. I went to get my mail on Saturday morning and there was a letter from the Lioness. A letter! My gosh! She had taken the time to write me a letter! It was always a treat to receive one of her letters. In my Maine days I wouldn't open it till I was alone and quiet in some peaceful place. I wanted to savor her words. So, I did the same for this letter. I waited till night and then lying in bed opened it. But it wasn't a letter. It was a copy of a magazine article about some germ theory with a small yellow sticky, "thought you might enjoy reading this article."

She didn't even take the time to write a half-page letter. I went nuts. That night I wrote a nasty email to the Lioness entitled, "fucked up" which spouted all my anger.

. . . received your article and you know what? I don't give a fuck. You obviously have no idea about the effect you have on me or you don't care. You bring me pain and why I let it happen indicates how fucked up I am. I'm going to be honest with you at the risk of alienating you forever.

Santa Fe was a fiasco for me. You didn't even want to spend one night alone. You invited Jen to join us. In the morning after my run, I was ready to pack it in, but you shocked me with the, "I really want to spend the day with you." I thought maybe you were remembering us. No way. I think the only reason you had sex with me was because I said, "I needed it." It was a nice release for past sins.

You had no intension of telling me you were going to be in Santa Fe on my last day. It was because I needed to talk that you fit me in. You said you didn't want me . . . I was crushed. Then back at the room, you asked, "can I kiss you?" I was pathetic for letting you. When I said, "I had waited so long for this," you probably had no idea what that meant. Do you know how difficult it is to make love and not be allowed to express feelings? I am Dionysian and you are Apollian and we shall never understand one another. You see me as an overzealous emotional being and I see you as a cold fish. Maybe this letter will help you to better love some other woman . . . signed Louling.

I didn't send the email. I decided to wait a day and see if I still felt like doing so the next day. I didn't. What if the Lioness died and the "Fuck you, email" was my last correspondence with her? I would feel awful. Besides I couldn't hurt her like that. Love had to be freely given. We couldn't expect anything in return. People could only give what they were capable of giving. She probably thought that she was doing a good thing sending the article. I was the one with the reaction. Making more out of it than I should have.

Instead, I sent a bland note saying that I was familiar with the topic.

I decided I would try some active imagination to get at the part of me that couldn't get over the Lioness. The part that could get so angry over a simple letter. There was obviously some irrational part stuck with memories of her. I lay in bed that night, got quiet and peaceful within myself. I imagined going deeper and deeper to where all the parts were.

"Okay, who's in there that can't let go of the Lioness? I want to talk with you."

The crying woman came to mind. Sometimes during the night, I would hear a woman crying. It must have been that part of myself that was hanging on to the Lioness. I felt sorry for her. I understood her pain. The Lioness had hurt her so much when she left years ago. She tried to be strong, but she was crying within. She knew she had to let her go, but it was so hard.

"I know she hurt you deeply, but I will help you find someone else," I said to her. "I'll help you find someone who is better for you. She doesn't love you but it's ok because I love you. I'll take care of and love you. We'll be fine without her. We'll find someone who wants us. We'll start by taking down her pictures. We won't email her as much anymore, and we won't tell her our inner feelings."

I felt good about this conversation, as if I had made contact. Then I asked to speak with the woman who kept eating and was never satisfied.

"Who's hungry? Who feels empty?" The woman with no heart responded. During one of my regressions in therapy, I had realized that I thought my heart was empty. There were no feelings inside. It had been a difficult session. It was this woman trying to fill herself with food.

I talked to her as well. "You can use my feelings. I really have feelings now. You felt bad about J moving to Texas, the thought of losing a true friend. You felt bad when the Lioness said she didn't love us. You have gotten closer to the family again. You listened to your brother when he was going through his breakup. You were there every day for him. You were good to your cousin's child. You played with her and bought her gifts. You have changed. The feelings are real. As a matter of fact, you feel too much now. You've made mistakes but it's ok. You feel, that's the important thing. You are a loving person, so you don't need to substitute food to fill the void. There is love in the void."

I fell asleep wondering if what I had done would work.

The next morning, I got up and didn't go immediately for food. I ate normally the rest of the day as well. Could it be working? Then I took the Lioness's pictures off the bureau and hid them in a drawer. I thought about tearing them up and throwing them into the ocean, but I couldn't do that yet. Instead, I took down the magnet hanging on the refrigerator with the letters FPG and purple grapes, symbolic of the Lioness. I continued not feeling that overwhelming hunger.

My energy returned. I redirected the sexual frustration and one morning I tore down the wallpaper in the bathroom. I bought paint and a lilac Monet wallpaper. Excited about redecorating, I even got paint and paper for the kitchen.

There was an email from the Lioness on my computer, and I didn't respond. She was so didactic. She bored me. More analytical questions!

\* \* \*

Delighting in this new sense of self, I invited J to come for dinner. It was just about a year since all the trouble had begun. J was dating another woman. We had finally become friends again. She offered to help me set up the VCR.

"You still can't deal with electrical equipment, can you?" She laughed.

"Some things never change," I responded. She asked about my trip to Santa Fe. When I told her how the Lioness had responded "Unsash yourself," to my invitation, J exclaimed, "Wow, quite a profound statement. Yet she continued to the fruition of the visit."

J had a way of hitting the mark. The statement did have deeper implications. Was it my subconscious wish that she let me go? And her subconscious saying, "Find a way to let yourself go. I can't do it."

Later, sitting on the floor looking at all our old furniture, J said, "It took a long time to get over you. I had to get rid of anything that reminded me of you. That's why I made you take it all. It was very difficult for me in the beginning. I would lie in bed and think I heard you moving around in another room. I would get up and look and then remember you were gone."

"I'm sorry," I said.

"I'm sorry, too," she said. "All our friends thought we would get back."

"Do you feel weird being with someone else after being with me for so long?" I asked.

"Sometimes. But it's nice being loved so completely." Her admission made me know I had done the right thing even if it caused us both so much pain. I realized I wasn't much different than the Lioness. I, too, had made physical love to a woman I stopped loving. I must have looked distraught for then J said, "You'll see her again. Maybe after January. Same time, next year."

"I don't think so. And I don't know if that's enough anymore. I know what's important now."

"What?" she asked.

"Love," I responded, and I could see the hurt in her eyes.

"Just back off," she advised. "You always came back to me when I did that."

The next morning as I was making breakfast, I saw two spiders crawling up the kitchen wall and a third one in my bedroom. Like the spiders, I spent most of November weaving and spinning the lines of creativity. While sitting on the parlor floor with my computer, I wrote till late at night, never tiring. I even signed up for a drawing and an Italian language course. I did watercolors of the beach. Some mornings I could even hear the sun rising just before awaking.

One day, I got a friendly email from the Lioness. I was glad that I hadn't sent the "Fuck you" one. She was still engrossed in completing deadlines for her writing course and unhappily dealing with family visits for the holidays. She felt blocked. I felt bad for her. Even though I still missed her, I was realistic that we would never be together.

Though I felt I was getting stronger each day, my dreams reflected my frustrations. I woke up out of breath, gasping. In one dream I was trying to make love to the Lioness. She kept saying "No." She was cooped up on some island. Her father came and saw us together. He warned me to stay away. I pursued when he left.

I wrote poems upon waking.

I did one more active imagination experiment before falling back to sleep early one morning. I called to the woman who had put the string around my heart. I told her that I didn't need to be punished anymore because I was a good person. I had done a lot of good work this year. I asked that she put her hands inside my heart and break the string. "I'm going back to sleep and when I awake the string will be broken," I said aloud and fell into a peaceful sleep. I wasn't sure if anything happened, but I believed something did. I knew I had to heal myself.

That evening, I tried to call the Lioness, but her phone was busy. It was still busy a half-hour later. I took this as a sign not to call and emailed instead. I had a business trip to Arizona planned for January. The Lioness was going to be out East so there was to be no visit. I asked her if she would be in the area visiting family. If so, she was welcome to stay at my place. She wrote back that her plans did not include being in my area, but that she appreciated the offer. She had celebrated the fifth anniversary of Carol's death with friends at a potluck dinner. Someone had brought earlier pictures of her and Carol, which she hadn't seen. It took her aback.

"How can she be dead and somehow so alive with me?" she asked.

I knew perfectly well how that could happen.

\* \* \*

Just before Christmas, I attended the company party with my brother. Martinis and dancing. When I got home, I was happy high and called the Lioness. It was only 10:00 pm her time so I was surprised to find her sleeping. Her reaction was not pleasant.

"Huh, who's this?" she moaned.

"Bad timing?" I asked.

"I'm in bed. I just got off the phone with a friend." She sounded out of it.

"Go back to sleep," I said and hung up. I decided not to call her again. It wasn't good for my ego.

She called me back the next night. It was an awkward conversation, all surface. I wasn't in the mood. I felt like I had already "shot my wad" and there was nothing left. She talked about the possibility of her moving after getting her degree. I wondered where.

We talked about our emails, and she apologized for not responding more quickly.

"Everything takes me such a long time to do," she complained.

"Since when?" I asked.

"I was always slow," she added.

"I guess I was always fast then," I responded.

"So, what are you doing for Christmas?" I asked.

"I'm spending Christmas with Jen and her friend," she said. "We're going to watch old movies and eat hors d'oeuvres. Which is fine with me. I hate doing all the food stuff." I wasn't thrilled to hear Jen's name.

"Well, maybe I'll call you over the holidays," I said, knowing full well, I wouldn't. There was no point. At the end of the conversation, I felt like she didn't want to hang up and wanted to say something to me but didn't.

I emailed her the next day that I wouldn't be calling any more. I told her that our last conversation felt superficial and I didn't think it was necessary to put either one of us through that again. I told her that the problem was my expectations but that I released them on my morning beach walk earlier in the day. "Let's just email and be friends. I'm releasing myself and you." I apologized for dragging her "into my own personal psychotherapy. I'm done with expectations. Aren't you glad and relieved? I am. Have a great holiday." I signed it, "a much lighter me."

She emailed back that she was sorry I wasn't satisfied with our phone conversation.

"It would be nice for both of us to be able to have a good time speaking on the phone now and again, but if that isn't working, then it I guess it doesn't work."

I was in a funk for the next few days. There was no one around to talk to so I wrote a poem. The best I had created so far. After the fourth revision, I sent a copy to the Lioness to critique. I had also been working on Part Three of the book about the Lioness. I wrote in my journal, "How do I get rid of her when I'm living her again?"

My dream that night: *I was leaning on a fireplace with my elbows. There was no fire. My head kept going down. The Lioness was in the back of the room. I knew she would come when she saw me crouching like this. She rushed down and touched my arm. At first, I had a grin on my face, and I said, "I'm all right." She pulled away, and I said, "I'm not all right."*

Writing was the only thing that made sense during that winter.

I told my sister that I had released the Lioness that snowy morning walking the beach.

"I feel different. I feel lighter," I said.

"The albatross is gone," she said. "You have been carrying a heavy weight all these years."

She was right. I had carried a torch for a woman who no longer existed. It took a while to accept that, but finally I did and the pain her interaction had caused stopped. I was freed to the here and now, and free to enjoy every moment of the day.

Positive things started happening. My brother from Staten Island came in and took me out for lunch. I got a card from the mother of a dear friend and another one from my drawing teacher thanking me for being an inspiration in class. Then an email from a Canadian friend I hadn't seen in a while and another from the Lioness, which I didn't rush to open. I went on a business trip to London. It was the first time I got to spend time by myself in this magnificent city. I visited the Tate Museum and leisurely strolled up and down the long blocks of London's heart. I savored a glass of wine at Covent Gardens while listening to classical music.

The depressive tone of the Lioness's next email actually made me feel sorry for her. Now that her class was over, she didn't think she would have the incentive to continue writing. I found that odd. Why did she need a class to write?

I wrote the last line in my 32$^{nd}$ journal, the one with the picture of the tiger lily on the cover. It read, "This is the end of the Lioness journal." It wasn't an easy break.

As time went on, I realized giving up the Lioness was giving up more than just someone I loved. We are defined by those that love us. It was giving up a person I felt accepted all of me. That was the difficulty. Would I be able to find such another?

I spent more time with my family and developed a strong bond with my cousin's youngest daughter. It amazed me that she really liked me. Every time I went to visit, she would run and jump in my arms. I started to understand what it meant to be a mother. New feelings opened up to me. The year of counseling had been good.

I still had bad days, but I was able to get through them by myself. Some days I felt so secure and strong, and some weak with tears, but a least I was in touch with my emotions. I still missed the Lioness. I thought about our lovemaking. But I yearned for closeness with another.

When I returned from the Arizona trip, there was a civil email from the Lioness. It made me want to talk to her, so I phoned. She didn't answer but called me right back.

"I was walking the dog," she said. We talked about our respective trips, a normal conversation. I'm not sure why, but at one point she asked me, "Are you lonely?"

"Yes, a bit," I admitted. Other than that, nothing heavy was said. When we hung up, I was pleased that I hadn't said anything stupid.

The weekend before Valentine's day, I saw the movie entitled *The End of the Affair* and became nostalgic for the Lioness. I decided to invite her to join me on my next trip to London, scheduled for March, the month of her fortieth birthday. Knowing she was a loner I didn't want her to spend such a special day alone. I emailed her the next day, "So what are you doing on your fortieth birthday? I'm leaving for London around the 17th. I have meetings on Monday, then I'm leaving for Zurich on Tuesday for a three-day conference on genetics. I return to London before coming home. This is way out, but I thought maybe you might like to join me. The hotel is paid by the company, and I have some extra frequent flyer miles that you could use for your flight. While I'm in Zurich, you could visit your friends in London. On my return, we could celebrate your birthday. Think about it."

After I send it, I knew it was a mistake. As much as I told myself I was over her, I kept finding her back in my thoughts. The next day in a confession to my sister, I said, "I did something really stupid or really romantic."

"I don't expect she'll say yes," she answered.

"Neither do I," I responded.

On Valentine's Day my brother surprised me with a gift. A beautiful gold bracelet. I was thrilled. He was fifteen years younger than I and we hadn't known each other growing up. Yet this year we had discovered each other, had become confidants.

The Lioness emailed the day after Valentine's. Her response was as expected.

"What an imaginative, extravagant idea! Unfortunately, the job I'd like to have, which will interest me and pay me enough so that I don't have to do it full time, can write, AND go to London every now and again, I do not have yet. I'm reluctant at not paying my own way. Also, I do have tentative plans for my 40th –to drive myself to Yosemite and hike and camp for a few days in the snow. Thanks for thinking of me."

In a way I was relieved. Her decline was kindly given. And I had enough things to worry about on this trip. Now I could concentrate on work presentations and not worry about whether the Lioness was happy. The only part that really hurt was that she preferred to spend her 40th alone and not with me. Even though I was strong, she still had the power to affect me.

For her birthday I only sent a card with a picture I had taken of a snowy beach scene. Inside I added the words of H.D., "I go where I am love and where I am loved, into the snow."

I woke up a few days later thinking about the quote. I had taken it from the introduction of Adrienne Rich's poetry book, *The Dream of a Common Language*. It contained one of my favorite poems about a Russian woman's climbing team who all died in a snowstorm during a hike. My mind wandered making unusual connections . . . snow . . . death . . . Lioness . . . refused to go to London . . . going alone . . . into the snow . . . looking for Carol . . . dead. . . .missing her . . . she's going to join Carol . . . she's going to commit suicide . . . like the women who hiked to their deaths . . . I gave her the book . . . I was scared to death I was picking up on the Lioness's thoughts. She's going to find Carol. I wasn't sure why I was thinking these negative thoughts, but it scared me so much I called my therapist and made an appointment.

"Why do I think these thoughts?" I asked her.

"Everything comes out in our emotions," she said. "It's your fear."

"Fear of what?" I asked.

"What are you afraid of?" she asked.

"I'm afraid she will commit suicide."

"How did she get the idea?" she asked.

"From the book I gave her."

"So, it's your guilt. Rejection sets you off."

"You're right. Rejection does set me off. But how can I be guilty of something that didn't happen." Her explanation didn't totally satisfy me.

"It doesn't have to happen," she answered.

"She tires me out. I don't think I will ever love like this again."

"No. You probably won't, but you'll love differently," she added.

"I'm not pursing her anymore. Unless she does."

"Why say, 'Unless she does'? You know she won't."

"Hope runs eternal."

"You have to change. Don't you think the Universe will provide for you?" Then she went on telling me how she had met her soul mate. She never thought she would, but she did, and he wasn't anything that she imagined he would be.

I knew she was right.

I asked if I could read her my favorite page from the novel I was writing.

"Yes, of course. I'd love to hear it." After I did so, I realized why the Lioness had come back into my life.

"I couldn't have written this part if I hadn't seen her again. She is a muse for me. Even if I'm not a muse for her."

I left her office and decided to trust the universe. Everything happened for a reason.

To test this new sense of independence, I called the Lioness the week before her birthday. Of course, it was after a dinner party and a lot of drinks! She answered in her usual sleepy tone, "I just went to bed. I have a headache."

"It's always something, Lioness," I said.

"Give me a break. I had therapy today and I cried during it. It gave me this wicked headache. How drunk are you anyway?"

"Well, I called you. That should give you a clue," I answered.

"I can't think. I didn't eat and my sugar is low," she added.

"Why didn't you eat?"

"I was upset from therapy."

"You need a mother."

"Right. That's just what I need."

"So how many women have you fucked since me?"

"None!" she laughed.

"Really? I'm impressed," I said. Then like a motor mouth I went on and on about my job, my apprehensions about the London trip, my dealings with J.

"Hey. I don't want to be your punching bag."

"Punching bag? Is that how I make you feel?"

"It was a joke. And a projection. When I'm anxious about something, I take it out on the person I'm with. It's my agenda, not yours. You always seem to be in control and way ahead of your co-workers."

"So why didn't you just say, 'Fuck of'? You get so serious these days. I like the spontaneous Lioness who bashed through life, who laughed, who made love, who made me light. Why are we so heavy now? Why don't you come visit after my London trip? Let's get to know each other. Let me mother you. We could hang out on the beach . . . "

"I don't want to be mothered by you. It's not part of the friendship I want to continue having with you," she responded with a bite. I knew I had hit a nerve.

"Sorry. I just meant I would cook and drive you around."

After we hung up, I sat on the chair and sobbed uncontrollably. I fell asleep on the couch. In the morning I looked down on the floor and saw a pearl lying there. I thought it must be from my earring, but it was from my necklace. The clasp had broken. I was lucky only one pearl had fallen off. And it broke in the house. A friend called. "Did I leave my glasses in your car?" I went out to the car to check. The back-car door was open, and the glasses were on the windshield. The left-over food was still sitting on the floor. It must have been one hell of a party!

The London trip went well. I was proud of myself for doing so many things alone. When I got back there was an email from the Lioness about her birthday excursion . . . "Found myself wanting to fuck the geology instructor's brains out. I know it's not about her, at all, really. Part of an addictive cycle. I'm beginning to see hints of how it might be wrapped up with mother-stuff. Some abandonment thing. 'If I could just fuck you and make you feel good, then you wouldn't leave me, and you'd give me the nurturing I need.' As a matter of fact, If you were here, I'd want to fuck your brains out too. But that's not really where I want to be coming from. Don't know why these feelings got so heavily triggered by this nice, unsuspecting, presumably straight girl. Or why it's so sexual! I'd rather be enthusiastic just about rocks!"

The jealousy was intense. The pain was excruciating. But I simply wrote back. "I certainly can identify with the addiction. I always want to fuck your brains out and mine!!!" I totally ignored that fact that she was attracted to another woman.

*　*　*

My sister asked me what I wanted for my fiftieth birthday in June. I had to stop and think. I didn't want any physical object. I didn't want to go anywhere. The only real thing I wanted was to finish the book. I had two months. Then I wanted to take a trip back to Maine and visit Mandala and the Co-op.

I went to dinner with my aunt and uncle and after a martini and glass of wine, I called the Lioness and left the following message, "So you didn't get to fuck the geologist? I didn't get to fuck the woman with blue hair in Switzerland, either. Call collect if you want." She called back later that night.

"So, what's going on?" she asked.

"I suffered all day after that email," I said.

"I didn't realize it would hurt you. You tell me all about other women you are attracted to."

"Yes. But it doesn't bother you. You don't have feelings for me. I have feelings for you. I'm jealous. It pains me to know you're attracted to other women."

"I didn't tell you to hurt you."

"You're not even aware of the effect you have on me. You're selfish. You give so little."

"Why do you say I'm selfish?"

"You never think about my concerns. How did you feel when I responded to your poetry?"

"I loved it. I love knowing some people get into my work," she replied.

"Then how do you think I felt when you didn't respond to my poem?" Quiet on the other side of the phone. "And the trip to London. Did you ever think it might be nice for me to have company? You only thought about how it would put you out."

"I didn't think about it that way."

"No, you never do. Even now, I'm all emotionally involved in this conversation and you're not. I'm not a mother figure to you. That's why you don't find me attractive."

"I find you attractive," she answered.

"How would I know that. The only emotion you show is when you sigh during our love making."

"I want to sleep with you again," she said softly.

"How can we do that unless one of us travels, and you keep saying 'no' to my invitations to come here. I can't invite myself to your place again."

"If and when I'm up to it, I'll let you know. I thought about asking you to visit. But I didn't want to get into a guilt thing. I just don't want a relationship now."

"I know that," I said. "I don't know what I want either. I just came out of an eighteen-year relationship. I'm not ready for a big commitment. All I can say is that you're the only person who has this effect on me. It's irrational. Seventeen years! How can I still be affected by you? And I cause no effect in you. Yet some woman you don't even know does."

"I don't know why the geologist caused such sexual feelings," she replied. "I'm not usually aware of these sensations."

"I'm always aware of such things. Our approaches to the world are very different. You obviously don't have feelings for me, or you would be jealous when I talk about other women."

"I get mixed up on the boundary. I don't want to give signals that I'm not sure I can deliver on. I don't want to get trapped in the abandonment issue. I slip into that pattern of doing what the other person wants just to get her attention. A mother issue. Maybe losing all the attention when my sister was born and trying desperately to get it back."

"Your mother had four children. It must have been hard for her to split her attention."

"It was hard for her," she agreed.

"But I can't imagine her abandoning you."

"No, you're right. Maybe it's the Oedipus thing. I remember writing to my therapist, 'Eros wants to make love to his mother. Why do you think I've been in counseling for so long?"

"Doesn't seem to be working. Counseling creates a false environment. In counseling you don't have to deal with the other person's reaction. The counselor remains blank. There's no consequence. You only grow in a relationship. In the give and take. And you won't let yourself indulge. I just don't understand why you slept with me. There are very few people in my past that I would sleep with. Again, it's something for you to think about. You once wrote, 'I didn't think a summer relationship would affect the rest of my life.' Sorry, Honey. It appears in some capacity, and I'm not sure why, myself, that we are connected for life."

When we hung up, I felt relieved. I had finally gotten to say things that I had been holding inside. And I didn't care. I emailed her that I enjoyed our conversation. I was glad we could be honest with one another. She emailed back that she enjoyed the conversation as well: "I only wish I could have hugged you at the end, but I wouldn't have wanted to stop there. And I'm not sure that works for you. To be fucking a woman (or, at present, not fucking a woman) who keeps not wanting to be your significant other is not the relationship you want or deserve. It may be too hard."

I got my period the next day, and I was five days early. I wondered how much of the conversation was due to hormones! I was glad that the Lioness hadn't taken offense at my words. I knew I needed someone who could match my emotional intensity. It would never be the Lioness. The next woman would be my forever. I was looking forward to meeting her.

I didn't email the Lioness for a whole month. I wanted to see if she responded on her own. She didn't. It put things into perspective for me. Besides, I was busy with reclaiming my house and cleaning it up for renting. I felt good about being a land baronessa and getting the cats back into my life.

When I finally emailed her, the Lioness emailed back that she had been thinking of sending me an email the same weekend, and then there was mine. She didn't say much except that she was exhausted and hadn't accomplished much. She was depressed. I emailed her back suggesting that she do something that would make her feel better, like hiking.

I, on the other hand, was getting so much done. I took two weeks off in May to write and was planning on another two in early June. I spent time with friends and went on two business meetings. My days were full. The writing satisfied me and filled me with a new confidence. I started envisioning the book published. The cover would be purple with red letters. I dyed my hair a rhubarb color, attended woman dances, and just had a good time chatting with new people. I didn't anticipate. I thought less and less about the Lioness. After seeing *Cinema Paridiso* I realized why. It was in the story of a guard who had to sit 100 days outside the princess's castle before she would agree to marry him. He would stand there through all kinds of bad weather and never leave his spot. He continued this sacrifice, but on the 99$^{th}$ day, he left and never looked back again. The moral for me was that if this man was able to endure all the pain and hardship, he really didn't need her to begin with. He found his inner strength, and it didn't require her love.

It was the eve of my 50$^{th}$ birthday party. I knew the Lioness would make some kind of contact, but I just wasn't sure how. I had been writing all day and only had one journal to go before tying in the Empress part to the Lioness part. It was about 10:00 pm when the phone rang.

"I wanted to wish you an early birthday. You know me I'm not good at getting cards out on time," said the voice. I recognized it immediately. "I also want to thank you for suggesting the hike. I did Wheeler's Point on Memorial Day. I wouldn't have thought of it myself."

"Great. Did it make you feel better? You still sound depressed," I replied.

"For a while, and then I got depressed over something else. I'm always depressed. That's why I'm still in counseling."

"Are you writing?" I asked.

"No." Followed by a lull. I didn't respond, after all it was her call. I was just going to respond to her questions.

"So, when are you going to Maine?" she finally asked referring to my last email mentioning my intention to return for a visit.

"Next week. Don't you think it's an appropriate trip? I'll have the first draft done by Sunday."

"Good. That's great, first draft for your 50$^{th}$."

"I planned it that way. A birthday gift to myself. I'm still working on the ending. That's still fuzzy."

"Well I think that's great," she answered.

"So how is the dog?" I asked.

"I'm taking him to the chiropractor."

"Why?"

"He's having a hard time walking. His side is weak, and he has torn ligaments in his knee. He has been low key and depressed for the last three years."

"He's like you." I laughed.

"Yeah. Except I was depressed years before I met you."

"I didn't know that. You didn't seem depressed in Maine."

"I hid it well. So how is your family? Your brother? Your mother?"

"They are all good. My brother still calls at 6:00 am. His wife moved out. My mom went to the doctors. She's getting short of breath. It maybe from the BP medication. We're taking her off it for a month. Coronary artery disease can be erratic in women. What about your family?"

"My sister and father are going to Croatia on a mission."

"Doesn't she have children? Will you be watching them?"

"My mother will be watching them. I'm too tired."

"Tired? What do you do all day? You're too young to be tired."

"It's been hot here, and I don't do well in the heat," she said.

"Why are you living in that part of the country, if you don't do well with heat? You're into self-torture, aren't you?"

"It's a dry heat. Better than New England," she defended her choice. Then I heard her scream into the room, "Get out of there! Get away! Stop eating that!" She dropped the phone, and I heard her running.

"Sorry," she said when she picked it back up.

"Cats in the garbage can?" I asked.

"Yeah." She laughed. "Someone puked, and it's in the garbage, and one of the cats was trying to get it."

"Cats are so independent. I'm glad to have mine back. Diva is old and scroungy, but I love her. And Loretta Lynne ... "

"Loretta Lynne Coal Bin?" she asked.

"You remember? I'm impressed."

"I remember." Lull.

"So, are you still temping?" I asked.

"Temping in Santa Fe," she responded as her voice dropped. "House keeping you busy?"

"Yeah. Physical labor is good after writing all day. It brings me back from space. That and sex. But I'm not having any sex. Next best thing."

"Sex is such a head trip."

"A good head trip. Are you on MCI?" I asked.

"No. AT & T."

"Expensive," I said thinking she was on for a long time.

"Yeah, I should go. So have a great day. What are you going to do on your birthday?"

"Do my beach walk, write, then a picnic party at my sister's.

"Well, have a great day." We said our good-byes. I didn't offer to call her back as in the past.

I felt drained when I hung up the phone. I cried. I cried from the depths. She would never say anything about us, and I couldn't. I was surprised to hear about her constant depression. She never showed it. Maybe all these years I subconsciously picked up on her depression and didn't know it. Maybe that's why I always felt like crying after interacting with her.

\* \* \*

I had been wanting small arm weights. On my birthday beach walk, I saw a pair of purple ones sitting under a bench. I looked in all directions. No one was in sight. I figured they were a gift from the gods. I took them home.

I decided on Sunday not to turn on the computer to check whether the Lioness had emailed. I didn't want to run the risk of encountering anything to ruin my good mood. It was a gorgeous day! The sun was shining bright, and I was happy as a pig in shit. All my friends were coming to the birthday picnic. As I headed out the hallway, something caught my eye. A Federal Express package leaned on the wall near the door. Funny, I thought, that wasn't there yesterday when I came home. And it was Sunday. How could that have been delivered? I leaned down to look closer. It was from New Mexico and had my name on it. I started to sink. I opened up the package. It was a book from the Lioness on how to read poetry. There was a postcard wishing me a very, very Happy Birthday. It read, "My hope for the book is that it will inspire your own writing. Much love, Lioness."

At first, I was so happy to receive her gift. Then I got depressed thinking she wouldn't be at the party. More than anyone else, I wanted her there.

"Is my life unique or what?" I asked my sister as I walked in the door. "What is it with the Lioness and me? Why do these things always happen?"

I left to get the ice and cried the whole time in the car. I was so down till everyone started coming, then I was so busy I forgot about her.

On Monday night, I called her to thank her for the thoughtful gift. I had finished part 1, 2, and 3 and was on a high. We talked for about two hours mainly about Maine and the fun times we had had. It was a comfortable conversation.

"I want to hear all about your Maine trip when you get back," she said.

"You'll be the first to hear. Who else would understand?" I responded.

"I couldn't take the Empress. All the dishonesty. She was beautiful though."

"You thought so, too?" I asked surprised.

"Yes, of course. That woman exuded sensuality. I just wished she would do something about it."

"Hmmm. I didn't think you found her attractive. I still remember the first time I saw her eyes. And then the time she was sitting on the chair in the full moon. God, it still makes me melt."

"Will you go see the High Priestess?" she asked.

"I don't know if she's still there."

"Maybe she'll be the right one for you."

"Oh, yeah. I'll go back and visit all my past loves till one clicks." We both laughed.

"Everyone there was so, so into being poor but not really poor," she criticized.

"I think they were trying to make a statement," I explained.

"I am a snob," she commented.

"At least you know it. So, when are you going to get a real job?" I asked. "All those degrees."

"I don't deserve a job," she responded.

"What are you talking about? No one has to deserve a job. We just choose what we want to do and do it. I do my job, but I take time to smell the roses now. You know peonies smell wonderful when you get up close."

"My mother likes peonies too," she replied.

"Speaking of loves and smelling the roses. Did you see *Cinema Paridisio*?"

"No. Why?" she asked. "It's about having a love forever." I explained about the guard and the princess . . . "And at the end, the commentator says to Alfredo, 'Don't ask me why he left.'"

"I know why," she responded. I didn't ask her to explain. I was afraid of her answer.

I didn't tell her how I really felt the morning I received her gift.

\* \* \*

The day of my Maine trip brought torrential rain. Almost hurricane like. The men installing the rugs in the house didn't finish till around 3:00, but I was determined to get on the road. Before I departed, I called my friend, Callas.

"I can't believe you are leaving in this rain," she exclaimed.

"I need to go," I said.

"Maybe Maine has the key," she responded.

I took my time driving there. The roads were flooding, and I was afraid of hydroplaning. I managed to get as far as Ogunquit by about 8:00 pm. By then it was dark, and I was tired. Luckily, I found a motel by the roadside charging only $48 for a room. It was still early in the season, so rates were cheap. The room was decent and the shower, modern. That was good enough for me.

I unpacked what I needed and then got into bed. I thought to myself, 'I hope I can get through this. I was strong during the drive, but now I'm feeling so weak.' I started crying for nothing, for everything.

Callas warned me that this would be an emotional trip. I didn't know why I felt I had to go to Maine this week, but I was certain that it was the right thing to do. Maybe I'd see why or maybe this would turn out to be another wild goose chase, a fantasy. Tomorrow was supposed to be sunny, but tonight it was raining, and my tears were falling. As a diversion, I reread the ending of *Narcissus and Goldmund*, the part where Goldmund returns to the monastery, completes his artwork, and then leaves to follow his soul's calling.

I awakened early and, while I drank my coffee, asked directions from the owner of the motel. It was still raining, but the radio announcer insisted it was going to stop. I didn't think so. I planned on breakfast around 9:00 am and sure enough at that time, I pulled into the parking lot of Moody's Diner, a classic local eatery, in Waldoboro. Good food. Inexpensive. Old town pictures hung on the walls. The homemade blueberry muffin was as good as expected.

On Route 1 just past the commercial area and before the bridge to Bucksport, I remembered a clearing over a hill opening to the view of a large green mountain covered with trees and surrounded by open blue sky. Every time I had passed that spot, I would get a rush of relief knowing I was almost home. I felt the same intensity of emotion during this trip even thought it had been almost twenty years since my last visit.

As I crossed the bridge, I wasn't sure which way to go. Right or left? It didn't look the same. My impression was that I had to go through the town to get to Orland. But the center of town was to the left, and I remembered going right to get to the Co-op. I went right, but then stopped at a Burger King and asked some woman, "Which way is the town of Orland?"

She pointed in the direction I was already headed. Well, my instincts were still strong even though everything looked different. New stores. Big buildings. Construction. It wasn't the quaint town I used to come to. I feared that maybe even the Co-op was gone. Then what would I do?

I drove up the road a bit and finally saw the sign on the right-T is is Co-Op, (the "h" was broken off). The sign was partly hidden by overgrown grass and brush. I turned into the drive- way and parked. There were more buildings than I remembered. The office had been turned into a living shelter, and across the street was a sawmill with many cars parked in the lot. Well, they finally had gotten that accomplished, I thought. There was also a restaurant-combo- food co-op. I went into the Co-op store where the crafts were sold. There were no customers. But it was still early in the season. A man with one arm was minding the shop. As I walked around looking at the crafts, I realized that they weren't of the same caliber when I was living there.

"So that white building is not the office anymore?" I asked him.

"No. Hasn't been for years. The office is over behind the Learning Center."

I asked if the Empress was still working there.

"Oh yes," he replied. "Do you know her?"

"Yes, I used to live here." Then an elderly gentleman came in. I recognized him right away with his jean-colored overalls and lifesaver sucking in his mouth. He used to work on the wood crew and was one of the guys the Empress could never control. Now he was in his seventies but looking strong as ever. I greeted him and said my name.

"People come back all the time. I worked with so many people over the years. Can't remember them all. I got a letter from some young woman just last week. Now what was her name?" he said as he pulled out his wallet to show me the letter. He sat down and struggled to find the note. "I buried my wife just two weeks ago."

"I'm sorry to hear that," I responded.

"Yeah, she was sick for a while. Here's the note. Her name was . . . "

"I didn't know her. Must have been after my time. I was here about twenty years ago."

"Yeah, I remember you. You lived out at the farm with the Empress and them, didn't you?" he smiled as if he knew what kind of an experience that was.

I left and walked over to the office. Four people were sitting behind the counter. One very heavy woman with a pretty face, two gray haired and bearded elderly gentlemen, and a middle-aged woman, who dragged her leg when she got up to greet me. All seemed poor and not in healthy shape.

"My name is Dorothy. I used to work here years ago. I'm looking for the Empress. Is she in her office?" I asked.

The middle-aged woman responded, "We're waiting for her too. She's scheduled to come in around 12:30. She works out at the farm in the morning."

Then I asked if Bear was around.

"She's around. I don't know where. Do you know where Bear is?" she asked the heavy woman.

"She's on the grounds. Maybe she's doing a dump run," answered the heavy woman. "What's your last name?" she asked looking at me. I told her.

"I know you. I'm Joseph's wife." Then I looked into her face and realized who she was. She and her husband had been involved in the building project. I used to eat at their house.

"You're Mary. I remember. You had a daughter, Angelica. She was about four or five back then."

"Yes. She's all grown up now. Has a child herself. Joseph died last month."

"Sorry to hear that," I responded.

"He had so much wrong with him, diabetes and then his heart. Remember Jack and Jill?" she asked.

"Yes, of course. We were good friends."

"She came back a few years back. They broke up. She's doing some volunteer work and moved back from California."

"Did the Hierophant die?" I asked.

"Yeah, she died about seven years ago. Ethel is living out with the Empress now. They raise Norwegian workhorses and goats. The Empress keeps bringing out animals, and Ethel takes care of them."

"Can you drive out there now?" I asked, remembering the road was primitive when I lived out there.

"I wouldn't," she advised. "Took my car out there for community supper last week and bottomed out."

"Thanks for warning. Is it ok if I wait for the Empress?"

"Sure," she answered.

For about twenty minutes, I sat at in one of the chairs with my feet on the desk and then decided to roam around. As I walked out the door, I saw a familiar face. It was Bear. She had aged. Her hair was all gray, and her clothes appeared that she hadn't taken them off in a week or two.

"Bear, it's me Dorothy," I said.

She squinted her eyes, "Dorothy, is that you?" We hugged.

"Are you up for a few days or just passing through?"

"I'll be here for a few days. Would you like to have supper with me?"

"Gee, that would be great, but it's Wednesday, and I take care of this elderly woman with Alzheimer's disease. She's Ethel's mother. I have to put her to bed and stay with her till she falls asleep."

"How about breakfast?" I suggested.

"Breakfast? Huh. Yeah. OK. Breakfast. Yeah."

"Do you want to meet at Duffy's?"

"Duffy's? I get up early. Have to work before leaving the farm. Let's meet at the Co-op."

"Okay, what time?"

"8:30," she said and then the elderly woman started asking her, "Are we going yet? Aren't we going? I gotta get going if we're going to get that haying done."

"Yeah, ok, we gotta go," Bear looked at me like things were not in her control. "Gotta keep her moving. You know what I mean." I nodded in understanding.

"See you tomorrow."

"Yeah, you should go out to the farm," she said. "It's different. The Empress should be out there."

"It's ok? I asked.

"Yeah, sure, go out there. She'll be glad to see you."

"What kind of car does she drive, in case she's on her way in?"

"That's hard to say. Could be the black truck or the jeep or the car," she giggled with a quizzical look on her face.

"It's ok. I'll figure it out."

"Sorry I have to go. Tomorrow I'll be free."

"It's ok, Bear. I understand."

I got into my car and started driving out to the farm. About ¼ mile down the road, a black truck passed by me with a dark woman in a headscarf. I knew it had to be the Empress. I turned around and went back to the co-op.

I waited in front of the office and shortly the Empress came walking down the covered porch to the office. She had aged and gained a lot of weight. She was carrying an arm full of things making her look even bigger than she was. She moved slowly as if she weren't well. I greeted her just before she went to open the door, and I couldn't believe the inappropriate comment that came out of my mouth.

"I see you've expanded around here. Now there is a sawmill and lunch shop. All these new buildings." She looked at me, and I knew she didn't recognize me at first. Then she did.

"It's been a long time. How long has it been?" she asked.

"About twenty years," I said and hugged her.

"How are you doing?" she asked.

"Good and you?"

"Okay. I've been better." Then her eyes gave me that deep spiritual look and she stared into my eyes as if she were trying to see if I was truly all right. I maintained a steady, confident look. She wasn't going to get into me this time. Finally, she stopped and said, "Are you staying for lunch?"

"Yes. I'll be here."

"Good. I'll be out in a while. I have some things to do. I'll see you for lunch."

And with that comment she walked into the office without inviting me to come in. That's strange, I thought. Wouldn't the normal reaction have been to invite someone you hadn't seen for years into your office to catch up? If this had happened to me a few years back, I would have been destroyed by her reaction. But I wasn't. Actually, I was amazed at how secure I felt. I said to myself at that point, 'You are not a part of these people's lives any more so just do your own thing. You're on your own in this nostalgic trip.'

I went to my car, got my camera, and started taking pictures of the buildings. I went to the red barn building where I used to do the lay out of the paper. It had two levels with a huge window that encompassed one whole side of the structure. The window was divided into small square panes, and in each pane, there was an old glass bottle or some antique. It was now called the Museum. Some great things were lying around, vintage costumes, Royal typewriters, old frames, antique furniture. I wanted to take something as a memory, but I couldn't bring myself to do so. I went upstairs. It was still bright and a great working space. I had spent many hours up there by myself in creative joy. It was a positive memory, and I felt good being there again. Then

I walked through the other buildings, the Pottery shed where the Lioness's cup was made and the Woodshed where I made wooden bread boards in the shape of her body.

In the Weaving Shop were two women. One was older and working at the wheel, and the other was young, maybe early twenties and sitting on the floor. They looked at me, and I felt like I was intruding.

"I'm just looking around," I explained. "I used to work and live here many years ago."

"I know who you are. You're Dorothy," said the younger woman. "I'm Angelica, Joseph and Mary's daughter.

"Wow! You remember me. You were just a small child when I was here. I can't believe you remember."

"I remember," she said. She had been a light- haired, delicate little girl. Now she was very heavy, dark-haired woman. I thought about the time I had accused the Lioness of having a crush on her because she spent so much time with the child. I was so jealous at the time that I said some stupid things.

"I remember everyone," she said filling me in on all the gossip. "Let's see who was here when you were. The Hermit left his order and was involved with AB for a while after she left Bad. Then he dated the High Priestess, too."

"AB! That wouldn't be a match!"

"No. She wasn't really interested in him. She's living with the Pig man now. The Hermit married someone else and has a child. Cowardly Lion came back a few years ago with his partner. The Hierophant died."

"What about that dog, Chico?" I asked. "I never liked him."

"Nobody did!" She laughed. "That dog was a pain in the you know what! He was mean. Used to bite. My father took him when he was dying and was going to put him to sleep. He was so sick. Couldn't walk, but that damn dog wouldn't die. We used a whole bottle of animal grunt on him, and he still wouldn't die. My father kept saying, 'Die you bastard. Die!'" We both laughed. "Secretary retired. She's still going strong in her eighties. You know the secretary."

"Yeah! Everyone was afraid of her. She was sarcastic. She ruled the roost."

"She was downright mean," she said going straight for the jugular.

"You're right. I was trying to be nice."

"The Empress is watching one of her nephews' kids," she continued. "Been around twelve years now. He was an alcohol syndrome baby. Skids got married and has two kids, but he's divorced."

"Your family lived at the Hospitality House?" I asked.

"Yeah."

"Is it still going?"

"Yeah, but now we call it the Hostility House."

"Oh!" I learned later that it was being run by the nun that the Hierophant lived with after she left the Empress so that was probably the reason for the name. I talked to her later in the week, and she told me that she kept all the finances separate from the Co-op. "They have a way of putting everything in the red. I'm keeping the two houses out of their mitts." She was also in charge of a second house in Ellsworth as well.

"What about you? What are you doing?" I asked Angelica.

"I have a little boy. He's in day care," she said as she gave me a picture to look at. "I went to college and lived away for a while. Then my Dad died, and my mom reminded me, 'You said you'd never leave me.' So, I moved back and live in the house next to hers. I work in the Weaving Shop."

How sad I thought. This girl has a college education and here she is working in this dead-end place.

After hearing all the gossip, I was ready to venture on.

"Well, I think I'm going to go visit the farm. Can I drive in?"

"My mom says 'no,' but you can," she replied.

I drove out to Duffy's for lunch but first parked across the street at the motel on the lake where I had lived one summer with the Lioness. The motel hadn't changed, a few small rooms next to the office and cottages down by the water. I walked down to the cottages on the path covered with reddish brown pine needles. Tall trees surrounded each cabin. I found the one we had lived in. Number 12. It was one big room with a small porch facing the lake. I tried to look in the window, but it was too dark to make out the details. I sat for a while on the porch and thought about all the lovemaking and friends visiting. It was a happy time. No cares.

After I had taken enough pictures, I drove across the street to the restaurant and ordered lunch. Homemade soup and BLT. The food was still good and cheap. I talked with a couple sitting at the next table. They owned an antique shop down Route 1. I was determined to enjoy my day. It didn't matter to me that the Empress had ignored me. I was making the best of this experience.

The turn off for the farm was a short distance from the restaurant. I parked down at the bottom of the hill and started my walk in. Hidden in between the trees was a green street sign which read, "Mandala WY" as if this were a real road. It was still dirt. Packed-down dirt, but dirt. On the right was an abandoned car covered with blue tarp, and on the left, the house that had always been there with a snow mobile parked on the side. The first hill was always the worst. I made mental notes of the rough spots in the road just in case I decided to drive in at some point. I would have to stay to the left on the way up to avoid some big rocks and holes. After the first hill, it wasn't so bad. Of course, I was in better shape that I had been back then. I had been running every morning about three miles so this was a piece of cake. In fact, I enjoyed the walk in. It seemed shorter than ever before.

Finally, I started seeing the tops of the barns. A huge beige horse with a thick mane and tail stared at me from a gated pen on the right. Another was loose on the road. His big backside pointed to me as he bent down to eat the green growth under the wooden fence edge. I hoped I didn't startle him coming up from behind. But he just kept eating and didn't care that I walked past. There were some new barns along the left side of the road leading into the commune and the rustic structure where Cowardly Lion and I had lived was now a large, red, clapboard-sided house. From my conversation with Angelica, I knew that this was the Empress's home now. I approached slowly since I was afraid there would be dogs.

Encircling the house was a broken-down fence enclosing a rather extensive amount of the land. Goats were grazing. As I got close to the house, two white, husky dogs came running and barking. They looked like mini Argus's. I was surprised but thankful to see them penned in. When I had lived in the community, we never penned in the dogs. A woman came out from the house.

"Are you Ethel?" I asked. "I'm Dorothy. I used to live out here about twenty years ago. I'm just looking around. I see you have more houses on the road in."

"Those are shelters we built," she replied.

"I saw Bear at the Co-op, and she said it would be ok if I roamed around. Is this the road to the house that the Empress used to live in?" I asked, pointing to a wooded path heading down toward the lake.

"Yes," she responded.

"And there's the eight-sided house. If I remember correctly, I can also get to the lake side house down here," pointing to another path in front of Bear's house. Before she could respond, Bear came out of her house.

"Hey, you made it in. Did you drive?" Bear asked.

"No, I walked. It was fun to do that again." Then Bear approached

Ethel and said, "Do you think we can get this motorcycle out of here. They're bringing a mulch dump and it's in the way of where they need to dump it."

"I don't know," she responded. "Do they have to put it there?"

"Well, yah. But I don't know how they'll do it with that big monster there," answered Bear as she shook her head. She turned to me, "Problems, always problems." I laughed. Nothing had changed.

"Can I see your house?" I asked Bear. "You still have that great view?" I said, looking down at the lake through two massive clumps of trees.

"Sure. Come on in." As we walked to the door, a heavy, aged, beige Labrador greeted us wagging his tail. He looked like an older version of Shannon.

"You still have a Labrador," I said. "I remember Shannon."

"Yeah. Poor old Shannon. He died. I had a few other dogs in between."

We walked inside, and she showed me the rooms.

"Wow, a modern bathroom, electricity, running water, and phone," I exclaimed.

"Yeah. I still have the outhouse but it's nice to have the bathroom. Sometimes I even answer the phone. This is where Hazel lives," she said, showing me a second bedroom. "I don't know if you met her at the Co-op. Nice woman. A little retarded. But nice woman. Someone left her on my doorstep with a note saying, 'I need a place for a few days.' That was ten years ago. She's been with me ever since."

"That's nice of you Bear," I said.

"Yeah, well, she's good company."

"I used to love this ceiling. Can I take a picture? It's so spiritual," I said looking up at the eight planks meeting in the center forming the octagon. There were boards tied in between the planks giving it a spider web effect.

"Sure, knock yourself out."

"I remember sleeping in front of this window with the view. All the stars. We had some great conversations here. How is Lady? Is she still with Tinman?" I asked.

"No, they broke up. She's still in Maine, though. She's ok."

"Do you know where the High Priestess is?" I asked.

"Gee, I haven't seen her in years. Secretary is living on the road opposite the Co-op. She'd know where the High Priestess is if anybody did. Secretary kept up with everyone. Go visit her. She'd love to see you. She'll be out in her garden. Still sharp as a knife. Got all her wits about her."

"How about the Doctor and the Painter. Do they still live in the area?"

"Haven't seen them in years. I think they moved away."

"Really? They built a house before I left."

"Oh yeah. I didn't know that," she responded.

"I'll find them. I'm going to go down to the lake houses and reminisce."

"Go ahead. They should be open. There's a couple living in the Hermit's old house and a bunch of the volunteers in the Empress's old place. There is an invisible fence keeping the dogs in at the Empress's house. I'm leaving after the mulch gets delivered. Have fun. See you at 8:30 tomorrow."

As I walked out the door and looked to the left, I saw a wooden sculpture. It was half done and resembled a standing bear.

"Is that a bear?" I asked.

"No. I'm not sure what it is. Maybe St. Francis. Who knows," replied Bear.

I took the path that led to the Hermit's house. It now had brown shingles. I walked up to the door to enter, but it was locked. Then I went around to the front to see if I could look in the window at the bed where the Lioness and I first made love. I could barely see in. So, I put my things on the picnic table and went down to the lake. There was the rock where Lioness stretched out and spread her beautiful ass in front of my face. I jumped on to the wooden dock and sat thinking about past sensuous times. A smile came over my face. It was a beautiful sunny afternoon, and I just sat quite a long while before walking around the building.

A kayak was tied to the grid fencing around the bottom of the porch. I tried taking it down, but it was too heavy. Then I started walking through the woods along the shore on a path that led to the Empress's house. The Hermit had always used it when he would come to say Mass. Half way, I passed by the cottage where I used to spend weekends alone trying to diet and pray and the clear round pool where I bathed many a morning.

I continued past the large rock with the two white praying statues, one kneeling, one standing. I stopped before getting too close to the house since I was afraid there would be no invisible fence along the lakeside. Instead, I returned to the Hermit's house, went up the hill and then back down the path that led directly to the Empress's place.

One could barely see the house since it was covered with leaves from the trees. Soon I was in front of the small square porch leading to the back door. The porch was not as high as it had been when I fell off it. Dirt had been put around it. A tiger cat came out to greet me and rolled around in the fallen leaves and dirt. I pet it, cautiously as I was still concerned about the dogs, but then I heard barking coming from inside the house. I walked to the back of the building and onto the dock. It seemed smaller than I had remembered. I sat down and just looked at the house. I could see the loft space where I had lived. The bottom floor had been boarded up with crisscross lathing. It was still a great house.

I resolved my prior life there. It came in the peaceful sitting. I knew that this chapter was closed and that this would be my last visit to this place. I was thankful for the experiences I had shared, but they were over. I never needed to come back again. I could never live like this now. It was not my cross to bear.

Walking up the hill, I realized why the Empress couldn't live there anymore. She couldn't do the walk. It was so steep, it took my breath away. And I used to do this climb several times a day without a second thought! As I walked out the road to the car, I looked back and said "goodbye." A trunk was coming in. It stopped next to me. The Empress and two young boys sat in the van.

"I'm doing the nostalgic tour," I explained.

"How was it?" she asked as she leaned out the window.

"Good."

"How long ago was it?" she asked.

"About twenty years."

"Seems like yesterday."

"Seems like a blink," I answered.

"You still look so young," she said.

"You probably looked young when you were fifty," I answered.

"This is my son and his friend."

"Nice to meet you, boys," I responded, not making an issue of her statement as I might have done in the past.

I was leaning on the truck and noticed the name of the community on the truck.

"Pretty fancy. You have your name on the truck now," I said.

She smirked like, "Yeah, big deal."

"Come and join us for community supper tomorrow night," she said as I was ready to take my leave.

"Maybe."

"Oh, good." And with that she drove on ahead, and I continued out. Gee, I thought, she could have invited me for a drink, and we could have talked. It would have been the perfect time. I was ready to be honest with her and tell her that I loved her at first sight and that sort of directed the rest of my relationship with her. But I realized she didn't want an explanation. There was no need for it. As my sister said later, "She wasn't honest with you back then, why would she want to be now?"

On the way back to the Co-op, I decided to try and find the Doctor and Painter's house. Instinctively I turned down the road opposite the store. I remembered that their house was on a primitive road off this main thoroughfare. The house where Hansel and Gretel lived should have been on the left, but in its place were a few new homes. Nothing really looked the same. I couldn't even tell which house had been Tee and Em's.

About two miles further, I was getting nervous that I was mistaken. Then I saw a small road with a sign that read, "Charlie Star Lane."

"Turn here," a voice from within whispered. So, I did. A man was working on the front side of his house. I stopped and asked, "Do you know if Doctor lives down this road? She used to have a practice in town."

"I don't know all my neighbors," he responded.

"She lived in an A-framed house with a lot of windows," I continued.

"There is a flat roofed house with a lot of windows just down the road a piece. I don't know if it is hers."

"Thanks," I responded and continued on slowly.

I came to the house he had described but it didn't look right except for all the windows. There were two cars in the driveway and a sign on the house with the word, "Wellspring." This was it! I was ecstatic, parked the car, and rang the doorbell. No one answered. I kept ringing. They had to be home. The cars were there, but maybe they had gone for a walk. Then I heard someone cough.

"Hey, Doctor, Painter. Are you home?" I shouted looking in the front windows. Finally, the door opened and out walked Painter.

"It's Dorothy, remember me?" I asked.

"Dorothy, of course I remember you!" We hugged and laughed. She was so glad to see me. "Look who's here!" she shouted back in the doorway. Doctor came out and gave me the same reception.

"Where are you staying?" Doctor asked.

"I'll get a hotel in town," I said.

"No. Stay here. Stay with us. Stay as long as you like," she assured me. It felt so good to be greeted like a real friend.

"Only if you let me take you for dinner," I said.

At supper, the friendship picked up where it had ended, and I got the update. They had separated themselves from the Co-op early on since it was too crazy for them. Doctor had her own practice, but a fire had destroyed all her equipment, and it was difficult for her to recover. She was doing some teaching at the University. Painter had completed quite a few art pieces. Her style was colorful and religiously symbolic. Doctor told me that when the Hierophant was dying, she had called the Empress and Bear into the room and told them that they had to change their ways, that they had to be more friendly and not alienate people. I admired Hierophant for her insight and strength. She always was a people person.

"Lots going on at Mandala. There's been some trouble out there," said Doctor. "The farm has been in the paper a few times. They had a couple of shootings. One of the fellows living there was on the Most Wanted list. And some woman got shot by her lover."

"Things have changed, haven't they?" I said, surprised to hear about this. When I lived out there, the volunteers were intellectuals or college students. Now the inhabitants were of a tougher nature. Most of them seemed poor or foreign from the group I had seen at the Co-op.

The next morning, I rose early and did my run, passing by small side paths with names like Bear Rock and Chickadee Lane. I turned around when the road dead- ended by a lake. I felt at home in the woods just like I did by the ocean. I didn't sense the alienation I had experienced when I was in the desert during my stay at the Lioness's. I forgot how quiet it was living in the woods. I hoped to see a bear or deer but didn't.

As scheduled, I pulled into the Co-op at 8:30 am and looked for Bear. She was nowhere around. Maybe she was not going to show up, I thought. I decided to wait till 9:00 am and if she didn't come, I would go have a good breakfast by myself at Duffy's. My mouth was watering for a homemade blueberry wheat muffin.

Finally, at about 8:50 am she strolled out. "You're here. I had to do some work in the office. Let's go in my truck."

I got my bag and jumped into her pickup. First stop was the building labeled Men's Shelter. She had to give instructions to a woman electrician who was doing some rewiring. The place looked pretty run down. One of the male inhabitants wanted a TV hook up in his room.

"Yeah, Okay, after she does some of this other work," patronized Bear.

The conversation with Bear was easy. She did most of the talking, and I learned Cleme was living in Connecticut working at a methadone clinic.

"She still comes to visit me," said Bear. "So, what did you do last night?"

"I went to the movies with Painter and the nun who runs the Hospitality House," I said.

"Did she say anything bad about us? I keep bringing people there and she keeps refusing them. Everything has got to be just so for her. She doesn't take drug addicts or alcoholics or . . . here I am bad-mouthing her."

"She didn't say anything bad about you," I responded not wanting to get involved in that triangle.

"Well, it has been a tough year. We had the police out at the farm a couple of times. One of the guys was a wanted criminal. Nice, quiet guy. You'd never know. But instead of the police coming out when he would be working in the garden, they came out at midnight. Startled the whole community. He had a gun and started shooting, and they shot back. One of the cops got hit. What a fiasco. They gave me a hard time for not doing a background search. But most of the time, nothing comes up on those searches."

"That must have been scary," I replied.

"Yeah, then we had this little boy living with us for about four years. He came with Ethel. That's another story. She was working in a hospitality house in Los Angeles and some dope addict had this child. Ethel took care of him. The mother was ok with that, but something happened, and Ethel left and brought him to us."

"You mean she took the child out of state?" I responded.

"Yeah, they finally figured it out and came and took the child. He was petrified. Ethel had to go to court. It just got resolved."

"Gee, it's tougher out here than when I lived here."

"I'll tell you. Never a moment's peace. Last night, someone dumped garbage in front of one of the houses we are building. So, when I leave you, I gotta go figure out what's going on and get that taken care of. Do you want to come with me?"

"No Bear. I'm not into that anymore," I said calmly.

"No? Huh?" she said and gave me that "are you sure" look.

"No, and I don't even feel guilty about it," I responded not wanting to get caught up in the whirlwind. She took out a map and showed me all the houses that they had built. I wondered how all that got done when I didn't see any workers around the Co-op.

"We're building sixteen more houses," she added.

"That's impressive," I said.

"Okay. So, what are you going to do?"

"I'm spending the day with Painter. We're going shopping in Camden."

"Oh. That will be fun. Well, I gotta go see about this garbage. Come out for community supper tonight. The food is great. You won't find better food anywhere."

"I'll be there. Good luck with the garbage," I said, feeling good about making contact with her again. Her heart was in the right place.

I drove out to Secretary's house. And sure enough, there was Secretary kneeling in the garden.

"Bear told me you'd be working in the garden," I said as I approached her.

After I stated my name, she remembered me. She still had beautiful, blue piercing eyes and looked great for her age. We talked about everybody, and I asked about the High Priestess.

"Last I knew she had divorced her husband and remarried. She was working at the Blue Hills Hospital, but I don't know if she is still there."

I had an hour left before I had to meet Painter, so I drove out to Blue Hills. As I used to take clients there for office visits, I knew exactly where it was. I went to the reception desk and asked if anyone by the name of High Priestess worked there. I described her age and looks. But no one knew of her. I drove back and met Painter. We shopped in all the stores in Camden and I managed to find a few gifts. Painter found a book entitled, "Menopause Madness," and we laughed hysterically reading each page out loud.

That night I drove out to the farm for community supper. I left my car near the first barn figuring if I wanted to leave early, it would be easier to get out. Supper had already started. There was a house full of people, including many young people with children. I said "Hi" to the Empress as she sat with an elderly woman. They seemed to be in a private conversation, so I didn't try to join them. That was our only contact. Instead, I found Bear and sat with her. She introduced me, "This is . . . from Chile and . . . from Peru. Poor . . . the cops picked him up as he was jogging and now, they are deporting him back to his country. Imagine, just 'cause he looked different, they picked him up. For no other reason."

"That's terrible," I said as I met his wife and child.

"They'll be gone in two weeks," she added. As I mingled, I was surprised to hear Bear encouraging one of the young women to have a baby. Things have really changed around here, I thought.

I was just about ready to go when I met a young man whose last name was the same as the Empress.

"You must be her nephew," I said.

"Second nephew. My mother is the Empress's niece. She's over there," and he pointed to a blonde, chubby woman.

'The Empress's niece?' I thought. She must be Sherry, the woman who came to Paris with us. I walked over to her.

"You're Sherry?" I asked looking at her.

"Dorothy?" she responded. And we both laughed and hugged one another.

"We were in Paris together," I said.

"Yes. You were a wild woman, I remember" she smirked and laughed even harder. "We had such a fun time. Remember my sister?" she said and pulled over the women standing next to her. "She was living in Germany, and I snuck her and her husband into the monastery. My aunt got livid."

"We had a great time. You know, I wasn't sure why I came out here tonight, but seeing you was worth the trip," I said. We hugged again, and I said my goodbye.

As I walked to the car, Bear followed me out.

"It was so good seeing you, Dorothy. Did you see the barn?"

"Yeah Bear, I saw the barn," I said.

"No, you gotta see the barn. Come on in. Let me show you. We have baby goats. They're so cute." She dragged me in. I couldn't care less as I wasn't really into barnyard animals.

"This is Billy, and this is Tom," she said as she introduced me to every other horse and then led me to the goat barn and did the same thing. I felt like she didn't want me to go. Then I thought, well, I am someone from the past, someone older that knew her, someone intellectual. She lives with a retarded woman and deals with these young people and all their problems. She used to live with Lady who was artistic and an intellectual equal. It must be difficult for her. She was the only one who had remained loyal to the Empress all these years.

Finally, I managed to get out of the barn.

"I heard you got the highest award from your order for your work here," I said.

"Yeah, they gave me $3000. I gave half to the community and the other half, well, I didn't keep it either," she said.

"I'm sure you didn't."

"The mother superior asked me if I thought about coming back," Bear said.

"And you said, 'Not even for a minute.'"

"How did you know? Every community has its good and bad. The nuns back home don't have perfect community either."

"You belong here Bear," I said and hugged her goodbye. Then I gave her my phone number. "In case you're in my area, call me," I said as I got into my car.

I felt bad leaving a good friend. I didn't think I would see her again.

Before bed, Doctor and Painter and I talked philosophy just like old times. I tried to explain the difference between a warrior and a martyr. "A warrior goes into battle for a cause, not his own, so he never has second thoughts and wins because his motive is pure. A martyr has a personal agenda and gets caught up in questioning the reasons for his actions at some point and causes his own demise or failure." Painter insisted that it wasn't failure.

The next morning, we had breakfast and Doctor wanted to make sure she got to say goodbye to me before I left. I put off my run to spend time with her. Painter made me a food care package and suggested a quicker route back.

I left feeling that I had accomplished what I had set out to even if it wasn't in the way I had anticipated. Sometimes one resolves an issue in the simple quiet self rather than in the overt interaction with the other. It was an important understanding.

On the way home I saw a sign over the highway which read, "Cat Mousam Road." Cat Mousam . . . That rang a bell. The Lioness had written a short story which she had sent to me. It was titled "Up on Cat Mousam." Funny, I never saw the sign before in all my trips to Maine. Funny, too, that when I called the Lioness to tell her about the trip, she asked me at the end of our conversation,

"Did you see Cat Mousam?"

"Yes, as a matter of fact I did. I realized that's where you got the name," I replied.

How did she remember it after all these years?

\* \* \*

I returned home a new woman, proud of myself for having faced my demons and surviving. Leaving a difficult relationship, expressing my feelings about the Lioness and accepting her rejection, traveling to Europe by myself, returning to Maine and ending the mystical hold, and first and foremost, giving myself the time and space to write had filled me with a new secure sense of self. I knew I didn't need anyone else to satisfy me, to entertain me, to guide me. I had found the muse and she lived inside me.

My cat, Diva, left me that summer. I slept with her the night before she died. We lay together on the porch floor on a blanket. She had suffered a stroke and couldn't move her back legs. She was the last remaining bond to J.

The next day I wrote in the journal, "In the morning I dyed my hair Malaysian cherry, and in the afternoon, I buried my cat, my friend of sixteen years. A fur ball of love. She licked my hand and purred till her very last breath. Funny, cherries don't grow in Malaysia." I emailed the Lioness that I understood how she must have felt sitting by her lover's side watching her die.

The next few weeks I did my usual—playing golf, visiting museums, dining with friends. In mid-July I volunteered to be a marshal at a local LPGA golf tournament, the day of the full moon.

As I marshalled the green of the second hole, four sisters sat down next to my post. At least, they looked like dykes to me. One was especially friendly, and I started flirting with her. She told me that the three other women lived in my town but that she lived about twenty miles away. Then she introduced me to the others. One sat quietly in a lawn chair a few feet back from the group. Her eyes were hidden behind dark sunglasses. Although she smiled and nodded her head when introduced, she didn't make any attempt to indulge in conversation. I wondered if she was the friendly woman's partner. After several golfers played through, they picked up their chairs and left.

When the last foursome teed off, I picked up my belongings and started following the golfers through the rest of the holes. I noticed the four women sitting at the 16th hole. I thought about joining them and maybe pursuing the friendly one. But the day was so beautiful. I was enjoying the sun, the grass, the birds. I felt so free. I didn't have to answer to anyone. Why did I want to tie myself up? I kept moving.

The next Saturday I was doing my early morning run on the beach route. A tall woman passed by walking quickly in the other direction. She turned her head, pulled out her earphone, and said, "Hey, aren't you the woman who was marshaling at the LPGA last weekend?"

"Yeah, that was me," I responded as I recognized her to be the quiet woman of the group. Neither one of us stopped.

That same night I went to a women's dance. I was standing at a table surveying the scene when I saw a familiar-looking face whiz down the middle of the dance floor. It was the tall woman again. I called to her, "Hey, aren't you the woman who was walking on the beach this morning?"

"Yeah, that was me," she responded and walked back toward me. We shook hands.

"I don't usually come to these dances, but some of my friends are supposed to meet me here. I'm early. I guess we went to the same high school. When did you graduate?"

"In '68. And you?" I asked.

"In '71," she replied.

"So, you're forty-seven. You must have been a freshman when I was a senior. What's your name?"

"Angretti. P Angretti."

"That name sounds familiar," I said.

"You probably know my brother, Lou," she suggested.

"Yes. He sold me my first house. He's a nice guy."

"Not really," she said and went on the explain, "I was helping my eighty-year-old grandfather, and Lou thought I was trying to get in good for the money. He told my grandfather I was gay."

"You're kidding! That wasn't his secret to tell. What did your grandfather say?"

Raising the palms of her hands in the air like she was a character from the *Sopranos*, she lowered her voice and said, "Hey, P, I heara you into the women. What's the matta ... " Just then one of her friends came over so I never got to hear the ending, though her imitation had me in stitches.

"I gotta go," she continued as her friend pulled her into the mass of dancing women. "Are you in the phone book?"

"Yeah," I said and shouted my last name. "But how will you remember my name?"

"That name is unforgettable. I'll remember. Maybe we could do a show."

"Or a walk," I chimed. "I want to hear the ending of the story!"

Before she scurried out of sight, I looked intensely at her face and thought, 'she's not blonde or blue eyed. She's not anything like my usual type. She has dark hair and eyes. Her face is chiseled like that of a beautiful Greek goddess. She's tall, very tall. I usually feel uncomfortable with tall women, but I didn't feel that way with her.

I stayed for a while longer and danced with other women. That night in my journal I wrote, "I met a woman that I think I can be friends with. She makes me laugh."

Little did I know she would become the great love of my life— the woman I planned to spend the rest of my life with. I could only imagine what new chapter she would inspire in me.

# Acknowledgements

I would like to thank the following women for their help on my book:

Susan Roche for her editing suggestions and her constant encouragement,

Nancy Coatta for designing a fabulous cover,

My sister, Sogno, for always listening,

Paula Nicoletti for her undying support and love.

And a special thanks to all the Muses, especially JB, who inspired me throughout my life.

Made in the USA
Coppell, TX
18 December 2020

45891772R00288